DOMINIC DELLICARPINI is the author of *Composing a Life's Work: Writing, Citizenship, and Your Occupation* and co-editor (with Jack Selzer) of *Conversations: Readings for Writing*. His research and publications focus upon the importance of writing and writing instruction for developing more active, informed, and engaged citizens. He has served on the Executive Board of the national Council of Writing Program Administrators and is co-founder of the National Conversation on Writing initiative. Dr. DelliCarpini teaches at York College of Pennsylvania, where he also serves as writing program director.

PENGUIN ACADEMICS

ISSUES

READINGS IN ACADEMIC DISCIPLINES

Dominic DelliCarpini

York College of Pennsylvania

Longman

Boston Columbus Indianapolis New York San Francisco
Upper Saddle River Amsterdam Cape Town Dubai London Madrid
Milan Munich Paris Montreal Toronto Delhi Mexico City
São Paulo Sydney Hong Kong Seoul Singapore Taipei Tokyo

"The Child is father to the man."
—William Wordsworth

For my son Derek, for teaching me what it means to be a man

Senior Editor: Brad Potthoff
Senior Marketing Manager: Sandra McGuire
Production Manager: Stacey Kulig
Project Coordination, Text Design, and Electronic Page Makeup: Electronic Publishing Services Inc., NYC
Senior Cover Designer/Manager: Nancy Danahy
Cover Image: Puzzle pieces © Michel Tcherevkoff/Stone
Senior Manufacturing Buyer: Dennis J. Para
Printer and Binder: Courier/Westford
Cover Printer: Lehigh/Phoenix Color Corp.

For more information about the Penguin Academic series, please contact us by mail at Pearson Education, attn. Marketing Department, 51 Madison Avenue, 29th floor, New York, NY 10010 or by e-mail at pearsonhighered@pearson.com.

Library of Congress Cataloging-in-Publication Data

Issues: readings in academic disciplines / Dominic DelliCarpini.
p. cm. —(Penguin academics)
ISBN 978-0-205-56857-4
1. College readers. 2. English language—Rhetoric—Problems, exercises, etc. 3. Report writing—Problems, exercises, etc. I. DelliCarpini, Dominic. II. Title.
PE1417.I88 2009
808'.0427—dc22 2009036747

1 2 3 4 5 6 7 8 9 10—CRW—12 11 10 09

Longman
is an imprint of

www.pearsonhighered.com
ISBN-13: 978-0-205-56857-4
ISBN-10: 0-205-56857-2

contents

Table of Contents by Discipline xiii

Table of Contents by Genre xix

Table of Contents by Interdisciplinary Topics xxiii

Preface xxix

Introduction 1

CHAPTER 1 Literacy Across Disciplines: What Does It Mean to Be "Literate" in the 21st Century? 27

21st Century Literacies: Curriculum and Assessment Framework 29

National Council of Teachers of English

This position statement by the national organization of English teachers can help you to understand the ways that "traditional" literacies continue to be important, yet how the definitions and range of literacy "required for full participation in a global, 21st century community" has been extended in recent times.

AASL Standards for the 21st-Century Learner 37

The American Association of School Librarians and the American Library Association

Among the literacies important for 21st Century students in our information age, the ability to access, evaluate, and incorporate information into our work is especially crucial. This document, endorsed by library science and educational technology specialists, lays out the standards for information-literate individuals.

Visual Literacy in the Age of Participation 39

Barbara Rockenbach and Carole Ann Fabian

This essay addresses the need for truly literate individuals to understand the ways that communication is dependent not only upon words, but upon images and the ability to participate in the creation and dissemination of ideas via current Web 2.0 technologies.

Expanding the Concept of Literacy 54
Elizabeth Daly

This essay suggests ways that the concept of a "text," in our visual culture, must be expanded to include multiple media, requiring students to be literate in the texts of the screen as well as in written, verbal texts.

America 101: How We Let Civic Education Slide—And Why We Need a Crash Course in the Constitution Today 67
Eric Lane

This essay calls for a return to the teaching of civics and current events in the classroom in order to promote civic literacy—the ability of students to participate knowledgeably in the work of our democratic culture.

Statistics and Quantitative Literacy 79
Richard L. Sheaffer

Among the various forms of quantitative literacy, this author suggests, the ability to understand and analyze statistics is especially important—both for a full education and for our informed participation in the work of a culture within which statistics bombard us regularly.

Humanism and Quantitative Literacy 98
Robert Orrill

This essay examines the boundary between the humanities and the sciences, suggesting that the humanities need to consider how "words and numbers mix in our public language."

CHAPTER 2 Looking Deep Inside Us: The Implications of Genetic Testing and Neuroimaging 113

Understanding the Human Genome Project and Neuroimaging 117
Online Resources

This feature suggests online sources that can inform you about scientific initiatives that promise to tell us a great deal about our own makeup, motives, and impulses. Perusing these sites can help you to prepare for the more specific debates across disciplines about the effects and uses of these scientific discoveries. Here, you will also learn how to access information about companies that are offering direct-to-consumer genetic testing, through which individuals can be provided with a report of their own genetic predispositions.

ASHG Statement on Direct-to-Consumer Genetic Testing in the United States 119
American Society of Human Genetics

This statement by a national organization of genetic scientists provides a position statement by research scientists about the application of their scientific discipline to business ventures.

Stem Cells and Genetic Testing: The Gap Between Science and Society Widens 128
Ricki Lewis

This essay suggests that the move from research science to applied science, in the case of stem cell research, has proceeded so quickly, and its promises have been so wide, that they will "ultimately feed the mistrust of science and scientists—and disappoint and mislead the public."

Mind Reading 134
Arthur L. Caplan

This essay, written by chair of the Department of Medical Ethics at the University of Pennsylvania, predicts that genetic testing and neuroimaging, despite potential problems, will dramatically improve the standing of mental health fields, basing them more firmly in biological sciences.

Therapeutic Promise in the Discourse of Human Embryonic Stem Cell Research 140
Beatrix P. Rubin

This essay studies the ways in which genetic research has been framed in language—as a project with great promise for curing disease—and how that use of language has been used to ensure continued funding for research.

Using the Best Interests Standard to Decide Whether to Test Children for Untreatable, Late-Onset Genetic Diseases 163
Loretta M. Kopelman

This essay analyzes a key ethical question raised by our new genetic knowledge: Should children be tested for their likelihood to suffer from an untreatable disease later in life?

Neuroimaging Techniques for Memory Detection: Scientific, Ethical, and Legal Issues 186
Daniel V. Meegan

This essay describes the scientific techniques surrounding neuroimaging and its ability to detect memories in the human brain, as well as the surrounding ethical and legal issues.

Neuroimaging and the "Complexity" of Capital Punishment 212
O. Carter Snead

This law professor investigates the growing interest in the potential for neuroimaging as evidence for both prosecutors and defense attorneys, and the reciprocal interest of cognitive neurosciences in "how their discipline might impact the law."

CHAPTER 3 Is the Concept of "Race" Real?: Theoretical Debates and Practical Implications 222

Background Readings on Race in America 224
Classic Texts Online

The Origin of the Concept of Race 225
Ashley Montagu

This noted anthropologist, in the context of the rise of Nazism, argues that "It should be pointed out that the very word 'race' is itself a racist term."

Ten Things Everyone Should Know About Race 236
Public Broadcasting System

In its 2003 series, "Race: The Power of an Illusion," the Public Broadcasting system sought to "clear away the biological underbrush and leave starkly visible the underlying social, economic, and political conditions that disproportionately channel advantages and opportunities to white people."

Race and the Law 239
Vincent Sarich and Frank Miele

In this piece, originally published as a chapter in their book Race: The Reality of Human Differences, *an anthropologist and a journalist collaborate to argue that "the latest genetic technologies are, for the most part, confirming not only the traditional anthropology but also the commonsense understanding of race" that is used in legal decisions.*

Does 'Race' Have a Future? 252
Philip Kitcher

In this piece, a philosopher asks not only if there is "a biological basis for dividing species into smaller units," but also examines the "uses" and "consequences" and the "prospects of doing better without racial categories."

Race and the Human Genome Project: Constructions of Scientific Legitimacy 277
Patricia McCann-Mortimer, Martha Augoustinos, and Amanda LeCouteur

This essay, written by two psychologists, examines the ways that scientific findings have been used—through specific rhetorical techniques—to change public understandings of race.

How Real Is Race?: Using Anthropology to Make Sense of Human Diversity 307
Carol Mukhopadhyay and Rosemary C. Henze

This piece, originally published in a journal devoted to the field of education, draws upon "scientific" perspectives on race to consider how race should be viewed "by teachers, students, and our society."

Race in a Bottle 323
Jonathan Kahn

This essay explores the ways that scientific research, and the public perception of that research, is being used by businesses to develop new products—in this case, pharmaceuticals geared toward specific races and ethnicities.

CHAPTER 4 What Does it Mean to Be (or Become) an "American"?: Citizenship and the Immigration Debate 333

The Elements of American Identity 335
Sheldon Hackney

This book chapter from One America Indivisible *argues that the conception of America is that "it is an idea and not just a place," and that democracy, with all its challenges, is what holds together an American society comprised of diverse cultures, wide disparities in wealth, and many individual stories.*

Teaching Citizenship and Values on the U.S.-Mexico Border 345
Susan Rippberger and Kathleen Staudt

Beginning from the fact that public schooling in both the United States and Mexico "has attempted to reinforce cultural and national values to create 'good citizens,'" this ethnography explores "possibilities for increasing mutual respect and collaboration" across the U.S.-Mexico border through a better understanding of the values learned through each country's schools.

Lessons of Belonging and Citizenship Among *Hijas/os de Inmigrantes Mexicanos* 367
Melissa Moreno

This article uses narratives of young adults from U.S.-Mexican communities to study how "citizenship surveillance" (constant questions about their citizenship status) affected their lives and their own understanding of their U.S. citizenship and their Mexican cultural alliances.

Preparing for Citizenship: Immigrant High School Students' Curriculum and Socialization 400
Rebecca M. Callahan, Chandra Muller, and Kathryn S. Schiller

This study explores the effect of high school civics classes and other predictors for engaged citizenship among children of immigrants as they pass from the K–12 system of public education into their lives as young adult citizens.

The Economic Logic of Illegal Immigration 418
Gordon H. Hanson

This essay examines whether there is any evidence to support the "strong consensus that if the United States could simply reduce the number of illegal immigrants in the country, either by converting them into legal residents or deterring them at the border, U.S. economic welfare would be enhanced."

The Real Problem with Immigration . . . and the Solution 433
Tim Kane and Kirk A. Johnson

This essay suggests that "the real problem presented by illegal immigration is security, not the supposed threat to the economy," and develops an argument as to what steps need to be taken in an age of terrorism to ensure the security of Americans.

Ethnic Identity and Imperative Patriotism: Arab Americans Before and After 9/11 445
Steven Salaita

This excerpt from Salaita's Anti-Arab Racism in the USA *considers the reception of Arab Americans in the United States both before and after 9/11, and examines the status of Arab Americans within the politics of minority groups more generally.*

CHAPTER 5 Studying the New Face of War: Definitions, Causes, and Effects Across Disciplines 462

Occasions that Justify War 464
Marcus Tullius Cicero

In this excerpt from his De Officiis (On Obligations), *this Roman statesman and rhetorician examines the limited situations within which war might be justified.*

Of War 470
Thomas Aquinas

In his classic formulation of "just war" theory from Summa Theologica, *Aquinas answers a series of ethical and theological objections that have been raised to waging of war, laying out the occasions within which war becomes a justifiable course of action.*

Toward the End of War?: Peeking Through the Gap 479
Pertti Joenniemi

This essay by a Foreign Relations scholar explores the changing definitions of war, especially those in a post–Cold War and post-9/11 world.

America and the New Dynamics of War 498
Jason Royce Lindsey

This political scientist explores the world of war as it relates to the United States' new ability to "deploy with less domestic political cost to the American government," a change that he argues is "profound for the United States and the world."

Making War on Terrorists: Reflections on Harming the Innocent 506
Thomas Pogge

This essay written by a professor of philosophy explores how the war on terrorism has led us to accept the killing of innocent individuals as morally justifiable.

Does War Beget Child Aggression?: Military Violence, Gender, Age, and Aggressive Behavior in Two Palestinian Samples 538
Samir Qouta, Raija-Leena Punamäki, Thomas Miller, and Eyad El-Sarraj

As social scientists, the authors of this essay use the methodologies of their disciplines—mental health—to add to what they call a "scarce and conflicting" pool of empirical evidence to support the common belief that "children and adolescents living in war zones are . . . a lost generation, aggressive and revengeful."

What Is War? 568
Mary Ellen O'Connell

In this opinion column, Mary Ellen O'Connell uses methods crucial to her discipline of legal studies to build a case that "the claim of global war"—and the denial of rights to enemy combatants based upon that claim—are not legally justified.

CHAPTER 6 Beyond Petroleum: Finding a Sustainable Energy Future 577

Beyond the Age of Petroleum 580
Michael T. Klare

This journalistic essay draws upon the expertise of those in public policy and governmental agencies to make its argument for a more coherent energy policy.

America Is Addicted to Foreign Oil 590
The Pickens Plan

T. Boone Pickens's Internet site demonstrates the ways that this businessman has used a variety of arguments—economic, environmental, and political—to build the case for his plan for a sustainable energy future.

Biogas as a Renewable Energy Source—A Review 594
M. Balat and H. Balat

As a "review" essay, this piece collects and synthesizes the scientific research on one possible solution to our energy needs—biogas, a byproduct of organic processes.

The Power and the Glory 612
Geoffrey Carr

This essay places the issue of alternative energy into the perspective of the applied sciences, discussing the ways that the need for new energy sources, in combination with the most promising technologies, provides an opportunity for investors who can most aptly predict the direction our energy decisions will take.

Power Play 618
Berenice Baker

This essay provides a good example of how a specific discipline—in this case, engineering—presents its research in more public forums.

Catch-22: Water Versus Energy 623
Michael E. Webber

This article explores another set of issues in the debate about how to address our needs for alternative energies—its effect upon our water supply.

The Clean Energy Scam 633
Michael Grunwald

This essay examines one movement within the rush to find sustainable energy sources—the use of biofuels—labeling these technologies "part of the problem."

How Biofuels Could Starve the Poor 642
C. Ford Runge and Benjamin Senauer

This essay, originally published in Foreign Affairs, *argues that the biofuel movement has not been driven by market forces or science, but instead by "politics and the interests of a few large companies."*

Credits 659

Index 663

contents by discipline

While the main Table of Contents presents the interdisciplinary readings in this book as a series of issues that have been addressed by multiple disciplines, the alternative tables of contents organize the readings in this book in other ways. These alternative tables can help in developing courses that are organized as a sequential study of disciplines or as a sequential study of genres. They can also help teachers and students find connections between and among the topics covered in this book.

This Table of Contents organizes readings by the **discipline or disciplines that primarily inform the piece, as well as by the intended audience in its original publication**. Since many of the readings draw upon multiple fields of study, some of the selections appear in more than one category.

Natural Sciences

Mathematics

Statistics and Quantitative Literacy 79
Richard L. Sheaffer

Life Sciences

Understanding the Human Genome Project and Neuroimaging 117
Online Resources

Biological Sciences

ASHG Statement on Direct-to-Consumer Genetic Testing in the United States 119
American Society of Human Genetics

Stem Cells and Genetic Testing: The Gap Between Science and Society Widens 128
Ricki Lewis

Therapeutic Promise in the Discourse of Human Embryonic Stem Cell Research 140
Beatrix P. Rubin

The Origin of the Concept of Race 225
Ashley Montagu

Ten Things Everyone Should Know About Race 236
Public Broadcasting System

Does 'Race' Have a Future? 252
Philip Kitcher

Race and the Human Genome Project: Constructions of Scientific Legitimacy 277
Patricia McCann-Mortimer, Martha Augoustinos, and Amanda LeCouteur

Physical Sciences

Biogas as a Renewable Energy Source—A Review 594
M. Balat and H. Balat

Catch-22: Water Versus Energy 623
Michael E. Webber

Social Sciences

Library Science

AASL Standards for the 21st-Century Learner 37
The American Association of School Librarians and the American Library Association

Civics

America 101: How We Let Civic Education Slide 67
Eric Lane

Public Policy

The Origin of the Concept of Race 225
Ashley Montagu

The Real Problem with Immigration . . . and the Solution 433
Tim Kane and Kirk A. Johnson

Toward the End of War?: Peeking Through the Gap 479
Pertti Joenniemi

Beyond the Age of Petroleum 580
Michael T. Klare

America Is Addicted to Foreign Oil 590
The Pickens Plan

Catch-22: Water Versus Energy 623
Michael E. Webber

Rhetoric/Public Policy

Race and the Human Genome Project: Constructions of Scientific Legitimacy 277
Patricia McCann-Mortimer, Martha Augoustinos, and Amanda LeCouteur

Anthropology

How Real Is Race?: Using Anthropology to Make Sense of Human Diversity 307
Carol Mukhopadhyay and Rosemary C. Henze

Economics

The Economic Logic of Illegal Immigration 418
Gordon H. Hanson

Behavioral Sciences

Does War Beget Child Aggression?: Military Violence, Gender, Age, and Aggressive Behavior in Two Palestinian Samples 538
Samir Qouta, Raija-Leena Punämaki, Thomas Miller, and Eyad El-Sarraj

Humanities

Rhetoric

21st Century Literacies: Curriculum and Assessment Framework 29
National Council of Teachers of English

Visual Arts

Expanding the Concept of Literacy 54
Elizabeth Daly

Humanities

Humanism and Quantitative Literacy 98
Robert Orrill

Bioethics/Rhetoric

Stem Cells and Genetic Testing: The Gap Between Science and Society Widens 128
Ricki Lewis

Bioethics

Mind Reading 134
Arthur L. Caplan

Rhetoric/Ethics

Therapeutic Promise in the Discourse of Human Embryonic Stem Cell Research 140
Beatrix P. Rubin

Ethics/Law

Neuroimaging Techniques for Memory Detection: Scientific, Ethical, and Legal Issues 186
Daniel V. Meegan

Ethics

The Origin of the Concept of Race 225
Ashley Montagu

Ethnic Identity and Imperative Patriotism: Arab Americans Before and After 9/11 445
Steven Salaita

America and the New Dynamics of War 498
Jason Royce Lindsey

Making War on Terrorists: Reflections on Harming the Innocent 506
Thomas Pogge

The Clean Energy Scam 633
Michael Grunwald

How Biofuels Could Starve the Poor 642
C. Ford Runge and Benjamin Senauer

Philosophy

Does 'Race' Have a Future? 252
Philip Kitcher

Civics

The Elements of American Identity 335
Sheldon Hackney

Ethnography/Sociology

Teaching Citizenship and Values on the U.S.-Mexico Border 345
Susan Rippberger and Kathleen Staudt

Sociology

Lessons of Belonging and Citizenship Among *Hijas/os de Inmigrantes Mexicanos* 367
Melissa Moreno

Applied Sciences

Journalism

Beyond the Age of Petroleum 580
Michael T. Klare

The Clean Energy Scam 633
Michael Grunwald

Education

AASL Standards for the 21st-Century Learner 37
The American Association of School Librarians and the American Library Association

Visual Literacy in the Age of Participation 39
Barbara Rockenbach and Carole Ann Fabian

America 101: How We Let Civic Education Slide 67
Eric Lane

Humanism and Quantitative Literacy 98
Robert Orrill

Statistics and Quantitative Literacy 79
Richard L. Sheaffer

How Real Is Race?: Using Anthropology to Make Sense of Human Diversity 307
Carol Mukhopadhyay and Rosemary C. Henze

Preparing for Citizenship: Immigrant High School Students' Curriculum and Socialization 400
Rebecca M. Callahan, Chandra Muller, and Kathryn S. Schiller

Business

Understanding the Human Genome Project and Neuroimaging 117
Online Resources

Race in a Bottle 323
Jonathan Kahn

America Is Addicted to Foreign Oil 590
The Pickens Plan

Medicine

Using the Best Interests Standard to Decide Whether to Test Children for Untreatable, Late-Onset Genetic Diseases 163
Loretta M. Kopelman

Legal Studies

Neuroimaging Techniques for Memory Detection: Scientific, Ethical, and Legal Issues 186
Daniel V. Meegan

Neuroimaging and the "Complexity" of Capital Punishment 212
O. Carter Snead

Race and the Law 239
Vincent Sarich and Frank Miele

What Is War? 568
Mary Ellen O'Connell

Economics

The Economic Logic of Illegal Immigration 418
Gordon H. Hanson

Business/Economics

The Power and the Glory 612
Geoffrey Carr

Engineering

Biogas as a Renewable Energy Source—A Review 594
M. Balat and H. Balat

Power Play 618
Berenice Baker

contents by genre

While the main Table of Contents presents the interdisciplinary readings in this book as a series of issues that have been addressed by multiple disciplines, the alternative tables of contents organize the readings in this book in other ways. These alternative tables can help in developing courses that are organized as a sequential study of disciplines or as a sequential study of genres. They can also help teachers and students find connections between and among the topics covered in this book.

This Table of Contents organizes readings by the **genre or mode of writing,** identifying pieces by their style and place of original publication. Since some genres cross categories, some of the selections appear more than once.

Academic Journals

Stem Cells and Genetic Testing: The Gap between Science and Society Widens 128
Ricki Lewis

Therapeutic Promise in the Discourse of Human Embryonic Stem Cell Research 140
Beatrix P. Rubin

Does 'Race' Have a Future? 252
Philip Kitcher

Race and the Human Genome Project: Constructions of Scientific Legitimacy 277
Patricia McCann-Mortimer, Martha Augoustinos, and Amanda LeCouteur

Teaching Citizenship and Values on the U.S.-Mexico Border 345
Susan Rippberger and Kathleen Staudt

Lessons of Belonging and Citizenship Among *Hijas/os de Inmigrantes Mexicanos* 367
Melissa Moreno

Preparing for Citizenship: Immigrant High School Students' Curriculum and Socialization 400
Rebecca M. Callahan, Chandra Muller, and Kathryn S. Schiller

Toward the End of War?: Peeking Through the Gap 479
Pertti Joenniemi

America and the New Dynamics of War 498
Jason Royce Lindsey

Making War on Terrorists: Reflections on Harming the Innocent 506
Thomas Pogge

Does War Beget Child Aggression?: Military Violence, Gender, Age, and Aggressive Behavior in Two Palestinian Samples 538
Samir Qouta, Raija-Leena Punamäki, Thomas Miller, and Eyad El-Sarra.

Biogas as a Renewable Energy Source—A Review 594
M. Balat and H. Balat

How Biofuels Could Starve the Poor 642
C. Ford Runge and Benjamin Senauer

Book Chapters

The Origin of the Concept of Race 225
Ashley Montagu

Race and the Law 239
Vincent Sarich and Frank Miele

The Elements of American Identity 335
Sheldon Hackney

Ethnic Identity and Imperative Patriotism: Arab Americans Before and After 9/11 445
Steven Salaita

Journalism/Popular Press Magazines

Race in a Bottle 323
Jonathan Kahn

Mind Reading 134
Arthur L. Caplan

Beyond the Age of Petroleum 580
Michael T. Klare

The Power and the Glory 612
Geoffrey Carr

Catch 22: Water Versus Energy 623
Michael E. Webber

The Clean Energy Scam 633
Michael Grunwald

Web Sites/Electronic Publications

21st Century Literacies: Curriculum and Assessment Framework 29
National Council of Teachers of English

AASL Standards for the 21st-Century Learner 37
The American Association of School Librarians and the American Library Association

Understanding the Human Genome Project and Neuroimaging 117
Online Resources

ASHG Statement on Direct-to-Consumer Genetic Testing in the United States 119
American Society of Human Genetics

Background Readings on Race in America 224
Classic Texts Online

Ten Things Everyone Should Know About Race 236
Public Broadcasting System

The Real Problem with Immigration . . . and the Solution 433
Tim Kane and Kirk A. Johnson

America Is Addicted to Foreign Oil 590
The Pickens Plan

How Biofuels Could Starve the Poor 642
C. Ford Runge and Benjamin Senauer

Trade Publications

Visual Literacy in the Age of Participation 39
Barbara Rockenbach and Carole Ann Fabian

Expanding the Concept of Literacy 54
Elizabeth Daly

America 101: How We Let Civic Education Slide 67
Eric Lane

Using the Best Interests Standard to Decide Whether to Test Children for Untreatable, Late-Onset Genetic Diseases 163
Loretta M. Kopelman

Neuroimaging Techniques for Memory Detection: Scientific, Ethical, and Legal Issues 186
Daniel V. Meegan

Neuroimaging and the "Complexity" of Capital Punishment 212
O. Carter Snead

How Real Is Race?: Using Anthropology to Make Sense of Human Diversity 307
Carol Mukhopadhyay and Rosemary C. Henze

Preparing for Citizenship: Immigrant High School Students' Curriculum and Socialization 400
Rebecca M. Callahan, Chandra Muller, and Kathryn S. Schiller

The Economic Logic of Illegal Immigration 418
Gordon H. Hanson

America and the New Dynamics of War 498
Jason Royce Lindsey

What Is War? 568
Mary Ellen O'Connell

Power Play 618
Berenice Baker

Reports/Statements by Professional and Disciplinary Organization

21st Century Literacies: Curriculum and Assessment Framework 29
National Council of Teachers of English

AASL Standards for the 21st-Century Learner 37
The American Association of School Librarians and the American Library Association

Statistics and Quantitative Literacy 79
Richard L. Sheaffer

Humanism and Quantitative Literacy 98
Robert Orrill

ASHG Statement on Direct-to-Consumer Genetic Testing in the United States 119
American Society of Human Genetics

The Economic Logic of Illegal Immigration 418
Gordon H. Hanson

The Real Problem with Immigration . . . and the Solution 433
Tim Kane and Kirk A. Johnson

contents by interdisciplinary topics

While the main Table of Contents presents the interdisciplinary readings in this book as a series of issues that have been addressed by multiple disciplines, the alternative tables of contents organize the readings in this book in other ways. These alternative tables can help in developing courses that are organized as a sequential study of disciplines or as a sequential study of genres. They can also help teachers and students find connections between and among the topics covered in this book.

This Table of Contents is organized **to show how topics speak to and with one another across disciplines.** Since there are many potential ways that these topics cross-fertilize, some of the selections appear in more than one category. And, of course, there are many other ways that the topics in this book might be brought into dialogue with one another; these suggestions represent just some of those ways students might examine issues in interdisciplinary ways.

Ethics, Race, and Ethnicity

Background Readings on Race in America 224
Classic Texts Online

The Origin of the Concept of Race 225
Ashley Montagu

Ten Things Everyone Should Know About Race 236
Public Broadcasting System

Race and the Law 239
Vincent Sarich and Frank Miele

Race in a Bottle 323
Jonathan Kahn

Teaching Citizenship and Values on the U.S.-Mexico Border 345
Susan Rippberger and Kathleen Staudt

Lessons of Belonging and Citizenship Among *Hijas/os de Inmigrantes Mexicanos* 367
Melissa Moreno

Preparing for Citizenship: Immigrant High School Students' Curriculum and Socialization 400
Rebecca M. Callahan, Chandra Muller, and Kathryn S. Schiller

Ethnic Identity and Imperative Patriotism: Arab Americans Before and After 9/11 445
Steven Salaita

Making War on Terrorists: Reflections on Harming the Innocent 506
Thomas Pogge

How Biofuels Could Starve the Poor 642
C. Ford Runge and Benjamin Senauer

Business Issues Across Disciplines

Statistics and Quantitative Literacy 79
Richard L. Sheaffer

Understanding the Human Genome Project and Neuroimaging 117
Online Resources

ASHG Statement on Direct-to-Consumer Genetic Testing in the United States 119
American Society of Human Genetics

Stem Cells and Genetic Testing: The Gap Between Science and Society Widens 128
Ricki Lewis

Therapeutic Promise in the Discourse of Human Embryonic Stem Cell Research 140
Beatrix P. Rubin

Race in a Bottle 323
Jonathan Kahn

The Economic Logic of Illegal Immigration 418
Gordon H. Hanson

America and the New Dynamics of War 498
Jason Royce Lindsey

Beyond the Age of Petroleum 580
Michael T. Klare

America Is Addicted to Foreign Oil 590
The Pickens Plan

The Power and the Glory 612
Geoffrey Carry

Power Play 618
Berenice Baker

Ethical Issues in the Sciences

Understanding the Human Genome Project and Neuroimaging 117
Online Resources

Stem Cells and Genetic Testing: The Gap Between Science and Society Widens 128
Ricki Lewis

Mind Reading 134
Arthur L. Caplan

Therapeutic Promise in the Discourse of Human Embryonic Stem Cell Research 140
Beatrix P. Rubin

Using the Best Interests Standard to Decide Whether to Test Children for Untreatable, Late-Onset Genetic Diseases 163
Loretta M. Kopelman

Neuroimaging Techniques for Memory Detection: Scientific, Ethical, and Legal Issues 186
Daniel V. Meegan

The Origin of the Concept of Race 225
Ashley Montagu

Ten Things Everyone Should Know About Race 236
Public Broadcasting System

Race and the Human Genome Project: Constructions of Scientific Legitimacy 277
Patricia McCann-Mortimer, Martha Augoustinos, and Amanda LeCouteur

Catch-22: Water Versus Energy 623
Michael E. Webber

The Clean Energy Scam 633
Michael Grunwald

How Biofuels Could Starve the Poor 642
C. Ford Runge and Benjamin Senauer

Influencing Public Policy

Therapeutic Promise in the Discourse of Human Embryonic Stem Cell Research 140
Beatrix P. Rubin

The Origin of the Concept of Race 225
Ashley Montagu

Race and the Law 239
Vincent Sarich and Frank Miele

The Elements of American Identity 335
Sheldon Hackney

Preparing for Citizenship: Immigrant High School Students' Curriculum and Socialization 400
Rebecca M. Callahan, Chandra Muller, and Kathryn S. Schiller

The Economic Logic of Illegal Immigration 418
Gordon H. Hanson

The Real Problem with Immigration . . . and the Solution 433
Tim Kane and Kirk A. Johnson

Toward the End of War?: Peeking Through the Gap 479
Pertti Joenniemi

America and the New Dynamics of War 498
Jason Royce Lindsey

Making War on Terrorists: Reflections on Harming the Innocent 506
Thomas Pogge

America Is Addicted to Foreign Oil 590
The Pickens Plan

Biogas as a Renewable Energy Source—A Review 594
M. Balat and H. Balat

The Clean Energy Scam 633
Michael Grunwald

How Biofuels Could Starve the Poor 642
C. Ford Runge and Benjamin Senauer

Studies of Human Behavior

Mind Reading 134
Arthur L. Caplan

Using the Best Interests Standard to Decide Whether to Test Children for Untreatable, Late-Onset Genetic Diseases 163
Loretta M. Kopelman

Neuroimaging Techniques for Memory Detection: Scientific, Ethical, and Legal Issues 186
Daniel V. Meegan

Race and the Law 239
Vincent Sarich and Frank Miele

Does 'Race' Have a Future? 252
Philip Kitcher

Preparing for Citizenship: Immigrant High School Students' Curriculum and Socialization 400
Rebecca M. Callahan, Chandra Muller, and Kathryn S. Schiller

Ethnic Identity and Imperative Patriotism: Arab Americans Before and After 9/11 445
Steven Salaita

Making War on Terrorists: Reflections on Harming the Innocent 506
Thomas Pogge

Does War Beget Child Aggression: Military Violence, Gender, Age, and Aggressive Behavior in Two Palestinian Samples 538
Samir Qouta, Raija-Leena Punamaki, Thomas Miller, and Eyad El-Sarraj

The Clean Energy Scam 633
Michael Grunwald

How Biofuels Could Starve the Poor 642
C. Ford Runge and Benjamin Senauer

Humanistic Examinations Across Disciplines

Humanism and Quantitative Literacy 98
Robert Orrill

Neuroimaging Techniques for Memory Detection: Scientific, Ethical, and Legal Issues 186
Daniel V. Meegan

Does 'Race' Have a Future? 252
Philip Kitcher

Race and the Human Genome Project: Constructions of Scientific Legitimacy 277
Patricia McCann-Mortimer, Martha Augoustinos, and Amanda LeCouteur

The Elements of American Identity 335
Sheldon Hackney

Lessons of Belonging and Citizenship Among *Hijas/os de Inmigrantes Mexicanos* 367
Melissa Moreno

Ethnic Identity and Imperative Patriotism: Arab Americans Before and After 9/11 445
Steven Salaita

Occasions that Justify War 464
Marcus Tullius Cicero

Of War 470
Thomas Aquinas

How Biofuels Could Starve the Poor 642
C. Ford Runge and Benjamin Senauer

Legal Issues

Understanding the Human Genome Project and Neuroimaging 117
Online Resources

Mind Reading 134
Arthur L. Caplan

Neuroimaging Techniques for Memory Detection: Scientific, Ethical, and Legal Issues 186
Daniel V. Meegan

Neuroimaging and the "Complexity" of Capital Punishment 212
O. Carter Snead

Race and the Law 239
Vincent Sarich and Frank Miele

The Real Problem with Immigration . . . and the Solution 433
Tim Kane and Kirk A. Johnson

America and the New Dynamics of War 498
Jason Royce Lindsey

What Is War? 568
Mary Ellen O'Connell

Educational Issues

All of Chapter 1: What Does It Mean to Be "Literate" in the 21st Century? 27
Literacy Across Disciplines

Stem Cells and Genetic Testing: The Gap Between Science and Society Widens 128
Ricki Lewis

Ten Things Everyone Should Know About Race 236
Public Broadcasting System

How Real Is Race: Using Anthropology to Make Sense of Human Diversity 307
Carol Mukhopadhyay and Rosemary C. Henze

Teaching Citizenship and Values on the U.S.-Mexico Border 345
Susan Rippberger and Kathleen Staudt

Lessons of Belonging and Citizenship Among *Hijas/os de Inmigrantes Mexicanos* 367
Melissa Moreno

Preparing for Citizenship: Immigrant High School Students' Curriculum and Socialization 400
Rebecca M. Callahan, Chandra Muller, and Kathryn S. Schiller

Medical/Psychological Issues

Understanding the Human Genome Project and Neuroimaging 117
Online Resources

Using the Best Interests Standard to Decide Whether to Test Children for Untreatable, Late-Onset Genetic Diseases 163
Loretta M. Kopelman

Mind Reading 134
Arthur L. Caplan

Neuroimaging Techniques for Memory Detection: Scientific, Ethical, and Legal Issues 186
Daniel V. Meegan

Race in a Bottle 323
Jonathan Kahn

Lessons of Belonging and Citizenship Among *Hijas/os de Inmigrantes Mexicanos* 367
Melissa Moreno

Does War Beget Child Aggression?: Military Violence, Gender, Age, and Aggressive Behavior in Two Palestinian Samples 538
Samir Qouta, Raija-Leena Punamäki, Thomas Miller, and Eyad El-Sarraj

Preface

This collection of readings is at once "disciplinary" and an "interdisciplinary." It asks students to consider the variety of communities to which they belong as readers and writers, and how each of those communities can be a resource to them as they develop their own writing. It also asks them to explore the variety of genres within which writing happens, from formal academic essays, to trade journals, to media stories and editorials, to electronic publication. In all these ways, it helps students to see why the reading, writing, and learning they are doing in college is connected to a whole spectrum of important academic, professional, and social dialogues.

What's Different About *Issues: Readings in Academic Disciplines*

Many textbooks that take a discipline-based approach to writing treat disciplines as methods of segmenting knowledge and academic work. This book focuses, instead, upon key connections: connections between and among disciplines, between and among academic writing and public genres, and between students' work as academic writers and their eventual work as professionals and citizens. In doing so, it can motivate students to write with real purposes, to see themselves as already involved in the work that these other writers have begun. Teachers can use this book in a number of ways in order to motivate engaged composing.

First, it treats writing *as a response to real issues that our culture faces*. Each chapter takes on a real challenge that we face as a culture: issues of 21st century literacies, race, the drive toward sustainable energy, the new definitions and implications of war, and the effects of scientific advances in genetics and neuroscience. Those focused and exigent topics can engage students in issues that they hear about every day in the news, while asking them to consider them more deeply through a sustained attention to the work of experts on those topics. Since this reader is organized primarily in an issues-based way, it can provide to students a wide spectrum of choices for their own writing.

This reader also *situates the responses of writers within a range of disciplinary communities*. That is, it demonstrates through its variety of authors and perspectives the ways that varied disciplines have taken on particular issues, the ways that those disciplinary communities have used their distinct perspectives and the methods of study to address those issues. By seeing how writers in the natural sciences, in the social sciences, in the humanities, and in applied sciences such as business, engineering, medicine, and law approach the same issues through different lenses, students can learn three related lessons: (1) that disciplinary communities have their own methodologies and their own priorities for learning, (2) that individual disciplinary communities regularly interact with other disciplinary communities, and (3) that academic studies have real implications beyond the academy.

This reader stresses those three elements in a number of specific ways, both through the range of readings included and in the limited, but crucial editorial apparatus.

The Range of Readings: Disciplines and Genres

Each chapter of *Issues: Readings in Academic Disciplines* provides a tour of disciplines and genres. Included in each chapter are readings that represent a wide range of disciplinary methods and goals, providing students with examples of disciplinary thinking. They will experience readings that use empirical methods of data collection in both the natural and social sciences; they will read pieces that use humanistic methods to explore the larger questions that face us as individuals and as a culture; and they will read pieces that apply advances in the sciences to the development of consumer products and services, to professional practices, and to ethical decision-making. Each of these readings provides not only topics that further their research and their own writing, but an education in the ways that these disciplinary communities function.

But the range of readings also shows the ways that these disciplines interact with one another: how the humanities critique the work of the natural sciences; how the natural sciences supply empirical data that can be translated into business decisions or public policy; how media draws upon the expert voices from the academy; and how the many public dialogues that take place in electronic forums have their basis in the work of experts across and among disciplines. Many of the pieces included here are already interdisciplinary, demonstrating how writers take into account not only their own fields of knowledge, but that pool of knowledge that comes from related disciplines. In this way, the focus of the book is as much interdisciplinary as it is disciplinary. Considering the use of this book in first-year college writing courses, this approach can be particularly useful, since those students are usually engaged in two related tasks: (1) learning about a variety of disciplines in their general education courses and (2) attempting to become members of the particular disciplinary community of their major field of study (or at least trying to choose one).

Thus, this reader can reach out to students right where they are at the time: attempting to find their ways into the intellectual culture of a college and trying to see how that learning is relevant to their future roles as professionals and as citizens. By reading this variety of discipline-based writing, they can learn the ways that one discipline explores another, and so see how a liberal education cuts across the sciences and the humanities, across theoretical and practical knowledge. In turn, we as teachers can help students see that the work of college is not defined by individual "knowledge silos," but by the broad-based perspectives on topics that come from interdisciplinary thought. This reader can thus help to situate first-year writing programs firmly into an institution's commitment to general education.

The range of readings is also varied by genre. In *Issues: Readings in Academic Disciplines,* students will find not only a variety of disciplinary perspectives, but a range of genres. Pieces included represent academic essays, journalistic texts, Web sites, opinion essays, trade journals, and visual rhetoric. In doing so, they can help writing teachers demonstrate that writing takes many forms, forms dependent upon purpose, audience, exigency, and venue of publication. The readings can also demonstrate the ways that academic research finds its way into more public genres: how journalists cite the work of disciplinary experts—and critique it; how Web sites and blogs respond to the contentions or researchers; how scientific discoveries are then translated into business and policy decisions through applied genres. In all these ways, the readings stress the connectedness of disciplinary and interdisciplinary knowledge, as well as the wide variety of forms of expression available in diverse genres.

This range of genres also allows you to help student writers think about stylistics. Since writers working in specific genres alter their stylistic technique to suit the genre—the chunking of text on Web sites, the use of a "lead" in journalism, the use of "review of the literature" and citations in an academic essay—you can use these examples to help students understand the underlying rhetorical principles as well as the actual stylistic moves that writers make. In this way, the collection is meant to enhance not only an understanding of issues and disciplines, but of how writing style adapts itself in each given case to find "the available means of persuasion."

Each of these goals and uses of the book are served by the editorial apparatus, which is primarily designed to make *Reading Across the Disciplines* adaptable to a wide range of course designs.

Editorial Apparatus

While the heart of this book is clearly the readings themselves, the arrangement of those readings and the accompanying editorial apparatus is meant to make it as usable as possible. Here are some features of the book's apparatus that can help teachers to adapt this book to their own central goals:

General Introduction

The general introduction to the book provides students with a basic understanding of disciplinarity, interdisciplinarity, and genre. It helps students to understand how disciplines are defined in a number of ways: by the topics that most interest its members, by the methods of study they use, by the types of evidence that they most value, and by styles of writing that are preferred by its practitioners. It also helps students to see that disciplines are not isolated, but interact directly and indirectly with other disciplines. In doing so, it stresses interdisciplinary thinking and writing as a way of enriching their own writing. And it explains the wider definitions of genre that go beyond "literary" genres to the varied modes of expression that underlie texts written for academic purposes, for professional purposes, and to forward opinions and perspectives. It also helps students to better understand multimodalities; that is, it helps them to recognize that while alphabetic rhetoric is still crucial, 21st-century writers must also take into account electronic publication and visual arguments of all sorts.

Alternative Tables of Contents

To allow this reader to be most adaptable to a wide variety of course designs, the text includes three alternative tables of contents. One provides ways to bring together the various issues covered in the book, for teachers who wish to create units based upon related topics. Another organizes the readings by disciplines, allowing teachers to develop courses that move from one disciplinary approach to another. And the third alternative table of contents organizes the book into genres, helping teachers and students to see the modes of delivery of various texts, from academic to public genres. These alternative tables of contents not only make the book versatile for teachers, but can help students to see the various ways that type of writing can be organized, and the various decisions that they need to make as writers.

Chapter Introductions

Each chapter introduction serves a number of purposes. It demonstrates the currency of the issues discussed in the chapter, and its importance for our culture. It also demonstrates why (and *how*) this issue is of concern for a wide range of writers from various disciplinary perspectives. And it provides an overview of the readings included in the chapter, showing both how they represent a range of disciplines and genres, and how those disciplines and genres interact with one another.

Headnotes

The headnotes for each reading provide important contexts that can help students to read each piece more effectively. They tell students a bit about the author and his or her disciplinary perspectives; they let students know about the place and time of original publication, helping them to consider purpose, audience, and exigency; and they suggest some key things to consider as they read each selection. These brief introductions thus allow students to think about the pieces not as isolated arguments, but situated ones.

Annotated Reading

In each chapter, one of the more substantial and complex pieces is accompanied by annotations that can serve three purposes: (1) it can assist the student in seeing the disciplinary methods used in formulating the argument; (2) it can help students analyze the rhetorical and stylistic moves made by the author to build that argument; and (3) it can help students see how an active, analytical reader uses annotation to better understand any given text. Annotations focused on each of these purposes are included for each of these pieces.

"Reading Analytically" Questions

Following each reading, students will find three questions that are meant to help them gather key information from the text to get at the heart of the argument being made by its author. These questions can also help students locate stylistic decisions made by the writer that are meant to make it convincing for its intended readers. These questions can be used for writing exercises and to initiate classroom discussions.

"Reading Across Interdisciplinary Communities" Questions

Also following each reading, students will find two questions that specifically prompt them to consider how that piece at once draws upon specific disciplinary methods and evidence, and interacts with other disciplines and readings in the chapter. These questions can be used to encourage students, both in their writing and in classroom discussions, to consider how disciplinary and interdisciplinary thinking informs each piece.

"Writing Across Disciplines" Writing Opportunities

At the end of each chapter, students will find five questions that are meant to help them move from reader to writer. These writing prompts suggest topics for additional research, ways to use disciplinary perspectives to investigate a topic further, and interdisciplinary ways to think and write—to use their own disciplinary perspectives to interrogate other discipline's understanding of the issue. These questions can be further customized by teachers to develop their own writing assignments.

In sum, the book seeks connections, not divisions. It helps students see the relationships that exist among academic disciplines, among various genres and audiences, between their work as students and their work as professionals and citizens, and between their reading and their writing.

MyCompLab

MyCompLab empowers student writers and facilitates writing instruction by uniquely integrating a composing space and assessment tools with market-leading instruction, multimedia tutorials, and exercises for writing, grammar and research.

Students can use MyCompLab on their own, benefiting from self-paced diagnostics and a personal study plan that recommends the instruction and practice each student needs to improve her writing skills. The composing space and its integrated resources, tools, and services (such as online tutoring) are also available to each student as he writes.

MyCompLab is an eminently flexible application that instructors can use in ways that best complement their course and teaching style. They can recommend it to students for self-study, set up courses to track student progress, or leverage the power of administrative features to be more effective and save time. The assignment builder and commenting tools, developed specifically for writing instruction, bring instructors closer to their student writers, make managing assignments and evaluating papers more efficient, and put powerful assessment within reach. Students receive feedback within the context of their own writing, which encourages critical thinking and revision and helps them to develop skills based on their individual needs.

Learn more at www.mycomplab.com.

Acknowledgments

I thank my reviewers, whose many suggestions have greatly improved the text: Ann Balay, Indiana University Northwest; Barclay Barrios, FAU; Lee Brasseur, Illinois State University; Benita Budd, Wake Technical Community College; Bill Condon, Washington State University; Stacy Donohue, Central Oregon Community College; David Elias, Eastern Kentucky University; Nat Hardy, Rogers State University; Karla Saari Kitalong, University of Central Florida; Erica Messenger, Bowling Green State University; Cleatta R. Morris, LSU in Shreveport; Gary A. Negin, California State University; Les Perelman, MIT; Shirley Rose, Arizona State University David Ryan, University of San Francisco; Guinevere Shaw, Bergen Community College; Marti Singer, Georgia State University; Chris Thaiss, UC Davis, and Christine Van Mierlo, St. Charles Community College. I would also like to thank the editorial team at Pearson Education, and especially Brad Potthoff and Joseph Opiela, for guidance on this project.

Introduction

What Are Disciplines and Why Do they Matter?

Disciplinarity. Interdisciplinarity. These are terms that you'll hear bandied about as you proceed with your college education. And they can sound pretty intimidating. The purpose of this introduction—and of this book—is to help you to better understand that these concepts aren't as complicated as they sound. It's also designed to show you that complex or not, understanding those concepts can be a great help to you as you read and write in your college classes, and on into your professions.

The readings in this book will help you to see that "disciplines" are really communities, groups of people with a shared set of ideas and beliefs about how we can make sense of the world around us. These "disciplinary communities" can help us as we do that important intellectual—and physical—work. As you read the examples of how various disciplines approach *inquiry* (another key concept that means asking serious questions in systematic ways), you'll gain a better understanding about why discipline-based thinking is such an important tool in your education.

So why are these inquiry-based communities called "disciplines"? Though the word "discipline" has taken on connotations that mean something like "keeping order in personal and social behavior," the original word has more to do with learning—of being a "disciple" or a "pupil" with the intention of learning more about a particular topic. In that sense, both teachers and students are "disciples" of a particular field, all coming together to learn as much as we can about the subject area. So when you and your teacher come together in a classroom, you are all students of the topic you are studying together, all "disciples" of that field. In order to go about that learning in the most productive and systematic way, communities of people interested in particular types of questions (and in asking questions in particular sorts of ways) come together to develop methods for orderly, productive thought. As a college student, your job isn't just to learn "content"—the *products* of that orderly thought by others in the disciplines you will study—but the *methods* that others in your discipline have used in order to generate those products. Knowing not only what others have learned in the past, but also how they went about it—the *processes* of learning within their field—can help you move beyond being a passive learner, and get you into the game. It can help you to "discipline" your methods of thinking in ways that will allow for the discovery of new ideas, new answers to questions. And in that way, "disciplined" thinking is anything but constrained or limiting thinking; it is, to the contrary, creative and inventive. The methods associated with the inquiry of various disciplines can be of great assistance to you as a writer, because they can help you to develop a rich set of ideas to draw upon as you write.

Learning about various disciplines and how they approach topics in specific, systematic ways can also help you become a more active and analytical reader of the kinds of texts you will read as a college student. By understanding the processes of thought that are used by practitioners in specific disciplines, you will be better able to judge the quality of the conclusions reached. Think of it this way; sometimes, in mathematics classes, you are asked not only to give the "answer" to problems that you are asked to solve. You are also asked by the teacher to "show your work." Why is that? What teachers can learn from looking at the "work" that leads up to the answer is whether you understand the disciplinary principles of that field, whether you are using valid, "disciplined" thinking in order to reach your conclusions. Similarly, your work as a college student is more than learning the "right" answer that some expert has presented to you and showing that you have memorized that answer. A more important part of your job is learning methods of systematic thinking that you can bring with you to other, similar problems. In doing so, you can learn the processes of thought, reading, and writing that will help you to investigate any given topic—processes that are likely to breed useful and pertinent information upon which you can build productive discussion, and in some cases (but not all), productive and reliable conclusions. That, in turn, will make you more active participants in the field, preparing you to produce writing that will be valued by those disciplinary communities.

Disciplines also share methods of communication. That is, not only do disciplinary communities need shared methods of inquiry (which are sometimes called "methodologies"), but they also share specialized vocabularies, ways of organizing writing done for other professionals in their field, and preferred stylistic choices. As with methodologies, a knowledge of these specialized terms and an understanding of why particular types of writing are organized and written as they are can have two benefits to you as a new "disciple" in that field: (1) it can help you read pieces in that field in the ways that they were intended, and so make reading challenging academic writing easier and more productive; and (2) it can help you to internalize key terms and organizational strategies that will make you a more capable writer in that field.

As a writer, you will also find that the *styles* we choose as writers need to be adjusted according to the disciplinary community into which we are writing. Perhaps you have been asked by an English teacher to "expand and elaborate" upon your ideas, to open an essay with an interesting anecdote, to vary your word choices or to use more complex sentence structures so as to avoid boring prose. Those are very good pieces of advice for some types of writing. But other types of writing have very different stylistic preferences. Would you begin a lab report with a story? Would you want to vary word choices in a technical document, changing the name, for example, of a particular part of a machine you're writing about in an engineering paper or a set of instructions? Would you want long, complex, and "flowery" sentences in a memo? Of course not. Knowing not only the preferences of particular disciplines, but also the communicative reasons behind those preferences, can help you to become more proficient at reading and writing in those disciplines. You should also pay attention to the various ways that writers in different disciplines and genres communicate, both in words and in images.

FIELDWORK AND METHODS

Ethnographic field methods, theoretically grounded in phenomenology, were the foundation for this four-year qualitative study of nationalism and schooling. We focused on two schools in El Paso and three in Ciudad Juárez, making an average of one visit per week while school was in session. We selected schools that were similar in terms of their proximity to the border. We also tried to choose schools that were comparable socially and economically, taking into account the different meanings of class and income within each nation. Even though the concepts of working-poor and middle-class status in the United States and Mexico are not parallel, especially since the Mexican economic crisis of the 1980s and subsequent devaluations of the peso, we looked for similarities in class disparities and relative class status among the different schools.

The opening of this "methods" section from Susan Rippberger and Kathleen Staudt's study of how citizenship is taught in the U.S. and Mexico (included in Chapter 4) describes the processes that were used to assure reliability of a study, and to communicate to other social scientists how to interpret the data that will be presented later in the paper.

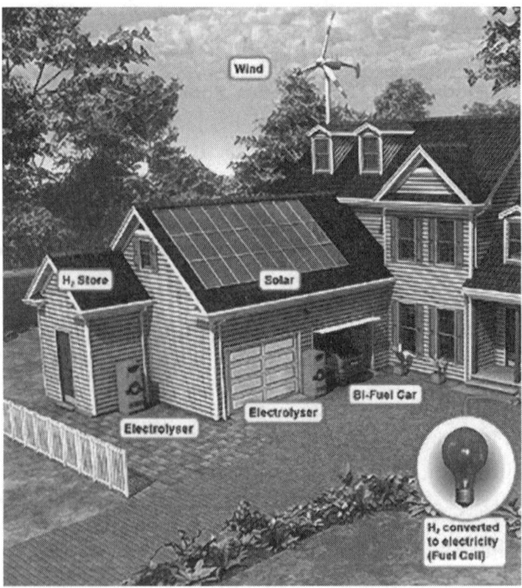

The picture to the left illustrates the many uses of a new type of technology in many facets of a household. Visuals like this are often used to build an argument graphically, especially in media and trade journals that are meant for a larger, less specialized audience.

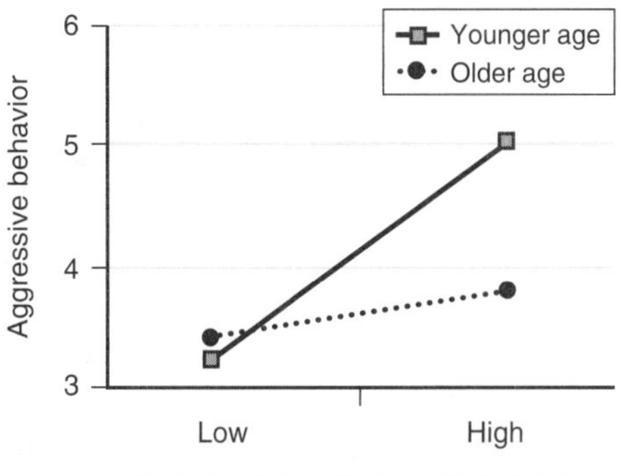

Graphs like the one to the left are used to present quantitative information and to show the correlation (or relationship) between different pieces of data. You will find many such graphs or tables in articles in the sciences, social sciences, and business.

Figure 1. The association between a child being victimized directly by military trauma and the child's aggression as reported by the parents as a function of the child's age.

As a college student, you will read and write in many disciplines, sometimes in a single day. That is, you will not only "major" in a particular field, but as part of your general or "liberal arts" education, you will study other fields as well. An English major might take courses in biology and history. A chemistry major might take courses in literature or business. A psychology major might also take courses in philosophy or political science. This "well-rounded" approach to education is not just about learning content from many fields; it is also about understanding how practitioners in those fields do research, make arguments based on that research, and present their findings in specific styles and types of documents. If you pay attention to the types of reading and writing that are highlighted in this book, you can take full advantage of the tour of academic disciplines you are taking as a college student, and learn how your own major field of study is similar to, and different from, those other fields you will study. You will also learn how the findings, methodologies, and writing styles of other disciplines can enrich your chosen field of study.

Knowing how other fields differ from your own, and where they intersect with your own, can be just as important as knowing the methods and language styles of your own discipline. This is why the concept of "interdisciplinarity" is another key element of your college education (and why it is central to this book as an "interdisciplinary" reader). While practitioners in particular fields of study tend to depend heavily upon their own processes of research, thought, and writing, they also can (and do) learn a great deal about their work from the methodologies and methods of other disciplines. Developing an understanding of how other disciplines do business can have several benefits: First, it provides a different lens from which to view the topic of study. So, if a scientist studying human genetics thinks about the kinds of questions that might be asked by a philosopher, she might then come to consider not only the scientific accuracy of her work, but the ethical implications of it. Conversely, if a philosopher wants to consider the ethical implications of genetic testing and mapping, he must first also understand not only the science behind genetics (at least to a degree), but the methods of thought and writing that helped lead to those scientific conclusions. And if either wanted to know about the impacts of these scientific findings upon individuals or upon our culture, they might then look to the methods and findings of social scientists like psychologists, sociologists, or political scientists. In these ways, *interdisciplinary* thinking enriches *disciplinary* thinking. And you'll see just those types of cross-disciplinary modes of thinking as you read the selections in each chapter of this book.

Not only does interdisciplinary thinking widen the lens through which we can inquire into various topics, but it can also help us to communicate across fields. One of the problems that educators have identified in the work done by academics is that sometimes we tend to stay within particular "knowledge silos," never taking the time to speak or write to those outside our own community. If we can't understand one another's assumptions, practices, and writing styles, we are less likely to benefit from the perspectives and insights offered by other fields. That can be problematic for a number of reasons. Most immediately, since as a student you will be a reader and a writer in a number of disciplinary areas—and probably are right now—knowing how to cross from one discipline to another while keeping your own disciplinary perspectives in mind can help you to enhance the work of that discipline, and help you enhance the thinking you do in your own. Further, when inquiry leads to action—which it often does—knowing how other disciplines arrive at their recommendations can help you to understand policy decisions and decisions we will be asked to make as citizens. After all, as citizens, we must pay attention (with some level of understanding) to the conversations going on in other areas, as they are likely to impact our lives and the good of our culture.

This book is designed to help you think in "interdisciplinary" ways. Each chapter includes a number of readings that all focus upon a similar set of public issues, but that are written from a number of disciplinary perspectives. Further, many of the readings included are already interdisciplinary; that is, the writers of these pieces have considered how the knowledge and processes of their own disciplines might be enriched by taking into account the knowledge from another discipline. As you read a number of pieces that inquire into those similar topics, you will be hearing a dialogue of disciplinary voices, each saying something like this: "I understand what you are saying from your (disciplinary) perspective; now listen to what I'm thinking based on mine." As you listen in to this cross-disciplinary set of perspectives, your challenge will be to first understand the ways each piece makes its argument, and second, to see how that argument is altered (or supported) by the other disciplinary perspectives. In effect, each chapter provides a set of related issues, and says with each new piece, "What if you looked at it this way?"

How to Use this Book Effectively

So what can you learn by reading and analyzing the writing in this book? You can learn how "disciplined" thinking can lead to writing that can be shared by others in specific communities of researchers—and so learn to better read and write within that discipline. You can also learn how to use those disciplined thought processes yourself, in order to be an active participant in that discipline. And, by comparing and contrasting the approaches taken to specific human issues and questions, you can learn how to think across disciplines, using interdisciplinary methods to see those issues and questions from a wider array of angles. This wider perspective will give you many options as you consider how you will get into the dialogue, how you will write about topics that most matter to you as an individual, and as an aspiring member of those intellectual communities. Among the many goals you might have as a college student, that is perhaps the most crucial.

To use the book effectively, then, you should read not only to take in content, but analytically. Analytical reading asks you to go beyond asking "what" a text says and to consider "how" it says it. In the end, that kind of analytical reading can also help you to ask whether the argument is sufficient, accurate, and credible; that is, it can help you make judgments about credibility that you will need to make as a college student. Reading analytically requires you to be an active reader who asks good questions about each text you encounter. Here are some questions you might ask in order to get the most out of each piece and to help you learn more about how each discipline functions:

- What is the purpose of this piece of writing? Where is that purpose stated?
- Who is the likely audience of this piece? What does that audience already seem to know and believe?
- What argument is this piece trying to make? What previous knowledge does it seem to be building upon? What previous knowledge does it seem to be challenging?
- What methods did the author use in order to gather data or information? In what ways does the author attempt to demonstrate the credibility of that method?
- What seems to be the most credible type of evidence for arguments in this discipline?
    - To what degree does it rely upon secondary sources (research and writing done by others)?
    - To what degree does it rely upon primary evidence (research and writing generated by one's own experiments, studies, or interpretation)?
    - To what degree does it value quantitative (number-based) information?
    - To what degree does it value qualitative (interpretive, holistic, observational) evidence?
    - To what degree does it value the words and thoughts of "classic" thinkers on a topic? Or does it seem to value more current thought on the topic?
- How do writers in this discipline tend to organize their writings? Are there common structures for a philosophical study? A scientific paper? An essay describing business trends?
- To what degree does this discipline tend to rely upon various types of visual aids: graphs, charts, illustrations, tables, and so on? Why are those elements important to making an argument in this discipline?
- Do writings in this discipline tend toward drawing conclusions, or simply providing discussions? Do they make recommendations or simply provide information and proposed understandings of a topic?

- How would you describe the writing style in this discipline? In particular, you might pay attention to some of the following features (and others suggested by your instructor):
  - Do sentences and paragraphs tend to be longer or shorter than in other disciplines?
  - Do writers in this discipline tend to use many direct quotations or not?
  - Does the writing style employ passive voice to depersonalize the methods and activities, or active voice?
  - Is first person (I, we) used at all? How is it used?

In addition to considering the "discipline" of each piece, it is also important that you pay attention to the *genre* and audience of the piece. Though the term *genre* is often used to describe types of literature (stories, poems, plays), it also connotes types of documents more generally. A Web site is a genre, as is a business letter or memo, an editorial, and so forth. One important thing to remember about genres is that they, in a sense, provide the expectations that a reader brings to them. When you sit down to read a newspaper article, you do not expect footnotes and works cited pages; but you'd be surprised not to find them in an article in a scholarly journal. When you go to a Web site, you would be both surprised and annoyed to find screen after screen of text to scroll through; but reading hundreds of pages of a book with few visuals may not surprise you. And no one wants a six-page memo or e-mail.

Since genre helps to determine the expectations of readers, it must also help to determine the ways that writers prepare documents for those readers. So, as you read as a writer—and that's one of the main purposes of this book—you should also be paying attention to the ways that writers keep the expectations of readers in mind as they present their work to their audience. Some of the documents in this book are meant for wide, public audiences. This is especially true of journalistic pieces, which tend to overview a topic, and provide pithy quotations from "experts" as well as definitions of complex concepts and terms. Other pieces are meant more for others within the discipline, and so are free to use "insider-language": concepts and ideas that assume a certain level of expertise of methods, prior knowledge, and/or assumptions of the field. Some documents rely upon formulae and data, while others are built upon logic or emotions. That is why reading the headnote of each piece, which tells you a bit about the author and the original publication context of the piece, is important; it can prepare you to read with that context in mind and to learn how to write for those types of audiences and purposes as well.

Genre often varies according to the community for which a piece is written. In that way, genre and discipline are related concepts. Each of those communities thus has its own genre preferences. Let's look at some of those communities and the writing that they do.

Disciplines as Intellectual Communities

While it is likely that you have a number of goals for yourself and your future profession(s), as a college student, you have a job right now: to learn as much as you can about your area of study. This *intellectual* work asks you go beyond your own ideas and ways of seeing the world and to consider the ideas and perspectives of others who are studying similar issues and questions. If you consider how your college or university is organized, you'll notice that it has been divided into various academic units: colleges of arts and sciences, of liberal arts, of nursing or engineering; departments of English, foreign languages, biological sciences, history, political science, and so forth. What all these academic units share is the desire to learn more about specific areas of human inquiry: they are all trying to answer current questions and solve current problems that face us all.

However, the divisions of a college suggest that the methods used to try to answer those questions—and sometimes the questions themselves—can be quite different. As places of "higher learning," colleges and universities divide themselves in these ways to form communities of like-minded individuals. But "like-minded" doesn't mean that members of these intellectual communities all agree. Quite to the contrary, the purpose of intellectual communities is to consistently critique and expand upon the work that that community finds important. Writing is one of the most important ways that this intellectual community does its work of constantly rethinking past assumptions. Writing done within these intellectual communities serves a number of purposes: it leaves a record of that work for current and future researchers in that area of study; it "shows the work" that led up to their contribution to ongoing discussions on a given topic, demonstrating that their contribution has validity and value for others in that community; and it lays the groundwork for further study of the topic, inviting others to expand upon what has already been established or to provide alternative perspectives.

As you read the pieces in this book, written by individuals in a variety of disciplines, you will notice that most of the scholarly studies begin by reviewing the past "literature" on a topic. A "literature review" doesn't use the word *literature* in the sense that you may have used it in the past, referring to works of creative writing. In academic writing, the "literature" on a given topic refers more generally to past writings on the topic. Rather than reinvent the wheel, researchers first pause to see what practitioners in their discipline have already done and written in relation to their topic, and summarize those findings near the beginning of their own document. In doing so, they are able to take the next steps in advancing knowledge on that topic rather than starting from square one. These reviews of the literature, which are usually chock-full of citations from previous researchers, usually end in what is sometimes called a "gap statement"—a statement by the writer about what has not yet been done, or done adequately, in the research of the field. In effect, the literature review says, "These things have already been established, and based upon that work and upon what has yet to be done, I offer what follows." If you think about that structure—the structure of most writing that seeks to advance our knowledge of a given topic, you can also better understand your own job as a writer: to first read and study the previous work, and then to add your own small contributions to the field.

FRAMING CONSIDERATIONS

Our work is rooted in a critical ethnography of education (Noblit, Flores, and Murillo 2004; Brookfield 2005; Wolcott 1994) that celebrates individual differences, pluralist forms of democracy, and emancipatory educational practices, particularly with regard to Latino learners (Darder and Upshur 1992; Valenzuela 1999). Methodologically, we found that phenomenology provides the philosophical foundation for qualitative inquiry, highlighting multiple voices, affirming local expertise, and rejecting traditional perspectives (Husserl 1970).

Notice how this first paragraph of a review of the literature from Susan Rippberger and Kathleen Staudt's study of how citizenship is taught in the U.S. and Mexico (included in Chapter 4) introduces the past publications on a topic. It allows the writers to demonstrate the work that has already been done by others and so situate their own work into an ongoing dialogue about how citizenship skills are taught in two different cultures. As the article proceeds, the authors discuss how their own study interacts with these previous works.

Sometimes that contribution takes the form of a replication study. A replication study borrows the methodology of another study—that is, it uses similar processes of research—and either (1) asks whether the conclusions drawn in the previous research are still true (after all, times change); or (2) it applies similar methods to a slightly different problem, and so builds upon useful and tested methods of research to examine similar problems. So, for example, a researcher interested in whether standardized tests are effective measures of student learning might replicate the methods of an older study of this question and, using the same methods, examine whether those conclusions still hold for contemporary students. Or, in the second case, a researcher might use the methodologies used to study that question and apply it to a different population, asking, for example, if standardized tests are as useful for, say, English language learners as opposed to native speakers. By building upon what already has been done, and using the methodologies that are accepted in a given discipline, new researchers (like you) can help to advance the understanding of the problems and questions that interest that group.

As a college student, you are entering a wide number of intellectual communities, both in your major field and in the various fields you will study as part of your "general education" (the core of courses all students at your institution are expected to study). As such, it is important that you think about the ways that each of these communities investigate issues and problems. This book can help you to do that if you read with an eye not only to the content of each article, but toward a better understanding of how people in these communities tend to build their arguments. And building an argument isn't just about methods, but about the evidence that is considered "valid" by that community. In the section below on the Fields of Knowledge-Making, you'll learn more about the methods and evidence that tend to be valued in different disciplines.

The pieces included in this reader don't always fall neatly into categories of academic communities. In some cases, they are interdisciplinary, bringing together the knowledge and methods of two—or even several—disciplines. And the genres included here also demonstrate that the knowledge generated by intellectual communities is often disseminated through more public genres. So an essay written for the Science column in *Newsweek* or *Psychology Today* has its roots in a given intellectual community, but translates the work of that community for a wider audience. Somewhere between specialized, scholarly journals and popular sources like newspapers, magazines, and open Web sites is something called a trade journal—a publication for professionals in a field, but not those who are actively involved in ongoing research.

These publications provide updates and ongoing development that can help those in professional communities continue to grow as members of that profession.

Disciplines as Professional Communities

We tend to think of the word *professional* as connoting those activities that provide income for practitioners; for example, professional athletes are paid for their work, whereas "amateurs" are not. And this is part of what we mean by "professional"—but only part. *Professional* also refers to those who "profess" a field of endeavor—that is, make claims to and for the validity and importance of that endeavor. So, a professor of chemistry professes the importance of the study of the structure and behaviors of elements and how they interact with one another. They suggest that this study is important enough to warrant a life's work that is devoted to this study.

But "professors" are not the only ones who "profess" the importance of a field of study and work. On the contrary, all "professionals" make a commitment to a community of people who share a belief in the importance of their work, and who use similar methods of study to advance the work of that profession. So businesspeople use methods like marketing analyses and business plans to test whether a business is viable; engineers use mathematical formulas and field tests to consider whether a machine or a building will withstand its proposed uses; nurses use both medical studies and interpersonal relations to consider how to best provide health care; and so on.

The point here is that learning the methodologies and procedures used by practitioners in a particular field is not limited to academic uses. As you move from student to professional, you will continue to be among communities of people who advance knowledge and practices in ways that serve both the disciplinary/professional community and those who this profession is meant to serve. This is one of the reasons why learning how to function in a disciplinary community while you are a college student is so crucial. To truly advance in your profession, you will want to do more than simply follow the pre-established methods of your field. You'll want to make contributions to that field by being an active member of it—asking good questions, proposing new solutions, and continuously studying the latest breakthroughs and controversies.

Being a good reader and writer is a large part of advancing in your field even beyond your college years. So forming good habits of reading and writing regularly will help you to keep up with your field, and is one very important part of your college education. Just as academics keep track of the advances in their intellectual communities, so do professionals keep track of the latest trends and advances in their "literature"—literature that is often collected in what are known as "trade journals." As noted above, trade journals are publications that offer to professionals surveys of new practices in the field, the up-and-coming areas of research that are most promising, techniques that are useful for professionals in the field, and so forth. Keeping up with the ideas in these publications is an important part of staying current in your field and so advancing your standing within your profession.

Knowing how to read these publications—and contributing to them as writers (because after all, all professionals are writers, too)—requires you to think about what each of these communities value in much the same way that you think about academic or intellectual communities. You need to read the pieces in trade journals not just for information and content, but to consider what types of things successful practitioners of the field do, what kinds of methods they use to study trends and practices in the field, and what type of evidence is offered to support their claims. By reading trade journals, you can also learn the specialized vocabulary of the field, or its "jargon." Though the word *jargon* is sometimes treated negatively—as in terms that are unnecessarily complex—the truth is that all fields need this kind of specialized vocabulary in order to do their work. Keeping track of the latest terms and buzz words can make you part of the ongoing dialogue in your profession, and so keep you up to date with the work of the field. And, since trade journals are often written in styles that are not quite as complex as academic journals, reading about the work being done in other related professions can also help you to think more about your own work and your own lives. More on that will appear in the sections below on civic communities and "interdisciplinarity."

This book contains many pieces of writing that were originally published in trade journals and on Web sites that are devoted to members of particular professional communities. By reading these works, you will learn how various professional disciplines converse through their publications. In those publications, they debate the validity of the knowledge that forms the basis for their work, offer new knowledge to others in the field, and provide both theories and practices that can keep one current in the field. As you read, then, you will be able to think not only about the work being done in particular disciplines, but how that work might affect your own studies, your own work, and your own future goals as a professional. And for those of you who are somewhat undecided about your future work, these readings can give you a taste of the kinds of things that professionals in this disciplinary community spend their time studying and doing, giving you a chance to consider what fields most interest you and fit your own talents and skills.

Disciplines and Civic Communities

There are many reasons why a college education can benefit you. It can make you a better reader and writer. It can help you to develop critical thinking skills. It can provide you with a base of knowledge that will be useful to you in your future work as a professional. And it can help you to interact as a contributing member of your fields of study and work. But a college education serves other purposes as well, among which becoming a better citizen is one of the most important.

What does it mean to be a "good" citizen, and why does disciplinary and interdisciplinary reading and writing contribute to that goal? There are many definitions and many reasons why the kinds of learning you can do by reading the selections in this book can help serve each of them—and how they can make you part of various civic communities that are also based in "disciplined" thinking and practices. Here are some thoughts on why being a good citizen can also be based in your ability to function within and across disciplines:

- *A good citizen is informed.* Staying informed on any given topic is no easy task, especially in our 21st-century world. Despite the fact that we have never had access to such a wide range of information—much of it is accessible in seconds through the Internet—staying up on a topic can be quite difficult. In fact, the glut of specialized information available to 21st-century citizens can be overwhelming, and the growing specialization of fields can frustrate even citizens who *want* to stay informed. But this process of staying informed can be much easier once you learn the techniques of reading in various disciplines. Once you have the capacity—and the confidence—to read documents that are outside your own main field of study, you can do a much better job of staying informed in the important issues of the day. For example, as I write this, the country is facing serious economic turmoil. For many Americans, the underlying financial processes that led to the current problems, and the potential solutions that are being proposed to solve them, seem mysterious and beyond them. But a good, interdisciplinary reader, by using techniques learned by reading across disciplines, can quickly engage in the ongoing dialogue, learn the key concepts and terms, and so contribute to the decision-making process—or at least make good decisions at the ballot box.

- *A good citizen knows how to communicate with other citizens.* There is perhaps no more important facet of a healthy society than the ability of its citizens to talk, discuss, and argue (in the productive sense of that word). But healthy argument is not possible unless the people involved share a knowledge of what makes an argument within a particular discipline valid, and others less valid. It is also crucial that citizens be informed enough about the arguments being made in particular fields to be able to speak that language—to be capable of understanding and using the key terms and concepts of that discipline. For example, the country is embroiled in discussions about global warming. In order to find our position in this debate, and to act (and vote) accordingly, a good citizen will learn enough about the science informing this debate to be able to converse with others on the topic, not based upon "liberal" or "conservative" allegiances, but upon a deeper knowledge of the problem and the preponderance of evidence on the topic. One of the reasons why arguments like this become "polemical"—divided rather than promoting serious discussion—is because the sides involved are not speaking with one another with a common body of knowledge and a common language within which to discuss the topic. If you learn to use the tools that this book offers to read analytically, you will be able to apply them to learning how to communicate with others in intelligent, productive ways.
- *Good citizens contribute their own knowledge and work to the greater good.* Though you are likely in college to advance toward a profession—as you should—it is also important to remember that the work you do in your profession contributes to the common good of our culture. Educated individuals are more than "workers" or "employees"; they are, instead, thinking individuals who can use their specialized knowledge and expertise to help both their professional community, and the larger community, function more effectively and more efficiently. As such, thinking about not only the processes you follow as a professional, but their implications in terms of the ethics, the advancement of science, the development

of stronger economic structures for the business world, and so on, are crucial to the strength of our democratic culture. By continuing to learn about the work of your field—and learning to use writing to make your own contributions to that field public—you are able to affect change that will make both local and national communities function better.

- *Good citizens offer their expertise to ongoing deliberations about how to improve our society.* In a large, diverse, and diffuse culture such as ours, writing is an especially crucial mode of democracy. Though we don't have the opportunity to sit in a "town hall" with the larger segments of our culture, we do have unprecedented opportunities to "deliberate"—to engage in considered and thoughtful discussions about future courses of action—with our fellow citizens. Blogs, wikis, Web sites, citizen journalism—as well as more traditional publication venues—allow you to do your civic duty in ways that go beyond voting and volunteering. Truly active citizens "give back" to the culture more than their time; they give back their learning and expertise. As you learn about the various disciplinary debates, you are gaining the expertise to involve yourself in those debates as active members, and so influence the course of the culture in some small, but significant way. That is the heart of democracy.

As you will notice as you read the selections in this book, if you are paying attention to the concept of the "civic community," many were written and published not only to advance the work of the individual or the specific field, but also the larger public good. And even those that were not written for that specific purpose have implications for our shared work as citizens. For example, though theories of race might in some ways be theoretical discussion for geneticists or sociologists, how we understand the concept of race will clearly change the nature of our culture. Though philosophical discussions about how the concept of war has changed in recent times might seem purely "academic," deliberating on the nature of war and how "war" in our time differs from what it meant to our parents and grandparents can certainly help us to make good decisions about our leaders—and let them know why we do, or do not, support their policies. And keeping up with the science surrounding genetic testing and neuroimaging can help us to consider how much we want others to know about our genetic and mental predispositions. In all these ways, being an *informed* citizen is being a *good* citizen; and being an informed citizen means knowing how to read and write in the specialized languages of varied disciplines. Otherwise, we are simply delegating our responsibility to others.

Interdisciplinarity and Liberal Education: Reading and Writing Across Disciplines

As should already be apparent, there are a number of important reasons for you to nurture your expertise not only in the content of your own field of study, but in the methods and forms of communication used in that field. It should also be apparent that reading more widely is also crucial for your participation in all of the communities to which you belong—your academic field of study, your current or future profession, and your role as an active and productive citizen. In many ways, "interdisciplinary" reading is at the heart of the liberal arts education that is provided by colleges.

Once again, let's start with some definitions. A "liberal" education has nothing to do with political labels: those who consider themselves "conservatives," "liberals," "moderates," and so forth all value what is called "liberal" education. A liberal education is one that is not limited to training you for a specific type of work (though that is part of it), but an education that widens your understanding (and your capacity to understand) fields of knowledge beyond the work you will eventually do. That wider education can make you more innovative and productive participants in those fields. That is, liberal education is about making you a reflective, thoughtful participant in areas of knowledge and practices of your profession, and the decisions of our civic community. Why is "interdisciplinarity" so crucial toward those ends? If you've been reading carefully, you can likely see that what has been discussed in each section above answers that question. So let's summarize and synthesize those ideas:

- As students entering academic communities, interdisciplinary practices can enrich your understanding of your own major field of study, and help you to invent new ideas for your writing.
- As future professionals, interdisciplinary knowledge can help you to apply the research of various fields to your own work, and to your own thinking and writing about that work. For example, a good businessperson will know how to use the methods of data

collection of the social sciences; a good scientist will understand the ethical implications of her work; a good psychologist will understand how political processes influence individual behaviors; and a good engineer will understand how their discoveries might translate into the current marketplace.

- As citizens, interdisciplinary knowledge can keep you from handing off responsibilities to the government and to "experts," and instead help you to be an activist—a citizen who is actively involved in processes through which public policies are made.

All of this, of course, is also about the ability to communicate with others. And the ability to communicate is about rhetoric. Here too, we need to understand our terms. Though *rhetoric* has gotten somewhat of a bad name in current uses—as a type of empty form of speech—it has long been a pillar of the liberal arts. Defined roughly as the "art of persuasion," rhetoric is about refining our communicative abilities in ways that can actualize our knowledge—that is, turn our knowledge into action. And as part of a larger community, the actions we want to create are not just our own; we want to persuade others to join us in what we take to be positive and worthwhile endeavors. Doing so starts with being informed. Rhetors, the ancient traditions told us, need to know about a great many topics, and also need the communicative abilities to discuss those topics with skill. As such, rhetoric is itself a discipline, a discipline with its own set of principles based in the methods for formulating an effective speech or piece of writing.

One key set of principles for developing an effective piece of communication is known as the five canons of rhetoric. These five sets of activities are methodologies for developing one's ability to speak or write intelligently on a topic. The five canons are:

1. invention: gathering knowledge on a topic;
2. arrangement: developing the knowledge on a topic into a productive pattern—organizing ideas;
3. style: finding the words and phrasings to express that knowledge of a topic;
4. memory: finding language devices to structure knowledge into key "talking points" or phrasings that can be used in a variety of occasions; and
5. delivery: presenting the argument itself in effective and audience-sensitive ways.

If you look carefully at those five canons, you will recognize the ways that interdisciplinary reading and writing can serve each of those important methodologies for constructing a spoken or written argument.

- *Invention* requires you to read widely, gaining a strong working knowledge of the area and its key principles.
- *Arrangement* requires you to understand the principles of organization that are accepted within various disciplines, across disciplines, and for the presentation of your arguments both in academic and public genres. Reading various types of documents with an eye to how arguments are arranged in that discipline is one of the best ways to develop your own organizational repertoire.
- *Style* requires you to learn not only the "basics" of good writing—sentence and paragraph structures, grammatical conventions, and so on—but the specialized forms of writing that are preferred in particular disciplines and genres. You can learn both by paying attention to not only what the authors you read say, but the language styles they use in saying it.
- *Memory*, while primarily meant for oral occasions, requires you to have facility with particular types of phrasings that are effective on particular occasions and for particular disciplines. You can learn this decorum by internalizing the key phrasings used in particular disciplines and genres.
- *Delivery* techniques, though different for oral and written occasions, are always about the "voice" or persona we are projecting. For spoken pieces, effective delivery requires using intonation and voice that will be useful for the occasion; for writing, similarly, it is about finding the structure, voice, and visual look of a document likely to be credible for its purposes. Written pieces have a "voice" and tone as much as oral pieces, and by analyzing the voice of pieces within particular disciplinary and public communities, you will better understand how to train your own voice to be effective in those communities.

In sum, a liberal education is built around your ability to read and write within many communities. If you learn methods for analyzing and employing the rhetorical mechanisms of these various communities through the reading you do across disciplines in this book, you will carry with you the ability to use those methods to engage with each intellectual, professional, and civic community you encounter. That is a liberal arts education.

Defining Disciplinary Communities: Four Fields of Knowledge-Making

Introduction: Divisions and Connections Among Disciplinary Communities

Let's be honest. Anytime we categorize things as complex as fields of knowledge, the divisions we create are necessarily somewhat artificial. After all, there are so many ways to categorize something that any method of division is bound to be less than perfect. For example, how would you categorize a college? Is it an institution of higher learning? Is it a business? A social setting? A community? A place for advancement of the arts and sciences? Career training? A home for academic research? The answer: all of the above. And depending upon how we characterize it, we'll have quite different understandings about its work and its purposes. That's why *how* we approach a topic is so crucial. If we ask whether a college is a successful business, we are asking a quite different question than if it is a successful institution of higher learning or a place for career training—though the answers can certainly be related.

Likewise, when we divide up fields of study, we are settling upon different ways to view different (and sometimes similar) topics. So, though the attempt to categorize fields of study is just one way of seeing academies and professions, these divisions serve some important purposes. This is especially true if we consider not only what *separates* them into communities of like-minded individuals, but the *connections* among the disciplines that demonstrate how one community draws upon and works with the others.

The four divisions discussed below can thus help you to consider how knowledge is constructed in these fields of endeavor: the various topics, the methods that are used to collect evidence, the values that define what kinds of evidence are considered most reliable, and the communication methods that are used in each of these four general areas of knowledge-making. They can also help you to see how, why, and when these four areas interact with one another. Though the brief discussions below clearly cannot do justice to these wide fields, they can help you to analyze these tendencies of the writers whose work appears in the readings that follow. Rather than see the readings that follow as falling into one category or another, you might instead use your understanding of these areas of knowledge to help analyze those tendencies, in varied combinations, in those readings.

The Natural Sciences

Let's begin with a key concept for those who profess the "natural" sciences as well as those who work in other fields: empirical evidence. Empirical evidence is data that derives from experimentation and observation. It is the key methodological element that underlies the sciences generally: that we should approach each question we ask objectively—without prior dispositions or belief systems—and base our discussion and conclusion upon what we observe, not what we "believe."

The natural sciences employ empirical methods to their study of natural phenomena, from chemical and physical reactions to the functioning of living organisms. Of course, those topics might be—and have been—examined in other ways as well. Religions, for example, explain natural phenomena in ways that are very different from the explanations offered by scientists. And philosophers or creative writers might ask us to consider "evidence" that goes beyond what we can observe. But to a natural scientist, at least when she is acting as a scientist within the scientific community, science is about disciplining oneself to draw conclusions based only in that which is observable and repeatable. It deals with the rule, not the exception.

As such, as you read the selections in this book, you might consider how the discussions of natural phenomena—genetics, racial categorization, human aggressiveness, and energy sources, for example—are based in evidence gathered using empirical methods. You can also think about how a writer's reliance upon empirical methods is used in order to build arguments.

The Humanities

The humanities encompass a wide range of disciplines and areas of endeavor—so wide that it is often difficult to define where the boundaries of these fields of study lie. In fact, the natural sciences are, in some ways, also humanities, since as "pure" sciences, they are about the business of studying the natural world (including the functioning of human organisms) in ways that are largely "disinterested"—that is, largely for the purpose of seeking the "truth," not for the direct purpose of how that knowledge can be put to use. Since just about all human topics are potential areas of study for those involved in the humanities, it is perhaps more fruitful to consider the perspective on those topics and the types of inquiry that practitioners use than to enumerate the fields that are included in it. Some fields of study traditionally included in the humanities are laid out by the National Endowment for the Humanities.

WHAT ARE THE HUMANITIES?

National Endowment for the Humanities

According to the 1965 National Foundation on the Arts and the Humanities Act, "The term 'humanities' includes, but is not limited to, the study of the following: language, both modern and classical; linguistics; literature; history; jurisprudence; philosophy; archaeology; comparative religion; ethics; the history, criticism and theory of the arts; those aspects of social sciences which have humanistic content and employ humanistic methods; and the study and application of the humanities to the human environment with particular attention to reflecting our diverse heritage, traditions, and history and to the relevance of the humanities to the current conditions of national life."

As you can tell from this definition, the lines between disciplines are never hard and fast. Thus "aspects of the social sciences which have humanistic content" are included here, as are areas of study often assigned to history or anthropology. The key is the "humanistic" content and methods. Those in the disciplinary community known as the humanities begin from the assumption that an understanding of human nature is good in and of itself, and is crucial to living a good life; as Socrates put it in Plato's *Apology*, "the unexamined life is not worth living." In sum, the humanities develop knowledge meant to encourage critical thinking about what it is unique about the human experience. These fields take on fundamental questions that, unlike the empirical sciences, are often difficult to address exclusively through observation.

The Social Sciences

One way to understand the social sciences is to see them as the intersection of the natural sciences and the humanities. Like the natural sciences, the social sciences generally have an investment in empirical knowledge—in observable, and often quantifiable data. In this way, the social sciences, which study the behavior of human beings as they function individually and in groups, treat humans as part of the natural world.

But the study of human beings is quite a bit thornier than the study of chemical, physical, or biological processes. Because of the many variables in human behavior, even the empirical evidence collected in social sciences research is much more open to interpretation than that in the "hard" or natural sciences. This is particularly true of strands of the social sciences such as political science, history, and sociology. Also usually included in the social sciences are psychology, anthropology, geography, communications, education, and criminal justice, among others fields.

Given the variables associated with human behavior, one of the keys to the methodology of some branches of the social sciences is in controlling enough of the variables to garner information that is as reliable as possible. For example, if one wanted to study the relationship of gender to attitudes about race, it would not be enough to survey men and women and then to draw conclusions about which are most likely to be racist; there are many other variables—class, educational level, life experience, age, parental influence, geographical location, and so forth that could also influence attitudes toward race. In order to create a study with some validity and reliability, a researcher would need to do his best to control for as many of those variables as possible so as to focus upon a single one, such as gender. Social scientists try to gauge statistical likelihoods that the correlation (or statistical relationship) between two or more variables is significant. This type of survey information is thus deeply dependent upon statistically accurate studies; it is also dependent upon writing survey questions that are not leading or biased. As such, articles in the social sciences usually include in-depth methodology sections that demonstrate the validity of their methods, samples of the survey instrument used, and in some cases, self-critique of the method and results. Likewise, future studies of similar issues will often begin with a statement about why the methodology used by the present study in some way corrects the methods used in previous, possibly flawed, studies.

Even beyond statistical analyses, the social sciences do their best to control for other forms of bias. Historical analyses attempt to avoid imposing present-day concepts and norms upon past civilizations. Anthropological studies attempt to avoid imposing the ideas of one culture upon another. And studies of criminal behavior attempt to avoid rash judgments about particular groups' criminal activities without controlling for other variables. In the field of education, the teaching methods that are studied and suggested are placed within cultural contexts, variables in the student population, and available technologies and other resources. In all cases, the attempt at scientific objectivity in the study of human behavior is the key challenge in the social sciences. As you read the pieces that use these methods, you should note the ways that they attempt to control for these variables as fully as they can.

The Applied Sciences

Like the social sciences, the "applied sciences" draw heavily upon the work of other disciplines. The applied sciences, however, focus upon the ways that the knowledge garnered from their own work and that of other disciplines *can be put to good use.* Look at it this way: What do engineering, nursing, business, education, and graphic arts all have in common? They, and many other applied sciences, all focus upon what can be done with theory-based knowledge; in that way, they often bridge the gap between academic communities and professions.

Of course, as noted at the beginning of this section, the four categories of knowledge-making that are discussed in this section, and which help to organize the chapters of this book, are rather porous. Each area has practical or applied elements to it. However, the difference between the fields devoted to *collecting* knowledge through their preferred methodologies, and those devoted to *making use of* that knowledge is still a distinction as we read and write in these fields. For example, whereas an academic paper in the natural sciences might end with a discussion of the methodology and results of a study, it is unlikely to conclude definitive statements about how the results might be used in business or in nursing. The applied sciences, however, work to demonstrate the practical value of that knowledge: how new technologies can increase profits; how sociological studies can improve nursing care; or how scientific discoveries can help us to build a better, more efficient automobile.

The hallmark of the writing that falls into the applied sciences is its translation of theoretical knowledge into action—and its evaluation of the success of those actions. Thus, a business plan might draw upon statistical information garnered from social sciences polling data to recommend an emerging market. New discoveries in physics might be translated into more efficient vehicles or better communications systems. The discovery of a new chemical process might lead engineers to build a machine that can better extract the raw materials for that process. And the discovery of information about the genetics of race might lead to differing classroom methods for teachers or prescription drug development—and marketing—for pharmaceutical houses. As you read the pieces in this book that take on those and other similar topics, you should pay attention to the ways that a focus upon the application of knowledge changes the purpose, organization, genre, and style of delivery. And, based upon your analyses of those pieces, you should consider how your own writing might be adapted depending upon whether you are writing for an academic, professional, or public audience.

In the end, that is the main purpose of the analytical reading that you will do in this book: to develop strategies for your own writing that are adapted to the specific discipline, occasion, genre, and audience for whom you are writing. If you read carefully, and pay attention to the ways that each author constructs arguments based upon those factors, you will become a more effective writer across the various occasions within which you will be asked to write in college and beyond.

CHAPTER 1

Literacy Across Disciplines

What Does It Mean to Be "Literate" in the 21st Century?

Not long ago, being a literate individual had a very simple definition: the ability to read and write. Those two skills still remain predictors of personal and public success, identifying those who are especially equipped to succeed personally and to be contributing members of the culture.

But in our more complex culture, new literacies—and a renewed interest in traditional ones—have emerged, gaining a great deal of attention across all disciplinary fields. The word *literacy* has been expanded to include concepts such as information literacy, civic literacy, historical literacy, computer literacy, quantitative literacy, religious literacy, scientific literacy, and so on. Clearly, literacy no longer refers only to linguistic abilities, but to any ability that is crucial for successfully negotiating a field or a set of tasks. As such, each field of study has attempted to define the particular abilities that are necessary for both professionals and nonprofessionals to understand and participate in that area of knowledge. After all, though professionals need an in-depth understanding of a field's assumptions, topics, evidence bases, and methods, all citizens need a working knowledge of these areas of study to engage in public decision-making—from voting intelligently to engaging in various types of duties that come with citizenship. The readings in this chapter thus form an important introduction to issues in the rest of the book, giving you a tour of the literacies associated with various disciplines. Though there are a great many literacies that could have been included here, the ones that are discussed in this chapter are meant to form strong connections with the readings throughout this book. They also invite you, as a researcher and writer, to respond to those views with your own—either by further developing the ideas of others, or by adding more items to the list of literacies necessary to be a productive individual in the 21st century.

The idea that the literacy needs of students are not being met is nothing new, really. In 1975, *Time* Magazine published a now-famous story entitled "Why Johnny Can't Write," in which the author claimed that "the U.S. educational system is spawning a generation of semiliterates." This piece set forth a wave of claims that the country was facing crisis, claims that have arisen again and again since. But what are the defining factors of literacy today? In 2008, the National Council of Teachers of English issued a statement on 21st century literacies as a "clarion call for changes underway today in literacy education," arguing that changes in the way we communicate "makes it clear that further evolution of curriculum, assessment, and teaching practices itself is necessary." As you read this piece, you might consider what literacies you, as a student in this new decade, need in order to function as a student, a citizen, and eventually, a professional.

We also live in what has been dubbed an "information age"—a time period in which the ability to manage and use the glut of information now available to us via electronic communication has become especially crucial. For this reason, another disciplinary group—professionals in library science—have also issued a series of statements on "information literacy." The statement on "Information Literacy Standards for Student Learning" draws upon the work of several organizations with a stake in the dissemination and use of information, laying out the literacies that they find to be crucial to functioning in our 21st century world. But "information" is not contained only in words, as several of the pieces in this chapter suggest. Barbara Rockenbach and Carole Ann Fabian argue that we have entered an "age of participation"—a Web 2.0 environment in which the Internet has become two-way and which allows us to participate in, rather than merely seek, information. In such a world, "users" of the Web are at the same time its creators. As we compose for blogs, social networking sites such as MySpace and Facebook, and information sharing sites such as Wikipedia, visual as well as verbal communication becomes crucial. Elizabeth Daly extends this line of thinking in "Expanding the Concept of Literacy," suggesting that the word *language* can no longer be limited to words, but now must also encompass multimedia texts. She concludes that "those who are truly literate in the twenty-first century will be those who both read and write the multimedia language of the screen."

Though these calls for new communication-based literacies are at the center of this debate, other disciplines have also participated in this national dialogue on literacy. In "America 101," Eric Lane calls for renewed attention to civic literacy"—the knowledge of our governmental processes and the ability to apply that knowledge to current debates and events. Richard L. Scheaffer brings the sciences into the debate, noting that "just as the information age is making the world more quantitative . . . the ability of people to deal with numerical issues of practical consequence is shrinking." He argues that since the ability to understand and analyze data is so crucial to the scientific method, students and citizens need this literacy to function well in our culture. Robert Orrill's "Humanism and Quantitative Literacy" takes the argument for quantitative literacy into the interdisciplinary realm, arguing that the "fractured condition of the American educational enterprise" has separated the study of the humanities from the sciences in ways that are detrimental to all.

As you read the many disciplinary and interdisciplinary pieces in this book, you might consider the ways in which the various fields interact with one another. Doing so will help you see why thinking both within and *across* disciplines is so important for full literacy as a student, a professional, and a citizen. The readings throughout this book will allow you to do just that.

NATIONAL COUNCIL
OF TEACHERS OF ENGLISH

21st Century Literacies: Curriculum and Assessment Framework

The National Council of Teachers of English (NCTE) states its mission as follows: "The Council promotes the development of literacy, the use of language to construct personal and public worlds and to achieve full participation in society, through the learning and teaching of English and the related arts and sciences of language." As such, this group of professionals treats its work as providing literacy education in both disciplinary and civic terms. It sees its area of expertise to be in the "learning and teaching of English and related arts and sciences of language" while making it clear that the purpose of this work is to help citizens achieve "full participation" in our culture.

As such, the framework for 21st-century literacy that follows describes the specific proficiencies that scholars in this discipline suggest are necessary to create engaged, literate individuals. As you read this set of educational outcomes, you might compare them to the definition of literacy that is forwarded in by others in this chapter as well as to your own educational experiences in English classes. Which of these outcomes do you think are most crucial for a literate individual? Which seem to have been most important in your own educational experience?

Adopted by the NCTE Executive Committee, November 19, 2008

Context for NCTE's 21st Century Literacies Framework

In the 1990s, the National Council of Teachers of English and the International Reading Association established national standards for English language arts learners that anticipated the more sophisticated literacy skills and abilities required for full participation in a global, 21st century community. The selected standards, listed in the appendix, served as a clarion call for changes underway today in literacy education.

Today, the NCTE definition of 21st century literacies makes it clear that further evolution of curriculum, assessment, and teaching practice itself is necessary.

> Literacy has always been a collection of cultural and communicative practices shared among members of particular groups. As society and technology change, so does literacy. Because technology has increased the intensity and complexity of literate environments, the twenty-first century demands that a literate person possess a wide range of abilities and competencies, many literacies. These literacies—from reading online newspapers to participating in virtual classrooms—

are multiple, dynamic, and malleable. As in the past, they are inextricably linked with particular histories, life possibilities, and social trajectories of individuals and groups. Twenty-first century readers and writers need to

- Develop proficiency with the tools of technology
- Build relationships with others to pose and solve problems collaboratively and cross-culturally
- Design and share information for global communities to meet a variety of purposes
- Manage, analyze, and synthesize multiple streams of simultaneous information
- Create, critique, analyze, and evaluate multimedia texts
- Attend to the ethical responsibilities required by these complex environments

Elements of the Framework

Applied to students of English language arts, the literacy demands of the 21st century have implications for how teachers plan, support, and assess student learning. Teachers benefit from reflecting on questions associated with 21st century literacy demands.

Develop proficiency with the tools of technology

Students in the 21st century should have experience with and develop skills around technological tools used in the classroom and the world around them. Through this they will learn about technology and learn through technology. In addition, they must be able to select the most appropriate tools to address particular needs.

- Do students use technology as a tool for communication, research, and creation of new works?
- Do students evaluate and use digital tools and resources that match the work they are doing?
- Do students find relevant and reliable sources that meet their needs?
- Do students take risks and try new things with tools available to them?
- Do students, independently and collaboratively, solve problems as they arise in their work?
- Do students use a variety of tools correctly and efficiently?

Build relationships with others to pose and solve problems collaboratively and cross-culturally

Students in the 21st century need interpersonal skills in order to work collaboratively in both face-to-face and virtual environments to use and develop problem-solving skills. When learning experiences are grounded in well-informed teaching practices, the use of technology allows a wider range of voices to be heard, exposing students to opinions and norms outside of their own.

- Do students work in a group in ways that allow them to create new knowledge or to solve problems that can't be created or solved individually?
- Do students work in groups to create new sources that can't be created or solved by individuals?
- Do students work in groups of members with diverse perspectives and areas of expertise?
- Do students build on one another's thinking to gain new understanding?
- Do students learn to share disagreements and new ways of thinking in ways that positively impact the work?
- Do students gain new understandings by being part of a group or team?

Design and share information for global communities that have a variety of purposes

Students in the 21st century must be aware of the global nature of our world and be able to select, organize, and design information to be shared, understood, and distributed beyond their classrooms.

- Do students use inquiry to ask questions and solve problems?
- Do students critically analyze a variety of information from a variety of sources?
- Do students take responsibility for communicating their ideas in a variety of ways?
- Do students choose tools to share information that match their need and audience?
- Do students share and publish their work in a variety of ways?
- Do students solve real problems and share results with real audiences?
- Do students publish in ways that meet the needs of a particular, authentic audience?

Manage, analyze, and synthesize multiple streams of simultaneously presented information

Students in the 21st century must be able to take information from multiple places and in a variety of different formats, determine its reliability, and create new knowledge from that information.

- Do students create new ideas using knowledge gained?
- Do students locate information from a variety of sources?
- Do students analyze the credibility of information and its appropriateness in meeting their needs?
- Do students synthesize information from a variety of sources?
- Do students manage new information to help them solve problems?
- Do students use information to make decisions as informed citizens?

Create, critique, analyze, and evaluate multimedia texts

Students in the 21st century must be critical consumers and creators of multimedia texts.

- Do students use tools to create new thinking or to communicate original perspectives?
- Do students communicate information and ideas in a variety of forms?
- Do students communicate information and ideas to different audiences?
- Do students articulate thoughts and ideas so that others can understand and act on them?
- Do students analyze and evaluate the multimedia sources that they use?
- Do students evaluate multimedia sources for the effects of visuals, sounds, hyperlinks, and other features on the text's meaning or emotional impact?
- Do students evaluate their own multimedia works?

Attend to the ethical responsibilities required by complex environments

Students in the 21st century must understand and adhere to legal and ethical practices as they use resources and create information.

- Do students share information in ways that consider all sources?
- Do students practice the safe and legal use of technology?
- Do students create products that are both informative and ethical?

Implications of the Framework for Assessments

Assessments need to take into consideration both traditional components and elements that may be different for 21st century student work.

Traditional elements of assessment of 21st century student learning

The traditional elements for assessing 21st century student work include relevance and reliability of information used in the work; significance of new information or understandings communicated throughout the process and in the final product; effectiveness of the work in achieving its purpose; impact of the work on the audience; creativity or aesthetics demonstrated in the final product; creativity, initiative, and effectiveness demonstrated in solving problems; efficiency and effectiveness of the student's process; and the student's legal and ethical process and behavior.

Newer elements of assessment of 21st century student learning

Assessment of 21st century products of learning may be different because of technological tools. Some elements to consider include:

- extent of students' access to 21st century tools both in and out of school
- range and depth of information readily accessible to students
- facility of students with technology tools
- extent to which tools can make artists, musicians, and designers of students not traditionally considered talented in those fields
- extent to which images and sound may amplify text
- extent to which student products can emulate those of professionals
- extent to which students receive feedback from experts in the field
- potential interaction with and impact on a global audience

- students' selection of tools or media that most effectively communicate the intention of the product
- students' level of ethical and legal practice as they remix products
- level of ethics and safety exhibited in students' online behavior

Assessment practices of 21st century student learning may need flexibility and responsiveness to situations such as:

- students' greater proficiency with tools or formats than the teacher, which may generate outcomes not anticipated in an assessment rubric
- technology glitches beyond students' control that negatively impact the quality of the final products
- scope of collaboration, in the classroom and globally, leading to a greater need for processes that assess progress and achievement of individuals and groups
- support and celebration of the increasing diversity in students' talents, imagination, perspectives, cultures, and lived experiences
- recognition that the processes of learning and doing are as important as the quality of the final product
- students' self-evaluation and reflection on process and product integrated into the learning process and contributing to students' continued growth
- ability of students, parents, and teachers to examine growth over time in authentic ways

Appendix: Selected NCTE/IRA Standards for English Language Arts Pertaining to 21st Century Literacies

1. Students read a wide range of print and non-print texts to build an understanding of texts, of themselves, and of the cultures of the United States and the world; to acquire new information; to respond to the needs and demands of society and the workplace; and for personal fulfillment. Among these texts are fiction and nonfiction, classic and contemporary works.
2. Students read a wide range of literature from many periods in many genres to build an understanding of the many dimensions (e.g., philosophical, ethical, aesthetic) of human experience.

3. Students apply a wide range of strategies to comprehend, interpret, evaluate, and appreciate texts. They draw on their prior experience, their interactions with other readers and writers, their knowledge of word meaning and of other texts, their word identification strategies, and their understanding of textual features (e.g., sound-letter correspondence, sentence structure, context, graphics).
4. Students apply knowledge of language structure, language conventions (e.g., spelling and punctuation), media techniques, figurative language, and genre to create, critique, and discuss print and nonprint texts.
5. Students conduct research on issues and interests by generating ideas and questions, and by posing problems. They gather, evaluate, and synthesize data from a variety of sources (e.g., print and non-print texts, artifacts, people) to communicate their discoveries in ways that suit their purpose and audience.
6. Students use a variety of technological and information resources (e.g., libraries, databases, computer networks, video) to gather and synthesize information and to create and communicate knowledge.
7. Students whose first language is not English make use of their first language to develop competency in the English language arts and to develop understanding of content across the curriculum.
8. Students use spoken, written, and visual language to accomplish their own purposes (e.g., for learning, enjoyment, persuasion, and the exchange of information).

Reading Analytically

1. The National Council of Teachers of English is explicitly trying to redefine the concept of literacy in this statement. After reading this document, write a brief definition of literacy as it is stated here, and compare that with more traditional definitions of literacy (the ability to read and write).
2. NCTE's new set of learning outcomes is responding to changing forms of communication used by students. Make a list of the differences in communications methods for your generation, and then evaluate which you feel are most important—and which least—to your own education and to the goals of a 21st century English class.
3. While this statement responds to new types of literacy that have become important in the 21st century, some have argued that such shifts have taken too much attention away from traditional

literacies such as the ability to write in standard English. Do you think that this statement neglects traditional roles of English teachers? Why or why not?

Reading Across Disciplinary Communities

1. Though this statement is directed to language arts teachers, it has a great many implications for teaching and learning in other fields of study as well—after all, writing and reading are at the heart of all disciplines. What specific learning outcomes noted in this piece might serve the learning goals of other disciplines? Which ones seem most important for your own field of study?
2. The mission of the NCTE suggests that this discipline is concerned with the "arts and sciences of language." In what ways is language an art? In what ways a science? To discuss this, draw upon both your own educational experiences and the specific learning outcomes that are listed in this NCTE curriculum framework.

THE AMERICAN ASSOCIATION OF SCHOOL LIBRARIANS AND THE AMERICAN LIBRARY ASSOCIATION

AASL Standards for the 21st-Century Learner

In our technology-saturated culture, a literate individual must know how to access, evaluate, and incorporate the wide range of information that is now readily available to us all. Though information is more readily available to us than ever before, knowing how to efficiently and effectively manage this wealth of resources can be quite difficult. These conditions have also deeply affected the work of a variety of disciplines involved with information management and retrieval. This statement of standards for information literacy represents the collaborative work of two such disciplinary communities, and is available from the American Library Association website (www.ala.org). Follow the link for its Professional Resources *page, and then the link for* Guidelines and Standards *and then* Other Standards *to find the* AASL Standards for the 21st-century Learner. *Just doing a Web search for that title will also turn up the document.*

The first of these disciplinary organizations, the American Association of School Librarians, states its mission as follows:

AASL works to ensure that all members of the school library media field collaborate to:

- *provide leadership in the total education program*
- *participate as active partners in the teaching/learning process*
- *connect learners with ideas and information, and*
- *prepare students for lifelong learning, informed decision-making, a love of reading, and the use of information technologies.*

The American Library Association, which has taken the lead in the development of information literacy education, and upon whose work this set of standards is based, sees its mission as providing "leadership for the development, promotion and improvement of library and information services and the profession of librarianship in order to enhance learning and ensure access to information for all."

As you consider this set of standards on information literacy, you might consider how the mission of each of these related, but separate, communities is reflected in the statement. In what ways has the work of librarians changed in an information age? Why is an organization devoted to technology now allied with librarians? In what ways do each of these organizations depict their work as serving the greater good of our civic community? You also might assess the ways in which changes in how we access information also changes our understanding of literacy, and how reading and writing are affected by the onset of technological changes and an information age.

Reading Analytically

1. Each of these standards attempts to define what a student who is "information literate" should be able to do. Choose one of the standards that you find to be particularly important, and describe the ways that this literacy might be useful for specific parts of your own research and writing.
2. Though we often think literacy to be a personal, individual attribute, some of the standards listed here refer specifically to group or collaborative activities. In what ways is research a personal activity? In what ways is it collaborative? Use specific examples to illustrate the principles of collaboration that are noted in this position statement.
3. Based upon this statement, outline a research process that you believe adheres to the principles reflected there. That is, if you

wanted to demonstrate that you are indeed information literate, what specific set of steps would you need to follow in order to complete a research project that demonstrates that set of competencies?

Reading Across Disciplinary Communities

1. Clearly, this set of information literacy standards is meant to apply to research in all disciplines. However, it is also itself a set of statements about the work of this particular set of disciplines—librarians, media experts, and experts in technology who are involved in the 21st century library. In what ways does this statement define the work of those disciplines? Illustrate, through specific claims being made here about information literacy, how this document helps to define the disciplinary communities involved, and their most important goals.
2. This statement is necessarily general, showing its applicability to the work of all disciplines. As such, these standards also need to be adapted to specific disciplines. Choose one of the standards that you find to be particularly important to your own field of study, and demonstrate how this set of skills serves the needs of students in that field.

BARBARA ROCKENBACH AND CAROLE ANN FABIAN

Visual Literacy in the Age of Participation

This piece begins by describing the conditions that suggest that we need to expand our understanding of both literacy and the ways that we now interact with information. The authors contend that in this "age of participation" or "Web 2.0" world, we no longer merely seek to consume information from electronic sources; we now contribute to those sources regularly and actively. Think of it this way: When we pick up a book or read from a Web site, we are ingesting what we find there. But when we write for a blog, change an entry in a wiki, or post thoughts to a social networking site like Facebook or Twitter, we are participating in creating the ideas that are out there. Further, we no longer merely interact in words, but have the capacity to converse in a variety of visual forms of communication. Since the world has changed in these ways, these authors argue, we need new literacies to work within it.

The authors of this piece, the director of Undergraduate and Library Research at Yale University and the director of Outreach and Communication for ARTstor Digital library, argue that this new set of conditions presents an opportunity for "knowledge workers" (and specifically for those with expertise in visual literacy) to find their way into this newly participatory information environment. As such, it demonstrates the ways that disciplines make their case for the relevance of their work within the larger community.

Every image sheds light on the assumptions of the day. Every image reveals, as well as defines, events. Every image must be read, must be interpreted. This is a perilous act, one that often leads us far away from the safe ground sought by most historians. Yet reading the image, like reading any text, is a way to engage the past and connect it to our lives.[1]

Louis Masur, Historian

Part One—A Landscape for Understanding Visual Literacy

1. The Age of Participation

We like to categorize and name things. Naming helps us to create meaning about ourselves and our role in the world. The naming of our times has followed a rich lineage starting with the Hunter/Gatherer Age, moving to the Agriculture Age, the Industrial Age, and most recently leading us to the Information Age. The Information Age has defined much of what we do in our professions for the last several decades, and most library and information science practice derives from notions of the Information Age. However, we are now faced with a changing world of information and services, one that potentially goes beyond information. Can we still characterize our times as the Information Age? The answer to that question has an influence on both user expectations and our role as information professionals, especially as we examine the skills and competencies the current age requires, among them visual literacy.

There is no shortage of theorists trying to determine the answer to the question of what to name the current era in which we live, floating names such as the Web 2.0 Age,[2] the Conceptual Age,[3] and the Age of Participation.[4] The Information Age, as we know it, began in the mid-twentieth century when the economic base of much of the world shifted from the production of physical goods (Industrial Age) to the production and manipulation of data or information. This shift really took hold in the mid-1980s with the development of the personal computer and blossomed further in the 1990s with widespread development and adoption of the Internet. Just a decade after what many are now calling Web 1.0, a potential new age is upon us.

The Information Age and associated Web 1.0 era is being eclipsed by a new Web 2.0 era. In 2004, Tim O'Reilly coined the buzzword Web 2.0 to describe a trend in the use of Web technology that aims to create communities for information sharing and collaboration. Also emphasized in the Web 2.0 world is creativity on the part of the users, or a desire and ability to contribute as well as consume. This means a world where the flow of information is a two-way rather than a one-way street, where receivers of information are no longer passive consumers but active contributors. These Web 2.0 concepts have led to the development of online communities and social networking Web sites such as Facebook, Flickr, MySpace, and Wikipedia, and more generally, applications such as wikis, blogs, and folksonomies.

Another theorist, Daniel Pink, has written in *Wired Magazine* and a book entitled *A Whole New Mind* about what he calls the Conceptual Age. He argues that as a result of outsourcing white collar or Information Age jobs to Asia, a general abundance of wealth and cheap goods, and the automation of number-crunching activities, we are moving from a left-brain dominant society to a right-brain society. In essence, creativity, emotion, and synthesis are in vogue:

> The Information Age we all prepared for is ending. Rising in its place is what I call the Conceptual Age, an era in which mastery of abilities that we've often overlooked and undervalued marks the fault line between who gets ahead and who falls behind . . . In a world upended by outsourcing, deluged with data, and choked with choices, the abilities that matter most are now closer in spirit to the specialties of the right hemisphere—artistry, empathy, seeing the big picture, and pursuing the transcendent.[5]

Therefore, according to Pink, our former linear world of information is changing. New abilities and new skill sets are perhaps not only valued but necessary in our current age.

A final way of characterizing our age, and one that particularly relates both to our times and the concept of visual literacy, is the Age of Participation. Jonathan Swartz describes the Age of Participation, which incorporates aspects of both the theories of Web 2.0 and the Conceptual Age, as follows:

> The old flow of information has been disrupted and an open and competitive network fuels growing opportunities for everyone—not simply to draw data or shift work around the world, but to *participate,* to create value and independence. If the Information Age was passive, the Participation Age is active.[6]

This focus on active users is essential to an understanding of our age. The existence of active, creative users willing to engage in the process of information creation presents new challenges and opportunities for information professionals. Across functional areas, librarianship is moving away from more controlled, passive, and didactic modes in which, rather than users seeking to be given information, we now have users who wish to be more active participants in the information-seeking process. For example, whereas bibliographic description of library materials was once solely the purview of library cataloging departments, we now see growing instances of library catalog records enhanced by user tagging and other social methods to make the materials more findable and more relevant to today's users. For example, the University of Pennsylvania has built a tool called PennTags to allow users to tag and group URLs, articles, and other information sources by their preferences. Our students now arrive on campus expecting a more dynamic interaction and a more active role in their learning process, requiring an instructional shift that affects faculty as well as librarians. The expectation of a more participatory process forces information professionals to rethink their role in the flow of information and suggests responsibility for nurturing a new range of skills and literacies such as higher-level critical thinking skills, problem-based inquiry, and visual literacy.

2. Visual Literacy Definition and Role in Age of Participation

There are many ways in which visual literacy has been defined in the last several decades. The term itself was first coined in 1968 by John

Debes, an employee of Kodak at the time who characterized visual literacy as follows:

> Visual Literacy refers to a group of vision-competencies a human being can develop by seeing and at the same time having and integrating other sensory experiences. The development of these competencies is fundamental to normal human learning. When developed, they enable a visually literate person to discriminate and interpret the visible actions, objects, symbols, natural or man-made, that he encounters in his environment. Through the creative use of these competencies, he is able to communicate with others. Through the appreciative use of these competencies, he is able to comprehend and enjoy the masterworks of visual communication.[7]

The focus in this definition is not on art or art historical reading of images, but on a set of capabilities that, for those familiar with the ACRL Information Literacy competencies,[8] should look familiar, allowing us to make the connection between visual literacy and the age of participation. Visual literacy has only become a focus of study in the information professions in the last decade. Notions of textual literacy have been with us for much longer and were embedded into the philosophy of libraries from the very beginning. Andrew Carnegie, creator of over 2,500 libraries around the world, states how textual literacy—the ability to literally read and understand complex works—was bound up with his founding principles from the beginning. "Show me the man who speaks English, reads Shakespeare and Bobby Burns and I'll show you a man who has absorbed the American principles. He will most likely read also the Declaration of Independence and Washington's Farewell Address."[9]

This link between libraries and textual literacy was important in the nineteenth and early twentieth centuries. However, literacies change over time as our culture changes or, as Richard Sinatra points out, "A culture's predominant mode of literacy depends on the technology and mass media it embraces."[10] The predominant technologies and mass media of our time are primarily visual. In addition to the visual mediums that have been with us for years (images in magazines, newspapers, on billboards, television and film) we now have the Internet, video games, and digital cameras in everything from our computers to our phones. The proliferation of digital mass media and our individual ability to not only observe but to actively create, use, and share it, is further extended by the emergence of online social networking environments such as Flickr, Yahoo images, YouTube, and Facebook. The library is now in a position of having to respond to these environments that are emerging outside of the academy. The democratization of Web 2.0 technologies suggests opportunities for libraries to think creatively about capturing users' attention. For example, the Library of Congress recently launched a pilot project to expose approximately 3,000 of its most popular images in The Commons on Flickr. Within days 650,000 images were viewed and 420 had been tagged by users; by March 2008 the Library of Congress reported that user-supplied tags helped the Library enhance sixty-eight bibliographic records.[11] In addition to changes in the external image landscape, the academic library is being called upon to provide and support the use of visual materials in unprecedented ways on campus: for example, evolving curricula draw on visual and textual materials across disciplinary boundaries and require the library to provide teaching/learning materials beyond traditional books and journals. The library, not always the site of image management, is now often building collections of images, subscribing to licensed resources of images and other media, and is often the creator and caretaker of institutional repositories of locally produced visual, textual, and media content.

The presence of an audience of users who expect to be active participants in their learning process and of a culture dominated by images suggests a need for renewed emphasis on visual literacy skills or competencies. The moment also presents an opportunity for art librarians expert in the area of visual materials to integrate their strengths in literacy instruction and their domain knowledge of the visual into more active, participatory teaching and learning approaches. One such approach might be the adaptation of the ACRL Information Literacy Standards to the specific competencies required for visual literacy in the arts.

Art librarianship has always been anchored to the visual—a variety of photographic or other-rendered representations of objects and built environments, most often still images but increasingly more time-based media, 3-D visualizations, and complex graphical works. Visuals are the currency of art education and scholarship. We have addressed the presence of images in our profession primarily through art historical techniques such as close analysis and other forms of systematic looking. This has been adequate for the classroom and the field of art and art history, yet our age calls for a different mode of visual analysis that acknowledges the ubiquity and importance of images in society. James Elkins, in his book *Visual Studies*,[12] provides an excellent and complex overview about concepts of visuality, visual culture, and visual studies. Among many provocative ideas, he distinguishes between the traditional domain-specific analysis of complex images and the more modern "infographic" decoding of contemporary images. In the former, an image is studied as a complex representation requiring the viewer to construct meaning over time through iterative looking, thinking, and contextual analysis. Think, for example, of the literacy required to "read" and understand Robert Campin's *The Annunciation Triptych* (Figure 1). An infographic image by contrast uses visuals as a textual shorthand to communicate simpler or more direct contemporary understanding of a message delivered as an image. Think, for example, of the American Institute of Graphic Arts (AIGA) inventory of symbol systems (Figure 2) that provides a universal graphic communication standard for directional and informational signage. Simple infographics like these can also be read within more complex iconographic works. For example, window surfaces in Rem Koolhaas's McCormack Tribune Campus Center are used as iconographic elements conveying a variety of meanings, such as referencing historical traditions of communication and ornamentation in architectural surface treatments (e.g., hieroglyphics), and the use of

Figure 1. Campin, Robert (ca.1375/9-1444). The Annunciation Triptych. *ca. 1425. Oil on wood, Overall (open): 25 3/8 x 46 3/8 in. (64.5 × 117.8 cm) Central panel: 25 1/4 × 24 7/8 in. (64.1 × 63.2 cm) each wing: 25 3/8 x 10 3/4 in. (64.5 × 27.3 cm). The Cloisters Collection, 1956 (56.70). Image copyright © The Metropolitan Museum of Art / Art Resource, NY The Metropolitan Museum of Art, New York, NY, U.S.A.*

Figure 2. Selection of icons from the AIGA inventory of symbol signs. http://www.aiga.org/content.cfm/symbol-signs

the dot-matrix patterning (similar to Lichtenstein's) to create large-scale portraits of architects. Within subject domains, there is also the "literacy" element of competence in recognizing core images or representational types. It is important to note that visual literacy takes on varied meanings within different disciplinary contexts. The visually literate scientist or engineer may possess entirely different visual mind-maps than visually literate humanists. It may not be possible to expect all learners to be competent in all areas of visuality, but basic skills can be taught and learned. In art/art history we might define competence to some extent as knowledge of canonical images, whereas in other disciplines it might be that radiographic visuals, astrological charts, geographic and cartographic imaging, or other normative image types are considered to be core elements of competence in their respective fields.

The 2008 *Horizon Report* lists four critical challenges for learning organizations in the coming five years. Among them is a call for institutions to "provide formal instruction in information, visual, and technological literacy as well as in how to create meaningful content with today's tools."[13] As art information specialists, we have a skill set that creates an opportunity to be leaders in the area of visual literacy across the disciplines. The call for a focus on visual literacy in higher education or the opportunity "to take a systematic institutional approach to defining core values that include visual acuity alongside the ability to read and write"[14] affords art information professionals the chance to lead their campus in these efforts. Because visual literacy is a life skill rather than just an academic exercise, it is one of the most important things we can teach students.

PART TWO—Visual Literacy in Art Librarianship Practice

3. Visual Literacy and the ACRL Information Literacy Competency Standards

A comparison between the textual and the visual can be drawn using the ACRL definitions of information literacy and one understanding of visual literacy; that is, visual literacy can be understood as a form of critical viewing in much the same way as information literacy can be understood as critical thinking. The ACRL Standards presuppose that there is an information need, a question to be answered. In visual literacy, the point of departure is a visual object to be understood. The Standards provide a methodological approach for uncovering, understanding, and appropriately using information; we think they provide for uncovering, understanding, and appropriately using visuals as well. The ACRL Standards approach can be useful in understanding both a specific visual and the more generalized understanding of visual cues in context. The Standards provide a systematic way of decoding what is seen and help learners construct meaning from visual points of departure.

Since the Standards are so widely known and accepted, it might be useful to parse each of them for their particular relevance to establishing a basic construct for visual literacy.

ACRL Competency Standard 1: The information-literate student determines the extent of the information needed.

Visual Literacy interpretation: Indicators for this competence would center on a user's ability to observe a visual object and the ability to first construct a question about that object, pose a problem set related to the object, and construct a problem-solving strategy to answer the questions and explore the visual "problem." In an active learning setting, the librarian can facilitate the users' discovery sequence—a process that asks them to use innate or learned skills for seeing, observing, and note-taking. Outcomes of this user-inquiry phase would be the articulation of questions and identification of problems that must be explored in order to understand the visual.

ACRL Competency Standard 2: The information-literate student accesses needed information effectively and efficiently.

Visual Literacy interpretation: When questions and problems are articulated, users working with the librarian can together begin to explore the relevant resources needed to answer their inquiries. Indicators would include identification of needed research resources for each area of inquiry, development of search strategies for each resource, understanding of the intellectual structure of the resources, tools needed for further examination and evaluation of the object, and preparation of documentation methodology. Outcomes of user inquiry could be identification of relevant resources, execution of search strategies, a preliminary annotated resource list, and proficiency in software, hardware, or other tools needed to fully support examination and study of the visual object.

ACRL Competency Standard 3: The information-literate student evaluates information and its sources critically and incorporates selected information into his or her knowledge base and value system.

Visual Literacy interpretation: Indicators for this Standard might include comparative analysis of the literature, an understanding of the relative merit of one source over another, cultural context of work and its effect on meaning, exploration of authenticity, issues of connoisseurship and provenance, and the ability to place the image within a meaningful context—aesthetic, historical, political, social or other. Outcomes would include image recognition and identification, the selection of the most relevant trustworthy source of support materials, and the identification of other visuals that place the subject visual within a broader context, interpretation, and contextual understanding of the image.

ACRL Competency Standard 4: The information-literate student, individually or as a member of a group, uses information effectively to accomplish a specific purpose.

Visual Literacy interpretation: Indicators would include use of the visual object to fulfill a particular curricular or creative purpose (as determined by the information seeker). Outcomes would include the ability to use appropriate technologies to create work products such as presentations, bibliographies, Webliographies, interactive environments, etc., intermingled with substantive content drawn from supporting literature and potentially, other visual material.

ACRL Competency Standard 5: The information-literate student understands many of the economic, legal and social issues surrounding the use of information and accesses and uses information ethically and legally.

Visual Literacy interpretation: For visual objects this is a standard of particular importance, since the rights framework for visual material, especially visual objects most often used in teaching and research settings, is so complex and, in many cases, not well articulated in legal documentation. Indicators for Standard 5 would include an understanding of intellectual copyrights as they apply to visual materials, architectural works, limitations on use of images in derivative works, economics of licensed use, understanding of creator rights organizations, and international differences in use of images. Expected user outcomes would include demonstration of appropriate use of conventions for citation, authorized use of images and observance of terms and conditions of use for works used in their work products, and an understanding and compliance with the economics/fees associated with use of images for educational as opposed to commercial purposes. When the outcome is itself a derivative work, these same indicators would also be relevant with the addition of an understanding of the rights of creators to their creative intellectual property and the legal framework that governs these as well.

4. Practical Applications of Visual Literacy as It Relates to Teaching Methodologies (conversation theory; constructivist theory)

Learning evolves from the concrete to the abstract; visual hierarchy begins with understanding and moves to an end goal of critical literacy skills. Therefore, teaching visual thinking needs to begin with practical exercises that encourage learners to participate in the learning process. It allows the learner to directly address a concrete problem and apply critical thinking skills to arrive at the answer. The idea is to prompt learners to be able to generalize and apply these skills across a broad range of visual encounters, ranging from a politician's Web site to an advertisement to a work of photojournalism. Several approaches make it possible for learners to discover the multiple meanings in images on their own.

Constructivist theory and active learning methods are often discussed in the K–12 learner context. However, it has been applied and well documented as an approach in museum education for all learners, and can be effectively applied in higher education as well. In all settings, direct student engagement in the process of learning is emphasized as a fundamental element for the acquisition of knowledge and the construction of meaning. That is,

> The learning of complex subject matter is most effective when it is an intentional process of constructing meaning from information and experience . . .
>
> Successful learners are active, goal-directed, self-regulating, and assume personal responsibility for contributing to their own learning.[15]

The ACRL Information Literacy Competency Standards for Higher Education give librarians a framework for teaching goals, and together with constructivist/active learning strategies, present a workable pedagogical approach for delivering library instruction to visual arts students. In addition, introducing artifactual evidence (the art object or its surrogate image) brings an immediacy and relevance to the research process that is somewhat obscured by more traditional approaches to instruction such as the narrative lecture or demonstration sessions.

> This connection of an object and a topic with the promotion of an activity having a purpose is the first and last word of a genuine theory of interest in education.[16]

A library-facilitated visual literacy experience would engage learners directly in a conversation about an image, drawing out initial reactions. Then, through a series of collective observations, questions, and responses, users begin to form an area of interest and a spark of inquiry that the librarian can use to guide further visual exploration in an attempt to eventually bridge to the textual resource arena. An important aspect of constructivist approach is its inherently non-linear structure resulting from inquiry that is directed by the learner, not the facilitator. The learners' prior knowledge forms the basis for the discovery process which grows from their frame of visual references. Learners enter the discovery conversation equipped with their own skills of observation and life experiences and from there push their limits beyond their known boundaries. Another important aspect of constructivist learning is the concept of "authenticity"—that is, the learning experience is tied to a real-life (and therefore authentic) purpose. In a higher-education setting, the exploration of an image is often tied to a curricular requirement, but transference of skills learned through this process would instill competencies that would support visual understanding in any experience. An ideal description of the process is provided for the classroom setting in *Constructivist Model for Learning*:

> The constructivist classroom presents the learner with opportunities to build on prior knowledge and understanding to construct new knowledge and understanding from authentic experience. Students are allowed to confront problems full of meaning because of their real-life context. In solving these problems, students are encouraged to explore possibilities, invent alternative solutions, collaborate with other students (or external experts), try out ideas and hypotheses, revise their thinking, and finally present the best solution they can derive.[17]

Conclusion

As art information professionals, we are in a unique position to educate our users about a vital and necessary skill set, visual literacy, relating to the current age in which we live. We have the background and understanding of visual rubrics as they relate to the fields of art and art history and, as we have outlined here, these rubrics can be expanded to other fields and disciplines. The confluence of our skills, Web 2.0 technologies, and most importantly, a desire on the part of our learners to be active participants in their own learning process, creates an environment where it is possible to imagine "the visual" catching and even eclipsing the textual in the area of information literacy. As Daniel Pink notes, "We've progressed from a society of farmers to a society of factory workers to a society of knowledge workers. And now we're progressing yet again—to a society of creators and empathizers, pattern makers, and meaning makers."[18] As never before, art information professionals are equipped to address a skill set that is increasingly relevant not only to the educational context but to a larger social, political, and economic context as well.

Notes

1. Louis Masur, "Pictures Have Now Become a Necessity: The Use of Images in American History Textbooks," *The Journal of American History* 84, No. 4 (March 1998): 1,410.
2. Daniel Pink, *A Whole New Mind: Moving from the Information Age to the Conceptual Age* (New York: Riverhead Books, 2005).
3. Tim O'Reilly, "What Is Web 2.0: Design Patterns and Business Models for the Next Generation of Software," http://www.oreillynet.com/pub/a/oreilly/tim/news/2005/09/30/what-is-web-20.html (accessed May 28, 2008).
4. Jonathan Swartz, *Jonathan's Blog*, Monday, April 4, 2005, http://blogs.sun.com/jonathan/date/20050404 (accessed January 21, 2008).
5. Daniel Pink, "Revenge of the Right Brain," *Wired* 13, no. 2 (February 2005), http://www.wired.com/wired/archive/13.02/brain.html (accessed January 29, 2008).
6. Swartz, *Jonathan's Blog.*
7. John Debes, "What Is Visual Literacy? International Visual Literacy Association," http://www.ivla.org/org_what_vis_lit.htm1969 (accessed March 15, 2008).
8. Association of College and Research Libraries, *Information Literacy Competency Standards for Higher Education* (Chicago: American Library Association, 2000), http://www.ala.org/ala/acrl/acrlstandards/standards.pdf (accessed May 28, 2008).
9. David Macleod, *Carnegie Libraries in Wisconsin* (New York: Arno Press, 1968), 17.
10. Richard Sinatra, *Visual Literacy Connections to Thinking, Reading and Writing* (Springfield, IL: Charles C. Thomas, 1986).
11. Raymond Matt, "More Photos in Flickr," *Library of Congress Blog*, http://www.loc.gov/blog/?p=268 (accessed May 10, 2008).
12. James Elkins, *Visual Studies: A Skeptical Introduction* (New York: Routledge, 2003), chapter 4.
13. "The New Media Consortium and the EDUCAUSE Learning Initiative," *The Horizon Report* (Austin, TX: New Media Consortium, 2008), 5–6, http://www.nmc.org/pdf/2008-Horizon-Report.pdf (accessed May 12, 2008).
14. Susan Metros and Kristina Woolsey, "Visual Literacy: An Institutional Imperative," *Educause Review* 41, no. 3 (May/June 2006): 6.
15. *Learner-Centered Psychological Principles: A Framework for School Reform & Redesign,* Learner-Centered Principles Work Group, Board of Educational

Affairs (BEA) American Psychological Association (November 1997), http://www.apa.org/ed/lcp2/lcptext.html (accessed July 29, 2008).

16. John Dewey, *Democracy and Education* (New York: MacMillan, 1916), 158.
17. *Constructivist Model for Learning,* North Central Regional Educational Laboratory. Learning Point Associates (2004), http://www.ncrel.org/sdrs/areas/issues/content/cntareas/science/sc5model.htm (accessed May 29, 2008).
18. Daniel Pink, "Revenge of the Right Brain," *Wired* 13, no. 2 (February 2005), http://www.wired.com/wired/archive/13.02/brain.html (accessed January 29, 2008).

Reading Analytically

1. Describe the change in conditions that, according to these authors, have been brought about by Web 2.0 technologies. How has the development of "online communities" such as blogs, wikis, and social networking sites affected the skills and tools that literate participants in these communities need?
2. Why have the changes in electronic environments discussed in the question 1 above made visual literacy especially important? In answering this question, draw upon both this article and your own experiences in online environments.
3. Note the way that these authors draw upon the standards for information literacy in the previous piece. Describe the ways that the authors adapt each of those standards to their own purpose and to build their own argument.

Reading Across Disciplinary Communities

1. Though this piece outlines kinds of literacy that are important for all individuals, the larger purpose seems to be directed toward a specific disciplinary community. To whom is this piece addressed? What is the argument that is being made to that audience about the work of those disciplinary fields? Try to summarize that argument concisely and demonstrate how it is built by these authors.
2. Though this piece is discussing the role of visual literacy generally, it also draws specifically upon the expertise of art librarians. According to these authors, why is this disciplinary community particularly well-equipped to assist others in the new Web 2.0 environment? List and discuss at least three key arguments and pieces of evidence.

ELIZABETH DALY

Expanding the Concept of Literacy

The author of this article is the Dean of the School of Cinema and Television in the Annenberg Center for Communication at the University of Southern California. As an expert in these media, she is particularly well-equipped to make an argument that traditional, text-based literacies are no longer adequate. Instead, she suggests, we must expand our notion of literacy to include multimedia languages.

As such, Eizabeth Daly, like each of the authors in this section, makes a case for the literacies associated with her own discipline. As you read, consider the ways that she makes her case for the "multimedia language of the screen," as she calls it. Consider, more specifically, how her definitions of "language" and "literacy" attempt to change and expand our notions of each, and how her definitions cohere with, or differ from, other definitions offered in this chapter.

When I ask people to define, in one or two sentences, the word *literacy*—what literacy is and what it enables people to do—the answers I receive are quite similar. To most people, literacy means the ability to read and write, to understand information, and to express ideas both concretely and abstractly. The unstated assumption is that "to read and write" means to read and write *text*. Although media and computer literacy are occasionally mentioned in these definitions, media literacy is most often defined as the ability to understand how television and film manipulate viewers, and computer literacy is generally defined as the skills to use a computer to perform various tasks, such as accessing the Web. If I also ask people about the nature of language, I usually receive the response that language enables us to conceptualize ideas, to abstract information, and to receive and share knowledge. The underlying assumption, so accepted that it is never stated, is that language means *words*.

Twenty-five years ago, a rather popular book was entitled *Four Arguments for the Elimination of Television.*[1] Clearly, that vision of the world was not realized: television has not been eliminated, and screens—from television screens to computer screens—now dominate our lives. This reality needs to be acknowledged. So, in the spirit of the title of the earlier book, I'd like to suggest four arguments for an expanded definition of *literacy*:

1. The multimedia language of the screen has become the current vernacular.
2. The multimedia language of the screen is capable of constructing complex meanings independent of text.
3. The multimedia language of the screen enables modes of thought, ways of communicating and conducting research, and methods of publication and teaching that are essentially different from those of text.
4. Lastly, following from the previous three arguments, those who are truly literate in the twenty-first century will be those who learn to both read and write the multimedia language of the screen.

These four statements are the foundational principles for the work being done at the Institute for Multimedia Literacy (IML) at the Annenberg Center at the University of Southern California (USC).

1. The multimedia language of the screen has become the current vernacular

I often ask colleagues to imagine that they are living and teaching in Padua around the year 1300. Inside the stone walls of that great university they lecture in Latin, but the people walking on the streets beneath their windows, including their own students, speak Italian. Eventually that vernacular has to be embraced (and, indeed, it was embraced) within the Italian academy. The corresponding argument today, simply put, is that for most people—including students—film, television, computer and online games, and music constitute the current vernacular.

Print first allowed for mass literacy, and it has been very effective, but to privilege a print language often means to ignore the success of the technologies—audio recording, radio, cinema, and television—that have come into existence since the primary modes of print were developed. These technologies have become, for average citizens, the most common methods of receiving information, communicating with one another, and entertaining themselves. It is not hard to see how the grammar of these technologies has long since invaded our collective thinking. Metaphors from the screen have become common in every aspect of daily conversations. *Close-up* is synonymous for "in-depth" and "penetrating." We speak of *flashing back* to our earlier lives. We *frame* events to put them in context. We *cut to the chase* when we are in a hurry. We *dissolve* or *fade out* or *segue* from one topic to another, and we have *background sound*. We spend many hours at our computers looking at and sharing *screens*. Students are accustomed to the direct emotional experience of music as one of the primary factors in creating their identities, and they spend hours playing computer games in online communities. In short, our shared experiences as human beings are more often than not derived from the images and sounds that exist on screens.

2. The multimedia language of the screen is capable of constructing complex meanings independent of text.

At USC, the highly ranked School of Cinema-Television is praised, envied, and admired but still held suspect. In the world of a research university, it remains an anomaly. No university is ranked nationally on the basis of such a school, nor is such a school considered to be critical, as are the Departments of Physics and English.

I believe the reason for this lack of status is not only because media creators and scholars deal with that "disreputable" world of entertainment but also, and even more important, because in their work in this discipline, they do not give primacy to print. They believe that images and sounds, integrated in a time-based medium, can be as important in creating knowledge and communicating ideas and information as text. At the most fundamental level, their work does not endorse the premise, widely held for the past two millennia, that comprehension of and expression through the printed medium defines what it means to be literate and, by extension, educated.

A few years ago, a colleague sent me an article that had appeared in the *Chronicle of Higher Education*. The author, a respected art historian, asserted that it was time for the academy to give up a deeply ingrained suspicion of images and realize that the visual could indeed contain intellectual content, that it might in some cases be equal to text. I assumed that the article was a reprint, written in the 1930s perhaps, but it was current. At that moment, I realized that we at the IML would need to defend not only the idea of a vernacular that was a cinematic/multimedia based language but also, more important, the value of that idea. We had a very long way to go to establish that such a language might have clear differences from, and even advantages over, print in some instances.

By arguing for the importance of the language of the screen, I do not intend to attack words or print. But print carries its own technological bias. Print supports linear argument, but it does not value aspects of experience that cannot be contained in books. Print deals inadequately with nonverbal modes of thought and nonlinear construction.

Like text, multimedia can enable us to develop concepts and abstractions, comparisons and metaphors, while at the same time engaging our emotional and aesthetics sensibilities. Rich media, with its multiple simultaneous layers, does much more than provide enhancements, illustrations, and tools for enriching, accessing, and transmitting the established literacy. Think for a moment of the still images that have defined many important moments in U.S. history the photo essays of the Great Depression; a sailor kissing a girl in Times Square at the end of World War II; a young Vietnamese girl fleeing napalm; a college student at Kent State kneeling over a body. As icons, they no longer require any explanation for most contemporary Americans, although a printed text or oral explanation might well complement and extend their meanings. However, even if we did not know the context of their creation, they would each carry strong meanings and convey powerful emotions. Multimedia and cinema, though sometimes enriched by language, embrace many other elements as co-equal—not only image but also sound, duration, color, and design. Think also for a moment of historic cinematic moments; the first moon landing; the planes slamming into the World Trade Center. What would it be like to try to fully share these and other momentous events without access to the language and power of the screen?

Print supports linear argument but it does not value aspects of experience that cannot be contained in books.

3. The multimedia language of the screen enables modes of thought, ways of communicating and conducting research, and methods of publication and reaching that are essentially different from those of text.

Since the Enlightenment, the intellectual community has valued the rational over the affective, the abstract over the concrete, the decontextualized over the contextualized. These values, combined with a deeply ingrained suspicion of practice and of the creation of product, make it difficult to bring the vernacular of contemporary media into the academy.

Accepting the language of multimedia as co-equal with text will require a major paradigm shift that challenges the domination of science and rationality, abstraction and theory. I am certainly not alone in thinking that this shift is long overdue. For example Stephen Toulmin, in his highly regarded 1990 book *Cosmopolis*, eloquently argued for the academy to move beyond the dominance of the Cartesian model.[2] But just how difficult this transition will be was made clear to me a few years ago when a senior academic figure explained why she found it difficult to judge the worthiness of artists for promotion and tenure. She said that she found their work too specific and lacking an abstract, theoretical base. It seemed that a professor was more valued if he or she wrote about art rather than made art.

The language of multimedia is, no doubt, more closely related to the affective and subjective language of art than to the rational and linear language of science. Sergel Eisenstein, the great Russian filmmaker, once described the language of art, as opposed to the language of science, as a language of conflict, a dialectical language as opposed to a linear one. When the language of science is applied to art, he argued, it ossifies art; for example, a landscape becomes a topographical map, and a painted Saint Sebastian becomes an anatomical study.[3]

The grammar of multimedia and the ways in which it creates meaning are only beginning to be systematically articulated. By contrast, the language of the cinema offers us an extensive body of theory, providing a starting point from which to think about multimedia. In 1923 Dziga Vortov, a Soviet documentary filmmaker and one of the Russian pioneers of cinematic language, wrote for the motion-picture camera a fanciful monologue that might well be applied to multimedia today: “I am a mechanical eye, I am a machine, show you a world the way only I can see it. Now and forever, I free myself from human immobility. I am in constant motion. I draw near and then away from objects . . . recording movement . . . of the most complex combinations. Freed from the limits of time and space, I put together any given points in the universe no matter where I’ve recorded them. . . . My path leads to the creation of a fresh perception of the world. I decipher in a new way a world unknown to you.”[4]

One of the fundamental cinematic building blocks, which also applies to much of multimedia, is *montage*, or the juxtaposition of elements, both within and between shots. For the filmmaker, this is the art of editing, and it is core to the creation of cinema. Montage offers a clear and important example of how differently text and multimedia construct meaning. Through montage, one is able to manipulate time and space and create sequences that could never exist in the physical world but that are thematically and conceptually related. Montage permits an interaction between the creator and the receiver, as well as among the elements of the creation. It not only allows but encourages the recombination of elements to create new meanings.

The famous demonstration of montage by Lev V. Kuleshov, another of the Russian pioneers, elucidates the concept. Kuleshov made a short film sequence that juxtaposed a well-known Russian actor's face against three different shots: a bowl of soup, a dead woman in a coffin, and a girl playing with a toy bear. When asked to describe what they had seen, viewers—according to V.I. Pudovkin, who was then a student in Kuleshov's workshop—insisted that the man was hungry when looking at the soup, joyous when watching the girl, and sad when viewing the dead woman. They described his various emotions with great detail, as proof of his outstanding talent as an actor. All versions were, however, the same shot of the man. Nothing in his image had changed. The meaning attributed to each sequence came only from the collision of the shots.

Multimedia, so ubiquitous to young people's experience, often seems to be particularly hard for them to analyze or deconstruct.

With the computer, we can now electronically construct images and sounds and manipulate space and time to create meaning in ways about which our Russian progenitors could only dream. The tools of keying, compositing, and morphing are more than ways of misrepresenting truth. They enable the construction of higher orders of meaning, nuance, and inference. Synthesizing and sampling, as well as simultaneity, are natural to multimedia, permitting a form of *bricolage,* a process through which, in the words of John Seely Brown, one is able to "find something (perhaps a tool, some open source code, images, music, text) that can be used or transformed to build something new."[5]

Interactivity as a core factor in multimedia is in some ways closely related to performance and can enable the viewer/reader/user to participate directly in the construction of meaning. It is perhaps worth digressing for a moment to note that whereas performance has long been devalued as "entertainment," the art of storytelling, always performative, has been a major way of transmitting culture and values throughout human history.

The very vocabulary of multimedia encourages approaches different from those used to write text. One "creates" and "constructs" media rather than writing it, and one "navigates" and "explores" media rather than reading it. The process is active, interactive, and often social, allowing for many angles of view.

The physical production techniques used to make multimedia and the practices of distributing it also differ from the models used to produce and publish text. First, and perhaps foremost, the production of multimedia is most often an act of collaboration. A film, large or small, is rarely made by one person. The "film by" credit is most often the manifestation of a particular business practice and does not reflect the true nature of authorship or the process of creation. This collaborative process may be reduced in scale in multimedia projects, but it is still typical. It lies in the very nature of the creative process and does not fundamentally change because of the difficulty or simplicity of the tools that are required.

Second, the final product—be it a film, a television program, or some other form of multimedia—is most successful when it emerges in large part during the process of creation. A script or scenario or storyboard provides a guide, but if one wants to go beyond the predictable and formulaic, there needs to be room for discovery and even serendipity during the production or creation of a film or multimedia document. One of the great U.S. filmmakers, Walter Murch, who edited *The English Patient,* among other well-known films, refers to this process as the "collision of intelligences" that produces something unforeseen by the creative team, a process that allows for and respects intuition. In some ways, this process constitutes a type of active research in which one studies what one is doing while doing it. Such work demands a climate open to experimentation and a willingness to explore and fail—an "ecology of experimentation," to borrow a term from a University of Michigan document.[6] It allows for rapid iteration and quick changes of direction.

Third, media forms are usually meant for public distribution and presentation. They are intended to be seen in environments beyond that of their creation. In the beginning at IML, both students and faculty felt that student projects were private and meant for viewing only by the student and the professor. Over the past semesters, however, we have seen the nature of authorship change. Students no longer write to please only the professor. They want to be understood by their peers and by others who will see and experience their projects. They consider themselves to be authors who possess expertise in a certain research area. Likewise, faculty in IML workshops are intent on making their own research projects accessible to those not in their discipline. Faculty in the humanities and in arts and sciences—from disciplines as diverse as quantum physics, art history, and philosophy—have found common ground, insights, and points of access into the pedagogical and research issues in one another's disciplines. Certainly not all work in a discipline will be understandable to those without training, but for interdisciplinary work, faculty must find a language to speak across the boundaries. Multimedia may well have the potential to provide a much-needed new space in which cross-disciplinary conversation can occur between the humanities and the sciences.

4. Lastly, following from the previous three arguments, those who are truly literate in the twenty-first century will be those who learn to both read and write the multimedia language of the screen.

After a hundred years, the language of cinema has been rather well defined, and a large body of critical literature exists. The production methodologies are also quite well understood and articulated, although that knowledge often seems to rest primarily within the oral culture of the filmmaking community. Even with this history and ample evidence of the skill required to construct media, the attitude widely held by both faculty and administration is that complex media texts do not deserve classroom or research time, especially if such study might take emphasis away from traditional activities such as essays and research papers.

Since the 1960s, universities and colleges and even high schools have taught so-called media or visual literacy courses. These courses, however, have had two limitations. First, they often seem to have an underlying assumption that television, cinema, and related media are inferior communication forms that may misrepresent reality, since media at its worst manipulates us and lies to us and at its best is superficial. These courses, so far as I can see, enforce the belief that real education remains in books and that real knowledge is rational and linear. Students are taught to read visual texts in order to defend themselves against the onslaught of visual culture. Second, these courses have been extremely one-sided in the definition of literacy, focusing on a "read only" approach. Full literacy demands the ability to write, as well as to read. I was recently told by a very well-known scholar that images are less useful than text because one can interpret images many ways but words are far more precise. I wondered if he had never had the experience that most us have on a daily basis—that of saying, "No, what I really meant to say was . . . "

The current situation is further complicated by the widespread assumption that students already have an adequate knowledge of screen language and multimedia. No doubt, young people today have less fear of the computer and more technical ability with software for rich media; multimedia is indeed their everyday language. However, they have no more critical ability with this language than do their elders—perhaps less. They need to be taught to write for the screen and analyze multimedia just as much as, if not more than, they need to be taught to write and analyze any specific genre in text. Generally, they have had instruction in text at the secondary level, but rarely have they received similar instruction for multimedia. Multimedia, so ubiquitous to their experience, often seems to be particularly hard for them to analyze or deconstruct.

Another consideration is that although the academic study of film, media, and audiovisual culture has established pedagogical precedents that provide theoretical building blocks for the critical application of film, television, and multimedia into higher education, it is common to see media integrated into disciplines across the curriculum without these important critical tools in place. Films or segments of films are screened in various classes "to engage students" in the subject matter. Often this usage appears to have occurred without appropriate regard for the nature of audiovisual media, its inherent meaning and structure, the cultural context of its creation, or the consequences of dissecting it.

Even the most cursory knowledge of media is not included in the general education curricula of most colleges or universities.

The most glaring examples of this practice have occurred during the past two decades in history departments, where film has become an integral part of the curricula. Despite initial resistance, dramatic narrative films are now recognized for their ability to bring the past "to life," creating an emotional impact that is thought to exceed that of written texts. However, most history and humanities faculty are not trained to address the rhetorical codes and narrative strategies of cinema. Thus, historical films are frequently analyzed empirically and are evaluated according to the same criteria as are conventional historical documents. Without a background in film theory and screen language, students and faculty do not read a film as the product of highly developed systems of signification embedded in a cultural context. By contrast, they have been taught these skills for textual narratives since their early stages of reading education.

To read or write the language of media and understand how it creates meaning within particular contexts, one needs some understanding of frame composition, color palette, editing techniques, and sound-image relations, as well as of the mobilization of generic and narrative conventions, the context of signs and images, sound as a conveyor of meaning, and the effects of typography. Such principles as screen direction, the placement of objects in the frame, color choices, morphing, cuts, and dissolves all do much more than make a screen communication aesthetically pleasing. They are as critical to the creation of meaning as adverbs, adjectives, paragraphs, periods, analogies, and metaphors are to text. Multimedia also requires that attention be paid to design, navigation, and interface construction. The mouse, the click, the link, and the database have already taken their place alongside more traditional screen descriptors.

Outside of schools of film, instruction in these formal elements of multimedia and cinematic construction is not provided in the same way that it is in English or foreign languages. In fact, even the most cursory knowledge of media is not included in the general education curricula of most colleges or universities. Higher education institutions require that students learn not only the content but also the formal techniques of such authors as Steinbeck, Hemingway, and Frost well enough to discuss both the content of their work and their creative style in light of an established body of literary theory. Such work is highly unlikely to be required in media of any kind. At best, one course in "the arts" may be required, but it is unlikely to be a course that requires the equivalent of a language lab.

At the IML, we are committed to empowering faculty and students to choose the best language for the task at hand. In some cases, this language may well be linear text, and in some cases, it may be one or more kinds of multimedia. To make that choice, a faculty member or student must have a command of the elements of multimedia and screen language and must understand how to use that command to create and disseminate knowledge.

The Institute for Multimedia Literacy

My work with multimedia literacy began a few years ago when one of the most famous alumni of the School of Cinema-Television, George Lucas, asked me a very provocative question. "Don't you think," he said, "that in the coming decade, students need to be taught to read and write cinematic language, the language of the screen, the language of sound and image, just as they are now taught to read and write text? Otherwise, won't they be as illiterate as you or I would have been if, on leaving college, we were unable to read and write an essay?"

As I flew back to Los Angeles that day, I knew that he was correct. What I did not fully realize, at 25,000 feet over the Pacific, was that what he had so casually suggested was likely to be highly disruptive within the academy. I was rather new to the university at the time and assumed that the proposal would be of considerable interest to colleagues. However, when I called a leading faculty member in the Department of English to suggest that we explore ways of incorporating teaching some basic multimedia writing in freshman composition, I was greeted with profound silence.

My colleagues in the School of Cinema, however, strongly endorsed the idea, and in the fall of 1998, we began what would become the USC Annenberg Center's Institute for Multimedia Literacy. We started with one course in which students who were not cinema majors were required to create a multimedia project, in their own discipline, that would have the intellectual rigor expected in a five-to-seven-page term paper but that could be "explored" (i.e., read) only on the computer screen. This multimedia project could not be printed out as hard copy. It had to employ sound and image; it had to be time-based; and it had to be interactive. Needless to say, we all found this assignment challenging. These first students came from anthropology, history, sociology, and English literature.

Today, we oversee classes that incorporate work in the extended literacy of multimedia throughout the undergraduate curriculum at USC, as well as in satellite classes at Berkeley, at Cal Tech, and in two Los Angeles–area high schools. Each semester, we offer a group of faculty the opportunity to participate in our program for the first time, while faculty from previous semesters continue to work with us. So far, more than two thousand students and forty faculty have been included. The faculty are assisted by teaching assistants and post-docs from the Division of Critical Studies in the School of Cinema. All are required to attend a summer workshop conducted by continuing post-docs but also, and most important, by faculty who have taught in the program previously. Peer mentoring operates at all levels. The goal is to help the incoming faculty members rethink the content of their courses. We ask them to clearly tell us what it is that they want to teach, and then we try to help them discover how the language of multimedia might further that goal. We also ask them to assess their current research to see how the language of multimedia might offer fresh perspectives or at least suggest a new approach to their current efforts. We hope that in doing so, they will connect their teaching to their research in more direct ways. In the workshop, they must author their own project, which must be specific to their discipline. At the same time, they are engaged in redesigning their syllabi to include multimedia projects.

Courses drawn into the program have ranged from gender studies to quantum physics, from Slavic studies to philosophy. The projects vary just as greatly in approach. Some are structured around Web sites, as in the case of the Slavic course in which the students developed a site enabling visitors to navigate the text of *Crime and Punishment* through maps of St. Petersburg. Another student site, created in an Asian American literature class, explicated the novel *Woman Warrior* by examining the abuse of women, from foot binding to corseting, using popular culture images that inculcated these practices into belief systems. Other classes have worked with databases, as in the "Culture of the 1960s" course in which the students collected oral histories. The faculty member will use this material both in his own research and in future classes. Most recently, we are seeing the creation of elaborate interactive games.

Over the past few years I have become more convinced than ever that the rapidly developing language of multimedia—the language of the screen—can bring important new approaches to research, publication, and teaching. Now we simply have to accept the challenge to embrace the paradigm shift that is required to bring this vernacular into the academy. Fortunately, I have colleagues who agree. For example Dr. Mark Kann, chair of the USC Political Science Department, recently stated: "It seems to me that at some point, multimedia expression is going to be like writing: it's something you don't leave college without. Kids are very sophisticated in navigating on computers and surfing the Internet. I think pretty soon they're going to have to be as sophisticated in expressing themselves using the media. And I wouldn't be too surprised if at some point a multimedia program that is the equivalent of freshman writing will start appearing at universities. It will become a requirement for graduation."

The concept of a language composed of elements other than word and text is neither fundamentally new nor particularly revolutionary. Rather, this concept is an evolutionary development of the ideas and practices that have been with us since people first struggled to leave records and tell stories. Technology is simply enabling these alternative ways of communicating to penetrate our lives more directly and in more powerful ways.

Notes

1. Jerry Mander, *Four Arguments for the Elimination of Television* (New York: Morrow, 1978).
2. Stephen Toulmin, *Cosmopolis: The Hidden Agenda of Modernity* (New York: Free Press, 1990).
3. Sergel Eisenstein, *Film Form*, trans. and ed. Jay Leyda (New York: Meridian Books, 1957), 46.
4. *Kino-eye: The Writings of Dziga Vertov*, ed. Annette Michelson, trans. Kevin O'Brien (Berkeley: University of California Press, 1984), 17–18.
5. John Seeley Brown, "Learning in the Digital Age," in Maureen Devlin, Richard Larson, and Joel Meyerson, eds., *The Internet and the University: Forum 2001* (Boulder, Colo.: EDUCAUSE and The Forum for the Future of Higher Education, 2002), 71–72, <http://www.educause.edu/forum/ffpiu01w.asp> (accessed January 21, 2003).
6. University of Michigan, *President's Information Revolution Commission Report*, April 2001, <http://www.umich.edu/pres/inforev2/> (accessed January 21, 2003).

Reading Analytically

1. Part of Daly's argument is based upon her ability to convince her readers that what we view on screen indeed constitutes a "language" with its own unique characteristics, and has a special importance in our times. What pieces of evidence and what logic does she use to build that argument? Present at least three examples of her attempt to make this case.
2. Another key argument that Daly is attempting to make here is that an educated or literate individual must possess the capability to interpret multimedia language, and that this capability is crucial to specific critical thinking abilities. Describe the logic and examples she uses to make this case.
3. In the last paragraph of her essay, Daly notes that "the concept of a language composed of elements other than word and text is neither

fundamentally new nor particularly revolutionary." Why would she make such a statement? How does she still manage to use this statement as a way to suggest the need for change?

Reading Across Disciplinary Communities

1. As Dean of the Annenberg Center for Communications at the University if Southern California, Daly also has an interest in promoting the work being done by her own institution and by others in her discipline. How does she use stories and other methods to enhance the *ethos* (or credibility) of her discipline and institution? What examples and stories do you find particularly compelling?
2. Though speaking from her discipline of media studies, and more specifically film and television studies, Daly's argument has implications for other disciplines as well. Consider how her suggestions for expanding the concept of literacy might affect another discipline. How would the teaching of history change under her definition of "multimedia language"? The teaching of social sciences like psychology or sociology? The teaching of literature? Choose one discipline that interests you, and try to apply this approach to it.

ERIC LANE

America 101

How We Let Civic Education Slide—And Why We Need a Crash Course in the Constitution Today.

This essay, like the others in this section, argues for a specific type of literacy that is crucial for 21st-century students—in this case, civic literacy, or the ability to understand the functioning of our government and its effects upon our lives as citizens. But unlike some of the other essays, this piece is not looking to new educational methods. Instead, it tends to look back to past forms of education—civics courses—as a model for curricula that we ought to revive. As such, Eric Lane, a Professor at Hofstra Law School and senior fellow at the Brennan Center for Justice, tells us that though "the average college senior knows astoundingly little about America's history, government, international relations, and market economy," "things weren't always this way."

Drawing upon statistics that demonstrate the lack of knowledge of our citizenry about American government, he argues for a return to educational practices that can remedy this lack of civic literacy. As you read, consider your own educational experiences and your own knowledge about government to determine if this argument seems reasonable, or if you might differ with his dismal depiction of the state of civic knowledge.

Starting this October, the United States Citizenship and Immigration Service will administer a new test for immigrants seeking American citizenship. The test is intended to be harder and more relevant than its predecessors. Replacing many of the more easily learned (and senseless) fact questions—"What are the colors of the flag?" "What colors are the stars on our flag?"—is a more meaningful series of questions about America's constitutional democracy. Heralded as a real measure of "what makes an American citizen," this new test asks, for example, "What is the supreme law of the land?" "What does the Constitution do?" "The idea of self-government is in the first three words of the Constitution. What are these words?" and "What is the rule of law?"

From the Framers onward, Americans have always considered civic literacy critical for a thriving democracy. "[A] well-instructed people alone can be permanently a free people," noted James Madison, the father of the Constitution and fourth president, in 1810. Americans continue to agree. A 1997 survey by the National Constitution Center (NCC) found that 84 percent of Americans believed that for the government to work as intended, citizens needed to be informed and active. Three-quarters of those polled claimed that the Constitution mattered in their daily lives, and almost as many people thought the Constitution impacted events in America today.

Yet, despite this nod to civic literacy, too few Americans could answer the questions on the citizenship test or similar questions. Forty-one percent of respondents to the NCC national survey were not aware that there were three branches of government, and 62 percent couldn't name them; 33 percent couldn't even name one. Over half of all those answering the NCC survey did not know the length of a term for a member of the Senate or House of Representatives. And another NCC study found that while 71 percent of teens knew that "www" starts an online web address, only 35 percent knew that "We the People" are the opening words of the Constitution. A study by the Intercollegiate Studies Institute found that "the average college senior knows astoundingly little about America's history, government, international relations and market economy, earning an 'F' on the American civic literacy exam with a score of 54.2 percent."

Things weren't always this way; civics and current events courses were once common, even required, in American schools. But since the late 1960s, civic education in the country has declined. The main culprit in this sad tale is our educational system. "Civic education in the public schools has been almost totally eclipsed by a preoccupation with preparing the workforce of a global economy," writes former Harvard University President Derek Bok. "Most universities no longer treat the preparation of citizens as an explicit goal of their curriculum." The congressionally required National Assessments of Educational Progress confirms Bok's point. A 1988 report found significant drops in civic knowledge since 1976; another in 2002 found "that the nation's citizenry is woefully undereducated about the fundamentals of our American Democracy." And while some have questioned the continuousness of the decline, there is little dispute with the troubling, perhaps ironic, conclusion: As the role of government has enormously expanded over the last 80 years, and as our voting rolls have opened to more and more groups of people, efforts to prepare our citizens for their civic responsibilities have fallen precipitously.

And this only addresses our basic civic literacy. Citizens still need a deeper understanding of the Constitution, an advanced set of knowledge to evaluate the operation of our government and weigh its successes and failures. A more advanced set of questions might ask: What is the vision of human nature that underlies the Constitution? What is the primary task of American government? Does the Constitution favor process over product and, if so, why? What is a special interest group? How does the Constitution define the common good?

Our civic ignorance is putting our constitutional democracy at risk. It is a significant part of the willingness of Congress and the public to defer to executive claims of authority since 9/11, with little understanding of its negative constitutional consequences. More generally, as the government continues to expand into our daily lives, our very freedom depends upon every citizen's ability to understand and respond to it. Civic education, retired Supreme Court Justice Sandra Day O'Connor recently noted, is our only hope for "preserving a robust constitutional democracy . . . The better educated our citizens are, the better equipped they will be to preserve the system of government we have." The only answer, then, is to reinject civic literacy into our educational system.

The ABCs of Civic Literacy

Preserving "a robust democracy," as Justice O'Connor called for, requires citizens to know and understand the Constitution, both its content and its context. At a minimum, every American should be able to answer every question asked of naturalized citizens in the new test, and they should know what their answers mean. For example, in this presidential election season, Americans should know that they vote for electors and not directly for the president, and why the Framers chose this method. Americans must also know the different branches of government, their respective governing roles, and why they have them.

But Americans must understand much more about the Constitution. What the Framers sent out from Philadelphia for ratification was more than just a description of the institutions and processes of a new government. It was a set of ideas and principles about government and democracy, the ones that have come to form our constitutional conscience.

The first is liberty. Initially, the idea of "liberty" held that Americans had a unique capacity to suppress self-interest for the public good in the conduct of public affairs. Through such "public virtue," Americans could live together harmoniously. Simple government was all they needed to protect their society from external threats and to regulate the behavior of those few miscreants who could not see the common need through the lens of their own self-interest. This attitude formed the Articles of Confederation, effectively depriving the Continental Congress of the power to unify or defend the country.

But by the Convention in 1787, that notion of liberty had proven unrealizable, even utopian. "We have probably had too good an opinion of human nature in forming our confederation," George Washington wrote in 1786, reflecting the chaos and oppression that had arisen from post independence experiment in simple majoritarian self-government. So the Framers recast the idea as a right to advocacy. This required that all of the nation's broad array of interests (as the Framers narrowly saw them) had to be represented in the nation's political processes. But it also demanded that for an interest to become law, it had to survive a complicated political process marked by a bicameral legislative body, separation of powers, and checks and balances. All of this required participation and debate, activities predicated on a robust civic literacy. The goal of the system was to protect liberty by thwarting majority impulses to dominate minorities.

Forty-one percent of respondents to a national survey were not aware that there were three branches of government, and 62 percent couldn't name them.

The Constitution, as first ratified, had no bill of rights; the Framers originally thought individual liberty could be protected through limiting federal powers and the complicated lawmaking processes the Constitution established. They also thought a bill of rights would offer little protection from a government intent on its violation (an observation often proven right by American history). But, during the ratification campaign, the Framers became convinced that a bill of rights was necessary both to further protect the liberty of Americans from majority politics and to assure ratification.

Liberty through representation also led to several other critical ideas captured by what one scholar has called "conflict within consensus." Self or group interests would be pursued within Congress, but within a consensus that we are bound to one another by our shared belief in our Constitution and its principles, that the realization of our self-interest cannot be the only measure of our government's legitimacy. From this flowed two other crucial ideas: compromise and tolerance. The Constitution itself was a set of compromises, and it assumed the vital need for compromise for the new government to function.

Through these principles—liberty, representation, compromise, tolerance—and their historical evolution, we formed our constitutional conscience. Madison described this as the "fundamental maxims of free Government," which become part of the "national sentiment" and "counteract the impulses of interest and passion." As with our own personal conscience, these principles must be first learned. And then they must be continuously relearned to resist the intense impulses of self-interest. That is why President Franklin Roosevelt thought that the Constitution is "like the Bible, it ought to be read again and again." It is also why upon his departure from office in 1989, Ronald Reagan cautioned Americans, "If we forget what we did, we won't know who we are." This all-encompassing vision of civic literacy is demanding. But the fragility of our democracy requires no less.

Throughout American history, citizens have been able to constantly reinvigorate and expand freedom, but only through an understanding and appreciation of our Constitutional processes and values. That is how a Constitution that did not free the slaves or provide the vote to women could be used as an argument for abolition and universal suffrage. And this is how Martin Luther King, Jr. could come to Washington to collect on the promise of both the Declaration of Independence and the Constitution for civil rights for all Americans.

A Failing Grade

Was there ever a Golden Age of civic literacy? Probably not, at least in absolute terms. But whatever grades Americans got in civic literacy prior to the mid-1960s, the last several decades have clearly seen these grades fall. In the past, university presidents considered ways in which the college experience could train students as civic leaders, argues Bok. Indeed, civic literacy was promoted at every level of educational instruction, partially fueled by an obligation to help the waves of immigrants then entering the country become Americans. But over the last several decades there has been far less educational focus on citizenship.

Since the late 1960s, fewer and fewer schools require civics courses, and fewer include civic components in their American history courses. This is particularly true in schools with less-privileged student bodies. A Mills College study by Professors Joseph Kahne and Ellen Middaugh points out that students in these schools are half as likely as students in wealthy school districts "to learn," for example, "how laws are made and how Congress works."

Several reasons account for this dangerous departure from past practices. One was a concern, beginning in the 1970s, that civic education equaled indoctrination and that civic pedagogy somehow conflicted with individual rights. Teaching about our constitutional democracy was seen, unfortunately, as imposing values on students. This was particularly true in the late 1960s, after the breakup of the grand postwar consensus and during the struggles of many groups to find their own group identities. Another reason was the view of political scientists that civics was "a low level subject matter" and that "students learned nothing from civics courses," according to Professors Richard Niemi and Julia Smith.

The same goes for current events classes. Those of us near or over 60 might remember the weekly classroom sessions in which the teacher led a discussion of what was going on in the world. These courses provided the opportunity to engage students in the larger world that they would soon enter and for which they would bear responsibility. They also provided students with the opportunity for critical thinking via the exploration of current events through a constitutional lens. After the 1960s, their abandonment is self-explanatory: Talking about current events became risky as the shared views of Americans became tattered. Heightened group self-involvement made reflection less possible and tension and anger inevitable. A discussion on topics such as the war in Vietnam, black power, women's rights, affirmative action, and even presidential politics was likely, at least in educators' eyes, to create disruptions rather than understanding.

Lacking a deep sense of civic life, we demand things without an appreciation of the give-and-take inherent in American politics.

At the same time, we stopped engaging with one another in civil society. We withdrew from a broader vision of what makes us American and started focusing more on what makes us different. We became more and more isolated and more and more disconnected from our constitutional conscience.

Concern over the decline in civic literacy has prompted some school systems to reintroduce civics-like courses over the last 10 years. But these efforts have been sporadic, uneven, and obstructed by other priorities. That was Bok's point about civic education being eclipsed by workforce preparation. O'Connor makes a similar point: The current emphasis on science and math "has effectively squeezed out civics education because there is no testing for that anymore and no funding for that." And this is unrelated to the cracking of the American consensus; in this era of No Child Left Behind, everyone is left behind when it comes to the unquantifiable learning necessary for civic literacy.

Complacency is now the main problem. Despite Benjamin Franklin's oftrepeated response to a woman's question concerning the nature of the new government—"a republic, madame, if you can keep it"—most Americans have absolutely no concern about its endurance. "Of course the Republic will survive, how can it be otherwise? We have always been free, and we will always be free," I have heard more than a few people—educated, politically conscious people—say. I recently tested this issue with a class of mine. Almost all of these students thought we were experiencing a decline in civil liberties and growing challenges to our constitutional system. But when asked how many thought it was even possible that today's democracy would be dramatically different 50 years hence, none said yes. They all thought that while there might be some reduced liberties and increased presidential power, none saw a democratic crisis ahead. Such complacency forecloses serious reform efforts. No crisis, no reform.

The Vices of Civic Ignorance

For most Americans, the connection between civic literacy and a healthy democracy is only rhetorical. If pressed, they would not know or appreciate what it means, nor would they concede that what they don't know does hurt them and all of us. But it does.

Two scholars, Michael Delli Carpini and Scott Keeter, detail this point in their 1996 study *What Americans Know About Politics and Why It Matters.* They find that civic literacy provides meaningful understanding and support for a number of constitutional values, including compromise and tolerance, and promotes meaningful political participation. They also argue that "a better-informed citizenry places important limitations on the ability of public officials, interest groups, and other elites to manipulate public opinion and act in ways contrary to the public interest."

The opposite is also true: Civic ignorance denies us the context through which to understand and measure the conduct of our elected officials. It unleashes our natural instincts to measure governmental processes and decisions, in the present tense alone, through the screens of our own self-interests. It curtails our ability to consider what might be good for a larger community or for the country. This is the path to democratic decline—and we are on it.

Take, for example, the war on terrorism and the Iraq War. After 9/11, Americans became appropriately worried about more attacks, and in turn they have, as they did in the past, looked to the President for protection. And President George W. Bush, as have earlier Presidents, responded. But his response has been based on a unique claim of unprecedented constitutional powers to engage our troops, wiretap our citizens, and torture our prisoners. "Monarchial prerogatives," the Administration has labeled them. While the excessiveness of this view has roiled some of the Administration's own loyalists, there has been no retreat from its assertion. There has been no need to. Congress has not asserted itself against this claim, in part because they would not take such a confrontational step without broad public support. And Americans have not been forceful in demanding that Congress protect our constitutional system. While there are various reasons for the public's acquiescence, it is hard to posit that civic ignorance doesn't rank high among them.

The drop-off in civic literacy has also helped fuel the erosion of the national political consensus that drove the soaring successes of post-war America. During that period the federal government grew from a distant star in a far-off galaxy to the daily light of our political life. As Richard Nixon noted in his 1970 State of the Union address, "Ours has become—as it continues to be, and should remain a society of large expectations.

Government helped to generate these expectations. It undertook to meet them." It undertook to meet them through responding to the consensus demands for a number of economic, civil, and environmental rights established through, for example, Social Security, Medicare, Medicaid, the Civil Rights Act, the Voting Rights Act, and a broad expansion of environmental protections.

But by 1970, this grand consensus was only a memory. Its dissolution came about for many reasons, but it is no accident that it coincided with the decline in civic education and civic literacy. In fact, the two have driven each other—political dissolution made it harder to speak about American civics, but the lack of such discussion guaranteed that Americans, particularly students, would enter the world with a dimmer conception of American life and a shakier commitment to a community beyond their narrow self-interests. In this disharmony, the spirit of "we" was replaced by a culture of "me" (or, sometimes, "us," as groups vied for advantage). We were (and are) living through "the growth of a politics based upon narrow concerns, rooted in the exploitative divisions of class, cash, gender, region, ethnicity, morality and ideology—a give no quarter and take no prisoners activism that demands satisfaction and accepts no compromise," as David Frohnmayer, the President of the University of Oregon, put it.

The result is a culture and government that can make only halting progress. Lacking a deep sense of civic life, we demand things for ourselves and our group without an appreciation of the give-and-take inherent in American politics. The expectation the Framers had of "mutual concessions and sacrifices . . . mutual forbearance and conciliation" became replaced by a civically illiterate nation, unappreciative and unforgiving of a government that was not fulfilling their demands.

Reviving Civic Literacy

The goal of civic literacy is to continuously reinvigorate our democracy through the promotion of meaningful civic engagement. It requires knowledge of the Constitution, its history, and its values, as they have evolved. We have to understand the fragility of our democracy and our obligation to maintain it. The only place to start is with the public schools. Public schools have an obligation to teach children about our history and civic institutions including the Constitution. This obligation trumps even math and science education: After all, what is the value of either math or science, if we don't have our democracy? Or as Amy Gutmann, the President of the University of Pennsylvania, asserted, "'political preparation'—the cultivation of virtues, knowledge, and skills necessary for political participation—has moral primacy over other purposes of public education in a democratic society."

What would an effective civic literacy program look like? This is not a road untraveled. Many groups have spent considerable time exploring the question and have offered a variety of very good proposals. One area of agreement in all the studies is that civic education must start early. Many of the lessons we need to learn from the Constitution—participation, compromise, tolerance—must become part of our attitudes and conscience to have real impact. And the sooner the effort begins and the more often it is repeated, the better it works.

Civic ignorance denies us the context through which to understand the conduct of our elected officials.

Accordingly, sometime in fourth or fifth grade students should take their first civics-oriented course. This course should also include some basics of American history; call it the American Constitution I. It should introduce the structural details of the Constitution and their significance, as well as the basics of the Declaration of Independence. Students should start to learn about the various visions that inspired them and how they changed. Certainly students at this age can appreciate the important story about how addressing self-interest and passion became the focus of the Constitution. And they can follow why compromise and consensus is so important. After all, they are exploring these very same conflicts within themselves, a platform that could be used for these lessons. The course should also reference relevant current events to capture students' attention (for example, if it is in a presidential year, a lesson could start by a teacher asking whether the students know what the president does and what an election is and work from that into the Constitution).

More sophisticated versions of this same course, which would also be required, should be offered again in middle school and high school—American Constitution II and III. The essential goal is a deep understanding and appreciation of our Constitution, but the courses should also provide students with capacity for the critical examination of the system. A line of discussion might be the value of the electoral college today, or the relationship between the First Amendment and campaign finance reform.

Starting in middle school and continuing through high school, students should also be required to take classes in current events, at least four semesters over this six-year period. Here the goal is not just (or merely) a discussion of today's events, but to use current events as a means of giving life to the Constitution. A discussion of the Iraq War could be used to talk about war powers, executive powers, legislative powers, separation of powers, decision-making processes, and the role of the courts. Schools should also encourage and aid student participation in extracurricular campus or outside organizations, such as internships and service clubs. We need far greater emphasis throughout our society on community and national service. The vigor of our democracy requires this understanding of appreciation of our constitutional values, and while they must be taught in the classroom, they can be experienced better outside it. Moreover, these classes should not be limited to the academically gifted. As professors Constance Flanagan, Peter Levine, and Richard Settersten demonstrate in a forthcoming work, the non-college-bound have the highest unemployment rates and the lowest voting rates among our population, and their departure from school marks the onset of their adulthood, diminishing their potential for civic engagement.

A Presidential Opportunity

The implementation of this or any such program will take hard work. Complacency about our democracy is its greatest enemy and, ironically, overcoming this complacency requires the very commitment to civic literacy that our complacency obstructs. This presidential election provides a great opportunity. Both candidates have demonstrated in their service and in their commitment to public service a unique understanding of the demands (bipartisan compromises, respect for the ideas of others, respect for our governing institutions) of our democracy. And both can translate their own learning and experience in these matters into a national discussion on civic literacy. If they don't, things probably will get worse. By all accounts, turnout among young voters is expected to be high, particularly for Barack Obama.

That said, high participation as a result of the appeal of a particular candidate can provide a platform for change, but is not change itself. In fact, it can have a negative effect. The candidate can lose, or he can win and then have to govern, making all the compromises necessary for an effective presidency. From either of these results, new voters will become disillusioned. Civic literacy pushes back against this response. A good civic education teaches that losing an election is not an excuse to disengage from the political system, that compromise is the currency of the system, that you have an obligation to remain involved, that you have to keep pushing to succeed, and that you have to accept a decision resulting from a legitimate process, even if you don't like it.

America, unlike most of world's nations, is not a country defined by blood or belief. Rather, it is an idea, or a set of ideas, about freedom and opportunity. It is this set of ideas that binds us together as Americans. That's why these ideas have to be taught. Our understanding and appreciation of them is how we grade our civic literacy. We are now failing, and heading toward what the philosopher Michael Sandel has called a "story-less condition," in which "there is no continuity between present and past, and therefore no responsibility, and therefore no possibility for acting together to govern ourselves." We need civic education to reverse this course.

Reading Analytically

1. Lane begins his essay with a discussion about a new test that will be administered to immigrants seeking citizenship. Why does he choose to begin with this story? What use does he make of this description of the new test?
2. One key claim that Lane makes is that the lack of civic literacy "is putting our constitutional democracy at risk." What evidence does he offer for this claim? Summarize at least three arguments that he makes to support this dire depiction of the state of our democracy.
3. Lane goes beyond depicting the problem of declining civic literacy, and offers what he takes to be possible solutions to that problem. Outline the program of reform that he is suggesting, and from your perspective as a student, evaluate whether you believe these solutions are useful, necessary, and feasible.

Reading Across Disciplinary Communities

1. Though civic literacy is clearly within the province of several disciplines—history, political science, philosophy, sociology, and others—Lane offers proposals that are clearly connected to his own discipline of law. What particular parts of his argument demonstrate his own disciplinary connections to legal studies? How might a program of civic literacy differ if it was offered by a political

scientist? A philosopher? A historian? On what points might these disciplines agree?

2. Despite the close connection of Lane's argument to disciplines like those named above, the concept of civic responsibility and good citizenship is also used as an argument for other forms of literacy. Review the arguments that are made for other forms of literacy in at least two other pieces in this section, and describe the ways in which those authors also frame their suggestions as crucial to a thriving democracy.

RICHARD L. SCHEAFFER

Statistics and Quantitative Literacy

It is difficult to go through a single day without encountering statistical information. Newspapers cite surveys and polls, doctors discuss the probabilities of specific causes for disease, social scientists predict the likelihood of particular phenomena based upon past correlation of causes and effects, and weather experts predict the likelihood of rain or snow on the evening news. In order to act as literate consumers of this glut of quantitative information, we need to know what all these numbers mean. Richard L. Scheaffer, in this essay, builds a case for statistical literacy based upon both the needs of citizens and the needs of professionals on the job. He also demonstrates the relationship between statistical literacy and curricula both in mathematics education and across the disciplines.

More specifically, Sheaffer builds an argument that statistical literacy should be a central—if not the central—component of mathematics education. While recognizing that current curricula do acknowledge the need for attention to statistical analysis, he suggests that even more time and attention must be paid to this particular facet of quantitative literacy. As you read, consider your own mathematics courses, measuring the degree to which they did—or did not—prepare you to competently interpret the statistics you encounter on a daily basis.

Abstract: Because much of the early work in quantitative literacy was led by statisticians—indeed, many K–12 programs in probability and statistics are named "quantitative literacy"—statistics bears a very special relation to quantitative literacy, with respect to both substance and education. This essay provides a perspective by leaders of statistics education on issues raised in the other background essays prepared for the Forum on quantitative literacy.

With contributions from Beth Chance, California Polytechnic State University; Cathryn Dippo, Bureau of Labor Statistics; Thomas Moore, Grinnell College; Jerry Moreno, John Carroll University; and Jeffrey Witmer, Oberlin College.

Setting the Stage

Who would disagree that college graduates, not to mention high school graduates, should be able to understand and correctly interpret disease or unemployment rates, the comparative costs of car or apartment rental agreements, and trends in the composition of the country's population? Yet many graduates are mystified by quantitative arguments, a mystification that ranges from minor confusion in some to functional innumeracy in others. Just as the information age is making the world more quantitative, however, the ability of people to deal with numerical issues of practical consequence is shrinking. It is past time to take seriously the challenge of improving the quantitative skills of graduates of U.S. high schools and colleges.

This first paragraph is meant to show exigency—the importance and timeliness of this topic and this article. How is that case made here?

Before examining the role of statistics in the movement to improve quantitative literacy, it is wise to consider definitions of the key terms under discussion because there have been many different interpretations, even among enlightened readers. In fact, at the level of education under consideration here (high school and undergraduate) what some would call "statistics" might be termed "data analysis" or "statistical thinking" by others. We need to sort out the definitions of at least three different terms, all dealing with the same substance.

It is important as a writer to begin with definitions of key terms so that you and your readers are using similar understandings of those key concepts.

Statistics often is thought of as the keeper of the scientific method (although this may sound a little presumptuous to physical scientists) because it is the discipline that studies how to understand the world through the rubric of setting hypotheses, collecting data relevant to those hypotheses, analyzing the data, and drawing conclusions about the hypotheses from analysis of the data. Here "data" is to be understood broadly, because it well may include judgments of experts as in a Bayesian analysis. Although statistics has many elegant theories, its practice usually outstrips theory in the sense

Though it might seem that *statistics* is a simple term, this paragraph shows that the word can be used in several ways.

that many practical problems do not fit nicely into the assumptions of any theory.

This difficulty leads directly to *data analysis,* which can be thought of as following the rubric of the scientific method but with emphasis on answering real questions rather than trying to fit those questions into established theories. In data analysis, exploratory techniques stand alongside confirmatory techniques. Empirical evidence that a technique works often is taken as "proof" among data analysts who might choose to use such a technique in practice. "An approximate answer to the right question is better than an exact answer to the wrong question" is one of the mantras of the data analyst, the supreme example of whom is the late John Tukey (Tukey 1962). In today's complex world, data analysis is what most statisticians actually practice, and so it is quite appropriate that the subject be referred to as data analysis in standards and guidelines.

This statement suggests the importance of the ability to analyze not only statistics, but the methods used to obtain them.

In reality, full-bore data analysis is more than most people need to deal with the statistical issues of everyday life and work. As a result, the third term, *statistical thinking,* comes into play. Statistical thinking is essential for anyone who wants to be an informed citizen, intelligent consumer, or skilled worker. It is the backbone of the contemporary emphasis on quality improvement because all levels of employees in a firm, from the CEO to the janitor, must have some notion of statistical thinking if a firm is to operate optimally. Using a quality-improvement definition, statistical thinking involves viewing life as made up of processes and viewing all processes as having variation. Once understood, variation can be broken down into that which can be reduced and that which must be managed.

This transition helps readers to see why it is important for citizens to have rudimentary skills of "statistical thinking," even if they are not full-scale experts. This then sets up the argument for including statistical thinking in the curriculum of schools and colleges.

This most basic of the three statistical terms might sound the most abstract, but we must keep in mind that processes can be simple and the sources of variation fairly obvious. Figuring out the gas mileage of a car is a process subject to variation, the most obvious sources of which are perhaps the grade of gasoline used and the style of driving. A person's health is likewise subject to variation, but here the sources of variation are many and sometimes difficult to detect. It is statistical thinking that keeps people from making rash decisions when accidents increase this month over last or one school has a slightly lower test score average than another

Notice how this paragraph shows the everyday uses of statistics—and so why people need to understand how to use and interpret them as a key "literacy."

school. The inherent variation in processes must be considered to determine whether change can be attributed to any cause other than pure chance.

Some might further differentiate between statistical thinking and *statistical literacy*, giving the latter a less formal definition than one involving processes and their variation. The ability to read a newspaper critically often is used as an attribute of a statistically literate person. The books by David Moore (2001) and Jessica Utts (1999) are good references for courses on statistical literacy, as is the Web-based Chance course (see www.dartmouth.edu/_chance). Because statistical thinking and statistical literacy are so close in the larger scheme of things, this essay uses the term statistical thinking when referring to this level of statistical education (which also may reduce the confusion over the many uses of the word *literacy*).

As to the definition of *quantitative literacy* (QL), two of the many possibilities adequately cover the topic for purposes of this essay. The British report *Mathematics Counts* (Cockcroft 1982) popularized the term *numeracy* and defined it in part as "an 'at-homeness' with numbers and an ability to make use of mathematical skills which enables an individual to cope with the practical demands of everyday life" (Cockcroft 1982, 11). More recently, the International Life Skills Survey, as quoted in *Mathematics and Democracy: The Case for Quantitative Literacy* (Steen 2001), offers a slightly broader definition of quantitative literacy as an "aggregate of skills, knowledge, beliefs, dispositions, habits of mind, communication capabilities, and problem-solving skills that people need in order to engage effectively in quantitative situations arising in life and work" (Steen 2001, 7).

In this paragraph, the author distinguishes between general "quantitative literacy" and the specific form of "statistical literacy." In the next paragraph, he goes on to elaborate on this connection.

There are strong ties between statistical thinking, data analysis, and quantitative literacy in terms of historical developments, current emphases, and prospects for the future. As pointed out in *Mathematics and Democracy* (Steen 2001), the American Statistical Association (ASA) conducted a National Science Foundation funded project called Quantitative Literacy in the mid-1980s that produced materials and workshops to introduce mathematics teachers at the middle and high school levels to basic concepts of data analysis and probability. The project was built around a hands-on, active learning format that involved student projects and appropriate use of technology.

Here, two more key literacies are tied together—quantitative literacy and civic literacy (the literacy needed to be a good, active citizen).

The ASA QL program was motivated by the Schools Project in England that had introduced statistics into the national curriculum, using the report *Mathematics Counts* (Cockcroft 1982) as one of the supporting documents. This report noted that statistics is "essentially a practical subject and its study should be based on the collection of data . . . by pupils themselves." To this end it urged "in-service training courses on the teaching of statistics not only for mathematics teachers but also for teachers of other subjects" as well as "teaching materials which will emphasize a practical approach" (Cockcroft 1982, 234). Even then, 20 years ago, the Cockcroft commission recognized that "micro-computers . . . offer opportunities to illuminate statistical ideas and techniques" (Cockcroft 1982, 235). All these points were taken to heart by the ASA QL team, and all are still valid concerns.

Another transition is formed here, building a logical flow of ideas: if citizens need statistical literacy, we need a curriculum that teaches students this literacy. This move forms the basis of much of what follows.

The emphasis on statistical thinking and data analysis that was introduced in Britain migrated to Canada and was picked up as a main theme for U.S. K–12 education by a Joint Committee of the ASA and the National Council of Teachers of Mathematics (NCTM). The ASA-NCTM QL project served as a model for the data analysis and probability strand in *Curriculum and Evaluation Standards for School Mathematics* published by NCTM (1989), a strand that is even stronger in the updated edition (NCTM 2000).

The movement to include data analysis and probability in the school mathematics curriculum thus has some of the same historical roots as the current QL movement, and has similar emphases. Properly taught, statistical thinking and data analysis emphasize mathematical knowledge and skills that enable an individual to cope with the practical demands of everyday life. They also develop knowledge, beliefs, dispositions, habits of mind, communication capabilities, and problem-solving skills that people need to engage effectively in quantitative situations arising in life and work. It is no accident that almost all of the examples given in the opening paragraphs of *Mathematics and Democracy* (Steen 2001) are statistical in nature. Simultaneous with the K–12 effort, many statisticians began emphasizing statistical thinking at the college level. As mentioned above in the discussion of statistical literacy, excellent textbooks and other materials as well as numerous college courses have been developed around this theme. These deal with issues of

Notice how this argument suggests why statistical literacy is important even for those in nonscientific disciplines. It may explain why you are required to take courses in science and mathematics in your college curriculum.

quantitative literacy in much more authentic ways than almost any mathematics text seems to. Because statistics and quantitative literacy share so much in common, we hope that statisticians and mathematics educators will work together to build a strong emphasis on QL in the school and college curriculum. Many statisticians would probably disagree with the statement in *Mathematics and Democracy* (Steen 2001) that QL is "not the same as statistics." Indeed, many think that a very large part of QL *is* statistics (statistical thinking or data analysis), just as the Cockroft commission thought that statistics was a large part of numeracy. In what follows, we take a more detailed look at the common ground between statistics and QL and suggest ways of building on that commonality for the good of all.

Here, the writer explicitly explains what is to follow, previewing the argument for the reader in ways that prepares them for what is to come. As a writer, it is important to help the reader to see the logical organization of your writing.

QL and Citizenship

Patricia Cline Cohen, quoting Josiah Quincy, notes in her essay that one of the duties of responsible government is to provide statistical knowledge about the general welfare of its citizens. Hard data "are to be sought and ought to be studied by all who aspire to regulate, or improve the state of the nation . . . " (Cohen, see p. 7). In fact, the very word "statistics" derives from its use to collect information on and about the state. A good example of the growth of statistics in government can be seen in the development and expansion of the U.S. Census Bureau over the years and the widespread uses to which its data are put. Developing an informed citizenry is one of the tasks of public education and, in light of the emphasis on data within the government, a large part of that task involves improving the quantitative literacy of all citizens. That statistics can be misused by politicians (and others) is one of the reasons citizens need some skill in statistical thinking and reasoning with data.

Here, the need for statistical thinking is framed as a key skill for citizens in a democracy to avoid being duped by politicians.

According to Cohen, statistics are a powerful tool of political and civic functioning, and at our peril we neglect to teach the skills required to understand them. In large measure, Cohen equates quantitative literacy with statistics and makes a strong case for including statistics in everyone's education. With this, statisticians certainly can agree. They would not agree, however, with Cohen's statement that "statistics has become a branch of mathematics." Statistics has many roots, including business, engineering, agriculture, and the physical, social, and biological sciences; it deals with many issues that would not be considered mathematical. Emphasis on context is one such issue; emphasis on the design of studies is another. Although statistics uses mathematics, the key to statistical thinking is the context of a real problem and how data might be collected and analyzed to help solve that problem. Some would say that the greatest contributions of statistics to modern science lie in the area of design of surveys and experiments, such as the demographic and economic surveys of the Census Bureau and the Bureau of Labor Statistics and the experiments used in many health-related studies.

Notice how the author shows how statistical literacy is important in many fields and disciplines.

In fact, statistics has much broader uses than its mathematical roots might suggest, and many, including the federal government itself, are attempting to enlighten citizens about the proper collection, analysis, and interpretation of data. One example of this is the effort of the FedStats Interagency Task Force to develop a statistical literacy program for users of the Federal Statistical System. A related effort is embodied in a recent report from the National Research Council entitled *Information Technology Research for Federal Statistics,* which talks about the importance of literacy, visualization, and perception of data:

Here, the author shows why statistical literacy involves more than just mathematical abilities, and includes other critical thinking skills.

> Given the relatively low level of numerical and statistical literacy in the population at large, it becomes especially important to provide users with interfaces that give them useful, meaningful information. Providing data with a bad interface that does not allow users to interpret data sensibly may be worse than not providing the data at all. . . . The goal is to provide not merely a data set but also tools that allow making sense of the data. (NRC 2000, 20)

These and other efforts by the federal government to improve statistical literacy are supported by Katherine Wallman, chief statistician of the US government, who said in a 1999 speech (Wallman 1999):

> Electronic dissemination is truly a boon to national statistical offices anxious to make their data more accessible and useful—and to user communities equipped to handle the wealth of available information. But this technology remains to a degree a bane, for while we have taken monumental strides in making our nation's statistics electronically available, attention to documentation in electronic media has lagged. And I continue

> to argue, as I have for almost a decade, that the gap between our citizens' computer literacy and their "statistical literacy" remains significant.

Citizens encounter statistics at every turn in their daily lives. Often, however, they are ill-equipped to evaluate the information presented to them. Fortunately, quantitative literacy initiatives show prospects of enhancing the statistical literacy of the next generation. Our ideal would be students who can use statistics to keep their fingers on the pulse of humanity, as envisioned by the great Belgian statistician and social scientist Adolph Quetelet:

> I like to think of the constant presence in any sound Republic of two guardian angels: the Statistician and the Historian of Science. The former keeps his finger on the pulse of Humanity, and gives the necessary warning when things are not as they should be. The Historian . . . will not allow humanity to forget its noblest traditions or to be ungrateful to its greatest benefactors. (Walker 1945, 10)

Note how these extended quotations help to support the author's argument.

QL and the Workplace

Everyone agrees that business needs workers with QL skills, but according to Linda Rosen and her colleagues in their essay, it is not at all clear what those skills are or how urgently they are needed. In fact, the types of skills needed vary from business to business, and it may require some serious research to sort out the best set of skills for the workforce of tomorrow. Rosen offers sound advice, emphasizing notions of communication and cooperation that are similar to skills that often are seen as part of QL itself. In particular, she urges advocates of quantitative literacy to better document the existing level and anticipated need of QL in the workplace, to raise general awareness about the importance of QL in today's workplace, and to engage educators to help upgrade the QL skills of the workforce based on identified quantitative needs (Rosen et al., see pp. 43–52).

Here, too, the author attempts to contrast mathematical literacy with statistical literacy, showing why the latter is more crucial.

These recommendations fit well with current efforts in the statistics community to build bridges between the academic community and business, industry, and government to ensure an effective statistics education for the workforce of the future. Somewhat surprisingly, however, the level of skills attached to quantitative literacy varies greatly among those quoted by Rosen, ranging from merely knowing basic arithmetic to making "judgments grounded in data." If such judgments are thought of in the sense of statistical thinking and data analysis, they are much deeper than basic mathematical skills and require an educational component that is not found in traditional mathematics courses. Statistical thinking has a stochastic component (could this variation be caused by chance alone?) that is essential to intelligent study of business, industry, and government processes.

Note here how the author starts from the thoughts of Rosen to build his own, more specific argument. While not refuting Rosen, he does suggest that the argument must go further.

It is important to realize that data, information, and knowledge are a part of a hierarchy: an event yields observations called *data*, which are collected and processed into *information*, which is analyzed and combined with human intelligence to produce *knowledge*. *Wisdom* is the product of knowledge, judgment, and experience. Such taxonomies are important in new fields such as data mining—the process of discovering knowledge through data. As these fields become increasingly important to society, the statistical aspects of thinking intelligently about data and its uses (and misuses) become critical. Most often, the teaching of statistics only reaches the information stage because moving to the higher stages of knowledge and wisdom requires setting the information inside a framework in which to make intelligent judgments. If statistical thinking is a part of the framework, issues such as context (including the surrounding science) and variation are taken into account. How to go beyond the information level in understanding the world around us is one way to phrase the key intellectual challenge of QL. Statisticians surely agree with those cited by Rosen who argue that the core mathematics curriculum must be "something more than arithmetic proficiency."

Although business leaders may be confused about the details of what QL is and how much of it they want, as Rosen suggests, most enlightened leaders of business and industry see the advantages of quantitative thinking quite clearly in at least one area, that of quality control and productivity improvement. The total quality management (TQM) effort is giving way to the Six Sigma improvement initiative, which has become extremely popular in the past several years. In addition to generating a great deal of discussion within statistics and quality-control circles, it has been one of the few technically oriented initiatives to generate significant interest from business leaders, the financial community, and the popular media. Hitching the QL wagon to the Six

Sigma star would be one way to move QL higher on the agenda of business leaders.

Here, the author summarizes the reasons why it is useful to see quantitative and statistical literacy as workplace skills. This then forms a natural transition to why it needs to be included in the curriculum—his next topic.

QL and Curriculum

A central theme of QL is that the meaning of "literate" must be expanded to include quantitative literacy and that the latter, like the former, must be addressed across the curriculum. This theme is clearly stated in the essay by Randall Richardson and William McCallum, who enunciate two main criteria for a QL curriculum: it must go beyond the basic ability to read and write mathematics to the development of conceptual understanding, and it must be engaged with a context, be it humanities, business, science, engineering, technology, or everyday life (Richardson and McCallum, see pp. 99–106).

Richardson and McCallum argue, along with many others, that QL cannot be regarded as the sole responsibility of teachers of mathematics, whether in high school or college. It is the responsibility of those in other disciplines to help provide basic tools and conceptual understanding and to model the use of mathematics as a way of looking at the world. In short, QL should be the focus of mathematics across the curriculum. The nurturing of QL across the curriculum, however, requires strong administrative support and significant institutional change.

Here, the author suggests that quantitative literacy should not be limited to mathematics courses; similar arguments are made in this chapter about writing and other literacies.

Those experienced with teaching statistics suggest that one way to garner administrative support and foster institutional change is to tie much of QL to the statistics curriculum, everywhere it is housed. The very lifeblood of statistics is context, and the current teaching of statistical thinking and modern data analysis is built around conceptual understanding (calculations are done by machine). Because it is *used* across the curriculum, in most colleges and universities statistics already is *taught* across the curriculum. It would make practical as well as pedagogical sense to anchor the expansion of QL to the statistics teaching efforts of colleges and universities. Indeed, some postsecondary institutions ranging from liberal arts colleges (Mt. Holyoke) to large research universities (Ohio State) have centered much of the quantitative

Here, the author shows how quantitative literacy could be incorporated across disciplines, since statistical information is included in the reading in all areas. You might compare this point to that which is made about the humanities and quantitative literacy by Robert Orrill in his essay, also included in this chapter.

reasoning component of their general education requirements on statistics courses.

QL and Mathematics

Closely related to the issue of curriculum is the relationship between QL and mathematics. Deborah Hughes Hallett asserts in her essay that QL is the ability to identify and use quantitative arguments in everyday contexts, that it is more a habit of mind than a set of topics or a list of skills. QL is more about how mathematics is used than about how much mathematics a person knows. For this and other reasons, a call to increase QL is a call for a substantial increase in most students' understanding of mathematics. It is, therefore, not a dumbing down of rigor but an increase in standards. According to Hughes Hallett, this increase is essential because "the general level of quantitative literacy is currently sufficiently limited that it threatens the ability of citizens to make wise decisions at work and in public and private life" (Hughes Hallett, see p. 91).

While the author suggests that mathematics is not the only place for teaching statistical literacy, he here argues that this is still one important site in the curriculum for doing so—if teachers reconstruct the way that they teach mathematics.

Statisticians will find it interesting (and gratifying) that probability and statistics are the only subject areas that Hughes Hallett mentions specifically. Indeed, she finds the absence of these subjects in the education of many students remarkable given that they are so "extensively used in public and private life." Simply requiring more students to study advanced mathematics is not the answer: they actually must be taught QL by solving problems in context. Courses must demand "deeper understanding," which will require a coordinated effort to change both pedagogy and assessment.

Although there is much to agree with in Hughes Hallett's essay, statistics educators would probably disagree with the claim that " . . . the teaching of probability and statistics suffers from the fact that no one can agree on when or by whom these topics should be introduced." The statistics community played an important role in developing the NCTM standards (1989, 2000) and offers strong support for the data analysis and probability strand contained in these recommendations. Similarly, ASA has been involved in the expansion of the data analysis and probability section of the National Assessment of Educational Progress (NAEP) framework for the 2004 examination. The NCTM recommendations for all grade levels, which are reflected in the NAEP framework, call for instructional programs from prekindergarten through grade 12 that enable all students to:

> . . . formulate questions that can be addressed with data and collect, organize, and display relevant data to answer them; select and use appropriate statistical methods to analyze data; develop and evaluate inferences and predictions that are based on data; understand and apply basic concepts of probability. (NCTM 2000, 48)

Here and in the parts that follow, the author uses the ideas and words of a leading disciplinary organization to support his views. This lends credibility to his argument.

With NSF support, ASA has developed a series of supplemental materials for teaching modern data analysis in the elementary, middle, and high school grades called, respectively, Exploring Statistics in the Elementary Grades, Quantitative Literacy, and Data Driven Mathematics. (See the education section at www.amstat.org or the Dale Seymour section of Pearson Learning at www.pearsonlearning.com.) These materials support and enhance the NCTM recommendations, and thus also the kinds of quantitative literacy that Hughes Hallett seeks.

The Advanced Placement (AP) Statistics course has become quite popular among high school teachers and students; its course description (see http://apcentral.collegeboard.com/repository/ap01.cd_sta_4328.pdf) reflects modern trends in data analysis that now are being emulated in some college courses. Statistics educators discovered long ago that classroom activities, laboratory activities, and group projects really work. The Mathematical Association of America (MAA) publication *Teaching Statistics: Resources for Undergraduate Instructors* showcases many examples of materials and programs that support this approach (Moore 2000). That the statistics community has rallied around these ideas is evidenced by the promulgation of good resources for hands-on, active teaching of statistics at both the school and college levels.

Notice how the author consistently argues for hands-on learning of statistics—showing that it is an applied science with direct applicability to other fields of study.

At the college level, both ASA and MAA have prepared guidelines concerning the undergraduate teaching of statistics. The ASA "Curriculum Guidelines for Undergraduate Programs in Statistical Science" encourages a broad range of programs that offer all students useful options beyond the traditional introductory course:

> Undergraduate statistics programs should emphasize concepts and tools for working with data and provide experience in designing data collection and in analyzing real data that go

beyond the content of a first course in statistical methods. The detailed statistical content may vary, and may be accompanied by varying levels of study in computing, mathematics, and a field of application. (ASA 2001, 1)

Reports from the MAA (CUPM 1993) recommend that all undergraduate mathematical sciences majors should have a datacentered statistics course. Taken together, the standards, guidelines, and curriculum materials fashioned by the statistics community (with support from the mathematics community) give solid evidence that many pieces of the "coordinated effort" needed to improve quantitative literacy are in place. The QL reform that may be coming should make good use of the projects and related ideas already afloat within the statistics education community.

To be honest, however, many statistics courses still are taught in a manner that misses the QL point. This is partly because tension always exists between breadth of coverage and deep understanding—the latter of most importance to QL. Although the statistics education community may have reached consensus on how to deal with the tension, this consensus does not always play out easily in the classroom. Courses serve many clients, some of whom demand coverage of many specific topics in statistical inference.

Here, the author offers a critique of current methods. Note how he introduces this point with a clear, direct transition in a quite personal voice.

Jan de Lange's paper, also about QL and mathematics, introduces two new and important ideas (de Lange, see pp. 75–89). First, it extends the definition of quantitative literacy to the term "mathematical literacy" because of the indisputable fact that much more in mathematics is useful besides numbers. Indeed, many aspects of statistical thinking (which de Lange includes under the name "uncertainty" as one of his core phenomenological categories) are not about numbers as much as about concepts and habits of mind. For example, the idea of a lurking variable upsetting an apparent bivariate relationship with observational data is a conceptual idea, part of statistical thinking but not particularly about numbers. The notion that designed experiments are more reliable than observational studies is another very important nonquantitative idea.

De Lange's second important idea is that if mathematics were properly taught, the distinction between mathematical content and mathematical literacy "would be smaller than some people suggest it is now." The issue is part of the aforementioned tension between breadth of coverage and depth of understanding, but it also suggests a resolution of the dilemma of QL courses. Separate courses in QL create serious problems. First, students are pigeonholed into those capable of taking "real mathematics" and those who will only need QL, thereby entrenching two classes of students in a structure that serves the nation poorly. Second, although all students need to be quantitatively literate, there is growing evidence that those who take regular mathematics courses (and who in a segregated system may not encounter much QL) are not learning many of the critical thinking skills they need.

Here, the author continues his argument for teaching statistics in context, not in isolation from other learning.

QL and Articulation

Articulation is a technical term in education which describes the ways that various courses fit together to create a coherent curriculum—how one course "articulates" with others.

Articulation of the K–16 mathematics curriculum is difficult to attain because it involves inextricably linked political and policy issues. Michael Kirst's essay (Kirst, see pp. 107–120) outlines the main areas of political tension: between professional leadership and political consensus, between flexible and specific standards, between dynamic standards and reasonable expectations for change, between professional leadership and public understanding of standards, between expectations and requirements. Progress toward improving articulation requires a clear signal up and down the line as to what is required. Part of that signal should be a clear message about QL.

As subject-matter standards and examinations have evolved in recent years, one of the widespread changes has been increased emphasis on data analysis and statistics; however, one of the main limiting factors is the quality of materials for teachers. "Any attempt to change mathematics curriculum," Kirst observes, "must involve rethinking textbook creation and adoption policies." Another limiting factor is the ever-present standardized examination. Multiple-choice basic skills tests do not adequately emphasize complex thinking skills such as statistical inference and multistep mathematical problem solving.

The statistics community would argue that an emphasis on statistics and QL in the mathematics curriculum could help alleviate some of these tensions. The movements to infuse school mathematics with data analysis and to enhance undergraduate statistics offerings owe much of their success to the fact that leaders from business and industry supported the efforts. It helped, of course, that these efforts began when quality improvement was a high national priority; that theme is still important for garnering support for statistics among business and political leaders. Another theme that allows statisticians to enter doors that might be more difficult for mathematicians to open is data: everyone is collecting tons of it and few know what to do with it. The public understands something of these issues. Indeed, many see the need for statistics education much more clearly than they see the need for mathematics education (although they might view statistics as a part of mathematics).

> Note how this shift to a direct and informal form of writing gathers attention. It gives the air of common sense.

Will college faculty buy into an articulated program in mathematics education that includes a strong component of QL? Statistics faculty are likely to do so, if the success of the AP Statistics course and the support for the changes promoted by the NCTM standards and the NAEP framework are any indication. AQL emphasis would not look as radically new to a statistician as it might to a mathematician.

QL and Assessment

Many of the exhortations in the background essays about the importance of assessment to a successful QL program are subsumed in the comprehensive and detailed paper by Grant Wiggins (Wiggins, see pp. 121–143). In Wiggins' view, echoed by others, "we have often sacrificed the primary client (the learner) in the name of accountability." Wiggins seeks to put the interests of the learner back in the center of assessment.

Assessment plays a central role in QL reform. Wiggins argues for a realignment of assessment with QL that puts more emphasis on open-ended, messy, and "authentic" assessment tasks. Much of this realignment will require challenging changes in the focus of traditional instruction, including much more formative (diagnostic) assessment. To develop reliable examples of high-quality assessment strategies that are focused on a few big ideas will require significant collaboration. In addition, instructors will need training to design, administer, and grade these new types of assessment.

> This short sentence allows the author to make his claim cogently. He goes on to show the reasons for this claim by showing how assessment must be "authentic"—it must measure the higher order statistical and critical thinking for which he advocates, not just basic skills.

Wiggins makes much of "context" but seems to use the term in at least two different ways. One relates to determining the source of a problem (who is asking the question, how was the information gathered, who is the answer for, what are relevant issues in the discipline that may affect the solution). Another suggests a more philosophical, historical point of view (where do laws or theorems come from, are they debatable, can you understand the history and how it affects our present state of knowledge). Although historical perspective is important, Wiggins seems to overemphasize the role of this type of context for beginning students. To statisticians, the first definition of context is absolutely essential for any problem; the second, although helpful for some problems, is not nearly as essential.

Data analysis problems usually have a built-in context that may make them easier for teachers to attack (although not many such examples are found in Wiggins' essay). They have less of the baggage of the years of formalism that has accompanied mathematics instruction and that can be difficult for new teachers to break free from.

Wiggins differentiates between "meaning making" and "statistical reasoning," whereas statisticians would not see these as so different. His interpretation of "meaning making" as "what is mathematics and why does it matter" seems a bit narrow. Many levels of reasoning and conceptual understanding are important in mathematics even when historical perspective is incomplete. The focus should be on students' abilities to reason with their own knowledge and "understand how it works," even if their ability to question and debate is limited. Mathematics that is relevant to students' direct experiences is more meaningful to many beginning students than philosophical debates. The important message is that different experiences are meaningful to different students, and teachers need to be ready to provide students with a variety of contexts.

Here, the author articulates his argument for a type of statistical knowledge that is useful and relevant, not just "school learning."

One of the main goals of mathematics education reform surely should be, as Wiggins claims, to make assessment design "more public, collaborative, and subject to ongoing peer review." This cannot be overemphasized, but teachers need more examples of how to do this, particularly for lower-level students. Although many of Wiggins' examples are quite grand, what teachers need are simpler tasks that could be assigned on a daily basis to help students learn to interpret and test their understanding. Fortunately, statistics educators have been thinking about authentic assessment for some time; B. L. Chance (1997) and J. B. Garfield (1994) give good overviews of current thinking on authentic assessment.

Conclusion

Statistics and quantitative literacy have much in common. Although few would disagree with

The author begins his conclusion by restoring the connection between statistical literacy and other forms of quantitative literacy. Note how he ends the paragraph with a call for collaboration between the two fields—usually a better form of argument than being divisive.

this, statisticians would probably argue that QL is mainly statistics while mathematicians and mathematics educators tend to argue that QL is only partly statistics. Statistics emphasizes context, design of studies, and a stochastic view of the world. Although statistics is clearly not the same as mathematics, nor even a part of mathematics, it uses mathematics as one of its main tools for practical problem solving. Being one of the most widely used of the mathematical sciences, statistics is well entrenched in many places across the curriculum. At the K–2 level, statistics already has embarked on a program that emphasizes active learning, much in the spirit recommended by modern cognitive science. All this suggests that students will reap dividends if the two disciplines work together.

Although statistics education has gained acceptance (even respect) over the past 15 years as a key component of the K–12 mathematics curriculum, this acceptance does not always translate into classroom practice. The taught curriculum is far from reconciled with the recommended curriculum. In addressing this challenge, statistics and QL should be mutually reinforcing. Simply put, statistics has opened the door for quantitative literacy. In his background essay on curriculum in grades 6–12, Lynn Arthur Steen argues that in a balanced curriculum, "[D]ata analysis, geometry, and algebra would constitute three equal content components in grades 6 to 8 and in grades 9 to 11" (Steen, see p. 66). "Real work yielding real results," he emphasizes, "must begin and end in real data" (see p. 59).

On the pedagogical side, statistics educators have learned to emphasize both engagement and relevance. There is ample evidence that both teachers and students like a hands-on, activity-based approach to data analysis (the type recommended earlier in this essay), and that students learn better through this approach. Two teachers using data analysis materials in an algebra course and a teacher of AP Statistics have noticed how data analysis not only adds valuable content to the curriculum but also improves attitudes:

> The [data analysis] materials allow the students to construct knowledge based on their experiences, and these materials provide activities and experiences to guide the students to good concept-based skills. The students understand what and why they are doing things.
>
> * * *
>
> Almost all of the students were amazed by the fact that some of the mathematical concepts that they study (logs and exponentials)

are actually used in such situations. I must also say that I find it very exciting to engage in these topics as well!

***

I would like to echo the comments about the value of an early statistics education. Yesterday, our AP Psychology teacher told me how much difference she sees between students with a stats background and students without. She said the difference was like "night and day," especially with project work. Our science teachers are saying the same thing. I guess what I am saying is what a lot of us already believe: a knowledge of statistics enriches every other discipline and life in general. Three cheers for statistics!

These quotations lend a positive tone and a sense of urgency to the topic, while showing how effective this program can be. Again, ending on a positive note is more likely to move his readers to action.

At the college level, statistics is one of the most widely required or recommended courses in the mathematical sciences, and the same emphasis on data analysis with hands-on activities and laboratory experiences is permeating these courses. AP Statistics is widely accepted, even emulated, by many college programs and can form one of the paths for articulating a QL message between schools and colleges. Strong ties between ASA and MAA can help cement the path.

As noted above, Adolph Quetelet emphasized the importance for science of both statisticians and historians of science. It seems appropriate, then, to end this review with a relevant observation from a historian of science, Theodore Porter:

> Statistical methods are about logic as well as numbers. For this reason, as well as on account of their pervasiveness in modern life, *statistics cannot be the business of statisticians alone,* but should enter into the schooling of every educated person. To achieve this would be a worthy goal for statistics in the coming decades. (Porter 2001, 61) (Italics added.)

Consider why this author decides to end his piece with a direct quotation. How does it capture the major argument that he is making?

References

American Statistical Association. 2001. "Curriculum Guidelines for Undergraduate Programs in Statistical Science." http://www.amstat.org/education/Curriculum_Guidelines.html.

Chance, B. L. 1997. "Experiences with Authentic Assessment Techniques in an Introductory Statistics Course." *Journal of Statistics Education*, 5(3). www.amstat.org/publications/jse/v5n3/chance.html.

Cockcroft, W. H., ed. 1982. *Mathematics Counts.* London: Her Majesty's Stationery Office.

Garfield, J. B. 1994. "Beyond Testing and Grading: Using Assessment to Improve Student Learning." *Journal of Statistics Education* 2(1). www.amstat.org/publications/jse/v2n1/garfield.html.

Mathematical Association of America. 1993. "Guidelines for Programs and Departments in Undergraduate Mathematical Sciences." http://www.maa.org/guidelines.html.

Moore, D. 1998. "Statistics Among the Liberal Arts." *Journal of the American Statistical Association* 93:1253–1259.

Moore, D. 2001. *Statistics: Concepts and Controversies,* 5th ed. New York, NY: W. H. Freeman.

Moore, D., and G. Cobb. 2000. "Statistics and Mathematics: Tension and Cooperation." *American Mathematical Monthly,* 615–630.

Moore, T., ed. 2000. *Teaching Statistics: Resources for Undergraduate Instructors,* MAA Notes No. 52. Washington, DC: Mathematics Association of America.

National Council of Teachers of Mathematics. 1989. *Curriculum and Evaluation Standards for School Mathematics.* Reston, VA: National Council of Teachers of Mathematics.

National Council of Teachers of Mathematics. 2000. *Principles and Standards for School Mathematics.* Reston, VA: National Council of Teachers of Mathematics.

National Research Council. 2000. *Information Technology Research for Federal Statistics.* www4.nationalacademies.org/cpsma/cstb.nsf/web/pub_federal statistics?OpenDocument.

Porter, T. 2001. "Statistical Futures." *Amstat News* (291) (September): 61–64.

Steen, Lynn Arthur, ed. 2001. *Mathematics and Democracy: The Case for Quantitative Literacy.* Princeton, NJ: National Council of Education and the Disciplines.

Tukey, J. 1962. "The Future of Data Analysis." *Annals of Mathematical Statistics* 33: 1–67.

Utts, J. 1999. *Seeing Through Statistics,* 2nd ed. Belmont, CA: Duxbury Press.

Walker, H. 1945. "The Role of the American Statistical Association." *Journal of the American Statistical Association* 40:1–10.

Wallman, Katherine K. 1999. "At the Intersection of Official Statistics and Public Policy: Confronting the Challenges." Amsterdam: Celebrating the Centenary of the Netherlands Statistical Office.

Reading Analytically

1. Scheaffer spends a good deal of time and ink toward the beginning of his essay defining what he means by statistical literacy and how it differs somewhat from other forms of quantitative thinking. Read those sections carefully, and try to articulate in your own words what this author seems to mean by statistical literacy.

2. One way that an author creates exigency—the importance of a topic—is by connecting the topic with other concepts that are valued by the audience. In this case, Scheaffer argues for the importance of quantitative and statistical literacy to our roles as citizens and as workers. Describe the main arguments he makes for the importance of these literacies in those two cases.
3. In building his case, Scheaffer draws upon several examples of programs that seemed to have helped to further statistical literacy. Describe those programs and detail the ways that he uses those examples to help further his argument.

Reading Across Disciplinary Communities

1. While we might, from the outside, consider quantitative literacy and statistical literacy to be the same thing, Scheaffer makes a strong effort to differentiate those two literacies. Why? In what ways does his argument for an increased attention to statistics differentiate one from the other? How does this also show the fine points of disagreement between two closely related disciplines, mathematics and statistics?
2. This chapter has a series of articles that argue for what each author believes to be the most beneficial curriculum for all students. That common curriculum is often called "general education"—the set of courses and outcomes that a college requires of all its students, no matter what their majors are. Examine your own college's general education requirements, and consider whether it ensures quantitative, literacy, statistical literacy or both. What other forms of literacy seem to be valued by the required set of courses of your institution?

ROBERT ORRILL

Humanism and Quantitative Literacy

We might tend to think of mathematics and other sciences as diametrically opposed to the study of humanities like literature, philosophy, or art. However, this author suggests that this division among disciplines—and specifically the rejection of quantitative thinking by those in the humanities—is counterproductive. Discussing what he calls the "fractured condition of the American educational enterprise," Orrill details the ways in which the division of the humanities from more quantitative disciplines has been a detriment to those who study the humanities.

To build this case, Orrill, executive director of the National Council on Education and the Disciplines, tells a number of stories and cites experts from the humanities to illustrate the ways in which the inattention to issues of quantitative literacy has weakened the disciplinary study of the humanities. As you read, consider how your own educational experiences did, or did not, offer you the opportunity to connect the various disciplines you studied. You might also consider the attitudes you encountered about scientific disciplines in humanities classes and vice versa. Did you find a tension between the two?

The President of Harvard College, seeing me once by chance soon after the beginning of a term, inquired how my classes were getting on; and when I replied that I thought they were getting on well, that my men seemed to be keen and intelligent, he stopped me as if I was about to waste his time. 'I meant,' said he, 'what is the number of students in your classes.'[1]

—George Santayana, *Character and Opinion in the United States*

With some hesitation, I invite you to consider Santayana's simple parable. This brief remembrance is one that he first recounted in a lecture delivered in England near the end of WWI. The incident itself, however, happened many years before, in the early 1890's, when Santayana was a junior member of Harvard's philosophy department. The impatient (and here unidentified) president in the story is Charles Eliot who, at the time this encounter took place, was widely regarded as the most influential educator in the United States. Although they are colleagues, there is no cordiality indicated in the meeting of the two men. Nor, almost three decades later, is there even a hint of any in its recollection.

The absence of good feeling in this encounter is, I believe, an emotional fact worth our close attention. In its details, of course, the incident does not seem to present a quantitative problem of any difficulty or interest. Hence my hesitation in calling it to your attention. Indeed, we know from other sources that Santayana would have had no trouble supplying the number that Eliot demanded from him. At this time, he tells us, the students in his classes numbered no more than a handful—there were only three or four undergraduates, for instance, in a course on the British Enlightenment that he had inherited from William James. So, in a strict sense, there is no quantitative issue here that involves anything other than the most rudimentary arithmetic.

Is this a case, then, in which Quantitative Literacy (QL) has little or no work to do? The answer depends, I believe, on how much we should make of the claim that QL informs us about numbers, not in the abstract, but in the many ways we meet them in life itself.[2] Here, for instance, what occurs in this encounter amounts to much more than an exchange of quantitative data. In Eliot's mind, as the young Santayana knows, three or four students in a class translates directly into a moral judgment—in sum, it means not enough, too few, a weak showing. Moreover, it further signifies that Santayana is failing to do his share and, very possibly, may be making less than a full effort. Taken in context, therefore, the number in question cannot be understood apart from its moral reverberations. In effect, numbers and feelings are so closely joined as to be inseparable and thereby combine in this instance, as they so often do in life, to make a moral event. How, if at all, should QL approach such events? Only arithmetically? Or is it attentive to them in a more complete sense and, if so, to what end? Addressing these questions here at Wingspread might help clarify the role of QL in a liberal education.

Here, in the beginning, something more might be said about Santayana's meeting with President Eliot. Briefly stated, what happens in this encounter? Outwardly, of course, very little. By chance, the two men come together, exchange a few words, and then go their separate ways. Inwardly, however, much changes for the young Santayana. Suddenly, he finds that the world is very different from what he thought it to be. In effect, the question that Eliot puts to him conveys that the worth of philosophy—or any subject—should be derived from the number of students that it can attract. For Santayana, this intrusion of market standards rendered the environment almost unrecognizable. What, innocently, he had believed to be a sanctuary of the intellect now confronts him—in the person of the president—with a setting dominated by the rule of quantification and a crude regime of numbers. From one moment to the next, then, his own alma mater, Harvard, had become a strange and oppressive place.

If he noticed Santayana's discomfort at all, it is unlikely that Eliot felt it to be of any significance. Doubtless, he considered the question he asked to be of the utmost importance and entirely in order. Writ large, in fact, it reflected a policy of "quantitative aggrandizement" then evident everywhere in American education.[3] In promoting this policy, Eliot himself had warned that the very survival of the American college depended on its keeping pace "with the growth of the country in population and wealth."[4] This meant, in practice, that the college must seek to have more of everything—money, students, buildings—and to gain these things it, above all, must include "all subjects" in its offerings and leave the choice among them entirely open to the election of students. Without a prescribed curriculum of its own, then, nothing could narrow a college's chances for growth. No matter that an absence of any uniformity in the learning of students made it difficult to give "clear meaning" or ascribe "exact significance" to the baccalaureate degree. For this, too, Eliot had a quantitative solution. As it had in the past, he said, the degree should still testify to the "main fact" that "the recipient has spent eight or ten years, somewhere between the ages of twelve and twenty-three, in liberal studies."[5]

Although much more could be said, this perhaps is where we should leave the Eliot-Santayana encounter. Suffice it to note that Santayana's discomfort in the American academic environment only intensified during the years that followed this incident. With a sense of profound relief, he eventually fled Harvard and thereafter rejected all offers either to return there or to accept a chair in any other American university. Moving on, though, I now want to discuss how this case is an illustrative one. Examining the historical record, we can see that many of Santayana's contemporary humanists shared the same feelings of discontent with Eliot's "new education;" and this, I believe, helps account for why they gave quantitative matters so little consideration in their approach to student learning. Without much exaggeration, one could even say that they entirely banished quantitative issues from their vision of a liberal education.

This, I might add, was essentially the character of my own educational experience. As an undergraduate, my studies were mostly of a humanistic nature; and, looking back, I cannot recall even once being asked to address a serious quantitative question in completing a large array of courses devoted to history, literature, philosophy, and the arts. This surely contributed to my becoming quantitatively oblivious; and later, as a teacher myself, I in turn never asked my students to attend to any of the quantitative problems lurking in the texts that we read together. Until very recently, in fact, I do not think that I noticed that they were there.

My own experience, then, suggests that an aversion to numbers has a long history in the so-called humane studies. Why this antipathy to quantification? What is its origin? In part, at least, its beginnings can be traced to the "anxiety" felt by Anglo-American humanists when, in the late 19th century, they looked ahead to the looming dominance of a mass democracy.[6] As they saw it, this threat of an overwhelming deluge of numbers placed civilization itself in grave peril. In 1884, for instance,

Matthew Arnold delivered a lecture in the United States that he entitled "Numbers; or the Majority and the Remnant." His main intent in this address was to warn his listeners about the dangers of becoming enthralled by the large numbers that made up so much of the data typically brought forth in praise of American life. To be sure, he said, these facts were undeniable and seemingly very impressive. Citing a fellow countryman, he told his listeners:

> The vast scale of things here, the extent of your country, your numbers, the rapidity of your increase, strike the imagination, and are a common topic for admiring remark. Our great orator, Mr. Bright, is never weary of telling us how many acres of land you have at your disposal, how many bushels of grain you produce, how many millions you are, how many more millions you will be presently, and what a capital thing this is for you.[7]

This, of course, is said ironically. In plain speech, Arnold means that all this talk of abundance is tiresome stuff. Worse yet, such boasting about material things weighs heavily on the spirit and is deadening to the soul.

More sermon than lecture, Arnold's talk holds fast throughout to a single message. The Americans may be a people of plenty, he says, but morally this has placed them at risk of identifying goodness with quantity—that is, of mistaking more for better and most for better yet. For correction, therefore, they should look to the lessons of tradition, to the wisdom that resides—as he famously put it—in "the best which has been thought and said." There they will be reminded that the "sages and saints" always have warned that the multitude is "unsound" and not to be trusted. More positively, they also will find the teachings that make up "the doctrine of the *remnant*." This guidance conveys the good news that a few, an elect, can protect against the failings of the many and spiritually uphold an entire culture. In some variant or other, of course, this belief that the masses should (and will) allow themselves to be led by a priesthood or an elect of some kind would long continue to influence the evolution of American education.

During his lecture tour, Arnold also emphasized that the doctrine he preached had a direct bearing on educational arrangements in the United States. It meant that the aim of the university, above all else, should be to nurture this much-needed "saving remnant." In turn, this task required that the work of the university should be devoted to the transmission of tradition and, therefore, that study therein should attend to a core curriculum that was literary, classical, and morally earnest in its orientation. Rejecting any such dwelling on the past, Eliot had said that the university should seek its fortune in the here and now, embrace American life, and grow along with it. Arnold, in contrast, urged that this teeming activity be kept out of collegiate education. Both held that students should be led "to think," but, for Arnold, thought was reflective, a turning inward, and directed in each person toward development of a "best self." If study remained true to this aim, the university could hope to produce a leavening cadre of "workers for good." Necessarily, of course, such an approach envisioned an exalted role for both faculty and students. For the sake of the culture at large, they were to serve as nothing less than a clergy of the intellect and keepers of the spirit.

In essence, what Arnold advocated was a somewhat spiritualized version of an Oxbridge college. During the years that followed, this in fact became the model that most humanists favored and hoped would prevail in American undergraduate education. More than any other option, this ideal provided their own basis for self-understanding and sense of vocation. They knew, of course, that their views were in conflict with the utilitarian model promoted at this time by Eliot and most other university presidents. In a concrete instance, we glimpsed this clash in the Eliot-Santayana encounter. On a larger scale, this also was the drama that Henry James saw unfolding when, in 1904, he revisited Harvard after an absence of twenty years. An admirer of Arnold, he had hoped on his return to find something resembling an American Oxford—quite literally, as he put it, to walk into a cloistered haven "inaccessible . . . to the shout of the newspapers, the place to perambulate, the place to think, apart from the crowd." In contrast with Eliot, then, he thought that Harvard should provide an "antidote" to the life that surrounded it. The image he invoked was that of a "university . . . stamped with the character and function of the life-saving monasteries of the dark ages."[8] But, instead, what he found happening on the ground was a dimming of this ideal. This weakening, moreover, was not due to the world pressing in and encroaching upon Harvard. On the contrary, much to James' regret, he saw that a "restlessly expansive Harvard" had acquired an impetus of its own and was now actively "stretching forth, in many directions, long, acquisitive arms."

The humanists, then, had wanted the American college to remain enclosed and be kept small. By 1900, however, most of them recognized that this was a lost cause. Enrollments in college were increasing almost everywhere; and the prevailing educational policy opposed all efforts to place limits on growth. With few exceptions, the humanists acquiesced in the face of these dominant trends; but they remained uncomfortable with the conditions that resulted. They were puzzled, most especially, by student motives for attending college. Why were they coming in ever-mounting numbers and what were they seeking? The answers to these questions turned out to be perplexing. All too few students, it seemed, shared the faculty outlook on the undergraduate experience. If asked, a humanist would have advised the student to think of college work as embarking on an "adventure of ideas"—or, as John Dewey put it, as setting out on a "voyage," a "travelling of the spirit."[9] As it happened, though, most students were not attracted to an intellectual journey of any kind. Instead, they had enrolled in college to secure social advantage, a required credential, or, in a large number of cases, with only the vaguest notion of what they wanted or needed. Moreover, many of these students came to college from high schools that had ill-prepared them to undertake challenging work. Taken together, all of this presented an awkward quandary that humanists found difficult to resolve.

Given these circumstances, what should the humanist do? In 1917, this was the question that Carl Becker put to himself in an irony-laden essay entitled "On Being a Professor." Then on the faculty of the University of Kansas, Becker later moved to Cornell and, over time, would become the most respected historian of his generation. Here, though, he presents himself as a bewildered Arnoldian—that is, as a humanist who belatedly has discovered that his educational aims are in conflict both with the "Zeitgeist" and the facts of the classroom. As a beginning teacher, Becker says, he believed that faculty and students together should think of "four years in college" as "a wonderful adventure in the wide world of the human spirit."[10] After teaching for two decades, however, he had come to accept that very few students joined him in this point of view. There simply could be no denying that most of those under his care, like humankind generally, did not "hunger and thirst after knowledge, anymore than after righteousness." For Becker, this was a troubling recognition. What, he asked, was his duty toward this growing body of students? Did he "best serve . . . by attending mainly to the great majority or by attending to the saving remnant." The answer to this question, Becker thought, determined whether the professor aimed "to make the university a school of higher education or merely a higher school of education."

But perhaps this question need not be asked. Maybe, Becker admits, the humanist lives too much in the past and wrongly clings to antiquated ideals. For a different approach, why not try to get in step with the new doctrine of "efficiency" recently imported into education from American industry?[11] This quantitative ethic, Becker finds, proclaims that the only questions worth asking about "any educational institution or course of study" are "whether it has a practical value, whether it has a measurable value, and whether its value is equal to its cost." To get "on the right track," therefore, humanists need first to stop bothering about all those "elusive" qualities of intellect and spirit that they, up to now, have believed to be at the heart of a true education. And why not do this? After all, could they any longer provide a compelling (or testable) definition of the wisdom and virtue they thought so important? If not, perhaps the "qualitative arithmetic" taught by the efficiency experts should be welcomed. In applying it, one:

> had only to count, an extremely easy thing to do, and very precise in its results. One had but to count the students in all the universities to determine which was the greatest university, the enrollment in all the courses to determine which was the best course. That student was the most liberally educated who obtained the best paying job. The ablest professor was the one who accumulated the most degrees, or printed the most books; while the most efficient was he who taught most hours in the day, or whose name was attended with the longest retinue of varied and noted activities.

Here, then, was a creed that promised an "easy solution" for "all the great problems of education"? To share in this new dispensation, the humanist had only to surrender the fundamental tenet that spiritual and material values should be considered of "a different order altogether" and, in consequence, also cease to insist—as they had long held—that the former can neither be "fostered nor measured by means . . . appropriate to the latter."

Becker, quite obviously, hopes that his fellow humanists will not be tempted to make any such move. His tone throughout bespeaks utter scorn for a doctrine that proposes to quantify what can only be qualitatively discerned. But nowhere does the essay become a call to battle. Instead, Becker counsels a policy of resignation. In the reigning climate of opinion, he says, conditions favor and support the efficiency experts. And, unhappily, the Zeitgeist "is useless to resist, however little one may enjoy it." So, for now, the humanist should expect that "efficiency" will continue to draw strength from its pledge "to bring education into harmony with the main trend of thought in society at large." Lacking any convictions of its own, Becker laments, the university will always try to mimic the practices that prevail in business, industry, and finance. Moreover, students themselves will prefer to be credited with a numbering of the hours of study they endure rather than be judged for the quality and spirit of their learning. Therefore, given these conditions, humanists must accept the fact that they will appear to be "late survivals" of an outworn tradition. Prudence dictates, then, that they seek a "sheltered corner" in the university and, from there, await the coming of a different time. And what about the spectre of efficiency? Becker's message, in the end, seems to be that this, too, will pass.

Many humanists shared Becker's discomfort with the "qualitative arithmetic" that ruled the university, but I do not suggest that all joined in his resort to quietism. Some, indeed, were quite forceful and direct in their opposition. Of these, Lionel Trilling should be counted among the most articulate. Arnold's biographer, Trilling was one of the most—perhaps *the* most—distinguished humanist of his time (roughly 1945–75). His cultural criticism was wide-ranging, and, running through it, one often finds an insistence on the greater value of the humanities relative to the number-driven social sciences. In fact, in his carefully-wrought essays, one sometimes can sense that he is morally incensed by the power that the social sciences have come to wield both in the academy and society at larger. This indignation perhaps reached a peak in a review of the Kinsey Report that he wrote shortly after this study appeared in 1948. Here Trilling addresses in detail what he sees as the ambitious intent of social science to "speak decisively" about a matter—sexual conduct—that, in its moral bearings, traditionally "has been dealt with by religion, social philosophy and literature."[12]

Trilling's approach to Kinsey's report is that of a cultural critic. Never, that is, does he directly reproach Kinsey for employing flawed statistical methods, making errors, or drawing wrong conclusions—though he leaves no doubt that he believes the report to be defective in all these ways. Instead, he accuses Kinsey of being duplicitous in that his report conceals its true aims from the public. The huge fault of the report, Trilling says, is that it claims to be indifferent "to all questions of morality at the same time that it patently intends a moral effect." Moreover, he adds, all social science shares in this same guilt when it refuses to honor—and make the best of—the subjectivity that necessarily pervades all of its investigative projects. Kinsey, then, stands out only as a very striking case of a much larger failing.

This failure is all the greater, Trilling argues, because it is one that social scientists could easily correct. All they need do, he asserts, is to give up the pretense of "objectivity" and accept that their work, unavoidably, is shot through with moral judgments from beginning to end. They refuse, however, to make any such admission, taking a stance instead based on claims that they—and others—make for the "neutrality" of numbers. Here, particularly, Kinsey serves to illustrate the point. As described by Trilling, Kinsey is a behaviorist to the core. This point of view commits Kinsey to the belief that human sexual experience can be reduced to physical acts of a range and kind observable throughout the natural world. So, having dismissed any semblance of social context or inner sense from his concept of experience, he further narrows the meaning of sex to only those acts that can be counted and numbered. These alone are the "facts," and there is no other admissible evidence of our sexual nature. In this way, Trilling points out, "the sexuality that is measured is taken to be the definition of sexuality itself."[13] From such a standpoint, then, "normality" in sexual behavior becomes entirely a matter of amount and frequency—and this, he observes, leads Kinsey to promote an ethic of "the more the merrier." What empirical finding, Trilling adds, could be more pleasing to the male animal?

In Trilling's estimation, furthermore, Kinsey's work is not only reductive. It also is redundant, and this perhaps is its most disturbing defect. Does the public really need such an extensive quantitative effort to provide it with sexual self-enlightenment? And why should the Rockefeller Foundation and the university have lent this project their authority and favored it with such lavish financial support? These questions, Trilling says, should come to mind when we consider that all the report tells "society as a whole is that there is an almost universal involvement in the sexual life and therefore much variety of conduct." This, after all, is something that could be gathered, at little or no cost, by turning to "any comedy that Aristophanes put on the stage." This, source, however, is one that now is little read and seldom consulted. Sadly, Trilling complains, the same must be said about our literary heritage in its entirety. No one, for instance, could imagine a foundation promoting a return, say, to Lucretius, even though this ancient poet tells us far more about the nature of human sexuality than can be found in the many pages of the Kinsey Report. This, Trilling says, reveals what has become the "established attitude" both among foundations and in universities. In these settings, as well as in the culture at large, quantitative data always trumps literary testimony. So, more than anything else, the Report should be viewed as symptomatic of the kinds of intellectual projects that really count and those which are only marginal. Most especially, the humanists must wake up to this fact and perhaps even be moved to lose their collective temper. Even though civility may suffer, Trilling concludes, such conditions call for resistance rather than restraint, redress rather than retreat.[14]

Here, with Trilling, we have come to the limits of this essay. Taken together, then, what do these case studies tell us? How do they add up? Most especially, what response might the advocates of QL want to make to them? These are questions that I hope we can discuss at Wingspread. For my own part, though, I believe it worth bearing in mind that humanists seem always to have kept a worried eye on quantification. Whatever else they reveal, these case studies do not bespeak indifference. All join Santayana in finding American culture pervaded by a "singular preoccupation with quantity." Often their reaction to this fact has been more emotional than judicious, as much moralistic as analytic. In their view, the cultural workings of quantification have been overbearing and bent on crowding out attention to spirit. To this felt threat, they have pushed back and attempted to hold the quantifiers at bay. In consequence, opposition to quantification has become deeply-seated in the heritage of humanism. Oddly enough, I believe that this adversarial legacy may present an opportunity for QL as it attempts to find allies among and across the liberal arts disciplines. Proponents of QL should consider inviting the humanists to turn first to their own texts as a means of revisiting their stance toward quantification. This, I believe, is much more likely to produce true engagement among humanists than asking that they retrain themselves in sophisticated quantitative methods. Whatever the outcome, humanists are more likely to enter the conversation—and remain involved—if they can begin on familiar ground. At the same time, this also would bring QL into contact with documents and texts about which it so far has had little to say. Here, then, might be found the makings of a genuine conversation.

No one can be sure, of course, that this conversation will be a productive undertaking. Even beginning a cross-disciplinary discussion of this kind will be difficult given the fractured condition of the American educational enterprise. Current circumstances, however, may not be entirely unfavorable to making a start. Albeit not yet in a single voice, many humanists now are calling for a thoroughgoing reconsideration of humanistic practice; and this self-questioning could open new, if still untried, paths through the academic hedgerows. Edward Said, for instance, has urged in a recent series of lectures that his fellow humanists turn from the old "unthinking Arnoldian way" and recognize that "the humanities and humanism are constantly in need of revision, rethinking, and revitalization."[15] Trilling's younger colleague, Said argues that humanists must work to shed the bias toward "withdrawal and exclusion" that has been inherent in their practice and to turn instead, as participatory democratic citizens, to a critical encounter with the "world of contemporary history, politics, and economics." In everyday practice, this means that humanists should attend to an almost limitless array of texts that takes in not just "rarified" literary masterworks but, among others, also includes documents such as policy statements, political pronouncements, and editorial arguments. Said emphasizes that the primary critical concern of the humanists must be with the "language" of these texts, but surely, in taking this direction, the humanist will encounter a language that is laced with quantitative concepts and replete with numbers. When this occurs, one might think that the humanist will be ready to enter into a conversation about how words and numbers mix in our public language in such a way as to act and react upon one another and together join in making meaning. This, anyway, is what I like to believe will happen.

Notes

1. The emphasis is Santayana's own.
2. On behalf of a Design Team, Lynn Steen writes that QL "clings to specifics, marshaling all relevant aspects of setting and context to reach conclusions." *Mathematics and Democracy: The Case for Quantitative Literacy*, 18.
3. Laurence Veysey, *The Emergence of the American University*, 338.
4. Charles Eliot, "What Is a Liberal Education," 1876.
5. Eliot, ibid. [In making this statement, Eliot assumes the existence of an integrated school-college continuum. He also supposes that the American high school eventually will become an educational institution comparable to the German *gymnasium* and the French *lycee*. It is interesting to note how many of the educational policies from this time are still in force even though many of the presuppositions underlying them have never panned out.]
6. Alan Ryan, *Liberal Anxieties and Liberal Education*, 53–94.
7. Matthew Arnold, "Numbers: Or, The Majority and the Remnant," in *Discourses in America*, 5.
8. Henry James, *The American Scene*, 45–46.
9. John Dewey, "A College Course: What Should I Expect from It?" *Collected Works, Volume 3, 1889–1892*, 52.
10. The leading advocates for "efficiency" were known as "educationists" and most held positions in major schools of education. Their agenda promoted displacement of disciplinary frameworks in favor of a curriculum organized around a quantification of common activities in categories of

"everyday life, e.g., such as health, family, and leisure." This assault on the disciplines led to an estrangement of liberal arts faculty from schools of education that persists to this day. For an extended discussion of this matter, see Robert Orrill and Linn Shapiro, "From Bold Beginnings to an Uncertain Future," *American Historical Review*, (June 2005), 727–751.

11. Carl Becker, "On Being a Professor," in *Detachment and the Writing of History.*
12. Lionel Trilling, "The Kinsey Report," in *The Liberal Imagination*, 216–234.
13. In a like manner, psychometricians define intelligence as those limited aspects of "intelligence" that their instruments enable them to measure.
14. A personal note. I have been on the receiving end of Trilling's anger and know at first hand that his own renowned civility, though admirable, also had its limits.
15. Edward Said, *Humanism and Democratic Criticism*, (2004), pp. 31–56. These lectures were delivered just prior to Said's untimely death.

Reading Analytically

1. According to Orrill, why do the humanities need to pay more attention to quantitative literacy? What would the benefits to those in the humanities be of a more comprehensive understanding of quantitative information? What is lacking in avoiding this area of knowledge?
2. One of the underlying arguments of Orrill's piece is the negative consequences of what he calls the "fractured condition" of American education. What evidence does he present in this essay for this claim that we have separated the fields of knowledge from one another to the detriment of our educational system? What benefits does he suggest would come from "cross-disciplinary" studies?
3. To whom does this piece seem to be addressed? If Orrill is suggesting the flaws in the humanities' ignoring of quantitative literacy, who does he believe needs to pay attention to these flaws? Who can help to solve them?

Reading Across Disciplinary Communities

1. Though Orrill argues for attention to quantitative literacy, his method of proof is clearly drawn from the kinds of textual analysis that are used in the humanities. How is his analysis of George Santayana's encounter with the president of Harvard College used to illustrate his overall point? Describe the message he is trying to portray through the use of this example.
2. Another method of argument used by Orrill is an historical analysis of the writings of other famous humanist authors, including Matthew Arnold, Carl Becker, and Lionel Trilling. Describe the ways in which Orrill

uses the words of these authors to demonstrate what he sees as a problem in the disciplines of the humanities.

Writing Across Disciplines
Interdisciplinary Writing Opportunities

1. Taken as a whole, the various pieces in this section suggest a variety of "literacies" that their authors imply are crucial for students in the world we now live. But, of course, curricula have limits—we can only have so many required courses. Based upon your own experiences, and drawing upon the arguments made in this chapter's readings, construct your own high school curriculum or college "general education" curriculum (the courses required for all students no matter their major). Make a list of courses that you would require, and write a description and justification for each course, drawing upon the readings in this chapter and perhaps other research you do.
2. Since this chapter brings together the thoughts of experts in various disciplines, all discussing the necessary literacies for students, it gives you the opportunity to think in interdisciplinary ways. To further investigate what education experts think about the various abilities that students need, interview professors in at least four different disciplines, asking them to discuss what they take to be the most crucial literacies for students. Then, write an essay that shows the similarities and differences in the idea of "literacy" across disciplines.
3. Though the readings in this chapter tend to separate out one type of literacy from another, it is clear that all forms of literacy cross disciplines. In fact, the idea of "interdisciplinary" study—applying the ideas from one discipline to the work of others—is considered to be an important way to increase our knowledge. Choose one of the forms of literacy that is discussed here, and demonstrate why it can be useful for those studying in another discipline. Why, for example, might visual literacy be important for scientists? Why is civic literacy important for a student of literature? Why is statistical literacy important for a philosopher? Try to focus upon your own field of study.
4. Though the traditional definition of literacy, the ability to read and write, has clearly been expanded by authors in this chapter, it does remain a crucial part of all disciplines. In fact, many schools have what are called writing in the disciplines (WID) or writing across the curriculum (WAC) initiatives. Investigate the ways in which your school assures that students, in first-year writing courses and/or in a WAC or WID program, assures students to write in various fields of study, and conduct interviews with writing teachers and/or teachers in other disciplines.

You might also do some research on WAC and WID initiatives at other schools as well to compare with those at your own institution.

5. There is no doubt that the onset of what has been called Web 2.0—the use of the Internet to allow for two-way communications through blogs, wikis, and social networking—has changed the ways that we write. Some suggest that these technologies have had a detrimental effect upon writing; others suggest that they have had a positive effect not only on writing, but on other forms of literacy. Conduct research on this topic, and build an argument that discusses the effect of these new technologies on student writing. You might begin by reading portions of the report called *Writing, Technology, and Teens,* issued by the National Commission on Writing and Pew Charitable trusts. (You can access this via the World Wide Web—just Google it.) You might also reference reports on this topic by organizations like the National Council of Teachers of English (one of which is included in this chapter) and other related organizations.

CHAPTER 2

Looking Deep Inside Us

The Implications of Genetic Testing and Neuroimaging

In 2003, the so-called Human Genome Project (HGP) completed its work. This 13-year effort, sponsored by the U.S. Department of Energy and the National Institutes of Health, had six key goals:

1. To *identify* all the approximately 20,000–25,000 genes in human DNA,
2. To *determine* the sequences of the 3 billion chemical base pairs that make up human DNA,
3. To *store* this information in databases,
4. To *improve* tools for data analysis,
5. To *transfer* related technologies to the private sector, and
6. To *address* the ethical, legal, and social issues (ELSI) that may arise from the project.

Though the first four goals lay out the scientific purposes of the project, the last two remind us that this work is indeed interdisciplinary—that the work of genetic scientists clearly has implications for other members of our culture and other areas of study. Goal 5 suggests that this work would find its way into the applied sciences, finding uses in areas such as medicine, business, engineering, and so forth. Goal 6 also reminds us that work of scientific disciplines is not isolated from applied social sciences such as nursing, philosophy, biotechnology, law, clinical psychology, business and medical ethics.

Another new technology, neuroimaging—which can test for the existence of memories in the brain—has similar implications for the applied sciences and raises similar ethical issues. Just consider, as Daniel Meegan notes in his article included in this chapter, the uses of (and ethical questions surrounding) a technology that "can identify the existence of a memory in the brain." Even if you do not consider yourself a scientist, this innovation deserves the attention of many fields of study—and of all citizens.

As much as one might believe that being informed is a good thing, there are of course concerns about whether the information made available by new tests might 1) effect our own psychological well-being; 2) make us feel more deterministic or less in control of our own destiny and/or 3) fall into the hands of those who will use it against us—to deny medical coverage, make hiring or firing decisions, and so forth. Since this fledgling industry still has little regulation, there are concerns about the use of this information and its reliability. This chapter focuses upon issues related to the proposed and actual uses of genetic testing and neuroimaging across disciplines, uses that are growing among science, medical, criminal justice, and business professionals.

So, for example, what are the implications of a company, DNA Direct (http://www.dnadirect.com) that offers a variety of genetic testing that "can offer peace-of-mind, prevention, and healing." Its Web site features information for both consumers and health-care professionals, including attention to pre- and post-test counseling. It also publishes its standards, noting that "DNA Direct is committed to providing responsible, reliable genetic information services and access to testing" and that they "have developed guidelines to enable our company to help consumers decide whether to pursue testing and to help them obtain value from testing." But is self-regulation enough? What happens when science becomes business? And, of course, interpreting the results of such tests require a good deal of the quantitative literacy that Richard Scheaffer (see Chapter 1) suggests most citizens lack; as geneticist Craig Venter notes, if you're "told that your probability of having a serious problem is 62 percent, what the hell does that mean?"

Services for genetic testing have implications for other social issues as well. In 2007, Henry Louis Gates, the director of the W. E. B. Du Bois Institute for African and African American Research at Harvard, endorsed a testing service called AfricaDNA.com, which is designed to allow participants to trace their genetic roots. Though Gates's purpose is clearly to provide information to an historically disadvantaged group, might the gathering of such information affect our understanding of race, a topic discussed in the next chapter of this book?

And what are the potential effects of our new ability to read and interpret the images within the brain? Neuroimaging, which studies the structures and functions of the brain, has some potential to demonstrate things such as the existence of specific memories and predispositions to violent behavior. That is, like genetic science, it may even be predictive of the probability of future behaviors or maladies as well as providing information about what is stored in the memory about past events—including, perhaps, memories of a crime witnessed or committed, a possibility that has garnered the attention of the criminal justice community.

So what are we to do with these new capabilities? In asking such a question, we can see the ways in which science filters into both private and governmental sectors—and why these innovations are being studied by various disciplinary fields. The articles in this chapter demonstrate just a few of those areas of study; as a writer, you can explore many more.

To prepare yourself to understand the larger implications of these technologies, you might first learn a bit more about how they work; the "Online Resources for Understanding the Human Genome Project and Neuroimaging" page that follows this introduction can guide you in doing so. Among those resources is a link to an article from the *Journal of the American Medical Association*, "Risks and Benefits of Direct-to-Consumer Genetic Testing Remain Unclear." In this piece, Bridget M Kuehn addresses the rapid growth of personalized gene-testing companies that offer everything from probabilities of suffering from diseases to, as a *Washington Post* story notes, finding "DNA-compatible mates who smell sexier to them, have more orgasms and produce healthier children."

Following the online resources, you will then find a position statement by the American Society of Human Geneticists. This statement of principles was agreed upon by a body of scientists who make this area of study their life's work, but who also are considering the uses of the science that they have helped to advance. This statement is thus an attempt by working scientists to address not only their own community, but the wider public, about the implications of what they do. Arthur Caplan adds his views on these new technologies—both genetic and neuroimaging—in an article published in a venue meant for the wider public, *The American Prospect.*

Still, as other pieces in this section suggest, the public is still often misinformed. According to Ricki Lewis in her article in the *American Journal of Bioethics,* the "gap between science and society" on this issue continues to widen. Beatrix Rubin asks if the discourse surrounding human embryonic stem cell research has used the idea of "therapeutic promise"—the idea that stem cell research will lead to cures for disease—to forward its own research agendas. Within the applied science of medicine, the availability of genetic testing to predict disease has raised questions about medical practice, questions explored by Loretta M. Kopelman in her study of whether children ought to be tested for predispositions toward late-onset diseases—even if those diseases are untreatable. Drawing upon what she calls "the professional consensus" on medical standards, she uses that disciplinary perspective to argue against the right of parents to order such tests. And still another field, criminal justice, has its eye on the potential for neuroimaging to influence its work; psychologist Daniel V. Meegan, for example, asks us to "imagine a neuroimaging test that can detect the presence of a crime memory." The stuff of science fiction films, he contends, is not so far from reality. As such, neuroimaging has garnered the attention not only of bioethicists and scientists, but of the legal community. In his essay for *Notre Dame Lawyer,* O. Carter Snead, a professor of that law school, lays out the implications for both criminal and civil law of the existence of such technologies, including both ethical and reliability issues.

Clearly, these articles raise some serious questions about not only the technologies, but their potential uses and abuses. Though they just scratch the surface of what one needs to know to truly understand the complex science, these pieces will introduce you to the varied implications of scientific discovery across disciplinary areas—from ethics, to applied sciences like business and nursing, to criminal justice, to the sociology of race. As you become interested in specific areas of this topic, you should continue your reading and research, based upon your own fields of interest. Then you can add your own thoughts and writing to the mix as well.

ONLINE RESOURCES

Understanding the Human Genome Project and Neuroimaging

The readings in this chapter investigate the effects of two major strands of science and technology that have begun to revolutionize our understanding of the makeup of human beings, our motives, and our actions. To better comprehend the scientific and ethical questions surrounding these discoveries that are discussed in this chapter, you might begin by gaining some basic knowledge about the technologies themselves. Here are some ways to do so:

1. **Search the Internet for "Human Genome Project":** There is a wealth of resources that describe the work of this effort, its history, and the attempts to ethically research and employ the fruits of this research. Since this effort was led by the U.S. Department of Energy and the National Institutes of Health, those sites can be particularly helpful in getting up on this topic.
2. **Search the Internet for "neuroimaging":** According to the Center for Cognitive Neuroimaging, this technology "makes it possible to 'see' the brain in action, to watch it engaging in the cognitions and emotions that are such an essential part of our mental life." While this clearly widens the horizon of how we understand human activity, it also raises many questions about how much we ought to know about the functioning of individual minds—and who will gain access to this information. But before you can truly engage in those debates, which form the topic of several of the selections in this chapter, you might visit the site for the Center for Cognitive Neuroimaging, the American Medical Associations' online resources on this topic, and other sites that can provide you with a primer on what this technology can do, how it works, and how it is expected to be developed and used.
3. **Search the Internet for "genetic testing services":** If you do this search, you will be able to access the sites for many "direct-to-consumer" genetic testing companies who offer services that are discussed in several of the articles in this section. Pay attention to the claims they make, the services they offer (everything from finding a good mate to understanding your cultural heritage or likelihood of disease). You might also note the marketing facets of these sites—including their emotional appeals and their use of visuals. One particularly interesting site is Africa.DNA, which is devoted to testing related to race issues (a topic that is broached in Chapter 3 of this book as well). If you get a feel

for how genetic testing is being marketed, you will be more ready to consider the arguments made about this service by various authors in this section—and be able to compare the claims to the science of genetic testing from the Human Genome Project.

4. **Read the article on direct-to-consumer testing by Bridget M. Kuehn, "Risks and Benefits of Direct-to-Consumer Genetic Testing Remain Unclear,"** available from the Journal of the American Medical Association site at http://jama.ama-assn.org/. To find the article from this site, use the search box and use the search terms "Kuehn direct genetic testing." You could also turn up this article by using a search engine with the search terms "Kuehn direct genetic testing JAMA."

   Once you locate this essay, you'll find that this senior staff writer for the *Journal of the American Medical Association* (JAMA) outlines key issues surrounding the marketing of genetic testing to individuals. Though JAMA is a trade journal for medical professionals, the style of writing is journalistic, accommodating a wider reading public. As you read, note the ways that the author brings together the expertise of medical professionals, government officials, and business practitioners in laying out the key issues in this debate, but does so in a style that it is easily accessible.

   One key issue that underlies Kuehn's piece is how patients will react to the results of genetic tests. This question can be viewed in a number of ways, including questions about whether patients have the knowledge to understand the results of these tests and their implications, and whether patients will be harmed (or helped) emotionally by the knowledge of their own genetic predispositions. As you read, one question that will likely be on your mind is quite personal: Would you want to know? You can also consider Kuehn's article in light of some of the direct-to-consumer sites that you found by searching "genetic testing services" in #3 above.

Reading Analytically

1. Kuehn's article is designed to lay out some key questions that need to be asked about the risks and benefits of direct-to-consumer genetic testing, questions that inform all of the readings in this section. Make a list of the questions that Kuehn raises here, and add to them any others that you feel also need to be asked.
2. The relationship between government regulation and the right of businesses to follow opportunities for profit is always a thorny one. After reading about actual and proposed regulations governing genetic testing, and visiting some of the direct-to-consumer sites, try to

articulate your own set of beliefs about what government ought, and ought not, do in order to regulate this growing industry.

3. One of the issues regarding patient reaction is whether the consumer is capable, without the intervention of medical professionals, of understanding the results of genetic testing. Yet Web sites like Web M.D. have long offered medical information to non-experts. Do a quick search of the web to see if the information there seems to you to be adequate, accessible, and credible, and write a brief position on this issue.

Reading Across Disciplinary Communities

1. The *Journal of the American Medical Association,* in which Kuehn's article appears and which also addresses neuroimaging, is both a trade journal—designed to bring news of the profession to practitioners in the field—and a journal that is read by members of the general public as well. Describe the ways that this author attempts, stylistically, to serve both those audiences, expert and non-expert. Point out particular lines in the essay that seem to straddle this line.
2. Think more about the audiences of this piece, audiences that may come from many different disciplinary groups. Then identify the parts that might most interest individuals from those groups. Consider in particular what parts and issues might interest elected officials or political scientists, nurses, philosophers, biologists, sociologists, psychologists, or business owners. You might also consider what issues should most concern any of us as we think as American citizens.

AMERICAN SOCIETY OF HUMAN GENETICS

ASHG Statement on Direct-to-Consumer Genetic Testing in the United States

This statement by a national organization of genetic scientists provides a position statement about the application of their research to business ventures. This organization lays out its mission and vision as follows:

ASHG MISSION

ASHG serves research scientists, health professionals, and the public by providing forums to:

- *Share research results at annual meetings and in* The American Journal of Human Genetics

- *Advance genetic research by advocating for research support*
- *Enhance genetics education by preparing future professionals and informing the public*
- *Promote genetic services and support responsible social and scientific policies*

Vision

Members of ASHG enter the 21st century with a commitment to become fluent in the language of the genome, understand human variation, and promote the public health. As we transfer new knowledge to the next generation of genetics professionals and the public, we will translate new ideas into improved clinical practice.

As you read this statement by the ASHG, consider how it fits into specific facets of that mission and vision. You might also consider, more generally, the obligations of this and other disciplines to the wider publics—the "civic communities" that are discussed in the Introduction to this book.

Direct-to-consumer (DTC) genetic testing has been gaining prominence over the past several years.[1] Proponents of DTC testing cite benefits that include increased consumer access to testing, greater consumer autonomy and empowerment, and enhanced privacy of the information obtained. Critics of DTC genetic testing have pointed to the risks that consumers will choose testing without adequate context or counseling, will receive tests from laboratories of dubious quality, and will be misled by unproven claims of benefit.

Currently, DTC genetic testing is permitted in about half the states[2] and is subject to little oversight at the federal level. In July 2006, the Government Accountability Office issued a report documenting troubling marketing practices by some DTC testing companies,[3] and the Federal Trade Commission (FTC) issued a consumer alert cautioning consumers to be skeptical about claims made by some DTC companies.[4] Internationally, several countries have issued reports cautioning against its use,[5–7] and several European countries have banned or are considering banning it entirely.

DTC testing has emerged during a period of rapid growth in the number of genetic tests. Today, there are more than 1,100 genetic tests available clinically, and several hundred more are available in research settings. Although most genetic testing is currently available only through a health care provider, an increasing variety of tests are being offered DTC, often without any health care provider involvement or counseling. The range of tests available DTC is broad, from tests for single-gene disorders, such as cystic fibrosis, to tests for predisposition to complex, multifactorial diseases, such as depression and cardiovascular disease. In addition to providing test results DTC, some companies also make recommendations regarding lifestyle changes on the basis of these results, such as changes in diet or use of nutritional supplements.

Ensuring adequate information, high-quality laboratories, and accurate claims and interpretation of test results is important for all genetic tests, including those provided DTC. At the same time, a one-size-fits-all approach is not appropriate for DTC tests, because the types of tests being offered are heterogeneous, and their consequences are wide ranging. A test may be used to diagnose disease, to predict risk of future disease, to determine the risk of passing on a disease to one's offspring, to aid in therapy selection, or to guide "lifestyle" choices such as diet and skin care. Different possible actions may result from different types of tests. For example, tests to determine whether someone is a carrier of a mutation for a particular disease may affect the choice of whether or whom to marry, whether to have children, and whether to terminate a pregnancy. Thus, the level of evidence required before a test is offered DTC, and the safeguards appropriate to ensure adequate consumer protection, will differ depending on what is being tested for and what the foreseeable consequences of testing are. Whereas the DTC model may be contraindicated for certain types of tests, the availability of other tests in the absence of a health care provider may not compromise, and may even foster, patient health. This policy statement does not attempt to set the dividing line between those tests that should be offered DTC and those that should not; rather, it sets forth principles that should govern all health-related genetic tests that are offered DTC.

Scope of this Statement

While DTC testing also encompasses paternity and ancestry testing, this policy statement addresses solely those genetic tests that make health-related claims or that directly affect health care decision making. In addition, although "DTC" is sometimes used to refer to tests advertised but not sold DTC, this policy statement focuses on tests that can be ordered directly by a consumer and whose results are reported

DTC without an independent health care provider—one not employed by the testing company—serving as an intermediary.

Context

DTC genetic testing differs from traditional genetic testing in that consumers order tests and receive test results without an independent provider serving as an intermediary. Whether a company is permitted to provide DTC genetic-testing services is a matter of state law. Currently, about half the states permit DTC genetic testing (see Ref. 2). Additionally, although some states require a provider to order a test on behalf of a patient, this requirement can generally be fulfilled by a physician employed by the laboratory. Some DTC companies offer genetic counseling, while others do not.

DTC tests are typically advertised and sold over the Internet. After the consumer orders the test, the testing company sends a sample-collection kit (e.g., buccal swab or blood-spot collection). The consumer sends back the sample, and the company performs the test and sends a test report via the Internet or the mail. This context has led to the concern that consumers will not receive adequate counseling—either in advance, to ensure that the test is appropriate, or on receipt of test results, to ensure that consumers comprehend the complex information and understand the consequences of testing for themselves and their family members.

Quality

Because of the fragmented regulatory environment for genetic testing in general, there is concern that the quality of the tests offered DTC may be inadequate. For a test to be of good quality, the laboratory performing it must be able to obtain the correct answer reliably, meaning that it detects a particular genetic variant when it is present and does not detect the variant when it is absent. A test's accuracy is referred to as "analytic validity." Further, there must be adequate scientific evidence to support the correlation between the genetic variant and a particular health condition or risk—the so-called clinical validity.

Currently, the federal government exercises limited oversight of the analytic validity of genetic tests and virtually no oversight of their clinical validity. Laboratories that perform clinical genetic testing must be certified under the Clinical Laboratory Improvement Amendments of 1988 (CLIA). However, although CLIA imposes basic requirements that address personnel qualifications, quality-control standards, and documentation and validation of tests and procedures, it does not address clinical validity or claims made by the laboratory regarding the tests. Nor does CLIA yet contain a "specialty area" for most genetic tests, which hampers the government's ability to determine whether tests are being performed correctly.[8] Although the Centers for Medicare and Medicaid Services (CMS) stated for several years that it intended to create a genetic-testing specialty, the agency suddenly reversed course in 2006, stating that no specialty would be issued.

The level of scrutiny by the U.S. Food and Drug Administration (FDA) differs markedly depending on whether the test is performed using a commercial "test kit" or a laboratory-developed test method. Whereas the FDA reviews the analytic and clinical validity and the labeling of commercial test kits before they are marketed and requires postmarket adverse-event reporting if there are problems with the kit, there is no premarket review of laboratory-developed tests, nor is there any requirement to report adverse events. Recently, the FDA indicated that it plans to regulate a small subset of laboratory-developed tests known as "in vitro diagnostic multivariate index assays,"[9] but this is a very narrow category of tests that will exclude the vast majority of genetic tests offered by clinical laboratories.

The lack of a coherent regulatory landscape to ensure quality is not unique to DTC genetic testing, since all other molecular and biochemical tests are also affected. However, quality concerns are particularly acute in the DTC context because of the low barrier to market entry, the complexity of the information that consumers need to understand to make an informed decision, and the lack of provider scrutiny. Consumers are at a significant risk of selecting tests with unproven benefit, of obtaining testing services from laboratories of dubious quality, and of making decisions without timely and accurate genetic counseling.

Claims

Claims made regarding DTC genetic tests may in some cases be exaggerated or unsupported by scientific evidence. Exaggerated or unsupported claims may lead consumers to get tested inappropriately or to have false expectations regarding the benefits of testing. Further, consumers may make unwarranted, and even irrevocable, decisions on the basis of test results and associated information, such as the decision to terminate a pregnancy, to forgo needed treatment, or to pursue unproven therapies.

Some DTC companies use privacy as a marketing tool, touting the benefits of obtaining genetic testing outside the health care system and thereby avoiding the risks of having genetic information contained in a medical record. However, these companies do not necessarily disclose their privacy policies or explain that a patient's subsequent disclosure of the test results to a physician may lead to the information becoming part of his or her medical record. Further, DTC companies are not necessarily subject to the health privacy regulations issued pursuant to the Heath Insurance Portability and Accountability Act (HIPAA), leaving consumers vulnerable to having their information used or disclosed in a manner that would be impermissible in the health care system.

Federal law prohibits companies from using unfair, deceptive, or fraudulent trade practices, including making false or misleading advertising claims. This law, in theory, prohibits clearly false genetic-testing claims. Several complaints have been filed and are pending with the FTC about a specific DTC genetic-testing company, and the FTC recently issued a consumer alert warning the public that "some of these [DTC] tests lack scientific validity, and others provide medical results that are meaningful only in the context of a full medical evaluation" (see Ref. 4). The FTC has not, however, taken direct action against any DTC genetic-testing company. Furthermore, with respect to tests for which some scientific support exists but for which claims are exaggerated or provide incomplete information, FTC regulators may be insufficiently knowledgeable to detect the misleading nature of such claims. It also must be recognized that there are limits to the government's ability to restrict commercial speech. Finally, although the FDA has the authority to regulate claims for products it regulates, the agency currently does not regulate most genetic tests and therefore does not regulate their claims.

On the basis of the foregoing analysis, the American Society of Human Genetics makes the following recommendations about DTC genetic testing.

Recommendations

I. Transparency

To promote transparency and to permit providers and consumers to make informed decisions about DTC genetic testing, companies must provide all relevant information about offered tests in a readily accessible and understandable manner.

a. Companies offering DTC genetic testing should disclose the sensitivity, specificity, and predictive value of the test, and the populations for which this information is known, in a readily understandable and accessible fashion.
b. Companies offering DTC testing should disclose the strength of scientific evidence on which any claims of benefit are based, as well as any limitations to the claimed benefits. For example, if a disease or condition may be caused by many factors, including the presence of a particular genetic variant, the company should disclose that other factors may cause the condition and that absence of the variant does not mean the patient is not at risk for the disease.
c. Companies offering DTC testing should clearly disclose all risks associated with testing, including psychological risks and risks to family members.
d. Companies offering DTC testing should disclose the CLIA certification status of the laboratory performing the genetic testing.
e. Companies offering DTC testing should maintain the privacy of all genetic information and disclose their privacy policies, including whether they comply with HIPAA.
f. Companies offering DTC testing and making lifestyle, nutritional, pharmacologic, or other treatment recommendations on the basis of the results of those tests should disclose the clinical evidence for and against the efficacy of such interventions, with respect to those specific recommendations and indications.

II. Provider Education

To ensure that providers are aware that genetic tests are being provided DTC and that some of these tests may lack analytic or clinical validity, professional organizations should educate their members regarding the types of genetic tests offered DTC, so that providers can counsel their patients about the potential value and limitations of DTC testing.

a. Professional organizations should disseminate information to their members explaining what DTC testing is, what tests are offered DTC, and the potential benefits and limitations of such testing for patients.

III. Test and Laboratory Quality

To ensure the analytic and clinical validity of genetic tests offered DTC and to ensure that claims made about these tests are truthful and not misleading, the relevant agencies of the federal government should take appropriate and targeted regulatory action.

a. CMS should create a genetic-testing specialty under CLIA, to ensure the analytic validity of tests and the quality of genetic testing laboratories.
b. CMS should ensure that all DTC genetic-testing laboratories are certified under CLIA and should maintain a publicly accessible list containing the certification status of laboratories.
c. The federal government should take steps to ensure the clinical validity of DTC tests that make health-related or health care-affecting claims.
d. The FTC should take action against companies that make false or misleading claims about DTC tests.
e. The FDA and the FTC should work together to develop guidelines for DTC testing companies to follow, to ensure that their claims are truthful and not misleading and that they adequately convey the scientific limitations for particular tests.
f. The Centers for Disease Control and Prevention (CDC) should conduct a study on the impact of DTC testing on consumers, to assess whether and to what extent consumers are experiencing benefit and/or harm from this method of test delivery. The CDC should also conduct a systematic comparison between the claims made in DTC advertising and the scientific evidence available to support these claims.

Conclusion

DTC genetic testing is a method of marketing genetic tests to consumers without the involvement of an independent health care provider. Potential benefits of DTC testing include increased consumer awareness of and access to testing. In the current environment, consumers are at risk of harm from DTC testing if testing is performed by laboratories that are not of high quality, if tests lack adequate analytic or clinical validity, if claims made about tests are false or misleading, and if inadequate information and counseling are provided to permit the consumer to make an informed decision about whether testing is appropriate and about what actions to take on the basis of test results.

References

1. Javitt GH, Stanley E, Hudson K (2004) Direct-to-consumer genetic tests, government oversight, and the First Amendment: what the government can (and can't) do to protect the public's health. Okla Law Rev 57:251–302
2. Genetics and Public Policy Center (2007) Survey of direct-to-consumer testing statutes and regulations. (http://www.dnapolicy.org/resources/DTCStateLawChart.pdf) (accessed July 31, 2007)
3. Government Accountability Office (2006) Nutrigenetic testing: tests purchased from four Web sites mislead consumers. (http://www.gao.gov/new.items/d06977t.pdf) (accessed July 26, 2007)
4. Federal Trade Commission (2006) At-home genetic tests: a healthy dose of skepticism may be the best prescription. (http://www.ftc.gov/bcp/edu/pubs/consumer/health/hea02.shtm) (accessed July 26, 2007)
5. Human Genetics Commission (2003) Genes direct: ensuring the effective oversight of genetic tests supplied directly to the public. (http://www.hgc.gov.uk/UploadDocs/DocPub/Document/genesdirect_full.pdf) (accessed July 26, 2007)
6. Ontario Ministry of Health and Long-Term Care (2002) Genetics, testing, and gene patenting: charting new territory in healthcare. (http://www.health.gov.on.ca/english/public/pub/ministry_reports/geneticsrep02/report_e.pdf) (accessed July 31, 2007)
7. Australian Law Reform Commission and Australian Health Ethics Commission (2003) Essentially yours: the protection of human genetic information in Australia. (http://www.austlii.edu.au/au/other/alrc/publications/reports/96/) (accessed July 26, 2007)
8. Hudson K, Murphy J, Kaufman D, Javitt G, Katsanis S, Scott J (2006) Oversight of US genetic testing laboratories. Nat Biotechnol 24:1083–1090
9. Food and Drug Administration (2006) Draft guidance for industry, clinical laboratories, and FDA staff: in vitro diagnostic multivariate index essays. (http://www.fda.gov/cdrh/oivd/guidance/1610.html) (accessed July 26, 2007)

Reading Analytically

1. What specific concerns are raised about direct-to-consumer testing in this position statement? In what ways do these concerns illustrate the special expertise of this group by offering potential side-effects that might not be realized by the general public?
2. One section of this statement is titled "Scope of this Statement." What is the purpose of this section? In what ways does this section function to limit the topic in ways that are useful to all writers?
3. Does this statement oppose direct-to-consumer genetic testing? Why does it present benefits as well as potential harm?

Reading Across Disciplinary Communities

1. Though this is a public document, it is also a document that is written by those in a scientific discipline. In what ways does this statement reflect the values of that discipline, and in particular, its belief upon observable and reliable data? How would you describe its style?
2. Though disciplinary groups often write to others within the discipline, they also offer their special expertise to other interested parties and other "stakeholders"—those who have a vested interest in the topic. Who is the intended audience for this piece? What clues in the text suggest that audience? Try to go beyond seeing this as for "the general public" to consider what particular groups seem to be addressed both directly and indirectly.

RICKI LEWIS

Stem Cells and Genetic Testing

The Gap Between Science and Society Widens

The author of this piece, Ricki Lewis, holds a Ph.D. in genetics and has worked as a science writer and educator. She is the author of Life, *an introductory biology text as well as* Human Genetics: Concepts and Applications. *She is a contributing editor to* The Scientist, *a newspaper read by scientists worldwide, focusing largely on innovations in biotechnology. This piece was first published in* The Journal of Bioethics.

Her essay argues that because findings about stem cell research have proceeded so quickly from the laboratory to the media, and because its reputed promises have been so wide, that this undue optimism will "ultimately feed the mistrust of science and scientists—and disappoint and mislead the public." Using both her knowledge of genetics and her experience in the social sciences as an educator, she provides a series of analyses of the ways that direct-to-consumer Web sites are framed—and so the tension between empirical science and applications in business. As you read, you might consider how you learn about science, and in particular, how media depictions of science influence your own understanding. If you are studying science, either as a major or a nonmajor, you might consider the differences between the ways that science is depicted in the media and how it is presented in the classroom.

The disconnect between what biomedical scientists know and what healthcare consumers believe and expect is growing, particularly for stem cell treatments and direct-to-consumer genome-wide DNA tests. The rush to "personalize" medicine, skipping traditional clinical trials and validation, is only going to ultimately feed the mistrust of science and scientists—and disappoint and mislead the public.

Induced Pluripotent Stem Cells and More

The ability to send a skin cell back in developmental time to reinvent itself is a giant step forward, if not unexpected since cell biologists started cataloging "stemness" genes years ago, President George W. Bush's partial claim to the idea notwithstanding (Lewis 2003). Even the obstacle that some of those reprogramming genes cause cancer will fade away with refined recipes for making the coveted induced pluripotent stem (iPS) cells.

Researchers have also quietly coaxed pluripotent cells from the likes of testes, teeth, fat, and bone marrow, as well as from the medical trash heap, including placenta and umbilical cord membranes and even menstrual blood. Stem-like cells also hail from fetal cells lingering in women's bloodstreams and self-fertilized eggs.

So far the new potential stand-ins for human embryonic stem (hES) cells seem to be the 'real deal,' as far as chromosomes, cells surfaces, self-renewal, and the ability to give rise to all three germ layers go. But who really knows? Why can we not activate the genes already in the nucleus of interest? How many different ways can we introduce four or five or more key reprogramming genes to get an exact combination, order, and ratio that jumpstarts development? While researchers try to figure this out and the media extols the coming cures, professional societies have been issuing statements to both temper the promise yet keep the door open on ES cells. The International Society for Stem Cell Research (Deerfield, IL) warns, for example, that "a great deal of work remains before these methods can be used to generate stem cells suitable for safe and effective therapies." Still, in just a few weeks, iPS cells, whatever they may actually be, have proven themselves able to recapitulate more than a dozen diseases *in vitro,* providing unprecedented glimpses of the genesis of pathology (Higgs 2008).

Their potential is staggering, but they are not quite ready for prime time in the clinic. However, you would never know it from the Web.

I recently lost a dear friend and patient (I was his hospice volunteer) to amyotrophic lateral sclerosis (ALS). Just after his funeral, I googled

"ALS and stem cells," knowing all too well that the one approved drug only modestly extends life in a few patients. Within seconds, the website for an Israeli company, Brainstorm Cell Therapeutics (New York, NY and Petach Tikva, Israel), materialized, sharing the good news that "patients treated with the company's NurOwn™ therapeutic cells are expected to enjoy a rapid recovery and much enhanced quality of life." ALS was one of several disorders featured on the website. *Are expected* were the operative words. In fact, the company, from which my inquisitive e-mails boomeranged, is "initiating a series of efficacy and safety studies toward a cure for amyelotrophic (sic) lateral sclerosis" that will place human bone marrow stem cells into the mouse model used to develop the one existing drug, and then test the rodents on a rotating rod, a standard technique. More acrobatic rodents would not have been much help to my friend.

More disturbing was EmCell (Kiev, Ukraine), a Ukrainian company that claims "the worlds (sic) largest clinical experience in embryonic stem cell transplants for various diseases and conditions." Their "16 years of international clinical experience in transplantation of human embryonic/fetal stem cells" raised the first red flag, since human ES cells debuted 10 years ago, not 16 (Lewis 1997). The second alert was the mention of "types" of ES cells, a contradiction in terms. But it was the description of their ALS therapy that revealed the mistaken identity.

The "embryonic stem cells" that EmCell uses to treat ALS come from "cell suspensions . . . obtained from growth zones of 4–8 weeks old cadaverous embryos' systems and organs" Maybe the methods were lost in translation, but a dissected full-fledged embryo does not yield hES cells, which arise in culture from inner cell mass cells. Would a desperate ALS patient who pays $15,000 for the treatment know that? EmCell is selling false hope that could taint the promise of actual hES cell therapies being developed at many companies.

The gap looms between experimental and medical science. I do not think it is ethical to market treatments that have not undergone randomized, controlled clinical trials, replication, and validation.

Direct-To-Consumer Whole Genome Testing

Marketing tests based on whole genome association (WGA) studies was perhaps inevitable, for the approach makes theoretical sense. Scan genomes of people who share a particular disorder for single nucleotide polymorphisms (SNPs, or single base differences) that they have but unaffected controls do not. The larger the populations screened, the more meaningful the resulting associations. Then translate the population odds ratios of the telltale DNA patterns into individual disease risk statements, stressing such words as *variant* and *wellness* and censoring use of *disease.*

Consumers submit DNA-bearing saliva, and algorithms based on published WGA studies spit back risk stats. The tests are exempt from United States Food and Drug Administration scrutiny because they are not medical, according to the language. Load up the website with an introductory genetics course, assemble an advisory board, and the United States Federal Trade Commission is satisfied, too.

But this is deceptive, because some people think it is too soon to hawk these WGA-based tests. The truth is, and the direct-to-consumer company websites actually say so in the fine print, we just do not know yet whether a population-based association can provide meaningful information for an individual. The many calculations of WGA studies produce some false positives, and associations have been known to dissipate as data accumulate. Consumers may not be aware of these limitations, nor realize that the terms *link, marker,* and *association* have precise scientific meanings. It is all too easy to see slick company websites and assume that tests based on results of association studies have been validated. They have not.

Several companies now offer services based on these WGA studies, not to be confused with the regulated tests for well-studied genes, such as *BRCA1* or the cystic fibrosis gene. We geneticists have mixed feelings about the new generation of tests.

When Navigenics (Redwood Shores, CA) unveiled its "Health Compass" at a special session at the American Society of Human Genetics (Bethesda, MD) annual meeting last fall (San Diego, CA, October 24–27, 2007), many in the packed room were so disturbed that even grad students ignored the free food. As soon as deCODE Genetics (Reykjavik, Iceland) announced a similar service, I sold my stock. Yet some very notable notables have leant their names to the advisory boards of these companies. Perhaps they figure the proverbial 'cat is already out of the bag,' so why not help provide the most accurate information? Even self-appointed scientist Al Gore has leant his voice and support to Navigenics.

When I caught a segment of the *Today Show* that featured yet a third company, 23andMe (Mt. View, CA), I decided to investigate further.

The founders of and the website for 23andMe were very impressive. The company seems to be making the best of technology that is, I believe, like the aforementioned stem cell therapies, not quite ready for prime time. Caveats and qualifiers abound. They use association studies published in the best journals, with the largest samples and most convincing statistics. Descriptions are clear, privacy protection paramount.

But, again, a gap glares for those in the know. Genetic counseling is mentioned only deep down in the "help" list on the 23andMe website. People receiving medical news from a physician often fall into a 'deer-in-the-headlights' trance. Wouldn't reading about one's DNA on a website, without benefit of face-to-face professional interpretation, lead to at least some misunderstanding? Navigencis *does* offer in-house 24/7 genetic counseling, but each web page has the disclaimer "Navigenics does not provide medical advice, diagnosis or treatment." Genetic counselors *are* medical professionals. It is confusing.

The 23andMe website states ". . . we cannot and do not diagnose diseases or medical conditions, provide medical advice or otherwise assess your health." Yet the first image that pops up is a "Personal Genome Service" that promises to "unlock the secrets of your own DNA. Today." Similarly, Navigenics' Health Compass reveals "what your genes have to say about the future of your health," but also runs a disclaimer that they do "not provide medical advice, diagnosis or treatment." Can they really have it both ways?

What, exactly, do these companies test for? The *Today Show* reporter learned his genetic associations to eye color, ability to taste bitter substances, and the consistency of his earwax, traits that could be more economically detected by looking in a mirror, tasting broccoli, and sticking a finger in an ear. But that is not all these companies offer. Instead of affirming that I have hazel eyes, love broccoli, and have thin earwax, I might learn that I have an elevated risk of developing multiple sclerosis, heart disease, colorectal cancer, and diabetes. At Navigenics I would learn my risk of developing obesity, lupus, and Alzheimer disease, and at deCODE Genetics, their under-$1,000 deCODEme "introduction to your genome" panel estimates risks of developing atrial defibrillation, psoriasis, and age-related macular degeneration. Oddly, all three companies analyze restless legs syndrome—now who would not want a heads-up on *that?* The top magazines and newspapers have been unable to resist sending intrepid reporters to part with some body fluid to have their genetic futures predicted—most receiving advice to do what they have been doing—eat veggies, get check-ups and various tests, exercise, and do not smoke.

What is a consumer to do with all this information? It beats me. But I am not alone.

The same journals that publish WGA studies are beginning to also publish challenges to their uses. A meta analysis of meta analyses determined that extrapolating from genomic profiles to assess health risks is premature (Janssens 2008). Kenneth Offit of Memorial Sloan-Kettering Cancer Center (New York, NY) contrasted the unregulated direct-to-consumer genome companies with the decade of prospective clinical trials that validated genetic testing for cancer predisposition (Offit 2008). Kathy Hudson and her team at the Genetics and Public Policy Center at Johns Hopkins University, who have been on top of direct-to-consumer genetic testing for years, recommend better FDA oversight, public registry of which tests are available for which conditions, and that the FTC monitor overblown testing claims (Katsanis 2008).

To end on an up note, perhaps the information that direct-to-consumer companies provide may inspire and empower healthcare consumers to alter their behaviors in ways that counter what their genes may set into motion. But that, too, needs to be validated. And so, like the stem cell saga, a gap between scientific progress and health consumer expectation gapes. It is not ethical to market DNA tests based on whole genome population-based studies without randomized, controlled clinical trials, replication, and validation.

Whether considering stem cells or DNA tests, that is simply the way that good medical science is done.

References

Higgs, D. R. 2008. A new dawn for stem-cell therapy. *New England Journal of Medicine* 358: 964–966.

Janssens, A. C. J. W. Gwinn, M. Bradley, L. A., Oostra, B. A., van Duijn, C. M., and Khoury, M. J. 2008. A critical appraisal of the scientific basis of commercial genomic profiles used to assess health risks and personalize health interventions. *American Journal of Human Genetics* 82: 593–599.

Katsanis, S. H., Javitt, G. and Hudson, K. 2008. A case study of personalized medicine. *Science* 320:53–54.

Lewis, R. 1997. Embryonic stem cells debut amid little media attention. *The Scientist* 11(19): 1.

Lewis, R. 2003. A state of stemness: What if? . . . *The Scientist* 17(1): 9.

Offit, K. 2008. Genomic profiles for disease risk: Predictive or premature? *Journal of the American Medical Association* 299(11): 1353–1355.

Reading Analytically

1. What does Lewis see as the main problems with the ways that genetic science is presented to the general public? How does she support these concerns in her essay? Despite its scientific bent, Lewis pauses to offer a personal narrative in this essay. What is the effect of that narrative? Is it appropriate to the piece and its discipline? Why or why not?
2. One of the keys to educating nonexperts or those in other disciplines is the ability to define terms in useful, accessible ways. What key terms are offered in this essay? Name at least three, and demonstrate how Lewis attempts to define them within her text.
3. One of the ways that Lewis makes her case about the growing disconnect between scientific discovery and the general public is through her analysis of Web sites that offer genetic testing. Using her model of analysis, go to another such site and do a similar analysis of what you find there.

Reading Across Disciplinary Communities

1. As an educator and a scientist, Lewis has one foot in each of two different disciplines. As a scientist, she clearly has a stake in accuracy and credibility of empirical information. (Remember the discussion of empirical science in the Introduction?) As an educator and the author of textbooks, she is also clearly concerned with making that science clear and palatable. What writing techniques does she use to serve both of those disciplinary goals? Give a few specific examples.
2. What cautions does Lewis offer about the ways that her own discipline, genetic science, stands to suffer through the entry of business fields into the mix? In what ways does she defend her own discipline by what she worries might be misuse by applied disciplines like business?

ARTHUR L. CAPLAN

Mind Reading

This essay, written by chair of the Department of Medical Ethics at the University of Pennsylvania, predicts that genetic testing and neuroimaging, despite potential problems, will dramatically improve the standing of mental health fields, basing them more firmly in biological sciences. Arthur L. Caplan, Emanuel and Robert Hart Professor at the University of Pennsylvania, is co-editor of Ethics at the End of Life: the Case of Terri Schiavo (2006). He holds a Ph.D. in History and the Philosophy of Science. This piece was originally published in The American Prospect, a periodical that calls itself "an authoritative magazine of liberal ideas, committed to a just society, an enriched democracy, and effective liberal politics."

Considering its topic, the background of the author as an historian and philosopher, and the magazine's mission, this piece can help us to better understand interdisciplinary connections between the fields of biology and social sciences—but to also see them in the political realm. In particular, Caplan looks at the ways in which social sciences stand to benefit by their connections to the empirical data garnered by a natural science, biology. This is one of the reasons why college majors in neuroscience often include faculty members from many disciplines, especially those in biology, psychology, and in some cases chemistry and philosophy. As you read, you might consider how each these disciplines, and other groups of disciplines as well, stand to benefit by this cross-fertilization. You might also consider if anything might be lost.

For too long, mental health has been a policy and ethical backwater. While mountains of articles have been written on the ethics of cloning human beings (hugely unlikely to happen anytime soon), the morality of using genetically engineered animals as sources of organs for transplants (ditto), and the moral defensibility of using treatments derived from embryonic stem-cell research to cure horrific diseases (a very long shot), hardly any literature exists on the ethics of current practices and policies in mental health.

All that is about to change. A technological revolution imminent in mental health will soon revolutionize how mental illness is widely perceived and elevate it to the forefront of health policy.

We have all heard, perhaps to the point of indifference, about the mapping of the human genome. With dramatic technological advances, we have jumped from having a rudimentary chromosomal map of our genes and those of other animals and plants to a finely tuned, high resolution blueprint of human DNA. Think of the transformation from a basic map of the world's continents and oceans to the ability to locate your own front yard through satellite imagery on Google Earth, and you'll begin to understand the enormity.

Most of the discussion about the benefits of mapping the human genome has focused on diagnosing physical disorders or the risk of acquiring them. Breast cancer, heart disease, deafness, cystic fibrosis, Fanconi's anemia, hemophilia, and similar maladies have been the poster children in the emerging era of precision genetic testing. But, as genomic knowledge expands and as more databases involving all aspects of the health of millions of people are correlated with an ever-increasing number of genes, mental illnesses will surely be the newest targets for genetic testing. This means that embryos, fetuses, children, and adults will soon be candidates for testing for a vast range of risks and predispositions: addiction, depression, anxiety, schizophrenia, phobias, paranoia, obsessive-compulsive disease, aggressive behavior, attention deficit disorders, and many other mental impairments. Doctors will soon be able to detect the risk of developing mental illnesses as accurately as they now detect many physical illnesses.

The expansion of genomics into mental health will bring much good in the form of prevention and early diagnosis. It will also bring much controversy. Among the many thorny questions to be answered: Should genetic testing for risks of developing mental diseases be entirely voluntary? How private should such tests be? How much counseling ought to accompany the tests, and who should do the counseling? How accurate must these tests be before being made available to doctors, employers, or to the public directly in home-test kits? And, critically, what exactly constitutes a "mental illness" for which testing would be worthwhile in the first place?

This is not the stuff of science fiction. At least one company, San Diego–based Psynomics, is offering a home-test kit for a gene associated with bipolar disease and depression. A buyer spits in a cup and sends the sample off to Psynomics for testing. It is not at all clear that the test is accurate enough to justify its widespread use. Nor are doctors ready to explain the results of the test to those who buy these kits. Nor is it clear how to protect someone from having their saliva taken and sent off without their permission—say by someone who swabs your mouth while you sleep or takes some of your DNA off a coffee cup or glass.

Right along with the explosion in knowledge about the genetic contribution to mental illness is another new and powerful, if less attention-grabbing, technology—neuroimaging. We have all seen the fascinating pictures of how our brains "light up" in response to certain stimuli or thought patterns. Scanning technologies far more powerful than the familiar CAT scan—tests like positron emission tomography, functional magnetic resonance imaging, multichannel electroencephalography, and near infrared spectroscopic imaging—already make it possible to "watch" neural activity in real time with impressive accuracy. Since the link between the brain and your behavior is a lot closer than it is between your genes and your behavior, imaging the brain through these and other technological advances is likely to prove to be the biggest boon ever to the mental-health field.

Long before symptoms actually appear, a brain scan may reveal early onset Alzheimer's, anti-social tendencies, or autism; show patterns predictive of depression or suicidal ideation later in life; or prove predictive of who will find themselves getting into trouble in junior high school. Conditions that are now difficult to diagnose, such as mild schizophrenia or Asperger's, may prove easily detected when imaging results confirm suspicions.

Where is neuroimaging taking us? Want to claim that you need extra time on an exam due to a learning disability? You may need to undergo a neuroimaging exam to confirm your diagnosis. Hope to convince a parole board that you are ready to be discharged from prison after having undergone extensive therapy for child molestation? An intensive brain examination taken while you are exposed to suggestive photos may prove your case and secure a release sooner than a therapist's diagnosis will. And before anyone prescribes an antidepressant to a very young person, both a neuroimaging study and genetic testing may be required to assess the child's risk profile for dangerous, adverse events and unwanted side effects that the drug might cause.

It is not just medicine that will be responding to the explosion of diagnostic power that will flow from advances in genomics and neuroimaging. The ability to detect an abnormal brain may begin to shift thinking in the courts and criminal-justice system away from a punishment perspective toward a more therapeutic or medical model. If you are facing the death sentence in a highly controversial case, how quickly can your lawyer introduce a picture of your brain that shows gross abnormalities inconsistent with personal responsibility? Similarly, mental-health workers may find themselves called upon more and more often to offer their prognoses about who is likely to steal, embezzle, or harass at work. Before long, neuroimaging exams may supplant many of the familiar psychological and aptitude tests used in schools and the workplace today. And how long will it be before exclusive private nursery schools and kindergartens add a request for a brain-scan analysis to their admissions requirements?

The range and complexity of ethical issues raised by neuroimaging are as impressive as any that have accompanied any recent technological development in health care. Who will be paying for all this testing? When will such testing be mandatory—upon entry to the military or the clergy, upon arrest, when seeking a marriage license? Who will do the testing, who will be able to see the results, and what standards will they answer to?

***

The technology rolling toward us will even change how we think about mental health and mental illness. Today, drug abusers stick themselves with needles, risking diseases and addiction to get high. Tomorrow, you may be able to feed a signal right into the pleasure centers of your brain, giving you a much greater high without all the mess and risk. Is that a good thing? What if someone chooses to stay in a virtual world, remain attached to a pleasure-stimulating machine, or try to use new drugs or devices to boost their performance, mood, or sex drive or even modify a personality trait they don't like? Is "cosmetic" mental health a field of which our children will partake? Will debates about what to do about mental illness expand far beyond those we currently recognize as mentally ill?

There is also, of course, a profoundly positive side to this story. Improvements in diagnostics will guarantee improvements in treatments for millions of people suffering brain-related disorders. Already, better neuroimaging permits doctors to implant devices aimed at treating Parkinsonism or epilepsy deep into the brain. More precision forms of psychosurgery and a wider range of implantable gizmos are very likely to follow.

Similarly, advances in our ability to "pinpoint" drugs to an individual patient's genetic or neural makeup will bring enormous benefits. Today, we must often rely on "one size fits all" drugs that can be associated with serious risks and side effects. Tomorrow, when treatments become more and more efficacious with fewer and fewer problems, issues of access to care and the moral imperative to pay for it will come center stage in health-policy debates.

What can be used to treat can also be used to enhance. So the nascent trend in high schools and colleges among students and faculty to try drugs that help focus attention, or to permit a person to stay awake and function with less sleep, is likely to evolve into an enormous societal debate about the use of drugs or implants to boost productivity. Our grandchildren may well find that certain career paths are not open to them unless they are willing to undergo psychosurgery or take powerful cognition-enhancing drugs.

If the technology is built, then the field of mental health will bear little resemblance to the struggling, underfunded, often stigmatized, and somewhat mundane set of activities grouped under the mental-health banner that we are familiar with today. Mental health is about to fulfill the old Freudian dream—resting psychiatry and psychology on a neuroscientific and biological foundation. That may not guarantee the delivery of the best mental-health care to those in need, but it will guarantee a revolution in the attitudes, expectations, and utilization of mental-health care services and knowledge. What once was a field fighting for parity and battling stigma is on the cusp of becoming a field where you would have to be crazy not to at least consider using what mental health will have to offer.

Reading Analytically

1. One of the main arguments Caplan makes is that neuroimaging is likely to benefit the fields of psychology and mental health. Upon what basis does he make that argument?
2. Implicit in the argument noted in the previous question is a social critique as well, a critique that fits well with the mission of this magazine as noted in the headnote. What criticisms of our treatment of the mental health field does Caplan offer? Who does he seem to blame for that treatment?
3. Despite his optimism, Caplan also offers some cautions about the growing technology of neuroimaging. What are those cautions, and upon what are they based?

Reading Across Disciplinary Communities

1. Though this piece is about science, it is also a political statement; in fact, the place of publication—this openly liberal publication—makes it immediately so. What facets of this piece stray away from "science" and move more toward politics? Give several examples.
2. Considering the above question, what are the implications of science entering into the political arena? Are there dangers when an empirical science becomes the topic of political debate? Or is science already political? Try to articulate your own position on the dangers, benefits, or both of science entering the area of politics.

BEATRIX P. RUBIN

Therapeutic Promise in the Discourse of Human Embryonic Stem Cell Research

This essay was written by an author who herself crossed disciplinary boundaries. Until 2001, Beatrix P. Rubin was a biologist involved in genetic research, after which she moved into the social sciences to study the therapeutic possibilities and the ethical issues surrounding applications of the human genome project. She is a researcher at the Collegium Helveticum, *where she works in the interdisciplinary project, "Tracking the Human." Rubin studied Biology at the University of Konstanz, the University of Oregon in Eugene, and the Technical University in Munich and completed a Ph.D. on the regeneration of the central nervous system at the University of Zurich.*

This essay studies the ways that genetic research goes beyond genetic science to consider the rhetoric surrounding science. More specifically, it considers the ways that activities such as the Human Genome Project have been framed in language—as projects with great promise for curing disease. The essay goes on to suggest that this use of language has been employed to ensure continued funding for research in the area. In this way, the article examines both the science and the rhetoric surrounding human embryonic stem cell research. As you read, you might consider both how the author conducts her rhetorical analysis—an activity that can make you a better, more analytical reader as well—and what ethical implications exist not only in the science, but the rhetoric surrounding it.

Abstract: In the recent past, biomedical research has been repeatedly promoted on the grounds that it will lead to novel cures. Future remedies have been proposed and propagated by diverse actors such as scientists, the media and patient representatives. Proposals for novel therapies based on human embryonic stem cells (hESCs) have framed the initiation, reception, and implementation of novel research in multiple ways. The Foucauldian notion of a *dispositif* as well as the concept of the "therapeutic promise" serve to draw attention to the central role of

> Michel Foucault is an influential French philosopher. His notion of the *dispoisitif* suggests that we can understand a social activity by studying the "discourse" surrounding it—that is, we can better understand a phenomenon by analyzing the ways people talk and write about it. In this essay, Rubin analyzes the discourse surrounding human stem cell research.

medical proposals in the discourse on hESC research. In particular the quest for therapies has rendered the human embryo accessible first as an object of experimental manipulation, then of public debate, and finally as the subject of regulation. This therapeutic promise has enabled a reorientation of hESC research towards medical applications, has guided public debate and, in so doing, has itself been enrolled as a legal norm. This paper highlights the work done by the therapeutic promise in initiating an alliance between bioethics and science in an endeavour that both shaped and ensured the continuation of hESC research.

This key term is at the heart of this article, as the idea that stemcell research can lead to therapies and cures drives much of the interest—and funding—for this research.

Introduction

When will stem cell research lead to new disease cures? Stem cell-based therapies are already in widespread clinical use, in the form of bone marrow and cord blood transplants. These procedures, which save many lives every year, demonstrate the validity of stem cell transplantation as a therapeutic concept. We are optimistic that similar successes will be possible with other types of stem cells for other diseases, but it is impossible to predict how soon this will happen, given the many technical challenges that must be overcome. The only safe prediction is that the sooner we begin, the sooner we will reach our goal ('Frequently asked questions': Harvard Stem Cell Institute, 2007).

This opening epigraph illustrates one of the ways we talk about stem cell research as having great promise for cures. Note that the author doesn't ask "if" it will do this, but "when." It is assumed that it will.

The proposals for a therapeutic future free of degeneration and disease which has become associated with human embryonic stem cell research have been embraced with great enthusiasm in various nations around the globe. Accordingly, the ethical evaluation and the political and legal regulation of its future design have led to extensive negotiations at the national and international level during the past 10 years. The versed reader might consider this as nothing out of the ordinary: those advancing the applications of biomedical research are recognized as inveterate exponents of far-reaching therapeutic proposals. Their recommendations have long been effective in guiding public perceptions of medical problems and in creating therapeutic solutions located in the future. These have, in turn, helped to solicit broad societal support manifest for example, in high levels of biomedical research funding. The facile conclusion could be that the proponents of human embryonic stem cell research have courted society anew by presenting just one more of a series of therapeutic futures. This assumption, however, ignores an important fact: human embryonic stem cell research (hESC research) and the novel therapies it should potentially lead to cannot be realized without access to the early human embryo in vitro. Without this, the much-vaunted and hoped for therapies based on hESCs cannot come into existence.

This paragraph lays out the problem: researchers need to convince the public that using human embryos for research is worthwhile, despite ethical concerns.

This article argues that in light of these circumstances the proposals of novel hESC-based therapies as they are envisioned by scientists and propagated, for example, by patient organizations and the media, engender debates different than those which have attended biomedical innovation in the past. These proposals no longer only represent a desirable medical future, but much more importantly, the aspirations surrounding their development turn the human embryo into the central object of the biomedical discourse. In this move, the embryo is rendered accessible in different ways: first as object of experimental manipulation within stem cell research, second as object of public/ethical debate, and thirdly as subject to legal regulation. In this paper, I introduce the term "therapeutic promise" to capture the central role that the medical proposals surrounding hESC research have played in (re)framing the management of the human embryo in these different contexts. The term 'promise' articulates all declarations of medical futures associated with hESC research, as well as all expectations towards such futures. The adjective 'therapeutic' points to the specific agency reflected in the term promise: to cure conditions heretofore considered incurable. The therapeutic promise is then understood in a Foucauldian sense as a *dispositif*. As such it organizes knowledge(s), values, and procedures around an overarching motif (Foucault, 1978, pp. 119–125). At the same time it is being organized by those knowledge(s), values, and procedures.

Here, the main thesis is stated: the use of the word *therapeutic* in the discussion and debate about stem cell research makes an implicit argument as to why we should allow it—it can lead to future cures. The article will thus study the use of that term in the scientific community and media, suggesting it is a *dispositif*—a term that carries with it a social goal and which helps to shape our understanding of the phenomenon.

With a focus on science and politics in the US and Europe, in particular Germany and the UK, the hypothesis put forward argues that in the discourse on hESC research the therapeutic promise, as an overarching motif, defies the boundaries between different political cultures.[1] It does so by connecting different realms of society in the quest for an ethically justified and hence obligatory medical future flowing from hESC research. In doing so, it both integrates and stabilizes the controversial experimental use of human embryos for stem cell research. The analytical focus on the different guises and functionalities of what I have termed the therapeutic promise suggests a specific analytical structure in which the discourse on hESC research can be divided into three temporally and structurally distinct phases, covering a period of about 40 years beginning in the 1970s. Whilst links clearly exist between these phases, this analytical framework provides an entry into how hESC research, itself premised on the human embryo, has been established through—or, put another way, contingent upon—the advancement of the therapeutic promise.

The goal, then, is to show that the potential gains (or "promise") outweigh the other ethical problems.

1. In phase I, the therapeutic promise served to redirect attention towards medical application, thereby initiating a therapeutic shift in ESC research in which the human embryo became an experimental object within stem cell science.
2. The second phase is characterized by a broad societal debate about the moral status of the human embryo, initiated and stabilized by the therapeutic promise. In so doing, it (the therapeutic promise) has become enrolled within public discourse as a legal norm regulating access to the embryo within national laws.
3. In the (still ongoing) phase III, the implementation of hESC research in the international setting under the rubric of regenerative medicine continues to be perturbed by the unresolved moral status of the human embryo. This is reflected in the divergent national laws regulating hESC research, which preclude an internationally coordinated effort within hESC research. In response to this moral impasse, the ethical and scientific enterprise under the guidance of the therapeutic promise engages in the identification of a novel category of biologically altered embryos. These are intended as a source for hESCs emancipated from the ethical dilemma posed by isolating cells from human embryos.

This list allows the author to lay out the stages in the process of convincing the public of the promise of stem cell research.

The remainder of this paper elaborates further on each of these phases, paying particular attention to the work done by the therapeutic promise in shaping and advancing hESC research.[2] The factors which contributed first to the exclusion and subsequently to the inclusion of hESC research within the realm of the scientific enterprise are first discussed. This analysis then frames the hypothesis that a medical (re)orientation, i.e. a therapeutic shift, became manifest in hESC research in the mid-1990s leading, in turn, to a change in the treatment of the human embryo. It will be argued that from this point onwards it became possible to (re)categorize the embryo as an experimental object for biomedical research and, with this, to pursue the isolation of hESCs. In the framework of the analysis developed in this paper, this shift is understood as the entry of the therapeutic promise into the discourse on hESC research.

This paragraph constitutes what some call an "advance organizer." It tells the reader what is to come in the rest of the paper, helping the reader see the overall organization of what is to follow.

Phase I: Therapeutic Shift of Embryonic Stem Cell Research

The starting point of the discourse on hESC research is generally considered to coincide with the first publication on the successful isolation and cultivation of hESCs (Thomson et al., 1998). The understanding has been that this publication comprehensively describes the scientific efforts aimed at establishing hESC research. Such a point of view, however, neglects the genealogy of hESC research, which took place against a legal and ethical background dominated by the different regulatory frameworks on in vitro fertilization (IVF). Until the advent of hESC research, the same therapeutic procedure, namely assisted human reproduction, which had brought about the human embryo in vitro had also defined the purpose for its existence and, from this, the scope of legal regulation. Against this background, the moral status accredited to the human embryo in vitro within most Western countries had either excluded or largely restricted its categorization as an experimental object of biological research. Thus prior to 1998 the experimental sciences themselves had to frame hESC research in such a manner that it turned into a scientifically worthwhile and ethically legitimate procedure, in spite of the prohibitive rules on embryo research.

Note how this paragraph gives some history of the debate.

Interestingly enough the scientific literature is practically devoid of reports on hESC research prior to 1998.[3] Given this, the scientific developments and domain-specific interests which have accompanied the derivation of hESCs have instead been retrieved and traced by speaking to experts in the field of developmental and stem cell biology. Between September 2004 and September 2005, 10 narrative interviews were conducted with scientists in France (two), Germany (three), and Great Britain (five). The interview cohort was selected on the grounds of their internationally recognized expertise in basic and applied research on different types of embryonic and adult stem cells. An important difference between the interviewees lay in their different level of experience in hESC research, which reflected their scientific interests and the regulatory frameworks for research on human embryos in different national settings. The interview cohort therefore afforded new insights into how the development of the hESC field was experienced/may be viewed differently within different research contexts. The interviews were based on a standard set of questions encompassing the scientific developments preceding, informing, and finally enabling the isolation of hESCs. Also discussed were factors 'external' to science per se, including how the rise of academic–industrial partnerships within biomedical research, the development of bioethics and increasing public deliberation of biomedical research are important for understanding the dynamics underlying hESC research. The interviews were recorded, transcribed and their content analysed following the method of Bogner and Menz (2004).

This paragraph lays out the methodology used by the author to conduct interviews—and thus to study the ways that scientists and others talk and write about stem cell research.

Stem Cell Research Forms Part of Developmental Biology

The interviews reveal the first successful isolation of hESCs as an enterprise which took place at the boundaries of an established discipline, that of developmental biology. The interests of this field had guided the isolation and analysis of embryonic stem cells for most of its course. The recent origins of ESC research can be traced back to the 1970s. Here, the source of stem cells with qualities similar to those of ESCs had not been embryos, but tumours of the reproductive organs (teratocarcinoma). The fact that these stem cells derived from tumours were designated pluripotent, i.e. able to generate cellular offspring of widely different function in cell cultures, was of scientific interest, because it provided a proof for their developmental plasticity. However, the therapeutic potential apparent in the cell cultures, which harboured a variety of functionally different cells, which might also be used in transplantation, did not resonate with the interests of the field. Indeed, one interviewee recalled how during the mid-1980s a scientific proposal to isolate therapcutically suitable cells was not deemed of interest for the scientific community (Interview 1). That is to say that although the capacity of these stem cells to generate organ-specific cells was recognized as a possibility, this was not yet imbued with clinical potential, rather it was understood exclusively in the context of mammalian development and, following from this, studied/considered useful only for the light it might shed on questions relating to development. This, of course, contrasts sharply with the contemporary situation, where the potential clinical use of the hESC is framed largely in terms of this capacity—a shift, I wish to argue, engendered by the therapeutic promise. The analysis developed here seeks to uncover and explain both the work and impact of the therapeutic promise—which although present in pluripotent stem cells of human origin in the 1980s (in the sense of the constitutive properties of these cells), was not yet recognized and as such, was not yet influencing the questions underlying and therefore the orientation of stem cell research (Cooper, 2004).

Note how the author shows the ways that the concept of therapeutic promise found its way into the discourse surrounding stem cell research—as a possible cure for these medical problems.

Within the framework of developmental biology the search for pluripotent stem cells, which were not derived from tumours, but of embryonic origin continued. It culminated in 1981 in the first successful isolation of such stem cells from mice embryos (Evans & Kaufman, 1981; Martin, 1981). Already then the methodological knowledge and with it the name and the functional properties of embryonic stem cells were introduced and defined. The stem cells of embryonic origin proved to have a wider developmental capacity in vivo, than the stem cells derived from tumours. This property was combined with techniques of genetic manipulation and mouse ESCs quickly became a powerful tool for studying mammalian development. At the same time, the interest in mouse ESCs, not as a tool but as a research subject, diminished. Researchers pursuing their analysis formed a small community representing a very specialized area of research within developmental biology.[4] It is clear from the interviews that this small field continued to be dominated by questions of cellular differentiation as related to development: the use of the ESC for cellular therapy did not arise (Interviews 3, 6 and 10).

Here, the author shows how the topic shifted from a study of developmental biology to the study of a field that could have real applications in medicine. This demonstrates one key difference between "pure science" (which simply seeks answers) and "applied science" (which, like medicine, applies those findings to actual practices).

Another decisive factor in the development of hESC research has been the focus on the mouse as a model to study mammalian development for methodological, as well as for ethical reasons. On the one hand, mice are much more amenable to meaningful experimental exploitation based on statistically significant numbers, the use of specific molecular tools, and the manipulation of the organism at all developmental stages.

On the other hand human embryos, if they were available at all, have always remained a rare and precious object of study, which did not allow for experimental manipulation that could provide similar insights into development as the mouse embryo. Their use had been placed outside developmental research and linked with clinical application, as expressed in the quote below:

> Yes, central questions of developmental biology, you should be studying in animals, not in the human. I mean, that has always been the basis of human embryo research: it should be of some clinical applicability, not just general knowledge, because you can get general knowledge about development from other species, without all the ethical issues in human embryos (Interview 6).

In conclusion, the fact that ESC research has emerged as a part of developmental biology determined its early course in several ways: first, it shaped the scientific interests that guided the development of the field. Second, it excluded an interest in the therapeutic applications, which might arise from ESC research. Third, it did not consider the ethical controversial analysis of the human embryo in vitro central to its interests.

This paragraph summarizes the first stage in the emergence of the concept of "therapeutic promise" as a key term—a term that has been used to gain acceptance for this research.

Origins of hESC Research

In 1995 the successful isolation of embryonic stem cells from a primate species marked an important change in the field of ESC research. It suggested that the isolation of ESCs from another primate species, namely human, should be feasible (Thomson et al., 1995). It is here, in this work that we see the entry of the therapeutic promise into the discourse on hESC research: the potential isolation of hESCs is not so much described as an advance for developmental biology, but much more as providing access to a novel type of stem cell based therapy. The latter indicates an important moment in the creation of a new and novel context for research with human embryos, one that is distinct from developmental biology: this is then elaborated and restated in 1998 (Thomson et al., 1998).

This is a key point. The author distinguished between two periods in the discussion of stem cell research. In the first, the purpose was understanding human development. In the current discussion, the discussion centers on claims that it has the potential to cure diseases.

The analysis of the scientific developments themselves does not deliver an explanation as to why a medical interest in the shape of hESC therapy became manifest in the mid- 1990s. However, it testifies to the fact that the therapeutic promise frames a rather unlikely scientific enterprise, namely the isolation of ESCs from human embryos. As discussed above, this represents an endeavour outside of the dominant framework of developmental biology. Equally, this enterprise also resided on the periphery of the moral landscape created by IVF regulations in Western countries, which had largely excluded an experimental use of the human embryo. In light of the organizational power that the therapeutic promise has demonstrated in promoting hESC research it is relevant to note how the organization of contemporary biological research on the one hand provided human embryos as an experimental resource and, on the other the material grounds for the realization of hESC research.

This reinforces the author's argument that most of the current discussion focuses on the promise of cures—and so allows biological research to gather public support.

As part of an international collaboration, the embryos used in the Thomson groups' initial experiments were mostly imported from Israel (Vogel, 2002). The research community there was in a position to provide human embryos due to a very different societal framing of embryo research as a worthwhile and ethically legitimate enterprise sustaining the population and the state (Prainsack, 2006). Furthermore, the methodological knowledge gained by the earlier isolation of ESCs from apes enabled Thomson to efficiently isolate a number of hESC lines based on a very small number of human embryos (Interview 3). In this context, attention now came to focus on the embryos from which hESCs were procured. Several interviewees (1, 7 and 10) alluded to problems encountered in earlier work when trying to isolate hESCs from 'inferior' quality embryos provided by IVF clinics, which reserved embryos of 'superior' quality for implantation. This point is echoed in the quote below, which emphasizes the importance of working with embryos in 'suitable' condition for the successful isolation of hESCs.

> And today it is quite clear that to isolate human embryonic stem cells is possible if you know what you are doing, but you have to have a good blastocyst (embryo) to do it (Interview 1).

From an analytical point of view, it is crucial that the human embryo is now identified unambiguously as an experimental object, consequently its 'quality'—in terms of its yield of hESCs—becomes a criterium by which its usefulness is defined and judged.

The word *unambiguously* demonstrates how ethical issues about the human embryo are now bypassed, as the embryo is treated simply as an object of study. Of course, many who argue against this research on ethical grounds would disagree.

The importance of the organization of biological research is not only reflected in the fact that human embryos could be provided through a collaborative effort, but also that the funding of this work could be secured. The fact that the contemporary biological sciences are routinely and continually scrutinized for potential commercial applications by universities (for example technology transfer offices), funding agencies, as well as representatives from the industrial sector, allowed Thomson to pursue his scientific interests: in spite of the fact that the political situation in the US made it impossible for him to acquire federal funds for research with human embryos, the close connection between academic research and the biotech industry allowed him to obtain support from the company Geron, which funded his research (Interview 8). The early link between hESC research and the biotech industry was secured by a number of far reaching patents. These were connected to the first patent issued in 1998 and covered potential commercial interests extensively (Loring & Campbell, 2006).

Here, the relationship between science and business is mentioned; if the stem cell research has promise for medicine, it can also become a profit center for biomedical companies. Note how the various disciplines interact here.

The initial efforts aimed at isolating hESCs mark the entry and indicate the agency of the therapeutic promise in the discourse on hESC research. They tie in with a general trend linking academic research, biotech industry, patient organizations and politics in the production and exploitation of economically relevant knowledge about health and disease (Rabinow, 1996, pp. 129–152). The emerging field of therapeutic hESC research no longer forms part of developmental biology. It is therefore not primarily interested in elucidating the mechanisms underlying the pluripotency of hESCs as they relate to an understanding of early human development. Instead its members seek to generate knowledge, which is first of all useful for the therapeutic applications of hESCs (Interview 3). Setting hESC research apart from the general trend alluded to above, however, is the fact that from the beginning it carried the burden of its contested resource. Within the framework of therapeutic research it has become possible to categorize human embryos as rare experimental objects for stem cell research. As such they have to be of good quality to guarantee a successful isolation. However, their experimental use in stem cell research has not yet acquired public approval and hence remains precarious.

Again, the idea that the various purposes of research have been brought together is noted.

Note how the author suggests that stem cells are a "contested resource." That is, they are necessary for this research, but the public and government needs to be convinced that using human embryos is worth the ethical risks or that resource will not be available.

Phase II: Hardening of Therapeutic Promise

Within the framework of this analysis, the publication of the derivation of the first hESC lines (Thomson et al., 1998) marks the beginning of the public phase of the stem cell discourse. From now on, the therapeutic promise, having emerged from the closed circles of the biological research community, has to function within the different regulatory regimes which are continuously being developed to monitor biological research activities and the medical futures embedded within them. If the structure of contemporary biological research linking academia and industry in a flexible network around the globe permitted the initiation of hESC research, this enterprise has been and continues to be shaped by the national political system within which it is situated. As Jasanoff has very convincingly shown, in Germany, Great Britain and the US, the governance of hESC research and cloning has relied on

> . . . very different national strategies of normalization, that is for making human biotechnology seem mundane and governable in the face of moral uncertainty and conflict (Jasanoff, 2005, p. 147).

Without denying the important discursive and regulatory differences between these and other countries of the West, the incorporation of hESC research in the ethical, political, and legal landscape of Western democracies has been greatly facilitated by the therapeutic promise as a common dispositif. At the same time the act of defining the status of the human embryo in vitro at the national level becomes increasingly interwined with the inscription of the therapeutic promise.

In this section, the author is showing how the discourse of "therapeutic promise" has become accepted over time—the idea has "hardened," or become commonplace.

The public debates on hESC research have been repeatedly construed as an 'abstract moral dilemma' (Manzei, 2005, p. 78), within which two 'goods' stand opposed: the dignity of the incurably ill, whose life might be saved by stem cell therapy, versus the protection of the dignity of the embryo, as a potential human existence. As Manzei has observed, one consequence of the narrow construction of the public debate has meant that many controversial issues comprising ethical, medical, and social problems, which will most likely arise through the application of stem cell therapies, have been sidelined (Manzei, 2005). From the analytical point of view advanced in this paper, the therapeutic promise thus remains largely unchallenged in the public debate;

such is the power of the promise that it is able to weather the bioethical storms provoked by the experimental use of the human embryo. In spite of the fact that the ethical dissent on the status of the human embryo is not solved, and likewise the ethical dilemma remains, the therapeutic promise is reinforced, as it is enshrined within national laws. In this regard the regulatory frameworks of Germany and the UK are understood as an attempt to introduce moral boundaries which conceptualize a nationally adapted exploitation of the human embryo in hESC research: on the one hand the human embryo in vitro is re-inscribed as a source for therapeutic means, whilst on the other hand the normative implications of the therapeutic promise, namely the obligation of research to develop cures for the incurably ill, is reinforced.

"Re-inscribing" means giving new meanings or new associations to a term; here, the author suggests that stem cell research has become nearly synonymous with its promise of potential cures.

'Promissory Capital' of Embryonic Stem Cell Research

In November 1999 the prestigious scientific journal Science awarded the distinction of a 'scientific breakthrough' to the publication by Thomson et al. (1998). The accolade came equipped with praise for the medical future hESC research holds for the aging patient. In the commentary the therapeutic promise is stated as follows:

> With dramatic results like these coupled with growing public acceptance, the stem cell field is poised for progress. If it lives up to its early promise, it may one day restore vigour to aged and diseased muscles, hearts, and brains—perhaps even allowing humans to combine the wisdom of old age with the potential of youth (Vogel, 1999, p. 2239).

Note how the author uses an analysis of these quotations from interviews to demonstrate the ways that scientists have come to talk about the "promise" of this research.

It is worth noting that this representation contradicts the view expressed in interview by an hESC expert who contended that, in fact, 'There was no Eureka moment in the field of stem cell research' (Interview 1). The incongruity apparent in the contrasting representations of research progress 'within' and 'outside' science apparent in the two preceding quotes is illuminating of the fact, that whilst not a scientific breakthrough an ethical breakthrough has occurred: the first widely publicized use of human embryos for experimental purposes outside the realm of IVF. From an analytical point of view, the introduction of the breakthrough metaphor can be considered as an attempt to situate hESC research within the biomedical landscape as a universal cure; if this necessitates societal reflection, it also carries with it a moral obligation to act upon the medical future which it holds:

> . . . actors are increasingly producing knowledge in the contexts of problem and application. To this extent, breakthrough has become the metaphorical location of values and activities whereby knowledge is rewarded and validated in relation to actual and clearly defined problems or impasses rather than, as in the case of discovery, being prized for its speculative or serendipitous character (Brown, 2000, p. 93).

In this context the 'breakthrough award' can be considered as one of many discursive instances which create a broadly shared view of hESC research through the therapeutic promise to which it is tightly coupled. This reinforces the 'promissory capital' (Thompson, 2005) of stem cell research. As Thompson has discussed in the context of reproductive medicine, the promissory capital 'signals a shift away from production, productivity, and profit toward knowledge, technologies of life and promise' (Thompson, 2005, pp. 258–260). In other words, if the hESCs remain as yet unknown, the future (clinical) potential with which they have been imbued ensures that they are considered a compelling subject of study. More broadly, this has contributed to the development of an emerging moral space, as Brown and Kraft (2006) have, in the case of umbilical cord blood banking, put it 'where failure (of parents) to invest now may result in moral recrimination later.' In the case of hESC research, moral recrimination is not limited to the decisions of the individual, but extends instead to society as a whole, reflecting that it is at this level that a proper framework for the conduct of this research should be decided upon.

Here, the summary of the issue helps us to see that despite the fact that we are unsure of whether stem cell research will keep its promises, we have come to accept that as a given.

Inscription of the Therapeutic Promise in Law

Although the public discourse under bioethical guidance has devoted a good part of its analytical power to investigating the legitimacy of employing human embryos for hESC research, it has, like the debates on IVF, not succeeded in resolving the dissent on the moral status of the human embryo in vitro. Within the public discourse the ethical dilemma has been decried, however a solution regarding the handling of the embryo that satisfies all parties concerned has not come about.

On the other hand, as discussed above, the novel medical options provided by hESC research have become so compelling that they constitute not only a subject of political debate, but also of legislative intervention. The argument is brought forward that in this context the development of the two diverging national laws reflects the regulatory space created by the policy on IVF on the one hand and the adherence to the therapeutic promise on the other. In the UK, the proponents of hESC research could refer to the debate on IVF, as a result of which embryo research had been framed as indispensable for medical progress and a corresponding legal framework had been developed (Mulkay, 1997, Parry, 2003). In this context, the legal regulation of hESC research was introduced as an amendment to the existing Human Fertilisation and Embryology Act 1990. In contrast, in Germany, legislation on IVF relied on a very different stabilization of the embryo as a 'liminal agent' (Jasanoff, 2005): by avoiding the creation of supernumerary embryos the use of human embryos outside procreation was strictly excluded. Here, the difficulty in transgressing the regulatory gap between the law on IVF and the needs of hESC research was reflected in a central phrase of the German debate 'that no embryo should die for German research.' As Sperling points out, the implicit normative character of German law on stem cell research limits and at the same time renders the experimental use of hESC lines, which were created before a certain cut off date, morally binding.

> By deeming research on some embryos as unethical, the law, also by implication, makes research on all other embryos ethical, and then not importing those embryos [cell lines, B.R.], which are seen as vital to the German polity, becomes almost immoral (Sperling, 2004, p. 146).

> Here, the author shows how the terminology surrounding stem cell research's potential has even influenced laws, which in some countries, give the right for such study only because of its promise of possible cures. The United States, under the Obama administration, has just reversed its position to allow for stem cell research funding. The reasons given were therapeutic promise and the need to keep up with cutting-edge science, which is discussed later in this article.

Common to both legal frameworks is not only the implicit, but also an explicit inscription of the therapeutic promise into the law where it becomes a central justification for research on human embryos or embryonic stem cell lines: therapeutic and diagnostic research is explicitly categorized to qualify for the use of human embryos (UK) or imported cell lines (Germany). This legal inscription might be subsumed under what Jasanoff refers to as the most influential form of boundary work being done in contemporary societies (Jasanoff, 2005, p. 27). In spite of the fact that the realization of national laws in the UK and Germany has taken on different pathways, I would argue that the therapeutic promise prevailed in ethical discourses within different national contexts as a strong and universally applicable moral coin. A coin of such value that it could not be refuted, but had to be traded for an equivalent counter value embedded in national traditions. The national style of governance determined the proper value of exchange, meaning the legal access granted to the human embryo (Great Britain) or to hESC lines created before a certain cut off date (Germany). The two different legal frameworks correspond to two of the five major cultural trading positions within a global moral economy as proposed by Salter and Salter (2007), each of which can be understood as follows:

> In cultural terms, the bioethical options are constructed so that as one moves from 1 to 5 the moral status (value) attached to the human embryo diminishes and the value attached to its scientific, commercial and social utility correspondingly increases (Salter & Salter, 2007, pp. 570–571).

Hence, whilst the diverging national frameworks reflect the intention to carry out hESC research—underpinned as this is by the 'therapeutic promise'—the extent to which access is granted in practice is determined by the differing value ascribed to the human embryo.

Phase III: Therapeutic Promise Organizes Research and Embryo at International Level

With ethical debates having taken place and legal frameworks agreed upon in each national setting, individual nation-states now embark upon a scientific and economic competition as individual players in a global race to realize hESC-based therapeutics. The conversion of the therapeutic promise into research programs and economic initiatives represents—for that promise—a return to its origins, as the research done to realize it becomes embedded once again within the global techno-economic system of biological research. Under the label of 'regenerative medicine,' hESC research is organized as a science-policy goal, with a view also to yielding (substantial) economic benefit. The hESC world begins to develop within a heterogeneous system of legal frameworks and international patents, which regulate hESC research in different nations. In

Note how this new term, "regenerative medicine," firmly establishes biological research into the realm of applied science (medicine) and business (biomedical firms)—it is seen as having potential in both areas.

the view of biomedical experts, the years 2004/2005 represented a starting point in the race to develop hESC research: on one hand the ethical debate has subsided and legal regulations, which categorize the permissible forms of hESC research are in place. On the other hand the first standardized laboratory protocols for the isolation and cultivation of hESCs have been developed and vast amounts of funding are being channeled into this emerging domain (Interviews 3 and 4). The pace and scope of the newly reconfigured and reoriented hESC research enterprise however varies across national boundaries, since it is contingent upon the particular ethical position and framework adopted by each nation. Some countries are better-placed than others: those nations not in at the beginning of this race will always lag behind (Interview 4).

Those nation-states which have adopted more restrictive legal approaches find themselves removed from the 'leading edge' of biomedical research and from realizing the therapeutic promise of the hESC. In some instances, this triggers political initiatives to address the perceived 'lag' or 'gap.' In this context the discussion of alternative sources of pluripotent stem cells, which might replace the human embryo, by the President's Council on Bioethics of the United States, can be regarded as an attempt to overcome the final roadblock on the way to not only a national, but also an international, implementation of hESC research (The President's Council on Bioethics, 2005). In response to a proposal discussed in this report and in order to disentangle hESC research from its ethical burden, a mouse embryo that lacks the capacity to implant in the uterus has been developed (see below). If the production of a biologically impaired embryo were to acquire validity as an ethically acceptable source of hESCs in the global moral economy, hESC research will have secured its material basis at the international level.

Here, the impact of this concept upon remaining a world leader in science is discussed—another topic that was addressed during the period that the United States had banned funding for this research on human embryos.

Flexible Therapeutic Promise: The Birth of Regenerative Medicine

The availability of an uncontested source of hESCs would be highly valuable to numerous institutions, which have been recently founded around the world primarily to carry out research in regenerative medicine.[5] The use of this 'de novo term' in the biomedical literature has increased rapidly over the past years: a scan of the public data bank PubMed has shown that it appears for the first time only in the year

2000 in six papers (mostly reviews). By October 2007 the number of publications has grown at an ever increasing rate to over 2,000.[6] As regenerative medicine became more prominent within the biomedical literature, this term also signified the creation of manifold links between the scientific research and the public discourse and the economic and political spheres, all of which now have at their disposal a common term designating the hESC future. With this move in which the therapeutic promise has now become a valid scientific and political concept, the need for hESC research becomes stronger. The dynamics are exemplified in a position paper published by the German Society for Regenerative Medicine, founded in 2004 to advance this novel type of medicine, which emphasizes the existence of an international competition under different regulatory restraints, the future economic potential which is essential to the German Biotech industry and, most significantly for the purposes of my argument here, the urgent search for remedies to counter the specific medical problems of a rapidly aging population (Arbeitskreis Regenerative Medizin, 2004). At this point, the therapeutic promise (re)connects to a theme that from its beginnings provided an important incentive for supporting research into hESCs: the intractable nature of the many diseases of old age and the quest for longevity—both of which were given political and economic force by the aging demographic in the Western world. This provided one driver for the foundation of Geron and also a context for the coining of the term 'regenerative medicine' by Michael Haseltine.

Researchers participating in the field of regenerative medicine operate in a complex environment shaped by national laws and a rapidly evolving and expanding patent landscape. These patents, whilst meant on the one hand to help exploit potential economic gains of the therapeutic promise, threaten to jeopardize scientific advance and technological innovation per se. In the US, patents issued early on in the derivation and application of hESCs are now being challenged on the grounds of lack of novelty. These early patents were widely criticized for the way in which they limited access to existing cell lines and impeded research into potentially economically relevant therapies, leading to the charge that 'they have stifled academic and entrepreneurial innovation' (Check, 2007). The extensive patenting on the one hand is contrasted on the other by a relatively modest industrial activity in the field of hESC

Here, there are concerns expressed about the ways that the entry of business motives into the arena might taint truly scientific approaches to the topic; you might consider how this is also an issue raised by the various Web sites that offer genetic screening directly to consumers. See the various readings on this topic in this section.

research (Giebel, 2005). This reflects the dichotomy between aimed for and economically feasible paths to innovation in stem cell research. Much like society at large, the economic system has engaged in a stem cell future, the actual potential of which remains both uncertain and some way off. In short, there is a mismatch between the timeframe for research that can determine the clinical potential of hESC-based therapies and those prevailing within industry with respect to realizing commercial returns on investment.

Creation of the 'Non-Embryo'

Furthermore, the implementation of hESC research through international collaborations is hampered by the different national laws on hESC research which reflect the dissent on the moral status ascribed to the embryo, as discussed earlier for the UK and Germany. That biomedical researchers are acutely aware of the ethical dissent on the human embryo is reflected in the fact that some have taken the initiative to circumvent the central ethical problem by devising experimental strategies which aim to avoid the destruction of the human embryo. Here one such approach is discussed. It involves the development of an embryo which has lost its ability to implant in the uterus due to a genetic manipulation, by a procedure termed 'altered nuclear transfer' (ANT). Interestingly, the generation of such an embryo has first been proposed and discussed by members of the President's Council on Bioethics (2005, pp. 36–50). In response to a proposal by council member William Hurlbut, an experimentally altered mouse embryo that possesses the suggested properties has indeed been generated experimentally (Meissner & Jaenisch, 2006). This embryo, which has forfeited its biological potential but can still be used to isolate ESCs, could be referred to as a 'non-embryo' in allusion to the term of the 'pre-embryo'—a term introduced in the British debate on IVF to circumscribe the first 14 days of human development. The delineation between not yet human and human which became associated with the term pre-embryo proved to be decisive in winning support for embryo research in the British debate on IVF (Mulkay, 1994). In the case of the 'non-embryo,' the discussion is continuing as to whether such a loss in developmental capacity conforms to a corresponding change in its moral status. The reactions to these sorts of experimental work within and beyond the scientific community have been rather mixed, with the ethical

Note here how important semantics and definitions can be. By terming this a "non-embryo" or a "pre-embryo," it bypasses claims of the potential for this embryo to become a human life.

assessment still ongoing (Ach et al., 2006). From an analytical point of view, these processes demonstrate once more the organizational power of the therapeutic promise and the ethical evaluation that it frames. It (the therapeutic promise) has installed itself so firmly in the discourse on hESC research that ethics is repositioned as a discourse guiding the conduct of embryo/hESC research and as such is endowed with the authority to lead the way on the search for the 'proper' hESC source. This process might be understood as what Franklin has described as 'the social being literally reinstalled within the biological' (Franklin, 2001, p. 342).

Conclusions

In this analysis the discourse on hESC research has been conceived as an instructive case for the manifold ways in which the proposals for novel therapies have framed and stabilized the initiation, reception, and implementation of a novel biomedical research domain in the Western system of science and policy. To do justice to the central role of the therapeutic proposals I have introduced the *dispositif* 'therapeutic promise' as an analytical tool to explore the work it does as mobilizing force in the discourse on hESC research. The aim has been to show that as such it has organized biological research, served as an ethical and legal guide and has driven research funding and economic proposals through the creation of a common beneficial and morally binding medical future.

The indicator for the organizational power of the therapeutic promise is the incremental enrollment of the human embryo as a unit of infinite 'biovalue' (Waldby, 2002) in national frameworks of hESC research. The fact that the national laws framing hESC research harbour divergent categorizations of the human embryo continues to perturb its appropriation as an experimental object of hESC research. In this context it remains to be seen whether and how bioethics and biomedical science will be successful in resolving the moral dilemma of embryo exploitation by introducing a novel category of ethically 'neutral' and therapeutically functional 'non-embryos.'

Hence it remains to be seen as to whether the therapeutic promise will ultimately tame the human embryo and introduce the 'non-embryo' as another 'liminal agent' (Jasanoff, 2005). Nevertheless, the argument made here is that the therapeutic promise has inscribed itself once again so firmly in the biomedical discourse so as to cast the development of hESCbased therapies as indispensable—scientifically, politically and economically. As a consequence it might guide biomedical research in the identification of novel venues to stem cell based therapies which avoid the use of the human embryo altogether. Extending the concept introduced by Rose and Novas, the diverse social actors, biomedical researchers, politicians, media representatives, members of ethics committees, lay people, to name just a few, might all be identified as 'ethical pioneers.' As pioneers they have been confronted with hitherto unknown ethical choices, created by a hope in a technology rather than an existing technology (Rose & Novas, 2005). Thereby they have established and continue to elaborate the therapeutic promise, as a multifaceted affirmation to a desired future.

This summarizes the main point of the article: the ways that this research has been framed in words have helped to push the research agenda forward.

This sentence expresses a key point in the article: the language surrounding stem cell research has tried to predict a better future—and to help bring it about—by convincing people of its therapeutic promise.

Acknowledgements

I would like to thank Professor Rainer Schweizer and PD Dr Hans-Peter Bernhard for the collaboration on the project which formed the basis of this publication. In this respect I would like to thank the cogito foundation and the University of St Gallen for the financial support, which enabled this work. In particular I would like to thank Sabine Maasen, Alison Kraft, Mario Kaiser, and the editorial team for critical reading and many important comments.

Notes

1. The countries of reference were selected because they possess sufficiently similar, but yet disparate political cultures (Jasanoff, 2005, pp. 21–31). This allows for indicating the role of the therapeutic promise, as a common motif in divergent paths of regulation. The author is well aware of the geographical limitations of this analysis and would like to refer the reader to other explorations for a global view on the reception and regulation of hESC research (Bender *et al.*, 2005).
2. A monograph discussing the single phases in more detail is in preparation.
3. In the period between the publication in 1981, which introduced for the first time the concept of embryonic stem cells in mice (Evans & Kaufmann, 1981) and the publication in 1998 on the isolation of human embryonic stem cells (Thomson *et al.*, 1998) a partially successful attempt at isolating embryonic stem cells from human embryos had been reported (Bongso *et al.*, 1994).
4. The absence of organized three-dimensional structures in the culture dish, which resemble those within the organism, was considered a major drawback in using embryonic stem cells for studies in developmental biology. With the

advent of hESC research the status of the field of mouse embryonic stem cell biology and of the scientists involved, has improved decisively. The knowledge generated in this field constitutes, for now, the most advanced source of therapeutically relevant know how.

5. Definitions and descriptions of regenerative medicine abound, but have a common theme, the treatment of degenerative processes: 'Regenerative medicine is the process of creating living, functional tissues to repair or replace tissue or organ function lost due to age, disease, damage, or congenital defects. This field holds the promise of regenerating damaged tissues and organs in the body by stimulating previously irreparable organs to heal themselves. Regenerative medicine also empowers scientists to grow tissues and organs in the laboratory and safely implant them when the body cannot heal itself' (National Institutes of Health, Fact Sheet, 2007).
6. The phrase 'regenerative medicine' has been used to search the PubMed data base (www.ncbi.nlm.nih.gov/entrez/query.fcgi). To account for the presence of the term in different contexts its occurrence in all fields of the publication record, including title, abstract, address, key words, and journal name has been recorded.

References

Ach, J. S., Schöne-Seifert, B. and Siep, L. (2006) Totipotenz und Potentialität: Zum moralischen Status von Embryonen bei unterschiedlichen Varianten der Gewinnung humaner embryonaler Stammzellen, Gutachten für das Kompetenznetzwerk Stammzellforschung NRW, in: L. Honnefelder and D. Sturma (Eds) *Jahrbuch für Wissenschaft und Ethik 11*, pp. 261–321 (Berlin and New York: Walter de Gruyter).

Arbeitskreis Regenerative Medizin (2004) Positionspapier Regenerative Medizin Perspektiven für die Regenerative Medizin in Deutschland, Kurzfassung November 2004, letztc Aktualisierung 5 January 2005. Available at: http://www.gesellschaft-regenerative-medizin.de/inhalt/grm/deutsch/presseinfo/041203_pi.shtml? navid ¼ 14 (accessed 19 October 2007).

Bender, W., Hauskeller, C. and Manzei, A. (Eds) (2005) *Crossing Borders. Grenzüberschreitungen* (Münster: Agenda Verlag).

Bogner, A. and Menz, W. (2004) ExpertInnen-Interviews: Konzepte, Gesprächsdführung, Auswertung, *Medien-Journal*, 28(2), pp. 11–26.

Bongso, A., Fong, C. Y., Ng, S. C. and Ratnam, S. (1994) Isolation and culture of inner cell mass cells from human blastocysts, *Human Reproduction*, 9(11), pp. 2110–2117.

Brown, N. (2000) Organising/disorganising the breakthrough motif: Dolly the cloned ewe meets Astrid the hybrid pig, in: N. Brown, B. Rappert and A. Webster (Eds) *Contested Futures: A Sociology of Prospective Techno-Science and Technology* (Aldershot: Ashgate).

Brown, N. and Kraft, A. (2006) Blood ties: banking the stem cell promise, *Technology, Analysis & Strategic Management*, 18, pp. 313–327.

Check, E. (2007) Patenting the obvious? *Nature*, 447, pp. 16–17.

Cooper, M. (2004) Regenerative medicine: stem cells and the science of monstrosity, *Medical Humanities*, 30, pp. 12–22.

Evans, M. J. and Kaufman, M. H. (1981) Establishment in culture of pluripotential cells from mouse embryos, *Nature*, 292, pp. 154–156.

Foucault, M. (1978) *Dispositive der Macht. Über Sexualität, Wissen und Wahrheit* (Berlin: Merve).

Franklin, S. (2001) Culturing biology: cell lines for the second millennium, *Health*, 5(3), pp. 335–354.

Giebel, L. B. (2005) Stem cells—a hard sell to investors, *Nature Biotechnology*, 23, pp. 798–800.

Harvard Stem Cell Institute (2007) *Frequently Asked Questions*. Available at: http://www.hsci.harvard.edu/faq (accessed 19 October 2007).

Jasanoff, S. (2005) *Designs on Nature: Science and Democracy in Europe and the United States* (Princeton: Princeton University Press).

Loring, J. F. and Campbell, C. (2006) Science and law. Intellectual property and human embryonic stem cell research, *Science*, 311, pp. 1716–1717.

Manzei, A. (2005) Über die Moralisierung der Bioethik-Debatte und ihre gesellschaftlichen Ursachen. Das Beispiel des Stammzelldiskurses in Deutschland, in: W. Bender, C. Hauskeller and A. Manzei (Eds) *Crossing Borders. Grenzüberschreitungen*, pp. 77–99 (Münster: Agenda Verlag).

Martin, G. R. (1981) Isolation of a pluripotent cell line from early mouse embryos cultured in medium conditioned by teratocarcinoma stem cells, *Proceedings of the National Academy of Sciences of the USA*, 78(12), pp. 7634–7638.

Meissner, A. and Jaenisch, R. (2006) Generation of nuclear transfer-derived pluripotent ES cells from cloned Cdx2-deficient blastocysts, *Nature*, 439, pp. 212–215.

Mulkay, M. (1994) The triumph of the pre-embryo: interpretations of the human embryo in Parliamentary debate over embryo research, *Social Studies of Science*, 24(4), pp. 611–639.

Mulkay, M. (1997) *The Embryo Research Debate: Science and the Politics of Reproduction* (Cambridge: Cambridge University Press).

National Institutes of Health (2007) *Fact Sheet Regenerative Medicine*, updated September 2006. Available at: http://www.nih.gov/about/researchresultsforthepublic/Regen.pdf (accessed 19 October 2007).

Parry, S. (2003) The politics of cloning: mapping the rhetorical convergence of embyros and stem cells in parliamentary debates, *New Genetics and Society*, 22(2), pp. 145–168.

Prainsack, B. (2006) Negotiating life: the regulation of human cloning and embryonic stem cell research in Israel, *Social Studies of Science*, 36, pp. 173–205.

Rabinow, P. (1996) *Essays on the Anthropology of Reason* (Princeton: Princeton University Press).

Rose, N. and Novas, C. (2005) Biological citizenship, in: A. Ong and S. Collier (Eds) *Global Assemblages: Technology, Politic, and Ethics as Anthropological Problems*, pp. 439–463 (Oxford: Blackwell).

Salter, B. and Salter, C. (2007) Bioethics and the global moral economy. The cultural politics of human embryonic stem cell science, *Science, Technology and Human Values*, 32(5), pp. 554–581.

Sperling, S. (2004) From crisis to potentiality: managing potential selves: stem cells, immigrants, and German identity, *Science and Public Policy*, 31(2), pp. 139–149.

The President's Council on Bioethics (2005) *A White Paper: Alternative Sources of Pluripotent Stem Cells* (Washington, DC).

Thompson, C. (2005) *Making Parents: The Ontological Choreography of Reproductive Technologies* (Cambridge, MA: MIT Press).

Thomson, J. A., Itskovitz-Eldor, J. *et al.* (1998) Embryonic stem cell lines derived from human blastocysts, *Science*, 282, pp. 1145–1147.

Thomson, J. A., Kalishman, J. *et al.* (1995) Isolation of a primate embryonic stem cell line, *Proceedings of the National Academy of Sciences of the USA*, 92(17), pp. 7844–7848.

Vogel, G. (1999) Breakthrough of the year. Capturing the promise of youth, *Science*, 286, pp. 2238–2239.

Vogel, G. (2002) In the Mideast, Pushing Back the Stem Cell Frontier, *Science*, 295, pp. 1818–1820.

Waldby, C. (2002) Stem cells, tissue cultures and the production of biovalue, *Health*, 6(3), pp. 305–323.

Reading Analytically

1. What do you take to be the key ethical issues that Rubin examines in this essay? Make a list of areas that she feels are particularly important to be brought to some level of scrutiny.
2. The key term that Rubin analyzes is "therapeutic promise." What does she mean by this term, and why is it such an important site for rhetorical analysis?
3. Part of Rubin's essay is devoted to presenting an historical overview of how the discussion about the use of human embryonic stem cells developed. Why does she present this extended historical narrative? What purpose does it serve for her larger argument?

Reading Across Disciplinary Communities

1. As is discussed in the headnote to this essay, Rubin is herself an interdisciplinary figure, having been trained in biology and human physiology, and then moving more closely into the social sciences. What parts of this essay seem to indicate her status as a natural scientist? What parts are more dependent upon her work as a social scientist?
2. Discussions about the use of human embryos for scientific research and medical therapies are also a key issue for religious communities. How could Rubin's essay be used by either side in this debate about the ethics of using human embryos for these purposes?

LORETTA M. KOPELMAN

Using the Best Interests Standard to Decide Whether to Test Children for Untreatable, Late-Onset Genetic Diseases

Questions about the implications of genetic testing are not limited to direct-to-consumer uses. The medical field also wrestles with similar questions, especially as it relates to identifying predispositions to diseases that have no cure. The question in those cases is whether it is beneficial to know about this predisposition even if nothing can be done. This thorny topic is taken on by Loretta Kopelman, who holds a Ph.D. in Philosophy, and is chair of the Department of Medical Humanities at East Carolina University.

In her essay, Kopelman uses methods from her discipline to analyze this key ethical question. Drawing upon the standards that are used in other cases, and in particular what is called the "best interests standard," she discusses how that set of criteria can be applied to genetic testing. As you read, consider the ways that using an established set of criteria can help a writer formulate a reasonable, logical evaluation on any given topic.

A new analysis of the Best Interests Standard is given and applied to the controversy about testing children for untreatable, severe late-onset genetic diseases, such as Huntington's disease or Alzheimer's disease. A professional consensus recommends against such predictive testing, because it is not in children's best interest. Critics disagree. The Best Interests Standard can be a powerful way to resolve such disputes. This paper begins by analyzing its meaning into three necessary and jointly sufficient conditions showing it:

1. is an "umbrella" standard, used differently in different contexts,
2. has objective and subjective features,
3. is more than people's intuitions about how to rank potential benefits and risks in deciding for others but also includes evidence, established rights, duties and thresholds of acceptable care, and
4. can have different professional, medical, moral and legal uses, as in this dispute.

Loretta M. Kopelman, "Using the Best Interests Standard to Decide Whether to Test Children for Untreatable, Late-Onset Genetic Diseases" from *Journal of Medicine and Philosophy* 32, 2007, pages 375-394. Used with permission.

Using this standard, support is given for the professional consensus based on concerns about discrimination, analogies to adult choices, consistency with clinical judgments for adults, and desires to preserve of an open future for children. Support is also given for parents' legal authority to decide what genetic tests to do.

I. Introduction

Since the early 1990s prestigious review panels and professional organizations world-wide have advocated predictive genetic testing for children at risk for preventable, early onset, or treatable diseases. In contrast, they recommend against and generally will not do predictive testing of children for untreatable, severe late-onset genetic diseases such as Alzheimer's disease and Huntington's disease except in unusual circumstances. These recommendations and the reasons for them are so uniform and respected, that I will call this *the professional consensus.*

Critics of the professional consensus disagree that it is generally best to postpone predictive genetic testing until subjects can decide for themselves if they want it. Because defenders and critics appeal to the Best Interests Standard to justify their positions, it is analyzed and used to examine their arguments. I begin by discussing the professional consensus.

II. The Professional Consensus

An assumption underlying the professional consensus is that predictive genetic testing of children should be undertaken when it is in their best interest, but not otherwise, even if parents request it. Testing may be best for them because useful means of prevention or treatment exist, such as medications, dietary interventions or surveillance for complications. For example, it would be important to test children for the adult-onset disease polycystic kidney disease because if the test is positive it is crucial to monitor and control their blood pressure.

In contrast, testing should generally not be done on healthy children for late-onset conditions when no useful means of treatment or prevention exist. Exceptions might be made for some clear and compelling reasons, such as parents mistakenly viewing their child's behavior as symptomatic of Huntington's disease (Fryer, 2000). Absent good reasons, it is more beneficial to children to wait and let them decide if they want testing when they are competent to do so.

Around the world, many organizations adopt this consensus and its reliance on the Best Interests Standard. For example, the authors of "Guidelines for Genetic Testing" by the Japan Society of Human Genetics explicitly identify the "the best interest of the subject" as the basis for their policy:

> If a surrogate representative makes the decision, because the subject is deemed to be unable to exercise autonomous decision-making, a decision for genetic testing must be made that protects *the best interest of the subject*. Therefore, the testing of children for adult-onset genetic disease that [have] no effective treatment or means of prevention should be avoided (emphasis added. Matsuda et al., 2000, Recommendation 8).

The American Medical Association's Council on Ethical and Judicial Affairs (CEJA) also recommends against testing unless it can be justified as being useful to the child, something CEJA regards as difficult to demonstrate where no treatments or prevention strategies exist (CEJA, 2007). The American Academy of Pediatrics' Committee on Bioethics (AAP, 2005) and the Canadian Pediatric Society (2003) also ground their support for the professional consensus on what is best for the child. The Working Party of the Clinical Genetics Society in the U.K. also agrees that predictive testing of children must not be done unless it is useful to them.

Further evidence of the widespread support for the professional consensus may be found in a comprehensive review of ethical and clinical position papers and guidelines from 1991–2005. Borry and colleagues (2006) undertook an analysis of 31 organizations and reported:

> The main justification for presymptomatic and predictive genetic testing was direct benefit to the minor through either medical intervention or preventive measures. If there was no urgent medical reason, all guidelines recommended postponing testing until the child could consent to testing as a competent adolescent or as an adult. (Borry et al., 2006, p. 374)

In addition, there is evidence that few laboratories are willing to test children for untreatable, severe, late-onset, genetic diseases (Wertz & Reilly, 1997). Most minors tested are carefully screened adolescents who are able to participate responsibly in decisions about testing (Duncan et al., 2005).

Critics who reject the professional consensus generally agree with defenders that policy should reflect what is best for children (Cohen,

1998; Pelias, 2006; Rhodes, 2006). They argue, however, that testing young children is often useful and affirm parental authority to decide what is best for their own children. They point out that parents often have to balance the interests of one person with those of other family members. There can be, of course, an important difference between the best interests of an individual child and the best interests of the family when it comes to many matters, including predictive genetic testing.

Agreement among critics and defenders about the relevance of seeking what is best for a minor offers an opportunity to evaluate their incompatible positions from the perspective of the Best Interests Standard.[1] In doing so, the discussion will focus on predictive testing for two late-onset, neurologically and psychologically devastating diseases, Huntington's disease and early-onset Alzheimer's disease. Predictive testing for Huntington's disease is accurate and children of affected individuals have a 50% chance of getting the disease. Early-onset Alzheimer's disease also may be predicted with considerable accuracy. Analysis of the Best Interests Standard is given in the next section and applied to this debate about predictive genetic testing for children in the sections that follow.

III. The Best Interests Standard

The Best Interests Standard is a widely recognized guidance principle for decision makers to use in making choices for children and other persons who lack capacity to make decisions. For example, the United Nations (1989) writes:

> *Article 3:* In all actions concerning children, whether undertaken by public or private social welfare institutions, courts of law, administrative authorities or legislative bodies, the best interests of the child shall be a primary consideration.

Recently, the Maryland Appellate Court wrote, "We have long stressed that the "best interests of the child" is the overriding concern of this Court in matters relating to children. . . ." (*Grimes v. Kennedy Krieger Institute*, 2001, pp. 852–3).

Many important policies also recommend using the Best Interests Standard in making decision for others including the Institute of Medicine in setting research policy for children (2004) and The President's Council in selecting care for the non-autonomous elderly (2005).

The Best Interests Standard is an "umbrella concept" because it unites under one principle different meanings and uses about how to make good decisions for those lacking decision making capacity. It is sometimes employed to express goals about what is ideal and sometimes to make practical judgments about what is reasonable given the circumstances.

In saying, "It is in the best interest of every child to have good health care," it is being used to express an ideal or goal. This usage is different from applying it to make practical decisions, where it may be impossible to provide what is ideal. It might be best for a child to have a kidney transplant, but may be reasonable and necessary to use dialysis if no kidney is available for transplant. While practical decisions using the Best Interests Standard should be informed by appropriate goals, their purpose is to find good and reasonable options, which are often less than perfect.[2]

The Best Interests Standard was introduced into the medical, moral, research, legal and other discourse to gain *some* protection of the interests of persons lacking decision-making capacity independent of the wishes of their guardians, not to get them "the best" by ignoring everyone else's interests.[3] In its practical uses, it does not require that everyone have "the best" since this would be incoherent or self-defeating.

In medicine, clinicians may decide it would be ideal to test all children for every treatable genetic disease, but if tests are expensive and resources scarce, they may justifiably decide to test only those at higher risk of getting the disease. Nor does this standard require that everyone else's interest, needs, duties, or allocation plans be ignored. Rather when we look at how this standard is used to make practical decisions, it calls for a good and reasonable choice to be selected from available options.

When the Best Interests Standard is understood in terms of how it is used, it is no more vague or likely to be abused than other guidance principles. It is more than someone's intuitions about how to rank benefits and hazards for others. Rather, this standard sits in a web of moral, legal, medical or social policies about duties to people who cannot make decisions for themselves, including policies about abuse and neglect, custody determinations, children's rights, parental obligations, professional duties, practice guidelines, legal precedents, and acceptable thresholds of care.

The Best Interest Standard is neither an entirely objective nor an entirely subjective principle, but has features of both. Judgments about what decisions are best for others have "subjective" features in the sense that they are, in part, shaped by the decision-makers' values, views, and perceptions about what is best. Some parents believe it is best for them to ignore the prevalence of late-onset disorders in their family while others prefer to discuss the matter with young family members.

The Best Interests Standard also has "objective" features in the sense that judgments about what is best for others should be shaped by sound scientific, logical, and medical analyses, predictions and judgments as well as well-considered policies about what constitutes acceptable care, abuse and neglect. A father may sincerely believe it is best to use prayer alone to treat his child's cystic fibrosis but his judgment about what is best should be challenged. He can lose custody temporarily or permanently and the courts will decide what option is best (Kraus, 1986; Kopelman, 1997). Obviously there is a gap between what parental decisions are barely "good enough" from a legal perspective and what is optimal or recommended by professional groups.[4]

The Best Interests Standard when used as a practical guide for decision makers should, I have argued elsewhere, be analyzed in terms of three necessary and jointly sufficient features (Kopelman, 2005, 2007, 2008). This analysis is intended to reflect its practical uses, including how it is used in many professional, moral or legal circumstances.[5]

1. First, decision makers should use the best available information to assess the incompetent or incapacitated person's immediate and long-term interests and set as their *prima facie* duty that option (or from among those options) that maximizes the person's overall or long term benefits and minimizes burdens.
2. Second, decision-makers should make choices for the incompetent or incapacitated person that must at least meet a minimum threshold of acceptable care; what is at least good enough is usually judged in relation to what reasonable and informed persons of good will would regard to be acceptable were they in the person's circumstances.
3. Third, decision makers should make choices compatible with moral and legal duties to incompetent or incapacitated individuals (those unable to make decisions for themselves).

IV. Using the Best Interests Standard

In the next sections, I will apply these three features of the Best Interests Standard to the controversy over predictive testing for children and argue this offers a powerful way to settle disputes about what is best for those unable to make decisions for themselves.

How to Rank Burdens and Benefits?

The first necessary condition of the Best Interests Standard (see above) concerns assessing potential benefits and risks on behalf of incompetent or incapacitated persons. We generally agree about what things are good, better or best in life; it is good for children to have proper medical care and an open future with greater rather than fewer opportunities; we agree that it is best to live a long life free of pain and suffering and full of pleasure and accomplishments; we agree it is good to learn to do what is socially beneficial and to help our families.[6]

For example, because it is clearly beneficial, parents and clinicians would be negligent not to test a child showing symptoms of a genetic disease. In other cases, reasonable and informed people of good will may disagree about how to maximize benefits and minimize burdens because they differ about the relevant values to use, the salient information, or how to rank potential benefits and risks (including their nature, probability, and magnitude).

In the case of the debate over the professional consensus, defenders and critics cite similar potential benefits and risks, but disagree about how to rank them. Potential benefits of finding a faulty gene(s) include that persons will have more information to make informed choices about life plans including reproduction, marriage, career, financial management, medical treatment, and end-of life options. Greater information and openness within families may help children adjust to the diagnosis early in life (Fryer 2000; Rhodes, 2006).

They also agree about the likely benefits of a test showing the absence of the faulty gene(s). This result would likely be a great comfort to many, relieve their anxiety in waiting for early signs, let people plan their lives differently, and avoid clinical monitoring or irrational identification (pre-selection) of a family member as fated to have the illness.

There are potential risks even of testing negatively, however, about which they agree. Family members may reject or resent the child who is spared the faulty gene(s) or have a false assurance that she is entirely healthy. The person is also at risk for having "survivor guilt" (Meiser & Dunn, 2000).

Finally, they agree risks exist if a positive result for a late-onset genetic disease is found which include: Parents may feel guilt, reject the child, confirm irrational beliefs about who will have the illness (pre-selection), or see him as more vulnerable than he really is. Risks to the child of finding the faulty gene(s) include low self-esteem, stigmatization, anxiety, or depression. Critics and defenders are also concerned about whether parental attitudes to the child will change. In addition both are aware of the social, economic, and personal hazards to the child once information about a positive result exists, including discrimination in employment or insurance. Table 1 summarizes many of the potential benefits and risks to testing.

TABLE 1 Suggested psychological benefits and dangers from childhood testing (Fryer, 2000, p. 284)[7]

Result	Possible Danger	Possible Benefits
Faulty gene absent	Rejection by family, especially if others affected	Avoid clinical monitoring Emotional relief
		Ability to plan life
		Avoids effects of later disclosure
	False reassurance about health status	Avoids "preselection" [irrational views about who is destined to have the disease]
		Relieves anxiety about possible early signs of this disorder
Faulty gene present	Impair child's self esteem	Child has time to adjust—avoids emotional problems of later disclosure
	Impair child's long-term adjustment	Enables parents to prepare child psychologically for the future, e.g. education, career, housing, etc.
	Impair relationship with parents (post-test changes in parental attitudes)	Child can take informed decisions from early age
	Stigmatization/overprotection	Allows openness in families
	Discrimination in education, employment, insurance, mortgage	Child doesn't miss opportunity for testing; relieves child's anxiety or uncertainty about the future
	Impair relationships with future partners	Relieves parent's anxiety or uncertainty . . .
	Removes autonomy to decline testing	
	Confirms any "preselection" [irrational views about who is destined to have the disease]	
	Could generate anxiety about early symptoms	

The controversy among defenders and critics about the professional consensus seems mired in competing intuitions about how best to rank these potential benefits and risks of predictive testing for children. Defenders argue that the potential benefits of such testing are speculative, while the risks are substantial. Critics argue defenders minimize benefits and cite hazards for which there is little evidence. In the remainder of this section, I consider arguments about how to rank these agreed upon potential benefits and risks, arguing they offer support for the ranking given by defenders of the professional consensus.

1. Honesty and openness

A dispute exists over how best to promote frankness and forthrightness. Some critics of the professional consensus use an argument from analogy to conclude testing children for untreatable late-onset diseases of children and informing them of results would promote these values.[8] A substantial body of evidence exists that properly informed children cope better with information about their serious illnesses and even impending death than those who are not informed. The failure to be candid about what is known by others isolates them from important support that discussions might bring. Thus, the argument goes, if children who are informed of their serious diseases or impending death do better than those who are not told, then children at risk of serious genetic diseases later in life would probably do better as well.

There are, however, problems with this argument from analogy since several important differences among these groups exist. First, the groups differ because one group is sick and the other healthy. Without genetic testing, no one has the results, so the conditions for the isolating and destructive effects of secrecy are not present. In contrast, when children face death, disabilities or serious illness, they know something is wrong and suffer more because they sense they are not being told something important (Bluebond-Langner, 1978).

Second, the professional consensus cannot be faulted for proposing a lack of candor because it encourages age-appropriate and open discussions among all family members, including children, about genetic diseases.[9] Parents can reinforce the idea that being at risk for a disease does not define the whole of someone's life. This gives minors under 18 years of age opportunities to think in general ways about the illness in their family, future plans, possible discrimination, reproductive options, career choices, economic risks of testing, etc.; they can decide for themselves if they want testing at 18 years of age.

Evidence about the benefits of informing children of their serious illnesses, disabilities or impending death, then, does not seem to support the judgment that similar benefits would accrue to healthy children tested for serious, adult-onset diseases for which there are no interventions and informed of the results. Thus this attack on the professional consensus' ranking potential benefits and risks fails.

2. Clinical judgment

The professional consensus against testing children for severe, untreatable late-onset diseases such as Huntington's and Alzheimer's relies to some degree on clinical judgment. Because so little testing of children for these diseases has been done, the professional consensus is not based on studies comparing outcomes for children who are tested and informed and those who are not. Rather it is based on clinicians' experiences with people who have these maladies and their abilities to identify conflict of interest, bias, and other factors that may distort people's reasoning when requesting this testing for their children.[10]

Some parents or minors who want testing, however, might agree the clinicians know more about most cases but claim to better understand the special features of their own case. Other critics respond that clinicians are mistaken and that testing for children should be encouraged (Rhodes, 2006).

In response clinicians may point out that the economic basis for professions is the "selling" of competent and unbiased information by members who are committed to acting in people's best interests. Professionals belong to societies that have special privileges and duties to ensure members are competent and act as they should. Clinicians "sell" the public (patients) their informed and good judgments and recommendations (get surgery, use steroids, etc.) and services. In contrast, "let the buyer beware" serves as the typical approach one should expect in non-professional, "market" driven situations. Clinicians, geneticists and genetic counselors and their professional organizations have an economic interest in "selling" their services, so their recommendations *against* their use are unbiased.

Moreover, other evidence exists that the professional consensus for children is evenhanded because it is consistent with recommendations for adults. The Huntington's Disease Society of America (1996) recommends *against* testing for anyone who cannot decide for himself, unless there are special reasons to do so, such as the person is showing symptoms. The American Geriatric Society (AGS) writes:

> At the present time, the role of genetic testing for the prevention, diagnosis, and treatment of late-onset disorders is uncertain.

> Until further information is available to clearly define the benefits of genetic testing for condition such as Alzheimer's disease, physicians should not routinely order genetic tests for late-onset disorders mentioned above (AGS, 2001, p. 225).

Thus the professional consensus' ranking of potential benefits and risks for children seems evenhanded and consistent with recommendation for adults. There is, however, another consideration regarding the benefits of preserving an open future for children.

3. Open Future

Defenders and critics disagree about whether testing and informing children of the results promotes the child's open future. Joel Feinberg (1980) and Dena Davis (1997) argue that parents should not close off possibilities for their child, such as having them sterilized or denying them life saving blood transfusions. According to the professional consensus when parents test their child for adult onset diseases such as Huntington's disease or Alzheimer's disease, they unjustifiably limit the child's options. Delay does not cause medical harm to children and by preserving their open future, we let them decide for themselves if they want predictive testing at a later time.

Critics may respond that predictive testing could enhance children's open future if they shape their choices in light of their special risks. Many decisions can be put off until the person can consent, such as reproductive decisions, but some cannot and learning of adult risk early in life may help them make rational decisions. A girl might decide to become a gymnast because skills peak early and this would not interfere with an adult on-set disease; a boy might decide to take the longed-for adventure earlier in life rather than later. Sufficient information for such plans, however, might be available if parents openly discussed the genetic diseases in their family. Yet Rosamond Rhodes contends that ". . . pediatricians should encourage parents to pursue genetic testing of children at a young age" (Rhodes, 2006, p. 609). "Putting off testing until the child reaches adolescence can also be expected to have a negative impact on the child. The delay amplifies the dread . . ." (Rhodes, 2006, p. 614). She argues that advocates of what I call the professional consensus minimize the harms of living with uncertainty and the benefits of allowing families to plan for family members' predicted future disabilities. Cynthia Cohen (1998) argues that defenders have overestimated the risks or underestimated the potential benefits of testing.

This attack on the professional consensus is undercut by two considerations, or so I will argue. First, most adults do not want testing when it is offered and second, serious concerns exist about discrimination once testing produces information about positive results for diseases like Parkinson's and early-onset Alzheimer's disease.

First, studies consistently show that only 10–20% of at-risk adults want testing for late-onset diseases when asked (Chapman, 1992; Lerman et al., 1996; Meiser & Dunn, 2000). In a comprehensive survey of the psychological impact of genetic testing on adults for Huntington's disease, Meiser and Dunn (2000) report:

> About 10–20% of people at risk request testing when approached by registries or testing centres. Most of the evidence suggests that non-carriers and carriers differ significantly in terms of short term, but not long term, general psychological distress. Adjustment to results was found to depend more on psychological adjustment before testing than the testing itself. . . . There is evidence that people who choose to be tested are psychologically selected for favorable responses to testing (Meiser & Dunn, 2000, p. 574).

Arguing by analogy this suggests that given the opportunity, 80–90 percent of children at-risk for genetic diseases when they become competent adults would rather not be tested. This supports the professional consensus that testing for untreatable adult onset diseases such as Alzheimer's and Huntington's diseases should be postponed until people are old enough to decide if they want it.

Critic Rosamond Rhodes acknowledges, "only 10–15% of at-risk adults opt for Huntington's disease genetic testing" (Rhodes, 2006 p. 615); but she attributes this to unreasonable fears which lead to uninformed choices about their education, finances and reproductive choices. Testing would be reassuring to many, she argues, since in some cases between 50–75% of those who are at-risk will hear good news. Rhodes concludes that adults *should* decide to be tested and pediatricians should encourage testing.

Yet if so many adults want the liberty to decline it seems reasonable to preserve this freedom for children, if possible, who as adults may also decide not to be tested. Moreover, the decision not to be tested does not seem irrational. Informed and reasonable people of good will may decide they do not want testing because they do not envision the results changing how they want to plan their lives; or they may fear the information would distress them and dominate their lives and so would rather live with uncertainty; or they may dread bad news more then they would be relieved by good news.

Recommendations that everyone should be tested, moreover, may not take into account personal differences. Meiser and Dunn (2000) report people who are by nature socially extroverted with good ego strength are more likely to request testing than those with tendencies to be depressive.

> People who reported being at risk of suicide or anticipated feeling depressed should the results be positive were significantly less likely to want the test, compared to those not anticipating suicidal or depressive feelings. . . . Interestingly, people who declined were more likely to have learned about their being at risk for Huntington's disease during adolescence rather than adulthood (Meiser & Dunn, 2000, p. 575).

Surprisingly, they also report that those finding out they were noncarriers sometime had trouble coping with the information.

Second, people may rationally decline genetic testing when it is offered because they fear a positive result will expose them to discrimination, especially in the workplace or in seeking insurance (Annas, 2001). If they are not tested, the information does not exist and people cannot discriminate against them. George Annas argues that fear of discrimination prompts commentators to seek specific legislative protections focusing on protection from genetic discrimination.

Concern is high enough about the problem that President George W. Bush called for specific protection against discrimination by insurance companies. Annas supports this idea but cites the difficulty of gaining such protections (such as defining a genetic test). Patricia Roche and George Annas (2006) document the struggles states are having trying to offer protection of genetic information. Nancy King (2007) argues that while there is uncertainty about the degree to which discrimination exists for those undergoing predictive genetic testing, "it may be time to say no to the genetic testing explosion—at least until we know what is hype and what is not" (King, 2007, p. 114).

Concerns about discrimination once information is available support the professional consensus. If testing of children for late-onset, serious, untreatable disease such as Alzheimer's or Huntington's disease could expose them to such risks of discrimination, and if there is no medical benefit to testing earlier, it seems better to wait and let them decide for themselves.

To summarize, it seems more likely that children's open future is enhanced by waiting until children are old enough to decide for themselves if they want predictive testing for diseases such as Alzheimer's or Huntington's. First, most adults do not want testing when asked. If most people do not want such testing, then you take away people's liberty to decide whether to test if you test them as children. Second, it also lets them decide how to evaluate the possibility of facing discrimination once the information exists.

4. New findings and policies

Even if it is reasonable to defend the professional consensus and its recommended ranking of potential benefits and risks, and I believe it is, there are obvious qualifications that need to be made. New information may quickly change recommendations about the potential benefits and risks of testing. As the field of genetic advances, it is likely that earlier monitoring or interventions will be found useful, undercutting policies discouraging certain testing (Fulda & Lykens, 2006; Green & Botkin, 2003). This would of course have implications for which conditions are regarded as untreatable, severe, or late-onset genetic diseases. There might also be policy changes such that attitudes to testing change; for example, people may gain confidence once good protections from discrimination exist.

This is no defense of "genetic exceptionalism" (the view that genetic tests and their results are fundamentally different from other tests). I agree with Green and Botkin (2003) that the dangers of pediatric predictive testing are not because genetic tests are unique, but because such precautions are needed for children whenever the results of studies may cause family discord, psychological distress, stigmatization, or discrimination.

To conclude, the professional consensus about how to rank potential benefits and risks of predictive testing of children for untreatable, severe, late-onset diseases such as Huntington's disease or Alzheimer's disease seems justified. Even though it does not rest upon large and persuasive studies, it is supported by clinical judgment, concerns about discrimination, analogies to adult choices, and desires to preserve of an open future for children to decide for themselves.

An Acceptable Threshold for What?

The second necessary condition of the Best Interests Standard (see above) acknowledges that reasonable persons of good will sometimes make different choices, but sets limits. A father who ignores sound medical advice and decides it is best to treat his son's sickle cell disease with herbal tea should be challenged since this behavior would almost certainly constitute medical neglect. As noted, when parental decisions about what they think is best endanger their children, the courts can intervene to take custody temporarily or permanently and decide what is best (Kopelman, 1997; Kraus, 1986). Endangerment is judged in terms of what is sound, logical, medical and scientific views, arguments and conclusions. Clinicians, judges, and others help set standards about when wards are neglected, abused, or otherwise endangered in their guardians' care (Kraus, 1986).

Parents have legal authority to decide what is best for their children and they do not lose authority if they provide care that is minimally acceptable. A choice is often judged "good enough" in relation to what reasonable and informed persons of good will would regard to be acceptable were they in the person's circumstances. Obviously differences can exist among an ideal choice, a reasonable decision, and what is minimally acceptable. For example, a judge would allow what is acceptable and not require what is ideal in deciding whether a morbidly obese child should be taken out of a loving but indulgent home. Yet the Best Interests Standard should not be regarded as the "good enough" standard since choices should be better than merely acceptable.

Even if one strongly disagrees with parents about the wisdom of testing their children for Huntington's disease or Alzheimer's disease, it is implausible that testing meets the legal threshold of endangering them the way denying them life-saving treatment would.[11] As critic Mary Kay Pelias points out, ". . . both society and the law operate from the presumption that parents act in the best interests of their children. These arguments are readily extended to support the right of parents to seek genetic testing for their own children, including testing for adult-onset diseases" (Pelias, 2006, p. 607).

Thus, even if the evidence about how to balance potential benefits and risks (the first necessary condition of the Best Interests Standard) supports the professional consensus *from a medical or moral perspective*; this is not necessarily the case from other vantages. Taken *from a legal perspective about competent parenting*, parents' choice for predictive testing of children for adult-onset disorders does not seem to meet the threshold of endangerment that is used to remove parental authority to decide what is best for their children. This does not mean their choice *is best* from a professional perspective.

Moreover, this does not mean parents can get testing whenever they wish since they must find professionals willing to do the testing.

Deciding whether to do predictive testing for children is a joint decision between clinicians and parents and clinicians should refuse to participate in something they regard to be wrong. Parents who want to test their children and not tell them the results have been criticized on all sides for the possible tensions and bias resulting from such secrecy (Rhodes, 2006). Even if this approach of testing and not informing the minor of the results is imprudent from a moral and medical standpoint, it would almost certainly not meet the legal threshold of endangering a child.

Which Rights or Duties?

The third necessary condition of the Best Interests Standard (see above) requires decision-makers to make choices for those who cannot make decisions for themselves that are compatible with more general duties to them. The Best Interests Standard is part of a larger picture about how to treat people and these more general values can offer important practical guidance, like a lighthouse guiding a ship.

For example, suppose parents think it would be best to enroll their seven-year-old child in genetic study to gather information to learn about genetic diseases in their community. The parents know that the study will use medical and school records and is not intended to benefit her. For five hundred dollars, they agree to enroll their child in a study where their child's blood samples are left indefinitely with the investigators who are at liberty to do whatever tests they wish.

Even if an institutional review board approves this study, one might still argue based on other articulated moral, social or legal duties to children, that such a study should not be done. It offers no direct benefit to the child and might place her at significant psychosocial risks of harm (psychological, economic, emotional, psychosocial, or other risks relating to confidentiality, loss of self-esteem, stigmatization, or workplace or insurance discrimination). Moreover, parents' agreement to enroll their child might be influenced improperly by the large amount of money they receive. (This example illustrates other possible breaches of duties such as those of the oversight committee members or investigators.)

Some controversies exist in this debate about how to understand children's rights. For example some defenders of the professional consensus argue against predictive testing on the grounds it fails to protect the children's "rights" to autonomy, confidentiality, and not to know they have a genetic disease (Working group, British Society, 1994). This argument is an easy target for critics who point out that children lack autonomy and autonomy rights and that parents have legal authority to act on their behalf, including how to protect their privacy and confidentiality (Pelias, 2006; Rhodes, 2006). This criticism, however, is not decisive. As noted, essentially the same point can be made without appealing to the child's so-called "autonomy" or "rights of autonomy," but stated in terms of the benefits of enhancing children's open future.

Older minors have some autonomy rights (to get certain medical treatments, marry, join the military, and so on) and reasonable and informed persons of good will may disagree about how much authority to give to their choices as they approach the age of majority.[12] Duncan and Delatycki (2006) propose rectifying the dearth of outcome data about predictive testing for children by testing, informing and studying results for older minors who request predictive testing for late-onset diseases. They argue there would be greater willingness to test older adolescents who seek such testing because they can participate in the decision.[13]

V. Conclusion

A new analysis of the Best Interests Standard is employed to evaluate the controversy over what I call "the professional consensus" (the view that it is generally not in children's best interest to be tested for untreatable, severe, late-onset genetic diseases such as Huntington's disease and Alzheimer's disease). When used as a practical guidance principle, the Best Interests Standard may be analyzed into three necessary and jointly sufficient conditions. Once these features are distinguished it can become a powerful tool for settling disputes about how to make good decisions for those unable to make them for themselves, including whether to support the professional consensus.

The first component guides decision-makers to assess potential benefits and risks and act to maximize the individual's interests and minimize the burdens. Critics and defenders cite the same potential benefits and risks of predictive testing for diseases such as Alzheimer's and Huntington's, but rank them differently.

I have supported the ranking of potential benefits and risks found in the professional consensus (generally, to delay predictive genetic testing for adult-onset conditions such as Huntington's and Alzheimer's disease) as being in children's best interest; it preserves an open future for children by allowing them to decide for themselves if they want testing, allows them to assess the hazards of discrimination once positive results exist, acknowledges that few adults want such testing when it is offered, and squares with clinical judgments about testing for adults.

The second component of the Best Interests Standard guides decision-makers to make choices for people who cannot decide for themselves such that these choices meet at least a minimum threshold of acceptable care. But acceptable for what? An acceptable threshold in one circumstance may not be in others. For example, a gap exists between what is minimally acceptable and an optimal choice, so what is good enough to fulfill the Best Interests Standard legally, may be morally or medically less than ideal. The professional consensus seems justifiable as a moral and medical recommendation but parents have legal authority to decide what is best for their child unless they endanger them. Choosing to have predictive genetic testing for your child almost certainly would not be considered endangerment in the legal sense for the purpose of taking custody from parents. Thus parents can authorize predictive genetic testing for late-onset diseases; however, they may have difficulty finding clinicians willing to do it since they believe it is not indicated and could be harmful.

The third component of the Best Interests Standard guides decision makers to make choices compatible with duties to those who cannot make decisions for themselves. Since these three conditions are necessary, even if there is a dispute about one of them, such as how to balance potential benefits and risks (the first necessary condition), we still draw conclusions about whether Best Interests Standard has not been fulfilled by seeing if the action falls below the threshold of acceptable care (the second necessary condition) or violates children's rights (the third condition). This analysis, thus, shows that it is a mistake, when one looks at how this standard is used, to suppose that it is merely a calculation of potential benefits and risks independent of people's duties or liberties.

The Best Interests Standard cannot be classified as simply either an objective or a subjective standard. It has subjective features in the sense that to some extent it reflects the values, views and perceptions of decision-makers selecting what they view as the best option for someone lacking capacity. It also has objective features in the sense that to some extent choices for others must meet standards of care, evidence and good judgment. For example, once the Best Interests Standard was introduced parents who were at liberty to select unproven over proven and life saving therapies for themselves, could no longer select them for their children because it constituted medical neglect.

Using this new analysis of the Best Interests Standard, I have supported the professional consensus against testing children for untreatable, severe, late-onset conditions such as Huntington's disease or Alzheimer's disease unless it can be justified as being useful to the child, something that is difficult to demonstrate when no preventive or treatment strategies exist. I have also argued that parents have the legal authority to authorize such testing for their child, if they can find clinicians willing to do the test. This discussion could be affected by the proliferation of prenatal predictive genetic tests and over the counter products since the market could make an end-run around the professional consensus.

Acknowledgments

I would like to thank Janet Malek, Leslie Frances, and Bonnie Steinbock for helpful comments that they made on earlier drafts of this article. I also benefited from a lively discussion of a talk based on this article at the American Philosophical Association in San Francisco on April 6, 2007. The mistakes are, of course, my own.

Notes

1. There are of course other perspectives about how to make these decisions, such as what is best for the family or society.
2. Elsewhere I have responded to criticisms of the Best Interests Standard. (See Kopelman 1997, 2005, and 2007). Some critics charge the Best Interests Standard is vague, open to abuse, or guides decision makers to do whatever they happen to think is best. Yet if we look at why it developed and how it is used, its meaning is clear (although there may be times it is hard to apply). For example some critics have defined the Best Interests Standard as requiring decision makers to do what is ideal and then argued the Best Interests Standard is unknowable, unattainable or self-defeating; others argue that it is too narrowly focused on the incompetent or incapacitated person's interests. Such analyses of the Best Interests Standard are unrelated to how it is used in practical settings. I also use this analysis of the Best Interests Standard to discuss an extremely difficult case where parents want life-saving interventions withdrawn from their son (Kopelman, 2008, forthcoming).
3. The Best Interests Standard has also been used to help interpret the research regulations such as in *Grimes v. Kennedy Krieger Institute, Inc.* 782 A. 2d 807, 366 Md. 20 (Court of Appeals of Maryland, 2001): at 852–853; and *T.D. v. N.Y. State Office of Mental Health,* 228 A.D.2d 95 (Court, 1996). The courts acknowledge both the importance of the Best Interests Standard

and that it cannot require what is ideal for the children in pediatric studies since that would have the effect of stopping research unless a case could be made that it is best for each child; the courts and regulatory bodies allow non-therapeutic or "no benefit" studies that have a low risk. For a further discussion of this see Kopelman, 2002.

4. The Best Interests Standard in its practical uses is tied to what a reasonable person would decide is best in similar situations. For example, the President's Council offers an analysis of the legal use of Best Interests Standard: "Best interest: a legal standard of caregiving for incompetent patients, defined by the courts in terms of what a "reasonable person" would decide in the same situation. A consideration of best interests generally attempts to weigh the burdens and benefits of treatment to the patient in his present condition, when no clear preferences of the patient can be determined" (President's Council, 2005, p. 231). Authors Hafemeister and Hannaford agree, writing that in judicial opinions the ". . . 'best interest' incorporates what a reasonable person in the patient's position would want" (Haefmeister and Hannaford, 1996, 19n). They point out that for medical decisions the courts frequently consider an incompetent person's diagnosis and prognosis and other objective medical criteria, the person's prognosis for suffering or enjoyment, and the likelihood that the person will have a tolerable quality of life.
5. This is discussed in detail in Kopelman, 1997, 2005, and 2007. As noted, it seems compatible with legal definitions of the Best Interests Standard in terms of a reasonable person standard. For example, see the President's Council (2005, p. 231) and Hafemeister and Hannaford (2000, 19n).
6. There is more of a consensus *that* we agree about these points than there is about *why* we agree.
7. Three alleged benefits of testing where the faulty gene(s) is present were omitted from Fryer's table because he acknowledges that they are controversial or doubtful. They are "16 years may not be a good age to be tested," "beneficence," and "lessen society discrimination." See Fryer (2000, p. 284).
8. See Fryer (2000) and Rhodes (2006). Karen Kovach also gave a version of this argument in her paper at the America Philosophical Association's meeting in San Francisco on April 6, 2007. She argued that the parents and children should decide about testing along with the clinician. While I agree and do not find this general stance to be controversial, the problem is that few clinicians will do the testing and that is how the problem arises. The issue is whether their resistance is justifiable.
9. This view is widespread and has been for many years. See for example the policy statements from the Working group of the British Society of Human Genetics, 1994, the AAP, 2005, and the CPS, 2003.
10. I have not found arguments about the disinterestedness of clinical judgment in the literature as such but they seem implied.

11. There has been little judicial attention to this issue of testing for untreatable, severe, late-onset genetic diseases perhaps because the two extremes (test everyone, test no one) are so implausible.
12. A correlative problem was discussed by the President's Commission in its discussion of making decisions for incompetent elderly persons with dementia. A majority of the commissioners recommended setting aside the once-competent person's advance directive if decision-makers decided it was now not in their best interest. A minority of the commissions sharply disagreed.
13. The Best Interests Standard is a relatively recent legal doctrine replacing the view that children are property of their parents. Other countries may give children fewer rights, not give the Best Interests Standard the same meaning, or interpret it differently. There seem to be some international differences about the professional consensus. Fryer (2000) finds geneticists in Canada, Northern Europe and the United States would generally not agree to test while those in other parts of Europe, Asia and Latin American would. Arguably the difference concerns how parental duties and authority are envisioned.

References

Alderson, P., Sutcliffe, K., & Curtis, K. (2006). 'Children's competence to consent to medical treatment,' *Hastings Center Report, 36*, 625–34.

American Academy of Pediatrics, Committee on Bioethics. (2005). Nelson, R. M., Botkjin, J. R., Kodish, E. D. et al., (Eds.) 'Ethical issues with genetic testing in pediatrics,' *Pediatrics, 107*(6), 1451–5. Policy statement issued May 1, 2005.

American Geriatric Society Ethics Committee. (2001). 'Genetic testing for late-onset Alzheimer's Disease,' *Journal of the American Geriatric Society, 49*, 225–226.

American Medical Association. (1995). *CEJM Report 4-A-95: Testing Children for Genetic Status* [On-line]. Available: http://www.ama-assn.org/ama1/pub/upload/mm/369/ceja_4a95.pdf, Accessed July 16, 2007.

Annas, G. J. (2001). 'The limits of state law to protect genetic information.' *New England Journal of Medicine, 345*, 385–388.

Bluebond-Langner, M. (1978). *The private worlds of dying children.* Princeton, NJ: Princeton University Press.

Borry, P., & Stultiens, L., Nys, H., Cassiman, J-J. Dieriokx, K. (2006). 'Presymptomatic and predictive genetic testing in minors: A systematic review of guidelines and position papers,' *Clinical Genetics*, 70(5), 374–81.

Canadian Pediatrics Society, Bioethics Committee. (2003). 'Guidelines for genetic testing of healthy children,' *Pediatric & Child Health, 8*(1), 42–45.

Chapman, M. A. (1992). 'Canadian experience with predictive testing for Huntington disease: lessons for genetic testing centers and policy makers,' *American Journal of Medical Genetics, 42*(4), 491–8.

Cohen, C. B. (1998). 'Wrestling with the future: should we test children for adult-onset genetic conditions?.' *Kennedy Institute of Ethics Journal, 8*(2), 111–130.

Cutler, S. J., & Hodgson, L. G. (2003). 'To test or not to test: Interest in genetic testing for Alzheimer's disease among middle-aged adults,' *American Journal of Alzheimer's Disease and Other Dementias*, 18(1), 9–20.

Davis, D. (1997). 'Genetic dilemmas and the child's right to an open future,' *Hastings Center Report*, 27, 7–25.

Duncan, R. E., Savulescu, J., Gillam, L., Williamson, R., & Delatycki, M. B. (2005). 'An international survey of predictive genetic testing in children for adult onset conditions,' *Genetics in Medicine*, 7(6), 390–6.

Duncan, R. E., & Delatycki, M. B. (2006). 'Predictive genetic testing in young people for adult-onset conditions: where is the empirical evidence?' *Clinical Genetics*, 69, 8–16.

Feinberg, J. (1980). The child's right to an open future. In: W. Aiken & H. LaFollette (Eds.) *Whose Child? Children's rights, parental authority, and state power* (pp. 124–153). Totowa, NJ: Littlefield Adams.

Foster, M. W., Royal, C. D., & Sharp, R. R. (2006). 'The routinisation of genomics and genetics: implications for ethical practices,' *Journal of Medical Ethics*, 32(11), 635–8.

Fryer, A. (2000). 'Inappropriate genetic testing of children,' *Archives of Disease in Childhood*, 83, 283–285.

Fulda, K. G., & Lykens, K. (2006). 'Ethical issues in predictive genetic testing: a public health perspective.' *Journal of Medical Ethics*, 32(3), 143–7.

Goldstein, J., Freud, A., & Solnit, A. (1975). *Beyond the Best Interests of the Child*. New York: Macmillan.

Green, M. J., & Botkin, J. R. (2003). 'Genetic exceptionalism in medicine: Clarifying the differences between genetic and non-genetic tests,' *Annals of Internal Medicine*, 138 (7), 571–5.

Grimes v. Kennedy Krieger Institute, Inc. 782 A. 2d 807, 366 Md. 29 (Court of Appeals of Maryland, 2001).

Hafemeister, T. L., & Hannaford, P. L. (1996). *Resolving disputes over life sustaining treatment: a health care provider's guide*. Williamsburg, VA: National Center for State Courts.

The Huntington's Disease Society of American. (1996). "Genetic Testing for Huntington's Disease [On-line]. Available: http://www.hdsa.org/site/PageServer?pagename=help_info_ed_faq, Accessed July 16, 2007.

Institute of Medicine of the National Academics. (2004). *Ethical Conduct of Clinical Research Involving Children*. Washington DC: The National Academics Press.

King, N. (2007). 'The ethics of genetic testing: Is more always better? *North Carolina Medical Journal*, 68, 112–114.

Kopelman, L. M. (1997). 'The best interest standard as threshold, ideal and standard of reasonableness,' *Journal of Medicine and Philosophy*, 22, 271–289.

Kopelman, L. M. (2002). 'Pediatric research regulations under legal scrutiny: *Grimes* narrows their interpretation,' *Journal of Law, Medicine & Ethics*, 30, 38–49.

Kopelman, L. M. (2005). 'Rejecting the 'Baby Doe' regulations and defending a 'negative' analysis of the best interests standard,' *Journal of Medicine and Philosophy, 30,* 346.

Kopelman, L. M. (2007). 'The best interests standard for incompetent or incapacitated persons of all ages,' *The Journal of Law, Medicine and Ethics, 35,* 187–196.

Kopelman, L. M., & Kopelman, A. E. (2008). 'Using a new analysis of the best interests standard to address cultural disputes: Whose data, which values?' *Theoretical Medicine and Biology,* January forthcoming.

Krause, H. D. (1986). *Family Law in a Nutshell,* (2nd ed.). St. Paul, MN: West Publishing Company.

Lerman, C., Narod, S., Schulman, K., Hughes, C., Gomez–Caminero, A., Bonney, G., Gold, K., Trock, B., Main, D., Lynch, J., Fulmore, C., Snyder, C., Lemon, S. J., Conway, T., Tonin, P., Lenoir, G., & Lynch, H. (1996). 'BRCA1 testing in families with hereditary breast-ovarian cancer. A prospective study of patient decision making and outcomes,' *Journal of the American Medical Association, 275*(24), 1885–92.

Matsuda, I., Niikawa, N., Sato, K., et al. (2000). Guidelines for genetic testing. *Japan Society of Human Genetics, Council Committee of Ethics* [On-line]. Available: http://jshg.jp/introduction/notifications/20001100e.htm, Accessed July 16, 2007.

Meiser, B., & Dunn, S. (2000). 'Psychological impact of genetic testing for Huntington's disease: an update of the literature,' *Journal of Neurology, Neurosurgery and Psychiatry, 69,* 574–78.

Morrison, P. J. (2005). 'Insurance, unfair discrimination, and genetic testing,' *The Lancet, 366,* 877–880.

Pelias, M. K. (2006). 'Genetic testing of children for adult-onset diseases: is testing in the child's best interests?' *Mount Sinai Journal of Medicine, 73,* 605–8.

President's Council on Bioethics. (2005). *Taking Care: Ethical Care-Giving in Our Aging Society,* presentation at The President's Council, Washington DC.

Rhodes, R. (2006). 'Why test children for adult-onset genetic diseases?,' *Mount Sinai Journal of Medicine, 73*(3), 609–16.

Roche, P. A., & Annas, G. J. (2006) 'DNA testing, banking, and genetic privacy,' *New England Journal of Medicine, 355,* 545–546.

T.D. v. N.Y. State Office of Mental Health, 228 A.D.2d 95 (Court 1996).

United Nations. (1989). The Office of the High Commission for Human Rights. 'Convention on the Rights of the Child,' Adopted and opened for signature, ratification and accession by General Assembly resolution 44/25 of 20 November 1989, *entry into force* 2 September 1990, in accordance with article 49. http://www.unhchr.ch/html/menu3/b/k2crc.htm (Accessed January 23, 2007).

Wertz, D. C., Fanos, J. H., & Reilly, P. R. (1994). 'Genetic testing for children and adolescents: Who decides?' *Journal of the American Medical Association, 272,* 875–881.

Wertz, D. C., & Reilly, P. R. (1997). 'Laboratory policies and practices for the genetic testing of children: a survey of the Helix network,' *American Journal of Human Genetics, 61,* 1163–8.

Reading Analytically

1. To understand the premise of this essay, one must first understand what is meant by the "best interests standard" as it is applied in medical fields. How is that standard defined? Draw upon specific portions of the essay that help to set up a working definition of the concept.
2. Because the standard for assessing the value in genetic testing for cases of untreatable diseases is multifaceted, various parts of that standard must be rank-ordered; that is, decisions need to be made as to which parts of the standard are most important in any given case. Outline the reasoning that Kopelman uses to suggest that hierarchy.
3. After reading Kopelman's piece, think about its message more personally. Would you want to know if you had the likelihood of having an untreatable disease? Why or why not?

Reading Across Disciplinary Communities

1. As a writer trained in philosophical method, Kopelman uses the methodologies of her discipline to construct her argument. In particular, philosophers are trained to examine questions with logic rather than just emotion. How is Kopelman's essay structured in order to demonstrate her logical reasoning?
2. The philosophical discipline also depends upon the use of previous thinkers, applying past writings to present situations. Provide three examples of how Kopelman uses summaries, paraphrases, and/or quotations from previous thinkers, and discuss the ways that she uses the ideas of those previous writers to support her own conclusions.

DANIEL V. MEEGAN

Neuroimaging Techniques for Memory Detection

Scientific, Ethical, and Legal Issues

This essay, written by a psychologist, brings together the scientific techniques surrounding neuroimaging and its ability to detect memories in the human brain with the surrounding ethical and legal issues that are of importance in those disciplines. It was first published in The American Journal of Bioethics, *a publication that is interdisciplinary in nature, combining "biology" and "ethics."*

The essay delves into the ethical implications of using new technologies for brain scanning, advanced by the growing field of neuroscience, for criminal investigation and prosecution. This question has many facets, including the reliability of this science as well as the relative rights of the accused and the victims. It is also a topic, as Meegan suggests, much on the mind of the larger public, driven by a number of films that explore the value and dangers of intruding into the human memory. As you read, you will need to weigh the various arguments presented, taking into account issues of privacy as well as the potential gains toward preventing and prosecuting criminals.

There is considerable interest in the use of neuroimaging techniques for forensic purposes. Memory detection techniques, including the well-publicized Brain Fingerprinting technique (Brain Fingerprinting Laboratories, Inc., Seattle WA), exploit the fact that the brain responds differently to sensory stimuli to which it has been exposed before. When a stimulus is specifically associated with a crime, the resulting brain activity should differentiate between someone who was present at the crime and someone who was not. This article reviews the scientific literature on three such techniques: priming, old/new, and P300 effects. The forensic potential of these techniques is evaluated based on four criteria: specificity, automaticity, encoding flexibility, and longevity. This article concludes that none of the techniques are devoid of forensic potential, although much research is yet to be done. Ethical issues, including rights to privacy and against self-incrimination, are discussed. A discussion of legal issues concludes that current memory detection techniques do not yet meet United States standards of legal admissibility.

In the 2004 film *Eternal Sunshine of the Spotless Mind*, a neuroscientist invented a technique whereby specific memories can be erased from one's brain. Although the ethical issues about the use and abuse of such technology were explored in the film, the film was not warning viewers of the imminent development of such technology. Indeed there are two characteristics of memory storage that make specific erasure difficult, if not impossible. First, memories are stored in a distributed fashion, and second, a memory network in one locus contains many memories. The first is a problem for erasure because to erase a memory trace in one locus leaves traces at other loci. The second is a problem for erasure because erasing a network erases more than just the desired memories.[1] Specific memory erasure can be viewed as a two-stage process: in the first stage, the neural basis of the memory is identified, and in the second stage, the memory is erased. Although the second stage is science fiction, neuroimaging techniques that could accomplish something resembling the first stage are currently in development, and, in one case, actually being used. Thus it is not too early to begin discussing the ethical and legal ramifications of such techniques.

Criminal investigation is the most obvious application of a technique that can identify the existence of a memory in the brain. If an individual is being investigated for the commission of a crime, then such a technique, it has been claimed, could identify them as guilty or innocent based on the presence or absence of a memory for the crime. Note that such a *memory detection* technique is different than lie detection because, in theory, the existence of a memory could be detected regardless of whether the examinee is lying. The development of neuroimaging techniques has made memory detection possible because existing behavioral techniques for the detection of memories rely on participant cooperation, which cannot be expected of the guilty person claiming innocence.

Imagine a neuroimaging test that can detect the presence of a crime memory. A positive result on such a test would support the conclusion that the examinee was guilty, and a negative result would support the conclusion that the examinee was innocent. The test has neither perfect specificity nor perfect sensitivity, however. A positive test result for an innocent examinee is called a *false positive,* and a negative result for a guilty examinee is a *false negative.* The validity of the test for guilt detection relies on a low false-positive rate, and the validity of the test for innocence detection relies on a low false-negative rate. The next section reviews three memory detection techniques with an emphasis on their vulnerabilities to false positives and false negatives.

Neuroimaging Techniques for Memory Detection

The two most obvious neuroimaging methods for memory detection are event-related variants of electroencephalography (EEG) and functional magnetic resonance imaging (fMRI). EEG measures brain electrical activity that reaches scalp electrodes, and fMRI measures regional blood oxygenation in the brain, which is correlated with brain activity. *Event-related* refers to a specific sensory stimulus event rather than an entire event, such as a crime, that would have a multitude of sensory stimuli associated with it. Event-related neuroimaging presents an event to a participant, and then measures the resulting activity. Memory research using event-related EEG (called the *event-related potential*, or *ERP, technique*) or event-related fMRI has sought to identify characteristic activity that occurs when an event has been presented to the brain prior to the test, as is the case with crime-relevant events and the criminal's brain. For all the effects described later in text, the activity resulting from *old* events (i.e., presented earlier) is quantitatively distinguishable from that resulting from *new* events (i.e., not presented earlier). Note that the utility of these effects are not compromised by the aforementioned characteristics of distributed memory networks. Even if a memory trace is distributed, a test need only find it in one place to demonstrate its existence; moreover, some of the effects described later in text indeed find distinguishable activity in multiple regions. The fact that many memories are stored in a single network is not a problem either, as long as the network is differentially active for old and new events.

Each of the effects reviewed will be evaluated on the following four attributes that characterize the ideal memory detection test for criminal investigations:

1. *Specificity:* Everyone has seen knives before, but only the guilty examinee has seen the specific knife that was used in the crime. If an effect occurs for new events that merely resemble old events, then there is a real risk of false positives. On the other hand, if an effect is very specific, then false negatives could result if the event is an inaccurate portrayal of the crime stimulus.
2. *Retrieval automaticity:* One of the problems that limits the validity of the polygraph is its vulnerability to countermeasures (National Research Council 2003). The neuroimaging effects described here distinguish between old and new activity, and an effective countermeasure would use mental control to make old and new activity indistinguishable. Old/new differences can be eliminated by making old events look new or by making new events look old. A memory effect that has automaticity is resistant to the former type of countermeasure. In other words, there is nothing that an examinee can do to make an automatic memory effect produce new-like activity for old events. A non-automatic effect, on the other hand, is susceptible to countermeasures and thus prone to false negatives. The second type of countermeasure, in which new events are made to look old, is also a very real possibility, especially for tests that lack specificity. For example, if the new (crime-irrelevant) events include a tree, then the guilty examinee can attempt to recall a tree from the

past, thereby producing old-like brain activity from which the brain activity produced by crime-relevant events will be indistinguishable.

3. *Encoding flexibility:* Encoding refers to the initial presentation of a stimulus. In the criminal investigation scenario, encoding occurred at the crime. All memory and neuroimaging research uses a prospective memory approach in which the encoding conditions are both known and controlled. This research has shown that the encoding conditions can have a profound impact on how a stimulus event is responded to on subsequent presentations. A criminal investigation necessitates a retrospective memory approach in which the encoding conditions are neither known nor controlled. For this reason, it must be assumed that the encoding conditions could have been poor. If a memory detection test is to ensure a low false-negative rate, then the effects must be robust in a variety of encoding conditions.
4. *Longevity:* Because considerable time might pass between the crime and the memory detection test, an ideal effect would remain measurable for long retention intervals. If an effect is known to decay to the point of immeasurability after a certain retention interval, then it should not be used for longer retention intervals. Otherwise the likelihood of false negatives is too high.

Priming Effects

The first effects I will describe are usually referred to as neural *priming* effects (Schacter et al. 2004) or *repetition suppression* effects (Grill-Spector et al. 2006). Just like priming a surface affects the way it receives paint, priming the brain with a stimulus affects the way it responds to the stimulus on subsequent presentations. Neuroimaging studies of priming have generally shown a reduction in activity for primed (old) events compared with unprimed (new) events, and the most consistent reductions are found in regions of the brain involved in the perceptual processing of sensory stimuli (Grill-Spector et al. 2006; Schacter et al. 2004).

Specificity

Priming effects are most robust when the event is perceptually identical to the prime stimulus (Koutstaal et al. 2001; Schacter et al. 2004). This has obvious implications for how priming effects might best be employed in criminal investigations. For example, if a knife was used in a crime, then a photograph of the actual knife would be more likely to elicit a priming effect than a pictorial representation of the knife, a photograph of another knife, or the word *knife*. Priming effects can also be attenuated when the prime and event, although the same object, are shown from different viewpoints (Vuilleumier et al. 2002). If priming effects are to be used in criminal investigation, then the selection of events should thus consider the most likely viewpoint of the perpetrator. In summary, priming effects are very specific, and thus there seems a greater risk of false negatives than false positives.

Retrieval Automaticity

Priming effects are thought to occur automatically (Wiggs and Martin 1998). Most priming research has used experimental tasks, often called *indirect memory tasks*, in which participants are not told that they are participating in a memory experiment, and they are given a task to do that is not explicitly mnemonic. Researchers generally assume that participants are not aware that they have seen an old event earlier. It is easy to envision a criminal investigation scenario, however, in which a guilty examinee is aware that they have seen a particular crime-relevant event earlier. Thus it is useful to consider research that has examined whether priming effects occur for *direct* memory tasks in which participants are explicitly told that some events are old. Although some studies have shown similar priming effects for direct and indirect tasks, other studies have shown differences (Henson 2003; Henson et al. 2002). More research is clearly necessary to understand the test conditions under which automatic priming effects can be reliably measured.

Encoding Flexibility

The priming literature has examined the impact of attending to the prime stimulus at encoding. Attending to an object is not the same as looking directly at it; one can look at one object but attend to another. Several fMRI studies have found that visible but unattended primes produce smaller priming effects than attended primes (Eger et al. 2004; Vuilleumier et al. 2005; Yi and Chun 2005; Yi et al. 2006; although see Bentley et al. 2003). In criminal investigations, even if it can be assumed that the perpetrator viewed an object, it might be unsafe to assume that they attended to it. Imagine a murder investigation in which the shirt worn by the victim might seem an obvious choice for a prime because the perpetrator must have seen it. However, the shirt was likely irrelevant to the task at hand, and thus could have gone unattended. The selection of events for a memory detection test should thus consider the likelihood that an object received the attention of the perpetrator.

Longevity

Behavioral priming effects can last an impressively long time (Cave 1997; Mitchell 2006). The question remains, however, whether neural priming effects last as long as their behavioral correlates. The first studies to confirm the longevity of neural priming used modest retention intervals of days (van Turennout et al. 2000, 2003), but a more recent study (Meister et al. 2005) found lasting, albeit less distributed, priming effects after a six-week retention interval.

Old/New Effects

Old/new effects are similar to priming effects in that they are differences in neural activity for old and new events. The primary difference is that old/new effects are thought to reflect memory retrieval processing rather than perceptual processing. When an old event is presented, there are two distinct types of retrieval processes that might be initiated (Yonelinas 2002). One type, called *familiarity,* is relatively fast and automatic and results in knowing that an event is old without remembering the context in which it was seen. The other type, called *recollection,* is relatively slow and effortful and results in remembering the context in which an old event was seen. ERP research has led the way in identifying distinct old/new effects associated with familiarity and recollection (Friedman and Johnson 2000; Rugg and Yonelinas 2003). The *mid-frontal* old/new effect, associated with familiarity, is a negative potential occurring between 300 and 500 milliseconds after event onset that is less negative for old than new events at mid-frontal electrode sites. The *parietal* old/new effect, associated with recollection, is a positive potential occurring between 400 and 800 milliseconds after event onset that is more positive for old than new events at parietal electrode sites.[2] More recently, fMRI research has also been successful at identifying brain activity uniquely associated with familiarity and recollection (e.g., Daselaar et al. 2006; Henson et al. 1999; Yonelinas et al. 2005).

Specificity

New events that are similar to old events are sometimes falsely recognized as old. Such false recognition is associated with the experience of familiarity (Yonelinas 2002), and mid-frontal old/new effects have shown old-like activity for similar-new events (Mecklinger 2006). Although this suggests a risk of false positives, there is reason to think that this problem is not as great as it may seem. False feelings of familiarity are a relatively rare occurrence in everyday life—it is not as if objects we encounter commonly elicit feelings of familiarity simply because of their resemblance to old objects. Scientists who wish to study familiarity in the laboratory thus create artificial situations in which participants are much more likely to experience familiarity and false recognition (e.g., Curran and Cleary 2003). Other research suggests that the mid-frontal old/new effect might be appropriately specific. For example, it is sensitive to study-to-test changes in stimulus format (Schloerscheidt and Rugg 2004) and context (Tsivilis et al. 2001).

Retrieval Automaticity

The automaticity of old/new effects has been assessed in studies that have used an *exclusion* methodology (Jacoby 1991). In exclusion tasks there are usually two types of old stimuli, one of which is to be classified as old (i.e., included) and the other as new (i.e., excluded). If brain activity associated with recognizing old events is automatic, then excluded events should show the same activity as included events. Existing studies suggest that this is the case for the mid-frontal old/new effect (Bridson et al. 2006; Czernochowski et al. 2005), but is not always the case for the parietal old/new effect (e.g., Dywan et al. 2002; Herron and Rugg 2003). These results are consistent with the suggestion that familiarity is automatic, but recollection is not (Jacoby 1991). Other results suggest that the parietal old/new effect might be immune to the types of deliberate misclassification that would be used by the guilty examinee trying to conceal his recognition of crime-relevant events (Johnson et al. 2003; Tardif et al. 2000).

Encoding Flexibility

ERP studies have examined two encoding manipulations: 1) *divided attention*, and 2) *levels of processing*. In divided attention studies (Curran 2004), optimal encoding is represented by a *single-task* condition in which items are studied for a later recognition test, and suboptimal encoding by a *dual-task* condition in which studying must be done simultaneously with a second task. In levels of processing studies (Rugg et al. 1998, 2000), optimal encoding is represented by a *deep* encoding condition in which semantic judgments are made about the items, and suboptimal encoding by a *shallow* encoding condition in which perceptual judgments are made. The results suggest that the mid-frontal effect is relatively insensitive to the encoding conditions, and that the parietal effect is relatively sensitive.

Longevity

ERP research has used retention intervals that are far too short to assess the practical longevity of old/new effects. In fact, the studies that have been designed to confirm that the mid-frontal old/new effect has longevity have used retention intervals of only one day (Curran and Friedman 2004; Wolk et al. 2006).

P300 Effects

Although related to the parietal old/new effect (Spencer et al. 2000), P300 effects have been used somewhat differently and thus will be treated separately here. The P300 is a positive ERP occurring between 300 and 1000 milliseconds after event onset that is maximal at mid-parietal electrode sites for events that are both infrequent and meaningful (Polich and Kok 1995). The classic P300 task, called the *oddball task*, requires participants to make one response to infrequent *target* events and another response to all other (*non-target*) events, thus producing a more robust P300 for targets than non-targets. Applications to memory detection were considered following the discovery that old non-targets could produce a target-like P300 (e.g., Allen et al. 1992; Farwell and Donchin 1991; Rosenfeld et al. 1988). In P300 memory detection tests, there are usually three types of events: targets and two types of non-targets. *Irrelevants* are frequent non-targets designed to be meaningless to all participants, and *probes* are infrequent non-targets designed to be meaningless to some participants and meaningful to others. In the crime investigation scenario, probes are crime-relevant events designed to be meaningless to innocent examinees and meaningful to guilty examinees. Studies employing this method have generally shown that probes elicit a target-like P300 for guilty examinees, and an irrelevant-like P300 for innocent examinees (e.g., Farwell and Donchin 1991).

Specificity

Most P300 studies have used words rather than pictures as events. Because words are recognizable stimuli to all literate examinees, it is only in the context of the test that targets, probes, and irrelevants take on their respective roles. Word stimuli thus make specificity a challenge. It is not so much a problem for targets and irrelevants because they are distinguished by frequency and task-relevance, which are known to be important factors in P300 generation. The task-irrelevance of probes, however, creates a risk that they could produce irrelevant-like effects for guilty examinees (i.e., false negatives). The solution to this problem is *context provision*. For example, in a recent PBS special featuring the Brain Fingerprinting test (Brain Fingerprinting Laboratories, Inc., Seattle WA),[3] the examiner read the following statement to examinees: "In this test, you will see an item that one of the suspects was wearing when he was apprehended, an item that was in the possession of the suspects when they were apprehended, the item the suspects were stealing, and where the crime was committed (the kind of place, dwelling or establishment)" (Innovation: Brain Fingerprinting 2004). These statements referred to the probestimuli; for example, the probe 'flashlight' was referenced by the statement concerning the item in possession of the suspects. This context provision was designed to increase the likelihood that 'flashlight' elicited a target-like P300 for guilty examinees.

The context provision approach is vulnerable to countermeasures. For example, if the guilty examinee simply ignores the contextual information, the meaningfulness of the probe 'flashlight' is likely to be comparable for guilty and innocent examinees, as everyone has had some experience with flashlights. To be fair, some word probes, even without context provision, are uniquely meaningful to guilty examinees. Nevertheless, words are inferior to pictures in terms of their potential for meaningfulness, and a photograph of the specific flashlight used in the aforementioned crime would presumably have been less likely to require context provision in order to have elicited a target-like P300 in guilty examinees.

Retrieval Automaticity

The P300 memory detection task described previously is an indirect memory task that does not force guilty examinees to be deceptive concerning their recognition of probes. In other words, when the task requires a target/non-target classification, probes are honestly classified as non-targets. Others, though, have used an old/new classification that forces the guilty examinee to dishonestly classify probes as new. Several studies have shown that the deliberate misclassification of old events as new (Johnson et al. 2003; Miller et al. 2002; Rosenfeld et al. 2003), or the exclusion of old events (van Hooff et al. 1996; van Hooff and Golden 2002), tends to attenuate the P300. The most likely cause of P300 attenuation in these studies is not dishonest responding, per se, but rather the mental effort involved in a difficult classification (Johnson et al. 2003).[4] In other words, it is more difficult to respond dishonestly than honestly. Because the probe P300 can be attenuated by dishonest responding to probe events, it is best to use an easy classification task that does not require examinees to be deceptive concerning their recognition of probes.

There are two countermeasure strategies that could be attempted by the guilty examinee in a P300 memory detection test: 1) to produce an irrelevant-like P300 for probes, and 2) to produce a probe-like P300 for irrelevants. There is no existing evidence to suggest that the former strategy is likely to be successful, as long as the probes are appropriately meaningful (see previous discussion) and the task allows honest classification of probes (see previous discussion). In other words, it is difficult to treat something meaningful as meaningless. The latter strategy, in which events designed to be meaningless are made meaningful, seems more intuitively plausible, and one study has provided evidence supporting this intuition. Rosenfeld et al. (2004) trained guilty participants, who had committed a mock-crime, to employ a countermeasure in which irrelevants were treated as task-relevant events. Although participants were still required to make an overt non-target response to irrelevants, they also made distinct covert responses to different categories of irrelevants, which resulted in a probe-like P300 for irrelevants.

The countermeasure strategy used by Rosenfeld et al. (2004) could be thwarted methodologically, however. The target, probe, and irrelevant events used by Rosenfeld et al. (2004), were organized into distinct categories. Countermeasure training involved informing guilty participants of the categorical nature of the test. They were then trained to make a particular covert response any time they saw an irrelevant from a particular event category. A simple way to prevent such a countermeasure is to eliminate the categorical nature of the test. Consider the following scenario. In preparation for a P300 memory detection test, a guilty suspect is being trained by a P300 countermeasure expert hired by his lawyer. The expert predicts that the weapon used in the crime will be used as a probe. If the test is known to have a categorical structure, then the expert can also predict that the target and irrelevants will be weapons. Thus the expert can train the suspect to use the countermeasure used by Rosenfeld et al. (2004); in other words, the suspect can be trained to make a distinct covert response every time he sees a weapon event. If, on the other hand, the test does not have a categorical structure, then advance training of this nature is impossible, and the only countermeasure available to the guilty examinee is to prepare to make covert responses to irrelevant events that cannot be predicted in advance. It is certainly possible that such a countermeasure strategy will result in a probe-like P300 for irrelevants, but this possibility has not yet been tested.

Encoding Flexibility

Farwell and Donchin (1991) provided a highly optimal encoding environment for probe stimuli. The participants were given detailed instructions before performing a mock act of espionage. The instructions included to-be-memorized details that would later become the probe events in a memory detection test. To ensure that the details were memorized, the participants were repeatedly tested until they had responded correctly at least five times to questions regarding each of the probes. Although this type of memorization might be representative of some types of premeditated crimes, there are many crimes that have far less optimal encoding conditions. Several recent studies have examined the effect of suboptimal encoding on P300 memory detection (Rosenfeld et al. 2006; 2007; van Hooff 2005; van Hooff and Golden 2002). In these studies, suboptimal encoding was represented by an *incidental* encoding condition and optimal encoding by an *intentional* encoding condition. The results have been mixed—incidentally encoded information sometimes does (Rosenfeld et al. 2007) and sometimes does not (van Hooff and Golden 2002) elicit a P300. Given that in many crime situations the perpetrator is not intentionally memorizing crime details, these results suggest that one cannot assume that all crime details will be salient enough to later elicit a measurable P300.

Longevity

In their oft-cited mock espionage experiment, Farwell and Donchin (1991) used a one-day retention interval. In a second experiment, they intended to test the efficacy of their procedure over longer retention intervals by using participants who had committed actual crimes sometime prior to the test. However, because the participants' memories for the crimes were revisited in an effort to determine the appropriate probes for the memory detection test, this experiment should not be considered a longevity test. More research is necessary to assess the longevity of P300 memory detection tests.

Scientific Issues

Previous research was reviewed in the preceding section. This section reviews what still needs to be done before these techniques can be put to use in criminal investigations. It also discusses the likelihood that future research will find that the techniques meet the standards required by criminal investigations.

Future Research

All of the research reviewed in the previous discussion was conducted in laboratory environments, and field tests will be an important component of future research. Because the application of P300 effects to memory detection was first considered at least 20 years ago, P300 effects have been tested in situations designed to resemble criminal investigations. By comparison, priming and old/new effects have been tested in situations that lack ecological validity. This is most obvious when considering automaticity, because memory researchers who use priming and old/new effects have not considered situations in which participants are trying to conceal their recognition of old events. Whereas memory research typically reports the combined effects of many participants, criminal investigation requires an assessment of individual examinees. Although priming and old/new effects have occasionally been used at the individual level in cases of amnesia (e.g., Düzel et al. 2001), P300 memory detection tests have been developed with the individual in mind (e.g., Farwell and Donchin 1991). Allen (2002) has provided invaluable information concerning the best way to implement the individual approach in memory detection. Lastly, it would be interesting to see whether variables that influence P300 effects, such as the infrequency of old events, have similar influences on priming and old/new effects.

Longevity and encoding flexibility have not been sufficiently tested for any of the effects reviewed in the previous discussion. Future tests of longevity require a lengthening of the retention interval so that it resembles that which is likely to occur in criminal investigations. As for encoding flexibility, there are many factors likely to affect encoding that have not yet been tested. These factors include the heightened emotional state of the perpetrator (something that cannot easily be reproduced in mock crimes), the possible presence of drugs (e.g., alcohol) in the nervous system of the perpetrator, and the age and health of the perpetrator.

Other issues arise at retrieval (i.e., when the memory detection test is administered) rather than encoding. For example, the emotional state of the examinee at the time of the memory detection test must be considered, because such factors have been shown to affect brain activity (Polich and Kok 1995). Also, an uncooperative examinee could sabotage a test by not following task instructions or by preventing reliable brain measurement (e.g., moving the head during an fMRI scan).

Forensic Potential

The existing research provides no conclusive evidence to suggest that any of the techniques are devoid of forensic potential. Nevertheless, much research is yet to be done. Some of the problems identified in the previous discussion, especially those related to specificity and automaticity, have the potential to be solved with methodological advancements. For problems associated with encoding flexibility and longevity, on the other hand, there is much less reason to be optimistic that methodological advancements will provide solutions. Among the sins of memory categorized by Schacter (2001), the sins of *absent-mindedness* and *transience* respectively describe the encoding flexibility and longevity problems. In other words, methodological advancements can do nothing about the fact that memory has a tendency to fail when the encoding conditions are poor and the retention interval is long. For this reason, it would not be at all surprising if further research using poor encoding conditions and long retention intervals provided evidence that false negatives were a genuine and insurmountable problem for memory detection.

Ethical Issues

Nothing was your own except the few cubic centimetres inside your skull.

—George Orwell, *Nineteen Eighty-Four* (1949, 25)

To those who live in free societies, Orwell's Oceania was the ultimate dystopia in which the Thought Police possessed effective means for identifying what was going on inside the minds of individuals based on their overt behavior. As suggested by the quote, the Thought Police did not have neuroscientific techniques for extracting the thoughts out of the brains of individuals. It is not surprising, then, that modern society is extremely wary of the prospect that neuroscience research is attempting to develop, or has developed, such techniques (Sententia 2001). Although one would like to think that free societies could be trusted to use such techniques appropriately, recent events (e.g., the use of torture in interrogations and the increased invasiveness of domestic surveillance by the United States since 9/11) make it clear that such thinking would be naive. It is important to note that EEG- and MRI-based techniques are impractical for surveillance because the former require the attachment of electrodes to the scalp and the latter require that the head remain stationary inside a strong magnetic field.

One might argue that the neuroscientific examination of a criminal suspect is inherently unethical because it violates the suspect's right-to-privacy. If our own thoughts are open to examination, the argument goes, then nothing is private. Although I appreciate this argument, its application to memory detection is dubious, for the following reason: memory detection is not mind reading. All of the techniques reviewed previously measure neural activity associated with the recognition of old events. Recognition is a thoughtless ability possessed by the most primitive of animals. Engineers build machines that perform recognition tasks, and although these machines are far from simple, their complexity is sensory/perceptual, rather than cognitive, in nature. In some cases (e.g., indirect tests of priming) the brain recognizes an event without the mind being consciously aware. So a true positive result on a memory detection test is achieved without reading the examinee's mind. All the test is doing is determining whether the brain has been exposed to crime-relevant information. Is this logically different than judging whether a suspect was present at the crime by using physical evidence found on the suspect's body (e.g., finding a strand of a rape victim's pubic hair amid the pubic hair of a suspect and using the hair as evidence)?

Thoughts aside, it could be argued that one's memories are private. Consider the analogy of the person as a camera, in which the eyes are the lens and the brain is the storage medium (e.g., memory card). It is disturbing to think that an investigator could access one's memory card, and the unethical use of such technology is an oft-explored theme in science fiction. However, the camera analogy breaks down in a way that should alleviate most concerns. First of all, imagine that the memory card is stuck in the camera and cannot be removed. Next imagine that there is no way to transfer the image files to another device. Lastly, imagine that there is no LCD (liquid crystal display) screen on the camera to allow one to view the image files. The only access to the files is to confirm their existence by taking the same picture again, in which case the camera can signal that it has taken the picture before. This is reasonably analogous to the access that a memory detection examiner has to an examinee's memories. It would be difficult to argue that this type of evidence gathering is more invasive to one's privacy than other accepted types of evidence gathering (e.g., tissue samples for DNA testing).

Compare the person-as-camera analogy to a situation in which the perpetrator records the crime on a video or still camera so that he can relive the crime later. Such a recording contains far more information than would be uncovered by a memory detection examination. Who, on ethical grounds, would object to the recording being used as evidence? One who argues that memories are private might also be logically forced to argue that such a recording is private.

Slippery-slope arguments are also invalid when applied to memory detection. For example, one might be concerned that methodological advancements in memory detection techniques might allow an examiner to read out the memory that is currently being retrieved by the examinee. But this is purely science fiction. Recall that multiple memories are stored in a single localized network. ERP and fMRI are only equipped to gauge the level of activation in such a network, and the level of activation provides only rudimentary information about one's memory state. Perhaps someday a completely different technique will be developed that enables memory reading. However, because such a technique would not simply be an improvement of existing techniques, there is no reason to be concerned that the current acceptance of ERP and fMRI techniques as ethical will later be regretted. In other words, ethical issues should be revisited each time a new technique is developed.

The compulsory examination of a suspect's memory for crime-relevant details could be viewed as violating the suspect's right against self-incrimination. On the other hand, if the examination is voluntary, the suspect should rightly be concerned about how the courts will perceive a refusal to be examined. Similar issues arise with uncooperative witnesses—should they be forced to submit to a memory detection test?

There are obvious ethical issues concerning whether memory detection will be used only for its stated purpose. An example of an inappropriate use in a forensic context would be including events that are relevant to a second crime for which there is no probable cause to think that the examinee was involved. Legal systems in free societies have a long history of successfully excluding evidence gathered in such an inappropriate manner. It is important that legal systems remain vigilant about ensuring that memory detection evidence is limited to the crime for which the examinee was knowingly examined.

Neurotechnologies carry considerable weight among those (e.g., jurors, judges, suspects, witnesses) who do not understand them (Wolpe et al. 2005). In the Harrington case (reviewed in following text), a key witness whose testimony contributed to a conviction later recanted his testimony when presented with the results of a post-conviction Brain Fingerprinting test. A guilty suspect who is unaware of the false-negative problem might volunteer a confession because he thinks he has no chance of producing a negative result. The courts have to decide whether such consequences amount to coercion.

Legal Issues

Legal Admissibility

P300 memory detection test results have already been considered by courts in the United States. In Harrington v. State of Iowa (2000), a negative result on a Brain Fingerprinting test (conducted 23 years after the crime) was submitted by the plaintiff as part of a post-conviction petition for a new trial in a murder case. In 2001, an Iowa District Court judge admitted the Brain Fingerprinting evidence based on his judgment that the evidence met the Daubert standard (Daubert v. Merrell Dow Pharmaceuticals, 1993), but denied the petition because he determined that the Brain Fingerprinting evidence (and other new evidence) would probably not have changed the outcome of the original trial. Subsequently, a key witness whose testimony contributed to the conviction in the original trial recanted his testimony. According to Brain Fingerprinting Laboratories, the recantation was triggered by the presentation of Harrington's Brain Fingerprinting test results to the witness. The witness's new testimony, along with other new information, was included in an appeal to the Iowa Supreme Court, the District Court's decision was overruled, and a new trial was ordered. When the prosecution decided not to retry the case, Harrington was released.

Let us examine the judge's decision to admit P300 memory detection test evidence based on the Daubert standard. In *Daubert v. Merrell Dow Pharmaceuticals* (1993), the Supreme Court of the United States recommended that judges consider four factors when deciding whether to admit expert scientific testimony: 1) Has the technique been tested? 2) Has it been subjected to peer-review and been published? 3) What is its error rate? and 4) Is it generally accepted in the relevant scientific community? To aid in making his decision, the judge in the Harrington case heard testimony from three P300 experts: Lawrence Farwell (who administered Harrington's Brain Fingerprinting test), William Iacono, and Emanuel Donchin. It became clear to the judge that P300 potentials were more likely to meet the standard than the other potentials used by Farwell's Brain Fingerprinting test, and thus the latter were excluded.[5] Although this exclusion was a wise decision, the judge failed to make the important distinction between P300 effects in general, and the specific use of P300 effects for forensic memory detection. P300 effects in general are very well established in the field of psychophysiology, and this was reflected in the testimony of the P300 experts. However, as should be clear from my earlier review, the use of P300 effects for forensic memory detection is far from established. Consider each of the four factors recommended in *Daubert v. Merrell Dow Pharmaceuticals* (1993). The P300 memory detection technique has not been tested in the field and has not been tested in laboratory or field situations with poor encoding conditions and long retention intervals (factor 1). It has been peer-reviewed and published (factor 2), but not to the point that it is generally accepted by the relevant scientific community (factor 4). Its error rates in relevant situations are unknown, and there is reason to believe that the false negative rate in relevant situations will be high (factor 3).

The decision by the Iowa District Court judge to admit P300 memory detection evidence based on the Daubert standard is not binding on any court in Iowa or elsewhere (Moenssens 2002). Nevertheless it sets a precedent that will surely be considered for future cases in which P300 evidence is submitted. Thus, with all due to respect to the judge, who surely made the appropriate decision given the limited evidence before him, I would like to offer the opinion that his decision was wrong. As of the publication date of this article, P300 memory detection tests do not yet meet at least three of the four criteria recommended in Daubert. The use of priming effects and old/new effects for forensic memory detection are even further away from meeting the Daubert standard.

Some jurisdictions in the United States use the standard recommended in *Frye v. United States* (1923), according to which the admission of scientific evidence should be based on whether the technique has "general acceptance" in the relevant scientific field. Although priming effects, old/new effects, and P300 effects have general acceptance as measures of mnemonic processing, their application to criminal investigations will not have general acceptance until the necessary research (reviewed previously) has been conducted. In other words, the memory detection techniques reviewed here do not yet meet the Frye standard.

The False-Negative Problem

What made the admission of P300 evidence in the Harrington case particularly shocking was that the retention interval was 23 years, and the peer-reviewed publication on which the Brain Fingerprinting test was based (Farwell and Donchin 1991) used a retention interval of one day. A negative result on a memory detection test with a 23-year retention interval is a completely meaningless piece of information for those trying to determine the examinee's innocence or guilt.

Based on the scientific evidence reviewed earlier, it is clear that the forensic application of memory detection is more likely to be limited by false negatives than false positives. Ideally, any forensic technique would have low rates of both false negatives and false positives. Nevertheless, because the criminal justice system is based on the principle that it is worse to convict an innocent person (a false-positive error) than to acquit a guilty person (a false-negative error), and the likelihood of the former might be low, memory detection has forensic potential as a prosecution tool. Assuming that future research using poor encoding conditions and long retention intervals confirms a high false-negative rate, the courts would then have to decide whether to allow evidence from a tool that cannot be used to support the innocence claims of defendants. This hypothetical imbalance would also have interesting implications for the commercialization of memory detection services because such an industry would have only prosecutors (and not defendants) as potential clients. Ethical issues related to rights against self-incrimination have caused some companies developing forensic neurotechnologies to claim that their products will only be used to exonerate the innocent (Pearson 2006). In this context, the false-negative problem creates a real dilemma for companies developing memory detection tools.

A False-Positive Problem?

Some may think that I have underestimated the likelihood of false positives. For example, even when a memory detection technique has the appropriate level of specificity, crime-relevant events are likely to produce old-like activity in some innocent examinees some of the time. There are at least three methodological constraints designed to address this problem. First, crime-relevant events (e.g., probes) should always be compared with crime-irrelevant events (e.g., irrelevants), and the latter are (in theory) just as likely as the former to produce old-like activity in innocent examinees. Second, there should always be multiple crime-relevant events, and when only a subset of these trigger old-like activity, a negative result should be concluded. The appropriate criterion for concluding a positive result based on the level of brain activity produced by crime-relevant events is yet to be determined. This criterion must take into consideration that the criminal justice system abhors false positives, and that reducing false positives by adjusting the threshold used for declaring a test result positive will increase false negatives. A third methodological constraint requires that the memory detection test be given to a control group of known innocent examinees. A positive result for any of the control examinees would suggest that the test is flawed. The use of control subjects is particularly important because of concerns about the subjectivity of event selection (United States General Accounting Office 2001); in other words, if event selection biases a test to a positive result, then the results of the control subjects should identify the bias. Note that, because a memory detection test cannot be given to a control group of known guilty examinees, it is difficult to know whether the test is biased to produce a negative result, thus compounding the false-negative problem.

A second example of a false positive is when an innocent witness to a crime, for whom all crime-relevant events would presumably produce old-like activity, tests positive. Such a witness would not be protected by the aforementioned methodological constraints. It is thus important that memory detection test results are always used in conjunction with other types of evidence that would exonerate the witness. In other words, a positive result should be considered evidence consistent with guilt rather than evidence of guilt (Illes 2004).

Successful memory detection requires that details of the crime are only known to the guilty examinee. If details are made public by the media or during legal proceedings, the selection of crime-relevant events becomes extremely difficult, if not impossible. Despite this problem, Brain Fingerprinting Laboratories has put itself in the ridiculous position of selecting probes in cases that have already been publicized in the media and in the courts. If investigators or defense lawyers plan to put suspects through a memory detection test, it is extremely important that details of the crime are not made publicly available. Once details have been made available, the selection of crime-relevant events becomes futile and a memory detection test becomes useless.

Advantages of Memory Detection Over Lie Detection

Some have erroneously implied or suggested that memory detection tests are actually lie detection tests (e.g., Farwell and Donchin 1991; Garland and Glimcher 2006; Rosenfeld 2005). As should be clear from the previous review, priming effects, old/new effects, and P300 effects measure recognition rather than deception. Moreover, they can (and should) be measured without dishonest responding. Lie detection is fraught with issues concerning what defines lying and truthfulness and whether there is a consistent neural state associated with each (Buller 2005; Illes 2004; Wolpe et al. 2005). These issues do not apply to memory detection, which measures simple brain responses consistently evoked by stimulus events depending on their familiarity. Lie detection is also infamously vulnerable to countermeasures (National Research Council 2003). Although much research is yet to be done, some or all of the memory detection techniques reviewed here may prove to be sufficiently automatic to be relatively invulnerable to countermeasures.

Notes

1. Memory *dampening* techniques, which are pharmaceutical in nature (Brunet et al. 2007; Doyère et al. 2007; Pitman et al. 2002), are different than erasure techniques in that they are designed to reduce the emotional intensity of memories (e.g., for the treatment of post-traumatic stress disorder). Such techniques are not hindered by the distribution and network characteristics of memory storage because the emotional component of memories is handled by localized processes that specifically act on those memories that are currently active (i.e., new or reactivated).
2. Two hypotheses stated here are not without controversy among memory scientists. Namely that: 1) familiarity and recollection are supported by distinct retrieval processes, and 2) the mid-frontal and parietal old/new effects represent familiarity and recollection, respectively. Nevertheless, the application to memory detection is unaffected by these scientific controversies. In other words, as long as an old/new effect distinguishes old from new events, it does not matter whether that effect is uniquely associated with a particular mnemonic process or experience.
3. The Brain Fingerprinting test is a P300 memory detection test originally developed by Farwell and Donchin (1991) and more recently commercialized by Brain Fingerprinting Laboratories, Inc., Seattle, WA (Rosenfeld 2005). The PBS special was part of the Innovation series, and originally aired in May 2004; available at: http://www.pbs.org/wnet/innovation/episode8.html (accessed December 7, 2007).
4. The attenuation of the P300 under high mental effort conditions suggests another possible countermeasure strategy in which the guilty examinee increases task difficulty by covertly performing a second task during the memory detection test (Bashore and Rapp 1993). One limitation of this strategy is that the constant performance of the second task should affect the P300 for all stimuli (i.e., not just probes), and thus the probe P300 should still look target-like.
5. The scientific problems associated with the potentials, other than the P300 potential, used in the Brain Fingerprinting test were reviewed by Rosenfeld (2005). Moenssens (2002), like the Iowa District Court judge, is under the mistaken assumption that the only science yet to be conducted before the Brain Fingerprinting test meets the Daubert standard relates to the these other potentials. I, on the other hand, submit that the use of P300 memory detection does not yet meet the Daubert standard.

References

Allen, J. J. 2002. The role of psychophysiology in clinical assessment: ERPs in the evaluation of memory. *Psychophysiology* 39(3): 261–280.

Allen, J. J., W. G. Iacono, and K. D. Danielson. 1992. The identification of concealed memories using the event-related potential and implicit behavioral measures: a methodology for prediction in the face of individual differences. *Psychophysiology* 29(5): 504–522.

Bashore, T. R., and P. E. Rapp. 1993. Are there alternatives to traditional polygraph procedures? *Psychological Bulletin* 113(1): 3–22.

Bentley, P., P. Vuilleumier, C.M. Thiel, J. Driver, and R. J. Dolan. 2003. Effects of attention and emotion on repetition priming and their modulation by cholinergic enhancement. *Journal of Neurophysiology* 90(2): 1171–1181.

Bridson, N. C., C. S, Fraser, J. E. Herron, and E. L. Wilding. 2006. Electrophysiological correlates of familiarity in recognition memory and exclusion tasks. *Brain Research* 1114(1): 149–160.

Brunet, A., S. P. Orr, J. Tremblay, K. Robertson, K. Nader, and R. K. Pitman. 2007. Effect of post-retrieval propranolol on psychophysiologic responding during subsequent script-driven traumatic imagery in post-traumatic stress disorder. *Journal of Psychiatric Research.*

Buller, T. 2005. Can we scan for truth in a society of liars? *American Journal of Bioethics* 5(2): 58–60.

Cave, C. B. 1997. Very long-lasting priming in picture naming. *Psychological Science* 8(4): 322–325.

Curran, T. 2004. Effects of attention and confidence on the hypothesized ERP correlates of recollection and familiarity. *Neuropsychologia* 42(8): 1088–1106.

Curran, T., and A. M. Cleary. 2003. Using ERPs to dissociate recollection from familiarity in picture recognition. *Cognitive Brain Research* 15(2): 191–205.

Curran, T., and W. J. Friedman. 2004. ERP old/new effects at different retention intervals in recency discrimination tasks. *Cognitive Brain Research* 18(2): 107–120.

Czernochowski, D., A. Mecklinger, M. Johansson, and M. Brinkmann. 2005. Age-related differences in familiarity and recollection: ERP evidence from a recognition memory study in children and young adults. *Cognitive, Affective, and Behavioral Neuroscience* 5(4): 417–433.

Daselaar, S. M., M. S. Fleck, and R. Cabeza. 2006. Triple dissociation in the medial temporal lobes: recollection, familiarity, and novelty. *Journal of Neurophysiology* 96(4): 1902–1911.

Daubert v. Merrell Dow Pharmaceuticals. 1993. United States Supreme Court, 509 U.S 579.

Doyère V., J. Debiec, M. H. Monfils, G. E. Schafe, and J. E. LeDoux. 2007. Synapse-specific reconsolidation of distinct fear memories in the lateral amygdala. *Nature Neuroscience* 10(4): 414–416.

Düzel, E., F. Vargha-Khadem, H. J. Heinze, and M. Mishkin. 2001. Brain activity evidence for recognition without recollection after early hippocampal damage. *Proceedings of the National Academy of Sciences USA* 98(14): 8101–8106.

Dywan, J., S. Segalowitz, and A. Arsenault. 2002. Electrophysiological response during source memory decisions in older and younger adults. *Brain and Cognition* 49(3): 322–340.

Eger, E., R. N. Henson, J. Driver, and R. J. Dolan. 2004. BOLD repetition decreases in object-responsive ventral visual areas depend on spatial attention. *Journal of Neurophysiology* 92(2): 1241–1247.

Eternal Sunshine of the Spotless Mind. 2004. Focus Features.

Farwell, L. A., and E. Donchin. 1991. The truth will out: interrogative polygraphy ("lie detection") with event-related brain potentials. *Psychophysiology* 28(5): 531–547.

Friedman, D., and R. Johnson. 2000. Event-related potential (ERP) studies of memory encoding and retrieval: a selective review. *Microscopy Research and Technique* 51(1): 6–28.

Frye v. United States. 1923. District of Columbia Court of Appeals, 293 F. 1013.

Garland, B., and P. W. Glimcher. 2006. Cognitive neuroscience and the law. *Current Opinion in Neurobiology* 16(2): 130–134.

Grill-Spector, K., R. Henson, and A. Martin. 2006. Repetition and the brain: neural models of stimulus-specific effects. *Trends in Cognitive Sciences* 10(1): 14–23.

Harrington v. State of Iowa. 2000. Pottawattamie County District Court, case number PCCV073247.

Henson, R. N. 2003. Neuroimaging studies of priming. *Progress in Neurobiology* 70(1): 53–81.

Henson, R. N., M. D. Rugg, T. Shallice, O. Josephs, and R. J. Dolan. 1999. Recollection and familiarity in recognition memory: An event-related functional magnetic resonance imaging study. *Journal of Neuroscience* 19(10): 3962–3972.

Henson, R. N., T. Shallice, M. L. Gorno-Tempini, and R. J. Dolan. 2002. Face repetition effects in implicit and explicit memory tests as measured by fMRI. *Cerebral Cortex* 12(2): 178–186.

Herron, J. E., and M. D. Rugg. 2003. Strategic influences on recollection in the exclusion task: electrophysiological evidence. *Psychonomic Bulletin and Review* 10(3): 703–710.

Illes, J. 2004. A fish story? Brain maps, lie detection, and personhood. *Cerebrum: The Dana Forum on Brain Science* 6(4): 73–80.

Innovation: Brain Fingerprinting. Thirteen/WNET New York, 2004.

Jacoby, L. L. 1991. A process dissociation framework: separating automatic from intentional uses of memory. *Journal of Memory and Language* 30(5): 513–541.

Johnson, R. Jr., J. Barnhardt, and J. Zhu. 2003. The deceptive response: effects of response conflict and strategic monitoring on the late positive component and episodic memory-related brain activity. *Biological Psychology* 64(3): 217–253.

Koutstaal, W., A. D. Wagner, M. Rotte, A. Maril, R. L. Buckner, and D. L. Schacter. 2001. Perceptual specificity in visual object priming: functional magnetic resonance imaging evidence for a laterality difference in fusiform cortex. *Neuropsychologia* 39(2): 184–199.

Mecklinger, A. 2006. Electrophysiological measures of familiarity memory. *Clinical EEG and Neuroscience* 37(4): 292–299.

Meister, I. G., J. Weidemann, H. Foltys, et al. 2005. The neural correlate of very-long-term picture priming. *European Journal of Neuroscience* 21(4): 1101–1106.

Miller, A. R., J. P. Rosenfeld, M. Soskins, and M. Jhee. 2002. P300 amplitude and topography in an autobiographical oddball paradigm involving simulated amnesia. *Journal of Psychophysiology* 16(1): 1–11.

Mitchell, D. B. 2006. Nonconscious priming after 17 years: invulnerable implicit memory? *Psychological Science* 17(11): 925–929.

Moenssens, A. A. 2002. Brain Fingerprinting: can it be used to detect the innocence of persons charged with a crime? *UMKC Law Review* 70(4): 891–920.

National Research Council. 2003. *The polygraph and lie detection.* Committee to Review the Scientific Evidence on the Polygraph. Division of Behavioral and Social Sciences and Education. Washington, D. C.: The National Academies Press.

Orwell, G. 1949. *Nineteen Eighty-Four: A Novel.* (Reprint, Markham, Ontario Penguin Books Canada, 1975).

Pearson, H. 2006. Lure of lie detectors spooks ethicists. *Nature* 441(7096): 918–919.

Pitman, R. K., K. M. Sanders, R. M. Zusman, et al. 2002. Pilot study of secondary prevention of posttraumatic stress disorder with propranolol, *Biological Psychiatry* 51(2): 189–192.

Polich, J., and A. Kok. 1995. Cognitive and biological determinants of P300: an integrative review. *Biological Psychology* 41(2): 103–146.

Rosenfeld, J. P. 2005. 'Brain Fingerprinting': a critical analysis. *The Scientific Review of Mental Health Practice* 4(1): 20–37.

Rosenfeld, J. P., J. R. Biroschak, and J. J. Furedy. 2006. P300-based detection of concealed autobiographical versus incidentally acquired information in target and non-target paradigms. *International Journal of Psychophysiology* 60(3): 251–259.

Rosenfeld, J. P., B. Cantwell, V. T. Nasman, V. Wojdac, S. Ivanov, and L. Mazzeri. 1988. A modified, event-related potential-based guilty knowledge test. *International Journal of Neuroscience* 42(1–2): 157–161.

Rosenfeld, J. P., A. Rao, M. Soskins, and A. R. Miller. 2003. Scaled P300 scalp distribution correlates of verbal deception in an autobiographical oddball paradigm: control for task demand. *Journal of Psychophysiology* 17(1): 14–22.

Rosenfeld, J. P., E. Shue, and E. Singer. 2007. Single versus multiple probe blocks of P300-based concealed information tests for self-referring versus incidentally obtained information. *Biological Psychology* 74(3): 396–404.

Rosenfeld, J. P., M. Soskins, G. Bosh, and A. Ryan. 2004. Simple, effective countermeasures to P300-based tests of detection of concealed information. *Psychophysiology* 41(2): 205–219.

Rugg, M. D., K. Allan, and C. S. Birch. 2000. Electrophysiological evidence for the modulation of retrieval orientation by depth of study processing. *Journal of Cognitive Neuroscience* 12(4): 664–678.

Rugg, M. D., R. E. Mark, P. Walla, A. M. Schloerscheidt, C. S. Birch, and K. Allan. 1998. Dissociation of the neural correlates of implicit and explicit memory. *Nature* 392(6676): 595–598.

Rugg, M. D., and A. P. Yonelinas. 2003. Human recognition memory: a cognitive neuroscience perspective. *Trends in Cognitive Sciences* 7(7): 313–319.

Schacter, D. L. 2001. *The Seven Sins of Memory*. New York: Houghton Mifflin.

Schacter, D. L., I. G. Dobbins, and D. M. Schnyer. 2004. Specificity of priming: a cognitive neuroscience perspective. *Nature Reviews Neuroscience* 5(11): 853–862.

Schloerscheidt, A. M., and M. D. Rugg. 2004. The impact of change in stimulus format on the electrophysiological indices of recognition. *Neuropsychologia* 42(4): 451–466.

Sententia, W. 2001. Brain Fingerprinting: databodies to databrains. *Journal of Cognitive Liberty* 2(3): 31–46.

Spencer, K. M., A. E. Vila, and E. Donchin. 2000. On the search for the neurophysiological manifestation of recollective experience. *Psychophysiology* 37(4): 494–506.

Tardif, H. P., R. J. Barry, A. M. Fox, and S. J. Johnstone. 2000. Detection of feigned recognition memory impairment using the old/new effect of the event-related potential. *International Journal of Psychophysiology* 36(1): 1–9.

Tsivilis, D., L. J. Otten, and M. D. Rugg. 2001. Context effects on the neural correlates of recognition memory: an electrophysiological study. *Neuron* 31(3): 497–505.

United States General Accounting Office. 2001. *Federal Agency Views on the Potential Application of "Brain Fingerprinting."* GAO-02–22.

van Hooff, J. C. 2005. The influence of encoding intention on electrophysiological indices of recognition memory. *International Journal of Psychophysiology* 56(1): 25–36.

van Hooff, J. C., C. H. Brunia, and J. J. Allen. 1996. Event-related potentials as indirect measures of recognition memory. *International Journal of Psychophysiology* 21(1): 15–31.

van Hooff, J. C., and S. Golden. 2002. Validation of an event-related potential memory assessment procedure: Effects of incidental and intentional learning. *Journal of Psychophysiology* 16(1): 12–22.

van Turennout, M., L. Bielamowicz, and A. Martin. 2003. Modulation of neural activity during object naming: effects of time and practice. *Cerebral Cortex* 13(4): 381–391.

van Turennout, M., T. Ellmore, and A. Martin. 2000. Long-lasting cortical plasticity in the object naming system. *Nature Neuroscience* 3(12): 1329–1334.

Vuilleumier, P., R. N. Henson, J. Driver, and R. J. Dolan. 2002. Multiple levels of visual object constancy revealed by event-related fMRI of repetition priming. *Nature Neuroscience* 5(5): 491–499.

Vuilleumier, P., S. Schwartz, S. Duhoux, R. J. Dolan, and J. Driver. 2005. Selective attention modulates neural substrates of repetition priming and "implicit" visual memory: suppressions and enhancements revealed by fMRI. *Journal of Cognitive Neuroscience* 17(8): 1245–1260.

Wiggs, C. L., and A. Martin. 1998. Properties and mechanisms of perceptual priming. *Current Opinion in Neurobiology* 8(2): 227–233.

Wolk, D. A., D. L. Schacter, M. Lygizos, et al. 2006. ERP correlates of recognition memory: effects of retention interval and false alarms. *Brain Research* 1096(1): 148–162.

Wolpe, P. R., K. R. Foster, and D. D. Langleben. 2005. Emerging neurotechnologies for lie-detection: promises and perils. *American Journal of Bioethics* 5(2): 39–49.

Yi, D. J., and M. M. Chun. 2005. Attentional modulation of learning-related repetition attenuation effects in human parahippocampal cortex. *Journal of Neuroscience* 25(14): 3593–3600.

Yi, D. J., T. A. Kelley, R. Marois, and M. M. Chun. 2006. Attentional modulation of repetition attenuation is anatomically dissociable for scenes and faces. *Brain Research* 1080(1): 53–62.

Yonelinas, A. P. 2002. The nature of recollection and familiarity: a review of 30 years of research. *Journal of Memory and Language* 46(3): 441–517.

Yonelinas, A. P., L. J. Otten, K. N. Shaw, and M. D. Rugg. 2005. Separating the brain regions involved in recollection and familiarity in recognition memory. *Journal of Neuroscience* 25(11): 3002–3008.

Reading Analytically

1. Before examining both the potential gain and the potential harm of applying this technology to criminal justice, the author must first describe how it works. What techniques does the author use to make this technology accessible to an audience beyond those in the field?
2. One key issue in evaluating the science of this technology is the "false negative" and "false positive" problems. What are those problems? Why is each significant in different ways?
3. After reading the various facets of the debate offered here, where do you tend to stand on the issue? Try to articulate your own position, drawing upon specific evidence from the article itself.

Reading Across Disciplinary Communities

1. Though this piece is written for a journal in bioethics, it must also cross into the discipline of legal studies. What are the key legal issues that Meegan raises? Try to explain each of those principles in your own words.
2. Scan the list of sources on the reference page, and make a list of the various disciplines that are represented there. What does this list tell you about the process of doing interdisciplinary research?

O. CARTER SNEAD

Neuroimaging and the "Complexity" of Capital Punishment

In this essay, a law professor investigates the growing interest in the potential for neuroimaging as evidence for both prosecutors and defense attorneys. He also examines the reciprocal interest of cognitive neurosciences and "how their discipline might impact the law." O. Carter Snead, a graduate of Georgetown University's School of Law is now a faculty member in Notre Dame's law school. He has also served on the President's Council on Bioethics.

This essay, written for an audience of lawyers and legal scholars, explores the viability of neuroimaging as a form of evidence. As such, it draws upon the expertise of this discipline to define the requirements of reasonable and admissible evidence as it relates to the current state of the technology. As you read, consider the standards of the law that are employed here, as well as the necessity of constructing a logical argument that is at the heart of this discipline.

"Can brain scans be used to determine whether a person is inclined toward criminality or violent behavior?"[1]

This question, asked by Senator Joseph Biden of Delaware at the hearing considering the nomination of John G. Roberts to be Chief Justice of the United States, illustrates the extent to which cognitive neuroscience[2]—increasingly augmented by the growing powers of neuroimaging—has captured the imagination of those who make, enforce, interpret, and study the law. Judges, both state and federal, have convened conferences to discuss the legal ramifications of developments in cognitive neuroscience. Scholarly volumes have been devoted to the subject. The President's Council on Bioethics convened several sessions to discuss cognitive neuroscience and its potential impact on theories of moral and legal responsibility. The United States General Accounting Office drafted a report surveying the views of government officials representing the CIA, Department of Defense, Secret Service, and FBI on the potential uses of "brain fingerprinting," a lie-detection technique that utilizes functional neuroimaging.[3] More recently, civil libertarians have expressed suspicion and concern that the United States government is using various neuroimaging techniques in the war on terrorism.[4] Members of the personal injury bar have urged the use of functional neuroimaging to "make mild and moderate brain and nervous injuries 'visible' to jurors."[5] Not surprisingly, members of the civil defense bar have published articles criticizing the reliability of such evidence and arguing that it should be inadmissible.[6] Criminal defense attorneys have likewise expressed a strong interest in using neuroimaging evidence to help their clients.

The attraction of the legal community to cognitive neuroscience is by no means unreciprocated. Cognitive neuroscientists have expressed profound interest in how their discipline might impact the law. Michael Gazzaniga (who coined the term "cognitive neuroscience") recently predicted that someday advances in neuroscience will "dominate the entire legal system."[7] Practitioners of cognitive neuroscience seem particularly drawn to criminal law;[8] more specifically, they have evinced an interest in the death penalty. Indeed, from their work in the courtroom and their arguments in the public square, a well-formed cognitive neuroscience project to reform capital sentencing has emerged.

This article seeks to identify, articulate, take seriously, and provide a critique of this project in light of its own objectives. In the short term, cognitive neuroscientists seek to assist defendants in their mitigation claims by invoking cutting-edge brain-imaging research on the neurobiological roots of criminal violence. Neuroimaging experts appeal to such evidence to bolster defendants' claims that, although legally guilty, they do not

For the long term, cognitive neuroscientists aim to draw upon the tools of their discipline to embarrass, discredit, and ultimately overthrow retribution as a distributive justification for punishment.

deserve to die because the abnormal structure and/or function of their brains diminishes their culpability.

For the long term, cognitive neuroscientists aim to draw upon the tools of their discipline to embarrass, discredit, and ultimately overthrow retribution[9] as a distributive justification[10] for punishment. The architects of the cognitive neuroscience project regard retribution as the root cause of the brutality and inhumanity of the American criminal justice system, generally, and the institution of capital punishment, in particular. In its place, they argue for the adoption of a criminal law regime animated solely by the forward-looking (consequentialist) aim of avoiding social harms. This new framework, they hope, will usher in a new era of what some have referred to as "therapeutic justice"[11] for capital defendants, which is meant to be both more humane and more compassionate.

This article provides a friendly critique of the cognitive neuroscience project. That is, the analysis proceeds from a position of sympathy and solidarity with the humanitarian impulses—and the general antipathy for the death penalty—that animate the cognitive neuroscientists working in this field. Thus, the wisdom and soundness of the cognitive neuroscience project will be appraised according to the metric of its own humanitarian ambitions: namely, success in helping convicted capital defendants persuade jurors and judges not to impose a sentence of death, thereby creating a more compassionate and humane legal regime for such defendants. Unfortunately, it seems unlikely that these ends would be achieved if the short- and long-term aims of cognitive neuroscientists were ever actually realized. To the contrary, it seems likely that the criminal regime desired by cognitive neuroscientists would, tragically and ironically, prove far harsher and less humane for capital defendants than the current system.

Why? Simply put, the project, taken as a whole, is utterly at war with itself. The short-term aim relies on a particular theory of mitigation that is firmly grounded in retribution—a principle whose foundations are explicitly rejected by the architects of the cognitive neuroscience project. Conversely, the long-term aim is devoted to dismantling the doctrinal foundation (i.e., retribution) upon which the short-term aspiration depends. Thus, the success of the long-term goal would necessarily defeat the short-term goal. Worse still, the extant mechanisms that the long-term project would explicitly leave in place (that is, those features of the capital sentencing framework animated solely by the consequentialist goal of avoiding societal harms) constitute arguably the single gravest threat to a capital defendant's life. If the capital sentencing regime were remade according to the aspirations of the long-term plan, this threat would be dramatically amplified precisely because of the research of cognitive neuroscientists. Indeed, it is only by virtue of the doctrine of just deserts that neuroimaging evidence of the roots of criminal violence can be understood as reducing a capital defendant's culpability. This conclusion accords with the (perhaps counterintuitive) fact that just deserts has served as arguably the most valuable limiting principle in the American jurisprudence of capital sentencing, and perhaps the criminal law more broadly.

As Paul Robinson has observed, within the context of sentencing, desert and dangerousness inevitably conflict as distributive criteria: "To advance one, the system must sacrifice the other. The irreconcilable differences reflect the fact that prevention and desert seek to achieve different goals. Incapacitation concerns itself with the future—avoiding future crimes. Desert concerns itself with the past—allocating punishment for past offenses."[12] The thrust-and-parry of this conflict is played out in dramatic fashion in the capital context. On the one hand, capital defendants introduce mitigating evidence to diminish their moral culpability, thus seeking a final refuge in the concept of retribution. On the other, the prosecution tenders evidence of future dangerousness, trying to stoke the consequentialist fears of the jury about violent acts that the defendant might commit if he is not permanently incapacitated by execution. In capital sentencing, pure consequentialism is the gravest threat to the defendant's life, while appeals to retributive justice are his last, best hope.

> ***Thus, in a final ironic twist, once retribution is replaced with a regime single-mindedly concerned with the prediction of crime and the incapacitation of criminals, the only possible use in capital sentencing of the neuroimaging research on the roots of criminal violence is to demonstrate the aggravating factor of future dangerousness.***

The long-term aspiration of cognitive neuroscience decisively resolves this conflict between desert and crime control in favor of the latter by removing any consideration of diminished culpability. In so doing, the long-term scheme eliminates the last safe haven for a capital defendant whose sanity, capacity for the requisite *mens rea,* competence, and guilt are no longer at issue. Thus, in a final ironic twist, once retribution is replaced with a regime single-mindedly concerned with the prediction of crime and the incapacitation of criminals, the only possible use in capital sentencing of the neuroimaging research on the roots of criminal violence is to demonstrate the aggravating factor of future dangerousness.

Imagine for a moment how a jury concerned solely with avoiding future harms would regard an fMRI or PET image that purported to show the biological causes of a non-excusing disposition to criminal violence. Likely, neuroimaging would radically amplify, in the minds of jurors, the aggravating effect of a diagnosis of APD (antisocial personality disorder) or psychopathy. In a sentencing system that focused the jury's deliberation solely on the question of identifying and preventing crime, the work of the cognitive neuroscience project's architects would be transformed from a vehicle for seeking mercy into a tool that counsels the imposition of death.

It is only through the lens of just deserts that such evidence could possibly be regarded as mitigating. This conclusion is bolstered by capital defense experts who have observed that "[e]vidence of neurological impairment . . . can be devastatingly damaging to the case for life. In presenting such evidence to a jury, counsel must be careful to avoid creating the impression that the defendant is 'damaged goods' and beyond repair."[13] In the regime contemplated by the long-term aspiration—where claims of diminished culpability are untenable—this is the only permissible inference that jurors can draw. Arguing for compassion or leniency in such a system would be as nonsensical as seeking mercy for a dangerously defective car on its way to the junkyard to be crushed into scrap metal. Reconciliation and forgiveness are not useful concepts as applied to soulless cars; they are only intelligible as applied to sinners.

The grave implications of the long-term aspiration for capital sentencing come into even sharper relief when one considers the role that retributive justice has played in modern death penalty jurisprudence. Contrary to the intuitions of the project's architects, retribution has served as a crucial limiting principle on capital sentencing. The Supreme Court, itself,[14] has referred to a "narrowing jurisprudence" of just deserts, which limits the ultimate punishment to "a narrow category of the most serious crimes" and defendants "whose extreme culpability makes them 'the most deserving of execution.'"[15] In the name of retributive justice, the Court has barred the execution of mentally retarded defendants,[16] children who were under the age of 18 when the offense was committed,[17] rapists,[18] and defendants convicted of felony murder who did not actually kill or attempt to kill the victim.[19] In each instance, the Court ruled that such defendants were not eligible for the death penalty because such punishment would be categorically disproportionate to their personal culpability. These same results could not have been reached if deterrence were the sole animating principle guiding the Court: General deterrence—i.e., whether the death penalty for a specific offense or a specific class of offenders will reduce crime overall—may be a contested issue. However, specific deterrence is always advanced by the execution of the convicted person, since execution guarantees that the same convicted person will not cause future harm.

In fact, the widely shared intuition that seems to be motivating the long-term aspiration—namely, that retributive justice is the primary source of the brutality and harshness of the modern American criminal justice system—may generally be misguided. Many features of the criminal justice system that are frequently criticized as draconian and inhumane are, in fact, motivated by a purely consequentialist crime-control rationale. Such measures include laws that authorize life sentences for recidivists (i.e., "three strikes" laws); laws that reduce the age at which offenders can be tried as adults; laws that punish gang membership; laws that require the registration of sex offenders; laws that dramatically increase sentences by virtue of past history; and, most paradigmatically, laws that provide for the involuntary civil commitment of sexual offenders who show difficulty controlling their behavior.[20] These laws are the progeny of the principle animating the long-term aspiration and some are worrisome examples of its possible implications.

Regardless of neuroimaging's capacity or incapacity to predict such criminal behavior reliably, there is already a powerful demand for the use of such techniques in crime control.

Paul Robinson has offered a provocative genealogy for such laws that provides further grounds for caution. He makes a powerful argument that abandoning retributive justice in favor of consequentialist values of rehabilitation laid the groundwork for the draconian measures described above. According to Robinson's account, once "the limited ability of social and medical science to rehabilitate offenders became clear," reformers tried to salvage what was left of the consequentialist project by turning to incapacitation as the principle means of avoiding future crimes.[21] He concludes that "the harshness of [the] current system may be attributed in largest part to the move to rehabilitation, incapacitation, and deterrence, which disconnected criminal punishment from the constraint of just deserts."[22]

Robinson points to the possibility that "if incapacitation of the dangerous were the only distributive principle, there would be little reason to wait until an offense were committed to impose criminal liability and sanctions; it would be more effective to screen the general population and 'convict' those found dangerous and in need of incapacitation."[23] The short-term project—using cognitive neuroscience to identify the roots of criminal violence—may someday create novel and powerful opportunities to interfere with individual liberty.

Questions of whether a given individual poses a continuing threat to society are central to the criminal justice system. In addition to capital sentencing, fact-finders are charged with making such determinations in the context of non-capital sentencing, civil commitment hearings, parole and probation hearings, pretrial detention, and involuntary civil commitment of sexual offenders. Regardless of neuroimaging's capacity or incapacity to predict such criminal behavior reliably, there is already a powerful demand for the use of such techniques in crime control. Moreover, far less reliable methods for predicting future social harms have already been accepted by the Supreme Court in the capital sentencing context. This problem would be dramatically aggravated by adopting a criminal framework that places an even higher premium on the prediction and prevention of violence than the present one does.

Notes

1. *Confirmation Hearing on the Nomination of John G. Roberts, Jr., to be Chief Justice of the United States: Hearing Before the S. Comm. on the Judiciary*, 109th Cong. 18 (2005).
2. Cognitive neuroscience can be described as the science of how the brain enables the mind. See, e.g., MICHAEL S. GAZZANIGA, THE MIND'S PAST xii (1998).
3. U.S. GEN. ACCT. OFFICE, INVESTIGATIVE TECHNIQUES: FEDERAL AGENCY VIEWS ON THE POTENTIAL APPLICATION OF "BRAIN FINGERPRINTING" (2001).
4. *See e.g.*, Press Release, Am. Civ. Liberties Union, ACLU Seeks Info. About Gov's Use of Brain Scanners in Interrogations (June 28, 2006).
5. Donald J. Nolan & Tressa A. Pankovits, High-Tech Proof in Brain Injury Cases, TRIAL., June 1, 2005, at 27.
6. *E.g.* J. Bruce Alverson & Sandra S. Smagac, *Brain Mapping: Should This Controversial Evidence Be Excluded?*, 48 FED'N INS. CORP. COUNS. Q. 131 (1998).

7. MICHAEL S. GAZZANIGA, THE ETHICAL BRAIN 88 (2005).
8. *See* Robert M. Sapolsky, *The Frontal Cortex and the Criminal Justice System*, PHIL. TRANSACTIONS ROYAL SOC'Y B: BIOLOGICAL SCI. at 1788.
9. In this article, "retribution," "retributive justice," and "just deserts" are used interchangeably to denote the concept that punishment should be distributed on the basis of the personal blameworthiness of the offender, in light of relevant mitigating and aggravating factors.
10. H.L.A. Hart distinguished the "General Justifying Aim" of punishment from its "distributive" principles. The former constitutes the ultimate legitimating goal of punishment, whereas the latter is a limiting or qualifying principle that informs the scope of liability (i.e., who may be punished) and the amount of punishment that may be meted out. *See* HART, PUNISHMENT AND RESPONSIBILITY 8–13 (1968).
11. *E.g.*, Jana L. Bufkin & Vickie R. Luttrell, *Neuroimaging Studies of Aggressive and Violent Behavior: Current Findings and Implications for Criminology and Criminal Justice*, 6 TRAUMA, VIOLENCE, & ABUSE (2005).
12. Paul H. Robinson, *Punishing Dangerousness: Cloaking Preventive Detention as Criminal Justice*, 114 HARV. L. REV. 1429, 1441 (2001).
13. Michael N. Burt, *Forensics as Mitigation*, http://www.goextranet/Seminars/Dallas/BurtForensics.htm (last visited July 28, 2007).
14. Atkins v. Virginia, 536 U.S. 304, 319 (2002).
15. Roper v. Simmons, 543 U.S. 551, 568 (2005).
16. Atkins, 536 U.S. at 321.
17. Roper, 543 U.S. at 571.
18. Coker v. Georgia, 433 U.S. 584, 592 (1977).
19. Enmund v. Florida, 458 U.S. 782, 801 (1982).
20. *See* Robinson, supra note 12, at 1429–31 & nn.2–7.
21. *See* id. at 1449.
22. Paul H. Robinson, *The A.L.I.'s Proposed Principle of "Limiting Retributivism": Does it Mean in Practice Anything Other than Pure Desert?* 7 Buff. Crim. L. Rev. 3, 14 (2003).
23. Robinson, supra note 12, at 1439–40.

Reading Analytically

1. This essay not only explores the use of neuroimaging in legal proceedings generally, but more specifically contextualizes the discussion within the issue of capital punishment. How does that context change the discussion?
2. What does Snead mean by "retributive justice"? Why is this concept an important element of his analysis?
3. This essay does not limit itself to a discussion of how neuroimaging can affect forensics, the disciplined study of past crimes, but how it might be used in a predictive way—to judge the propensity to commit

violent crimes. In what ways does that added element change the terms of the discussion?

Reading Across Disciplinary Communities

1. While it takes on a topic similar to the one in the preceding essay, its author (a legal scholar) and its publication (a college law journal) create a different context, and so shift the focus from the science to the legal issues. Of course, both articles need to include both disciplinary perspectives. But how is the central focus different here than in the previous piece?
2. Early in the article, Snead notes that "the attraction of the legal community to cognitive neuroscience is by no means unreciprocated." What does he mean by this? Why does the neuroscience community see value in its legal uses?

Writing Across Disciplines: Interdisciplinary Writing Opportunities

1. In order to fully understand the potential and implications of findings of the Human Genome Project, you and your classmates will need more information on this initiative's goals and accomplishments. Beginning with the online resources offered at the beginning of this chapter, do some research on the various findings of this government program, and write an essay that describes what you take to be the most important discoveries of this project, and the key implications of those discoveries. You might develop an oral report for your classmates as well; in sharing these reports, you can act as a community of scholars to better understand the implications of this project.
2. How does the work of the Human Genome Project change the way we understand human nature? Using some of the philosophical methods of inquiry gleaned from the writing styles and organization of writers from that discipline, write an essay that describes how some finding of the Human Genome Project can affect the way we understand what it means to be human. You might also consider how it affects tenets of religious beliefs about human beings, either from your own set of beliefs or from beliefs from a particular religion that you research.
3. As is discussed by many of the writers in the chapters on race, violent conflict, or what it means to be an American, those concepts are directly influenced by genetic research. Drawing upon studies in biology and other natural sciences, discuss the ways that recent genetic studies have, or should, influence the way we view some facet of human difference and similarity or the causes of human conflict.

4. In their essays, Ricki Lewis and Beatrix P. Rubin discuss the effect of the language used to describe the "promise" of genetic research—and the sciences more generally—to influence our views on these disciplines. Continue this work by doing a survey of media depictions—both in the mainstream media and on Web sites, blogs, and wikis—of genetic research. What do you take to be particular ways that these findings are framed in language that affect public opinion, and public policy, on genetic research.
5. One of the key issues raised in this chapter's readings surrounds the applied uses in business ventures of the availability of genetic testing. Starting with the online resources offered at the beginning of this chapter, perform a survey of Web sites that offer "direct-to-consumer" genetic tests, and discuss the marketing techniques that are developed to move genetics from a theoretical, academic set of studies to a source of profit through business. There are many questions you might take on as you complete this study; focus on one or some of the following: Do you believe that these business ventures are ethically sound? What problems might they cause? What benefits do they offer? How do the sites themselves seem to address issues of reliability, effects upon the consumer, and ethics? Do you find any of the problems that are suggested by Bridget Kuehn or the American Society of Human Genetics reflected in these sites? Anything to refute their critiques? Would you consider using any of these services? How might these tests affect our racial or ethnic relationships or self-identity for those who use these services? As you develop your topic, try to draw upon issues that are germane to your own major of field of study.

3 CHAPTER

Is the Concept of "Race" Real?

Theoretical Debates and Practical Implications

It seems like a simple enough question: Do races exist? As we look around us and see human diversity—differences in skin color, facial features, common practices, language variations, and so forth—it seems reasonable to answer that question in the affirmative.

But as the selections in this chapter suggest, the question is anything but simple. In fact, thinkers from a variety of disciplinary communities continue to examine that question in a wide variety of ways. Scientists have debated whether biological and genetic studies, especially in light of the mapping of human DNA through the Human Genome Project (discussed in Chapter 2 of this book), suggest that the concept of race is more "socially constructed" (developed through social practices) than it is a function of actual human physiology. Philosophers have examined the ethical implications of using race as a form of categorizing people. Historians have traced the roots of the concept of race through key moments in our past. Anthropologists, sociologists, and other social scientists have studied human behaviors in past and present cultures to examine the implications of race upon cultural norms and behaviors. And applied sciences—medicine, business, and so forth—have asked whether the category of race should be considered in the work they are attempting to do.

The readings in this chapter demonstrate the variety of ways that experts across disciplinary fields have written about topics generated by this deceptively complex question. By reading carefully, you can generate topics for your own further research and study; you can also learn more about the ways that researchers within (and across) various disciplinary communities have attempted to explore the nature of the question and its implications for our personal and public decision-making. As you read, consider how the question might influence your own areas of study.

The chapter begins with an excerpt from Ashley Montagu's influential book, *Man's Most Dangerous Myth: The Fallacy of Race,* first published in the wake of Hitler's fascism in 1942; this excerpt, from the sixth edition, which was published in 1997, continues to argue that racial categorization is a dangerous concept, one that is inherently racist. To the contrary, Vincent Sarich and Frank Miele argue, as the subtitle of their book suggests, for "the reality of human differences," suggesting that DNA evidence has been misread to suggest that race is a human construct. In "Race and Law," a chapter from their book *Race: The Reality of Human Differences,* they counter those that suggest that race is but an illusion, arguing against the version of race forwarded by the PBS miniseries, "Race: the Power of an Illusion," an excerpt of which is also included in this chapter. Philip Kitcher, a professor of philosophy, then brings his disciplinary perspective to the debate, suggesting that though races are not "natural" (i.e., biological), that "settling the issue is harder than it might appear," and that the debate on race should "involve people who have usually been left out of the discussion"—that is, that it should be interdisciplinary, not merely settled in the sciences.

After these introductory readings, which lay out some of the key issues of the "race question," authors from a variety of disciplinary communities address the effects of race upon a wider set of stakeholders. These readings thus represent "applied" disciplines—disciplines that go beyond theoretical debates to examine the implications of the race question upon policies, practices, and business decisions. Patricia McGann-Mortimer, Martha Augoustinos, and Amanda LeCouteur in "'Race' and the Human Genome Project: Constructions of Scientific Legitimacy," demonstrate one of the key uses of genetic testing (the topic of Chapter 2 of this book)—to help us better understand whether race is a biological fact or a social construct. In their piece, these authors conduct a rhetorical analysis of the ways that the authoritative language of science and "scientific truth" can be used to create legitimacy for a wide range of practices and policy decisions. Carol Mukhopadhyay and Rosemary C. Henze, in "How Real is Race? Using Anthropology to Make Sense of Human Diversity," complicate this question. They argue that though biological conceptions of race are not "scientifically valid," the categories remain important social constructs for practitioners in the field of education. Finally, an article by Jonathan Kahn explores another set of implications raised by the "science" of race and ethnicity, this one affecting those in business fields. Kahn's article explores a growing trend in medicine and the pharmaceutical fields to create race-based drugs, examining both the potential and the dangers of this use of racial categories.

Taken as a group, the readings in this chapter not only provide a sampling of the ways that key questions about race and racism have been examined by writers, but also illustrate how each disciplinary perspective adds new knowledge to inquiries into the topic. As you explore the ways that each author constructs their argument, uses evidence, and organizes the pool of knowledge upon which he or she draws, consider what perspectives that your own experiences, your own academic field of study, and your own political and social beliefs bring to this issue.

CLASSIC TEXTS ONLINE

Background Readings on Race in America

No matter whether we see race as biologically real or not, there is no denying that race relations have traditionally been an area of concern in our culture. From the civil rights movement to the election of our first African-American president, race is no doubt real in the social sphere.

To gain some historical perspective on this topic, as well as statements on race relations by famous leaders and authors, you might do some online searches to make use of the rich resources available for those interested in this topic. There are many, many possibilities, but here are some starting points:

Martin Luther King, Jr. resources: A search for "Martin Luther King, Jr." will provide access to some of his key speeches, in written, audio, and video versions. One particularly useful Web site is called The King Center.

Malcolm X resources: Malcolm X was a radical, but foundational voice in the civil rights movement. A search for "Malcolm X" will turn up a variety of written transcripts, video, and audio versions of his moving speeches. One particularly useful Web site is called Brothermalcom. It provides a useful start for further research.

The 1964 Civil Rights Act: A search for the "1964 Civil Rights Act" will provide you with background on this key piece of legislation and how it attempted to protect the rights of African Americans as well as other minority groups. It can also help you to further understand how the issue of race has been treated within legal circles.

The U.S. Census: One key way that racial and ethnic categories have been institutionalized has been through the United States Census. Try searching "U.S. Census and race" or "U.S. Census and ethnicity," and you will find a great many resources on this topic.

Jim Crow Laws: Searching "Jim Crow laws" will give you some background on the past ways that African Americans were treated as a category of human beings within the law, and so provide background on current debates.

Uncle Tom's Cabin: This classic and controversial text by Harriet Beecher Stowe is available online: search "Uncle Tom's Cabin etext."

Invisible Man: Available by searching "Invisible Man Project etext," you can access portions of this classic Ralph Ellison text, including the famous "Battle Royal" chapter.

ASHLEY MONTAGU

The Origin of the Concept of Race

This piece was originally published in Montagu's influential book, Man's Most Dangerous Myth: The Fallacy of Race. *First published in 1942, in the context of the rise of Nazism's racist principles, the book is now in its sixth edition (1997); the excerpt included comes from that edition. A noted and prolific author, Montagu (whose birth name was Israel Ehrenberg) received an undergraduate degree in psychology from the University of London and a Ph.D. in anthropology from Columbia University. His work spanned a number of disciplinary fields, drawing especially upon biology and social sciences to develop his wide array of works, many of which focused upon questions of race. Montague's writings drew upon his scholarly studies, but spoke to much wider audiences as he became a public voice and social critic in debates about race.*

In this chapter, he argues that "the very word 'race' is itself a racist term not simply because it represents a congeries of error, or that it is spurious 'reality' with no objective existence, but in addition, and most importantly, because its baleful influence constitutes a threat to the very existence of humanity." As you read this piece, you can learn about many of the key points in the long-standing cultural debate on race and racism; you can also see how academic, disciplinary research can play an important role in shaping public attitudes well beyond the academy.

The idea of "race" represents one of the most dangerous myths of our time, and one of the most tragic. Myths are most effective and perilous when they remain unrecognized for what they are. Many of us are happy in the complacent belief that myths are what uncivilized people believe in, but of which we ourselves are completely free. We may realize that a myth is a faulty explanation leading to social delusion and error, but we do not necessarily realize that we ourselves share in the mythmaking faculty with all people of all times and places, or that each of us has his own store of myths derived from the traditional stock of the society in which we live, and are always in ready supply. In earlier days we believed in magic, possession, and exorcism; in good and evil supernatural powers; and until recently we believed in witchcraft. Today many of us believe in race. Race is the witchcraft, the demonology of our time, the means by which we exorcise imagined demoniacal powers among us. It is the contemporary myth, humankind's most dangerous myth, America's Original Sin.[1]

In our own time we have lived to see the myth of race openly adopted by governments as an expedient fiction. Myths perform the double function of serving both as models of and models for cultural attitudes and behavior. Thus myths reflect the beliefs and give sanction to the actions of society, while at the same time providing the forms upon which belief and conduct are molded. Built, as they are, into the structure of social relationships, racial myths often have a force which exceeds even that of reality itself, for such myths, in addition to the social encouragement they receive, draw upon both false biology and even worse theology for their sustenance. As Calas has said, myths are idealizations of social conditions, so that with regard to the matter of inequality, the main function of myths is to explain the origin of differences in ways that satisfy the needs of the group.[2] In short, the functional role of the myth is to provide a sanction for a course of action. Myths that account for social differences correspond to, and often have the force of, legal fictions, while legalistic attempts to justify the status quo endow the myth with an aura of historical sanctity. As such, myths are almost impervious to rational thought, for it is the nature of myth to be elaborated, but never proved. Myths, therefore, are of great value since they make thinking, as a problem-solving exercise, unnecessary.

The monstrous myths that have captured the emotions of people and shackled their minds still afflict the minds of millions in so-called civilized societies. The ambiguities and uncritical use of our language give rise to ambiguities of their own and constitute the compost upon which myths proliferate and are sustained. In the reality of the mythologies which every society creates for itself, the unreal becomes more real than the real, ritual investing them with an importance that renders them sacred. Developing as they do, myths achieve an integrity, a validity, a power, which is quite impregnable to any attempted demonstration of the unreliability of their component parts. We realize that many people have different investments in their beliefs, that humans are governed more by emotion, custom, and precedent, than by logic and reason, that errors and illusions, serving some explanatory purpose, frequently become endemic myths shared in common in the world of unreason and political fantasy. Myths that at one time may have served a socially useful purpose may live on into a time when they have not only become useless, but thoroughly baneful, decayed, degraded, and degrading. As Paul Gaston has said, in his admirable book, *The New South Creed,*

> Myths are not polite euphemisms for falsehoods, but are combinations of images and symbols that reflect a people's way of perceiving truth. Organically related to a fundamental reality of life, they fuse the real and the imaginary into a blend that becomes a reality itself, a force in history.[3]

And as George Tindall put it, charged with values, aspirations, ideals and meanings,

> Myths may become the ground for either loyalty and defense on the one hand or hostility on the other. In such circumstances, a myth itself becomes one of the realities of history, significantly influencing the course of human action, for good or ill. There is, of course, always a danger that in ordering one's

vision of reality, the myth may predetermine the categories of perception, rendering one blind to things that do not fit into the mental image.[4]

The function performed by myths is akin to that of religion, namely, the unification and intelligibility of experience. Racism often has its roots in religion, and like religion, can easily be accommodated to many diverse situations.[5]

The belief in race, as in Nazi Germany, became a secular religion whose myths recreated reality. The systematic murder of millions of human beings in the name of race was the final expression of the hideously brutal power of racial myths, of demonological mindedness.

The power of myths and their related ideologies lies not in their objective truth but in their being perceived as true. Of the myth of race it may be said that everyone seems to know, and is only too eager to tell. All but a few persons take it completely for granted that scientists have established the "facts" about race and have long ago satisfactorily recognized and classified the races of humankind. Scientists in the past did little to discourage this view, and, indeed, in most cases were even more wrongheaded than the layman on the subject. Exalted in their citadels of infallibility, scientists by their consensus gave security and comfort to those who believed in a hierarchy of races. Under such circumstances, it is not difficult to understand why so many people continue to believe that race is a reality, a fact, that some "races" are superior to others.

A scientific fact has been defined as a collective judgment of a specialized community. But the collective judgment of the specialized community of anthropologists during the nineteenth, and well into the twentieth, century was abysmally wrong concerning the "fact" of race. For this the scientists who subscribed to the concept of race cannot be faulted, for it was a product of a social environment which, through the distorting glass of prejudice, saw people divided by caste and class, and segregated by race. In a society that segregated people by caste and class, "race" was the term that categorized the most visibly distinguishable groups of people. As Lancelot Hogben, the eminent social biologist and early critic of the concept of race, remarked in 1932:

> Geneticists believe that anthropologists have decided what a race is. Ethnologists assume that their classifications embody principles which genetic science has proved to be correct. Politicians believe that their prejudices have the sanction of genetic laws and the findings of physical anthropology to sustain them.[6]

In reality, none of them had any grounds for such beliefs other than those which emanated prejudices.

In some nations, for example in Hitler's Third Reich, the myth of race also functioned as an ideology and continues to do so most prominently in such countries as South Africa, Australia, Brazil, and the United States of America, where it has come to be known as "the great divide."

An ideology is a prescriptive doctrine or system of belief that is not supported by rational argument, and flourishes in an environment of adverse political and social conditions. An ideology often originates with a charismatic leader or elite claiming exclusive authority as representing something like revealed truth; as such, an ideology may determine the lives and conduct of a whole population, providing its members with justifications, conviction, and moral fervor for their actions, regardless of the course of events.[7]

The myth of race refers not to the fact that physically distinguishable populations of humans exist, but rather to the belief that races are populations or peoples whose physical differences are innately linked with significant differences in mental capacities, and that these innate hierarchical differences are measurable by the cultural achievements of such populations, as well as by standardized intelligence (IQ) tests. This belief is thoroughly and dangerously unsound. It is the belief of racists and racism. Caught up in the vicious circle of prejudice, words become things, things become weapons—and the more weapons one has, the more convinced one is of the right to use them. But this is to anticipate.

It was as long ago as 1848 that John Stuart Mill wrote, in his *Principles of Political Economy,* "Of all the vulgar modes of escaping from the consideration of the effect of social and moral influences on the human mind, the most vulgar is that of attributing the diversities of conduct and character to inherent natural differences."[8] And even more forcibly, twenty-five years later in 1873, in his *Autobiography,* Mill wrote,

> I have long felt that the prevailing tendency to regard all the marked distinctions of human character as innate, and in the main indelible, and to ignore the irresistible proofs that by far the greater part of those differences, whether between individuals, races, or sexes, are such as not only might but naturally would be produced by differences in circumstances, is one of the chief hindrances to the rational treatment of great social questions, and one of the greatest stumbling blocks to the human improvement.[9]

Another political economist, Walter Bagehot, in 1869, similarly wrote: "When a philosopher cannot account for anything in any other manner, he boldly ascribes it to an occult quality in some race."[10]

Writing in 1915, Lord Bryce, author of *The American Commonwealth*, put the matter clearly: "No branches of historical inquiry," he wrote,

> have suffered more from fanciful speculation than those which relate to the origin and attributes of the races of mankind. The differentiation of these races began in prehistoric darkness, and the more obscure a subject is, so much the more fascinating. Hypotheses are tempting, because though it may be impossible to verify them, it is, in the paucity of data, almost equally impossible to refute them.[11]

Such views in the course of the years have had their effects, but nothing like the effect that the persisting myth of race has had upon the ignorant and the ill-educated. Taking it for granted that different populations could be classified into distinct groups—so-called "races"—anthropologists, on the basis of such differences as head shape, hair form, skin color, and similar traits drew up long lists of races. It was a game the classifiers played in all seriousness as if it were anything other than the postprandial indulgence it was, and the compilations of races that resulted numbered from half a dozen to two hundred.[12] Though taken seriously for a time were, these lists were ultimately a complete failure, primarily because they were based on a fundamental misconception of the nature and variability—and intractability—of the materials they attempted to put into some kind of order.

It was easy to see that an African black and a blonde Swede must have had a somewhat different biological history, and the difference in appearance considered sufficient to distinguish them as belonging to two different races. In biology a "race" has been customarily defined as a subdivision of a species that inherits physical characteristics distinguishing it from other populations of the species. By that definition then, do not "Blacks" and Swedes belong to different races? The answer, as we shall see, is that even in terms of the biological definition, they do not.

Is there a "black" race, or a Swedish race? There is not, any more than that there is a "white" race, a "yellow" race, or a "red" race. Both "black" and "Swede" are collective terms which lump together groups and individuals who differ from each other in physical and often in cultural traits. Furthermore, the variability in physical traits *within* any population is usually greater than it is *between* populations, while even more interesting and significant is the strikingly small number of gene differences between such populations, a fact evident in the gradational or climal variability which characterizes the populations of humankind.

For example, Richard Lewontin, professor of genetics at Harvard University, has carried out a most important investigation of genetic diversity in the human species. Taking the blood groups and various enzymatic traits for which the genetics is known, by means of a mathematical-genetic analysis Lewontin found that the mean proportion was 85.4 percent. The difference between populations within a race accounted for less than 8.3 percent, so that only 6.3 percent is accounted for by racial classification. Lewontin concludes,

> It is clear that our perception of relatively large differences between human races and subgroups, as compared to the variation within these groups, is indeed a biased perception and that, based on randomly chosen genetic differences, human races and populations are remarkably similar to each other, with the largest part by far of human variation being accounted for by the differences between individuals.
>
> Human racial classification is of no social value and is positively destructive of social and human relations. Since such racial classification is now seen to be of virtually no genetic or taxonomic significance either, no justification can be offered for its continuance.[13]

Such facts render the concept of race and the continuance of race classification erroneous and obsolescent—important subjects we shall discuss in detail. For such reasons, among others, modern biologists find that the use of the concept of race should be discontinued.[14]

The truth is that the "deceptively clear label," as Lucien Febvre called the concept of race,[15] obscures and renders divisible what is indivisible. This is not to say that there are no genetic or physical differences between various populations, but it is to say that they are by no means as large or significant as most scientists once supposed. Misleading simplifications embodied in word-labels, especially when they are given the respectability of long-usage and established authority, tend to be accepted uncritically, and do not constitute a substitution for critical examination and. We must constantly be on our guard against subscribing to a lexicon of unsound terms of which we elect ourselves the guardians, and make ourselves the prisoners of our own vocabularies.

In the biological sense there do, of course, exist distinctive human populations that exhibit an interesting variety of physical differences. These differences are superficial, and far fewer in number than the traits we have in common. It is well to remember that what makes us alike is very much more important than what makes us different. In a racist society which segregates people by race and divides them by class, in which exclusiveness is the unstated rule, it is not surprising that the classifiers would, often without being aware of it, bring their class-structured ways of thinking to the classifications of the "races of mankind." The consciousness of class and classificatory schemes were closely related. Embedded in this, of course was the tacit assumption that with the biological ranking there naturally went a socio-cultural grading, which combined with the physical ranking, from "high" to "low," or superiority to inferiority, enabled one to assign populations and individuals to their "proper" levels. "The higher races" were "superior," and "the lower races" were "inferior." In this way was established the basic axiom of physical anthropology, namely, the belief that distinctive human characteristics and abilities are determined by race, a view that was and is essentially racist. Since the meaning of a word is the action it produces, this was racism.

Racism is conduct based on the belief that physical and behavioral differences characterizing individual members of different groups or populations are determined by genetic, that is, innate factors, and that these differences enable one to rank each individual and group in the scale of humanity according to the attributed predefined values of those differences. The implication is that in such individuals and groups the genes that are supposed to determine their physical traits, such as skin color, hair form, head shape, and the like, are linked with the genes that determine the qualities and limits of their mental capacities or abilities, and that linked with these traits is the ability of the population or group to achieve a high level of civilization. Thus, three criteria are involved in the racist view: (1) physical traits, (2) mental capacities and abilities, and (3) the ability to achieve a high level of civilization. To put it briefly, the racist believes that physical characteristics, capacity, and creativity, are genetically related, fixed and unchangeable. He may never have formulated his belief in these words but in this own mind, however, vaguely this is what it amounted to.

This is the triad that constitutes the basic belief of the racist, and it is entirely unsound, for there is absolutely no genetic linkage between genes for physical traits, mental capacities, or civilization-building abilities. As we shall see, human beings are born everywhere with potentialities or capacities which must be stimulated and guided by learning if they are to become abilities. A capacity is a potentiality. An ability is a trained capacity. Allowing for individual differences existing in every population, the full range of abilities that has been developed in any society—given the same opportunities for development—is within the capability of every human population, for educability is the species trait of humanity. What human beings have learned to do in any culture, human beings can anywhere learn. We shall discuss these matters more fully in later pages.

Here it should be pointed out that the very word "race" is itself a racist term not simply because it represents a congeries of errors, or that it is a spurious "reality" with no objective existence, but in addition, and most importantly, because its baleful influence constitutes a threat to the very existence of humanity, much of which has already vanished as a direct result of racism. In a large number of cases it has led to wars and unjustifiable conquests, costing the lives of many millions, and the destruction of untold numbers together with their cultures in their own homelands. Such destructive conduct continues to the present day in North and South America, Australia, Africa, India, Sri Lanka, Ethiopia, the Middle East, the Philippines, in Poland, the Balkans, and the former USSR, now Russia and the independent republics of Eastern Europe and Northern Asia.

To summarize then, humankind may be regarded as comprising of a number of populations or peoples the members of which often differ physically and superficially from one another. These differences have come about as a result of the long isolation of such populations during which the physical differences have evolved. The cultural differences have come about as the result of differences in the history of experience to which each population has adaptively responded. Both the physical and the cultural differences are neither fixed nor permanent, but are subject to change. We see this occurring very rapidly when boundaries that formerly separated people are reduced and populations come into contact. In spite of occasional appearances to the contrary, humanity is moving toward unity without uniformity, toward the condition in which the differences that today separate humanity will be regarded as points of interest and value, not as excuses for fear and discrimination, but as no more important than the differences which separate the members of the same family.

The classificatory definition of humanity as *Homo sapiens*, properly interpreted, is appropriate because it gives quite accurate status to a unique class of creatures—human beings—characterized by an educability, a capacity for wisdom and intelligence approached by no other creature. These traits, *not* the external physical traits constitute the principal, the distinctive qualities, that make *Homo sapiens* human. When human beings are defined on the basis of the differences in physical traits we narrow the definition of their humanity. And that is, perhaps, the most telling criticism of the concept of race.

Notes

1. For excellent discussions of contemporary mythmaking and myths, see Barrows Dunham, *Man against Myth* (Boston: Little, Brown, 1947); Bergen Evans, *The Natural History of Nonsense* (New York: Alfred A. Knopf, 1964); Read Bain, "Man, the Myth-Maker," *Scientific Monthly* 65 (1947): 61–69; David Bidney, "The Concept of Myth and the Problem of Psychocultural Evolution," *American Anthropologist* 62 (1950): 16–26; D. H. Monro, "The Concept of Myth," *Sociological Review* 42 (1950): 115–32; Lewis S. Feuer, "Political Myths and Metaphysics," *Philosophy and Phenomenological Research* 15 (1955): 332–50; Harry A. Murray, ed., *Myth and Mythmaking* (New York: Braziller, 1960).
2. Nicholas Calas, "Myth and Initiation," *Chimera* 4 (1946): 21–24.
3. Paul M. Gaston, *The New South Creed: A Study in Modern Mythmaking* (New York: Alfred A. Knopf, 1970).
4. George M. Tindall, *The Ethnic Southerners* (Baton Rouge: Louisiana State University Press, 1976).
5. Alan Davies, *Infected Christianity: A Study of Modern Racism* (Kingston & Montreal: McGill Queen's University Press, 1988); Ervin Staub, *The Roots of Evil: The Origns of Genocide* (New York: Cambridge University Press, 1989); Michael Barkun, *Religion and the Racist Right: The Origins of the Christian Identity Movement* (Chapel Hill: University of North Carolina Press, 1994).
6. Lancelot Hogben, "The Concept of Race," in *Genetic Principles in Medicine and Social Science* (New York: Alfred A. Knopf, 1932), 122–44; see also L. Hogben, *Nature and Nurture* (New York: W. W. Norton, 1933).
7. Louis J. Halle, *The Ideological Imagination* (New York: Quadrangle Press, 1972). For an illuminating study of the causes of the ideological appeal of Naziism, see Peter H. Merkl, *Political Violence Under the Swaztika: 581 Early Nazis* (Princeton: Princeton University Press, 1975); Paul Massing, *Rehearsal for Destruction* (New York: Harper & Brothers, 1949); George L. Mosse, *Toward the Final Solution: A History of European Racism* (Madison: University of Wisconsin Press, 1985).
8. John Stuart Mill, *Principles of Political Economy* (London: Longmans, 1848).

9. John Stuart Mill, *Autobiography.*
10. Walter Bagehot, *Physics and Politics* (New York: Alfred A. Knopf), 3; Ashley Montagu, "The Language of Self-Deception," in *Language in America*, eds. Neil Postman, Charles Weingartner, and Terence P. Moran (New York: Pegasus, 1969), 82–95.
11. James Bryce, *Race Sentiment as a Factor in History* (London: University of London Press, 1915), 3.
12. As an example see A. C. Haddon's *The Races of Man* (Cambridge: Cambridge University Press, 1924). This was a book by a very noble man, a great scholar and founder of the anthropology department at Cambridge University. For a sympathetic biography of Haddon (1955–1940) see A. Hingston Quiggin, *Haddon the Head Hunter* (Cambridge: Cambridge University Press, 1942). Among many hundreds of scholarly articles and some twenty books, Haddon was the co-author with Julian Huxley of the admirable and influential *We Europeans: A Survey of "Racial" Problems* (New York: Harper & Bros., 1935).
13. Richard Lewontin, "The Apportionment of Human Diversity," in *Evolutionary Biology*, vol. 6, eds. T. Dobzhansky, M. K. Hecht, and W. C. Steere (New York: Appleton Century-Cotts, 1972), 396–97.
14. See Ashley Montagu, *An Introduction to Physical Anthropology*, 3rd ed. (Springfield, IL: Thomas. 1960); A. Montagu, "A Consideration of the Concept of Race," *Cold Spring Harbor Symposia on Quantitative Biology* 15 (1950): 315–36; A. Montagu, "The Concept of Race," *American Anthropologist* 64 (1962): 929–45; Livingstone, "On the Non-Existence of Human Races," *Current Anthropology* 3 (1962): 279–81; A. Montagu, ed., *The Concept of Race* (New York: Free Press, 1964).
15. Lucien Febvre, *A Geographical Introduction to History* (New York: Alfred A. Knopf, 1925).

Reading Analytically

1. In this excerpt from Montagu's *Man's Most Dangerous Myth*, the author attempts to redefine race as a "myth" rather than a reality. Why does Montagu believe that racial categorization is largely a "myth," and in what ways does he suggest that myths are particularly dangerous?
2. Since one of Montagu's main purposes in this book is to critique arguments that race is a "real" concept, instead suggesting that it is a dangerous "myth," it is important to know with some precision what counterarguments he is refuting. List at least three beliefs about race that Montagu seems to be refuting, and discuss the specific critique he offers to those counterarguments.
3. One of the main contentions that Montagu makes is that "the very word 'race' is itself a racist concept." Do you agree? If we abandon the

concept of race, what are the gains and losses? How would it affect, for example, the concept of "multiculturalism"?

Reading Across Disciplinary Communities

1. As an anthropologist, scientific "facts" are particularly important; that is, an anthropologist must not only make arguments, but base them in empirical (observable) evidence. What types of science-based arguments does Montagu make in support of his understanding of race? After you have summarized those arguments, consider how other authors in this chapter offer other facts. Try to sort out how these various types of "facts" can help you to draw your own conclusions about the nature of racial categories.
2. Though Montagu is, by education, an anthropologist, he does not limit the evidence he uses to make his case to anthropological evidence. Scan the piece for the various experts and studies he cites to find at least three different disciplinary fields that are included in his evidence base. Then, for each of those three, discuss the ways that this field of study can contribute to the public debate about the concepts of race and racism.

PUBLIC BROADCASTING SYSTEM

Ten Things Everyone Should Know About Race

In its 2003 series, "Race: The Power of an Illusion," the Public Broadcasting system sought to "clear away the biological underbrush and leave starkly visible the underlying social, economic, and political conditions that disproportionately channel advantages and opportunities to white people." Drawing upon research garnered from experts in a variety of disciplines (some of whose work can also be found on this Web site at http://www.pbs.org), the accompanying Web site published this "fact sheet" on race, a set of "facts" that are questioned by Vincent Sarich and Frank Miele in the reading that follows.

One of the questions that such "fact sheets" raise is, of course, whether a concept as complex as race can be reduced to a list of "facts." As you read this list of items, you might consider whether or not they represent truly established facts, or whether they are only presenting one take on the question of race. Continue to consider the facts that are presented here as you read other selections in this chapter, asking not only about their accuracy, but their implications for how our culture will make policies and behave toward one another.

Our eyes tell us that people look different. No one has trouble distinguishing a Czech from a Chinese. But what do those differences mean? Are they biological? Has race always been with us? How does race affect people today?

There's less—and more—to race than meets the eye

1. **Race is a modern idea.** Ancient societies, like the Greeks, did not divide people according to physical distinctions, but according to religion, status, class, even language. The English language didn't even have the word 'race' until it turns up in 1508 in a poem by William Dunbar referring to a line of kings.
2. **Race has no genetic basis.** Not one characteristic, trait or even gene distinguishes all the members of one so-called race from all the members of another so-called race.
3. **Human subspecies don't exist.** Unlike many animals, modern humans simply haven't been around long enough or isolated enough to evolve into separate subspecies or races. Despite surface appearances, we are one of the most similar of all species.
4. **Skin color really is only skin deep.** Most traits are inherited independently from one another. The genes influencing skin color have nothing to do with the genes influencing hair form, eye shape, blood type, musical talent, athletic ability or forms of intelligence. Knowing someone's skin color doesn't necessarily tell you anything else about him or her.
5. **Most variation is within, not between, "races."** Of the small amount of total human variation, 85% exists within any local population, be they Italians, Kurds, Koreans or Cherokees. About 94% can be found within any continent. That means two random Koreans may be as genetically different as a Korean and an Italian.
6. **Slavery predates race.** Throughout much of human history, societies have enslaved others, often as a result of conquest or war, even debt, but not because of physical characteristics or a belief in natural inferiority. Due to a unique set of historical circumstances, ours was the first slave system where all the slaves shared similar physical characteristics.

7. **Race and freedom evolved together.** The U.S. was founded on the radical new principle that "All men are created equal." But our early economy was based largely on slavery. How could this anomaly be rationalized? The new idea of race helped explain why some people could be denied the rights and freedoms that others took for granted.
8. **Race justified social inequalities as natural.** As the race idea evolved, white superiority became "common sense" in America. It justified not only slavery but also the extermination of Indians, exclusion of Asian immigrants, and the taking of Mexican lands by a nation that professed a belief in democracy. Racial practices were institutionalized within American government, laws, and society.
9. **Race isn't biological, but racism is still real.** Race is a powerful social idea that gives people different access to opportunities and resources. Our government and social institutions have created advantages that disproportionately channel wealth, power, and resources to white people. This affects everyone, whether we are aware of it or not.
10. **Colorblindness will not end racism.** Pretending race doesn't exist is not the same as creating equality. Race is more than stereotypes and individual prejudice. To combat racism, we need to identify and remedy social policies and institutional practices that advantage some groups at the expense of others.

Reading Analytically

1. Perhaps the first thing to consider after reading this selection is its complex genre: a "fact sheet" in the context of a Web site that supplements a miniseries. As a quick summary of principles, it has the advantage of providing an overview of the topic. In what ways is that appropriate to its Web site delivery and the expectations of Web users? What, if anything, is lost in this type of argument?
2. Since this selection is meant to present, in summary fashion, "ten things everyone should know about race," it must not only be a quick overview, but must use a style that is designed to make the information included seem simply factual. What features of this presentation make it easily scanned by readers who are used to reading quickly on the Web? What types of sentence structures are used to make the information appear like indisputable facts?
3. After reading the various "facts" that are presented, keep a running log of these contentions and after each, add a note based upon the other arguments that are offered by authors in this chapter. Pay special attention to the arguments of Vincent Sarich and Frank Miele, as they specifically critique this PBS series.

Reading Across Disciplinary Communities

1. Since this is a public genre, not an academic one, the PBS Web site does not (at least in this portion), provide a great deal of supporting evidence for its list of what amounts to ten specific theses. As you read each of the ten items, make a list of the disciplines that would be able to weigh in on each of the contentions most reliably. You might think of it this way: If you wanted to question the truth of any of the selections, to what type of expert might you go?
2. Think about your own major field of study, or one that you are considering. Which of the items listed here might be of most interest to that field? Why? What types of research might you do to check the accuracy of that claim?

VINCENT SARICH AND FRANK MIELE

Race and the Law

In this piece, originally published as a chapter in their book Race: The Reality of Human Differences, *an anthropologist and a journalist collaborate to argue that though "an increasing number of anthropologists . . . have signed on to proclamations that categorically state the term [race] has long ago ceased to have any scientific legitimacy," "the latest genetic technologies are, for the most part confirming not only the traditional anthropology but also the commonsense understanding of race" that is used in legal decisions. Vincent Sarich is Emeritus Professor of Anthropology at the University of California, Berkeley; Frank Miele is senior editor for* Skeptic Magazine.

As you read, you might consider how the genre of the piece is influenced by these two disciplinary backgrounds. You can also compare the arguments made here not only with the PBS fact sheet on race, but also with the argument that race is a "myth" made by Ashley Montagu—since this piece argues for the "reality" of race. One question to consider is how two anthropologists, Montagu and Sarich, can use the same body of disciplinary evidence to reach such very different conclusions.

In contrast to a recent (2003), highly acclaimed PBS documentary that termed race "an illusion," a myth constructed by Europeans in the Age of Exploration to justify colonialism and slavery, we argue that race is real.

We begin the case for race by noting how one of the most contentious facets of our society, our legal system, has no trouble in recognizing either the existence of race or the ability of the average citizen to do so. Further, DNA markers have been used to identify the race of perpetrators.

We have an inborn tendency to sort people into groups. The latest evidence shows how this tendency can mirror biological reality.

Some twenty years ago, coauthor Vincent Sarich received a call from a San Francisco attorney who was serving as defense attorney in a racial discrimination case brought by a man who claimed he had been discriminated against because of his American Indian ancestry. As part of their discussion, the question of legal "standing" arose; that is, did the plaintiff actually have the requisite racial ancestry—was he, in fact, an Indian? Vince naively asked for the legal definition of "race" and was told there wasn't one. Still, in the spirit of scientific inquiry, he observed the proceedings until the first break, at which point he told the attorney that, in his opinion, the attorney's client had no chance of arguing successfully that the plaintiff lacked standing. To Vince's eyes, the plaintiff obviously "looked" Amerindian. End of case.

As we began working on this book, we discussed the issue of the legal definition of "race" and asked the opinion of an attorney who specializes in civil rights law, which touches on this issue. He informed us that there is still no legal definition of "race"; nor, as far as we know, does it appear that the legal system feels the need for one. Thus, it appears that the most adversarial part of our complex society, the legal system, not only continues to accept the existence of "race" but also relies on the ability of the average individual to sort people into races. Our legal system treats "racial identification" as self-evident, whereas an increasing number of anthropologists (the profession, one would think, with the pertinent expertise) have signed on to proclamations that categorically state the term has long ago ceased to have any scientific legitimacy.

Why this clash? To us the answer is simple: The courts have come to accept the commonsense definition of race, and it is this commonsense view that, as we show, best conforms to reality. A look at two recent (2000) cases is illustrative. In both *Rice v. Office of Hawaiian Affairs* and in *Haak v. Rochester School District*, neither side raised any questions about the existence of human races or the ability of the average citizen to make valid judgments as to who belongs to which race (even if the racial categories are euphemistically termed "peoples" or "populations"). No special expertise was assumed or granted in defining or recognizing race other than the everyday commonsense usage, as given in the *Oxford English Dictionary*, that a race is "a group of persons connected by common descent" or "a tribe, nation, or people, regarded as of common stock." The courts and the contending parties, in effect, accepted as givens the existence of race and the ability of the ordinary person to distinguish between races based on a set of physical features.

Rice v. Office of Hawaiian Affairs *Race by Any Other Name is Still Race*

In the first case, the United States Supreme Court reversed a judgment of the 9th Circuit Court of Appeals. The petitioner, H. F. Rice, had challenged the State of Hawaii for not allowing him to vote in an election for the nine trustees of the Office of Hawaiian Affairs, an agency that administers programs designed for the benefit of "Hawaiians."

Originally, "Hawaiian" was defined as "any descendant of the races inhabiting the Hawaiian Islands, prior to 1788" [the year the first European, Captain James Cook, reached the islands]. That was later changed to "any descendant of the aboriginal peoples which exercised sovereignty and subsisted in the Hawaiian Islands in 1778, and which peoples thereafter have continued to reside in Hawaii." The term "Native Hawaiian" was defined as "any descendant of not less than one-half part of the races inhabiting the Hawaiian Islands previous to 1778—provided that the definition identically refers to the descendants of such blood quantum of such aboriginal peoples which exercised sovereignty and subsisted in the Hawaiians in 1778, and which peoples thereafter continued to reside in Hawaii."

The tortuous, convoluted text in the Hawaii statutes is not just the usual legalese. Both the drafters of the amendments and the court in its decision admitted that the substitution of "peoples" for "races" was cosmetic, not substantive, and that "peoples" does indeed mean "races." The sole reason for the changes was to banish any mention of the offending word, "race," and substitute a palatable euphemism.

Rice, everyone agreed, was a Hawaiian citizen but without the requisite ancestry to be recognized as "Hawaiian" under state law. The state therefore argued that denying Rice the vote in the OHA election was justified, and the 9th Circuit concurred when Rice challenged.

However, the U.S. Supreme Court reversed the 9th Circuit by a 7–2 margin (Stevens and Ginsburg dissenting), citing in particular the 15th Amendment: "The right of the citizens of the United States to vote shall not be denied or abridged by the United States or by any State on account of race, color, or previous condition of servitude." The Court found the Hawaiian law unconstitutional because it defined voter eligibility on the basis of race.

The 15th Amendment is explicit—race means what the average person thinks it means—and the majority of the Supreme Court read it that way. In the end, the tortuous, convoluted verbiage introduced into the Hawaiian statutes to avoid the offensive term "race" accomplished nothing.

Haak v. Rochester School District
What We See Is What You Get

In the other case, the 2nd Circuit Court of Appeals ruled that a white fourth-grade student named Jessica Haak could not transfer from her home district to an adjoining, primarily white district because the transfer program was enacted for the explicit purpose of lessening racial isolation among the six districts involved. The plaintiffs, Haak's parents, challenged on the grounds that denying the right to transfer based upon racial classification violated the clause in section 1 of the 14th Amendment, which makes it unconstitutional for any state to "deny any person within its jurisdiction the equal protection of the law." The district court ruled in Haak's favor, but the 2nd Circuit overturned that decision, noting that although the U. S. Supreme Court had had many opportunities to rule that race could not be used as a factor in deciding who attended which school, it had never taken the opportunity to establish a precedent by doing so.

In *Haak,* neither side even raised the issue of who belonged to which group (race or ethnicity). A "minority pupil" was defined as "a pupil who is of Black or Hispanic origin or is a member of another minority group that historically has been the subject of discrimination." Interestingly, however, neither the application to transfer under the program, the program brochures, nor the acknowledgment letter sent to parents who apply provides any standard by which to establish a student's race or ethnicity. Parents are expected to self-screen their children. Once the applicant is met in person by a program administrator, a question may be raised as to the student's race as a result of the student's "name, manner of speaking and phrasing, and personal appearance during an interview or orientation." Even so, it seems that Haak, who is white, was accepted into the program by the school's assistant principal and sent an official letter of acknowledgment. That acceptance was revoked after a second administrator saw Haak in person and verified her race as Caucasian/White according to the school district's records, therefore making her ineligible for the transfer program.

The critical points here are that in both *Rice* and *Haak*, neither side raised any questions about the existence of human races or the ability of the average citizen to make valid judgments as to who belongs to which race. No special expertise was assumed or granted in defining or recognizing race other than the everyday usage of the term. In *Rice*, the court, in effect, took judicial notice of the commonsense definition of race. In *Haak*, the court accepted physical appearance as a valid means by which the average citizen can recognize races and distinguish among them.

The Hawaii statutes at issue in *Rice* were inventively drafted to include the word "ancestry" for fear that the term "race" would be grounds to strike down the law. Notwithstanding the convoluted definition of having Hawaiian "ancestry," the definition maps quite well to the commonsense definition of "race." In short, the courts accepted the existence of race, even if the legislature was afraid to use the offending word. The Supreme Court struck down the Hawaii law because its definition of being Hawaiian based on ancestry was for all intents and purposes the equivalent of the commonsense definition of race and so was expressly prohibited by the 14th Amendment.

In *Haak*, the plaintiffs did not dispute that the school administrator (or anyone else, for that matter) correctly identified or was able to identify Haak's race. Rather, they contested the constitutionality of a law that discriminates on the basis of race. The ability to determine race was assumed and accepted by both parties and by the court.

Should the Criminal Justice System Recognize that Race Is Real?

A critical question is whether the courts recognize the existence of race as a mere social construct or as an underlying biological reality. In taking statements from witnesses and in courtroom testimony, the criminal justice system routinely, and with little or no complaint, accepts statements such as "The perpetrator was identified as a male, Caucasian, about twenty-five years old," or "The little girl I saw abducted in the parking lot looked like she was Hispanic or a fair-skinned African American." But consider a recent example in which accepting the existence of race as a biological reality, rather than "race" as a social construct of Western society, became a matter of life and death.

Throughout 2002 and the first half of 2003, Louisiana police were hunting for a serial killer who had murdered at least five women in the

Baton Rouge area. Relying on tips and two eyewitness accounts of a white male allegedly driving a white pickup truck containing the body of a slumped, naked white female on the night of one of the murders, police focused the search on white males. A host of experimental research has demonstrated that eyewitness testimony of an unexpected event that is viewed only briefly is notoriously unreliable in far more than racial identification. Perhaps the best-known real-life example is the number of observers who report planes bursting into flames before they crash; later examination of the wreckage shows that there was no in-flight explosion. However, in the Louisiana serial-killer case, another eyewitness, a neighbor of one of the victims, frustrated that the police were restricting their search to whites, circulated a flyer with a composite sketch of the perpetrator the neighbor thought he saw—a black male who it turned out closely resembled Derrick Todd Lee.

The state police crime lab had linked all five cases to the same perpetrator by using the minimum of thirteen DNA markers required by the FBI forensic crime lab for individual identification. (DNA markers are sequences in the complete human genome that can identify a person's ancestry or parentage.) If the thirteen markers in samples taken either from two of the victims or, more likely, from a victim and a suspect, are the same, the probability that they come from the same individual is virtually certain, about the same probability as flipping a coin thirteen times and getting the same result or verifying a thirteen-digit credit card or bank account number. The odds of misidentification are effectively about one in a billion.

In the Baton Rouge case, samples of the perpetrator's DNA (probably from semen, though not specified in the reports we read) were taken from the victims' bodies. Holding firm in their belief that almost all serial murderers are white, the police swabbed the cheeks of more than 600 white male suspects for DNA analysis to see if they matched the samples taken from the victims.

We should note here that this method of individual DNA matching, sometimes called "DNA fingerprinting," has also cleared suspects and provided grounds for appeal. Since 1992, the Innocence Project at Yeshiva University's Cardozo School of Law, headed by Barry Scheck and Peter Neufeld (best known as defense attorneys in the O. J. Simpson criminal trial), alone has freed over thirty-five people wrongly convicted, including a number of African Americans. DNA is also used in paternity testing; evaluating kinship in inheritance disputes; and missing-persons cases, especially in identifying kidnapped children who may be unable or afraid to speak to the police on their own behalf. In 1993 a two-year-old was returned to his parents two years after being kidnapped only after police established scientifically who the child was by using genetic fingerprinting. DNA profiling is so accurate that it is highly recommended by law enforcement departments around the United States to protect individuals in the event of abduction or kidnapping.

Thirteen markers are sufficient to determine a reliable individual match, but more are needed to sort individuals by race correctly. Technically, the thirteen markers used by the FBI for individual DNA fingerprinting are termed "short tandem repeats" (STRs). They are repetitions of the same sequence of base pairs in junk (noncoding) DNA. Junk DNA is just that. It is not responsible, to the best of our knowledge, for any trait or variation within a trait. There is more junk DNA than one might think. The current estimate is somewhere over 90 percent of the total. However, it is possible that science has yet to determine the function of some so-called junk DNA. The particular thirteen STRs used in the FBI Combined DNA Index System, or CODIS, were selected because they can be rapidly determined from very small amounts of DNA, using commercially available kits; more important to the discussion here, laboratories worldwide are contributing to the analysis of STR allele frequencies in different human populations.

The seventy-three genetic markers used in the DNAPrint methodology (commercialized by DNAPrint Genomics), on the other hand, are termed "single nucleotide polymorphisms" (SNPs, pronounced "snips"). Each SNP is a specific place on the DNA molecule that can have one or more of the variant nucleotides (adenine, guanine, cytosine, or thymine [A, G, C, T]) in the population, termed "alleles." Certain alleles are more common in some races than in others, and sometimes, much more so. These have been called "ancestry informative markers" (AIMs). Just one or two or six AIMs are not enough to establish a person's race, that is, genetic ancestry. The more AIMs examined, the greater the probability of accurately determining the person's race. (The same holds true for physical racial characteristics and for blood groups—the more predictors, the greater the accuracy of the prediction—but AIMs are much more powerful). Repeatable, independent academic research has established that with 100 genetic markers, it is possible to sort people whose known ancestors are from Africa, Europe, Asia, or the Americas with almost 100 percent accuracy. DNAPrint Genomics has reduced the number of AIMs required to seventy-three and extended the methodology to determine the percentage of racial background in people of mixed ancestry.

After examining seventy-three DNA markers, Tony Frudakis of DNAPrint Genomics told the Baton Rouge serial-killer task force in the first week of March 2003 that it should shift its focus from white suspects to an African American of average skin tone, because his analysis indicated the perpetrator had 85 percent sub-Saharan African and 15 percent Native American ancestry. The seventy-three-marker DNAPrint, which became sufficiently developed for this type of investigation only in early 2003, determines an individual's proportion of East Asian, Indo-European, Native American, and sub-Saharan African ancestry and then compares these proportions against a database of 300 to 400 people already typed to produce a comparable skin tone. A suspect fitting the racial profile, thirty-four-year-old Derrick Todd Lee of St. Francisville, whose DNA matched that found at the crime scenes and who was indeed recognizably black, was arrested and charged with first-degree murder, rape, kidnapping, and burglary.

The methods of behavioral profiling that have been highly promoted in both blockbuster movies and "real crime" TV shows misled the police in the Baton Rouge case, because their compilation of cases supposedly solved showed the vast majority of serial killers to be white males ages 25–35. The DNAPrint methodology is correct at a rate as high as that for the individual DNA fingerprinting that is accepted as legally valid. As of mid-2003, there had been no independent confirmation of the DNAPrint methodology, but Frudakis told ABC News in June 2003 that in 3,000 blind tests (in which each person's self-reported race was unknown to technicians doing the DNA analysis), there was not a single error.

The Baton Rouge case is not the first time police have used DNA samples to identify or narrow the list of potential suspects. For over a year, Britain's Forensic Science Service (FSS) has employed what the agency terms "DNA photofitting," in which the genetic markers in the suspect's DNA found at a crime site are compared against a database of DNA markers that are more common in one race than in others. FSS even tests the suspect's sample for a gene associated with red hair.

If "race" were a mere social construction based upon a few highly visible features, it would have no statistical correlation with the DNA markers that indicate genetic relatedness. The maximum degree of genetic relatedness an individual has is with himself or herself—or with an identical twin (or two identical triplets, and so on). There is also a certain amount of "family resemblance" in facial features and the like, especially in groups that tend to marry among themselves. If the commonsense recognition of races based on a relatively small set of physical features reflects an underlying biological reality, then those visible features should be correlated with genetic resemblance (as measured by DNA markers) as well as with self-reported ancestry.

Unless race is a biological reality that gives important information about an individual's degree of genetic resemblance to the various human populations and the sequence in which those populations evolved by separating from other populations, it would be inconceivable to achieve the level of accuracy obtainable through the DNAPrint methodology. Indeed, given a sufficient number of markers, such analysis is capable of not only identifying race but predicting skin tone as well. To say the least, it also calls into question the "experiment" in the PBS *Race* documentary, in which students of different racial appearance were surprised to find that the similarity among them in mitochondrial DNA (mtDNA, which is inherited only along the maternal line) did not agree with either physical features or ancestry.

"Episode One: The Difference Between Us" of the PBS program showed an experiment in which students of different racial backgrounds obtained a buccal swab (a tissue sample collected by wiping the inside of the cheek with a cotton swab) to get a sample of their mtDNA. Then the students examined six selected mtDNA markers and used them to guess which other students' DNA would be most like theirs. They made their picks based upon the usual set of physical features and ancestry used in the commonsense definition of race. If race has any biological reality, their guesses should have been fairly on target. The students registered surprise when the two methods of racial sorting—physical features and ancestry on the one hand, and mtDNA markers on the other—did not agree. The transcript concluded: "If human variation were to map along racial lines, people in one so-called race would be more similar to each other than to those in another so-called race. That's not what the students found in their mtDNA."

The program's take-home message is that straightforward experimental evidence reveals "race" is a mere social construct, a snare and delusion, and that race has no real substance in biology. This unwarranted conclusion is clearly contradicted by the DNAPrint methodology previously described (see also Chapters 4 through 9). The PBS experiment, in effect, stacked the deck. First, the number of markers used in the experiment was below the standard of thirteen required by the FBI crime labs for even individual identification. A good analogy would be political-opinion polling. In order to get a valid result, the pollster must sample enough people.

Second, the experiment relied solely on mtDNA, which is inherited only along the maternal line. There is no reason physical racial markers should necessarily be inherited along only one of the two parental lines. To use the political-polling analogy, interviewing only women does not produce a valid sample of all voters. Males and females differ, on average, in that men tend to vote for conservative candidates, and women to support more liberal ones.

With enough markers and comparison of mtDNA and Y-chromosome DNA (which traces only the paternal line), scientists can even obtain biological verification of history. In India, for example, the Y-chromosome DNA reflects the Aryan invaders, whereas the mtDNA shows a greater presence of females from the indigenous population. Among Ashkenazi Jews, the Y-chromosome DNA reflects a Middle Eastern component; the mtDNA shows that these Jewish males interbred with local European women. The same is true for the Lemba, an African tribe that follows certain Mosaic practices and whose traditions have long professed a Jewish origin. The Y-chromosome data showed the male Jewish ancestry of the Lemba, and the mtDNA revealed their African maternal roots. Another example comes from Latin America, where there is a greater contribution of European Y-chromosome DNA versus Amerindian mtDNA. The usual pattern found in recorded history is that a small number of intruding males in a dominant position, either as powerful conquerors or rich merchants, mate with a much larger number of indigenous females. The top prize in this regard, perhaps, goes to Genghis Khan and his Mongol Golden Horde. One Y-chromosome study has shown that one in every 200 males alive today, mostly in Asia, is descended from the Great Khan.

How—and Why—Do We Know Race?

The fact is that the latest genetic technologies are, for the most part, confirming the classification schemes of not only traditional anthropology but also the commonsense understanding of race. Ordinary people can and do divide *Homo sapiens* into a number of reasonably discrete groups on the basis of reasonably objective criteria. No special expertise is required. A series of experiments in cognitive psychology carried out by social anthropologist Lawrence Hirschfeld showed that as early as age three, children readily classify people on the basis of racial characteristics, without having to be taught to do so. He presented the children with a series of drawings. Each drawing consisted of the figure of an adult (termed the target figure) and two figures of children, each of which shared one of three characteristics—race, body build (light or heavy build), and occupational uniform (postal or medical worker)—with the target. They were asked which of the two figures looked like the target did as a child; which of the two figures looked like it was the target's offspring; and which of the two figures looked most similar to the target. In the minds of the children being tested, race was predominant over the other two categories. The children "expected that race was more likely to be inherited and to remain unchanged over the life span than either occupation or body build." After almost fifteen years of such research, Hirschfeld concluded that children do not have to be taught to believe in the reality of race, nor do they believe it is just some superficial quality. Rather, they believe that "race is an intrinsic, immutable, and essential aspect of a person's identity," and "they come to this conclusion on their own."

Why can we do this? Why, in fact, are we so good at it? The reason is no mystery, or at least it shouldn't be. *Homo sapiens* is a socially interactive species and was so even before we became quite so sapient. The common ancestor we share with chimpanzees and all our ancestors along the way must have been able to recognize the members of their social group as individuals and, by extension, tell the difference between any of them and members of another group. So can baboons, wolves, dogs, killer whales, and lions (but not the other big cats, who are solitary) make such distinctions. The evolution of interactive sociality strongly selects for individuals who are able to recognize other similar individuals and adjust their behaviors with respect to who else is involved. The physical evidence for the evolutionary importance of this ability can be seen in the large amount of brain tissue devoted to these tasks at the base of our brains. As Hirschfeld concluded, "Because human groupings (i.e., collectivities of people based on gender, race, native language, or kinship status) are integral parts of nearly all social environments, acquiring knowledge of such groupings is a necessary part of the child's early development."

When they discuss evolution and social behavior, philosophers and ethicists never seem to tire of warning their readers against falling into what is known as "the Naturalistic Fallacy," namely that if some scientific research were to prove (or, at least, seem to imply) that there is a natural tendency for humans to be aggressive or rapacious, or even prejudiced, therefore we ought to be that way and consequently either approve of or ignore such behavior. The same ethical philosophers have shown much less interest in disabusing their readers of "the Moralistic

Fallacy," that is, arguing that since, according to many moral codes, humans ought not be aggressive, rapacious, or prejudiced, therefore, we *are* not—the scientific evidence be damned. We have already noted the recent tendency of proceeding from what one thinks ought to be to what is. One corollary of the Moralistic Fallacy has been the argument that since "race" is merely a social construction, and a very evil one at that, used to justify European colonialism and the enslavement and extermination of native peoples, the study of "race" inherently leads to the justification of "racism" in both thought and deed. And that did happen. In this realm *Homo sapiens* has hardly justified the species name *sapiens*—the "wise ones"—and one can depressingly wonder when, if ever, the species will become wise in this realm.

The race problem, or as social constructionists would prefer to put it, the "problem of race," will yield only through a broader and deeper historical and evolutionary perspective. . . .

We believe that recognition and study of racial differences are not racist if we insist on the realization that everyone can gain on an absolute basis even as differences between individuals and between groups might remain the same or even increase. In our view, the most important thing government can do is to remove all reference to group identity from both statutory and administrative law and to focus instead on enhancing the potential for achievement by individuals.

Imposing equality requires the use of government force, thereby reducing individual freedom. This is not only ethically unacceptable, but it also hamstrings individual initiative and the intellectual and economic growth that come with it. It also means insisting on maintaining a lie and thereby eroding freedom of speech and academic inquiry when research suggests otherwise.

But we also recognize that there is no such thing as a free lunch or even a free lunchroom. The meritocracy has its costs. As evolutionist Ernst Mayr noted, "Equality in spite of evident nonidentity is a somewhat sophisticated concept and requires a moral stature of which many individuals seem to be incapable."

Around 5 million years ago, out on the African savanna, our ancestors separated from the apes. Since that time, our cranial capacity has increased threefold. One would have to assume a concomitant, if not necessarily commensurate, increase in our cognitive ability. Around 50,000 years ago, modern *Homo sapiens* started to diverge into the racial lineages that definitely still exist and that are readily recognizable today. The task that lies before us in this millennium is to see how realistic, sophisticated, and ethical we humans can be in the minefield that is race, while coming out alive having traversed it.

The use of the DNAPrint methodology in identifying the Baton Rouge serial killer is described in Dana Hawkins Simons, "Getting DNA to Bear Witness: Genetic Tests Can Reveal Ancestry, Giving Police a New Source Of Clues," *Silicon Investor*, Science and Technology section, 6/23/03 (http://www.siliconinvestor.com/stocktalk/msg.gsp?msgid=19042492); Josh Noel, "Florida Lab Pointed to Race—Serial Killer Search Changed Course" (http://www.2theadvocate.com/cgi-bin/print_me.pl); ABC News, "Racial Profiling—Will a New DNA Test Shatter Serial Killer Profile?" (http://abcnews.go.com/sections?GMA?Primetime/forensics_serialkiller 030613.html); Nancy Touchette, "Genome Test Nets Suspected Serial Killer," *Genome News Network* (http://www.genomenewsnetwork.org/articles/06_03/serial.shtml); "Law Enforcement Independently Validate DNAPrint's Forensics Tests," *Forensic Nurse* (http://www.forensicnursemag.com/hotnews/31h2272358.html). The underlying methodology of DNAPrint is described in *DNA Witness 2.0 Validation Studies* (Sarasota, FL: DNAPrint Genomics in conjunction with National Center for Forensic Science and San Diego Police Department Crime Lab, no date). Descriptions of the methodology that have appeared in peer-reviewed scientific journals include Michael Bamshad et al., "Human Population Genetic Structure and Inference of Group Membership," *American Journal of Human Genetics* 72 (2003):578–589; and M. D. Shriver et al., "Skin Pigmentation, Biogeographical Ancestry, and Admixture Mapping," *Human Genetics* 112, 4 (2003):387–399.

The research on how children develop the concept of race without being taught can be found in Lawrence A. Hirschfeld, *Race in the Making: Cognition, Culture, and the Child's Construction of Human Kinds* (Cambridge: MIT Press, 1996), pp. 97, xi.

Reading Analytically

1. Since this piece argues for the "reality" of race, and its usefulness as a social category, Sarich and Miele must counter arguments that biological and genetic studies have suggested that race is a specious concept. What types of evidence do they present to build their counterargument?
2. The authors of this piece present two legal case studies as a key element of the argument that they are making. What specific facets of each case are used to illustrate that race is more than, as PBS suggests, an "illusion"? Note in particular the ways in which the authors

frame these legal decisions in order to build their case, pointing out lines that interpret the cases in ways meant to support their thesis.

3. In the final line of this excerpt, Sarich and Miele state that "the race problem, or as social constructionists would prefer to put it, 'the problem of race,' will yield only through a broader and deeper historical and evolutionary perspective." What is the difference between seeing the question as the "race problem," or as the "problem of race"? What are the implications of this difference as seen in the rest of this piece that lead up to this conclusion? Find specific lines in the piece that are meant to support that conclusion.

Reading Across Disciplinary Communities

1. Though Sarich is an anthropologist, the findings of anthropological studies are only one mode of evidence in the piece. What other fields of study are used in building this case? In what ways does Sarich use an anthropological eye even as he examines findings from those other fields of study?
2. As a journalist, Frank Miele is trained in using the words of expert voices to develop his own credibility as an author. What types of experts does he cite in this piece? How does he use direct quotations to build the credibility of his thesis? Provide at least three examples and discuss their effect upon the argument that this excerpt is building.

PHILIP KITCHER

Does 'Race' Have a Future?

In this piece, a philosopher asks not only if there is "a biological basis for dividing species into smaller units," but also examines the "uses" and "consequences" and the "prospects of doing better without racial categories." In this way, this essay demonstrates the ways that two disciplines—biology and philosophy—can interact with one another from their unique perspectives. Philip Kitcher holds a Ph.D. from Columbia University in Philosophy/History and the Philosophy of Science. As such, much of his work uses his philosophical training to interrogate the ethics and methods of other disciplines.

As you read this piece, you might consider how Kitcher at once draws upon scientific evidence and at the same time provides the kinds of larger questions that are typical of humanistic inquiry (as discussed in the

Introduction to this book). You might also consider how his arguments, like those of Sarich and Miele, question whether biology-based understandings of race are in and of themselves sufficient to eliminate the concept of race as a viable system of categorization.

I

There are simple and powerful arguments against the biological reality of race.[1] Although the phenotypic characteristics, the manifest features that have traditionally been used to divide our species into races, are salient for us, they are superficial, indicating nothing about important differences in psychological traits or genetic conditions that constitute some racial essence. Throughout history, allegations of deep differences in temperament and capacity, claims grounded in no evidence, have done incalculable harm. Contemporary genetic studies of human populations have revealed that there are no alleles distinctive of this race or of that, and, although a few researchers like J. Philippe Rushton—"ogre naturalists," as Ian Hacking aptly dubs them—continue to seek such simple genetic differences, there is a widespread consensus among anthropologists that races are not "biologically real."[2]

If you have a particular view of natural kinds, the line of reasoning I have just sketched will appear overwhelming. Suppose you believe that natural kinds are distinguished by some special underlying feature that explains the behavior of members of the kind—like atomic number, for example, in the case of the elements—then you will infer directly

An earlier version of this article was prepared for a symposium at the Eastern Division of the American Philosophical Association in December 2005. I am grateful to my co-symposiasts, Anthony Appiah and Tommie Shelby, for their exceptionally thoughtful presentations, to Macalester Bell for some insightful advance suggestions, and to members of the audience for their questions and comments. A later version was presented at a conference on "Race in the Age of Genomic Medicine," brilliantly conceived and organized by Koffi Maglo, at the University of Cincinnati, where I had the opportunity to learn from scholars in a variety of fields. Although all the speakers at that conference have influenced the final version, the greatest impact on my thinking came from presentations by Marcus Feldman, Keith Ferdinand, and Charles Rotimi. I also owe a large debt to Ian Hacking, both for his incisive writings about issues of classification over many years, and for sharing with me some important forthcoming work. Finally, I would like to thank the Editors of *Philosophy & Public Affairs*, for suggestions that have helped me to improve this article.

Source: Philosophy and Public Affairs Volume 35, Number 4, Fall 2007.

from the absence of special genetic or chromosomal markers of race to the biological insignificance of racial divisions. But there is a serious mistake here. The essentialist/explanationist approaches to natural kinds that have dominated much philosophical discussion in past decades have always been woefully inadequate as accounts of biological kinds.[3] Indeed, anyone familiar with the writings of two of the greatest evolutionary biologists of the last century, Theodosius Dobzhansky and Ernst Mayr, can only wonder at philosophical insistence on the idea that natural kinds have essences.[4] As Dobzhansky and Mayr tirelessly pointed out, biological taxa are not demarcated by essential differences; in general, there is no analogue of atomic number, no genetic feature, say, that separates one species of mosquito or mushroom from another; there are occasional exceptions, cases in which species of lizards are formed by hybridization or species of grasses result from doubling, or tripling, of chromosomes, but these are relatively rare.

Many of the premises from which eliminativists about race begin are correct, and important enough to repeat, again and again: there are no genes distinctive of the groups we call races, no biological markers of psychological or behavioral differences. In their studies of nonhuman organisms, however, biologists typically do not appeal to distinctive genes in their demarcation of taxa. Once this fact is appreciated, the question of race as a biological category should be recast. Is there a biological basis for dividing species into smaller units, and does appeal to this basis generate a division of our own species into races?

II

The obvious way to approach this question is to begin from the ways in which species are differentiated. Here, as I have argued elsewhere, we discover a number of species concepts, and the significance of this point will occupy us later. For the moment, however, I want to consider the approach to species most popular among naturalists (especially naturalists who study animals that reproduce sexually). Dobzhansky introduced, and Mayr articulated in great detail, the *biological species concept,* according to which species are clusters of populations that would freely interbreed in the wild, separated from other such clusters by *reproductive isolation.*[5] The notion of reproductive isolation is more delicate than philosophers typically appreciate. It does not entail that interbreeding is impossible: the fact that tigers and lions can produce hybrid progeny under conditions of captivity does not undermine their status as distinct species. Nor does it mean that interbreeding never occurs in the wild: there are well-studied cases of "hybrid zones" at the boundaries of species ranges. The important point about these hybrid zones is that they remain stable and relatively narrow; outside the special conditions, usually marked by a low density of the pertinent organisms, breeding is within the species.[6]

What causes reproductive isolation? Sometimes rather striking features of the organisms like incompatibility of the genitalia or a barrier to proper incorporation of genes into the zygote. Most often, however, the mechanisms are subtle. The courtship behavior of the male fly is rejected by the female of a different species, or the species are simply active at different times or in different places. In the Caribbean, lizard species of the genus *Anolis* sometimes differ in the fact that one species lives in the crowns of trees, another on the trunks, and yet another on the ground around the bases.

Much more could be said about this approach to species, but our interest lies with infraspecific units. As Dobzhansky and Mayr both saw, there are occasions on which we might want to divide a species into varieties or "local races," *species in statu nascendi.*[7] Consistent with the general approach to species, the obvious criterion to employ is one of *reduced* interbreeding. If we discover a population within a species that is mostly inbred, that is, it is considerably more probable that members of the population will mate with one another than with outsiders, then we have an embryonic version of the condition, reproductive isolation, that distinguishes species. Naturalists identify such populations as subspecies, or races.

I want to refine this conception a bit by recognizing explicitly something implicit in the biological practice: the populations are identified, of course, by phenotypic traits, differences that are sometimes slight, and it is assumed that these differences have arisen over generations of inbreeding. The notion of race is thus that of an inbred lineage, where the inbreeding may initially have resulted from geographical isolation that eventually gives rise to differences in phenotype and to some interference in free interbreeding, even when the geographical isolation is overcome. That notion is available for generating infraspecific units within any species, including *Homo sapiens.*

About a decade ago, I proposed that this was the way to make sense of race as a biological category. Quite independently, Robin Andreasen has deployed a different approach to species (the "cladistic species concept") to argue for a similar thesis.[8] Andreasen and I are united in accepting the biological facts to which eliminativists point; we insist on the absence of deep essential differences among biological races. More recently, Michael Hardimon has refined my conception of race in connection with our own species, suggesting that our ordinary concept of race is that of a relatively inbred lineage that emerges from a particular geographical region and manifests distinctive superficial traits that people find salient.[9] Two points are worth making about Hardimon's careful analysis. First, a similar refinement would be available along the lines marked out by Andreasen. Second, there are obvious prospects for a historical explanation of the emergence of racial concepts. The sorts of phenotypic features often used to demarcate races—skin color, hair texture, and so forth—have always been salient for humans (witness literary descriptions from ancient times); racial concepts were forged in the age of discovery, when clusters of these traits came to be associated with groups of people who had descended from ancestors in a particular region.

Suppose, then, that careful study of patterns of human mating discloses that there are inbred lineages, coming from particular regions and having acquired, over generations, slight differences in phenotypic features that people find salient. Suppose, further, that when the lineages come into contact, rates of inter-lineage mating remain significantly lower than those of intra-lineage mating. There are genuinely biological phenomena here, and a division of our species can be grounded in those phenomena.

But to leave matters at that is unsatisfactory. For the causes of the incipient reproductive isolation may be social. Recall the subtleties of isolating mechanisms, and the species of lizards differentiated by their positions on the trees. Perhaps people in one line of descent do not mate as frequently with those in another line of descent because their paths rarely cross, or rarely cross in contexts conducive to courtship, and perhaps the separation of places of activity comes about because those in one group have once made judgments about those in the other, judgments based on no evidence but profoundly consequential in fixing the socioeconomic status of the descendants of the judged. The biological phenomenon, the incipient isolating mechanism, is an effect of social attitudes, the result of marginalization and prejudice. These people belong to a different race because they were once *labeled*—mistakenly, ignorantly, unreasonably—as intrinsically different, for that initial labeling has given rise to the separation of their way of life from that of the labelers.

If that is so, races are both biologically real and socially constructed.[10]

III

I have outlined a view of human races that views them as biological kinds, not in the traditional, thoroughly misguided and harmful, way, but in line with the practice of naturalists who try to bring order to the organisms they observe and study. I could now go on to elaborate the view, and to support it with what evidence there is about human practices of mating. Instead, I want to argue that matters are far more complicated than I have portrayed them.

The simple eliminativist argument with which I began goes astray because of a mistaken premise about natural kinds: natural kinds have essences, and, in particular, biological kinds have genetic essences. The mistake is corrected by turning from a bad philosophical account of kinds to taxonomic practice in biology. But the account I developed also made philosophical presuppositions about natural kinds, presuppositions I now find dubious.

Those presuppositions stem from a realist view of natural kinds. Realists believe that nature is divided, independently of us, of our cognitive capacities and our interests. One of the important tasks of the natural sciences is to trace the divisions—in Plato's famous metaphor, to carve nature at its joints—and, in a discussion of progress, I once proposed that conceptual progress consists in adjusting language to those objective fault-lines.[11] If you accept a view like this, then you will be interested in the general types of divisions that various sciences draw, in the ways the fault-lines run. Once you see a particular type of division, division by microstructure, say, or division by interruption of free reproduction, then you will trace that sort of division wherever you can, and take the resultant boundaries to demarcate natural kinds. Interruption of free reproduction is important to biologists, and we should thus look for it within *any* group of organisms. A refusal to apply that principle of division to *Homo sapiens* would have to rest on an illicit separation of our species from the rest of the living world.

This picture no longer seems to be persuasive. I find it hard to envisage nature as prescribing the forms our language should take, as coming nicely organized with fence-posts that our concepts must respect. There is, as I see it, no feasible project of inquiry (singular) that aims at a complete account of our world, but rather many *inquiries* driven by specific questions we find it important to answer. We make conceptual progress by devising concepts that prove useful for us, with our particular capacities and limitations, to deploy in answering the questions that matter to us, and we should recognize that those questions are historically contingent and culturally variable. To use an analogy I find useful, there is a nondenumerable infinity of possible accurate maps we could draw for our planet; the ones we draw, and the boundaries they introduce, depend on our evolving purposes.[12]

Abandoning a strong realism about kinds does not mean giving up completely on realism. There is a world, one world, containing what is completely independent of us, and that world resists some of our efforts to draw boundaries within it; indeed, it resists the overwhelming majority of divisions we might try to find. There are nondenumerably many choices for demarcating objects within it, however, choices that the world would not resist. Other sentient and sapient beings with different capacities might be led to different choices; similarly for human beings with different interests. Even given a choice of boundaries for objects, a decision about where Manhattan stops or just how much space is included within a star, there are nondenumerably many ways to sort objects into kinds, and these, too, depend on our capacities and our purposes. In the sense that the world contains the so-far undifferentiated totality of what is independent of us, there is just one world. In the sense that the world is a collection of objects, assorted into types, there are many worlds, and we choose the one, or ones, in which we live.

The position I am sketching, probably too indistinctly, plainly recapitulates the views of Nelson Goodman.[13] Yet there are affinities with earlier authors, especially with James and Dewey, both of whom want to combine a version of realism with an insistence on the indefinitely multiple possibilities of classification.[14] That insistence, rather than the famous, and famously problematic, slogan about truth, seems to me to be the core insight of pragmatism with respect to issues about truth and realism. So, for brevity, I shall call the position I have sketched a *pragmatist* account of natural kinds (I use an indefinite article because it may not be the only one deserving the label).

This version of pragmatism about kinds can be defended by focusing on the pluralistic character of taxonomic practices in the sciences, especially within biology. A couple of decades ago, John Dupré and I argued, independently, that there were lots of different ways in which the world of living things can be divided up, according to the things human beings find salient and according to the purposes they have.[15] Dupré called his view "promiscuous realism" and I referred to mine as "pluralistic realism"; in essence, we continued to take the Platonic metaphor of a beast with joints seriously, and campaigned for multiple-jointedness. So, for example, I proposed that there were many different species concepts, appropriate for different purposes of inquiry. Both Dupré and I, however, tended to think in terms of manageable pluralism, or limited promiscuity; for my part, I took the Biological Species Concept to be one among a number of contenders. The real trouble, however, is that the Biological Species Concept itself allows for indefinitely many ways of development, depending on how one approaches the notions of population and of reproductive isolation. Even worse, it is quite evident that the multiplicity of species concepts I considered, and the folk divisions that Dupré rightly emphasized, pick out only a tiny subset of the possible ways in which people might shape their divisions of the natural world to different purposes. Promiscuity becomes rampant, and, as you appreciate that, the thesis that there is a vast number of ways to carve the beast at its joints, a vast number of privileged fault-lines in nature, topples over into the position that there are no privileged fault-lines at all, that the divisions are drawn to suit our purposes. Really promiscuous realism drops the realism and becomes pragmatism.[16]

I shall say no more by way of motivation and defense. My aim is to explore the consequences of this pragmatic approach to kinds for the naturalistic proposal about races outlined above. The first thing to note is that pragmatism renders suspect a crucial part of the argument for grounding races in biology. Once you move to pragmatism, you lose the general license to introduce a subdivision of *Homo sapiens* on the grounds that the principle of division accords with the infraspecific distinctions biologists make in other cases. The fact that it is useful for certain purposes to use reduced gene flow in a widespread species of oaks to talk about local varieties, or local races, does not mean that it will be useful to mark out similar divisions in the case of our own species. Pragmatism insists that the usefulness be demonstrated in the particular case at hand.

Here I find common ground with some criticisms that people have offered against the biologically grounded proposals made by Andreasen and me, criticisms that are especially cogent against my version. A common objection runs something like this: "You point to reduced interbreeding between human lineages that have been geographically separated and inbred during long periods. But this is likely to be a temporary phenomenon. Sooner or later, and hopefully sooner, the social barriers will be broken down; people will respond to the beauties of others without regard to the trivial differences of the phenotypic markers used in racial discriminations. Nobody seriously thinks that, in the human case, we can talk of *'species in statu nascendi'*—indeed, it would be a horrific thought."[17] I agree that the phenomenon of reduced interbreeding is likely to be temporary, and, indeed, I think the significance of elaborating the biological approach to race is to raise consciousness about the phenomenon so as to hasten the day when the social barriers disappear. I have been inclined to respond to the criticism by leaning heavily on a realist conception of kinds. Biologists pursuing evolutionary studies have shaped their concepts of species and subspecies to conform to the genuine fault-lines in nature; even in cases where there is no intention of pursuing an evolutionary project, of picking out incipient speciation within *Homo sapiens,* there are similar fault-lines; hence, without supposing that the notion of biological race in human beings is valuable to the same ends, it is still a legitimate biological category.

This response will not do. Given pragmatism about kinds, it is necessary to point to particular purposes that drawing racial divisions in this way would serve, purposes that can themselves be defended. If no such defensible purposes can be identified, then we should simply acquiesce in eliminativism. Indeed, the criticism can surely be strengthened. Given the immense harm that use of racial concepts has generated in the past, insisting on race as a legitimate biological category, even though that concept is linked to no valuable biological project, can seem irresponsible and even perverse. Moreover, even if the concept of race plays a role in some lines of biological inquiry, the values of those lines of inquiry, and of pursuing them through retention of the concept of human race, would have to be sufficiently great to outweigh the potential damage caused by deploying this concept in the other contexts in which it plays so prominent a role, namely in our social discussions.

In assessing this criticism, I think it helps to start with some clear instances of related biological categories that can be defended on pragmatic grounds. With respect to sexually reproducing organisms, a division according to reproductive isolation is valuable in pursuing certain kinds of evolutionary questions, precisely because, when two populations become reproductively isolated, changes in gene frequencies within the one are no longer reflected within the other. The ways in which descendant populations respond to selective pressures may thus be quite different. When the focus shifts to asexual organisms, it is not possible to make the division in exactly the same way, nor is it always appropriate to suggest that the distinctions be made according to the features that accompany division by reproductive isolation in the closest sexually reproducing relatives of the asexual organisms under study (a suggestion that Mayr has repeatedly offered in his attempts to claim a universal priority for the Biological Species Concept).[18] Consider, for example, asexual microbes, including some viruses, bacteria, and parasites.[19] Here taxonomic divisions are reasonably based on the molecules that give these organisms their distinctive ways of attacking the bodies of their hosts, or on the genotypes that underlie the production of those molecules. In effect, you look at what the microorganism *does* to the plant or animal it infects and then group together those microbes with the same crucial structures. It would be mad dogmatism to worry, in this context, about protecting some principle that genuine taxa can only evolve once: if a virus is completely wiped out, but researchers at a bioterrorism agency subsequently use the recorded sequence of its genome to synthesize an exactly similar organism, we would quite properly see them as having subverted the original program of eradication and as having reintroduced the very same virus. For the purposes that drive taxonomy here are medical; we need ways of classifying the microorganisms in terms of the structures that underlie the tricks they use to do harm to their hosts.

The challenge for someone who intends to defend a biological approach to human races is to develop a similar account for the utility of picking out those inbred lineages that descend from populations once geographically separated, in which, as a result of the separation, there are differences in superficial phenotypic traits, characteristics which, despite their superficiality, are salient for human beings.

IV

Contemporary research on genetic variation within human populations offers what initially appears to be a way of meeting that challenge.[20] Our recently acquired capacities for genomic analysis, coupled with a commitment to understanding human diversity, have enabled biologists to identify subspecific units within the human species—"clusters" as the researchers call them—based on measures of overall genetic similarity. In effect, studies of this kind are using techniques of statistical analysis that critics of the biological species have previously deployed at the phenotypic level, to discern groups that have probably been separated from other such groups for a large part of their ancestry. It is crucial to emphasize that the recognition of different clusters in no way contradicts the received wisdom that there are no racial essences: as the researchers point out, 93 to 95 percent of human genetic variation is found within the clusters (rather than between clusters); each cluster, then, is itself genetically quite heterogeneous.

Faced with the statistical analysis, and especially with the illuminating figures that present the data, it is tempting to say that here we have a completely objective division of the human species into infraspecific groups. We have put the question, and nature has spoken: there are races, or something akin to them. That conclusion, however, has to be hedged with qualifications. First, it is important to understand the question that has actually been put. Given rich data about individuals and bits of their DNA sequences, computer programs have sought divisions, *being told in advance how many clusters they are to find.* So, for example, we might ask, "If our species were to be divided into just two groups on the basis of genetic similarity, how would geographical populations be assigned to those groups?" and we would discover that the two clusters are "anchored by Africa and America" (Eurasian populations would be lumped with the African ones). Ask for three groups, and Eurasia is split off; ask for four, and East Asian populations form a distinct fourth group; ask for five, and Oceania is separated from the other East Asian populations.[21] So there is a genuine issue about *level* or *fineness of grain*, one that can only be settled on pragmatic grounds: the clusters, or races, will be picked out by fixing the number so that the resulting division best accords with the inquiries we find valuable.

Picking out new clusters preserves, in an important sense, the boundaries that have already been drawn. You may find new subdivisions within a previously identified unit, but you do not generate new clusters that straddle earlier ones. If two populations are assigned to different clusters at one value of the parameter, they remain separated at all higher values. On this basis, one might conclude that the pragmatic component in dividing the species is relatively insignificant, just a matter of finding the appropriate level in an objective tree-structure. There is, however, a second way in which the goals of inquiry affect the whole enterprise, one that elaborates the general points of the previous section. Why, we might ask, does clustering according to genetic similarity identify the significant units within the human population? The obvious answer is that hypotheses about genes, about genetic differences and genetic similarities, play important explanatory roles in addressing questions that matter to us, so that division on a genetic basis yields categories that are more valuable than, say, dividing people up according to the curvature of their eyebrows or the length of time for which they can stand on one leg. Yet here we should tread carefully, for the emphatic disavowal of racial essences already signals the fact that the clusters demarcated on the basis of genetic similarity are not going to play a significant role in the explanation of shared phenotypic features or susceptibilities to various types of disease. Indeed, the authors of the study *do* tread very carefully, linking the categories they introduce, not to some ("ogre naturalist") project of understanding differences in phenotypes, but to understanding the history of human migrations.[22] The fact that contemporary science takes the question "How did our species reach its current distribution?" as a significant one does not entail that there is a list, Nature's Agenda, on which it figures. It is posed because we find it significant: because of a fact about us. In principle, we might discover, on reflection, that it is not something we need to know, and, if that were to occur, then the enterprise of tracing genetically similar "clusters" would lose its principal rationale.

The pragmatic dimensions of our concepts are frequently invisible to us because we are so used to certain kinds of inquiries that they come to feel natural, externally given. Only when science changes dramatically, or when we realize that some lines of research have damaging social effects, do we pause to wonder if those inquiries are genuinely justified. On the face of it, the genetically similar clusters discerned in the brilliant work of Rosenberg, Feldman, and their associates are well adapted to the pursuit of important issues about human history. The pragmatism I commend would simply involve awareness of the fact that importance is conferred by us, and that the status can, in principle, be retracted.

V

The difficulty with biological projects of subdividing our species is that they appear to introduce a conceptual framework that can easily revive unjust and damaging social practices. Although contemporary research may speak of "clusters" rather than "races," it is relatively easy to foresee that the old, loaded word will often substitute for the aseptic scientific terminology.[23] As the researchers themselves note, self-reported ancestry (itself entangled with folk racial categories) can sometimes serve as a good proxy for an identification grounded in genetics.[24] The places where divergence is most likely to occur are in practices of classification that appeal to extraneous and superficial markers, where tangled prejudices easily come into play. Yet, of course, where prejudice still exists, overtly or disguised, there is ample motivation for assimilating the scientific classification as a cover for continued assertions about the reality of race.

This means that the notion of race is likely to continue to straddle the divide between well-motivated science (for example, the quest to trace patterns of human migration) and social applications. Any pragmatic assessment of its value will have to deal in a synthetic and balanced way with both types of context. We shall need an overall evaluation, one that takes into account all its potential uses and abuses. Recent debates about the continued deployment of 'race' and cognate terms are full of contending voices that emphasize selected aspects of the picture.

One might maintain, at this point, that these contending voices can be ignored, at least insofar as we are concerned with the legitimacy of a notion that has shown itself valuable in connection with a serious scientific project: once we know that talk of "clusters" is valuable in the study of human migrations, debate ends and the concept stands vindicated.[25] That version of pragmatism strikes me as too anemic. As I insisted above, the significance of scientific questions is conferred by us, and, in recognition of the problems associated with continued usage of a concept, it might be reasonable to suggest that, when all the consequences of using that notion are taken into account, we would be better off to give up on particular lines of research.

I anticipate obvious questions and worries. Does this strong pragmatic test set standards for justified scientific research that are impossibly demanding? I believe not. We would rightly worry about the continued deployment of a concept in fundamental physics, if thinking about nature in terms of that concept could lead, relatively directly, to the discovery of principles about the release of energy that would make massively destructive bombs available to anyone.[26] Similarly, if a concept, valuable to some investigators pursuing a particular research question, might cause, in the social world into which that concept is likely to make its way, considerable burdens for many people, then one ought *at least* to raise the question of whether such research is warranted. I emphasize that this is not a matter of *censorship*—the idea of a "thought police" that supervises research and issues interdictions against some programs is obviously counterproductive (as well as being distasteful); the ethical question "Should this research be done?" needs to be differentiated from the sociopolitical question "Should there be a public ban on exploring some types of investigations?"[27] We might answer both questions in the negative.

Many areas of scientific research would survive this stronger pragmatic test, for, although there are often uncertainties about the intellectual and practical consequences, the occasions on which one can confidently predict that damage is likely to be done are quite rare.[28] When such occasions arise, the obvious tactic is to try to find ways of insulating the research so that potentially damaging consequences do not occur. Precisely this sensible tactic is prefigured in the use of the term 'clusters' by the researchers on human migrations. Unfortunately, the pressure on science journalism, even in the most apparently respectable media, to sensationalize recent findings, led quickly to the demolition of the barrier that the investigators had hoped to erect.[29] So, to recapitulate my earlier conclusion, we need a thorough survey that considers all the potential uses and abuses.

VI

There is at least one type of social issue for which we might seem to require a notion of race based on separation of inbred lineages. People belong to two kinds of lineages, one biological and one cultural. The former relates us to our biological ancestors and descendants, the latter to those who pass on to us parts of our distinctive mix of ideas and ideals, lore and law, as well as to those to whom we pass on our traditions. When the biological line in which we stand belongs to a population whose lineages are inbred, and when the principal *cultural* ancestors and descendants of people in these lineages tend to be people who belong to the *biological* lineages, then we have a use for the notions of race and ethnicity, the one pointing to the line of biological descent and the other to the line of cultural descent. This provides a basis for exploring mismatches between race and ethnicity, to pose questions about the desirability of viewing members of a particular race as bearers of its culture. At the heart of claims about cosmopolitanism lies the thought that *cultural descent* should be liberated from the patterns associated with *biological descent*, that individuals should not be confined to the ethnicity associated with their race.[30]

There are genuine questions in this area, ranging from large issues about the survival of cultural traditions and the responsibility of biological descendants to preserve the lore of their ancestors to debates about the desirability of transracial adoption. 'Race' and 'ethnicity' provide convenient shorthand terms for exploring them, and for marking out the places in which concerns about the coincidence of biological inheritance and cultural inheritance coincide. All this, however, may seem far too slight to serve as a counter to the damage that is likely to be done by retaining a notion of race. For, after all, there are obvious and familiar costs to the continued use of racial distinctions.

The most obvious of these is the practice of stereotyping, whether it is manifest in the police practice of rounding up the usual suspects or in a teacher's forming a premature judgment about a young schoolchild. Sometimes the stereotype is imposed on the basis of a folk generalization, a claim that people of a certain race are more likely to have some undesirable trait, where not only do the appliers of the stereotype have no evidence for that claim but there is also in fact, absolutely no evidence for it to be found. On other occasions, however, there may indeed be a correlation that would stand up to serious investigation: evidence would disclose that people with a particular cluster of superficial phenotypic traits, who belong to a relatively inbred lineage that was once separated from other such lineages for many generations, are more likely to have the trait in question. Even here the practice is pernicious, for the correlation is readily mistaken for a causal diagnosis. Despite all our knowledge of the triviality of the genotypic differences between racial groups, the singling out of some racial groups as more likely to engage in criminal behavior (say) encourages the myth that there are deep features of membership in such groups that explain the increased probability. So the practice of stereotyping fosters backsliding into the ugly racial theses that have disfigured past centuries, and they recur in modern dress as searches for behavioral genes associated with criminality, genes alleged to be differentially distributed among the races.

In fact, the practice is even more hideous than I have represented it as being, for a better explanation of the correlations involves the *past* application of racial concepts. Where the correlations are sustained, where, for example, young men with particular phenotypes are more likely to engage in criminal behavior than young men with other phenotypes, nothing hangs on the phenotypes themselves, the textures and colors of skin and hair, nor on the distribution of alleles responsible for such traits. The accidental association occurs because of a past history of poverty and deprivation, one that continues into the present: young men with dark skin are not more likely to commit crime because of the darkness of the skin or because the alleles that code for proteins that increase melanin concentrations in the skin have some psychological side effect, but because they are poor, undereducated, given fewer opportunities, and so on. Behind these conditions, of course, we can trace a past history of discrimination. So, at the root of the causal story are past practices of identifying some people by the superficial characteristics, viewing them as belonging to a special race, and, in consequence, cramping and confining their aspirations and their lives. Crude essentialist notions of race, often committed to prejudiced speculations about the "biological bases" of various cognitive and behavioral traits, have played crucial roles in these practices. Application of the notion of race is thus ultimately responsible for the correlations adduced to "defend" the current practices of stereotyping; the old errors have unjustly generated conditions that now differentially affect people with different phenotypes, and racial stereotyping is likely to maintain the difference, enabling future generations of stereotypers to mount the same defense.

To abandon the recording of data in terms of racial categories would undermine an ability to support stereotyping by appeal to evidence of correlations, but it would probably not terminate the *beliefs* that prompt the application of stereotypes. Folk generalizations are likely to live on, and even to be reinforced by resentment of the decision not to collect data couched in racial categories. The eliminativist thought that the damage done by current employment of the concept of race can be undone by jettisoning the concept is surely too simple. Conceptual reform is no substitute for the serious work of ameliorating social conditions, and it is an empirical issue how much good conceptual reform alone can do.

Moreover, we may look at the harms and injustices caused by past use of racial concepts somewhat differently, inquiring whether retention of some, appropriately sanitized, notion of race is needed to correct them. Might sociological research not require a concept of race to identify the damage that has been done by various forms of racial discrimination? Perhaps repairing that damage may require policies of compensation, explicitly crafted in racial categories: think of programs of affirmative action. Even more importantly, the political struggle for remedying the injustices of the past may turn on developing racial concepts that foster forms of solidarity among those who now suffer from the effects of those injustices, as well as from the racism that is still perpetrated. Tommie Shelby has argued eloquently for redeploying a notion of race in these ways.[31]

Although the harm that accrues from the use of racial stereotypes surely outweighs the usefulness of deploying the notion of race to explore issues about race and ethnicity, not to mention the value of the concept of human race in biological inquiries, the pragmatic evaluation of the concept turns on a host of intricate questions for which it is hard to assemble empirical evidence.

In any event, however, scientific work in the past few years has added further complications.

VII

Although there are no distinctive *alleles* found in the relatively inbred lineages we might mark out as races, there is significant variation in the *frequencies* with which alleles occur in different human groups.[32] It is well known, for example, that the allele for Tay-Sachs occurs with greatest frequency among Ashkenazi Jews (as well as in some French Canadian populations), and that the mutations associated with cystic fibrosis are most common among people whose ancestors hail from northwestern Europe. Recently, however, it has become evident that the alleles that affect receptivity to bone marrow transplants are distributed in ways that reflect some traditional racial divisions; in particular, because of the variance in African American populations, it is important not only to use a racial category in classifying potential donors but also to appeal to people, identified by race, to donate. For those involved in trying to help people who urgently need a bone marrow transplant, the eliminativist proposal appears dangerously misguided. As Hacking rightly notes, they view the continued employment of racial categories as a matter of life and death.[33]

This is a striking instance of what we can expect to be a general phenomenon, one likely to become ever more evident. Because of the geographical isolation of some populations for long stretches of our human past, there are differences in the frequencies with which different alleles occur within those populations. As genomic studies reveal the variations in DNA sequences, and in the frequencies with which particular sequences occur in different relatively isolated populations, and as the medical significance of certain variants becomes known, it is to be expected that differential diagnosis can be facilitated by data on the rates at which particular sequences are found in different races. In many instances, the statistical information might be superseded by identifying the patient's sequences at the pertinent loci, but when treatment is needed immediately, or when the recommended approach depends on information about others (as in the example of transplants), the partitioning of the statistics according to race may be crucial.

In fact, there is an important difference between the issues that arise in tailoring prescriptions to patients who have different genotypes and recruiting donors for transplant programs. Suppose a doctor must prescribe for a patient. *Assume* it is already known that the disease for which relief is sought is associated with two different genotypes, one that is very common in one racial group (a lineage that has been relatively isolated for a significant chunk of human history) and another that is very common in a different racial group. There are two treatments, one good for cases that are associated with the first genotype and the other good for cases associated with the second genotype. Initially, knowing the person's race would seem valuable in deciding which treatment to prescribe. Yet a moment's reflection reveals a better approach: for the patient is *at hand* and (insurers permitting) can be tested to determine which genotype is present. Prescription can go better by moving beyond the racial classification to finer-grained sorting by genotypes.

In recruiting transplant donors, however, the people an agency wishes to attract are *not at hand*. Instead, one must appeal to markers that raise the probability of finding matches for members of particular groups, markers that are available to the intended audience. So, registry websites contain phrases like the following:

> Because tissue type is inherited, patients are most likely to match someone of their same race and ethnicity. There is a special need to recruit more donors who identify themselves as: Black or African American, American Indian or Alaskan Native, Asian, Hawaiian or Other Pacific Islander, Hispanic or Latino.[34]
>
> We are currently trying to recruit more African, African Caribbean and Mixed Race potential donors in our efforts to offer patients the CHANCE OF LIFE.[35]

Because African, African American, and African Caribbean populations are genetically diverse for the pertinent loci, the chances of finding a match are smaller than those for many other groups. This intensifies the need to recruit a large number of potential donors. If everyone had been tested, and knew *and remembered* his or her genotype at those loci, then the appeal could be couched in terms of requests for those with particular allelic combinations to volunteer. But it is utterly unrealistic to hope that we can replace self-identification by race with anything like that. From a practical point of view, the use of the racial category is necessary.

Moreover, recruitment by race may have a special force. When the racial groups involved have a history of marginalization (or worse), members of those groups may see themselves as joining together to tackle a problem that arises from their genealogical relationship. Here, in a medical context, racial solidarity may play a valuable role.[36]

I have starkly distinguished recruitment of donors from prescription of medicines by taking advantage of convenient idealization: I assumed that the causes of differential effectiveness were genetic, and that these were already known. In many instances, however, doctors are aware of an effect that correlates with racial classifications, but are ignorant of the causes. They see the decision to prescribe differently for members of different races, where races here are demarcated in everyday ways and are available to patients in their own self-identification, as an interim measure, valuable in a condition of imperfect information. Perhaps at some future time the causal factors responsible for differential reactions to alternative drugs will be understood, perhaps they will be genetic, and the physician's decision can be taken in the more fine-grained way I imagined. In arriving at that knowledge, however, epidemiological data will be required, and the crude correlation may prove helpful in arriving at the causal explanation. So the use of racial categories here is not just a stopgap measure to treat patients, but part of an investigative strategy for doing better.

Recent debates about "race-based medicine" (see, for example, the BiDil® controversy) bring out two further complications. First, skeptics about the role of race in medicine argue that the racial classifications that appear in the alleged correlations are unlikely to be good indicators of genetic differences. Their caution is justifiable, given that the racial groups across which differential responses are supposed to occur—"African Americans" and "Whites"—are unlikely to accord very closely with clusters demarcated by genetic analysis; these are just the sorts of cases in which social criteria are likely to distort class membership and prevent self-identified ancestry from serving as a good proxy for genetically distinctive populations. So, although critics may concede the point that relying on a crude correlation is the best available strategy for treating patients in the here and now, they are skeptical of the value of racial categories as vehicles for refining our ignorance about the causal factors responsible.

The second complication arises as a response to this line of criticism. It is quite possible that *environmental* differences may affect aspects of the human phenotype that determine the efficacy of a drug, and that those environmental differences may themselves be caused by the social practice of assigning people to different races. It is very clear that African Americans (the people inclined to designate themselves in this way) are markedly less well served by U.S. medicine than other major groups. Quite plausibly, part of that difference results from their having been identified in this way from the time of their birth, through chains of causation that give rise to unhealthy living conditions, limited prospects, and alienation from institutions that tend to promote the health of more fortunate people. To the extent to which hypotheses of this sort are correct, self-identified racial membership is an important causal variable, not because it serves as a proxy for *genes*, but because it is a reliable indicator of ways in which racial discrimination survives in environmental conditions that decrease health.

"Race-based medicine," conceived as the reiteration of the familiar theme that different races have different alleles and thus different propensities for disease, is rightly criticized. Understood differently, it may involve an appreciation of the ways in which social discrimination acts through the physical environment to diminish health. More than a temporary measure, a way of coping with sick people in a situation of relative ignorance, it can be viewed as a commitment to understanding the causes of differential morbidity and mortality, and even as a method of creating trust among people who have been neglected by and who have become alienated from the institutions of U.S. medicine, a tacit promise that, at last, their plight is being taken seriously.[37]

VIII

Let us take stock. In rejecting a realist approach to natural kinds, I have suggested that the legitimacy of notions of race has to depend upon the suitability of those notions to our purposes. At first sight, the damage that racial concepts have caused, and continue to cause, makes it look as though we come to eliminativism by a nonstandard route. I have been trying to suggest, however, that matters are far more complicated than they initially appear. Not only are there uses that pull in different directions, but there are also serious, unresolved empirical issues, I believe, about what conceptual reform might accomplish.

How, then, to go on from here? My answer is in the spirit of the pragmatism I have been espousing, and also of the plea for a more democratic science that I have tried to defend in recent years.[38] The phrase "the suitability of the notion of race to our purposes" is radically incomplete as a characterization of any test to which racial concepts might be subjected. For, although one can pick particular contexts and uses as they seem salient—as I have done by pointing to questions about human migrations, about race and ethnicity, about racial stereotypes, and about medical uses of racial categories—these are a poor substitute for a systematic survey of the variety of uses to which racial concepts might be put, an investigation of their effects, and an exploration of what might be achieved by eliminating the concepts. There is much here that is unknown, unknown not simply to academic philosophers but to anyone. A responsible verdict on the notion of race must await the elaboration of information about all the uses, their consequences, and the prospects of doing better without racial categories.

Although that is necessary, it is hardly sufficient. For the fact that notions of race have surfaced both in scientific inquiry and in socially consequential debates means that the continued viability of these notions should not be decided by any group of academic researchers. As so often, the glib first-person plural, "our purposes," disguises the heterogeneity of perspectives that different groups of people might bring, even when presented with the ideal elaboration of information. If there are any groups whose voices should be heard in rendering the verdict the pragmatic test demands, then they should surely be those who have suffered most from the past employment of the categories. This strikes me as a clear case in which the declaration of independence of scientific inquiry rings hollow, an exemplar of the need for that involvement of the judgments of informed outsiders for which I have argued elsewhere. 'Race' is a viable concept just in case it would be hailed as such by a set of ideal deliberators, inclusive with respect to variant human perspectives, fully informed by the systematic elaboration I have seen as a necessary part of the pragmatic test, and mutually engaged. At present, we can only speculate about how that discussion would come out.

Are races natural kinds? I believe not, because I am dubious of the notion of natural kind. There are biological phenomena that can be connected with infraspecific distinctions biologists find it useful to make in nonhuman cases, and, more to the point, that are valuable for research on human historical geography. That does not clinch the case for making infraspecific divisions within our own species. There is a genuine issue about whether the category of race is worth retaining. I hope to have said enough to show that settling that issue is harder than it might appear, that there are considerations pulling in different directions. Beyond that, I have tried to argue that the pragmatic test of racial concepts will depend upon systematic explorations, and the amassing of information nobody yet has, and, most importantly, that it should involve people who have usually been left out of the discussion.

Notes

1. These have been well presented by many anthropologists in recent decades; see, for example, F. B. Livingstone, "On the Nonexistence of Human Races,"

in *The Concept of Race*, ed. Ashley Montagu (New York: Free Press, 1962). Useful recent summaries are provided by Stephen Molnar, *Human Variation* (Englewood Cliffs, N.J.: Prentice-Hall, 1992); and by Jared Diamond, "Race without Color," *Discover* 15 (1994): 82–89. Appiah offers lucid philosophical presentation in his contribution to Anthony Appiah and Amy Gutmann, *Color Conscious* (Princeton, N.J.: Princeton University Press, 1997).

2. Ian Hacking, "Why Race Still Matters," *Daedalus* 134 (2005): 102–16; J. Philippe Rushton, *Race, Evolution, and Behavior* (New Brunswick, N.J.: Transaction Press, 1995).
3. Hacking has made it extremely clear that what philosophers call the "Kripke-Putnam" theory of kinds comprises two related, but distinct, approaches (and explicitly not a fully developed theory). See his forthcoming essay, "Putnam's Theory of Natural Kinds and Their Names Is Not the Same as Kripke's," where he points out how Putnam looks to underlying structures as sources of explanation rather than as essences.
4. Their articulation of a nonessentialist approach to species begins in two classic works of the neo-Darwinian synthesis. See Theodosius Dobzhansky, *Genetics and the Origin of Species* (New York: Columbia University Press, 1937; reprint 1982), especially chap. X and Ernst Mayr, *Systematics and the Origin of Species* (New York: Columbia University Press, 1942; reprint Harvard University Press [Cambridge, Mass.: 1999]), chap. II–V. Mayr reiterated his main arguments, and his defense of the "biological Species concept," throughout his long career.
5. In Mayr's classic formulation, "Species are groups of actually or potentially interbreeding natural populations, which are potentially isolated from other such groups," *Systematics and the Origin of Species*, p. 120; it should be noted that this is the abbreviated version of Mayr's definition, even though it is typically repeated as Mayr's analysis.
6. See M. J. Littlejohn and G. F. Watson, "Hybrid Zones and Homogamy in Australian Frogs," *Annual Review of Ecology and Systematics* 16 (1985): 85–112; and N. H. Barton and G. H. Hewitt, "Analysis of Hybrid Zones," *Annual Review of Ecology and Systematics* 16 (1985): 113–48.
7. The term is introduced in Theodosius Dobzhansky and Boris Spassky, "*Drosophila paulistorum*, a cluster of species *in statu nascendi*," *Proceedings of the National Academy of Sciences* 45 (1959): 419–28. It is taken up in Mayr, *Animal Species and Evolution* (Cambridge, Mass.: Harvard University Press, 1963), and in Theodosius Dobzhansky, *Genetics of the Evolutionary Process* (New York: Columbia University Press, 1970); but it is effectively present in the discussions of notions of race from *Genetics and the Origin of Species* and *Systematics and the Origin of Species* on.
8. Robin Andreasen, "A New Perspective on the Race Debate," *The British Journal for the Philosophy of Science* 49 (1998): 199–225.
9. Michael Hardimon, "The Ordinary Concept of Race," *Journal of Philosophy* 100 (2003): 437–55.

10. It is worth emphasizing that there is nothing paradoxical here. We can apply either label depending on how deeply we intend to probe the causal history of our practices of racial classification.
11. See Philip Kitcher, *The Advancement of Science* (New York: Oxford University Press, 1993), chap. 4. In a forthcoming essay, "Plato's Joints," Laura Franklin-Hall subjects Plato's metaphor to devastating scrutiny.
12. See Philip Kitcher, *Science, Truth, and Democracy* (New York: Oxford University Press, 2001), chap. 5. I attempt to explicate the analogy further in "Scientific Realism: The Truth in Pragmatism" (forthcoming).
13. The obvious link is to his *Ways of Worldmaking* (Indianapolis, Ind.: Hackett, 1978). But the same general view is also present much earlier in the dependence of kinds on practices of projection that appears in Nelson Goodman, *Fact, Fiction, and Forecast* (Indianapolis, Ind.: Bobbs-Merrill, 1956).
14. See William James, *Pragmatism*, Lecture VII; John Dewey, *The Quest for Certainty*, chap. 5, *Experience and Nature*, chaps. 1–2.
15. John Dupré, "Natural Kinds and Biological Taxa," *Philosophical Review* 90 (1981): 66–90, and *The Disorder of Things* (Cambridge, Mass.: Harvard University Press, 1993); Philip Kitcher, "Species," *Philosophy of Science* 51 (1984): 308–33.
16. Some critics of my proposals about species came close to seeing this point; see, for example, P. Kyle Stanford, "For Pluralism and Against Realism about Species," *Philosophy of Science* 62 (1995): 70–91.
17. Concerns along these lines were offered independently by Anthony Appiah, Amy Gutmann, and Michele Moody-Adams.
18. See *Systematics and the Origin of Species*, p. 122, for recognition of the problem with asexuality; for a succinct statement of Mayr's later attempts to deal with it, see *The Growth of Biological Thought* (Cambridge, Mass.: Harvard University Press, 1982), pp. 283–84.
19. For penetrating discussion of the taxonomic issues that arise with respect to bacteria, see Laura Franklin-Hall, "Bacteria, Sex, and Systematics," forthcoming in *Philosophy of Science*.
20. The landmark article is Noah Rosenberg et al., "Genetic Structure of Human Populations," *Science* 298 (2002): 2381–85. Effectively, this article is the culmination of the "respectable" biological theorizing about infraspecific—"racial"—divisions that proceeds from the work of Dobzhansky and Mayr to the contemporary achievements of L. L. Cavalli-Sforza and Marcus Feldman. Feldman is in fact the last-named author of the Rosenberg et al. study.
21. Interestingly, as the authors point out, the sixth population is a relatively isolated group from Pakistan; at this stage the association of clusters with major geographic regions breaks down. See Rosenberg et al., "Genetic Structure of Human Populations."
22. Here they continue in a direct way the inquiries carried out by Cavalli-Sforza. It is also worth noting that the kinds of rationale for introducing genetically based classifications that emphasize the causal role of genes in giving rise

to human phenotypes (rationales most evident in the writings of "ogre naturalists") are quite alien to biologists like Cavalli-Sforza and Feldman, both of whom have been persistent and subtle critics of tendencies to crude genetic determinism.

23. As it did, almost instantly. The *New York Times* rightly saw this as extremely important scientific work, and, ignoring the cautious language of the article, reported it as a regrounding of the concept of race.
24. Rosenberg et al., "Genetic Structure of Human Populations."
25. I am indebted to an Editor of *Philosophy & Public Affairs*, who suggested that I should confront directly the issues raised in the next few paragraphs.
26. This possibility is explored in Dürrenmatt's play *Die Physiker*. I have elaborated on the moral in chapter 8 of *Science, Truth, and Democracy*.
27. See *Science, Truth, and Democracy*, chap. 8, and also "An Argument about Free Inquiry," *Noûs* 31 (1997): 279–306.
28. This also means that we only rarely have to confront the obviously difficult issues about how to weigh intellectual values (greater understanding of some aspect of nature) against practical concerns.
29. In the *New York Times* article that rightly celebrated the beautiful research, the term 'cluster' immediately gave way to 'race.' (It is unclear whether the substitution resulted from a connection that might appear natural to well-meaning people, or whether it should be charged to culpable carelessness.) I heartily sympathize with the tactic pursued by Rosenberg, Feldman, and their colleagues, but any effective use of this tactic will have to come to terms with the ways in which social interests and prejudices distort the transmission of knowledge. I discuss related issues in "Knowledge and Democracy," *Social Research* (2006). It is also worth noting that Möbius, the central figure of Dürrenmatt's *Die Physiker*, also tries an insulating strategy—and that he fails.
30. I discuss issues of this sort at greater length in sections VI and VII of my essay "Race, Ethnicity, Biology, Culture," in *Racism*, ed. Leonard Harris (Amherst, N.Y.: Prometheus Books, 1999), pp. 87–117; reprinted as chap. 11 of Philip Kitcher, *In Mendel's Mirror* (New York: Oxford University Press, 2003).
31. Tommie Shelby, *We Who Are Dark* (Cambridge, Mass.: Harvard University Press, 2006). In his APA symposium presentation, Shelby gave a concise but forceful account of the uses of racial categories, along the lines I give here.
32. To acknowledge this is *not* to embrace essentialism. I note this because discussions with philosophers who have made outstanding contributions to our understanding of racial concepts have convinced me that there are serious misunderstandings of any proposals that recognize this kind of genetic variation—in some instances, I have even found an inability to hear the words that present recent genomic findings. For those who have difficulty, Hacking's lucid explanation in "Why Race Still Matters" ought to be required reading.
33. Ian Hacking, "Why Race Still Matters," *Daedalus* (2005): 102–16, at p. 108.
34. http://www.katiasolomonfoundation.org/CordandMarrowDonation.html. I conjecture that the appeal statement uses both terms 'race' and 'ethnicity' not

because of any confusion about the relation of the cultural concept of ethnicity to genotypes, but because the foundation simply wants to maximize the number of responses.

35. http://www.aclt.org/details/d.aspx/16. Capitals in original.
36. Here, evidently, I echo the arguments that Shelby has constructed for the *social* uses of solidarity.
37. This point parallels Shelby's case that racial notions may be needed to understand, and correct, patterns of past prejudice. In the medical context, it has been made very eloquently by Keith Ferdinand.
38. Philip Kitcher, *Science, Truth, and Democracy*; also "What Kinds of Science Should Be Done?" in *Living with the Genie*, ed. Alan Lightman, Dan Sarewitz, and Christina Dresser (Washington, D.C.: Island Press, 2003), pp. 201–24.

Reading Analytically

1. At the end of his first section, Kitcher asks a key question: "Is there a biological basis for dividing species into smaller units, and does appeal to this basis generate a division of our own species into races?" Separate these two questions and consider how they are different from one another, and how the second question is dependent upon the first. Then discuss how these two questions frame the rest of his essay.
2. Several key terms are crucial to Kitcher's argument. Using context clues from Kitcher's essay, define the following terms as they are used by the author. That is, do not use "dictionary definitions," but find language within the essay itself that helps you to understand these terms: *eliminativists, reproductive isolation*, *taxonomic*, and *pragmatism*.
3. Kitcher moves from a study of how races are defined to a discussion, via pragmatism, of the effects of those definitions and divisions. In the end, which of the two perspectives on the title question, "Does 'Race' Have a Future?" does he seem to favor? Where does he indicate that preference?

Reading Across Disciplinary Communities

1. One of the tasks of the humanities is to provide broader perspectives on the work of other disciplines, asking questions that would otherwise go unasked. What type of questions does Kitcher ask of the sciences that might not be asked by scientists themselves?
2. As a philosopher, Kitcher uses forms of evidence that are based not only in empirical evidence, but in logical reasoning about that evidence. List at least two instances in which Kitcher pauses to build a logic-based study of some tenet of scientific fact. Then describe the method he uses to help the reader follow his process of logic.

PATRICIA MCCANN-MORTIMER, MARTHA AUGOUSTINOS, AND AMANDA LECOUTEUR

Race and the Human Genome Project

Constructions of Scientific Legitimacy

This essay was written by three psychologists who study the uses of language or "rhetoric." They examine ways that scientific findings have been used to change public understandings of race. All three authors were members of the Department of Psychology at the University of Adelaide, in the Discourse and Rhetoric Unit.

As psychologists who are interested in the ways that language affects human behavior, the authors here construct a study of not just the physical facts about race, but of the ways that the language is a primary feature in how we see the world. As such, this piece can help us to see how the social sciences interact with the biological sciences; the piece can also provide some experience with the ways that one does "rhetorical analysis"—studying how words are used persuasively. That type of analysis can be applied to each of the readings in this section to consider how each author attempts to construct the concept of race in ways that support his or her argument.

Abstract: At the public announcement of the completion of a draft map of the human genome (June 2000), Craig Venter, Head of Celera Genomics and chief private scientist involved with the Human Genome Project, claimed that 'race' was not a scientifically valid construct. This statement, based on an analysis of the genomes of five people of different ethnicities, has not served to end the considerable discussion and debate surrounding the concept of 'race.' Using a social constructionist and critical discursive approach, this study analyses text and talk associated with the debate on the scientific validity of the concept 'race.' Given the problematic and highly contested nature of this concept, the present research examines, closely and in detail, a range of ways in which constructions of truth are worked up in scientific discourse. In particular, we analyse the ways in which empiricist and contingent repertoires within scientific discourse are mobilized to establish and contest claims of objectivity and facticity. We also examine a range of rhetorical devices deployed by protagonists in the debate to warrant particular truth claims including quantification rhetoric and the 'Truth Will Out Device' (TWOD). We conclude that despite the promissory representation of the Human Genome Project as having produced scientific evidence to discredit the biological legitimacy of 'race,' the concept is likely to persist in both popular and scientific usage.

This last sentence of the abstract captures the thesis of the piece: Though much biological research suggests that race is not a significant category, it is still likely to persist in human usage. This shows how the natural sciences and social sciences both have a stake in the concept of race—one looking at the human being's physical makeup, the other looking at how humans interact.

The recent completion of a map of the human genome has been described as one of the most important and significant scientific developments in history. Advances in molecular genetics and the biosciences not only offer new possibilities for human biological intervention; they also have the potential radically to transform the ways in which we come to construct what it is to be human. Our notions of self, personhood and identity will increasingly be shaped by the knowledge this research disseminates about the genetic bases of human behavior (Novas and Rose, 2002). Among the heightened expectations generated by the Human Genome Project (hereafter, HGP), scientists optimistically claimed that the project would provide definitive answers to enduring questions concerning the scientific status of 'race' as a biological category. Indeed, following the completion of a draft map of the human genome in June 2000, Craig Venter (Head of Celera Genomics, and chief private scientist involved with the HGP) claimed that his analysis of the genomes of five people of different ethnicities had demonstrated that 'race' was not a scientifically valid construct. Typically, however, Venter's claim has not served to end the debate regarding the validity of the concept of 'race.' Using a discursive approach to examine the nature of fact construction, this article focuses on some instances of text and talk associated with the ongoing debate about the scientific validity of the concept 'race' that were generated in the public domain following Venter's claims. Given the highly contested nature of the concept, the present research aims to examine, closely and in detail, some of the ways in which constructions of truth about 'race' are typically worked up in scientific and media discourse. In particular, we analyse the ways in which empiricist and contingent repertoires are mobilized to establish and contest claims of objectivity and facticity. We also examine a range of

This sentence suggests one potential outcome of mapping the human genome—determining if race is a true biological category or just a social invention.

rhetorical devices that were typically deployed in the debate to warrant particular claims about genetics and 'race.'

This begins to lay out the methods that the writers will use to examine their question. "Empiricist" repertoires suggest the work of natural scientists; "contingent" repertoires suggest the work of social scientists and humanists. Thus, this article looks at the concept of race in an interdisciplinary way.

The Concept of 'Race'

Like the concept of gender, 'race' is entrenched in both popular usage and scientific discourse as a taken-for-granted, essentialist category. Essentialist views of 'race' emerged and proliferated in the first half of the 19th century and held that different 'races' constituted fixed and distinct biological entities or species (Richards, 1997). European imperialist expansion and colonial rule over indigenous peoples during this period created ideal conditions for the proliferation of essentialist beliefs. Such views were widely held among anthropologists, ethnographers and biologists between 1850 and 1910, and coincided with Social Darwinist beliefs about a natural biological hierarchy between different racial groups (Richards, 1997). Social Darwinism generated a fertile ground for the emergence of scientific racism and, in particular, the empirical investigation of biological and psychological 'racial' differences. This research program was vigorously pursued in the US between 1910 and 1940, particularly as 'race psychology' came to dominate the concerns of US psychologists. After the 1940s, however, influential scholarly critiques of scientific racism led to the eventual demise of this research focus.

Central to the decline of scientific racism was the discrediting of the validity of 'race' as a scientific category by geneticists during the 1930s (Cunningham-Burley and Kerr, 1999; Richards, 1997). The view that 'race' was not a scientifically valid concept was further consolidated in the 1950s. Gannett (2001: S482) cites the UNESCO Statements on Race in 1950 and 1951 as marking 'a consensus among social scientists and natural scientists that population geneticists had successfully demonstrated that "race" is a social construct without biological foundation.' Richards (1997) argues that, by 1968, 'the concept of "race" was at best a convenient short-hand term for reproductively isolated populations . . . of dubious applicability to humans among whom such populations were extremely rare' (pp. 252–3). Despite the emergence of such constructions, and the fact that a majority of scientists from many disciplines saw 'race' studies as scientifically obsolete, debate over the scientific status of the concept has continued (Billig, 1998). The debate has been resurrected several times during the latter part of the 20th century, most notably in the controversy over 'race' and intelligence that was invoked by Jensen in the 1970s, and again in the 1990s by Hernstein and Murray's populist writings on the 'bell curve,' and Rushton's views on racial differences. In psychological research in particular, the concept of 'race' continues to be used unproblematically as a 'natural' kind variable in ways that reinforce the commonplace view that it is a biological and genetic reality (Tate and Audette, 2001).[1]

This paragraph reviews the historical changes in our concept of race, which moved toward a belief that race is not biologically valid—that humans are more alike than different, despite racial categories.

Given the entrenched use of 'race' as a commonsense, 'natural' category to classify people in both everyday and scientific discourse, it is perhaps not surprising that Venter's statement regarding the scientific illegitimacy of the concept was met with skepticism and incredulity by scientists and members of the public alike. All indications suggest that the controversy over the scientific legitimacy of 'race' will continue well into the 21st century.

Race and the Human Genome Project

Throughout the last decade, the HGP was presented to the public as a research enterprise that was essential for the development of significant technological, scientific, and medical advances. Graphic metaphors were employed both by scientists and the media, in presenting this scientific knowledge for public consumption. The mapping of the human genome was depicted, for example, as a search for 'the essence of human life' and as the decoding of the 'book of life' (Nelkin and Lindee, 1995; Nerlich et al., 2002; Petersen, 2001). This promissory construction of the HGP not only emphasized how knowledge generated by this project would revolutionize science, but also stressed its enormous potential for alleviating human suffering associated with a range of medical and genetic disorders. At the same time, however, considerable controversy and criticism surrounded the project on a number of fronts. Most notable were concerns about the ethical and social consequences associated with the potential uses (and abuses) of genetic information and genetic interventions. Many critics also pointed to the proliferation of reductionist explanations for an array of human behaviors. During the last decade, numerous studies have purported to have discovered genetic links to a growing number of behavioural and personality characteristics. These have included traits such as creativity, aggressiveness, tendency to worry (McCann-Mortimer et al.), extroversion, novelty seeking, high anxiety, sociability, and sexual

This "promissory" characterization of genetic research is also discussed in the article by Beatrix Rubin included in Chapter 2 of this book.

orientation (Rifkin, 1998). Nelkin and Lindee (1995), amongst others, argued that genetic essentialism was pervading popular culture and everyday public understandings of human behaviour. Analyzing diverse sources such as television, advertising, newspapers, magazines, film and literature, they demonstrated the increasing pervasiveness of genetic essentialism as a powerful discourse which 'reduces the self to a molecular entity, equating human beings, in all their social, historical, and moral complexity, with their genes' (p. 2). Moreover, persistent and entrenched social problems such as poverty, educational underachievement, mental illness, delinquency, alcoholism, violence, and criminal behaviour, were being increasingly attributed to 'deficient' or 'problematic' genes by experts, rather than to the social conditions in which people lived (Nelkin and Lindee, 1995; Rifkin, 1998).

Note how the review of the literature gives important background from previous research—research upon which the writer will build. As you do research projects, that is the purpose of your initial research—to learn the state of the conversation on a topic.

Controversy also surrounded the Human Genome Diversity Project (HGDP), a sub-program of the HGP with the scientific goal of sampling and mapping the DNA sequences of diverse population groups. The project's emphasis on possible DNA group differences led to significant concerns about the potential of the project 'to contribute to racism' (Gannett, 2001). The project particularly targeted Indigenous groups for DNA sampling, though this was met with strong resistance from some Indigenous organizations who were aggrieved at not having been consulted. Some have branded the HGDP the 'vampire project' and described it as a form of 'genetic colonialism' (Dodson and Williamson, 1999). These concerns were hardly surprising given that research on human variation that has been categorized as 'racial' has a long history of being misused to justify oppressive social practices and to legitimate inequalities between groups. Indeed, a report issued by UNESCO's International Bioethics Committee in 1996 argued that the genetic information generated by the HGDP had the potential to be misappropriated for racist ends by those seeking whatever scientific support they could find to legitimate discriminatory beliefs (Gannett, 2001).

In contrast to concerns about the project's potential to support racist ideologies and practices, its advocates argued that the HGDP would prove once and for all that discrete biological 'races' do not exist (Gannett, 2001; Kohn, 1995); that 'race' was a *social* and not a valid *scientific* construct. According to Kohn (1995), scientists

This shows the key controversy between those who feared that mapping the human genome would suggest that race (and perhaps racism) was scientifically justifiable, and those who believed it would show that race is just a social construct, a set of categories with no real scientific merit.

involved with the HGP claimed that, far from contributing to racism, the project would 'make a significant contribution to the elimination of racism' (p. 37) by demonstrating the biological unity and genetic heterogeneity of different population groups. Indeed, at the public announcement of the completion of a draft map of the human genome, this promise was partly kept.

On 26 June 2000, Frank Collins, leader of the publicly funded Human Genome Project, and Craig Venter, Head and Chief Scientist of the privately funded company, Celera Genomics, met at the White House with President Bill Clinton to announce their historic milestone to the world. President Clinton utilized a series of vivid metaphors to emphasize the scientific significance of the working draft, describing it as 'the most important, most wondrous map ever produced by humankind', and 'the language in which God created life' (see Nerlich et al., 2002). Clinton, together with the HGP scientists, also presented this scientific advance as having widespread potential benefits such as eliminating endemic illnesses like cancer and heart disease. Moreover, Venter declared that the project had helped to 'illustrate' that the concept of 'race' 'had no genetic or scientific basis'. This scientific claim was re-affirmed in another Celera press release, issued when the genome map was published in *Science* and *Nature* in February 2001. The focus of the present article is a critical analysis of some of the text and talk that was generated in the wake of this scientific claim. As with previous recurring controversies over the scientific legitimacy of the 'race' concept, protagonists on both sides of the debate claimed the scientific high ground, drawing on empiricist explanatory repertoires to defend their positions. Our analysis aims to explore some of the discursive practices and rhetorical strategies that were typically deployed in the debate to warrant the facticity of positions, and to undermine potential opposing arguments.

> This is a key moment in this research, a type of proclamation that race is not biologically real. Still, some of the authors in this section suggest that this is not the last word on the topic.

> Here, the purpose of this article is explicitly stated: to examine the various arguments made, and to analyze the rhetoric used to make those arguments. As you read, consider how those rhetorical analyses are made.

Science in the Media

As with many of the research findings generated by the HGP, the ensuing debate over 'race' was largely conducted publicly within the context of media reports and articles written for mass consumption. Recent research has emphasized the increasing importance of the media's role in disseminating science news, and in shaping public understandings of science. The public's increasing engagement and fascination with the science of genetics has been attributed, in part, to this media reporting. It is widely accepted that science journalism acts as a gatekeeper between scientists and the general public, and that science news may be reified or challenged according to the particular 'framing' employed by the science writer (Conrad, 1997, 1999, 2001; Van Dijk, 1988).

Here, you can see how not only disciplinary discourse, but *genres* (kinds of writing, as discussed in the introduction to this book) matter. Since the media translates complex ideas into more understandable forms for the general public, media reporters and writers have a huge role to play on how science finds its way into the wider understanding of citizens. You might compare this with the role of media in religious matters in the essay from Religion in the News, included in Chapter 5.

Van Dijk (1988) has identified three major devices that are used in media articles that present scientific news to the public. These include: offering supporting evidence from a range of reliable sources, giving indicators of 'precision and exactness such as numbers,' and directly quoting expert sources (pp. 84–7). According to Conrad (1999), scientific experts are chosen to give perspective, balance, context and legitimacy, and exactly who is consulted can depend on their status, their accessibility and their ability to deliver a good quote. It has also been argued that science journalists sometimes choose experts according to whether their aim is to validate, or to problematize, the new scientific information. Thus, particular experts may be chosen because they are known to be strong proponents of a particular position, or because they could be expected to challenge and contradict the new findings (Conrad, 1999). These claims about features of media dissemination of science news are relevant to the present study as several of the texts under analysis were media reports pertaining to the controversy over 'race' and the HGP. Before turning to the texts in question, we also need to consider existing work in the sociology of science that has explored the specific and particular linguistic features of scientists' discourse.

Scientists' Discourse

There is now a considerable body of social constructionist inquiry that has examined the discursive and rhetorical features of scientific discourse (e.g. Gilbert and Mulkay, 1984; Knorr-Cetina, 1981, 1996; Latour and Woolgar, 1979; Woolgar, 1988). Central to our analysis is Gilbert and Mulkay's (1984) classic study of biochemists' formal and informal accounts of competing theoretical hypotheses in oxidative phosphorylation research. Gilbert and Mulkay (1984) identified two recurrent interpretative repertoires that biochemists deployed in their writings and talk about research developments in their field, the 'empiricist' and 'contingent' repertoires. These two repertoires were selectively employed by scientists in various contexts in order to accomplish specific actions. As its name implies, the empiricist repertoire comprised lexical, grammatical and stylistic features that accorded agency and primacy to empirical data. Typically, data were depicted as emerging procedurally from rigidly conducted experimental procedures. Scientists primarily deployed the empiricist repertoire in formal accounts such as scientific papers, which were always constructed 'in an impersonal style, with overt references to the author's actions and judgements kept to a minimum . . . in which the physical world seems regularly to speak, and sometimes to act, for itself' (Gilbert and Mulkay, 1984: 57). Within this empiricist repertoire, scientists' actions were depicted as almost forced upon them by the phenomena of the natural world.

Notice how scientific writing—writing that attempts to be as objective as possible—is distinguished from the types of "contingent" or more personal depictions of issues in wider publics (as in the media).

In direct contrast to the empiricist repertoire, scientists deployed what Gilbertand Mulkay labelled the 'contingent repertoire' in their informal talk about their scientific theories and practices. In this talk, scientists openly acknowledged the contingent nature of their activities and theoretical preferences, and emphasized how these were significantly shaped by personal and social factors such as 'speculative insights, prior intellectual commitments, personal characteristics, indescribable skills, social ties and group membership' (p. 56). It was also observed that, not uncommonly, these two contradictory repertoires occurred alongside each other in a range of situations; for example, in the context of speaking at a conference or during interviews with the researchers.

Scientists used the empiricist repertoire largely to justify and validate their own views and beliefs. In contrast, scientific opponents whose views were regarded as incorrect were described in terms of the contingent repertoire. Scientific errors by others were generally attributed to such personal and social factors as: tunnel vision, political maneuvering, massaging the data (e.g. for publication, career advancement or to win grants), dogmatism, laziness, irrational thinking and reading misleading publications. Accounts of scientific error thus tended to invoke the contaminating intrusion of non-scientific and nonexperimental factors—in other words—the doing of bad science. This erroneous science was seen in contrast to that performed by the speakers, who depicted their own views as invariably correct and unmediated representations of the natural world.

This paragraph demonstrates how some of the "pure science" forwarded by practitioners of science can be watered down or changed in translation to a mass audience.

One of the significant features of the scientists' talk was the way in which they shifted flexibly between the empiricist and contingent repertoires in different contexts to justify and validate their scientific views and evaluations. When scientists were faced with contradictions that were made apparent through the concurrent deployment of these repertoires in their talk, they resorted to claiming that gradually, over time and given enough sound empiricist research, the truth of the natural world would reveal itself. Gilbert and Mulkay named this regular practice the 'Truth Will Out Device' (TWOD). The TWOD invokes the idea that empirical science progresses gradually, and although scientists may be temporarily misled by contaminating non-scientific factors, eventually these are corrected by virtue of the way in which objective facts inevitably assert themselves. Thus, the steady and gradual progress of science was viewed as an inherent safeguard against erroneous factual claims.

Our analysis will demonstrate the continuing relevance of Gilbert and Mulkay's findings to the understanding of some discursive practices associated with the current debate over 'race' as a scientific category. We demonstrate how the deployment of empiricist and contingent repertoires functions in the construction of truth and error claims in the debate, and how protagonists on both sides reaffirm their belief that 'science' will eventually solve the enduring controversy over 'race'.

Notice how this author uses the methods of analysis from a previous study and applies it to a new topic. This can be a very useful tool for you as a writer as well.

The data

Data for the analysis were obtained via Internet searches for all available published texts pertaining to 'race' and the HGP, beginning with the public announcement of the completion of a draft map of the human genome in June 2000, and up to and including April 2002. The study included texts drawn from diverse sources such as newspapers, commentaries in scientific journals, scholarly magazines, press releases, and information from the Applera/Celera website. Although all texts were written for a wide general readership (even commentaries appearing in scientific journals), it is important to emphasize the heterogeneous nature of these materials, as not all articles were written in the genre of media scientific reporting. From these combined sources about 50 texts were collected, and from these, a final 20 were chosen for detailed analysis primarily on the basis that they contained material that was deemed central to the debate about 'race' and the HGP.

Given the problematic, and highly contested, nature of the concept 'race,' the present research aims to examine the detail of how constructions of truth about 'race' are worked up in talk and texts. Our focus, too, on the rhetorical organization of the texts requires attention to how arguments are constructed to defend against, or to attack, alternative views, rather than to ascertain the truth or falsity of claims about 'race.' Specifically, our analysis aims to:

1. Demonstrate how the term 'race' is constructed and contested in texts and talk associated with the completion of the mapping of human genome.
2. Demonstrate the ways in which texts are organized, and 'rhetorical devices' are deployed, to establish an appearance of objectivity, facticity and 'out-there-ness' in scientific discourse associated with the contested concept 'race.'
3. Explore the broader functions of the discursive practices used in constructions of 'race' in these texts.

This list is designed to show clearly the purposes of the current article. It can help readers to see what is to come in the article.

It is important to emphasize, again, that our analysis does not seek to determine the 'truth' about 'race,' but rather to analyze, in fine detail, the ways in which truth claims were warranted and made to appear 'solid' and factual in various texts that constitute the current debate over the scientific status of 'race.'

Analysis and Discussion

The debate over 'race' has centered on opposing constructions that have posited 'race' as a natural, biological (essentialist) category, versus a social construct that does not have a factual, scientific basis. Although this article analyses the contours of the most recent manifestation of this controversy, embedded as it is within the reported biotechnological advances associated with the HGP, it is significant to note that the arguments and discursive practices we identify, appear to be generally characteristic of previous debates on how 'race' should be constructed. We will analyse a number of texts sampled from the current debate beginning with Venter's (2000) statement, to examine the discursive practices characteristically deployed in conflicting constructions of 'race.'

'Race' As a Social Construct: Constructions That Minimize Group Differences

Venter's (2000) press release describing the completion of a draft map of the human genome consisted of 10 short paragraphs and was 1130 words in length. The statement made reference to the historical significance of this scientific milestone, and to the future potential of this genetic knowledge for curing disease and medical conditions. Venter's statement, however, also attended to the longstanding scientific controversy over 'race,' and addressed some of the major criticisms that the HGP had attracted from its inception, including fears that it would lead to the proliferation of biological reductionist explanations of human behavior, and to the possible discriminatory use of genetic information.

In Extract 1, Venter orients to the scientific controversy over 'race' by reporting on the findings of the project in relation to the concepts of 'race' and 'ethnicity.' This information is presented relatively early in the press release, in the second paragraph. What can also be seen in Extract 1 is an instance of the use of an empiricist discourse of science which, as Potter (1996) has observed, is a practice that helps build a sense of facticity by making 'descriptions separate and external to the actor' (1996: 121).

EXTRACT 1

Note the method used by the authors to analyze the discussion about race and genetics; they first present specific textual examples, and then analyze the rhetoric of each to demonstrate how the ideas are constructed in persuasive words.

The method used by Celera has determined the genetic code of five individuals. We have sequenced from the genomes of three females and two males who have identified themselves as Hispanic, Asian, Caucasian, or African American. We did this initial sampling, not in an exclusionary way, but out of respect for the diversity that is America, and to help illustrate that the concept of race has no genetic or scientific basis. In the five Celera genomes there was no way to tell one ethnicity from another.

This extract can be considered in terms of its similarities and differences to the descriptions provided by Gilbert and Mulkay (1984) of scientists' reports of their theories and experimental procedures in formal and informal contexts. First of all, we can see the use of a grammatical form that is typical of formal reporting in scientific papers: 'The method used by Celera has determined . . .' (l. 1). This impersonal style minimizes the involvement of the author, their actions, commitments, and interpretations. The orientation to 'method,' here, is also characteristic of formal scientific writing, carrying with it assumptions of a standard, universal procedure for generating scientific knowledge. These are key features of the empiricist repertoire.

Note how this demonstrates the usual discourse used by scientists—impersonal, direct, declarative, and unemotional. How is that different from other styles of writing?

It is of interest, though, that immediately following this impersonal scientific statement, a plural pronoun is used to describe some details of the method: 'We have sequenced . . .' (ll. 2-3), 'We did this initial sampling . . .' (l. 6). Standard, impersonal, formal alternatives can be imagined for each of these statements: 'The genomes . . . were sequenced,' 'This initial sampling was done . . .,' but these impersonal forms are not used here. By the fourth sentence in the extract (ll. 9–10), we see a reversion to the impersonal form of construction. We are informed that, 'there was no way to tell one ethnicity from another' (compare, as potential alternatives, forms that continue the 'we' usages: 'We could not find any way to tell . . .'; 'We could not tell any differences . . .'). The extreme-case formulation of this statement of results ('there was *no way* to tell') also works to counter potential alternative readings of the genomic code 'evidence' in relation to 'race.' As Pomerantz (1986) pointed out, the use of extreme terms to modify descriptions is a common practice that is designed to strengthen an argument, particularly when an issue is in dispute. What can be seen happening, in between the two impersonal, empiricist framings of standard scientific procedure and results, is a nice piece of interest management of the part of the author. He inoculates against possible charges that the project involves some sort of racist profiling ('We did this initial sampling, not in an exclusionary way, but out of respect for the diversity that is America . . .'), and in the process, provides a nationalistic warrant for doing so. But what is also achieved, very neatly, with this construction of stake or interest is a confession of motivation, of what is driving the research project. First of all, 'respect for . . . diversity . . .' drives the project. This assertion serves to counter potential claims that genetic differences might have been present, but were suppressed in a motivated way. Presumably those who are respectful of diversity would not try to ignore its effects if there was evidence of them in the genetic code. However, at the same time, this confession of motivation leaves open the possible charge that *political values* are driving the project. Indeed, we see later how such attributions were mobilzed by Venter's critics.

This suggests that despite the scientific purposes, there does seem to be other motivations at work here too; that is, it is not only "empiricist" (based on observable data) but "contingent" (based on social purposes and goals).

Second, we are told that the project was motivated by a desire 'to help illustrate that the concept of "race" has no genetic or scientific basis.' This admission is also potentially problematic in the sense that it flouts the 'value-free,' objective, received view of the nature of science, and yet its framing in positive terms ('to help'), and in relation to a social problem that social scientists, at least, have focused on resolving for generations, works to counter potential criticism along this line. This formulation can also be seen to be producing a quality of what Potter (1996) refers to as 'out-there-ness' in relation to the description of 'race' as having no genetic basis. Celera's procedures and the findings from them are described as 'illustrat[ing]' something that chronologically pre-exists them. To illustrate, or throw light on, or draw a picture of a thing, is strongly suggestive of that thing's independent existence 'out there.' Also of significance in this extract is the manner in which the sample of five individuals whose genomes were mapped is described. We are told that these individuals have *self-identified* as Hispanic, Asian, Caucasian or African-American (ll. 5–6). What we can see here is a description of 'racial' categories being worked up as something that is social, that can be self-selected by individuals as preferred social identities.

In the next extract from Venter's press release (paragraphs 6 and 7) we can see other types of discursive and rhetorical work through which the factual status of 'race' as having no genetic basis is built up. In particular, Extract 2 contains the frequent use of numbers and quantification in ways that enable descriptive contrasts. The use of such contrastive procedures, that Potter (1996) has labelled 'maximization and minimization,' is a central feature of rhetoric.

Note how the authors first introduce the purpose of the next extract, to prepare the reader for their argument. This allows the reader to observe the issues that the authors wish to stress.

EXTRACT 2

We are clearly much more than the sum totals of our genes, just as our society is greater than the sum total of each of us. Our physiology is based on the complex and seemingly infinite interactions among all of our genes and the environment, just as our civilization is based on the interactions among all of us.

One of the wonderful discoveries that my colleagues and I have made while decoding the DNA of over two dozen species from viruses to bacteria to plants to insects, and now to human beings, is that we are all connected through the commonality of the genetic code and evolution.

When life is reduced to its very essence, we find that we have many genes in common with every species on Earth and that we are not so different from one another. You may be surprised to learn that your protein sequences are greater than 90% identical to proteins from other mammals.

In this extract we can see 'informal quantification' being used to maximize the extent of similarity between the 'genes,' 'DNA' and 'genetic code' of human beings and other living things. Terms such as 'greater,' 'seemingly infinite,' 'all,' 'every,' 'many' and 'commonality' work to reinforce the idea that 'we are not so different from one another.' (ll. 12–13). A more specific quantitative characterization is provided in relation to 'protein sequences,' where humans and other mammals are described as being 'greater than 90% identical'. This characterization of extreme quantifiable similarity is interesting in its selectivity. We are now talking, not of genes and genetic code, but of 'proteins' and 'protein sequences.' In this sense, the specific form of quantification is used as part of a process of ontological gerrymandering, in which a particular range of phenomena are picked out as relevant to the description in order to advance the argumentative case. As Potter (1996: 187) has pointed out, such gerrymandering practices are immensely powerful: 'The choice of boundaries and the huge range of descriptive terms available mean that highly contrasting versions of the "same thing" can be produced while resisting criticisms of inaccuracy, falsehood or active confabulation.' Indeed, what Venter accomplishes in this process of gerrymandering is to emphasize the 'essential' (l. 9) commonality of all living things ('every species on Earth'; l. 11). As we shall see, this emphasis on biological continuity—that, deep down, we are very similar and that surface characteristics belie fundamental similarities—is a repertoire commonly mobilized by those questioning the biological status of 'race.'

Note how, in a rhetorical analysis, the authors focus on specific word choices. As a writer, you too should consider carefully the connotations of the words you choose.

Although Venter argues for the *essential* biological continuity of all life forms here, it is of significance that he also orients to potential criticisms that the genome project will engender genetic reductionism. In ll. 1–4, he attends to this concern when he states, categorically, that: 'We are clearly more than the sum totals of our genes . . . Our physiology is based on the complex and seemingly infinite interactions among all our genes and the environment'. In this way, biogenetic explanations are undermined as being 'clearly' insufficient explanations.

The last extract that we consider from Venter's statement comes from paragraph 9 of the press release. Here we can see another offensive orientation to one of the central criticisms that had been leveled at the project; the potential for appropriation of genetic information for discriminatory purposes. We can also see some key features of both the empiricist and contingent repertoires that Gilbert and Mulkay described as characterizing scientists' reports about their own (correct) and others' (erroneous) work.

EXTRACT 3

some will want to use this new knowledge as a basis of discrimination . . . While those who will base social decisions on genetic reductionism will ultimately be defeated by science, new laws to protect us from genetic discrimination are critical in order to maximize the medical benefits from genomic discoveries.

In l. 1, there is a reference to an erroneous or ab-use to which an indefinite 'some' will want to put the knowledge generated by the HGP. These erroneous applications are attributed to a contingent factor—to the moral shortcoming of 'social' (and, by implication, illegal) discrimination. We can also see, in l. 2, an example of a key feature of the empiricist repertoire of science: the TWOD. Gilbert and Mulkay (1984) described the TWOD as a form of accounting that scientists typically drew upon to explain the existence of opposing views. The outcome of a mapping of the human genome was, as mentioned previously, expected to bring an end, once and for all, to debate about the genetic basis of the concept of 'race.' Maps, produced via the standard and universal procedures and method of science, can be read; the facts should be available for observation by anyone trained in the appropriate method. Patently, the availability of such a map has not produced a resolution but, 'ultimately' (l. 3), we are assured here, the facts will assert themselves. Those who hold the wrong (and morally and legally deficient) view will 'be defeated by science' in the end.

> Notice how the authors transition from an analysis of Venter's press release to an analysis of how other writers in the media have used it in their own writing. Remember that one of the purposes of this article is to show how scientific ideas move from professional, disciplinary writing to more public audiences.

Venter's press release has been cited widely by journalists and scientists writing in the media. His statements have been both supported and contested. A close analysis of some examples of these evaluations of Venter's claims about the HGP and 'race' demonstrates the ways in which the empiricist and contingent repertoires described by Gilbert and Mulkay are drawn upon by both sides of the debate. The following extract comes from an article entitled 'Do Races Differ? Not Really, DNA Shows' by a *New York Times* science writer (Angier, 2000).

EXTRACT 4

. . . scientists' growing knowledge of the profound genetic fraternity that binds together human beings of the most seemingly disparate origins.

Scientists have long suspected that the racial categories recognized by society are not reflected on the genetic level.

But the more closely that researchers examine the human genome—the complement of genetic material encased in the heart of almost every cell of the body—the more most of them are convinced that the standard labels used to distinguish people by 'race' have little or no biological meaning. They say that while it may seem easy to tell at a glance whether a person is Caucasian, African or Asian, the ease dissolves when one probes beneath surface characteristics and scans the genome for DNA hallmarks of 'race.'

As it turns out, scientists say, the human species is so evolutionarily young . . . it has simply not had a chance to divide itself into separate biological groups or 'races' in any but the most superficial ways.

In this extract, what we can see is a series of contrast structures being developed in order to build a persuasive case that apparent surface differences between 'racial' groups belie deeper/underlying similarities. In ll. 1–3, the contrast being introduced is that between 'profound' likeness/similarity and seeming disparity. We have the contrasts: like versus unlike and deep versus surface at work. Then, in ll. 4 and 5, comes a contrast between scientists' knowledge on the one hand, and society's understanding on the other. In ll. 6–10, these contrasts are brought together to build a compelling case: scientists/researchers use 'close' 'exam[ination]' of material that is 'encased' at the deepest of levels, 'in the heart of almost every living cell of the body.' 'Society,' by contrast, uses labels in order to 'distinguish' people in a way that lacks 'biological meaning.' This non-scientific form of distinguishing, 'telling at a glance' (l. 11), only 'seems' meaningful; it is inferior to scientific knowledge because it is based on 'surface characteristics' (l. 12), it is superficial (l. 17).

Note again the close attention to the word choices. As a reader, you should also pay attention to the ways that writers use specific words to make their case and influence opinions.

Atkinson's (1984) classic text on political rhetoric emphasized how the use of contrasts in this way makes a message more persuasive and convincing. Edwards and Potter (1992) claim that the building of contrasts is a rhetorical process whereby a 'factual' version is constructed in opposition to an 'alternative, which is itself formulated in an unconvincing or problematic manner' (p. 163).

In another extract from this text we can see some more uses of quantification rhetoric to strengthen the claim that 'race' does not have a significant genetic basis.

EXTRACT 5

The human genome is large, though, composed of three billion-odd subunits, or bases, which means that even a tiny percentage of variation from one individual to the next amounts to a sizable number of genetic discrepancies. The question is, where in the genome is that variation found, and how is it distributed among different populations? Through transglobal sampling of neutral genetic markers . . . researchers have found that, on average, 88 percent to 90 percent of the differences between people occur within their local populations, while only about 10 percent to 12 percent of the differences distinguish one population, or race, from another. To put it another way, the citizens of any given village in the world, whether in Scotland or Tanzania, hold 90 percent of the genetic variability that humanity has to offer.

This account presents a version that minimizes the amount of variation between 'races,' and maximizes the amount of difference that occurs between people 'within local populations.' A contrast is made between small percentage characterizations of genetic difference due to 'race' (ll. 10 'only about 10 percent to 12 percent') and large percentages due to local population variability (l. 8 '88 percent to 90 percent'). This contrast is framed within a claim of extreme order of absolute quantity for the human genome—that it is composed of 'three billion odd subunits or bases' (ll. 1–2). The case is made, using a contrast between this extreme figure and a minimized 'tiny percentage of variation from one individual to the next,' that even small variations between individuals 'amounts to a sizeable number of genetic discrepancies.' The inference is that racial differences, if genetically based, should be traceable to similar 'sizeable' genetic differences between 'races.' However, as we are told in ll. 7–11, and then again in l. 14, such large differences in genetic markers are not to be found within 'races.'

Of interest too, in this extract, is the particular range of phenomena picked out in the description of the process of measuring genetic differences between people: 'through transglobal sampling of neutral genetic markers' (l. 7). This description selects one realm—'neutral genetic markers'—to make the case for little genetically based 'racial' difference. Again, this would seem to be an instance of ontological gerrymandering in which rhetorical boundaries are drawn in the way most advantageous to the argument being made. The next text that we will examine also comes from an advocate of the position that 'race' is not a scientifically valid construct. In this case, the text is another Celera press release, this time authored by Culliton (2001) who cites in length, a member of the Celera Review Board (Dr Harold P. Freeman) on the eve of the publication of the human genome map in the highly reputable journals *Science* and *Nature:*

EXTRACT 6

Mapping the DNA sequence variation in the human genome holds the potential for promoting the fundamental unity of all humankind. Throughout recorded history and up to the present time, countless human conflicts have occurred based on how groups of people have seen, classified and behaved toward another group . . . In the past, some scientists used observations of racial differences to support racist doctrines. Racism, rooted in the erroneous concept of biological racial superiority, has powerful societal effects and continues to influence science. Race as used in the United States is a social and political construct derived from our nation's history. It has no basis in science. The biologic concept of race is now believed to be untenable. The power of science can be used to eliminate public perceptions of racial superiority and inferiority, which are the basis of racism itself. In this way, the mapping of the human genome could be pivotal in promoting the concept of one race, the human race.

In this text we can see another example of the use of the contingent repertoire to explain the erroneous views of others. In ll. 5–9, the case is made that those who promulgate biological bases for 'race' are

The authors begin their analysis by summarizing their point about the extract: that it is "contingent" (has a persuasive social purpose) and that it is a refutation (explaining why others' views are "erroneous").

motivated by racism, even within the realm of science. There is much focus, too, in this account on history and the past. A sense of how bad things were in the past is repeatedly worked up. History is depicted as a time of 'countless human conflicts,' of 'racism.' We are presented with a contrast between these historical evils and errors, and the true understandings of contemporary science (l. 12: The biologic concept of 'race' is no longer believed to be tenable). A similar contrast structuring is deployed to work up an opposition between science and the 'social and political' (ll. 10–11: Race . . . is a social and political construct . . . It has no basis in science). Using yet another form of contrast structuring, science is positioned as superior to lay understanding. Science is described as having agency—'power . . . to eliminate' false 'public perceptions' (l. 13). The humanistic promise of progress from ignorance to understanding, from conflict to harmony and happiness, of widespread human betterment, is a strong feature of this account. The mapping of the human genome is depicted as holding the potential for the achievement of 'unity' amongst 'humankind'/'the human race.' The rhetorical self-sufficiency of arguments that are framed in terms of values such as 'unity' has been commented upon by analysts such as Billig (1991) and Wetherell and Potter (1992). These arguments are difficult to undermine, they enjoy something of the status of socially accepted clichés and, because they involve principles that are beyond question, require no further warrant. A pattern of contrast structuring involving science and society or 'culture' was also present in many of the analysed texts. In the following example, a geneticist writing in *Science* (Paabo, 2001) provides another favourable account of the findings of the HGP.

EXTRACT 7

Fortunately, from the few studies of nuclear DNA sequences, it is clear that what is called 'race,' although culturally important, reflects just a few continuous traits determined by a tiny fraction of our genes. Thus, from the perspective of nuclear genes, it is often the case that two persons from the same part of the world who look superficially alike are less related to each other than they are to persons from other parts of the world who may look very different.

Here, 'race' is depicted as a cultural concept (l. 2) (compare 'a social and political construct,' l. 10 in Extract 6); it has no scientific significance. This claim is reinforced by a minimization of references to genetic bases for racial differences: '*just a few* continuous traits determined by *a tiny fraction* of our genes' (ll. 3–4). Again, the general style of writing is in terms of declarations that permit no doubt as to their veracity: 'it is clear that' (l. 1–2); 'Thus . . . it is often the case that . . .' (ll. 4–5). And, once again, we can see a contrast being worked up between surface appearances, 'look superficially alike' (ll. 5–6), and what is true at a deeper, genetic level.

These constructions ("It is clear that," etc.) are often used to suggest the absolute certainty of the author and to convince the reader that there is no room for debate. Are these constructions effective? Ethical?

To summarize, the textual extracts examined above illustrate what is a recurring trope in arguments that 'race' has no basis in genetics: that superficial, physical (surface) differences belie the underlying genetic unity of all human beings. There is a common rhetoric of quantification, too, running through these texts in which scientists and reporters argue that the concept of 'race' has no genetic basis. This quantitative characterization typically involves a diminution or minimization of the importance of differences based on 'race.' For example, racial differences are described using terms such as 'surface,' 'superficial,' 'external,' 'very minimal,' 'seemingly disparate,' 'few' and 'tiny fraction.' By contrast, talk of human similarity emphasizes the *relationship* of human beings with terms such as 'fundamental unity,' 'profound genetic fraternity,' 'commonality,' 'universality,' 'connected,' 'related' and 'bind together.' Contrasts play an important role in these descriptions. Surface appearances are contrasted with deeper genetic 'perspectives' or ways of looking for the facts. Science is contrasted with the social and political; that is, with *interested* forms of making sense of the world. Typically, too, science is contrasted with 'public' knowledge, which is portrayed as inferior.

This concept of quantification is based upon the theory that "numbers don't lie" and that science is the strongest truth. Do you find this is effective? Is it always the case? What would people in other disciplines suggest?

'Race' as a biological construct: Constructions that emphasize group differences

In this section we examine several texts that disputed claims that the mapping of the human genome had proved that 'race' had no basis in genetics. Not surprisingly, one feature shared by these texts was an emphasis on the differences rather than the similarities between 'racial' groups. The first of these extracts comes from an article entitled, 'The straw man of "race"' (Entine, 2001), published in a monthly

The authors now go on to analyze a set of texts that take the opposite position. Note how the same evidence from science can thus be used to make two contrary cases. What does that tell you about the power of language?

journal, *The World and I* (described as 'academic–scholarly' by Ulrich's Periodicals Directory, 2002; Bowker, 2002).

EXTRACT 8

The fact that 99.8 percent of the population shares the same genes does not 'prove' or even necessarily suggest that there are no population or 'racial' differences. The percentage of overall differences is a far less important issue than which genes are different. Even minute differences in DNA can have profound effects on how an animal or human looks and acts . . .

The argument set forth here is designed directly to counter the standard terms of the opposition's claims. We can see the author orienting to the other side's deployment of quantification rhetoric (l. 1: The fact that 99.8 percent of the population shares the same genes) in order to undermine this claim or re-frame its meaning (l. 2: does not 'prove' or even necessarily suggest). This offensive rhetorical action is accomplished, in part, by disputing the ontological terrain. The author refuses to accept the selective boundaries of the phenomenon of debate as they have been presented by the opposition: 'The percentage of overall differences is a far less important issue than which genes are different' (ll. 3–4). He then engages in his own contrast between minimized genetic differences (l. 5: 'Even minute differences in DNA') and maximized external/observable differences (ll. 5–6: 'can have profound effects on how an animal or human looks and acts').

Note how the authors use the analysis of direct quotations to make their case.

In the next extract, Entine quotes Arizona State University evolutionary biologist Joseph Graves Jr, an expert with category entitlement, to provide corroboration or the view that physical differences between human groups are significant and that genes are implicated in these differences. It is significant also that Entine makes explicit reference to Graves' 'racial' identity, describing him as 'African-American' (ll. 3–4). This description here is rhetorically significant in that it constructs Graves as an expert whose views are counter to what one normally would expect from a minority group member. Thus this description inoculates against potential criticisms that this expert may have a particular stake or interest (an 'axe to grind') in arguing for the significance of group differences (Potter, 1996).

Again, note how the introduction to the quotation alerts readers as to what they should be paying attention to the way that you introduce a quotation in your own writing is crucial.

EXTRACT 9

'Evolution has shaped body types and in part athletic possibilities. Don't expect an Eskimo to show up on an NBA court or a Watusi to win the world weightlifting championship, adds Graves, who is African American. Differences don't necessarily correlate with skin colour, but rather with geography and climate. Endurance runners are more likely to come from East Africa. That's a fact. Genes play a major role in this.' [188 lines omitted] 'The fact that monolithic racial categories do not show up consistently in the genotype does not mean there are no group differences between pockets of populations,' agrees Arizona State University Evolutionary biologist Joseph Graves Jr. 'There are some group differences. We see it in diseases.'

Entine directly quotes Graves who asserts that 'There are some group differences' (l. 9) and as 'a fact' that genes 'play a major role in this' (l. 6–7). Note, also, how visible physical characteristics that are commonly used to define 'racial' groups such as 'skin colour' (l. 5), are downplayed in contrast to criteria such as 'geography and climate' (l. 5) in this account. Again we see here an instance of ontological gerrymandering in which a specific set of criteria is selected as relevant to the description in order to argue for a particular position. Although 'skin colour' proves to be problematic, in that this marker does not 'necessarily correlate with' (l. 4) group differences, in contrast, 'pockets of populations' (l. 10) do demonstrate such differences, according to Graves, particularly in the incidence of disease (l. 12). Indeed, references to ethnic group differences in the incidence of certain kinds of disease, and responses to certain medical treatment, were commonly deployed by experts who sought to defend the legitimacy of identifying biological group differences (see Extract 10). Attributions of stake and interest, suggesting that the genome scientists were motivated by factors other than purely scientific ones (i.e. contingent factors), was another common offensive device mobilized to undermine the claim that 'race' was not a biological construct. In the next extract, drawn from the beginning of Entine's article, we can see a contrast being worked up between (false) ideology and (true) science.

Here, the analysis shows the ways that the words of others can be framed to stress the author's point.

EXTRACT 10

Ideological doublespeak on evolution is now infiltrating genetic science. The latest volley in the hundred-years war can be traced to statements issued earlier this year by the National Human Genome Project Director Francis Collins and Craig Venter of Celera Genomics. When these two distinguished scientists unveiled their crude maps of the human genome, they went out of their way to emphasize that, in the words of Venter, 'race has no genetic or scientific basis.' Venter's unambiguous declaration created hardly a ripple in social science circles which have long embraced this position.

Ideology is described here as duplicitous (l. 1); it is 'doublespeak,' not 'truth,' and it is difficult to detect or counter (it 'infiltrates'; it is not easy to observe). The use of the descriptor, 'distinguished' (l. 5), in relation to the 'opposition' scientists is interesting here. Presumably, the usage is designed to be sarcastic given the propinquity of the next descriptor, 'crude' (l. 6), used to refer to the maps of the McCann-Mortimer et al. human genome they have generated. Furthermore, the scientists, Venter and Collins are described as having gone 'out of their way to emphasize' (l. 7) their conclusion that 'race' has no genetic basis. The extremity of their actions suggests inappropriate motivation or interest. Here, too, (ll. 8–9) we see science being contrasted with social science—an inferior form of knowledge because of its purported interest-driven 'embracing' of the social/political. The next text arguing against claims such as Venter's that 'race' has no basis in genetics is an extract by a science writer from an article that appeared in the national broadsheet, *The Weekend Australian* (Brooks, 2000). We can again see, here, a contrast being built up between the political and the scientific; between interest and factuality.

EXTRACT 11

'A politically correct statement,' some scientists say. 'A factual statement,' say others. Confusion reigns. What did Venter mean? Surely not that the physical differences of different ethnic backgrounds are not genetic? It's established scientific fact that African-Americans have a higher precedent of sickle anaemia because the same gene made their African

ancestors resistant to malaria; that most Ashkenazim Jews' genes came from a tiny population that moved to Europe and caused an evolutionary bottleneck; and that many Japanese livers contain an enzyme that is inefficient at absorbing alcohol.

The extract begins (ll. 1–2) by presenting the conflicting responses that the HGP findings had elicited from scientists: 'a politically correct statement' by opponents, on the one hand, and a 'factual statement' by proponents, on the other hand. The ironic questioning that occurs in ll. 3–4 ('What did Venter mean? Surely not that the physical differences of different ethnic backgrounds are not genetic?'), carries the implication that Venter's statements defy commonsense belief. These questions are followed by a statement of what is 'established scientific fact' (l. 5), and a three-part list (African-Americans have . . . most Ashkenazim Jews' genes came from . . . many Japanese livers contain') is deployed to add a sense of generalized support to this empiricist warrant. Three-part lists are described by Jefferson (1990) as commonplace rhetorical constructions that are robust against attack, in their suggestion of the generality of the principle they are illustrating. This list of 'established scientific facts' about group differences echoes the scientific claim in Extract 9 regarding group differences in the incidence of disease.

In a further extract from this article, we can see the author working up the notion that interest rather than science was the motivation for Venter's claims.

EXTRACT 12

Brandon Wainwright, the Brisbane-based deputy director of the Human Genetic Co-operative Research Centre, believes . . . 'There may end up being DNA sequences that are specific to race, specific to population.' Wainwright says Venter may have made the statement to avoid the spectre of genetic racism. Dr. John Morrison, research scientist and geneticist at Monash Medical Centre in Melbourne agreed that Venter would have wanted to avoid the genome project sparking fears about race.

In this extract, two scientists with well-detailed category entitlements to speak on issues of genetics are reported indirectly (ll. 4–5 and ll. 7–8) as suggesting that Venter might have had political reasons for claiming that the concept of 'race' had no genetic basis; more specifically 'to avoid the spectre of genetic racism,' and 'to avoid the genome project sparking fears about race.' Such suggestions about the research claims of those with whom one disagrees are typical of the contingent repertoire of scientific explanation. Invoking political reasons as a motivation works, here, to undermine the basis upon which Venter has claimed to be speaking—that of empiricist truth.

> You can see here how even claims to scientific or "empiricist" truth can be contested by those outside the discipline.

The last extract we consider comes from an article entitled 'Under the skin,' published in *New Scientist* (Ananthaswamy, 2002). This article is of particular interest because, unlike the other texts that we have examined in this section, it does not seek to question the scientific illegitimacy of the concept 'race.' Indeed, it argues that conventional 'racial' groupings are scientifically erroneous, but that nevertheless, it may still be possible to identify human groups according to 'genetically similar clusters' (p. 34).

EXTRACT 13

So the races we think we see have little relevance to biology.
But is there a better way to get at humanity's underlying genetic
variations? David Goldstein of University College London
thinks so . . .
and that finding it is mainly a matter of studying the right
genetic markers.
'We are all using too small a number of markers,' he says. 'My guess
is that when we use a large enough set of markers and an
exhaustive enough set of individuals, the results will stabilise.
In fact, I'm quite sure that they will.'

What we can see in this extract is another example of the TWOD that Gilbert and Mulkay identified in their scientists' talk. A genetics researcher, Goldstein is reported as arguing that, over time, given the identification of the 'right genetic markers' (l. 5–6) and a sufficient sample size of both markers and individuals (ll. 8–9: 'a large enough set of markers and an exhaustive enough set of individuals'), more scientifically valid human groupings will *eventually* be identified along genetic/biological lines. Note also how in l. 10 he qualifies his initial hedging in ll. 7 and 8 ('My guess is') that scientific researchers will ultimately find such genetic markers to, 'In fact, I'm quite sure that they will.' In this way, Goldstein offers up hope that science will, given time and the application of the correct method, discover how correctly to identify valid human groups according to genetic variations.

The texts we have examined in this section have sought to challenge and undermine claims by HGP scientists that 'race' was not a biologically valid construct. We demonstrated how such underminings were accomplished through the deployment of constructions that emphasized the magnitude and significance of observable physical differences between human groups, and how genes or biology must be implicated in such differences. Typically, these constructions were framed within the empiricist repertoire of science as various experts with category entitlement were enlisted by authors to cite 'facts' about group differences across several domains such as athletic ability and the incidence of disease. We also demonstrated how contingent factors were commonly mobilized by critics to suggest that Venter was motivated by contaminating non-scientific factors, such as 'political correctness,' to make this statement about 'race.' Typically, again, contrasts between science and politics were instrumental in accomplishing such attributions of stake and interest.

Note how this paragraph pauses to summarize and clarify the purpose of the whole section.

Concluding remarks

In this article we have seen how protagonists on both sides of this debate typically drew upon the rhetoric of science to legitimate their position, primarily by means of invoking the empiricist repertoire. In pursuit of their claims to scientific 'truth,' both sides employed 'defensive' rhetorical devices such as quantification to warrant the 'factual' nature of their position. Science is, not surprisingly, equated with the empiricist, experimental tradition in which quantification is a highly valued aspect. As Potter et al. (1991: 359) have pointed out, 'Quantification is an extremely powerful tool, but one which is socially constituted and rhetorically exploitable.' Indeed, we have seen how those questioning the scientific status of 'race' used both formal and informal quantification in ways that *minimized* differences and *maximized* the similarity between conventional 'racial' groups. In contrast, those maintaining the biological and scientific validity of 'race' deployed quantification in ways that served to *emphasize* the significance and magnitude of group differences.

These sentences reiterate one of the main points of the article: that scientific data and facts can be used to construct very different conclusions, depending upon what is selected and how it is framed.

When 'offensive' rhetorical devices, such as charges of stake and interest and references to commonsense or what 'everybody knows,' were deployed to undermine alternative versions of what 'race' is, arguments were typically framed in terms of 'poor science' or 'contingency.' As previously discussed, Gilbert and Mulkay (1984) found that scientists typically attributed the views of their opponents to a range of contaminating, non-scientific factors. Our analysis identified several such contaminating factors that were attributed to the erroneous views of those wanting to uphold the biological legitimacy of 'race,' including discrimination (Extract 3), scientific racism and faulty public perceptions (Extract 6). Similarly, proponents of the view that 'race' is a valid biological concept attributed the erroneous views of their opponents and, in particular, Venter, to contingent factors such as ideology (Extract 9), 'political correctness' (Extract 10) and the desire 'to avoid the spectre of genetic racism' (Extract 11). Such practices, therefore, appear to be the norm in scientific controversies.

Our analysis also demonstrated instances of the TWOD (Gilbert and Mulkay, 1984) being deployed by protagonists on both sides of the scientific controversy over 'race.' Indeed, Venter's press release can be seen to be a public declaration of the TWOD. It was a declaration that science and, more specifically the HGP, had finally solved the enduring controversy over the scientific status of 'race'; that the 'truth' or objective facts about 'race' had now come to the fore through the mapping of the human genome. Moreover, Venter's statement also functions to assert that the 'truth' about the biological illegitimacy of 'race,' that can be verified through the scientific sequencing and mapping of DNA, will ultimately defeat those who are motivated by discrimination. Venter, like other experts (Extract 6), assures us that science has the inherent power to eliminate and defeat such enduring social inequities. Clearly, however, as we have demonstrated, Venter's claim finally to have solved the question of 'race' was not universally accepted, but was subject to considerable scientific challenge.

In addition to the mobilization of contingent factors and oppositional sets of numbers, another discursive practice used to contest Venter's views involved shifting the ontological boundaries of the concept 'race.' Central to this definitional shift was the argument that, although conventional 'racial' categories as typically understood may not be defined by particular genetic markers, 'pockets of populations' living in particular geographical locales could be so defined. This view resonates with current thinking in population genetics, which, since the 1950s, has replaced a traditional typological concept of 'race' with a populational one (Gannett, 2001). The decline of scientific racism in the 1950s has been partly attributed to this shift to population thinking by geneticists and anthropologists. However, as Gannett (2001) has argued, there are no ethical guarantees that population thinking, particularly as it is applied to the study of human biological diversity, will be 'an effective arbiter of boundaries between what counts as "good" (objective and morally responsible) science and "bad" (false and racist) pseudo-science' (p. S481). Despite the empirical 'facts' mobilized by human genome diversity researchers to emphasize the genetic continuity and heterogeneity in humans, an objective of such research is to identify 'statistical differences among populations' in gene frequencies associated with particular characteristics such as disease incidence. As Gannett (2001: S490) argues, 'group DNA differences will always be culturally meaningful and socially relevant—even if these groups in no way correspond with traditional racial divisions, and even if these DNA differences are quantitative not qualitative.' Regardless of how 'groups' are defined, and no matter how small the reported differences between groups, such group differences can always be (mis)appropriated to legitimate racist and discriminatory practices. It will take much more than the rhetorical power of scientific 'truth' to eradicate racism.

This concluding set of remarks suggests not only the point of the article, but a social position about racism—that as long as contrary arguments can be made using scientific data, science alone can't stop racism. Is this conclusion appropriate to the purpose of the article?

Note

1. This is by no means limited to the discipline of psychology, however. 'Race' continues to be treated as a natural variable in many disciplines. See, for example, critiques on the use of 'race' in public health and epidemiological research by Bophal and Donaldson (1998) and Fullilove (1998), and Lin and Kelsey (2000).

References

Ananthaswamy, A. (2002, April 20) 'Under the Skin: Our DNA Says There's No Such Thing as Race. So Why do Doctors Still Think it Matters,' *New Scientist* 34–7.

Angier, A. (2000, August 22) 'Do Races Differ? Not Really DNA Shows,' *New York Times*, Science Desk; Section F, Fl.

Atkinson, J.M. (1984) *Our Masters' Voices: The Language and Body Language of Politics*. London: Methuen.

Billig, M. (1991) *Ideologies and Beliefs*. London: Sage.

Billig, M. (1998, July) 'A Dead Idea That Won't Lie Down,' *Searchlight* available at [accessed 20 March 2002]: www.searchlightmagazine.com

Bophal, R. and Donalson, L. (1998) 'White, European, Western, Caucasian, or What? Inappropriate Labelling in Research on Race, Ethnicity, and Health,' *American Journal of Public Health* 88: 1303–7.

Bowker, R.R. (ed.) (2002) *Ulrich's Periodicals Directory*. Available at: www.ulrichsweb.com [accessed 28 March 2002].

Brooks, S. (2000, July 1–2) 'Genes East, Genes West,' *The Weekend Australian*, p. 30.

Conrad, P. (1997) 'Public Eyes and Private Genes: Historical Frames, News Constructions, and Social Problems,' *Social Problems* 44: 139–54.

Conrad, P. (1999) 'Uses of Expertise: Sources, Quotes, and Voice in the Reporting of Genetics in the News,' *The Public Understanding of Science* 8: 285–302.

Conrad, P. (2001) 'Genetic Optimism: Framing Genes and Mental Illness in the News,' *Culture, Medicine and Psychiatry* 25: 225–47.

Culliton, B.J. (2001, February 12) *Whose Genome is it Anyway?* Press release. Available at: http://www.celera.com/genomics/news/articles/02_01/whose_genome.cf [accessed 9 September 2001].

Cunningham-Burley, S. and Kerr, A. (1999) 'Defining the "Social": Towards an Understanding of Scientific and Medical Discourses on the Social Aspects of the New Human Genetics,' *Sociology of Health and Illness* 21: 505–16.

Dodson, M. and Williamson, R. (1999) 'Indigenous Peoples and the Morality of the Human Genome Diversity Project,' *Journal of Medical Ethics* 25: 204–8.

Edwards, D. and Potter, J. (1992) *Discursive Psychology*. London: Sage.

Entine, J. (2001, January 9) 'The Straw Man of "Race,"' *The World and I* 16: 294–318.

Fullilove, M.T. (1998) 'Comment: Abandoning "Race" as a Variable in Public Health Research—An Idea Whose Time has Come,' *American Journal of Public Health* 88: 1297–8.

Gannett, L. (2001) 'Racism and Human Genome Diversity Research: The Ethical Limits of "Population Thinking,"' *Philosophy of Science* 68: 479–92.

Gilbert, G.N. and Mulkay, M. (1984) *Opening Pandora's Box: A Sociological Analysis of Scientists' Discourse*. Cambridge: Cambridge University Press.

Jefferson, G. (1990) 'List Construction as a Task and a Resource,' in G. Psathas (ed.) *Interaction Competence*. Lanham, MD: University Press of America.

Knorr-Cetina, K. (1981) *The Manufacture of Knowledge: An Essay on the Constructivist and Contextual Nature of Science*. Oxford: Pergamon Press. 430 *Discourse & Society* 15(4)

Knorr-Cetina, K. (1996) *Epistemic Cultures: How Scientists Make Sense*. Cambridge, MA: Harvard University Press.

Kohn, M. (1995, December) 'Can Science Handle Race?,' *New Statesman and Society* 8: 37.

Latour, B. and Woolgar, S. (1979) *Laboratory Life: The Social Construction of Scientific Facts.* London: Sage.

Lin, S.S. and Kelsey, J.L. (2000) 'Use of Race and Ethnicity in Epidemiologic Research: Concepts, Methodological Issues, and Suggestions for Research,' *Epidemiologic Reviews* 22:187–202.

Nelkin, D. and Lindee, M.S. (1995) *The DNA Mystique: The Gene as Cultural Icon.* New York: Basic Books.

Nerlich, B., Dingwall, R. and Clarke, D. (2002) 'The Book of Life: How Completion of the Human Genome Project was Revealed to the Public,' *Health: An Interdisciplinary Journal for the Social Study of Health, Illness and Medicine* 6: 445–69.

Novas, C. and Rose, N. (2002) 'Genetic Risk and the Birth of the Somatic Individual,' *Economy and Society* 29: 485–513.

Paabo, S. (2001) 'The Human Genome and our View of Ourselves,' *Science* 291: 1219–21.

Petersen, A. (2001) 'Biofantasies: Genetics and Medicine in the Print News Media,' *Social Science and Medicine* 52: 1255–68.

Pomerantz, A.M. (1986) 'Extreme Case Formulations: A Way of Legitimating Claims,' *Human Studies* 9: 219–29.

Potter, J. (1996) *Representing Reality: Discourse, Rhetoric and Social Construction.* London: Sage.

Potter, J., Wetherell, M. and Chitty, A. (1991) 'Quantification Rhetoric—Cancer on Television,' *Discourse & Society* 2: 333–65.

Richards, G. (1997) *'Race,' Racism and Psychology: Towards a Reflexive History.* London: Routledge.

Rifkin, J. (1998) *The Biotech Century: Harnessing the Gene and Remaking the World.* London: Gollancz.

Tate, C. and Audette, D. (2001) 'Theory and Research on "Race" as a Natural Kind Variable in Psychology,' *Theory and Psychology* 11: 495–520.

van Dijk, T.A. (1988) *News as Discourse.* Hillsdale, NJ: Erlbaum.

Venter, C.J. (2000, June 26) *Remarks at the Human Genome Announcement.* Press release, Applera/Celera Genomics. Available at: http://www.applera.com/press/prccorp062700a.html [accessed 16 May 2002].

Wetherell, M. and Potter, J. (1992) *Mapping the Language of Racism: Discourse and the Legitimation of Discrimination.* London: Harvester: Wheatsheaf.

Woolgar, S. (1988) *Science: The Very Idea.* Chichester: Ellis Horwood.

Reading Analytically

1. One of the key purposes of this essay is to analyze "the ways in which constructions of truth about 'race' are typically worked up in scientific and media discourse." What do the authors mean by calling truth a "construction"? What does that suggest about how language and rhetoric function?

2. What are the key differences and similarities that the authors offer in regard to scientific discourse and media discourse?
3. One of the key ways that scientific discourse functions, both in the disciplines themselves and in the media, is through what the authors call "quantification." What does that term mean, and why is it such a persuasive device for scientists?

Reading Across Disciplinary Communities

1. As psychologists of language, these authors look analytically at the language within which the discussion of race is framed by scientists. Describe the ways that they conduct these analyses through the use of specific examples.
2. Using methods of language or "rhetorical" analysis, analyze how one of the other authors in this chapter frames the debate about racial categories; be sure to provide specific examples from the piece and demonstrate the ways that the phrasing is meant to persuade us of the author's perspectives.

CAROL MUKHOPADHYAY AND ROSEMARY C. HENZE

How Real Is Race?

Using Anthropology to Make Sense of Human Diversity

This piece, originally published in Phi Delta Kappan, *a journal devoted to the field of education, draws upon "scientific" perspectives on race to consider how race should be viewed "by teachers, students, and our society." As such, this essay demonstrates how scientific information can be applied to a specific profession—teaching. Carol Mukhopadhyay is an anthropologist at the San José State University and Rosemary C. Henze, also at San José State, is a professor of linguistics.*

This piece, beginning with the contention that "race isn't biologically real," first provides evidence for their claim, and second, shows how that fact can be demonstrated to students in the classroom. As you read, you might consider how the methods the authors suggest take into account both the lack of scientific support for racial categories and the very real social facets of race—both of which are discussed in this section. You might also pay attention to the ways that this piece, written for an audience of those in the applied social science of teaching, moves from a theoretical discussion to a practical set of applications.

Surely we've all heard people say there is only one race—the human race. We've also heard and seen overwhelming evidence that would seem to contradict this view. After all, the U.S. Census divides us into groups based on race, and there are certainly observable physical differences among people—skin color, nose and eye shape, body type, hair color and texture, and so on. In the world of education, the message of racial differences as biological "facts" is reinforced when we are told that we should understand specific learning styles and behavior patterns of black, Asian, Native American, white, and Latino children and when books such as *The Bell Curve* make pseudoscientific claims about race and learning.[1]

How can educators make sense of these conflicting messages about race? And why should they bother? Whether we think of all human beings as one race, or as four or five distinct races, or as hundreds of races, does anything really change? If we accept that the concept of race is fundamentally flawed, does that mean that young African Americans are less likely to be followed by security guards in department stores? Are people going to stop thinking of Asians as the "model" minority? Will racism become a thing of the past?

Many educators understandably would like to have clear information to help them teach students about human biological variability. While multicultural education materials are now widely available, they rarely address basic questions about why we look different from one another and what these biological differences do (and do not) mean. Multicultural education emphasizes respecting differences and finding ways to include all students, especially those who have been historically marginalized. Multicultural education has helped us to understand racism and has provided a rich body of literature on antiracist teaching strategies, and this has been all to the good. But it has not helped us understand the two concepts of race: the biological one and the social one.

In this article, we explain what anthropologists mean when they say that "races don't exist" (in other words, when they reject the concept of race as a scientifically valid biological category) and why they argue instead that "race" is a socially constructed category. We'll also discuss why this is such an important understanding and what it means for educators and students who face the social reality of race and racism every day. And finally, we'll offer some suggestions and resources for teachers who want to include teaching about race in their classes.

Why Race Isn't Biologically Real

For the past several decades, biological anthropologists have been arguing that races don't really exist, or, more precisely, that the concept of race has no validity as a biological category. What exactly does this mean?

First, anthropologists are unraveling a deeply embedded ideology, a long-standing European and American racial world view.[2] Historically, the idea of race emerged in Europe in the 17th and 18th centuries, coinciding with the growth of colonialism and the transatlantic slave trade. Attempts were made to classify humans into "natural," geographically distinct "races," hierarchically ordered by their closeness to God's original forms. Europeans were, not surprisingly, at the top, with the most perfect form represented by a female skull from the Caucasus Mountains, near the purported location of Noah's ark and the origin of humans. Hence the origins of the racial term "Caucasian" or "Caucasoid" for those of European ancestry.[3]

In the late 19th century, anthropologists sought to reconstruct human prehistory and trace the evolution of human cultural institutions. Physical and cultural evolution were seen as moving in tandem; "advances" in human mental capacity were thought to be responsible for human cultural inventions, such as marriage, family, law, and agriculture. If cultural "evolution" was propelled by biological evolution, according to this logic, the more "advanced" cultures must be more biologically and intellectually evolved. Physical indicators of evolutionary rank, such as skull size, were sought in order to classify and rank human groups along an evolutionary path from more "primitive" to more "advanced" races.

Nineteenth-century European scientists disagreed on when the "races" began. Theologians had long argued that there was "one human origin," Adam and Eve, and that certain races subsequently "degenerated" (predictably, the non-Europeans). Some evolutionary scientists, however, began to argue for multiple origins, with distinct races evolving in different places and times. By the beginning of the 20th century, European and American science viewed races as natural, long-standing divisions of the human species, evolving at different rates biologically and hence culturally. By such logic was racial inequality naturalized and legitimized.

When contemporary scientists, including anthropologists, assert that races are not scientifically valid, they are rejecting at least three fundamental premises of this old racial ideology: 1) the archaic subspecies concept, 2) the divisibility of contemporary humans into scientifically valid biological groupings, and 3) the link between racial traits and social, cultural, and political status.

1. *There were no distinct, archaic human subspecies.* The first premise anthropologists reject is that humans were originally divided, by nature or God, into a small set of biologically distinct, fixed species, subspecies, or races. Anthropologists now know conclusively, from fossil and DNA evidence, that contemporary humans are one variable species, with our roots in Africa, which moved out of Africa into a wide range of environments around the world, producing hundreds, perhaps thousands, of culturally and genetically distinct populations. Local populations, through natural selection as well as random genetic mutation, acquired some distinctive genetic traits, such as shovel-shaped incisor teeth, hairy ears, or red hair. Adaptation to human cultural inventions—such as agriculture, which creates concentrations of water that allow malaria-carrying mosquitoes to breed—also produced higher frequencies of sickle-cell genes (related to malaria resistance) in human populations in some parts of Africa, India, Arabia, and the Mediterranean.[4] At the same time, continuous migration and intermating between local populations prevented us from branching off into distinct subspecies or species and instead created a richer and more variable gene pool, producing new combinations and permutations of the human genome.

   Human prehistory and history, then, are a continuing story of fusion and fission, of a myriad of populations, emerging and shifting over time and space, sometimes isolated temporarily, then fusing and producing new formations. There have been thousands and thousands of groups throughout human history, marrying in and, more often, out; they have disappeared and reemerged in new forms over time.

   In short, there are no "basic" or "ancient" races; there are no stable, "natural," permanent, or even long-standing groupings called races. There have never been any "pure" races. All human populations are historically specific mixtures of the human gene pool. This is human evolution, and we see these same processes at work in the 19th and 20th centuries and today. "Races" are ephemeral—here today, gone tomorrow.
2. *Contemporary humans are not divisible into biological races.* When anthropologists say races aren't biologically real, they also reject the

idea that *modern* humans can be divided into scientifically valid, biologically distinct groupings or races. For races to be real as biological categories, the classification must be based on objective, consistent, and reliable biological criteria. The classification system must also have predictive value that will make it useful in research.

Scientists have demonstrated that both the concept of race and racial criteria are subjective, arbitrary, and inconsistently applied.[5] U.S. racial categories, such as the ones used in the Census, aren't valid in part because the biological attributes used to define races and create racial classifications rely on only a few visible, superficial, genetic traits—such as skin color and hair texture—and ignore the remaining preponderance of human variation. Alternative, equally visible racial classifications could be constructed using such criteria as hair color, eye color, height, weight, ear shape, or hairiness. However, there are less visible genetic traits that have far greater biological significance. For example, there are at least 13 genetic factors related to hemoglobin, the protein that helps carry oxygen to tissues, and there is also significant variation in the ABO, RH, and other blood systems. We could create racial classifications based on genetic factors that affect susceptibility to diabetes or to certain kinds of breast cancer or to the ability to digest milk. In sum, given the variety of possible biologically based traits for classifying human beings, the criteria used in U.S. racial categorizations are highly arbitrary and subjective. Our discussion here focuses on the U.S. concept of race. While racial concepts are no doubt similar in Canada and Europe, this is not true in other parts of the Americas.[6]

The number of potential biologically based racial groupings is enormous. Not only are there millions of genetic traits, but most genetic traits—even culturally salient but superficial traits such as skin color, hair texture, eye shape, and eye color—do not cluster together. Darker skin can cluster with straight hair as well as with very curly hair or with hairy or nonhairy bodies; paler skin can cluster with straight or curly hair or with black or blond hair or with lighter to darker eyes. Each trait could produce a different racial classification. For example, if one used height as a criterion rather than skin pigmentation, then the Northern Afghan population would be in the same racial category as the Swedes and the Tutsi of Rwanda. There are huge numbers of genetically influenced traits, visible and nonvisible, which could be used to classify humans into biologically distinct groups. There is no "natural" classification—no co-occurring clusters of racial traits. There are just alternatives, with different implications and uses.

Racial classifications are also unscientific because they are unreliable and unstable over time. Individuals cannot reliably be "raced," partly because the criteria are so subjective and unscientific. Robert Hahn, a medical anthropologist, found that 37% of babies described as Native American on their birth certificates ended up in a different racial category on their death certificates.[7] Racial identifications by forensic anthropologists, long touted as accurate, have been shown to be disturbingly unreliable, even in relatively ethnically homogeneous areas, such as Missouri and Ohio.[8] Forensic evidence from such urban areas as San José, California, or New York City is even more problematic.

Racial categories used by the U.S. Census Bureau have changed over time. In 1900, races included "mulatto, quadroon, or octoroon" in addition to "black." Southern Europeans and Jews were deemed to be separate races before World War II. Asian Indians ("Hindus") were initially categorized as "Caucasoid"—except for voting rights. The number and definitions of races in the most recent U.S. Census reflect the instability—and hence unreliability—of the concept of race. And U.S. racial classifications simply don't work in much of the rest of the world. Brazil is a classic, often-studied example, but they also don't work in South Asia, an area that includes over one-fifth of the world's population.

Historical and contemporary European and American racial categories are huge, biologically diverse macro-categories. Members of the same racial group tend to be similar in a few genetic ways that are often biologically irrelevant. Moreover, the genetic variability found within each racial grouping is far greater than the genetic similarity. Africa, by itself, is home to distinct populations whose average height ranges from less than five feet (the Mbuti) to over six feet (the Tutsi). Estimates suggest that contemporary racial variation accounts for less than 7% of all human genetic variation.[9] U.S. races, then, are not biologically distinct or biologically meaningful, scientifically based groupings of the human species.

3. *Race as biology has no scientific value.* An additional critique of the concept of race is that racial categories, as defined biologically, are not very useful in understanding other phenomena, whether biological or cultural.

   There is no substantial evidence that race, as a biological category, and "racial" characteristics, such as skin color, hair texture, and eye shape, are causally linked to behavior, to capacities, to individual and group accomplishments, to cultural institutions, or to propensities to engage in any specific activities. In the area of academic achievement, the focus on race as biology can lead researchers to ignore underlying nonbiological causal factors. One classic study found that controlling for socioeconomic and other environmental variables eliminated purported "racial" differences in I.Q. scores and academic achievement between African American, Mexican American, and European American students.[10]

Health professionals have also critiqued the concept of race. Alan Goodman and others have shown that race does not help physicians with diagnosis, prevention, or treatment of medical diseases.[11] Racial categories and a false ideology of race as "biology" encourage both doctors and their patients to view medical conditions as necessarily genetic, ignoring possible environmental sources. Hypertension, infant birthweights, osteoporosis, ovarian cysts—all traditionally viewed as "racial" (i.e., genetically based)—now seem to reflect environmental rather than racially linked genetic factors. The Centers for Disease Control concluded in 1993 that most associations between race and disease have no genetic or biological basis and that the concept of "race" is therefore not useful in public health.

As a result of recent evolution and constant interbreeding between groups of humans, two individuals from different "races" are just as likely to be more similar to one another genetically than two individuals from the same "race." This being so, race-as-biology has no predictive value.

If Not Race, Then What?

Classifications are usually created for some purpose. Alan Goodman and other biological anthropologists suggest that investigators focus on using traits relevant to the problem at hand. For example, if a particular blood factor puts an individual at risk for a disease, then classify individuals on that basis for that purpose.

Some suggest using the term "population" or "breeding population" to refer to the multitude of small, often geographically localized, groups that have developed high frequencies of one or more somewhat distinctive biological traits (e.g., shovel-shaped incisors) in response to biological, historical, and cultural factors. But others point out that there could be thousands of such groups, depending on the classifying criteria used, and that the groups would be merging and recombining over time and space. Moreover, the variability "captured" would reflect only a fraction of the variability in the human species.

Most anthropologists now use the concept of "clines" to help understand how genetic traits are distributed.[12] New data indicate that biological traits, such as blood type or skin color, are distributed in geographic gradations or "clines"; that is, the frequency of a trait varies continuously over a geographic area. For example, the genes for type B blood increase in frequency in an east-to-west direction (reflecting, in part, the travels of Genghis Khan and his army). In contrast, skin pigmentation grades from north to south, with increasing pigmentation as one gets closer to the equator. The frequency of the gene for sickle cell decreases from West Africa moving northeast.

Virtually all traits have distinct geographic distributions. Genes controlling skin color, body size and shape (head, limbs, lips, fingers, nose, ears), hairiness, and blood type are each distributed in different patterns over geographic space. Once again, for biological races to exist, these traits would have to co-vary, but they don't. Instead, biological traits produce a nearly infinite number of potential races. This is why anthropologists conclude that there are no scientifically distinguishable biological races—only thousands of clines!

So What Is Race Then?

We hope we have made the point that the concept of separate, biologically distinct human races is not scientifically defensible. Unfortunately, racial ideology, by focusing on a few physical attributes, traps us into a discourse about race as biology rather than race as a cultural construction. The concept of race is a cultural invention, a culturally and historically specific way of thinking about, categorizing, and treating human beings.[13] It is about social divisions within society, about social categories and identities, about power and privilege. It has been and remains a particular type of ideology for legitimizing social inequality between groups with different ancestries, national origins, and histories. Indeed, the concept of race is also a major system of social identity, affecting one's own self-perception and how one is perceived and treated by others.

But race does have a biological component, one that can trick us into thinking that races are scientifically valid, biological subdivisions of the human species. As noted earlier, geographically localized populations—as a result of adaptation, migration, and chance—tend to have some characteristic physical traits. While these may be traits that characterize an entire population, such as hairy ears, it is more accurate to talk about the relative frequency of a particular trait, such as blood type O, in one population as compared to another, or the relative amount of pigmentation of individuals in a population, relative to other populations. Some traits, such as skin color, reflect climatic conditions; others, such as eye color and shape, probably reflect random, historical processes and migration patterns. The U.S. was peopled by populations from geographically distinct regions of the world—voluntary immigrants, forced African slaves, and indigenous American groups. Therefore, dominant northwestern European ethnic groups, such as the English and Germans, were able to exploit certain visually salient biological traits, especially skin color, as markers of race.

The effectiveness of these physical traits as markers of one's race depended, of course, on their being preserved in future generations. So dominant cultural groups created elaborate social and physical barriers to mating, reproduction, and marriage that crossed racial lines. The most explicit were the so-called anti-miscegenation laws, which outlawed sex between members of different races, whether married or not. These laws were not declared unconstitutional by the U.S. Supreme Court until the 1967 case of *Loving v. Virginia*.[14] Another vehicle was the cultural definition of kinship, whereby children of interracial (often forced) matings acquired the racial status of their lower-ranking parent; this was the so-called one-drop rule or hypodescent. Especially during the time of slavery, the lower-ranking parent was generally the mother, and thus the long-standing European cultural tradition of affiliating socially "legitimate" children with the father's kinship group was effectively reversed.

In contrast, there have been fewer social or legal barriers in the U.S. to mating and marriage between Italians, British, Germans, Swedes, and others of European ancestry. Consequently, the physical and cultural characteristics of European regional populations are less evident in the U.S. With intermarriage, distinct European identities were submerged in the culturally relevant macroracial category of "white"—more accurately, European American.

Thus even the biological dimension of contemporary racial groupings is the result of sociocultural processes. That is, humans as cultural beings first gave social significance to some physical differences between groups and then tried to perpetuate these "racial markers" by preventing social and physical intercourse between members of the groups. Although the dominant racial ideology was about maintaining racial "purity," the issue was not about biology; it was about maintaining social, political, and economic privilege.[15]

Why Is This Understanding Important for Educators?

We hope we've convinced you that race isn't biologically "real" and that race in the U.S. and elsewhere is a historical, social, and cultural creation. But so what? What is the significance of this way of viewing race for teachers, students, and society?

1. *The potential for change.* First, it is important to understand that, while races are biological fictions, they are social realities. Race may not be "real" in a biological sense, but it surely is "real" socially, politically, economically, and psychologically. Race and racism profoundly structure who we are, how we are treated, how we treat others, and our access to resources and rights.

   Perhaps the most important message educators can take from the foregoing discussion is that race, racial classifications, racial stratification, and other forms of racism, including racial ideology, rather than being part of our biology, are part of our culture. Like other cultural forms, both the concept of race and our racial classifications are part of a system we have created. This means that we have the ability to change the system, to transform it, and even to totally eradicate it. Educators, in their role as transmitters of official culture, are particularly well poised to be active change agents in such a transformation.

   But how, you may well ask, can teachers or anybody else make people stop classifying by race? And are there any good reasons to do so? These familiar categories—black, white, Asian, Native American, and so on—seem so embedded in U.S. society. They seem so "natural." Of course, that's how culture works. It seems "natural" to think of chicken, but not rats, as food. But, as we have shown above, the labels and underlying constructs that we use to talk about human diversity are unstable, depending on particular social, political, and historical contexts. Individuals in positions of authority, of course, have the ability to change them institutionally. But ordinary people also have the ability to change how they classify and label people in their everyday lives.

   Several questions arise at this point. Do we as educators consciously want to change our way of conceptualizing and discussing human biological variation? What makes the "race as biology" assumption so dangerous? Are we going to continue to classify people by race, even while recognizing that it is a social construct? What vested interests do people have in holding onto—or rejecting—racial categories? How can we become more sophisticated in our understanding of how systems of classification work while also becoming more critical of our own ways of classifying people? Are there alternative ways of thinking about, classifying, and labeling human beings that might be more empowering for students, teachers, and community members? By eliminating or changing labels, will we change the power structures that perpetuate privilege and entitlement? Moving beyond race as biology forces us to confront these and other issues.

2. *The dangers of using racial classifications.* Categories and classifications are not intrinsically good or bad. People have always grouped others in ways that were important within a given society. However, the myth of race as biology is dangerous because it conflates physical attributes, such as skin color, with unrelated qualities, such as intelligence. Racial labels delude people into thinking that race predicts such other outcomes and behaviors as achievement in sports, music, or school; rates of employment; pregnancies outside marriage; or drug use. Race was historically equated with intelligence and, on that basis, was used to justify slavery and educational discrimination; it later provided the rationale that supported the genocide of Jews, blacks, Gypsies, and other "inferior" races under Hitler. So using racial categories brings along this history, like unwanted baggage.

   Macroracial categories are dangerous in that the categories oversimplify and mask complex human differences. Saying that someone is Asian tells us virtually nothing concrete, but it brings with it a host of stereotypes, such as "model minority," "quiet," "good at math," "Inscrutable," and so on. Yet the Asian label includes a wide range of groups, such as Koreans, Filipinos, and Vietnamese, with distinct histories and languages. The same is true for "white," a term that homogenizes the multiple nationalities, languages, and cultures that constitute Europe. The label "African American" ignores the enormous linguistic, physical, and cultural diversity of the peoples of Africa. The term "black" conflates people of African descent who were brought to the U.S. as slaves with recent immigrants from Africa and the Caribbean. These macroracial labels oversimplify and reduce human diversity to four or five giant groups. Apart from being bad science, these categories don't predict anything helpful—yet they have acquired a life of their own.

Macroracial categories, such as those used in the U.S. Census and other institutional data-collection efforts, force people to use labels that may not represent their own self-identity or classifying system. They must either select an existing category or select "other"—by definition, a kind of nonidentity. The impossibility, until recently, of selecting more than one ethnic/racial category implicitly stigmatizes multiracial individuals. And the term "mixed" wrongly implies that there are such things as "pure" races, an ideology with no basis in science. The recent expansion of the number of U.S. Census categories still cannot accommodate the diversity of the U.S. population, which includes people whose ancestry ranges from Egypt, Brazil, Sri Lanka, Ghana, and the Dominican Republic to Iceland and Korea.

3. *How macroracial categories have served people in positive ways.* Having noted some negative aspects, it is equally important to discuss how macroracial categories also serve society. Recall that labels are not intrinsically "good" or "bad." It depends on what people do with them. During the 1960s, the U.S. civil rights movement helped bring about consciousness and pride in being African American. This consciousness—known by terms such as ethnic pride and black power—united people who had been the victims of racism and oppression. From that consciousness sprang such educational interventions as black and Chicano history classes, ethnic studies departments, Afrocentric schools, and other efforts to empower young people. The movement to engender pride in and knowledge of one's ancestry has had a powerful impact. Many individuals are deeply attached to these racial labels as part of a positive identity. As one community activist put it, "Why should I give up being a race? I like being a race."

Racial classification can also have positive impact by allowing educators to monitor how equitably our institutions are serving the public. Racial categories are used by schools to disaggregate data on student outcomes, including achievement, attendance, discipline, course placements, college attendance rates, and other areas of school and student performance. These data are then used to examine whether certain groups of students are disproportionately represented in any outcome areas. For example, a school might discover that the percentage of Latino students who receive some type of disciplinary intervention is higher than that for other school populations. The school can then consider what it can do to change this outcome. Teachers might ask, is there something about the way Latino students are treated in the school that leads to higher disciplinary referral rates? What other factors might be involved?

The racial classifications that educators use to monitor student outcome data reflect our society's social construction of race. As such, the categories represent groups that have been historically disenfranchised, oppressed, or marginalized. Without data disaggregated by race, gender, and other categories, it would be difficult to identify problems stemming from race-based institutional and societal factors that privilege certain groups, such as the widespread U.S. practice of tracking by so-called ability. Without data broken out according to racial, gender, and ethnic categories, schools would not be able to assess the positive impact intervention programs have had on different groups of students.

4. *Shifting the conversation from biology to culture.* One function of the myth of race as biology has been to distract us from the underlying causes of social inequality in the United States. Dismantling the myth of race as biology means that we must now shift our focus to analyzing the social, economic, political, and historical conditions that breed and serve to perpetuate social inequality. For educators, this means helping students to recognize and understand socioeconomic stratification, who benefits and who is harmed by racial discrimination, and how we as individuals and institutional agents can act to dismantle ideologies, institutions, and practices that harm young people.

There is another, more profound implication of the impermanence of race. Culture, acting collectively, and humans, acting individually, can make races disappear. That is, we can mate and marry across populations, thus destroying the racial "markers" that have been used to facilitate categorization and differential treatment of people of different ancestry and social rank. An understanding of human biological variation reveals the positive, indeed essential, role that intermating and intermarriage have played in human evolution and human adaptation. Rather than "mongrelizing" a "pure species," mating between different populations enriches the genetic pool. It is society, rather than nature—and socially and economically stratified societies, for the most part—that restricts social and sexual intercourse and severely penalizes those who mate across racial and other socially created lines.

Suggestions and Resources for Educators

Anthropological knowledge about race informs us about what race is and is not, but it cannot guide educational decision making. The underlying goal of social justice can help educators in making policy decisions, such as whether to use racial and ethnic categories to monitor educational outcomes. As long as we continue to see racially based disparities in young peoples' school achievement, then we must monitor and investigate the social conditions that produce these disparities. We must be careful, however, to avoid "biologizing" the classification; that is, we must avoid assuming genetic explanations for racial differences in behaviors and educational outcomes or even diseases.

As we pursue a more socially just world, educators should also continue to support young people's quest for knowledge about the history and struggles of their own people, as well as those of other groups, so that students in the future will not be able to point to their textbooks and say, "My people are not included in the curriculum." In the process, we can encourage both curiosity about and respect for human diversity, and we can emphasize the importance that historical and social context plays in creating social inequality. We can also encourage comparative studies of racial and other forms of social stratification, further challenging the notion that there is a biological explanation for oppression and inequality. In short, students will understand that there is no biological explanation for a group's historical position as either oppressed—or oppressor. We can encourage these studies to point out variations and fine distinctions within human racial groupings.

In addition to viewing the treatment of race and racial categories through a social-justice lens, we would apply another criterion that we call "depth of knowledge." We believe that it is important to challenge and inspire young people by exposing them to the best of our current knowledge in the sciences, social sciences, and other disciplines. Until now, most students in our education system have not been exposed to systematic, scientifically based teaching about race and human biological variation. One reason is that many social studies teachers may think they lack sufficient background in genetics and human biology. At the same time, many biology teachers may feel uncomfortable teaching about race as a social construct. The null move for teachers seems to be to say that we should all be "color blind." However, this does not help educate students about human diversity, both biological and social. In rare cases when students have the opportunity to engage in studies of race, ethnicity, culture, and ways to end racism, they are both interested and intellectually challenged.[16] One high school teacher who teaches students about race said he wants to dispel the notion that teaching about diversity is "touchy feely." "We don't just want to touch diversity; we want to approach it academically. . . . We feel we have a definite discipline."[17]

Rather than shield students and ourselves from current scientific knowledge about race, including its contradictions and controversies, we submit that educators should be providing opportunities for students to learn what anthropologists, geneticists, and other scientists, including social scientists, have to say about human biological variation and the issue of race. Particularly in middle schools, high schools, and beyond, students should be involved in inquiry projects and social action projects, in critical examination of the labels we currently use, and in analysis of the reasons for and against using them in particular contexts. Rather than tell students that they should or should not use racial labels (except for slurs), educators should be creating projects in which students explore together the range of possible ways of classifying people and the implications and political significance of alternative approaches in different contexts.

Notes

1. Richard Herrnstein and Charles Murray, *The Bell Curve: Intelligence and Class Structure in American Life* (New York: Free Press, 1994).
2. Audrey Smedley, *Race in North America: Origin and Evolution of a Worldview* (Boulder, Colo.: Westview Press, 1998).
3. Jonathan Marks, *Human Biodiversity: Genes, Race, and History* (New York: Aldine de Gruyter, 1995).
4. Leonard Lieberman and Patricia Rice, "Races or Clines?," p. 7, available on the Anthropology Education Commission page of the American Anthropological Association website, www.aaanet.org/committees/commissions/aec. click on Teaching About Race.
5. George J. Armelagos and Alan H. Goodman, "Race, Racism, and Anthropology," in Alan H. Goodman and Thomas L. Leatherman, eds., *Building a New Biocultural Synthesis: Political-Economic Perspectives on Human Biology* (Ann Arbor: University of Michigan Press, 1998).
6. Jeffrey M. Fish, "Mixed Blood," in James Spradley and William McCurdy, eds., *Conformity and Conflict*, 11th ed. (New York: Allyn & Bacon, 2002), pp. 270–80.
7. Alan Goodman, "Bred in the Bone?," *Sciences*, vol. 37, no. 2, 1997, p. 24.
8. Ibid., p. 22.

9. Leonard Lieberman, "'Race' 1997 and 2001: A Race Odyssey," available on the Anthropology Education Commission page of the American Anthropological Association website, http://www.aaanet.org/committees/commissions/aec. click on Teaching About Race.
10. Jane Mercer, "Ethnic Differences in IQ Scores: What Do They Mean? (A Response to Lloyd Dunn)," *Hispanic Journal of Behavioral Sciences,* vol. 10, 1988, pp. 199–218.
11. Goodman, op. cit.
12. Lieberman and Rice, op. cit.
13. Carol Mukhopadhyay and Yolanda Moses, "Reestablishing 'Race' in Anthropological Discourse," *American Anthropologist,* vol. 99, 1997, pp. 517–33.
14. Janet Hyde and John DeLamater, *Understanding Human Sexuality,* 6th ed. (New York: McGraw-Hill, 1997).
15. Smedley, op. cit.
16. Karen Donaldson, *Through Students' Eyes: Combating Racism in United States Schools* (Westport, Conn.: Praeger, 1996); and Rosemary C. Henze, "Curricular Approaches to Developing Positive Interethnic Relations," *Journal of Negro Education,* vol. 68, 2001, pp. 529–49.
17. Henze, p. 539.

Reading Analytically

1. One of the ways that this piece is organized is by section titles, many of which take the form of questions. Look over the section titles and write an analysis of how the shape of the argument is built upon these various pieces of the whole, and how questions are used to keep the audience engaged.
2. If you were to situate the attitudes toward race that are presented by these authors, what other pieces in this section seem closest to the perspectives presented here? Which authors might object, and why?
3. Is the amount and type of evidence presented here sufficient to build the perspective on race that is offered? What are the main sources of evidence? Upon what disciplines does that evidence draw?

Reading Across Disciplinary Communities

1. While a good deal of theoretical information from the field of anthropology and other sciences needs to be presented in this piece before it moves on to the application of those theories in the final sections, the authors are careful to keep the audience—who are practicing teachers—engaged. What methods do they use to keep that audience focused? What particular lines or phrasings, even in the earlier sections, remind the readers that this piece will have practical implications for their work?

2. As is discussed in the introduction to this book, one of the ways to think about disciplinary groups is as "professional communities." Clearly, this piece points to the professional community of teachers. What other professional communities might benefit from a deeper understanding of racial concepts? List at least two, and describe the kinds of practice-based writing you might do to help inform them about race in ways that would advance that profession.

JONATHAN KAHN

Race in a Bottle

This essay was first published in Scientific American, *a magazine that presents news and research from the scientific disciplines to a nonexpert audience. It explores the ways that scientific research, and the public perception of that research, is being used by business to develop new products—in this case, pharmaceuticals geared toward specific races and ethnicities. Jonathan Kahn, a scholar of history and law, provides an overview of the issues involved when scientific research finds its way into applications in the applied science of business. Kahn holds a Ph.D. in history from Cornell University, and a Doctor of Jurisprudence (Law) from Boalt Hall School of Law. He has written widely on issues pertaining to legal rights as related to new discoveries in genetics.*

This piece raises questions about what happens when discoveries in specific academic fields find their way into applications in business. As you read, you might consider both the ethical implications of marketing pharmaceuticals to specific groups based upon scientific discoveries, and how this piece can help us to understand what takes place in the translation from the "pure" sciences to the applied sciences—a question raised in the chapter on genetics and neuroscience as well.

Two years ago, on June 23, 2005, the U.S. Food and Drug Administration approved the first "ethnic" drug. Called BiDil (pronounced "bye-dill"), it was intended to treat congestive heart failure—the progressive weakening of the heart muscle to the point where it can no longer pump blood efficiently—in African-Americans only. The approval was widely declared to be a significant step toward a new era of personalized medicine, an era in which pharmaceuticals would be specifically designed to work with an individual's particular genetic makeup. Known as pharmacogenomics, this approach to drug development promises to reduce the cost and increase the safety and efficacy of new therapies. BiDil was also hailed as a means to improve the health of African-Americans, a community woefully underserved by the U.S. medical establishment. Organizations such as the Association of Black Cardiologists and the Congressional Black Caucus strongly supported the drug's approval.

A close inspection of BiDil's history, however, shows that the drug is ethnic in name only. First, BiDil is not a new medicine—it is merely a combination into a single pill of two generic drugs, hydralazine and isosorbide dinitrate, both of which have been used for more than a decade to treat heart failure in people of all races. Second, BiDil is not a pharmacogenomic drug. Although studies have shown that the hydralazine/isosorbide dinitrate (H/I) combination can delay hospitalization and death for patients suffering from heart failure, the underlying mechanism for the drug's efficacy is not fully understood and has not been directly connected to any specific genes. Third, and most important, no firm evidence exists that BiDil actually works better or differently in African-Americans than in anyone else. The FDA's approval of BiDil was based primarily on a clinical trial that enrolled only self-identified African-Americans and did not compare their health outcomes with those of other ethnic or racial groups.

So how did BiDil become tagged as an ethnic drug and the harbinger of a new age of medicine? The story of the drug's development is a tangled tale of inconclusive studies, regulatory hurdles and commercial motives. BiDil has had a relatively small impact on the marketplace—over the past two years, only a few million dollars' worth of prescriptions have been sold—but the drug has demonstrated the perils of using racial categories to win approval for new pharmaceuticals. Although African-Americans are dying from heart disease and other illnesses at younger ages than whites, most researchers believe the premature deaths result from a complex array of social and economic forces [see "Sick of Poverty," by Robert Sapolsky; Scientific American, December 2005]. Some medical professionals and policy experts, however, have pointed to BiDil as proof that genetic differences can explain the health disparity. Worse, some pharmaceutical companies are now using this unfounded argument to pursue other treatments targeted at various ethnic groups, a trend that may segregate medicine and fatten the profits of drugmakers without addressing the underlying causes that are killing so many African-Americans before their time.

Birth of BiDil

The BiDil saga began more than 20 years ago with a pair of studies designed to gauge the effects of vasodilating drugs—which widen blood vessels—on heart failure, a debilitating and ultimately fatal disease that afflicts millions of Americans. Until then, doctors treated heart failure with diuretics (to reduce the accumulation of fluid that results from inadequate pumping) and digoxin (to increase the contraction of the heart muscle) but had little else at their disposal. In the early 1980s Jay Cohn, a cardiologist at the University of Minnesota, hypothesized that administering two vasodilators, hydralazine and isosorbide dinitrate, might ease the strain on weakened hearts by relaxing both the arteries and veins. Together with the U.S. Veterans Administration, Cohn designed and conducted two trials to assess this theory.

The first Vasodilator Heart Failure Trial (V-HeFT I) tested the H/I combination against a placebo and a drug called prazosin, which is used to treat high blood pressure. The results seemed to show great promise for the combination. The second trial, V-HeFT II, tested H/I against enalapril, a first-generation angiotensin-converting enzyme (ACE) inhibitor. (ACE inhibitors lower blood pressure by curbing the production of vessel-constricting peptides.) As it turned out, enalapril proved more effective than H/I for treating heart failure. From that point forward, ACE inhibitors became the new first-line therapy for heart failure patients. Doctors began recommending hydralazine and isosorbide dinitrate—both available as inexpensive generic pills—for those who did not respond well to ACE inhibitors.

Cohn, however, remained committed to developing a treatment that combined hydralazine and isosorbide dinitrate because he believed in its effectiveness. In 1987 he applied for a patent on the method of using the drugs together to treat heart failure in all people, regardless of race. (He could not get a patent on the drug combination itself because both medicines were already available in generic form.) He then licensed the patent rights to Medco, a small pharmaceutical firm in North Carolina, which took steps in the early 1990s to put the H/I combination into a single pill—and BiDil was born.

Medco and Cohn brought BiDil to the FDA for approval in 1996. In early 1997 the agency refused to approve the drug. Ironically, most of the doctors on the FDA's review panel thought BiDil did in fact work and said they would consider prescribing it. The problem was not with the drug but with the statistical data from the V-HeFT trials, which were designed not to meet the regulatory standards for FDA approval but to test the hypothesis that vasodilators could treat heart failure. After the rejection, Medco's stock plummeted by more than 20 percent, and the company let the patent rights revert to Cohn. By 1997 half of the 20-year life of the original BiDil patent had already passed, which may explain Medco's reluctance to sink more money into the drug.

BiDil's Racial Rebirth

It was only at this point that race entered the story. After the FDA's rejection of BiDil, Cohn went back to the V-HeFT results from the 1980s and broke down the data by race, examining how well African-Americans had responded to the competing treatments. Such retrospective "data dredging" can yield useful insights for further investigations, but it is also fraught with statistical peril; if the number of research subjects in each category is too small, the results for the subgroups may be meaningless. Cohn argued that H/I worked particularly well in the African-Americans enrolled in the V-HeFT studies. The clearest support for this claim came from V-HeFT I, which placed only 49 African-Americans on H/I—a tiny number considering that new drug trials typically enroll thousands of subjects. In 1999 Cohn published a paper in the Journal of Cardiac Failure on this hypothesized racial difference and filed a new patent application. This second patent was almost identical to the first except for specifying the use of H/I to treat heart failure in black patients. Issued in 2000, the new patent lasts until 2020, 13 years after the original patent was set to expire. Thus was BiDil reinvented as an ethnic drug.

Race-specific patent in hand, Cohn relicensed the intellectual-property rights to NitroMed, a small Massachusetts firm. The FDA then gave NitroMed the go-ahead to conduct the African-American Heart Failure Trial (A-HeFT), a relatively small study involving 1,050 self-identified African-Americans. In A-HeFT, half the heart failure patients took BiDil while the other half received a placebo; at the same time, the patients in both groups continued taking their already prescribed treatments for heart failure (for example, about 70 percent of the subjects in both groups were on ACE inhibitors). The results were strikingly positive: the mortality rate in the BiDil subjects was 43 percent lower than that in the placebo group. In fact, BiDil appeared so effective that A-HeFT's Data Safety Monitoring Board suspended the trial early, in July 2004, so that the drug could be offered to the subjects in the placebo group as well. NitroMed's stock surged on the news, more than tripling in value in the following days. The next June the FDA formally approved BiDil with a race-specific label, indicating that it was for use in black patients.

But researchers have good reason to believe that BiDil would also be effective in nonblack patients. Indeed, Cohn himself has said he believes the drug should work in people of all races. So why did the developers of the drug test it in only one ethnic group? The answer seems to be driven more by commerce than by science. If the FDA had approved BiDil for the general population, the patent protection for the drug's manufacturer would have expired in 2007. Restricting the clinical trial to African-Americans maximized the chances that the FDA would approve the race-specific use of BiDil, giving NitroMed an additional 13 years to sell the H/I combination without competition.

Segregated Medicine

Science and commerce have always proceeded together in advancing medicine, but in the case of BiDil the balance seems to have gotten out of whack. There can be no doubt that Cohn and the other medical professionals behind the drug's development sincerely want to improve the lives of the many people suffering from heart failure. In this respect, the approval of BiDil is certainly a good thing. But Cohn and NitroMed have also used race to obtain commercial advantage. The patented drug costs about six times as much as the readily available generic equivalents. The high cost has already made many insurers reluctant to cover BiDil and may place it beyond the reach of the millions of Americans without health insurance. Moreover, the unprecedented media attention to the race-specific character of the drug may lead many doctors and patients alike to think that non-African-Americans should not get the drug, when, in fact, it might help prolong their lives.

Perhaps most problematically, the patent award and FDA approval of BiDil have given the imprimatur of the federal government to using race as a genetic category. Since the inception of the Human Genome Project, scientists have worked hard to ensure that the biological knowledge emerging from advances in genetic research is not used inappropriately to make socially constructed racial categories appear biologically given or natural. As a 2001 editorial in the journal Nature Genetics put it, "scientists have long been saying that at the genetic level there is more variation between two individuals in the same population than between populations and that there is no biological basis for 'race.'" More recently, an editorial in Nature Biotechnology asserted that "race is simply a poor proxy for the environmental and genetic causes of disease or drug response. . . . Pooling people in race silos is akin to zoologists grouping raccoons, tigers and okapis on the basis that they are all stripey."

The FDA's approval of BiDil was based on accepting NitroMed's argument that the drug should be indicated only for African-Americans because the trial population was African-American. This labeling sends the scientifically unproved message that the subject population's race was somehow a relevant biological variable in assessing the safety and efficacy of BiDil. Most drugs on the market today were tested in overwhelmingly white populations, but we do not call these medicines "white," nor should we. The FDA's unstated assumption is that a drug that proves effective for white people is good enough for everyone; the same assumption should apply when the trial population happens to be black. Otherwise, the FDA is implying that African-Americans are somehow less fully representative of humanity than whites are.

In November 2004 Nature Genetics published an article by Sarah K. Tate and David B. Goldstein of University College London entitled "Will Tomorrow's Medicines Work for Everyone?" The paper noted that "29 medicines (or combinations of medicines) have been claimed, in peer-reviewed scientific or medical journals, to have differences in either safety or, more commonly, efficacy among racial or ethnic groups." Journalists immediately quoted the study as providing further evidence of biological differences among races; for example, an article in the Los Angeles Times, after discussing BiDil, referred to "a report in the journal Nature Genetics last month [that] listed 29 drugs that are known to have different efficacies in the two races." (The italics are mine.) Similarly, a story in the Times of London asserted that "only last week, Nature Genetics revealed research from University College London showing that 29 medicines have safety or efficacy profiles that vary between ethnic or racial groups." And a *New York Times* editorial entitled "Toward the First Racial Medicine" began with a discussion of BiDil and went on to note that "by one count, some 29 medicines show evidence of being safer or more effective in one racial group or another, suggesting that more targeted medicines may be coming."

One small problem: these newspaper stories totally misrepresented the Nature Genetics piece. Tate and Goldstein asserted that the racial differences in drug safety or efficacy have only been claimed, not proved, and in the next sentence they go on to say, "But these claims are universally controversial, and there is no consensus on how important race or ethnicity is in determining drug response."

In only four of the 29 medicines identified, Tate and Goldstein found evidence that genetic variations between races could possibly be related to the different responses to the drugs. (All four are beta blockers used for treating high blood pressure and other cardiovascular ills; some research indicates that these drugs work better in individuals carrying a gene variant that is more common in people of European ancestry than in African-Americans.) For nine of the medicines, the authors found "a reasonable underlying physiological basis" to explain why blacks and whites may respond differently to the drugs; for example, some scientists have speculated that ACE inhibitors may be more effective in people of European descent than in African-Americans because of variations in enzyme activity. (Other researchers have contested this hypothesis.) For five of the drugs, Tate and Goldstein found no physiological reasons to explain the varying responses; for the remaining 11 they concluded that the reports of differing responses may not be valid.

Racial Injustice

Nevertheless, the appeal of race-specific drugs is growing. In 2003 VaxGen, a California biopharmaceutical company, made an abortive attempt to use a retrospective analysis of racial subgroups to salvage a proposed AIDS vaccine called AIDSVAX. Although the clinical trial for AIDSVAX showed no decrease in HIV infection rates in the study population as a whole, VaxGen claimed a significant reduction in infection among the black and Asian participants. But only a few hundred blacks and Asians were involved in the study, meaning that a handful of infections could have skewed the results. The claim of race-specific response was undercut later that year when another trial in Thailand showed that AIDSVAX was ineffective there as well. In a similar case, AstraZeneca, the British pharmaceutical firm, argued that its lung cancer drug, Iressa, worked better in the Asians enrolled in a 2004 clinical trial, which showed that the medicine did not improve survival rates overall. (Unconvinced, the FDA changed the labeling for Iressa, disallowing its use in any new patients.) More recently, AstraZeneca has conducted trials of Crestor, the company's multibillion-dollar cholesterol-lowering drug, in African-Americans, South Asians and Hispanics. Consumer groups have claimed that Crestor is less safe than other cholesterol-lowering drugs, but AstraZeneca says the race-specific studies demonstrate the safety and efficacy of the medicine.

Researchers using race to develop drugs may be motivated by good intentions, but such efforts are also driven by the dictates of an increasingly competitive medical marketplace. The example of BiDil indicates that researchers and regulators alike have not fully appreciated that race is a powerful and volatile category. When used to bolster the commercial value of a drug, it can lead to haphazard regulation, substandard medical treatment and other unfortunate unintended consequences. The FDA should not grant race-specific approvals without clear and convincing evidence of a genetic or biological basis for any observed racial differences in safety or efficacy. Approving more drugs such as BiDil will not alleviate the very serious health disparities between races in the U.S. We need social and political will, not mislabeled medicines, to redress that injustice.

Reading Analytically

1. Kahn begins his essay with a specific case of FDA approval of a drug. In what way does he use this case as illustrative of a wider point that he is trying to make? What is that point?
2. Since the original place of publication, *Scientific American,* is at once within the discipline of the sciences and also, as a popular publication, partially journalistic, Kahn must find a middle ground. Give some examples of how Kahn, a specialist in history and law, uses voices from the scientific community to bolster his piece, while still keeping it readable for his nonexpert audience.
3. Does this piece seem to be "antibusiness"? That is, does the message here seem to suggest that when science is used in the marketplace, it becomes tainted? In what ways does it suggest that claim, and in what ways does it stop short of making that case?

Reading Across Disciplinary Communities

1. The mixture of disciplines in this piece is striking. The author is an expert in history and law, but he is writing as a journalist about science for a publication that is primarily about scientific discovery. Where do you see, in this piece, the expertise of the author, as a historian, a legal scholar, or both coming through? How does he present the state of science on this topic? What evidence does he draw upon?
2. In some ways, the situation within which this author is writing, as described in the previous question, is similar to your own. Though he is not a full-scale expert on the topic or in the discipline of the topic, he

still manages to write a very credible piece. What can you learn from reading this about methods that you can use as a student of a particular field who does not yet have full knowledge of that field? What techniques might be useful to you in your own writing?

Writing Across Disciplines
Interdisciplinary Writing Opportunities

1. As the readings in this chapter suggest, race is a concept that has an effect upon just about every disciplinary community. Drawing upon your own major, or a major that you are considering, research the various ways that writers in that discipline have written about issues of race, and write a brief essay that identifies the key questions, approaches, and methods that people in your discipline have used to explore the topic. Be sure to cite specific examples of studies of race that specialists in your discipline have developed.
2. The title question of this chapter asks if "the concept of race" is real. Many of the pieces in this chapter debate that question, drawing upon human genetics, social roles, and philosophical concepts. Because of this wide range of perspectives, it is very difficult to answer this question with any degree of certainty. Still, writers like the ones in this section have attempted to take a position on the question. Join those writers by offering your own argument: Drawing upon some of the pieces in this section, and other materials you might research, argue for or against the viability and usefulness of race as a category. Why should we continue to treat race as an important concept? Or why should we abandon that concept and think differently? Or perhaps should we develop a new definition of race? As you develop your own argument, show why retaining or abandoning this concept would have positive or useful effects.
3. Race is not only a theoretical concept, but also one that has real effects upon the ways we interact with one another. That is, whether race is biologically viable or socially constructed, there is no denying that race has its effects upon many facets of our lives. Drawing upon your own field(s) of interest or expertise, illustrate the effect that racial categories have upon some social issue. You might consider, for example, race's effect upon education, upon medicine, upon specific laws, upon economics, upon political views or elections, upon self-image, or upon policies of businesses. Research the specific effect of race on that area of human behavior, and illustrate in your essay the ways that racial categories have had an influence upon the ways our culture functions.

4. Race is not only a public issue, but also a private one. That is, whether race is "real" or not, it clearly does have a large impact upon the way we develop our own sense of self. Using methodologies common in the social sciences—surveys, focus groups, interviews, case studies, and so forth—develop an essay that discusses the impact of racial identity upon the self-image of some group of people. You might consider the racial identity of individuals in your hometown community, your family, your college or high school, or members of any other group to which you belong.
5. Since race has such a broad influence upon other social issues, you might use the concept as a way of studying many of the other issues discussed in this book. Research and write an essay on the ways that race influences our views of "terrorism" and war: how it is influenced by the findings of recent scientific discoveries in genetics or neuroscience; how concepts of race have influenced, or have been influenced by, ideas about racial or ethnic categories, or whether our beliefs about war are specific to what it means to be an "American." Starting from the key questions about race asked in this chapter, demonstrate how those questions influence some other set of social issues.

CHAPTER 4

What Does it Mean to Be (or Become) an "American"?

Citizenship and the Immigration Debate

The United States of America has always defined itself as a nation of immigrants. Indeed, the promise of America is inscribed on one of its best-known icons, the Statue of Liberty:

Give me your tired, your poor,
Your huddled masses yearning to breathe free,
The wretched refuse of your teeming shore.
Send these, the homeless, tempest-tost to me,
I lift my lamp beside the golden door!

But times change, and immigration has become the subject of much debate among our citizenry. In a time fraught with economic hardships, fears of terrorism, and waves of illegal immigration, some see immigration not as a fulfillment of the ideal of the "melting pot," but rather as a weakening of our cultural unity and domestic security.

Rather than consider this debate polemically—as a debate about whether immigration is "good" or "bad"—the readings here will first ask you to step back and ask (through the various disciplinary communities who have studied and written on these issues) some foundational questions: What does it mean to be an American citizen? How does one become a "good" American citizen? And is immigration still good for America? As with all topics that are broached by scholarly disciplines, the readings in this chapter avoid rushing to judgment, but instead offer a variety of perspectives on the topic that are based on research, reflection, and complex arguments. As such, the perspectives on immigration offered will challenge you to step back from answering the practical question ("What should we do about immigration policies and illegal immigrants/immigration?") until you have a larger understanding of the contexts and complications of this issue. By reading the work of others on the topic, and then by adding your own voice to the subjects broached here through your own research and writing, you will see the inherent complexity of topics such as this one. You will also see how individual disciplines use their own methods to explore such wide-ranging issues.

The chapter begins with a discussion of "The Elements of American Identity," an excerpt from *One America Indivisible.* This study by Sheldon Hackney explores the stories that make up the American character, as well as the contradictory elements of a culture that is based more in an idea than in an ethnic culture. Following this introductory piece, the remainder of the pieces in this section address specific facets of immigration and citizenship, facets that are of particular interest to disciplinary communities. First, two readings address issues related to the amalgamation of Mexican immigrants into our citizenry. Two social scientists, Susan Rippberger and Kathleen Staudt, detail the results of a study that examined key cultural differences that separate Mexican and American citizens along the U.S.-Mexico border, differences that need to be taken into account as we consider how Mexican immigrants might best find their way into American citizenship and culture. Melissa Moreno, a specialist in education and ethnic culture, adds to this discussion, providing ethnographic research to explore the impediments and pathways to "belonging" to the American citizenry among Mexican immigrants. Rebecca M. Callahan, Chandra Muller, and Kathryn S. Schiller widen the lens, exploring the effects of high school civics classes upon immigrants from many cultures as they enter adulthood—adding another dimension not only to the discussion of immigration, but also to the discussions of civic literacy that are broached by Eric Lane's "America 101" in Chapter 1 of this book.

Another disciplinary perspective is added to this debate through Gordon H. Hanson's "The Economic Logic of Illegal Immigration." Rather than treat immigration as a cultural issue, he instead explores the economic impact of illegal workers in the United States. Perhaps what is most interesting about this piece is the way that it begins from a set of commonplace ideas and widely accepted assumptions, and uses quantitative data to examine the accuracy of those assumptions. This approach also helps to illustrate the value in the types of "quantitative literacy" called for in two selections in Chapter 1 of this book. But Tim Kane and Kirk A. Johnson refuse to accept this simple economic formula, contending that the "real problem" with illegal immigration isn't just its effect upon the economy, but its effect upon *our* (i.e., current citizens') security. As such, these two fellows at the conservative think-tank, the Heritage Foundation, lay out a set of principles that they believe can protect both economic and security interests of current American citizens. Finally, Steven Salaita, a professor of American and Ethnic literature, provides another perspective on immigration. Using his background in the humanities—and his own background as an Arab American—he examines the effects of the 9/11 tragedy upon the "mainstream perceptions of Arabs and Arab Americans."

In sum, the pieces in this section provide a range of analytical methods that can be used to examine a cultural issue such as immigration, ranging across fields as diverse as history, the humanities, education, political science, sociology, and economics. As you sample some of these approaches, you can gain a better sense of the varied ways that disciplinary communities each bring their own expertise to the varied topics we undertake as a culture.

SHELDON HACKNEY

The Elements of American Identity

This essay from One America Indivisible *argues that America is "an idea and not just a place." Hackney suggests that democracy, with all its challenges, is what holds us together despite our diverse cultures, wide disparities in wealth, and individual stories. As such, it begins your examination of the questions related to immigration and citizenship that hold the readings in this chapter together by asking you to think first about the American ideal. A professor of history at the University of Pennsylvania, Hackney brings to this question a broad vision of the concepts that underlie the American* ethos, *helping us to see the varying ways we can consider what holds our culture together—from the ideal of amalgamation captured in the "melting pot" to the pluralist ideals that value multiculturalism and the hybrid nature of our culture.*

These ideas are crucial to the debate about what it means to be an American, and to the practical discussions about how to best treat the question of immigration in all its complexity. Depending upon how we see America—as having, in his words, "one story or many"—we may form very different attitudes toward the contemporary policy on immigration, on education of immigrants, and on citizenship and noncitizen workers, all topics broached by writers in this chapter.

Democracy as Religion

By far the most powerful popular conception of America is that it is an idea and not just a place or an ethnic group. It is the idea of democracy. In this broadly shared view, the essence of America is its political system and the political values set forth in the Declaration of Independence and the Constitution. This includes a commitment to representative government responsive to public will and a commitment to the worth of the individual as the measure of public action. We speak frequently and loosely of an "American Dream," meaning the opportunity to improve oneself and the material conditions of one's life, to be free of arbitrary and unnecessary constraints, and the opportunity to participate in the process of self-governance. By now, of course, we have accumulated more than two hundred years of shared experience; we use a common language and occupy a common territory. We are tied together by common laws and civic rituals; we enjoy a common cultural life and an integrated economy. Nevertheless, the most widely recognized tie that binds us together is the view of America as the embodiment of the democratic idea.

The only problem with this is the problem that is inherent in our democracy itself, the problem that flows from the fact that we committed ourselves in the beginning to both liberty *and* equality. How can we honor both of those transcendent ideals at the same time?

Source: One America Indivisible: A National Conversation on American Pluralism and Identity.

Liberty Versus Equality

In a society with a great deal of liberty, one will soon have a lot of inequality. People make different choices, have different amounts of luck, different desires, different talents, start in the race at different points on the track. They therefore will have very different degrees of success in life, especially success measured by material rewards.

Americans have handled the apparent contradiction between their two fundamental principles by saying that "equality" refers not to equality of condition but to equality of opportunity, equality before the law, and equal access to the political process. Much of our political dialogue historically has been about whether or not equality of opportunity actually exists at a particular time and in a particular situation.

Conservatives generally argue that equal opportunity actually exists and that therefore the inequality of condition that is observable is justified. Liberals generally argue that there are all sorts of unfair barriers and impediments to equal opportunity and that therefore the inequality of condition that is observable is not justified. The liberal cure throughout most of the twentieth century, of course, is some sort of government action to improve equal opportunity.[1]

Unfortunately, as we are increasingly aware, people with more economic resources have much more power to influence the political process than those with fewer economic resources. Equality of opportunity, then, "justifies" economic inequality, but economic inequality erodes democracy by providing unequal access to the political system.[2] Because democracy is the core value of our society, the political inequality produced by the unequal distribution of wealth is a serious and continuing tension in our system; witness the current journalistic muckraking about money in politics and the heated arguments about campaign finance reform. This is the source of much of the cynicism affecting public life now.

The tension between liberty and equality cannot be resolved. However, by linking the two ideals, and allowing them to limit or attenuate each other, we have a civic ideal toward which we can constantly strive, producing eventually perhaps an optimum blend of mutual responsibility and individual responsibility that a wholesome community requires.

The Yin and Yang of American National Character

Assuming that we can learn somehow to synthesize the apparently opposed goals of liberty and equality, and that we can solve the various dilemmas of multiculturalism arising from our need to be both "just American" and a special kind of American at the same time, the question then becomes, "Is civic nationalism enough to hold us together?"

Most Americans want more commonality than is provided by civic nationalism alone, and most believe that there is an American culture—"conventional ways of believing and behaving"—that is shared across regional, religious, ethnic, and racial lines. If pressed to enumerate traits of character exhibited by "typical" Americans, Americans produce lists with a high degree of overlap.

The problem is that for almost every trait one can cite as being characteristically American, there is its opposite as well. One can construct a veritable yin and yang of American national character.

Americans believe in equality and are instinctively suspicious of people who "put on airs." Yet, Americans are also fascinated by celebrities. We hold Harry Truman in great respect because he seemed to be an ordinary man who rose to the challenge of being president at an extraordinary time. Conversely, we remain fascinated with John F. Kennedy because he seemed so uncommon. We love to see exceptional people do exceptional things, and we are just as eager to see them crash after attaining exalted heights. Icarus would be a media darling in contemporary America.

Americans proclaim that hard work is its own reward, but we are also constantly on the lookout for get-rich-quick schemes. From the gold rush to the land rush to their modern-day equivalents on Wall Street and in Las Vegas, we think there must be a way to get rich without having to sweat. The lottery is a poor man's investment in the American Dream.

Americans thus may be motivated by greed, but we are also the most philanthropic people on the face of the globe. While "tax" is a dirty word in our political lexicon, charity is considered a supreme virtue. As comparative data demonstrate, we are the least taxed of the industrial nations, and we provide the lowest levels of public services.[3] Yet, no nation can match us for private giving. We are materialistic, but we have the highest percentage of church members among the developed industrial nations. New Age cults and mysticism thrive amongst people who are pursuing the main chance.

We are heterogeneous in almost every imaginable way, and tolerance of difference is thought to be a virtue; yet we have sprouted the hate-mongering Ku Klux Klan, the separatism of the Nation of Islam, the Know Nothings, the Anti-Masons, the militias, and assorted other nativist groups.

Ninety percent of Americans describe themselves as middle class, and middle-class virtues are enshrined in our Puritan heritage. Yet, we are also the land of instant gratification, of Minute Rice and fast food, of hot tubs and easy credit, of Hollywood escapism and theme park fantasies.

We think of ourselves as a practical and self-reliant people, but we have been host to more utopian experiments in communal living than any other nation on earth.

Competition is such a natural thing to Americans that almost every activity is organized into a contest so that we can find out who is the best at it. The Frisbee made its first appearance as a toy. Soon there were games—distance and accuracy contests—then sports—ultimate Frisbee and Frisbee golf—then leagues and national competition. You can't determine who is the best individual without *organizing* a competition, of course. It is the league or the tournament that recognizes and creates the merit of the individual. Here again we confront the simultaneous reciprocal relationship between the individual and his or her organizations.

Optimism is properly considered a traditional American trait. As historians have noted, the rigors and dangers of immigration filter out the lethargic and gloomy. On the other hand, there is also a long and honored tradition in Puritan America of the jeremiad. Judging from the best-seller lists over the last generation, Chicken Little can always get a respectful hearing in America.

Bearing in mind the questionable claim of such cultural traits to being useful in distinguishing Americans from others, it is nonetheless interesting to know how Americans think of themselves. Participants in the National Conversation mentioned a number of other characteristics they thought were especially American: a high value placed upon free speech and the other individual freedoms protected by the Bill of Rights; a tendency to favor the underdog; a belief that people should have a second chance and that social mobility is a good thing; the expectation of progress and that "things should work"; the belief that striving for success is the normal condition of life, and that individuals are obliged to attempt to improve themselves and their circumstances; that choices should be available; that education is a ladder for social mobility; and that individuals have a duty to contribute to their communities.

This list gleaned from pilot and trial conversations is completely compatible with the findings of pollster Daniel Yankelovich. Some American values are persistently stable: freedom, equality before the law, equality of opportunity in the marketplace, fairness, achievement based on education and hard work, patriotism, democracy, the special moral status of America, caring for community, religion, and luck.[4]

Of course, the participants pointedly and repeatedly made clear that we do not always live up to our ideals, either in our individual private lives or in our collective public life. Specifically, the taint of racism and intolerance is clearly seen as the chief flaw yet to be overcome. Until it is, the universal values of the democratic idea will remain a distant dream, but a dream that can pull us onward toward a closer and closer approximation of the Promise of American Life set forth in our founding documents.

One Story or Many?

When one moves from individual traits to the task of imagining the group, one discovers three conventional categories currently in use.[5] First, most writers agree that the dominant cultural style at least until the 1960s was Anglo American (growing out of British and later out of more general European heritage), and that members of other groups were expected to conform to it.

The second category is pluralism. The social revolution of the sixties not only opened up the mainstream of opportunity to members of ethnic and racial minorities, but it replaced the notion of a single acceptable cultural style with the idea that America contains a multiplicity of equally legitimate cultural heritages—pluralism. The theory of pluralism is rooted in the work of Horace Kallen and was popularized first by Randolph Bourne in the second decade of the twentieth century, but it did not achieve a widespread following until the sixties.

The third category, America as a melting pot, goes back even farther. It is an idea that has existed since Hector St. John de Crevecoeur in the Revolutionary era defined "this new man, this American," as a product of the mixture of the various European "races." Despite its early formulation, and its use occasionally by writers in the nineteenth century, the idea of the melting pot did not become popular as a goal of social policy until Israel Zangwill's play, *The Melting Pot,* in 1908 struck a responsive chord amidst national anxieties about the lack of social cohesion resulting from the flood of "new" immigration from eastern and southern Europe in the late nineteenth and early twentieth centuries.

Anglo conformity does not work as a model because it does not allow the sort of dual and mixed identities that many Americans want, and because it denigrates the non-European heritages of many Americans.

The melting pot metaphor accounts for the huge amount of assimilation that has actually occurred in the United States, but it does not accommodate itself to the persistence of pre-American cultural identities that is also part of our reality. Cultural pluralism, on the other hand, comes in many forms, but in its most equalitarian form it does not recognize the historical fact of the primacy of British, European, and Western Civilization's cultural parentage. All heritages are equally legitimate, but all were not equally influential.

Furthermore, there is a separatist version of pluralism that views the United States as simply a holding company for a collection of nations, an umbrella organization for diasporic national fragments whose members get their identities from, and owe their loyalties to, non-American states. Such a vision of America is not acceptable to most Americans.

In addition, no brand of pluralism incorporates the existence of a core of common beliefs that all Americans are expected to share, and with regard to which they are all equal. Without a specific notion of what the common core is, the idea of pluralism offers no hope of cohesion, and no basis for the sort of social consensus that is necessary for collective political action. For all of these reasons, existing theories of pluralism are inadequate.[6]

Americans want a way to think about cultural diversity that is not provided by any of these existing models but goes beyond them. They want a model of America that provides a generous notion of an American identity that all citizens share or should share, a space in which everyone is an equal, and in which the same rules and expectations apply to all. At the same time, they want room for cultural differences to thrive, to be respected by all, and to be kept alive from generation to generation.

Diane Ravitch usefully distinguishes among three "ways of life." Assimilation, either of the equalitarian variety or the Anglo-dominance variety, views the goal to be a society without significant cultural subgroups. Cultural pluralism, whose founding theorist was Horace Kallen, views American society as a democracy of nationalities. "Dynamic pluralism," Ravitch writes, "describes the ways cultures blend and change one another, creating the restaurants in central Texas that serve both bratwurst and tacos, the Puerto Rican bagel factory in Manhattan, and the near-universal popularity of jazz, ragtime, salsa, reggae, the blues, and the polka, all of which began as ethnic musical expressions."[7] Furthermore, Ravitch argues, one does not have to choose among these options. They coexist. They coexist in the society, and they may coexist in a single individual.

The influence of cultures on each other is a phenomenon that is older than human history. The blending and melding, the borrowing and lending over the long course of history occurred most often along trade routes and within the border regions that join contiguous but different cultures. Such cultural borderlands are currently an active and productive field of scholarship. Even the scholars engaged in postcolonial studies are beginning to illuminate the two-way traffic of cultural influence. The striking thing about the contemporary world, however, is that the movement of peoples, the linkages forged by international business, and the global reach of communications have made cultural borderlands ubiquitous. Even the most insular communities in the United States are being affected by the interaction of heterogeneous cultural influences. "World music" is but a metaphoric example.

Dynamic pluralism thus can be thought of as an important element of a new conception of the American identity that is emerging out of the verbal effervescence created by the National Conversation and out of recent scholarship.[8]

First, the new conception is rooted in "civic nationalism," a belief in our democratic governance system and the universal political values to which we committed ourselves in the Declaration of Independence and the Constitution.

Second, there is a sense that out of our history has come a set of meanings and attitudes and preferences and typical behaviors that amount to a national character. However difficult it is to specify it with accuracy, it is nonetheless real, and it is recognized by other Americans, and especially by foreigners encountering Americans.[9]

Third, the new way of thinking about the American collectivity allows for both a common American identity and identities of descent. The arena of commonality is fundamentally important. Based upon civic nationalism, a loose sense of national character, and an inclusive but singular national story, this common identity has been omitted from previous notions of pluralism. It is also important, of course, that the common identity provides room for particularistic identities that can comfortably coexist with the common identity.

This newly emerging identity accommodates itself to the American devotion to mobility, both geographic and social. It permits change over time—change in the boundaries and in the meaning of identities, as well as in their creation and demise. It accounts for both assimilation and for the persistence of pre-American identities.[10]

Most important, this new way of thinking about the American identity recognizes the hybridity of American culture. That is, it reflects the understanding that when various world cultures encountered each other in North America over long periods of time, the relationships were not simply those of dominance and submission but of mutual influence. The resulting American culture therefore may be built on a British and European base, but it is more accurately understood as a hybrid of many cultures and not simply a variant of any one of its root cultures. Furthermore, it continues to evolve in a dynamic fashion.

We also have a history that belongs to all Americans, whenever their ancestors happened to have migrated to these shores.[11] As Abraham Lincoln pointed out in his first inaugural address, in the midst of the secession crisis, we are a single people bound together by "the mystic chords of memory, stretching back from every battlefield and patriot grave to every living heart and hearthstone all over this broad land."[12]

Though the phrases are less memorable, Alasdair MacIntyre, the contemporary philosopher, was expressing the same idea when he wrote:

> Like members of all other societies, we need to share in a common conversation and to understand each other as participating in a common enterprise whose one story is the story of us all, so that our present conversation emerges from the extended, complex but nonetheless in some ways continuous debates of the past. Yet those of us in America who come together do so from a variety of cultures, with a heterogeneous variety of pasts and a variety of stories to tell. If we do not recover and identify with the particularities of our own community—North American Indian, Spanish Catholic, New England Protestant, European Jew, Irish, Black African, Japanese, and a host of others—then we shall lose what it is that we have to contribute to the common culture. We shall have nothing to bring, nothing to give. But if each of us dwells too much, or even exclusively, upon his or her own ethnic particularity, then we are in danger of fragmenting and even destroying the common life.[13]

Notes

1. Lamar Alexander and Chester E. Finn Jr. (eds.), introduction to *The New Promise of American Life* (Indianapolis: Hudson Institute, 1995).
2. Sydney Verba, Kay Lehman Schlozman, and Henry E. Brady, *Voice and Equality* (Cambridge: Harvard University Press, 1995).
3. Lipset, *American Exceptionalism,* passim.

4. Tommy Ehrbar, "The Character of America," *Pitt Magazine* (December 1995): 26–29.
5. For a somewhat different but very well-informed discussion of categories and of the theory of pluralism, see Joseph B. Gittler, "Humanocentrism: Multiculturalism Supplemented and Complemented," *International Journal of Group Tensions* 25, no. 1 (Spring 1995): 3–25. Several scholars, like Gittler, conflate the categories of "Anglo-dominance" and "melting pot." I see their logic but think there is a clear distinction between the two.
6. Ibid. for an exhaustive critique of pluralism.
7. Diane Ravitch, "The Future of American Pluralism," *The New Promise of American Life,* 80–82. See also Lawrence H. Fuchs, *The American Kaleidoscope: Race, Ethnicity, and the Civic Culture* (Middletown: Wesleyan University Press, 1990).
8. See especially David Hollinger, *Postethnic America* (New York: Basic Books, 1995). A similar approach is employed by Gary Nash in his excellent presidential address to the Organization of American Historians, "The Hidden History of Mestizo America," *Journal of American History* (December 1995): 941–962. In the book that contains an important revision of his earlier views, *We Are All Multiculturalists Now,* Nathan Glazer expresses his basic agreement with Hollinger's fluid, voluntaristic, and open "postethnic" perspective, though he observes that Hollinger does not appreciate fully the condition of African Americans in American life and culture. See pp. 159–160.
9. See, for instance, Michael Lind, *The Next American Nationalism* (New York: Free Press, 1995). See also my interview with Lind in "The Next American Nation: A Conversation with Michael Lind," *Humanities* (May–June 1996): 4–8, 42–45.
10. Jean Bethke Elshtain, *Democracy on Trial*; Robert Wiebe, *Self Rule: A Cultural History of American Democracy* (Chicago: University of Chicago Press, 1995); Christopher Lasch, *Revolt of the Elites and the Betrayal of Democracy* (New York: W. W. Norton and Company, 1995): John Patrick Diggins, *The Lost Soul of American Politics* (New York: Basic Books, 1984); Michael J. Sandel, *Democracy's Discontent*; Mary Ann Glendon, *Rights Talk: The Impoverishment of Political Discourse* (New York: Free Press, 1991); Patrick Kennon, *The Twilight of Democracy* (New York: Doubleday, 1995); Lamar Alexander and Chester E. Finn Jr. (eds.), *The New Promise of American Life.*
11. See, for example, Martin Peretz, "Kitsch and Culture," *New Republic,* December 23, 1996.
12. See Michael Kammen, *Mystic Chords of Memory: The Transformation of Tradition in American Culture* (New York: Alfred A. Knopf, 1991) for a magisterial cultural analysis that aims at explaining the creation of an American tradition and the forming of our national identity.

13. Alasdair MacIntyre, "How to Be a North American," (lecture presented at the National Conference of State Humanities Councils, Chicago, November 14, 1987), Humanities Series, publication no. 2–88 (Federation of State Humanities Councils), 11–12.

Reading Analytically

1. Hackney begins this excerpt from his book, *One America Indivisible,* with the contention that America "is an idea and not just a place or an ethnic group." What does that mean? How does he explain the underlying "ideas" of the American culture by using this overarching belief?
2. According to Hackney, what kinds of contradictions exist in American ideals such as equality or democracy? How can the concept of "civic nationalism" help to overcome these inherent contradictions?
3. In what ways does Hackney suggest that pluralism and diversity can in fact help to create a cohesive culture? What does he mean by "dynamic pluralism"? What historical precedents suggest that this conception of American culture could help to create unity while also respecting diversity?

Reading Across Disciplinary Communities

1. As a historian, Hackney brings to this discussion the belief that the study of the past can inform the present and future. In what parts of this piece does he demonstrate that belief? Where does he use his knowledge of historical precedent to help his readers think about contemporary America? Name and explain at least three examples of his use of this disciplinary method.
2. Though this is a study of promise of the American ideal, Hackney also carefully avoids being foolishly utopian in his vision. What problems with the American culture does he identify as a historian, and how does he manage to remain fundamentally optimistic despite these challenges?

SUSAN RIPPBERGER AND KATHLEEN STAUDT

Teaching Citizenship and Values on the U.S.-Mexico Border

Beginning from the fact that public schooling in both the United States and Mexico "has attempted to reinforce cultural and national values to create 'good citizens,'" this ethnography explores "possibilities for increasing mutual respect and collaboration" across the U.S.-Mexico border through a better understanding of the values learned through each country's schools. As social scientists, these authors use one of the key methodologies of that discipline, ethnographic fieldwork. In this methodology, researchers study cultures through direct observation of phenomena in those cultures. But this observation is also informed by the need to create reasonable comparisons between the cultures, and so must control as many variables as possible. Hence, the authors note that they selected schools that were "similar in terms of their proximity to the border" (one on each side of the Mexico-U.S. border) and that "were comparable socially and economically." This methodology illustrates the science *in the social sciences—the attempt to control as many variables as possible to breed empirical results. Of course, as a* social *science—the study of human beings—only so many variables can be controlled.*

As you read this piece, you might consider not only its content—which is invaluable in helping to understand differences in culture that both immigrants and current citizens face in trying to create a cohesive, if diverse, American society—but also its methods. The latter will help you better understand how the disciplines of the social sciences collect and present evidence as they build arguments.

Abstract: In the United States and Mexico, public schooling, as a government institution, has attempted to reinforce cultural and national values explicitly through civics lessons and implicitly through attitudes and classroom management. This study shows how schools on each side of the U.S.-Mexico border attempt to teach distinct national and cultural norms. Based on fieldwork in Ciudad Juárez and El Paso schools, our research illustrates the blending and separation of cultural values in a large metropolitan border area. It looks at overt civic rituals in schools, such as the flag salute, and at more tacit normative training associated with classroom organization and management strategies. We link teaching practices to cultural concepts of time, personal interaction, and nationality. The development of themes regarding human relationships and time, sociability and individualism, and nationalism and hegemony opens up some commonly held assumptions of U.S. and Mexican cultures for a more critical view.

In both the United States and Mexico, public schooling has attempted to reinforce cultural and national values to create "good citizens." The curriculum in each country reflects and transmits these values both directly and indirectly as schools attempt to socialize children for national purposes. But these purposes become complex and sometimes contradictory in areas of the border where Mexico and the United States are mutually influential and interdependent (Martínez 1994), and where a majority of the population on the U.S. side is of Mexican descent. In such binational border areas, each nation tries to promote a unified collective culture, but cultural separation is unrealistic and difficult to maintain.

The metropolitan area comprising El Paso, Texas, and Ciudad Juárez, Chihuahua, with over 2 million people, offers a unique cultural setting for study. These two cities were originally one Mexican town, El Paso del Norte, but were divided in 1848 when the United States annexed the northern part of Mexico's territory under the Treaty of Guadalupe Hidalgo. To the north of the Rio Grande (originally named the Rio Bravo, and still called by that name in Mexico) the town became El Paso; to the south, Ciudad Juárez. Today, over 80 percent of the inhabitants of El Paso are Mexican Americans or Mexican immigrants. El Paso's continuing Latino majority has resulted in Latino political representation, including, most recently, several bilingual mayors of Mexican heritage, one of whom received an education in the Ciudad Juárez schools.

In both El Paso and Ciudad Juárez, bilingualism is very common, and the area is a blend of both cultures. People from the two cities cross the border on a regular basis for family gatherings, business, shopping, and work. In addition, there is a large population of migrants who live on both sides of the border. We found many attempts to keep the two cultures artificially separate—physically, through border patrols and six chain-link fences that divide the densely populated downtown areas of the two cities,[1] and academically, through classroom interaction and lessons on patriotism. Yet it is common to hear Mexicans say that Ciudad Juárez has become too Americanized, while those in the United States often describe El Paso as very Mexican, linguistically and culturally.

In this binational area, we examine schooling, nationality, and culture through a critical lens (Darder 1995). Rather than affirm cultural assimilation that often reinforces educational inequities (Rendón and Hope 1996; Howard 1999), we focus on possibilities for increasing mutual respect and collaboration across the border. While our research is specific to El Paso–Ciudad Juárez, we hope to shed new light on transnational communities and metaphorical borders throughout the United States.

Drawing on four years of qualitative research in the two cities, we compare curricular civic rituals such as the flag salute as well as more normative training associated with classroom organization and management strategies. We explore cultural expressions of time, personal relationships, and nationalism as they play out in the classroom. Through the development of each theme, we attempt to reinterpret some of the one-sided beliefs about U.S. and Mexican cultures that often reinforce hegemonic attitudes and practices rather than create community. Citizenship training in school reinforces that which cultures value. Many of these values, taught in civics education, are designed to fit children into the mainstream national culture so that they learn to be productive members of the larger society. They learn to support a system that, depending on their social class or ethnicity, may or may not benefit them economically or socially (Allen 2004; Spring 2005). . . .

Fieldwork and Methods

Ethnographic field methods, theoretically grounded in phenomenology, were the foundation for this four-year qualitative study of nationalism and schooling. We focused on two schools in El Paso and three in Ciudad Juárez, making an average of one visit per week while school was in session. We selected schools that were similar in terms of their proximity to the border. We also tried to choose schools that were comparable socially and economically, taking into account the different meanings of class and income within each nation. Even though the concepts of working-poor and middle-class status in the United States and Mexico are not parallel, especially since the Mexican economic crisis of the 1980s and subsequent devaluations of the peso, we looked for similarities in class disparities and relative class status among the different schools.

In El Paso we concentrated on two primary classrooms in each school, one bilingual (Spanish/English) and the other monolingual (English). In the three Ciudad Juárez schools, we focused on two primary classrooms in one school and on English as a second language (ESL) lessons in the other two schools. We visited each of these schools weekly for four years, taking photographs, videotaping, and conversing with educators and students, recording our observations and conversations in journals.[2] Regular visits gave us the opportunity for follow-up questions and informal conversations with participants. We also tape-recorded formal interviews with the principal and two teachers in each school.

In addition to open-ended interviews and conversations, we filmed approximately twenty-five hours at the five El Paso and Ciudad Juárez schools. The videotapes, edited to an hour, became part of our original plan for a layered phenomenological analysis.[3] In this edited video we compared bilingual and monolingual elementary classrooms in El Paso with elementary classrooms and ESL lessons in Ciudad Juárez. The first edited version of the video with the original classroom voices and sounds was shown to the El Paso and Ciudad Juárez students, teachers, and administrators that we had filmed. Each time we showed the video, we tape-recorded and took notes on viewers' responses to the video.

Later we added a voice-over narration (one version in English, another in Spanish) that we shared and discussed at each of the schools we visited and also at binational educational conferences and in university education classes. Responses to the video formed an additional layer of information, complementing our interviews and observations. Many of those who viewed the video had attended school in both Ciudad Juárez and El Paso and had firsthand knowledge of the differences between the two educational systems. Some recognized a school in the video that they had attended and sang along with the national anthem or saluted the flag in fond memory. Their comments after viewing the video were used to adjust, confirm, or complement our own analysis.

In the border setting, we found students, both wealthy and poor, who cross the border daily to attend school, some in carpools and others on foot. Most go from Ciudad Juárez to attend El Paso schools, but there are also El Paso parents (both Anglo and Latino) who send their children to private schools in Ciudad Juárez because they want them to be fluent in Spanish. Other students attend El Paso and Ciudad Juárez schools at different times in their lives as their families move back and forth across the border. Many of these students are, in fact, U.S. citizens, but they live primarily in Ciudad Juárez and identify as Mexican. Ciudad Juárez schools allow these "illegal aliens" to attend Mexican schools, not charging them international fees.

In each city we saw major variations between schools in resources, classroom management, class size, degree of space between teachers and students, and teaching styles. In Ciudad Juárez, where schools have two shifts, we visited both morning and afternoon classes.[4] Morning classes for the most part enroll children who have greater academic preparation and more consistent care at home. Generally their family incomes are higher, their uniforms are cleaner, and they have more parental support for learning and schooling than children in afternoon classes. Morning classes also tend to be slightly more orderly and academic than afternoon classes. In the United States, student preparation and parent support vary as well, with some classrooms more orderly and others more chaotic.

Findings: Transnational Themes in U.S. and Mexican Classrooms

Making cross-national comparisons in a bilingual, binational area is by definition challenging. In this case it was especially so because the two cities were originally one city and retain many close ties. While we found similarities, we also found many interesting differences. Different conceptions of values regarding people, time, collectivity, and national uniqueness emerged repeatedly from our observations, interviews, and conversations in schools. Teachers, administrators, students, and parents on both sides of the border shared many of the same universal values, but on each side we found a general hierarchy of values uniquely ordered by each culture.

Three themes stood out as most compelling: (a) human relationships versus time, (b), sociability versus individualistic behavior, and (c) nationalism versus hegemony. A critical look at each theme helps dispel stereotypes and clarify opportunities for greater understanding between schools on both sides of the border. This information can help administrators and teachers understand their own values and those of their students better so they can prepare policies and lessons that are more relevant and meaningful to their students.

Human Relationships Versus Time

As we observed classroom interaction and organization, we noticed that both human relationships and notions of time are important to people in Ciudad Juárez and El Paso, but in different ways. In the El Paso schools we visited, time, especially punctuality and clock-driven agendas, seemed to take precedence over personal contact and human relations. By contrast, we found that while Ciudad Juárez teachers valued both time and people, they placed human relationships and a more organic flow of activities above considerations of scheduling. We do not wish to suggest that U.S. people are cold and unsupportive of one another, nor do we mean to fortify the stereotype of a Mexican "mañana syndrome" in which time and punctuality are irrelevant. But our observations do point to a general preference for either interaction or efficiency in each culture.

We were surprised to find that in the Ciudad Juárez classrooms we visited, there was rarely a clock on the wall. In only two classrooms did we observe clocks, and both were items that appeared to have been brought in by the teachers as wall decorations as much as for keeping time. Very few children wore wristwatches; the teacher was usually the only one in the classroom with a watch. In the El Paso schools we visited, by contrast, there was a clock in every classroom and others in the halls, and many children wore watches. Children received lessons in telling time, and clocks were used as a basis for different classroom activities such as counting by fives, estimating, and drawing pie graphs. The abundance of clocks and watches in El Paso and the lack of them in Ciudad Juárez may have been partly due to different levels of resources, but these patterns were too common to be purely a matter of economics.

Similarly, we saw very few calendars in Ciudad Juárez classrooms, although primary teachers occasionally started assignments by having students write the date at the top of the page. The El Paso primary teachers frequently started the day with a group discussion based on the calendar date, day of the week, season, and sometimes weather, all training children to think in terms of linear time.

In the Ciudad Juárez schools we observed that buzzers announcing class and recess are set off at approximate times, whenever the principal feels it is appropriate. Teachers respond to buzzers dismissing students soon thereafter, as they bring their work to a close. In the El Paso schools we visited, teachers usually follow a schedule based on distinct time frames. If buzzers are used, they are often preset to go off at exact times, whether appropriate to the lesson or not. On many occasions we saw students shove their unfinished work in their desk and rush out to recess at the sound of the recess buzzer. Although Mexico's curriculum is centralized and prescribed, the teachers we observed often deviated from the standard by taking the time they needed to fully develop a lesson.

In El Paso, quiet and order were greatly valued in support of "time on task." One El Paso teacher noted these patterns in the video, commenting, "We are so time-oriented." Others agreed and parodied themselves in mock teacher voices: "You have thirty seconds to get back to your seats—one, two . . ."

A South American civics teacher, who saw the video at a conference, reflected on the abundance of watches in the El Paso classrooms. She suggested that the educational process was more mechanical there than in Latin America, and time was more organized, tending to make robots out of children. "Teachers," she said, "were not looking at peak interests, or learning frameworks for students, but at the clock." Her analysis built on different cultural notions of time (*temporalidad*), especially the difference between linear and cyclical concepts of time that may determine practice in the two countries. She suggested that the use of time, space, and participation in Mexico is part of the learning process, recognizing a locus of learning within the student. On another level, the emphasis on schedules over people can be seen as training students for adulthood in the United States, with its ethic of work and productivity.

In the Ciudad Juárez schools we worked with, people and human relationships seemed to be more important than time on task. On several occasions we watched as a teacher spent her recess and part of the class time consulting with parents, with us, or with other teachers. On other occasions, teachers left their classes to introduce us to the principal or guide us around the school; children often approached us during class to greet us or talk with us. At one point, when we apologized to the teacher for disrupting her class, she told us that the children would find someone else to talk to if we were not there. She allowed students to come up in the middle of the lesson to ask questions, get help with pencil sharpening, or ask permission to go to the restroom, activities defined as disruptions in El Paso schools. In contrast, children in the El Paso schools we visited stayed in their seats much more and appeared more distant from the teacher and from us as visitors. Even as we observed in classrooms, teachers and students rarely spoke with us.

In each city, cultural norms of time and relationships affect teaching, which in turn tends to reinforce these cultural norms. The emphasis on schedules in El Paso may socialize children in ways that support a national economy based on efficiency and productivity. In the Ciudad Juárez schools we visited, learning appeared to focus more on concepts of social discourse and interaction, perhaps reflecting adult social roles and work relations.[5] These differing models of efficiency (based on time) and sociability (based on relationships) have an impact on the learning process in each country and form part of the hidden expectations within schooling.

Sociability versus Individualism

A second, related area of difference had to do with the emphasis placed on behaving as an individual or as a member of a group. Teachers we observed in El Paso teach more directed lessons, interacting most often in teacher-student dyads. In Ciudad Juárez, we saw teachers giving directed lessons, but more often they were interacting with students, going from desk to desk to help groups of children. The students tended to group themselves informally, helping each other and sharing ideas, space, and materials.

While U.S. culture is often considered to emphasize individuality, the El Paso schools we observed required greater conformity and control. Students must always be supervised, and they are increasingly held accountable to state and national standards through high-stakes testing. Interestingly, uniforms in Ciudad Juárez were seen as a symbol of belonging, but in El Paso teachers told us they represented conformity and control more than group identity.[6] Ciudad Juárez students who watched the video we made first noticed the obvious differences, such as greater resources and lack of uniforms on the U.S. side. They asked questions about the El Paso students: "Do they share desks like we do?" "Do they wear uniforms like us?" And if students do not wear uniforms, "How can people identify where you go to school?"

The Ciudad Juárez teachers we observed tended to nurture a collectivity or community, but also allowed more chaotic or independent behavior in the classroom. This often had the appearance of "letting kids be kids." Ciudad Juárez teachers who saw the video noticed that students in the El Paso classrooms seemed more self-controlled; when the teacher left the room, they stayed seated, working quietly. In Ciudad Juárez, students became boisterous and less connected to the lesson when the teacher left the classroom. Ciudad Juárez teachers also noticed that the teaching interaction was different in the United States: El Paso teachers were always supervising, and children were kept on task and could not deviate from their lesson.

The El Paso teachers who viewed the video also noticed this difference. Many mentioned that the classes in Ciudad Juárez were too noisy. "Shh!" one said, reacting to background noise in the video. They were surprised that the students in Ciudad Juárez could walk up to the teacher during the class to "distract her," in their words. El Paso teachers also asked what the lessons were about in the Mexican classrooms. "Everyone seemed to be doing something different," observed one. "Is it a lesson?" another asked, voicing her cultural expectations of what a lesson should look like. A graduate student in education commented that the rooms in Ciudad Juárez were noisy, but that it could be "learning noise . . . kids working in groups, helping each other, discussing the project to get the job done."

One reason for the apparent chaos and greater freedom for children, a Ciudad Juárez teacher told us, is that she wants her students to like school. "There are no bad children," she explained. "Just some who have more trouble settling down." This same teacher often warned students that if they did not finish their work, they would not be able to go out for recess, and that if they did not get their name listed on the "happy face" side of the chalkboard, they would not get a candy when they went home.[7] These warnings were motivational rather than punitive, since all the children eventually went out to recess, work done or not, and all received candy, happy face or not. She said that she wanted them to go home with a good feeling about school, so they would return happily. Attendance is important to Ciudad Juárez teachers, as classes that do not maintain at least thirty students can be closed and the teacher transferred to another classroom or school.

Classes in Ciudad Juárez average thirty to thirty-five students. Classes in El Paso are smaller, with fifteen to twenty students per room. Large classes and meager resources in Ciudad Juárez may contribute to the sociability of students, who must often share space—sometimes three to a desk—and work together in groups. An El Paso teacher gasped on seeing the video of large classrooms in Ciudad Juárez. "Thirty-two kids! And no helpers?" An El Paso graduate student who had gone to primary school in Ciudad Juárez made the point that you need to be social to survive in Mexico, as you must share everything with your classmates.

All who watched the video noticed the disparity between the two cities in schooling resources, reflecting different levels of government spending on education.[8] They suggested, however, that the lack of financial resources may contribute somewhat to the greater sense of community, collegiality, and creativity in Ciudad Juárez classrooms. Children had to share more, helping each other with materials and ideas, and sit closer, sharing desks. Teachers had to be more creative in order to provide students with meaningful, participatory lessons. The greater creativity, sharing, and independence can also make the classroom appear to be less organized, something noticed by El Paso teachers.

Several El Paso graduate students commented on the waste of supplies and materials in El Paso schools, especially in contrast to the scarcity in Ciudad Juárez schools. An El Paso graduate student who attended primary school in Ciudad Juárez mentioned that U.S. children do not value what they are getting; if they had to pay for pencils, photocopies, and other materials as the Mexican children do, they might be more appreciative. One of the main differences, he explained, is that students and teachers in the United States often take materials and schooling for granted, while students and teachers in Mexico do not.

In El Paso schools we observed less student participation and the students seemed comfortable in a more controlled atmosphere. Given the greater sociability, teachers and students in the Ciudad Juárez classrooms we visited seemed more comfortable with grouping; students even grouped themselves without direction from the teacher. An El Paso teacher commented that on the U.S. side of the border the students do not work in groups unless the teacher structures it, and even then they sometimes resist. She explained that the students look to the teacher in the El Paso classes, that the teacher-student dyad is the norm all the way to university. Several students noted that El Paso teachers have the power to decide who succeeds and who does not, based on their impressions and sometimes their prejudices.

In both cities, teachers displayed a range of personal styles—many very warm and caring, others distant and caring, some not caring at all. Still, most video viewers perceived the physical and emotional relationship between students and teachers to be closer in Ciudad Juárez (and sometimes in the El Paso bilingual classes with Mexican American teachers). Ciudad Juárez teachers we worked with used affectionate terms with their students, like *hija/hijo* (daughter/son), and they touched students more. They made requests personal, for example, "Put the date on your paper *for me*." One of the Ciudad Juárez teachers noticed that the El Paso children did not seem as comfortable approaching teachers. Several others agreed, noting that Ciudad Juárez students seemed much freer in approaching their teachers. They felt that El Paso teachers in the study more often imposed a barrier that children could not pass, suggesting a greater distance between students and teachers.

Students in a graduate seminar on education at the University of Texas at El Paso who saw the video found the concept of personal space particularly interesting, especially with respect to how it affects the subjects being taught and the teaching process. One saw personal space as precisely defined on the U.S. side so that students will fit in, like pieces of a machine: you fit into your "place" in the world of jobs. Another added that the personal space resembled the cubicles of the comic strip "Dilbert," where people are kept separate and isolated from one another for the purposes of capitalist productivity. We concluded that this type of isolation and personal accountability was aligned with teacher control, where adherence to lesson plans and time frames may have taken precedence over individual learning.

Individual accountability, a uniquely U.S. concept, is related to individual responsibility and is monitored in classrooms by teachers and in schools through national testing.[9] In the Ciudad Juárez schools we researched, students were asked to be responsible for their work, but rarely were they singled out. For example, an ESL teacher walked around the room to check whether all the students had finished their homework. He discreetly encouraged those who had with "Muy bien," and gently chided those who had not with "That's a problem, without doing the homework, we can't progress." He then gave a mini-lecture at the front of the class, not pointing out any individuals but talking in general terms about winners and losers and asking students which they wanted to be. In response, they all shouted "Winners!" He reminded them that teachers are not there to babysit or to chastise, but to help them learn and enjoy learning. In this classroom, the teacher's use of praise and reprimand was social rather than individual.

Teachers in Ciudad Juárez are not held responsible if students fail, as they are in El Paso. Both countries have end-of-year centralized, standardized tests. In El Paso, these tests are used to hold schools and teachers accountable for students' learning; test scores are often published in newspapers and are used to compare schools and classrooms citywide. This is not the case in Ciudad Juárez. Reflecting these societal attitudes, Ciudad Juárez teachers in our study described failure or success as integrated and social, taking into account each child's ability and effort, parental encouragement, the social setting, and the teacher's input. They understand that there are many possible factors contributing to student failure: the child's inattention, a learning disability, the parents' lack of care and encouragement, and so on.

In the schools we visited, we found that social collectivity was reflected in the architecture and in the physical organization of each classroom. Each Ciudad Juárez school we saw had a patio in the center of the school that was used as a playground and as a common meeting place for children and adults. One Ciudad Juárez teacher noted that the school architecture reflects the more people-oriented way classes are run and schools are set up. The El Paso schools we visited had very few informal central meeting places, although auditoriums and the administrative office served as common ground. For recess, El Paso schools usually separate children in side or rear playground areas supervised by teachers or aides.

Different attitudes toward sociability and individuality are reflected in the flag ceremonies held in each country's schools. In the El Paso schools that we observed the flag salute took place in individual classrooms at the beginning of each day, and it was sometimes followed by singing the national anthem. Across Mexico, the ceremony honoring the flag ("honores a la bandera") is more elaborate. The whole school, including students, faculty, administration, and staff, meets each Monday morning in the central patio, where students line up by classroom. A uniformed, militaristic drill team brings in the flag, while the rest of the school stands at attention. The pledge, the national anthem, and general announcements follow. A first-grade teacher in Ciudad Juárez described the Mexican ceremony as family-like and the U.S. flag salute as more solitary. An El Paso education student also commented that the El Paso classroom flag ritual seemed abstract, devoid of community or ceremony, while the Ciudad Juárez flag ritual was holistic and ceremonial.

Our findings suggest that El Paso schools value individualism in theory, but in practice they require more uniformity than Ciudad Juárez schools. The El Paso schools we observed tended to stress order, efficiency, and accountability, calling for greater teacher control and greater student conformity. In Ciudad Juárez schools, students are also held accountable, but in a different way; they must take responsibility for their own learning. Our findings also suggest that the Ciudad Juárez schools tended to be more collectively oriented, but children were allowed quite a bit more individual freedom.

Mexican Nationalism versus U.S. Hegemony

A third theme brought out by the research was how each country influenced the other, and how each simultaneously bought into and resisted this cross-national influence. We observed this in the classroom, through lessons in language, traditions, and citizenship training, as well as in business and social life. Obvious examples of cultural blending include celebration of the other country's holidays and mixing and borrowing elements of language. Less obvious is how schooling reinforces cultural and national norms as defined by dominant governmental structures, thus serving to resist cross-national influence (Fuhrman and Lazerson 2005).

We looked into apparent contradictions in cultural perspectives and what it means to live in a border area where U.S. culture dominates in some instances and Mexican culture dominates in others. Even though students and teachers often passively accept national values embedded in the curriculum, many are aware of the paradox inherent in trying to keep the two cultures separate. A fourth-grade Ciudad Juárez teacher commented on the social science textbook she uses, which professes a national unity represented symbolically by *one* flag, *one* language, and *one* monetary system. She told us, "No es cierto. Aquí en la frontera vemos la bandera mexicana y la bandera estadounidense diario, escuchamos español e inglés, y usamos dólares y pesos."[10]

Another example of two-way cultural influence is the celebration of holidays. U.S. holidays such as Halloween, Thanksgiving, and Christmas have become very popular in Ciudad Juárez. However, Mexican cultural holidays like El Día de los Muertos (Day of the Dead, November 2) and La Fiesta de la Virgen de Guadalupe (Festival of the Virgin of Guadalupe, December 12) have also experienced a conscious revival in the last few decades, both in Ciudad Juárez and across the border in El Paso. Within the last five years the Day of the Dead celebrations have grown to include citywide altar competitions and overwhelming community support. Not only families but also schools, museums, and libraries celebrate these Mexican holidays on both sides of the border, even though formal school curricula may only include national holidays.

One Ciudad Juárez elementary teacher told us that she tries to reinforce Mexican holidays, since there is an inclination to accept holidays borrowed from U.S. culture. We visited a first-grade class on December 12, the day to honor the Virgin of Guadalupe, a revered religious and cultural figure who is the patron saint and empress of Mexico. Talking about this holiday's cultural significance for Mexicans, the teacher described how *matachin* (traditional native) dancers take part in the celebration. Later that day, the children planned a Christmas celebration, voting on their favorite party food. They suggested hot dogs, *hamburguesas*, pizza, and nachos, all U.S. in origin. In this case, even in a lesson where the teacher tried to keep the cultures separate, the children brought in elements of U.S. culture.

El Día de los Reyes (day of the three kings or wise men) is celebrated on January 6 and was once the traditional day of gift giving in Mexico. However, many people in Ciudad Juárez, and El Paso as well, now open presents on December 25, then celebrate El Día de los Reyes with the traditional *rosca*, a crown-shaped sweet bread with a tiny plastic doll inside representing Jesus.[11] In Ciudad Juárez some lament that the more commercial U.S. holiday, Christmas, with Santa Claus and decorated pine trees, is displacing the more traditional Mexican celebrations surrounding El Día de los Reyes and the New Year.

In El Paso, we observed that Mexican Americans often identify with Mexican culture, yet also see themselves as fully American. For example, we noted more city murals depicting the Virgin of Guadalupe in El Paso than in Ciudad Juárez. In Ciudad Juárez there is no such dual allegiance: even though residents of that city may appreciate and borrow from U.S. culture, they identify as Mexican.

In a border area, the two languages, U.S. English and Mexican Spanish, affect each other in subtle ways. Spanish contains many borrowed words like *fensa* for fence (instead of *barandal*) or *yonke* for junkyard (instead of *chatarra*). In El Paso we observed that code switching in the course of conversation is frequent. While many Anglos are at least partially fluent in Spanish, some resent the fact that El Paso is truly bilingual. They have trouble understanding, for example, why El Paso employers require those they hire to speak both languages. Businesses in El Paso, however, understand that they serve a binational, bilingual population, and some even accept pesos. Many businesses operate on both sides of the border, especially U.S. and Mexican-based restaurant chains such as Taco Tote, Cafe Dali, Barrigas, McDonald's, and Peter Piper's Pizza.

Bilingualism, a reality and a necessity on the border, is central to educational equity and economic prosperity. Nonetheless, bilingual education is defined differently in each city depending on which language is perceived to have higher economic status. The schools we observed in Ciudad Juárez provided English as a Second Language (ESL) as an enrichment program to help all students gain an economic or social advantage. Originally ESL was taught in private schools or in after-school courses, but during the 1990s, through a special state program, ESL was offered at most public schools in Ciudad Juárez.[12] Spanish as a second language, though, is not as valued in Ciudad Juárez. Indigenous children who are monolingual speakers of Rarámuri receive a compensatory bilingual program (Rarámuri-Spanish) in their rural communities in central Chihuahua.[13] But until the mid-1990s, if they migrated to Ciudad Juárez they could not enroll in public schools because there were no bilingual classes using the indigenous language.

In the United States, where English is valued more highly than Spanish, bilingual education is a compensatory program. In general, students are provided academic instruction in their own language along with structured ESL lessons until they are able to function in an all-English learning environment.[14] Unfortunately, poorly implemented bilingual programs can have the effect of segregating students, and often there is no consistency in the educational path of children who switch into and out of bilingual programs.[15] In addition, English-only movements and anti-immigrant sentiment have weakened both equity and excellence in education for nonmainstream students (Macedo, Dendrinos, and Gounari 2003; Valenzuela 1999). Recently, some El Paso schools have been promoting dual-language programs as enrichment for both English and Spanish speakers. In dual-language classrooms there is a mixture of English-dominant and Spanish-dominant students, and both languages are used and valued—especially important in a border area.

While El Paso and Ciudad Juárez are similar culturally and linguistically, citizenship training in their schools is very different. These differences are expressed not only in the subtle attitudes toward time and personal relationships, as described above, but also in direct citizenship training through history and civic education lessons. The Ciudad Juárez schools we visited taught patriotism based on national history much more than did the El Paso schools. El Paso and Ciudad Juárez teachers and administrators in our study both remarked that Mexicans are much more patriotic than people in the United States. Throughout Mexico, schools are named after national military heroes and events such as Benito Juárez, Nicolás Bravo, 16 de Septiembre, and 20 de Noviembre.

El Paso graduate education students, commenting on the video, noted that transmission of civic values seemed more formal in Ciudad Juárez, and that there seemed to be more pride in expressing nationalism. A state-level administrator in Ciudad Juárez explained the importance of the flag ceremony as a lesson in civics, order, organization, precision, and community. "It is a ritual that is to be respected without question" he observed. "The U.S. flag salute, on the other hand, is short, unorganized, individual, and not particularly impressive."

Teachers from both Ciudad Juárez and El Paso expressed the importance of helping students understand the meaning behind patriotic creeds and ceremonies. A first-grade teacher from Ciudad Juárez stressed the importance of understanding the words in the Mexican pledge and the national anthem, posting them in the classroom. Speaking of the *Star-Spangled Banner*, a U.S. teacher remarked, "I always have to teach the meaning of the song; 'ramparts,' for instance, is very hard." El Paso school teachers saw Mexico's civic ceremonies as more formal and militaristic than their own. But they expressed regret that El Paso schools do not teach as much patriotism or national history as the Mexican schools.

Our research suggests that Ciudad Juárez schools define citizenship in terms of patriotism and love of country, equating good citizenship with nationalistic behavior: respecting the flag, the president and other authority figures, and knowing Mexico's history. In El Paso classrooms, on the other hand, we found that citizenship is defined as "good" behavior, meaning obedience and even passivity. El Paso teachers told us that good citizenship means "listening to teachers," "no bad words," "no fighting," "following instructions," "no tattling," and "doing homework," all behaviors that reinforce teacher control (figs. 1, 2). At an assembly in an El Paso elementary school, the principal lectured students on being good citizens at school so they could be good citizens when they grow up; following rules now is like following laws later, he asserted. A Canadian ESL teacher in Mexico City who viewed the film

Figure 1. Civic bulletin board in the hallway of an El Paso elementary school, 2001. Photograph by Kathleen Staudt.

Figure 2. Close-up of civic bulletin board shows the personal nature of civics education in an El Paso elementary school, 2001. Photograph by Kathleen Staudt.

was particularly critical of one of the El Paso teachers in our study who maintained tight control over her class (and who not coincidentally was voted teacher of the year). He saw her as very rule-oriented—even the lesson she taught was on rules. He said, "If she came to Mexico, she would go crazy. She'd say, 'Nobody's following the rules here!'"

We found that the national culture taught in public schools is unique for each city, and that students learn to respond to the subtle cultural norms found in classroom rules and day-to-day educational processes. Even though students may be bilingual and feel comfortable in social situations on both sides of the border, the classroom presents a more closed cultural environment. For this reason, immigrant students attending school in the United States may not understand all the overt cultural events and subtle cultural cues they receive, as they have received a different kind of nationalistic training.

Conclusions and Implications

Cross-cultural comparisons are not simple, particularly in a border region with a fluid interchange of cultures, divided by a political line that serves as both a point of contact and a point of separation. Our research indicates that schools on the Ciudad Juárez–El Paso border reflect border society and are places where society is recreated as a cultural blend. This blending is perpetuated by bilingual classes, by the attitudes and practices of U.S. teachers schooled in Ciudad Juárez, and by the flow of students who cross the border daily to attend school or who live alternately on both sides, depending on their parents' work location. Notwithstanding this cultural mix, the schools on each side of the border represent and transmit a national culture. Here a critical ethnography of education renders a more plural and contested picture of border education, open to possibilities for a more equitable education for immigrant students in U.S. classrooms (Spring 1991).

Teachers in our study often seemed constrained by cultural mores, passively reinforcing national cultural expectations. Part of the constraints they face includes the structure of education itself, based on traditional views that encourage assimilation and conformity to a dominant culture rather than pluralism. Educators that we spoke with in both Mexico and the United States often assumed, for example, that "American" (U.S.) students are Anglo, or that Mexican students are mestizo. These assumptions are not just misperceptions; they are often based on a politically motivated desire to assimilate students into one nationality, privileging those in the mainstream. More often, though, assimilation practices have the effect of isolating students who do not fit the mainstream profile (Valdés 2005). Imposition of national standardized testing and demands for accountability represent attempts to increase U.S. government control in schools. Along with the back-to-basics and English-only movements, such trends threaten to ignore diversity and to eradicate individuality and creativity from the curriculum (Valenzuela 2005).

Our framework of phenomenology, rejecting traditional assumptions and giving all voices equal weight, highlights a need for greater understanding, equity, and transformation. Seeing border education through a lens of critical ethnography forestalls stereotypes of first- and third-world countries.

Informal influences in the society may work to undermine nationalistic training in the schools. While schools and other government agencies attempt to cement a separate national culture, businesses, families, and friends ensure that the cultures blend. This blending has traditionally stopped at the school door, as expectations for classroom learning follow a more nationalistic format and a centralized curriculum in each country. Students who have previously attended Ciudad Juárez schools are not always aware of the cultural mores demanded in El Paso schools, and they may become marginalized by expectations they are not aware of. School environments, not as culturally or politically open as the social venues students frequent, can be confusing and discouraging places for immigrant students. And their El Paso teachers may fail to understand the rich but subtle expectations and academic processes that children from Ciudad Juárez bring to El Paso classrooms.

Our study shows that cultural interpretations of time, relationships, and national identity within classrooms have served to initiate children into the larger national and cultural context, yet a more balanced perspective might serve both border cities. Schools on both sides of the border might benefit from finding a balance between order and chaos, between precise scheduling and more humanistic development of classroom lessons. A balance between individual freedom and community responsibility is not necessarily for the purpose of nation building, but for greater learning and a more caring educational environment. Along these lines, teachers may acknowledge a need for less external control, or conformity, perhaps questioning whom this benefits. Teachers in El Paso could teach a greater love of the country's history and democratic institutions, while teachers in Ciudad Juárez may wish to teach a more critical perspective on the same topics. U.S. schools might incorporate a more critical perspective on U.S.-Mexico history, one that deals with some of the problematic relationships such as the invasion of Mexico and the loss of territory to the United States during the U.S.-Mexican war.

Findings of our study may help determine how this border area compares to other transnational communities and shed light on symbolic borders nationwide. These issues speak to the larger national issues of bilingualism and multiculturalism and the need for less assimilationist policy and greater understanding and pluralism, the basis for democracy. El Paso is a city whose population is overwhelmingly of Mexican heritage, divided more along class than ethnic lines. It is more connected geographically and culturally to Ciudad Juárez than to other U.S. cities. In this context, education can benefit by embracing and building on the city's rich bilingual and bicultural heritage, possibilities made more visible through a lens of critical theory and phenomenology.

While dominant cultures influence educational systems, it is important to acknowledge and respond to the pluralism within educational settings—particularly in El Paso, where 70 to 99 percent of the students are of Mexican heritage, depending on the school. It can only enhance students' learning to understand and respond to their unique cultural learning patterns. Understanding cultural differences in schools as well as the interconnectedness between the two cites can help educators on both sides of the border respond to their students' educational needs by creating a curriculum, teaching style, and teacher training programs that acknowledge and build on both educational systems for mutual benefit.

Notes

1. In rural areas, surveillance and artificial boundaries are much less intense.
2. Along with the five schools we focused on, we made monthly visits to another seventeen schools in El Paso and twelve in Ciudad Juárez as part of our work in university-community collaboration projects. Here we observed classrooms, student assemblies, and district board meetings and talked informally with students, parents, teachers, and administrators, recording our observations and informal conversations in journals.
3. We want to acknowledge Tobin, Wu, and Davidson for their 1989 work with video ethnography, using viewers' interpretations of video footage as an additional source of information and analysis.
4. The two shifts, morning and afternoon, function as two separate schools, each with its own name, principal, faculty, staff, and students.
5. See Freire (1994) and Vygotsky (1978) for further discussion of social learning.
6. Uniforms are required for public schools in Mexico; although the advantages and disadvantages of requiring uniforms in public schools have been discussed for decades, in the last ten years or so a sizable number of U.S. public schools have started to encourage or require them.
7. Often called "assertive discipline," this method of class management builds on behaviorism, rewarding "good" behavior symbolically by listing those who exhibit such behavior on the chalkboard under a caricature of a happy face.

8. In Ciudad Juárez, at the time of this research, the government spent the equivalent of approximately US$100 to US$500 per student per year. This amount includes teachers' salaries, free textbooks, and some school upkeep. Parents are asked to contribute money at the beginning of each year for classroom supplies. In El Paso, the amount spent is approximately $5,000 per student per year. Teachers in Ciudad Juárez make the equivalent of approximately $6,000 to $10,000 yearly; El Paso teachers earn approximately $25,000 to $45,000 yearly.
9. The term "accountability" with regard to schooling is unique to the United States. At binational conferences since the 1980s, scholars have struggled to find appropriate Spanish translations; one often used is "personal responsibility."
10. "That isn't true. Here on the border we see the Mexican flag and the U.S. flag every day, we hear Spanish and English, and we use dollars and pesos."
11. The one who finds the "baby Jesus" in a slice of *rosca* hosts the celebration of El Día del Candelaria in February, formally ending the Christmas season.
12. This program was terminated several years later because of political difficulties.
13. The Rarámuri are a native Mexican population also called the Tarahumara.
14. See Nieto (2004) for information on bilingual programs that are designed to meet the needs of diverse student populations.
15. See Valdés (1998) for research on current shortcomings of bilingual education programs.

Works Cited

Allen, Danielle S. 2004. *Talking to Strangers: Anxieties of Citizenship since Brown v. Board of Education*. Chicago: University of Chicago Press.

Anderson, Benedict. 1991. *Imagined Communities: Reflections on the Origin and Spread of Nationalism*. New York: Verso.

Apple, Michael W. 1990. *Ideology and Curriculum*. 2nd ed. New York: Routledge.

Brookfield, Stephen D. 2005. *The Power of Critical Theory: Liberating Adult Learning and Teaching*. San Francisco: Jossey-Bass.

Calvo Ponton, Beatriz. 1989. *Educación normal y control político*. Mexico City: Centro de Investigaciones y Estudios Superiores en Antropología Social.

Carlsson-Paige, Nancy, and Linda Lantieri. 2005. "A Changing Vision of Education." In Noddings 2005, 107–21.

Cherryholmes, Cleo. 1988. *Power and Criticism: Poststructural Investigations in Education*. New York: Teachers College Press.

Darder, Antonia, ed. 1995. *Culture and Differences: Critical Perspectives on the Bicultural Experience in the United States*. Westport, CT: Bergin & Garvey.

Darder, Antonia, and Carole Upshur. 1992. *What Do Latino Children Need to Succeed in School? A Study of Four Boston Public Schools*. Boston: Mauricio Gastón Institute for Latino Community Development and Public Policy.

Denzin, Norman K., and Yvonna S. Lincoln, eds. 1998. *Collecting and Interpreting Qualitative Materials.* Thousand Oaks, CA: Sage.

Foley, Douglas E. 1990. *Learning Capitalist Culture: Deep in the Heart of Tejas.* Philadelphia: University of Pennsylvania Press.

Freire, Paulo. 1994. *Pedagogy of Hope: Reliving Pedagogy of the Oppressed.* New York: Continuum.

Fuhrman, Susan, and Marvin Lazerson, eds. 2005. *The Public Schools as an Institution of American Constitutional Democracy.* New York: Oxford University Press.

Halstead, J. Mark. 1996. "Values and Values Education in Schools." In *Values in Education and Education in Values,* ed. J. Mark Halstead and Monica J. Taylor, 1–14. London: Falmer Press.

Howard, Gary R. 1999. *We Can't Teach What We Don't Know: White Teachers, Multiracial Schools.* New York: Teachers College Press.

Husserl, Edmund. 1970. *The Crisis of European Sciences and Transcendental Phenomenology: An Introduction to Phenomenological Philosophy.* Trans. David Carr. Evanston, IL: Northwestern University Press.

Ladson-Billings, Gloria. 2005. "Differing Concepts of Citizenship: Schools and Communities as Sites of Civic Development." In Noddings 2005, 69–80.

Levinson, Bradley, and Dorothy Holland. 1996. "The Cultural Production of an Educated Person." In *The Cultural Production of the Educated Person: Critical Ethnographies of Schooling and Local Practice,* ed. Bradley A. Levinson, Douglas E. Foley, and Dorothy C. Holland, 1–54. Albany: State University of New York Press.

Macedo, Donaldo, Bessie Dendrinos, and Panayota Gounari. 2003. *The Hegemony of English.* Boulder, CO: Paradigm.

Marshall, Catherine, and Gretchen B. Rossman. 1999. *Designing Qualitative Research.* 3rd ed. Thousand Oaks, CA: Sage.

Reading Analytically

1. Summarize these researchers' findings as they relate to "human relationships versus time," describing the ways that these two cultures differ in this facet of their educational and cultural systems.
2. One of the ways that these researchers drew conclusions about the "individualism" or "sociability" of these two cultures was by observation of the physical makeup of the classrooms. What features of the two cultures' classrooms seemed particularly telling to these researchers? Describe the ways that these social scientists interpreted those features as significant.
3. According to this article, what is the difference between *nationalism* and *hegemony*? How do the authors define those two terms? In what specific ways do they distinguish one from the other, using particular features from their observations?

Reading Across Disciplinary Communities

1. Read over the introduction and "Fieldwork and Methods" section of this article. Summarize the methodology that was used in order to conduct this research, and then attempt to explain the reasoning behind at least two specific parts of the methodology used. That is, try to explain why this method was chosen and how it was meant to breed reliable results.
2. While part of the work of this discipline is descriptive—presenting findings of the observational, ethnographic fieldwork—the conclusion also interprets those findings and makes recommendations. What are those recommendations? What does the fact that recommendations are made tell you about the work of the social sciences more generally?

MELISSA MORENO

Lessons of Belonging and Citizenship Among *Hijas/os de Inmigrantes Mexicanos*

This article uses narratives of young adults from American and Mexican communities to study how "citizenship surveillance" (constant questions about their citizenship status), differing ideologies of citizenship, and contradictions in cultural norms affected their lives and their understanding of their U.S. citizenship and their Mexican cultural alliances. In some ways, the methodologies of this social scientist are similar to those of Susan Rippberger and Kathleen Staudt in the previous piece. But whereas those authors used ethnographic fieldwork—observation of the culture—Moreno uses another method important to the social science: interviews and focus groups.

Perhaps what is most interesting in this piece is the way that Moreno presents the words of her interviewees as a form of insight into the beliefs and experiences of these immigrants. As you read, you might consider whether the interpretations and conclusions that Moreno draws from these words are reasonable, and whether there are other conclusions that could be drawn—or future studies planned—based upon these statements by Mexican immigrants to the United States.

Abstract (Summary): Narratives of immigrant Mexican offspring concerning national belonging are important because they attest to the power and inequalities immigrant families and communities experience in their quest for social mobility and well-being in the U.S. As members of a significant racialized and marginalized group, their narratives speak to what Suzanne Oboler (2006: 10–11) calls the "dilemma of belonging" and the structural conditions that Latino families and community members face in attempting to become socially, culturally, and politically embedded in society. [. . .] anti-immigrant legislation such as House Bill 28, filed in 2006 by Leo Berman in the Texas House of Representatives, sought to deny health care and educational financial aid to U.S.-born children of undocumented immigrants. Such legislation structures the exclusion of many children in their struggle to belong in the only society they have known.

Introduction

> I constantly reflect and think about who I am, where I belong, who thinks I belong . . . who thinks I don't belong, and why they think that (Interview with Consuelo, 2005).

This opening epigraph sets the tone for the essay that follows, which investigates "lessons of belonging."

National belonging and citizenship identity are highly contested for *Hijas/os de inmigrantes Mexicanos* (daughters and sons of Mexican immigrants in the U.S.). This article is based on a larger study I conducted on how U.S.-born young adults learn to form a sense of national belonging in relation to their U.S.-Mexican communities in the greater borderland areas[1] of California. My social analysis, based on ethnographic histories, interviews, and fieldwork participation with *hijas/os de inmigrantes Mexicanos*, shows how meanings of citizenship are broadly learned and negotiated in a xenophobic U.S. society.

This article begins not only by stating the purpose, but by introducing the method of study that led to its conclusions. Note also how a word like "xenophobic" (fear or hatred of foreigners) sets the tone for the argument, suggesting that Americans are not welcoming to "outsiders."

For example, Consuelo was one of several *hijas/os de inmigrantes Mexicanos* who openly related how ideologies and everyday life experiences with family shaped a sense of citizenship (i.e., social, cultural, and civic). Narratives of immigrant Mexican offspring concerning national belonging are important because they attest to the power and inequalities immigrant families and communities experience in their quest for social mobility and well-being in the U.S. As members of a significant racialized and marginalized group, their narratives speak to what Suzanne Oboler (2006: 10–11) calls the "dilemma of belonging" and the structural conditions that Latino families and community members face in attempting to become socially, culturally, and politically embedded in society.

This line suggests that the main goal of Immigrants is similar to that of all Americans who share this "quest" (a noble journey) toward the "pursuit of happiness."

I will provide a context for the use of cultural citizenship as a framework for this study. Based on the narratives of *hijas/os de inmigrantes Mexicanos* related to their families, I examine the power associated with citizenship surveillance,[2] ideologies of citizenship, and national cultural contradictions. I offer multilayered meanings and implications of social and cultural "citizenship as a lived experience" (Ibid.: 4–5), so that educators and advocates of Latino families can better understand and sustain a meaningful education for young Latinas/os faced with inequalities in schools and society (Benmayor, 2002; Bañuelos, 2006; Seif, 2004).

Note the use of first person here, as she discusses her methodology—what she did in this study. Authors often use first person in this case, in order to distinguish their own actions from that of the subjects.

Notice how this brief description of the methodology of the primary research is also contextualized within the work of other experts (The author's secondary research).

Theoretical Perspectives on Citizenship

This section, on "theoretical perspectives," shows how authors often begin an essay by looking at the underlying concepts related to the topic within a discipline, before going on to their own work. This places the author's work within the larger work of the disciplinary community, as discussed in the introduction to this book.

Meanings of citizenship are often framed by discourses and practices of inclusion and exclusion that are operationalized in schools, culture, and society. A sense of belonging and citizenship is learned through various social interactions in multiple institutions. Lessons of belonging are part of the "journey to citizenship," which is denned as "the story of how migrant people come to know themselves and others through proud experiences of solidarity, contest, and contradictions as they move across different institutions" (Hall, 2002: 2). In Mexican communities in the U.S., the journey to citizenship includes how "people of Mexican descent are bombarded with questions and inquiries about citizenship on the borderlands" (Bejarano, 2005:194). Their journey to citizenship is defined by the conditions of a xenophobic culture (Villenas and Deyhle, 1999), barriers to obtaining citizenship rights (Fox, 2005; 2006), U.S.-Mexico border human rights violations (Chavez, 2006; Palafox, 2001 a, b), and anti-immigrant legislation (Cano, 2006; Jonas, 2006). For example, anti-immigrant legislation such as House Bill 28, filed in 2006 by Leo Berman in the Texas House of Representatives, sought to deny health care and educational financial aid to U.S.-born children of undocumented immigrants.[3] Such legislation structures the exclusion of many children in their struggle to belong in the only society they have known.

This paragraph begins the "review of the literature" that places the current study within the context of the work of others in the discipline.

Anti-immigrant political discourse and policy practices of elite "experts"[4] in national institutions often sustain hegemonic or domineering processes of cultural reproduction that normalize[5] some national citizens over others (Anderson, 1983; Maira, 2005; Ong, 1999). Cultural reproduction is the process of transmitting the dominant group's values and beliefs, which often exclude the participation of marginalized people in traditional institutions (Bourdieu, 1972; 1977). As Ladson-Billings (2004), Omi and Winant (1989), and other scholars argue, U.S. society has historically used cultural reproduction to normalize citizens with upper-class, white European dispositions while other members have been racialized as second-class or "other" status (Almaguer, 1994; Menchaca, 1995). Leo Chavez (2001, 2003), Nicholas De Genova (2004), Kevin Johnson (1997, 2003), and other scholars explain that essentialist and homogenizing discourses circulated by experts have categorized members of Mexican communities as "un-American." For example, in "The Hispanic Challenge," Huntington's (2004) anti-immigrant discourse pivots on how Mexican immigrants living in the U.S. threaten the nation because they resist social integration and are culturally and linguistically different from Protestant Anglo-American citizens. This kind of discourse overlooks the social and educational inequalities encountered by children of U.S.-Mexican families, as well as the disparity within the U.S.-Mexico political economy (Suarez-Orozco, 2001; Rumbaut and Portes, 2001), that pose challenges to accessing the institutions that often facilitate social integration. However, even when sons and daughters of Mexican immigrants gain access to education in leading universities—and assimilate culturally or learn to become bicultural—they continue to encounter the dilemma of belonging because they do not have access to legal citizenship (Seif, 2004; S.I.N. Collective, 2007). In this sense, the citizenship experience for young people in U.S.-Mexican immigrant families and communities has more to do with the availability of institutional resources (i.e., educational, health, etc.) and of national citizenship than with an individual desire to resist or embrace sociocultural integration as implied by elite "experts" (e.g., Lawrence Harrison, Samuel Huntington, Patrick Joseph Buchanan, etc.). Yet, the discourse of conservative policymakers and academics dominates national public debates surrounding citizenship legislation (Giroux, 2003; Urrieta, 2005).

> This is a key term. As a reader, it is important to understand key terms like this that help to set up the author's understanding of the situation. "Marginalized" means "outside the mainstream of the culture."

> This repeated term is also crucial. It suggests that Mexicans are seen as "marginalized" by being identified as a nonwhite race.

> Notice how this argument suggests that "discourse" (the way we talk about something) affects our views on that topic—in this case, immigrants.

From the standpoint of many U.S.-born sons and daughters of Mexican families, the meaning of citizenship and the politics of belonging have a significant impact on their daily lives with family and community members. Their citizenship is not a simple issue of being, or not being, a legal citizen, or of individual rights. Rather, it is about the everyday politics surrounding the citizenship practices and identity of their families and community members whose citizenship statuses vary (De Genova, 2004; Seif, 2004). By resisting hegemonic processes of cultural reproduction, marginalized families are social actors engaged in the cultural production of citizenship (Bourdieu, 1977; Levinson and Holland, 1996). In this way, people create and perform everyday practices and identities that are meaningful to their cultural group(s) for the purpose of participating (socially, culturally, civically, and politically) in their communities and society. In some ways, cultural production of citizenship concerns learning different means of living, about the self in relationship to others, and about action and responsibility (Bañuelos, 2006; Benmayor, 2002; Delgado-Bernal, 2001; Freire, 1970; Giroux, 1983; Hooks, 1994; Villenas, 2002).

This paragraph begins by transitioning from causes (marginalization/racialization) to effects: the "impact on their daily lives."

Social science researchers use the concept of cultural citizenship to explain the cultural production of citizenship, particularly within racialized ethnic communities (Flores and Benmayor, 1997; Maira, 2004; 2005; Ong, 1999; Rosaldo, 1997). This concept seeks to explain citizenship by going beyond traditional notions that are solely based on individual and legal citizenship (Rosaldo, 1997). It addresses multiple sociopolitical conditions surrounding underrepresented communities with immigrant and non-immigrant members, many of whom contend with the effects of global migration and the dilemmas of belonging in society (Flores, 1997; Maira, 2004; Seif, 2004). The concept of cultural citizenship allows researchers to highlight cultural production and agency, particularly among social actors in Latino communities. Rosaldo has broadly defined cultural citizenship as "the right for people to be different and still belong to the nation" (in Ramirez, 2002: 65). In essence, these scholars emphasize the idea of claiming identity, space, and rights.

Note the way that this argument is here placed within the disciplinary context of "social science researchers."

Researchers use cultural citizenship to index the ways in which institutional structures limit how racialized subjects belong in the nation and global society. For example, Maira (2004; 2005)

This paragraph introduces and explains another key concept, "cultural citizenship," which is then used throughout the rest of the argument.

and Ong (1999) examine the effects of cultural reproduction and hegemonic forms of authority on various Asian immigrant groups. Using a Foucauldian notion of power, their conceptualization of cultural citizenship explains how globalization limits citizenship practices and how agency is bounded by "governmentality" and "surveillance." Ong (1999:264) defines cultural citizenship as a "dual process of self-making and being-made within the webs of power linked to the nation-state and civil society." In this way, cultural citizenship accounts for an array of social, cultural, and political entities that shape various dimensions of citizenship practices among immigrant families and communities.

In terms of the conceptual limitations of cultural citizenship, Fox (2006) points out that research based upon cultural citizenship theory tends to overlook distinctions between "claiming" and "gaining" citizenship rights, particularly within a context of challenges posed by national legal citizenship. For Fox (2005: 76), "rights and empowerment can encourage the other, and indeed overlap in practice, but they are distinct. In other words, some must act like citizens (claim rights) so that others can actually be citizens (have rights), but acting like a citizen is not the same as being a citizen." Thus, those with legal citizenship status or those working toward it often must civically and politically perform as citizens for others in their community to gain citizenship rights. I believe, following Maira (2004: 222), that legal citizenship is not always separate from cultural citizenship in that "issues of economic and legal citizenship spill over into cultural citizenship." In other words, cultural citizenship intersects with other forms of citizenship (i.e., social, civic, political, and legal).

Note how this quotation is incorporated into Moreno's own argument about citizenship.

Note the way that this paragraph ends with a clear, focused summary of the other experts' work that has been cited.

Benmayor (2002), Coll (2004), Ramirez (2002), and Seif (2004) have examined the intersections of citizenship. They use the lens of cultural citizenship to examine narratives that explain how social actors who intend to create social and institutional spaces of belonging for themselves and community members employ cultural and political practices. Some also explain how subjects have a complex citizenship relationship to multiple nation-states because ideologies, values, and belief systems are contested among family, community members, and members of the dominant culture (Hall, 2002; Maira, 2004; Ramirez, 2002). These studies focus on how human agency is linked to the cultural production of citizenship and to the institutional structures that culturally reproduce citizenship.

In this article, I use a cultural citizenship framework to interpret the narratives of the university-educated, U.S.-born *hijaslos de inmigrantes Mexicanos* who contributed to my larger study. This framework explains lessons about national belonging in the context of immigrant families. I conceptualize cultural citizenship as a constructivist process in which young people learn about the institutional power linked to citizenship. This process involves learning to "define themselves, define their membership, claim rights, develop a vision of the type of society they want to live in," "interpret their histories," and "forge their own symbols and political rhetoric" (Flores, 1997:263). In this way, cultural citizenship consists of broad ways of teaching and learning an ethic of belonging through relational moments, including shared practices, platicas (dialogues), and stories about critical and formative events that occur within families (Benmayor, 2002; Delgado Bemal, 2001; Fráquiz and Brochin-Ceballos, 2006). I identify lessons of belonging through experiences with citizenship surveillance, citizenship ideologies, and cultural contradictions related to national citizenship.

This paragraph shows how authors move from the review of the literature—which summarizes past work on a topic—to their own argument and purpose. This is a common way that scholars build upon previous research to develop their own contributions to a topic. The use of first person distinguishes the work of others from the work of the author herself.

Methodology and Contributors to the Study

A "methodology" section describes the primary research of the author—how the study was conducted and how reliability was ensured.

The social analysis of citizenship conceptions and practices offered here is based on narratives of young adults who self-identify with their U.S.-Mexican communities, grappling with their citizenship practices and identity. The larger study drew on ethnographic methods and conversations that took place between 2000 and 2006 with 10 volunteers, all university-educated, young-adult contributors (23 to 29 years old). Each had participated in a common nonprofit Latino youth leadership organization[6] (for over 10 years), attended leading universities, and were U.S.-born sons and daughters of Mexican immigrants living in the borderland areas of California. This research involved conversations over five summers, one year of field participation, in-depth structured and unstructured recorded interviews, and focus group dialogues. The data were organized through a constant comparative approach (Strauss and Corbin, 1997; Strauss, 1987) and interpretive research analysis (Denzin, 1997; Denzin and Lincoln, 2000). Contributors to the study were "educated"[7]

Note how the author carefully describes the demographics of the people who were interviewed in this study.

and in many ways had successfully negotiated institutions of higher education with the support of their families and community members. They articulated how notions of citizenship were implicated in their day-to-day lives.

As bilingual and bicultural graduates of leading universities (e.g., the University of California at Los Angeles, U.C. Berkeley, U.C. Santa Cruz, Stanford University, and Dartmouth College) and longtime youth leaders, they saw themselves as future leaders and voices for one of the largest marginalized ethnic groups in the nation. They defined themselves as "community participants," who intended to "give back" to their communities, while attempting to socially and politically embed themselves in society. Despite early challenges to learn about, access, and use U.S. and Mexican social and cultural capital, this group of immigrant Mexican daughters and sons did their best to assert a sense of belonging by creating and drawing on relational and institutional resources.

It is important that the limitations and scope of a specific study are noted. Here, the author lays out the specific parameters of the study—what *is* and *is not* being studied. Focusing and limiting a topic is very important to allow a writer to cover a topic in enough detail.

Although the leadership organization played a significant role in the process of citizenship identity formation, this article primarily focuses on citizenship formation as it relates to family history. Central to this piece is how, during the contributors' coming of age in their families, they contended with moments of citizenship surveillance and negotiated citizenship ideologies, while broadly learning the difference between what it means to be a citizen and to act like a citizen. Their narratives provide an understanding of how various degrees of citizenship status and structural entities have shaped their lives. They reveal how citizenship is a social and legal construction that is constantly negotiated in everyday life.

This final line previews the findings of the article, and so sets the context for what follows.

Negotiating Citizenship Surveillance

This key term, borrowed from previous researchers, forms an important basis for the argument that follows.

For many members of racialized ethnic communities, the journey to citizenship is shaped by moments of "citizenship surveillance" (Chavez, 2006; Johnson, 2003; Maira, 2004; 2005). Citizenship surveillance entails negotiating one's national (legal) citizenship identity during moments in public when one is not identified as a normalized citizen of the nation or is challenged as not being a legitimate citizen that belongs in society. Over their lifetimes, the *hijaslos de inmigrantes Mexicanos* in this study, their families, and friends faced moments of citizenship surveillance. Encounters with citizenship surveillance taught them that their citizenship identity was not normalized, regardless of their legal citizenship status and the ways they and their families acted like citizens (e.g., as loyal workers, civic participants, voters, etc.). Moments of citizenship surveillance often led them to recognize a disjuncture and disconnection between citizenship ideologies of "justice" and the lived experience of citizenship in U.S. society (see also Urrieta, 2004).

For example, in reference to citizenship surveillance, Consuelo, a key contributor to this study, told how she and her family had contended with white men she believed to be vigilantes. Dressed in plain clothes, they had flashed some kind of badge at her family. In 1993, after her first quarter at U.C. Santa Cruz, Consuelo visited her family in the greater borderlands of California. After the visit, the family escorted her into the airport, where vigilantes identified them as non-American citizens. This event shows how the "right to belong" in the nation is often not granted automatically for many Latino families, regardless of their legal citizenship status (Rosaldo, 1997:34–35). Consuelo recounted her family history of contending with citizenship surveillance, saying:

Providing a specific example helps to clarify the concept being discussed.

> It was random. We didn't know if it was real or not. They [the vigilantes] were like, "Your papers please." I was like, "What? Excuse me?" They looked at my dad, and he started reaching [for his wallet]." I said to my dad, "Espérate, espérate, espérate (wait, wait, wait)." I said to them, "I don't think you are supposed to be doing this here. We are at the airport. Why are you asking us about our citizenship? You are not supposed to be doing this." "No," [the men said]. "We are asking you to identify yourself and we need your papers and their papers too." I was like, "We are U.S. citizens! My brother and I were born here. My parents are residents, but I don't think you should be asking us. I don't think you should be doing this . . . ." At that time, civilians at airports [were] doing that [inspecting]. It was like now with the Minutemen, but back then it was happening at the airports . . . . Then, they took my parents' micas (citizenship documents). I know my parents were very, very nervous. I was shocked. It was like they were saying, "Do you belong here!"

This extended quotation, like the many that follow, are used as a key evidence base. Since the article is based on interviews, the words of the immigrants themselves are crucial to understanding their process of trying to assimilate as citizens.

Consuelo described a form of status domination exercised by the presumed vigilantes who were interrogating her family. This act symbolized the kind of citizenship assault that the contributors, their families, or friends were periodically subjected to. As Bejarano (2005) and Villenas (2002) have argued, rather than being identified as normalized citizens, the "brown bodies" of Latino youth and their families often mark them erroneously as illegitimate citizens in schools and society.

With a history of experiencing citizenship surveillance, Mexican immigrant offspring and members of their communities feared the long-term effects of the Minutemen project (Chavez, 2006), anti-immigrant legislation such as H.R. 44378 (Cano, 2006; Jonas, 2006), the implementation of Operation Return to Sender[9] (Prado, 2007), and other anti-immigrant measures such as Texas House Bill 28. Moments of citizenship surveillance have a greater impact on some Latino families than on others, and social safety nets are weakened as mobilizations of surveillance and deportations take place. As Maira (2004: 228) argues, such moments of citizenship surveillance do not "signify a racial, historical, or political rupture," but rather are moments "of renewed contestation over ongoing issues of citizenship" that have existed politically for years, but are now more intensified.

Here, the author uses the previous argument to show that this problem has continued to become more serious over time.

After this episode of citizenship surveillance, Consuelo explained how she questioned the authority of the vigilantes and how they attempted to silence her, especially after they learned she was "only" 17 years of age.

> They [vigilantes] were like, "How old are you?" I was like, "I'm 17!" They said, "I don't think you are old enough to know what we are supposed to be doing or not." I was like, "We are here at the airport because I am going back to college. I know that you are not supposed to be doing this. This is not right." They said, "You need to show your identification." "I am a U.S. citizen! I already told you."

The vigilantes used Consuelo's "underage" status to dismiss her questions and assertions about their citizenship surveillance. Challenging their "authority," as Consuelo did, could be interpreted as invoking an aspect of American culture by practicing freedom of expression. However, others could view it as the sign of a disloyal or unpatriotic citizen, especially if those challenged supposedly represent "the law." Monsivais (2002) argues that adults habitually castigate young people over the right to speak, particularly in public spaces. Unlike Consuelo, for children and young people whose parents are unauthorized or undocumented, moments of citizenship surveillance are intensified because they are rendered silent, fearing that they and their parents could be deported (Bejarano, 2005).

Gender and racialized ethnic identity often compound how moments of citizenship surveillance are negotiated. As a young woman of color resisting this form of public assault, Consuelo attempted to counter it by identifying herself as a university student. She was college educated, and yet was asked to prove her citizenship. Although women of color are not identified by society as educated subjects or authorities in public spaces (Anzaldua, 1987; Hurtado, 1996; Villenas and Moreno, 2001), Consuelo voiced how she strategically negotiated the moment of citizenship surveillance. She intended to defend her family, including her elementary-school-aged brother, when saying:

This transition links the general concept of "citizenship surveillance" to other contributing factors—gender and race. As such, as a social scientist, the author tries to account for all variables.

> That was the first time that I actually spoke up right away. Usually, things happen, and I don't say anything until afterwards. Then I'm like, oh, I should have said this, this, and this . . . . I saw my parents' reaction, and I was like, "Wait, I don't think that you are supposed to be doing this!" I spoke. I said, "You are not wearing a uniform; how do I know that you are agents?" I even told them my brother's age. I said, "He's not supposed to carry an ID. He's only in elementary school, and you expect him . . ." My dad was like, "Ya, ya no mas (there, there, that's enough)." They were like, "Okay this time, but you need to get. . . ." Later, I wrote about it for a college class.

Consuelo refused to be silenced by the vigilantes and she attempted to maintain her dignity and that of her family. With higher levels of education and literacy, many Latina/o college students learn to assert themselves in public, as Consuelo did. As college students, most of them intend to become educated citizens to serve the public and their communities, and to be recognized as legitimate members of society (Benmayor, 2002; Delgado Bernai, 2001; Gándara, 1995). Seif (2004:213) states that, "for Latinos from working-class backgrounds, educational struggles and achievements" are often "key to positions of influence in California" and even legislative politics. However, poor-quality K–12 education often fails young Latinas/os and creates barriers to attaining higher education (Garcia and Figueroa, 2002; Valenzuela, 1999; Urrieta, 2004). As Seif (2004) explains, unofficial citizenship status often prevents young undocumented Latinas/os from gaining access to colleges and university education. Such exclusion prevents a vast number of young Latinas/os from fully asserting their sense of belonging in society.

Notice how the author generalizes from the specific examples to wider claims.

Consuelo's case was about learning one's relationship to the nation-state. In an interview, her brother Rafaël explained how this moment of interrogation made their family deeply question their symbolic attainment of the "American Dream." He described the "pride and hope that going to college represents for so many Mexican-origin students and parents" (Benmayor, 2002: 96) and how Consuelo's attainment of a college education had in many ways symbolized their achievement of the American Dream. Yet, this encounter with the vigilantes made their family reevaluate their membership in society and recognize what Urrieta (2004) calls their "disconnection in American citizenship." Rafael described their moment of critical reflectivity as follows:

Note how the introductory phrase explains the importance of the quotation that follows. It is important to tell readers why the quotation is being included, so as to help them notice the key points that a writer is trying to make.

> I remember my sister was like, "You guys can't do this." She had it in her to stand up. . . . This [my sister going to college] was confirming that my parents had done everything right for the last 17 years. It had [confirmed the American Dream before this interrogation]! We were at the airport, and we were going to send her back to school, and we were dressed up and all excited. . . . It was like we were being accepted and then that happened. It was so dramatic! We had done everything right! "Yeah, you did everything; now prove that you are allowed to be here. . . ." Everything was working out, and maybe white Americans were not that bad, and then that happened. . . . I remember thinking (whispers), "American citizen, American citizen, American citizen," and just getting ready for when they asked. . . .

Consuelo and Rafael understood this moment of citizenship surveillance as a disjuncture in their sense of citizenship. This was the case insofar as their family, like other Latino families, had a long history of being socially and politically embedded in their local community. They frequently participated in organizing efforts (e.g., voter registration drives, community services, tutorials, teach-ins, self-help committees) intended for the well-being of their diverse neighborhood. Yet, this moment of citizenship surveillance was deeply disturbing, as they were not identified as normalized citizens of the local place and nation-state.

Rafael critically reflected on his journey to citizenship, particularly in hearing about deportations, the border patrol, and noticing that his mother always carried proof of his citizenship. These events shaped his understanding of normalized versus subjugated citizen identities during his coming of age. Rafael explained:

> I had heard of INS raids by the border patrols. They had never done anything to us, but I heard stories. I had heard stories of parents being deported and kids being left behind. . . . I remember as kids we would tell each other bits and pieces of what we heard of the border patrol and made it worse, either on purpose or because we were so confused. Maybe because I'm so close to the border, there is a bit of menace. . . . Still, in my gut, whenever I see that shade of green or that border patrol truck, I kind of stop for a second. It's like the border patrol; you know what I mean. . . . I am 23 years old, I am a citizen, and I went to Dartmouth, but still! . . . Growing up, mom always carried our birth certificates with her in her purse as a custom of hers. It was something I always thought of as weird. It is like, "I am an American, but how legitimate is my ability to be here if my mom is carrying proof?"

Notice how the quotations are also interpreted after they are presented, using the specific examples to illustrate the wider principles that have been argued by previous authors—in this case, Villenas and Deyhle.

The border patrol stories as described by Rafael were a "cultural and material assault on their dignity and livelihood" (Villenas and Deyhle, 1999: 419) and functioned as a form of social discipline. His mother's perceived need to carry their birth certificates speaks to the ways in which "citizenship policing profoundly shapes the mothering experiences of working-class Latina mothers" (Villenas and Moreno, 2001: 671). In many ways, this family's experience with citizenship surveillance represented more than an individual struggle; it represented the struggle of an entire Latino community (Flores, 1997). Given the situations surrounding citizenship surveillance and subjugation, Consuelo observed: "You would think there would be more places of belonging for young people living with these kinds of stresses. It is a different world out here."

Although these university-educated young adult Latinas/os intend to act like citizens by asserting their sense of belonging in various social, civil, and political events, they are not always publicly identified as such. Often, they are positioned as the defendants for their families, needing to "talk back" to authority figures (Hooks, 1994). Yet, talking back, as one of the "forms of publicly declared resistance," is contingent on the "mode of domination" experienced (Scott, 1990: 198). Like other Latino families, Consuelo's family, with legal citizenship, recognized that they had a privilege to talk back, insofar as they did not have to worry[10] about the intense circumstances (e.g., incarceration and deportation) that unauthorized or undocumented members in the community did (Bejarano, 2005).

Everyday Lessons of Citizenship Ideologies

Citizenship ideologies are intensely calculated in education, culture, and society (Urrieta, 2004). Ideologies are disseminated through discourses oiplaticas (conversations) that inform everyday practices of community participation (Gonzalez, 2001). In this study, learning and grappling with the significance of citizenship meant encountering multiple and intersecting ideologies of citizenship, specifically "good citizenship," "liberal citizenship," (Abowitz and Harnish, 2006), and "cultural citizenship" (Flores and Benmayor, 1997; Rosaldo, 1997). Good citizenship refers to knowledge about the civic and political world; liberal citizenship is about knowledge regarding equality to exercise freedoms in society; and cultural citizenship means knowledge about issues related to the dilemmas of membership and identity of ethnic community in the nation (Abowitz and Harnish, 2006). Contributors to this study implicitly used these citizenship ideologies when explaining how their parents sought to impart a political awareness of state and national issues that affected U.S.-Mexican cultural communities in the context of national cultural politics and debates on immigration.

Note how each new term introduced is carefully defined.

Cultural citizenship expressed through social and political discussions in the home space can give insight into a group's marginal positionality in the nation-state. For example, Arturo, who attended the University of California at Berkeley, recalled that his parents had discussed issues with him such as California's anti-immigrant Proposition 187, restrictive driver's license legislation, and human rights violations near the U.S.-Mexico border. He said,

Again, one of the most effective ways to define terms is through specific examples.

> The news is always on. . . . We talk about social justice or injustice . . . like immigration. For example, a couple of years ago, there were beatings in [Riverside] California. It was a discussion, a sensitive one, where my family felt angry. Yes, we did. I mean they [the victims] are humans, and a piece of paper determines whether you are beaten or not. . . . It's a big thing. . . . We discuss that [injustice] all the time. . . . My family has discussed politics and propositions like 187, and even that whole new ID act that came through. . . . We do talk. My parents are not highly educated, but they are up to date with things that are up in the community.

Arturo's references to Proposition 187, the beatings, and the denial of diver's licenses to undocumented immigrants reflect his parent's teachings on social justice and injustice. Many educators assume that immigrant working-class Latino parents without formal education are deficient (Villenas, 2002) and apathetic to politics in everyday life. However, parents like Arturo's seem to facilitate difficult dialogues in their home space regarding the tension-filled national debates about Latino immigration and human rights violations inflicted on Mexican people (Palafox, 2001b).

In the home space, cultural citizenship is sometimes taught alongside liberal citizenship (Abowitz and Harnish, 2006). The latter concerns the different citizenship "rights" and "freedoms" experienced by parents and children according to their national status. In the context of U.S. nationalism, and despite their status as legal residents, Arturo's parents did their best to teach him the meaning of citizenship; they highlighted the rights and freedoms they lacked, in comparison with those of U.S. citizens. He illustrated the social and cultural logic embedded in the meaning of citizenship that his parents had imparted. For them, citizenship had to do with respeto (respect), dignity, freedom, and democracy, convictions shared by many Latino families (Gonzalez, 2001). Arturo said he and his brother learned from his parents that:

The key terms introduced earlier in this section are now used to frame the rest of the examples and arguments being made by Moreno.

> "It is your country. . . . You have every right to exercise your rights, but act properly. You can't go on and expect to claim rights only when it's good for you and then exercise them against what you are claiming or speaking about. . . ." My dad always repeated a saying by Benito Juárez, "el respeto al derecho ajeno es la paz (the

> respect of others' rights is the path to peace)." That is, respect other people for who they are and their opinions. He [Arturo's father] said, "People's actions might not always reflect what we believe in, but nonetheless, we need to understand why they are doing it. We don't have to agree with it, but it doesn't hurt to know why . . . ." My parents said we have the right to express our opinion. "Tu sipuedes hijo. Tu si, parque a ri, que to van hacer (Yes, you can, son. Yes, because what can they do to you). No one is going to threaten you; no one can take your citizenship away." I say to my dad, "No one can take away your green card. Express your opinion. Just because it has an expiration date does not mean that you won't get it back." They are always with this guard. . . . Thanks to my parents' sacrifices, we [my sibling and I] are able to think this freely.

Arturo's parents draw upon their Mexican national cultural logic to encourage him to practice the liberties they lack or feel uncomfortable expressing publicly. This cultural logic took the form of Benito Juárez' admonition to respect the rights of others. The "guard," or reservations of Arturo's parents concerning publicly expressing political opinions, was premised on citizenship surveillance; nonetheless, they educated him to assert his dignity, pride, and sense of belonging. In their efforts to teach their children membership, many Latino families draw upon a cultural logic that is often connected to liberal citizenship. In this sense, liberal citizenship is part of family education, despite perceptions that Latino families are uneducated about notions of democracy and resistant to social and political integration.

Note the use of Spanish words (which are then defined) to show the cultural flavor contained in the language.

In the sociopolitical context of *familia* (family), many Latinas/os are taught "resilience in the face of public discussions about Latinos as 'Other,' 'problem,' and 'noncitizen'" (Villenas, 2002:16). The young adults in this study recalled that when they were youths, their families had taught them resiliency and encouraged them to practice good citizenship by participating in school and community organizations and engaging civically in their local communities. This encouragement was meant to deflect what Stanton-Salazar (2001:251) calls "alienated embeddedness" in school and public spaces. For example, Bella, a graduate of Stanford University, received encouragement from her parents to practice good citizenship through her involvement with community organizations:

> They never said no [you cannot go and be active], unless they said, "You've got to take care of the kids because I've got to go

to work." They were always really supportive, even now. . . . When I am involved in big [political] events, they will drive down three hours to come to that event. . . . They are very supportive of the space that I am trying to create. That is what I am trying to do. They realize how important it is.

In Bella's case, her good citizenship contrasted with the "individualist ideologies" in the U.S. (Stanton-Salazar, 2001: 213) that are rooted in the belief that subjects make it "on their own." Instead, she learned the value of being involved and creating networks of relationships, sharing social and cultural capital, and accessing institutional resources. Ironically, members of the dominant culture also value these practices, even though they claim individualistic ideologies. Contributors to this study understood the role of their parents in protecting them from such "individualist ideologies." Participation was encouraged in multiple community organizations and in the assigning of roles and responsibilities within the family. Again, the discourse that Latino parents and their children do not care about teaching and learning "good citizenship" is shown to be untrue.

The author refutes the arguments and assumptions of others through the evidence presented.

Contributors to this study recognized that many young immigrant and nonimmigrant Latinas/os found it challenging to seek familial and institutional resources. They knew of tension-filled relationships between other hijas/os de inmigrantes Mexicanos and their parents. For those other hijas/os, socialization into individualistic ideologies created social distance among family members and sometimes ruptured possibilities for unity between parents and children, as well as solidarity among community members. Contributors to this study also recognized that institutional forces strained familial lazos de confianza (bonds of trust) (Stanton-Salazar, 2001; Vélez-Ibánez, 1996). For these reasons, in their community and educational work they sought to create curricula and programming that strengthened Latino households and communities.

For the daughters and sons of immigrants in this study, their parents and culture were significant agents that informed their good citizenship as it related to a work ethic. They shared narratives about the role of their mothers in learning to define themselves as hard-working citizens (Delgado Bernal, 2001; Gándara, 1995). For example, Octavio described how his mother's culture shaped his good citizenship in terms of his work ethic and political engagement:

My Mexican culture has contributed to my activism. I connect that to my mother teaching me the importance of working very hard.

She instilled in me a strong work ethic. "Whether you are a skilled laborer or doing any type of work in your life, you work hard. If you are going to mop, you're going to mop really well. In fact, it is going to be the best "trapiada" [mop] ever. That is what you're going to do, because there is no other way to do it. . . ." In my activism and in the work that I do, I have chosen to do it with all of my corazon [heart]. . . . She has raised five boys on her own and I have seen her lead and teach by example. . . . She is not the most [formally] educated person, but she has taught me so much about life, to value work and to believe in what you are doing. Work as hard as you can to get what you need out of life and remember to contribute to the greater good. This is what has influenced my activism.

This interpretation demonstrates how the words of those interviewed fit within the values of "good" American citizens.

Octavio attributed his ethic of hard work, good citizenship, and contributing to the greater good to his mother. Yet this strongly upheld, national ethic of hard work often overlooks that work alone does not always provide social mobility; it also ignores the role of national citizenship, economic inheritance, and access to institutional opportunities (social, cultural, educational, and financial capital) in advancing social mobility (Bourdieu, 1977; Ong, 1999).

In their efforts to socially integrate and practice good and liberal citizenship, these *hijas/os de inmigrantes Mexicanos* narrated how their mothers informed their values and perceptions of themselves as citizens deserving opportunities. Their mothers shaped the practices used to navigate institutions and public spaces (i.e., schools, work, social environments) to seek resources for themselves and others in their communities (Villenas and Moreno, 2001). Delgado Bernal's (2001: 632) studies offer similar narratives in the sense that they "voiced a strong commitment to their families or the Mexican communities from which they came, a commitment that translated into a desire to give back and help others." In my study, Consuelo spoke of how her mother taught her the importance of seeking opportunities for herself and community members:

Since I was a little girl, my mom would always say, "I don't know what to tell you, how to teach you to do things, or how you can get to places or resources. So you need to go out and ask someone. I can't help you because I didn't grow up here, but there are people out there who can help you. . . . You have

> the opportunity that I didn't have in Mexico. Now it is your responsibility to go out and find out . . . how to get an education, how to get help not just for yourself, but for our family and community." She always taught me that things were not going to be handed to me because I smile. You have to work for it. You have to ask for it, and if you don't know what to ask, then you need to find someone to help you formulate those questions.

Her mother provided important *consejos* (advice or homilies) (Delgado-Gaitan, 1994) on the value of identifying individuals able to help Consuelo locate educational resources or teach her to ask questions leading to educational opportunities. Given the educational and economic inequalities her mother had experienced in Mexico, Consuelo's mother encouraged her to seek opportunities that would enable her to become an educated citizen who could serve the public. In some ways, the skills and knowledge associated with liberal citizenship—assuming one has the freedom to ask questions and seek opportunities—equal the freedom normalized citizens enjoy (Abowitz and Harnish, 2006).

Consuelo and others like her learned to ask questions to find resources for themselves and others and to reflect on their own social position. The lessons they learned differed from those voiced by participants in Gándara's (1995: 30) study, whose parents stressed doing things on their own and not asking for help, especially outside the family. In the present study, contributors described how their parents taught them to constantly inquire about resources and in the process educate themselves.[11]

Though some Latinas/os experience forms of exclusion and citizenship surveillance, they also learn lessons of belonging in their home space through notions of cultural, good, and liberal citizenship. These lessons are about desiring freedoms, valuing community membership, the work ethic, serving the greater good, and seeking resources for self and other community members. For many, the journey to citizenship involves engaging in a practice of constant self-reflectivity and self evaluation about their form of belonging, as well as their family's membership in the nation-state.

The concluding paragraph summarizes the section's findings, and reinforces the overall point of the article.

Being a Citizen and Acting Like a Citizen

This section frames the actions of immigrants as a "Journey to citizenship," reinforcing the desire of immigrants to assimilate despite the challenges of the "journey." This refutes those who suggest that Mexican immigrants do not wish to be part of American culture.

In their family journey to citizenship, contributors to this study learned to value their citizenship partially through their knowledge of their parents' struggle to attain residency or naturalized citizenship. Their self-identities as citizen-actors hinged on learning the power and possibility of their citizenship practices and identity in everyday life.[12] Their language of empowerment enabled them to reflect upon their approaches to advocacy. Beyond their broad notions of citizenship, they recognized the implications of having community members with legal citizenship and others without it. They thus became familiar with the challenging barriers and limitations faced by those lacking authorized status or legal citizenship. Legal residents were seen as valuable members who contributed to the well-being of their communities and sustained the political economy of the nation. These community members practiced citizenship by participating locally in social, cultural, and economic activities, all the while contending with issues concerning their legal citizenship status.

Their parents' citizenship status informed their sensibilities and dispositions; they learned to value working with immigrants across a spectrum of citizenship statuses. For example, Tomás, who received a degree in political science from U.C. Berkeley, indicated that his mother had been an undocumented immigrant. Gaining knowledge of her status implicitly informed his values about citizenship differences:

> My mom wasn't a citizen until a couple of years ago. For many years, I didn't understand why my dad was voting and why my mom was not. . . . In working with citizens and noncitizens or undocumented workers in the community, I started to be more sensitive to [their citizenship status] . . . . How is someone living in this country for 20 years and who has been advocating for and empowering other people not a citizen here just because there is a legal document saying that you aren't?

Notice how the quotations in each section are organized in ways that support the overall point of that section.

The last statement recognizes a tension inherent in citizenship differences. Implicitly referring to his mother and others, Tomás pointed to the dilemma and disjuncture in how one can learn to practice social and cultural citizenship, while legal citizenship is a binding mechanism for many. He thus acknowledged the contributions of Latino community members who "act like citizens" by contributing and educating others, without "being citizens" in the legal sense (Fox, 2005: 76). In the past, members who acted like citizens have aided others to become or be citizens in the long term.

Arturo's parents pointed to the ways in which their citizenship status caused their lives to be organized differently from his. Even after receiving a "green card," his father often calculated his actions, especially his back-and-forth travels across the U.S.-Mexico border. For Arturo, self-surveillance and fear affected his father and other undocumented members of his community:

> My parents remind us—my brother and I—of our upbringing and how different we have it from them. Some things have resulted in certain sacrifices, of course, by mostly them. I think it helps us not just to discuss it [citizenship], but also to really digest it. It helps me now in my field, for example, working with some people who are technically not legal residents. Every time I speak to someone [who is undocumented], I want to go out of my way to help them because my dad was one. He suffered frequently and he didn't get resources because of that. Today my dad has his green card. Still, every time he crosses the border, I can't help looking into his eyes and thinking there is always that fear. You know, it aches inside of me.

Arturo expressed deep compassion for his father and recognized that his own rights as a citizen in society had emerged from his father's endurance of financial and other hardship in attaining residency. In this sense, he learned that his own sense of "being a citizen" had emerged because his father had "acted as a citizen" by being responsible and accountable to family, work, and state for countless years (Fox, 2005: 76). Together, Tomás and Arturo highlight the realities that many U.S.-Mexican young people share by being part of families and communities made up of members with mixed citizenship statuses.

The U.S. government has managed the citizenship process for people depending on their nation's historical relationship with the U.S. (Chavez, 2001; Johnson, 1997; 2003). From his political science studies and his work in a nonprofit, Tomás explained how he had learned about differences in

Here, the focus on one group of immigrants is reinforced by differentiating Mexican immigrants from the experiences of another group.

citizenship processes. He attempted to explain the differences in citizenship recognition for Vietnamese and Mexican people:

> I understand different citizenship nuances in working with undocumented immigrants . . . and not just those from Mexico. I worked with Vietnamese who were noncitizens and their situation was completely different than for Mexicans. If you were a noncitizen from a Vietnamese community, the [U.S.] government was not going to send you back. They were going to get you processed as quickly as possible. . . . That affects the ways that communities of color don't want to work with each other. . . . In this case, because the Vietnamese are given money to open up businesses and things like that. . . . With the Mexican community essentially it is, "we want you out . . ."

With some experiential and academic knowledge about the political dynamics involved in attaining citizenship, Tomas questioned how the U.S. has played a role in determining distinct forms of citizenship among different national groups (e.g., Cubans, Central Americans, etc.). In the case of Vietnamese immigrants, many have been "allowed" to enter the country with official refugee status because of the U.S. military involvement during the Vietnam War era (Oropeza, 2005). In this sense, the political history between the U.S. government and other nations creates a hierarchy of citizenship differences among ethnic groups that affects their interrelations (Chavez, 2001; Johnson, 1997; Oropeza, 2005).

Some contributors described the social meanings and everyday political lessons learned by their parents' process of attaining residency or naturalized citizenship. For example, Consuelo's parents only held residency. Their hesitance to pursue naturalized citizenship was due to the heavy bureaucratic process and financial burden on the family, which is the case for many Latino families. Before her parents attained residency status, Consuelo, then only a girl, carried a sense of burden by constantly acting as her parents' "voice" or representative:

> There were times when I felt like I had to be their voice and did not realize that they had their own voice. My parents were involved in organizations at church, school, and their community. They had their own voice, but I always thought I was their voice. . . . My mom has been living here for many, many years. . . . All that my mom has to do [for citizenship] is take a class, which

she has studied for a hundred million times. She can answer all the questions and maybe get that document.

As a young adult, Consuelo reevaluated her limited notion of citizenship as national citizenship status, without which a person was powerless. Such a notion of citizenship often leads some *hijaslos de inmigrantes Mexicanos* to associate their parents' identity with subjugated experiential knowledge. Since her childhood, Consuelo had recognized that, regardless of her parents' citizenship status, they "acted as citizens" without "being citizens." They had a long history of mobilizing the community and had even held the county accountable for hazardous conditions that had caused a death in their neighborhood. Consuelo's parents participated in ongoing community organizing efforts that were often linked to local and state-level politics (e.g., community housing conditions and health initiatives for all children). Consuelo's parents participated in Parental Involvement in Children's Education (PICE) for more than 15 years, and in 2006 they received the PICE award of the year. Due to her educational opportunities and ability to critically self-reflect, Consuelo reexamined her approach to advocacy with immigrant mothers. Instead of always speaking on their behalf, she began to encourage them to voice their concerns; her support for their efforts in community projects was unwavering.

Bella also came to value her family's everyday citizenship practices of serving the public by creating and maintaining healthy families. Bella said of her mother's involvement:

> My mom is involved with the Latina Association Child Care Providers. . . . She is involved with trying to make sure that the city does not cut funding for childcare for low-income families. We actually talk about this stuff. We don't actually sit down and plan, but we share about it. Also, it's not just about me being an educator and a community organizer, but also about my brother who is a teacher, my sister who is a teacher, my other brother who is a teacher, my other brother who is a Little League coach, and my other brother who is starting a basketball league for his kids. . . . It has to come together and empowers everyone.

The tone and voice of the quotations lend authenticity to the argument being made by Moreno.

Bella and the other *hijaslos de inmigrantes Mexicanos* valued everyday forms of community participation and the network of relationships they used to engage in a culture of service.

This line suggests that Bella's experience can be generalized to the experiences of others—making the example illustrative of a larger trend.

While exerting their agency, they and their families did sometimes encounter challenges in local politics. Beyond upholding the value of acting like citizens, they encouraged their parents and community members to be citizens—that is, become naturalized U.S. citizens. For example, Bella's father has had a long history with migrant farm labor, which in many ways delayed his attainment of national citizenship. Bella described her father's complex past[13] by highlighting the significance of legal citizenship in their family history:

> My dad emigrated in 1965 from Guanajuato, Mexico, and he didn't become a citizen until 1995. He was here for 30 years before he became a citizen. My dad was 20 years old. Vino a trabajar (he came to work) and support the family. I remember when he became a citizen. I was a junior in high school. That was the one day they actually let me stay [home] from school. It wasn't to stay home; it was para acompanarlo (to accompany him) to the citizenship ceremony. It's emotional because I remember sitting there in a huge room in the Los Angeles Convention Center. I was sitting there, and it just hit me: "I am an American and my dad is becoming an American because he has lived here." My dad has lived in the U.S. longer than he lived in Mexico. After the ceremony, the first thing he said was "I have to vote." He already had his life set. . . . [He owned] his house, and his kids went through college. . . . On his way out, he said the Pledge of Allegiance. It was such a moving experience for me. I was like, "My dad is . . . American in many ways, even though he grew up in a rancho (farm village)."

Even when the U.S. has not been accommodating to people such as Bella's father, he and other Mexican immigrants have displayed American loyalty upon attaining legal citizenship. After many years of exploitative labor, Bella's father defied the general notion that Mexican immigrants resist applying for national citizenship. Indeed, he longed to apply for citizenship, but prohibitive costs and fear of deportation made the process challenging. The 1986 Immigration Reform and Control Act (IRCA) made it possible for thousands of undocumented immigrants to apply for citizenship (Johnson, 1997). Still, the process took many years to complete. Bella's family's journey to citizenship illustrates how her father's naturalized citizenship symbolically legitimized their American national identity.

Bella's knowledge of her parents' family history regarding citizenship contributed to her sense of well-being and social mobility. Her narrative was contextualized within the larger struggle of working-class families who were familiar with notions of social mobility and, to some extent, the American Dream. Bella described how her father's history informed her own sense of citizenship:

> When you look back at our lives, what has molded us the most is that our parents felt empowered about our future. They passed that on to us, and that is why we are so active. My parents had nothing, but they dared to dream, and they reached their goals [voice cracks], and as humans, that is all we have [cries]. . . . I get emotional because my dad had it hard as hell. He didn't go to school, and he was able to raise eight children that are now college educated. Damn, that is amazing! For me, that is where my sense of citizenship comes from. Yes, it is all about my culture, background, and everything. . . . "Who did I learn citizenship from?" I have to say from my parents and from my experiences.

Bella expresses the possibility of social mobility for immigrant parents and children. Her narrative captures how some immigrant parents and their children come to know themselves as national citizens. The idea of social mobility is deeply embedded, despite the limitations imposed by an anti-immigrant climate and the inability of many immigrants to attain either legal citizenship or mobility. Though not accepted as normalized U.S. citizens, they remain loyal to U.S. society.

Again, notice how after each quotation, Moreno takes the time to show its significance. It is important that we not only include key quotations, but that we tell our readers why they have been included.

Arturo recognized that attaining U.S. national citizenship is a struggle. He observed that citizenship for Mexican people was not normalized in society, even after obtaining legal citizenship. Given his father's labor background, Arturo proposed that citizenship should be defined in terms of a labor contribution within the nation:

> My dad did not get his residency until 1994, when he was 56 years old. He came from Michoacán, Mexico, when he was 18 years old. . . . He went through many hardships, deportations, and abuse. . . . When I consider everything that my dad has gone through, it's amazing. I don't know if I would be capable of being like that if I had experienced what he did. He once told me, "When I came to this country, I gave my youthful years. I gave my strength. I worked here. I got married here. I had my children here. I built my life here and I am proud of being Mexican. . . . Now, does he feel represented? No. They [the public]

> do not know that he has a son who graduated from the University of California at Berkeley, who started a master's program, and is incredibly active in the nonprofit sector impacting other people's lives. No. And, they do not know that he has an 18 year old who is about to start U.C. Berkeley. No, they do not see that he has given his labor. . . . I know my dad thinks this is a great place. Now, he is defining it as a great place in comparison to the place he was bom and the opportunity he had here versus what he had in the town he grew up in. He identifies as Mexican because he was born there. . . . He does love this country very much.

Arturo's narrative describes the dilemma of belonging and the ways his father grappled with the complexity of U.S. and Mexican citizenship identities. Arturo was critical of the social devaluation of his father's citizen-worker practices, despite having lived most of his life in the U.S. Caught between nations, immigrants learn to construct their citizenship identity during their formative years. As Ramirez (2002: 70) puts it, "dominant notions of citizenship supported by government policy in the United States and Mexico influence the way" citizenship is understood and experienced. Governments in these neighboring nations have historically upheld political and ideological projects that sustain nationalist identities, which in turn facilitate their roles in the global political economy (Barry, 1995; Gutiérrez, 1995; Jonas and Tactaquin, 2004; Sánchez, 1993). These projects, and the histories of *hijaslos de inmigrantes Mexicanos*, show that despite the inseparable quality of the U.S.-Mexican political economy, and of cultural realities, they are replete with tensions and disparities.

Here, the primary research (the interviews) is blended with the secondary research (the other experts' findings). This is a common and useful way to place your writing within the larger context of a discipline.

Conclusion

The meanings of cultural and legal citizenship are intertwined and learned according to space, place, and time. In this article, I show how citizenship is constituted in and through a family journey to citizenship. As Villenas and Deyhle (1999: 441) indicate, "families are the starting point for surviving and effecting resistance to cultural assault, to valorizing and (re)creating a family education that stresses dignity and pride." A family's citizenship education and history with national

This line clearly restates the key point being made in this article.

legal citizenship inform the ways in which *hijas/os de inmigrantes Mexicanos* understand citizenship. I have attempted to represent the nuances of citizenship as a lived experience through the "cultural citizen narratives" they offer (Benmayor, 2002). Their narratives illustrate the nexus between citizenship ideologies and identity. They show how questions of citizenship for U.S.-born young adults are not always answered by their legal status; rather, their journey to citizenship is about the ways their family and community members build their sense of citizenship in everyday life.

Contributors' narratives show how cultural and legal citizenship overlap, while indicating a disjunctive or disconnect with national citizenship. Even with national citizenship and a university education, members of immigrant families are still confronted by citizenship surveillance and must deal with the dilemma of belonging. For families with members lacking national citizenship, the problem is exacerbated; it is a concern of many Latino families and community members across citizenship statuses.

For educators and educational researchers, multilayered understandings of citizenship are necessary for analyzing and organizing inclusive pedagogies of citizenship in schools and society. Traditional citizenship theories and philosophies often overlook the dynamic intersections between citizenship discourses, practices, and identity, which are embodied by subjects who are not normalized as citizens, such as *hijas/os de inmigrantes Mexicanos.* We must continue to highlight contradictions in citizenship that subjugate members who negotiate their struggle toward belonging and citizenship in schools and society. Both analytical and colloquial meanings of citizenship are essential for examining the overlap and distinctions between legal and cultural conceptions of citizenship; they are also necessary for addressing how citizenship is a legal construct and a citizen-identity project. Given the legislative practices used to mobilize against immigrant communities, including Latinos, educators and researchers must continue to perform research and educate others about citizenship and educational inequalities on the ground.

The author concludes with a statement about why these findings are important, and how they can be used by specific parties.

Notes

1. The borderlands of California in this study refer to the Oxnard, Santa Ana, and San Diego areas.
2. Sunaina Maira (2004; 2005) interrogates the meaning of citizenship surveillance within the context of South Asian Muslim immigrant youth. For

Maira, citizenship surveillance is operative when one's belonging to the nation-state becomes suspect.

3. Anti-immigrant groups often refer to U.S.-born children of undocumented immigrants as "anchor babies." However, such children have been unable to offer an "anchor" in the U.S. for their parents. Under "Operation Return to Sender," carried out by the Immigration and Custom Enforcement (ICE), in some cases both parents and their U.S.-born children have been deported; sometimes, parents have been deported and their children left behind.
4. Elite "experts" include academics and policymakers whose political discourse is legitimized by institutional knowledge that informs political debates. Luis Urrieta, Jr. (2005), further discusses this power dynamic.
5. Foucault (1977) explains how discourses reinforce, justify, and normalize some individuals while others are subjugated as illegitimate subjects.
6. This Latino youth leadership organization, in which they had participated for 10 years or more, focused on empowering youth to civically engage in their schools, other organizations, and local communities by teaching them public speaking and parliamentary procedure, and to facilitate group collaborations, undertake short- and long-term goal setting, and pursue various orientations of self and group leadership.
7. In Cultural Production of the Educated Person: Critical Ethnographies of Schooling and Local Practices, Levinson, Foley, and Holland explore how multiple cultural productions in schools, families, and communities define the "educated person." Villenas (2002) defines the educated person as "well-educated children who have respect, moral values, and loyalty to family." In this article, "educated" refers to moral and formal education.
8. Federal House Resolution 4437, the Border Protection, Antiterrorism, and Illegal Immigration Control Act of 2005, was introduced by James Sensenbrenner in December 2005. To understand the intent of the legislation, see Cano (2006) and Jonas (2006). It sought to criminalize undocumented immigrants, as well as individuals and organizations that provided services to them. Although this legislation was never reconciled with the Senate version, the political climate led to many more deportations under Operation Return to Sender. For an annual report on deportations, see www.ice.gov/doclib/about/ice07ar_final.pdf.
9. Operation Return to Sender, launched in June 2006, resulted in over 18,000 arrests nationwide (Marin Independent Journal, March 7, 2007).
10. According to Sunaina Maira (2005) and Kevin Johnson (2003), after the U.S.A. PATRIOT Act of 2001 and other proposed anti-immigrant legislations, Latino and Muslim immigrants and non-immigrants have been more afraid to speak out because due process and free speech have been curtailed in exchange for a presumed sense of safety for the larger majority.
11. They also articulated lessons learned from adults encountered in their schools and in the youth leadership organization.

12. Their sensibilities and dispositions were similar to those expressed by the hundreds of thousands of Latinas/os across generations during the immigrant marches of 2006.
13. Bella's father's journey to citizenship was linked to the Bracero Program, the guest worker program that existed between 1942 and 1964.

References

Abowitz, Kathleen Knight and Jason Harnish. 2006. "Contemporary Discourses of Citizenship." Review of Educational Research 76, 4 (Spring): 653–690.

Almaguer, Tomás. 1994. Racial Fault Lines: The Historical Origins of White Supremacy in California. Berkeley: University of California Press.

Anderson, Benedict. 1983. Imagined Communities: Reflections on the Origin and Spread of Nationalism. London: Verso.

Anzaldúa, Gloria. 1987. Borderlands/La Frontera: The New Mestiza. San Francisco: Aunt Lute Books.

Appadurai, Arjun. 1990. "Disjuncture and Difference in the Global Cultural Economy." Public Culture 2: 1–24.

Bañuelos, Esthela, L. 2006. "'Here They Go Again with the Race Stuff': Chicana Negotiation of the Graduate Experience." Dolores Delgado Bernal, C. Alejandra Elenes, Francisca E. Godinez, and Sofia Villenas (eds.), Chicana/Latina Education in Everyday Life: Feminista Perspectives on Pedagogy and Epistemology. New York: SUNY Press: 95–112.

Barry, Tom. 1995. Zapata's Revenge: Free Trade and the Farm Crisis in Mexico. Boston, MA: South End Press.

Bejarano, Cynthia L. 2005. Qué Onda: Vrban Youth Culture and Border identity. Tucson: The University of Arizona Press.

Benmayor, Rina. 2002. "Narrating Cultural Citizenship: Oral Histories of First-Generation College Students of Mexican Origin." Social Justice 29,4: 96–121.

Bourdieu, Pierre. 1977. "Cultural Reproduction and Social Reproduction." Jerome Karabel and A.H. Halsey (eds.), Power and Ideology in Education. New York: Oxford University Press: 487–510.

———. 1972. Outline of a Theory of Practice. Cambridge: Cambridge University Press.

Cano, Gustavo. 2006. "Political Mobilization of Mexican Immigrants in American Cities and the U.S. Immigration Debates." Mexico-North Research Network, Washington, D.C., and the University of Nebraska Omaha. At www.mexnor.org.

Chavez, Leo R. 2006. "Spectacle in the Desert: The Minuteman Project on the U.S.-Mexican Border." David Pratten and Atreyee Sen (eds.), Global Vigilantes: Anthropological Perspectives on Justice and Violence. London: C. Hurst and Company Publishers.

———. 2003. "Immigration Reform and Nativism: The Nationalist Response to the Transnationalist Challenge." Matthew C. Gutmann, Felix V. Matos Rodriguez, Lynn Stephen, and Patricia Zavella (eds.), Perspectives on Las Américas: A Reader in Culture, History, and Representation. Maiden: Blackwell Publishing.

———. 2001. Covering Immigration: Popular Images and the Politics of the Nation. Berkeley and Los Angeles: University of California Regents.

Coll, Kathleen. 2004. "Necesidades y Problemas: Immigrant Latina Vernaculars of Belonging, Coalition, and Citizenship in San Francisco, California." Latino Studies 2: 186–209.

De Geneva, Nicholas. 2004. "The Legal Production of Mexican/Migrant 'Illegality.'" Latino Studies 2: 160–185.

Delgado Bernai, Dolores. 2001. "Learning and Living Pedagogies of the Home: The Mestiza Consciousness of Chicana Students." International Journal of Qualitative Studies in Education 14, 5:623–641.

Delgado-Gaitan, Concha. 1994. "Consejos: The Power of Cultural Narratives." Anthropology of Education Quarterly 25, 3:298–316.

Denzin, Norman K. 1997. Interpretive Ethnography: Ethnographic Practices for the 21st Century. Thousand Oaks, CA: Sage Publications.

Denzin, Norman K. and Yvonna S. Lincoln (eds.). 2000. Handbook of Qualitative Research. Second Edition. Thousand Oaks, CA: Sage Publications.

Flores, William V. 1997. "Citizens vs. Citizenry: Undocumented Immigrants and Latino Cultural Citizenship."

Flores, William V. and Rina Benmayor (eds.). Latino Cultural Citizenship: Claiming Identity, Space, and Rights. Boston: Beacon Press: 255–277.

Flores, William V. and Rina Benmayor (eds.). 1997. Latino Cultural Citizenship: Claiming Identity, Space, and Rights. Boston: Beacon Press.

Foucault, Michel. 1977. Discipline and Punish. Harmondsworth: Penguin.

Fox, Jonathan. 2006. "Refraining Mexican Migration as a Multi-Ethnic Process." Latino Studies 4: 39–61.

———. 2005. "Unpacking "Transnational Citizenship.'" Annual Review of Political Science 8: 171–201.

Fráquiz, María E. and Carol Brochin-Ceballos. 2006. "Cultural Citizenship and Visual Literacy: U.S.-Mexican Children Constructing Cultural Identities Along the U.S.-Mexico Border." Multicultural Perspectives 8.1: 5–12.

Freire, Pablo. 1970. Pedagogy of the Oppressed. New York: Continuum Publishing Company.

Gándara, Patricia. 1995. Over the Ivy Walls: The Educational Mobility of Low Income Chicanas. New York: SUNY Press.

García, Eugene E. and Julie Figueroa. 2002. "Access and Participation of Latinos in the University of California: A Current Macro and Micro Perspective." Social Justice 29, 4:47–59.

Giroux, Henry. 2003. "Zero Tolerance, Domestic Militarization, and the War Against Youth." Social Justice 30, 2: 59–65.

———. 1983. Theory and Resistance in Education: A Pedagogy for the Opposition. Boston: Bergin and Garvey Publishers Inc.

González, Norma. 2001. I Am My Language: Discourses of Women and Children in the Borderlands. Tucson: University of Arizona Press.

Gutiérrez, David, G. 1995. Walls and Mirrors: Mexican Americans, Mexican Immigrants, and the Politics of Ethnicity. Berkeley: University of California Press.

Hall, Kathleen D. 2002. Lives in Translation: Sikh Youth as British Citizens. Philadelphia: University of Pennsylvania Press.

Hooks, Bell. 1994. Teaching to Transgress: Education as the Practice of Freedom. New York: Routledge.

Huntington, Samuel. 2004. "The Hispanic Challenge." Foreign Policy 141 (March/April): 30–46.

Hurtado, Aída. 1996. The Color of Privilege: Three Blasphemies on Race and Feminism. Ann Arbor: University of Michigan Press.

Johnson, Kevin R. 2003. "September 11 and Mexican Immigrants: Collateral Damage Comes Home." De Paul Law Review 52 (Spring).

———. 1997. "The New Nativism: Something Old, Something New, Something Borrowed, Something Blue." Juan F. Perea (ed.), Immigrants Out! The New Nativism and the Anti-Immigrant Impulse in the United States. New York and London: New York University Press: 165–188.

Jonas, Susanne. 2006. "Reflections on the Great Immigration Battle of 2006 and the Future of the Americas." Social Justice 33, 1: 6–19.

Jonas, Susanne and Catherine Tactaquin. 2004. "Latino Immigrant Rights in the Shadow of the National security State: Responses to Domestic Preemptive Strikes." Social Justice 32, 1–2: 67–91.

Ladson-Billings, Gloria. 2004. "Culture Versus Citizenship: The Challenge of Racialized Citizenship in the United States." James A. Banks (ed.). Diversity and Citizenship Education. San Francisco: Jossey-Bass/Wiley Imprint: 99–126.

Levinson, Bradley A. and Dorothy Holland. 1996. "The Cultural Production of the Educated Person: An Introduction." Bradley A. Levinson, Douglas E. Foley, and Dorothy C. Holland (eds.), The Cultural Proauction of the Educated Person: Critical Ethnographies of Schooling and Local Practices. New York, Albany: SUNY Press: 1–54.

Maira, Sunaina. 2005. "The Intimate and the Imperial: South Asian Muslim Immigrant Youth After 9/11." Sunaina Maira and Elisabeth Soep (eds.), Youthscapes: The Popular, the National, the Global. Philadelphia: University of Pennsylvania Press: 64–84.

———. 2004. "Youth Culture, Citizenship and Globalization: South Asian Muslim Youth in the United States after September 11." Comparative Studies of South Asia, Africa and the Middle East 24: 219–231.

Menchaca, Martha. 1995. The Mexican Outsiders: A Community History of Marginalization and Discrimination in California. Austin: University of Texas Press.

Monsivais, Alejandro C. 2002. "Ciudadanía y juventud: elementos para una articulación conceptual." Perfiles Latinoamericanos. Revista de la Sede Académica de México de la Facultad Latinoamericana de Ciencias Sociales 20, 20: 157–177.

Oboler, Suzanne (ed.). 2006. Latinos and Citizenship: The Dilemma of Belonging. New York: Palgrave, Macmillan.

Omi, Michael and Howard Winant. 1989. Racial Formation in the United Sates from the 1960's to the 1990's. Second Edition. New York, London: Routlege.

Ong, Aihwa. 1999. "Cultural Citizenship as Subject Making: Immigrants Negotiate Racial and Cultural Boundaries in the United States." Rodolfo D. Torres, Louis F. Miron, and Jonathan X. Inda (eds.), Race, Identity, and Citizenship. Maiden, MA: Blackwell Publishers: 262–294.

Oropeza, Lorena. 2005. ¡Raza Si! ¡Guerra No! Chicana Protest and Patriotism During the Vietnam War Era. Berkeley: University of California Press.

Palafox, Jose. 2001a. "Introduction to 'Gatekeeper's State: Immigration and Boundary Policing in an Era of Globalization.'" Social Justice 28, 2: 1–5.

———. 2001b. "Opening Up Borderland Studies: A Review of U.S.-Mexico Border Militarization Discourse." Social Justice 27, 3: 56–72.

Prado, Mark. 2007. "30 Illegals Targeted in Canal Raid: People Pulled from Homes During Immigration Sweep." Marin Independent Journal (March 7).

Ramirez, Renya. 2002. "Julia Sanchez's Story: An Indigenous Woman Between Nations." Frontiers 23, 2: 65–83.

Rosaldo, Renato. 1997. "Cultural Citizenship, Inequality, and Multiculturalism." William V. Flores and Rina Benmayor (eds.), Latino Cultural Citizenship: Claiming Identity, Space, and Rights. Boston: Beacon Press: 27–38.

Rumbaut, Reuben G. and Alejandro Portes. 2001. "Introduction, Ethnogenesis: Coming of Age in Immigrant America." Ethnicities, Children of Immigrants in America. Berkeley: University of California: 1–19.

Sánchez, George. 1993. Becoming Mexican American: Ethnicity, Culture and Identity in Chicana Los Angeles, 1900–1945. New York: Oxford University Press.

Scott, James. 1990. Domination and the Arts of Resistance: Hidden Transcripts. New Haven: Yale University Press.

Seif, Hinda. 2004. "'Wise Up!' Undocumented Latino Youth, Mexican-American Legislators, and the Struggle for Higher Education." Latino Studies 2: 210–230.

S.I.N. Collective. 2007. "Students Informing NOW (S.I.N.) Challenge the Racial State in California without Shame . . . SIN Vergüenza." Educational Foundations (Winter/Spring): 71–90.

Stanton-Salazar, Ricardo D. 2001. Manufacturing Hope and Despair: The School and Kin Support Networks of U.S-Mexican Youth. New York: Teachers College, Columbia University.

Strauss, Anselm. 1987. Qualitative Analysis for Social Scientists. New York: Cambridge University Press.

Strauss, Anselm and Juliet Corbin. 1997. Grounded Theory in Practice. Thousand Oaks, CA: Sage Publications.

Suarez-Orozco, Marcelo M. 2001. "Globalization, Immigration, and Education: The Research Agenda." Harvard Education Review 71, 3: 345–365.

Urrieta, Luis, Jr. 2005. "The Social Studies of Domination: Cultural Hegemony and Ignorant Activism." The Social Studies (September/October): 189–192.

———. 2004. "Disconnections in 'American' Citizenship and the Post/Neo-Colonial: People of Mexican Descent and Whitestream Pedagogies and Curriculum." Theory and Research in Social Education 32, 4: 433–458.

Valenzuela, Angela. 1999. Subtractive Schooling US.-Mexican Youth and the Politics of Caring. New York: SUNY Press.

Vélez-Ibáñez, Carlos. 1996. Border Visions: Mexican Cultures of the Southwest United States. Tucson: University of Arizona Press.

Villenas, Sofia. 2002. "Reinventing Education in New Latino Communities: Pedagogies of Change and Continuity in North Carolina." Stanton Wortham, Enrique G. Murillo, Enrique G. Murillo, Jr., and Edmund T. Hamann (eds.), Education in the New Latino Diaspora. Westport: Ablex Publishing: 17–35.

Villenas, Sofia and Donna Deyhle. 1999. "Critical Race Theory and Ethnographies Challenging the Stereotypes: Latino Families, Schooling, Resilience, and Resistance." Curriculum Inquiry 29, 4: 413–445.

Villenas, Sofia and Melissa Moreno. 2001. "To Valerse par Si Misma: Between Race, Capitalism, and Patriarchy: Latina Mother-Daughter Pedagogies in North Carolina." International Journal of Qualitative Studies in Education 14, 5: 671–687.

Reading Analytically

1. Early in her essay, Moreno spends a good deal of time attempting to define varying understandings of the concept of citizenship. Why does she find it important to do so? What are some of the complications in attempting to define what she means by *citizenship?*
2. One of the key concepts of this article is *citizenship surveillance.* What does Moreno mean by this term? Provide some specific ways she defines the term and some examples of how she saw this phenomenon in action.
3. Another key component of this piece is its study of "citizenship ideologies"—the differences in the way citizenship is understood by those in the study. Describe at least three differing ideologies—underlying beliefs—that inform the understanding of citizenship by those interviewed by Moreno.

Reading Across Disciplinary Communities

1. You have likely been asked to interpret parts of literary works by analyzing the words of the author or of characters in a work of fiction. How does the interpretation of words by a social scientist differ from the interpretation of words in a literary work? How are they similar? Try to cite specific interpretations by Moreno to illustrate your point.
2. One of the keys to the effective practice of the social sciences is retaining objectivity in one's observations and interpretations. Does Moreno seem to retain that objectivity? What signs are there that she does, or does not, present her findings in a scientific, objective form?

REBECCA M. CALLAHAN, CHANDRA MULLER, AND KATHRYN S. SCHILLER

Preparing for Citizenship

Immigrant High School Students' Curriculum and Socialization

This study explores the effect of high school civics classes and other predictors for engaged citizenship among children of immigrants as they pass from the K–12 system of public education into their lives as young adult citizens. As Eric Lane argues in "America 101" (included in Chapter 1 of this book), civics classes are an important part of socialization of all citizens—both those born here and those who immigrate here. This study, however, examines the longer-term effects of those classes, not merely upon political knowledge but upon actual engagement in the culture as immigrants become adult citizens.

As an attempt to fill in the "gap in the literature" on civic education, this piece illustrates not only the work of education scholars, but the ways that scholars interact with one another to further the work of a field. As the author's note in the abstract to this piece, "Although prior research suggests that high school civics education, academic achievement, and a sense of connection increase political participation in early adulthood, we do not know if these processes apply to immigrant youth." That "gap statement" defines the way that scholarly authors build upon previous work while finding a niche for their own contributions. In this case, the study builds upon what we know about civics classes generally, and applies that knowledge and methodology to the study of immigrant youth. As a student writer, this can be an excellent way for you to participate in discipline-based writing: building upon a previous study and changing its goals slightly, changing its population under study, or replicating a national study on a local level. Doing so can help you to learn more about methodologies of your discipline as well as the types of topics that most interest scholars in your area of endeavor.

Immigrant adolescents are one of the fastest growing segments of our population, yet we know little about how schools prepare them for citizenship. Although prior research suggests that high school civics education, academic achievement, and a sense of connection increase political participation in early adulthood, we do not know if these processes apply to immigrant youth. Using longitudinal, nationally representative data from the Adolescent Health and Academic Achievement study (AHAA) and the National Longitudinal Study of Adolescent Health (Add Health), we employ multilevel models to investigate the effects of formal and informal school curricula on early adult voting and registration. We find that children of immigrant parents who take more high school social studies coursework have higher levels of reported voter registration and voting. In addition, attending a high school where students have a greater sense of connection or where parents have more education are important predictors of registration and voting, regardless of immigrant status.

The American common school emerged in the mid-19th century as a means to prepare and educate an active citizenry for participation in a democratic society. With the rise of the urban center as an immigrant receiving ground, the role of schools in transforming immigrant students into civic participants grew in importance (Tyack, 1974). A historical function of U.S. public schools has been to prepare youth, and immigrant youth in particular, to participate in civic society, to participate in the democratic process in general, and to vote in particular (Cremin, 1951; Goodlad, 1984). According to Census 2000, one in five school-age children is an immigrant, or a child of immigrant parents[1] (Hernandez, 2004); this dramatic increase in the immigrant student population brings the role of schools in preparing students for the democratic process to the forefront. U.S. schools often serve as a social and educational nexus in the community where immigrant students, and even their parents, can come for socialization into the American mainstream (Olsen, 2000). The struggle to balance immigrant students' unique educational and linguistic needs has been with the U.S. common school since its earliest incarnation (Deschenes, Cuban, & Tyack, 2001; Tyack, 2003). Ultimately, schools both educate immigrant students through traditional coursework, and socialize them via the formal and informal processes provided within the school context.

Social studies coursework is one element in students' development as participating citizens in U.S. society; also important is integration into the social and academic fabric of the school. For the purposes of the present study, social studies coursework includes history, government, geography, political science (including civics and economics), international relations, and sociology/psychology. For immigrant students, whose parents are by definition new to the dominant society, the school likely not only provides the academic and civic training necessary for active adult integration, but also provides the forum for social integration on which to build future civic participation (Parker, 2001). Social studies coursework thus has the potential to carry even greater weight for immigrant students because it may provide the political guidance and knowledge not necessarily available in the home. The common school prepares immigrant youth not only through Americanization and socialization, but also through academic preparation and linguistic training.

Research suggests that both high school civics classes (Atherton, 2000; Chaffee, 2000) and higher levels of academic achievement (Nie, Junn, & Stehlik-Barry, 1996) contribute to active political participation during young adulthood via heightened civic awareness (Niemi & Junn, 1998). A sense of belonging to a larger community also contributes to higher levels of civic participation during young adulthood as well (Smith, 1999). However, relatively little research has explored how these processes work for immigrant students as they move from the K–12 school system into adulthood, when they adopt the responsibilities that come with age. The literature exploring immigrant voting behaviors pertains primarily to the immigrant adult community (Barreto & Munoz, 2003; Cassel, 2002; Cho, 1999; Jones-Correa, 2001; Junn, 1999; Ramakrishnan & Espenshade, 2001), with relatively little work exploring these behaviors among immigrant young adults who have participated in the civic training provided by our high school system. This study explores the effects of adolescents' school experiences, both individual and as a function of the school social environment, on the voting behaviors (voter registration and voting) of young adults. We consider whether these experiences may differently influence the voting behaviors of children of immigrant and native-born parents.

Schooling and Citizenship Education

One focus of social studies coursework is the education of young adults who will actively participate in their community via voting and other civic activities. The social studies education adolescents receive during high school has been linked to their future political participation (Atherton, 2000; Chaffee, 2000; Niemi & Junn, 1998). However, the curriculum does not act in isolation; students' social positioning and socio-economic status also affect the results of citizenship education (Parker, 2001). In addition, demographic variation across U.S. schools suggests variability in the quality and quantity of the curriculum students, and immigrant students in particular, receive (Cosentino de Cohen, Deterding, & Clewell, 2005). In an article summarizing findings from a larger project including three separate survey studies of high school and college-age youth, Sherrod (2003) reports that political knowledge during adolescence predicts voting and other behaviors during young adulthood. Key here is the role of knowledge gained, at least in part, from social studies coursework (Sherrod, 2003). For immigrant adolescents and others outside the high school mainstream, then, a strong social studies foundation is critical for future civic integration and active participation.

In addition, research stemming from the IEA Civic Education study, which included over 140,000 14-year-old youth in 28 countries, explores the relationship between the social studies classroom and students' reported intent to participate in the civic processes as adults (Torney-Purta, Lehmann, Oswald, & Schulz, 2001). Specifically, school context and academic press, the degree to which other students in the school plan to pursue higher education, contributes to building civic knowledge (Torney-Purta, 2002). Results from the IEA Civic Education study indicate a need to connect the school climate and the social studies curriculum to young adult civic behaviors, including voting and registering to vote.

Although social studies education is designed to prepare youth, including relative newcomers, for future civic participation, it is important to note that the curriculum itself is stratified. In a large scale study using High School & Beyond survey data, Gamoran (1987) found that while social studies coursework maintains a small effect on achievement test scores, there was little variation in the quantity of coursework completed. His analyses, however, account for neither student performance in the social studies coursework under study, nor the type of social studies coursework taken. In addition, Oakes (1985) indicates marked differences in content across courses, suggesting that some social studies courses contain relatively more challenging, academically engaging content than others. Honors social studies courses are arguably more academically challenging, and possibly more engaging, for immigrant students than courses that simply fulfill graduation requirements. Furthermore, elective social studies coursework may distinguish the student completing graduation requirements from the student searching for an academic challenge (Oakes, 1985). While history courses are almost always a high school graduation requirement, additional social studies coursework (e.g., political science and international relations) offers access to more specific or deeper content, preparing students for civic participation as well as entry into higher education.

Community Service and Social Integration: Predictors of Young Adult Civic Involvement

High schools not only prepare adolescents academically and cognitively for entry into the adult world, but also provide opportunities for social integration and community involvement via volunteer and community service activities. Active community service during adolescence has been argued to promote civic involvement during adulthood as measured by both voting and registering to vote. However, whether the community service is required as opposed to voluntary has proven contentious. In an analysis of the effects of different types of high school community service on voting at age 26 using NELS survey data, Hart, Donnelly, Youniss, and Atkins (2007) found that voluntary, mixed, and required community service during high school all predict voting, even when controlling for civic knowledge and other relevant background characteristics. Previously, scholars had expressed concern regarding the potentially detrimental effects of mandating community service in high school, possibly contributing to decreased levels of civic involvement during young adulthood (Finn & Vanourek, 1995). Hart et al. (2007) are able to distinguish between the types of community service adolescents perform, ultimately confirming the benefits of service, regardless of whether it is required. In another recent investigation of the effects of high school activities on young adult civic outcomes, McFarland and Thomas (2006) found that community service participation during adolescence strongly predicts civic participation during young adulthood. Using both NELS and Add Health survey data in multilevel models predicting an index of adult political participation, the authors explore the effects of involvement in voluntary organizations during high school while controlling for peer practices, parent education and a variety of school and individual background characteristics.

Along with community service, identification with and participation in a larger social community predict civic integration (Delli Carpini, 2000; Youniss, McLellan, & Yates, 1997). As a template for adult society, the high school community provides the boundaries within which adolescents can begin to develop a sense of community and belonging to a group outside the home. The social climate of the high school has the potential then to influence the early adult civic behaviors and choices of its citizenry. While adults' social integration and connection to the larger community affect civic integration and participation (Putnam, 2000), whether the social connection of adolescents to their school community promotes their future civic participation in adulthood has yet to be explored. For immigrant adults, belonging to a group and participating in its organized activities results in increased civic engagement (DeSipio, 2002; Leal, 2002). However, we do not know if immigrant adolescents' connections to school and the socialization that is inherent in the school process promote adult civic participation.

Connection to school is mediated by many factors, school composition being one. In fact, school racial and ethnic composition affects student achievement through academic as well as social interactions (Rumberger & Willms, 1992). It follows then that the linguistic and immigrant composition of the school may also play a role in immigrant young adults' civic integration. Nearly two-fifths (37%) of individuals who speak a language other than English live in relative linguistic isolation (Shin & Bruno, 2003), suggesting that many immigrant adolescents attend schools with a considerable immigrant population. We hypothesize that in schools with high immigrant concentrations, immigrant students may be more likely to receive curriculum designed to meet their specific linguistic and academic needs, including instruction about citizenship. In these high immigrant contexts, immigrant students may also feel more closely connected to their classmates and to the school overall.

Research Questions

The literature points to the formal and informal facets of schools and schooling as predictors of civic participation in young adulthood, yet does little to differentiate the strength of each for different groups of students within the larger society. We focus our analysis on the predictors of civic participation among a group highly dependent on the school system for their inauguration into American civic life: immigrant adolescents and young adults. Concern for immigrant adolescents as they transition into active roles as young adults in our society leads to our primary questions of interest. We focus our attention on three main research questions: First, does the social studies curriculum affect voter registration and voting? We consider multiple aspects of the curriculum, including the amount of coursework and students' performance in the courses. Second, turning attention to whether the process operates differently for immigrant students, does the effect of social studies vary for immigrant as opposed to third-plus generation youth? Finally, we ask whether the school context influences voting behaviors. We are especially interested in the school contextual effects for immigrant students in a school. . . .

Results

The main goals of these analyses are to investigate whether (a) high school experiences, and social studies coursework in particular, predict participation in two major forms of civic life (voting and registering to vote); (b) the children of immigrants are more or less likely than their schoolmates with native-born parents to participate; and finally, (c) these effects vary with school composition and context. Baseline research found that children of immigrants are significantly less likely to register to vote than those of non-immigrants (71.0% compared to 77.5%) and similarly less likely to vote in the most recent presidential election. Children of immigrants are also much more likely to be of Asian, Mexican, or other Latino/a descent and, on average, have parents with lower levels of formal schooling. Not surprisingly, children of immigrants also have significantly lower average AH-PVT scores than those of non-immigrants in their high schools. The generally higher levels of math courses taken by children of immigrants can be accounted for by the large percentage of Asians (over 30%) in this group. In contrast, children of immigrants tend to take fewer social studies courses than their schoolmates but get similar grades in those courses. Interestingly, children of immigrants are significantly more likely to have performed community service than their other schoolmates.

Registering to vote

We first examine factors that are associated with registering to vote, which is the most basic and frequent form of civic participation. Using four separate models, we predict the likelihood of registering among U. S. citizens who attended U. S. high schools with children of immigrants. Beginning with Model I, we find no statistically significant difference between the children of immigrants and their schoolmates in the likelihood of registering to vote. The coefficients indicate that African Americans were about 60% more likely (1.603 = exp [.472]) than whites to register to vote and Asian Americans were about 56% less likely (.561 = exp [-.578]) than whites to do so. Background variables indicate that young adults whose parents have higher levels of education, older respondents and those who attended church services at least once a week were more likely to register.

In Model II we added indicators for participants' academic and social experiences in high school to estimate their effect on voter registration net of students' background. Interestingly, formal course enrollment—either type of math courses or number of social studies courses—did not predict registering to vote. In contrast, students who earned higher grades in social studies courses were more likely to register; an increase of one grade point predicted a 29% increase in the odds of registering. Similarly, those who felt connected to their high school or performed community service as adolescents were more likely to register to vote, with an increase in odds of 12% per standard deviation increase in feeling connected. Community service was one of the strongest predictors of registration. Our estimates suggest that "volunteers" are about 72% more likely to register than schoolmates who did not undertake community service. In general, estimated effects of social background remain substantively unchanged from Model I and the estimated overall difference between the children of immigrants and their schoolmates in the likelihood of registering to vote also remain non-significant.

However, we are not only concerned with overall rates of registering to vote, but whether factors related to registering differ between children of immigrants and their schoolmates. In Model III we included interaction terms between immigrant status and (1) being of Asian descent, (2) parents' education level, (3) the number of social studies credits taken, and (4) participation in community service as an adolescent. A significant interaction term would suggest a difference between children of immigrants and others in the association of that factor with registering to vote. Again, exploratory analyses indicated that the coefficients for these four variables differed significantly between the two groups of students.

One of the most dramatic results in comparison to earlier models is that third-plus generation Asian Americans are no more or less likely to register than children of white native-born parents, shown by the non-significant coefficient for this group in Model III. In contrast, the children of Asian immigrants are much less likely to register to vote, as shown by the significant interaction term.[1] Thus, it is only among Asians who are children of immigrants that we estimate differences in reported voting registration. Model III also shows that it is only children of native-born parents for whom we estimate a significant effect of parents' education on registration; parents' level of education does not seem to predict registration for children of immigrants.

Turning to school experiences, we estimate that when children of immigrants accumulate more social studies credits they are more likely to register to vote in young adulthood. Specifically, the interaction term between immigrant status and social studies credits suggests that for each additional credit earned, children of immigrants become 22.5% ($1.225 = \exp[-.024 + .227]$) more likely to register to vote. In contrast, children of native-born parents who performed community service in high school were 87% more likely to register than their peers who did not perform community service. Although children of immigrants who performed community service were also more likely to register, the estimated effect of community service on registering was much more modest for this group (they were only 14% ($1.146 = \exp[.625 - .489]$) more likely to register than their peers who did not perform community service).

In summary, racial/ethnic status and formal schooling in social studies are related to the likelihood of registering to vote for the children of immigrants; in contrast, socioeconomic status and community service experience has a stronger association with registering to vote for their third-generation plus schoolmates.

In the final model we added indicators for high school context to examine whether school environments may influence civic participation in young adulthood. First, the location and type of high school attended predict voter registration. Estimates shown in Model IV suggest that young adults who attended high school in the South were 39% more likely to register than those who attended schools in other parts of the country, and those who attended private high schools were 58% less likely to register to vote than those who attended public high schools.

In Model IV we also estimated the effects on voter registration of the school environment as measured by characteristics of the student body. Schools where students' parents have higher average levels of education may promote voter registration for all students in the school. For every standard deviation increase in the average level of parents' education in the school, we estimate a 33% increase in the young adult's odds of registering. This effect is only somewhat weaker, and is in addition to the estimated effect of individuals' own parents' education. Interestingly, the effect of having attended a high school in which students felt connected is almost twice as strong (22% change in odds per standard deviation) as that of an individual's own feeling of connection (13% per standard deviation). Thus, although we estimate no differences between immigrant and native-born young adults, the social environment of the school in which adolescents spend a large amount of their time is related to their likelihood of registering to vote later in life.

Voting in the 2000 election

We find similar patterns in the likelihood of participants voting in the 2000 Presidential Election, which occurred just prior to the Wave III in 2001. The similarity is not surprising given that individuals must register to vote in order to participate in the election.[2] However, the differences in models for these two outcomes highlight their distinctive natures. As with registering, Asian Americans were less likely to vote. Respondents who were older, those with more educated parents, with higher AH-PVT scores, and those who attended religious services during high school were more likely to vote in early adulthood.

The first substantive difference between the two outcomes is apparent in Model II, in which AH-PVT, which measures both verbal ability and scholastic aptitude, remains a statistically significant predictor of voting after controlling for formal schooling experiences.

More important for our research question about how schools shape immigrants' voting, Model III does not show statistically significant differences between children of immigrants and their native-born schoolmates in the relationships between either being of Asian descent or not, and participating in community service as adolescents or not. In other words, the children of Asian immigrants were least likely to vote compared not only to native-born whites but also to native-born Asian Americans and white immigrant groups, but there were no significant differences between groups. Furthermore, the estimated effect on voting of participating in community service during adolescence is similar for children of native born and immigrant parents alike.

However, the interactions between immigrant status and both parents' education level and social studies credits earned remain statistically significant and follow the same pattern as for registering to vote.

Finally, Model IV indicates that only two attributes of adolescents' high schools predict early adult voting. Even after controlling on students' own family background, adolescents who attended high schools where the average parents' education level was higher were more likely to have voted in 2000 than those who attended schools with lower average levels of parents' education. And, those who attended schools where students reported feeling more connected to the school were also more likely to vote.

In summary, generally the factors that predict young adults' voting are similar to those that are associated with registering. Although the coefficient for immigrant status alone is not statistically significant in any model, children of immigrants do appear to differ from their schoolmates in which factors are associated with their likelihood of civic participation. First, while the children of Asian immigrants were less likely to register to vote than children of other immigrants or children of native-born Asian Americans, they were no less likely to go to the polls in a Presidential election. Second, community service is more weakly related to registering to vote among children of immigrants than for their schoolmates.

Third, parents' education level matters less, and formal social studies coursework matters more for children of immigrants compared to their schoolmates. These interaction effects make the lack of a significant coefficient for immigrant status possibly misleading because our estimates suggest that there may be differences between immigrant and native-born students in the contribution of school and parents to the development of civic participation.

Figures 1 and 2, which show expected levels of civic participation for otherwise "average" respondents, illustrate these differences. Figure 1 shows that children of immigrants are both less likely to register and to vote than those of native-born parents with similar levels of education. At low levels of parental education, there is virtually no difference between children of immigrants and native-born parents in the probability that they register or vote in early adulthood. The difference between the two groups increases as parents' education increases because children of more highly educated native-born parents have higher levels of civic

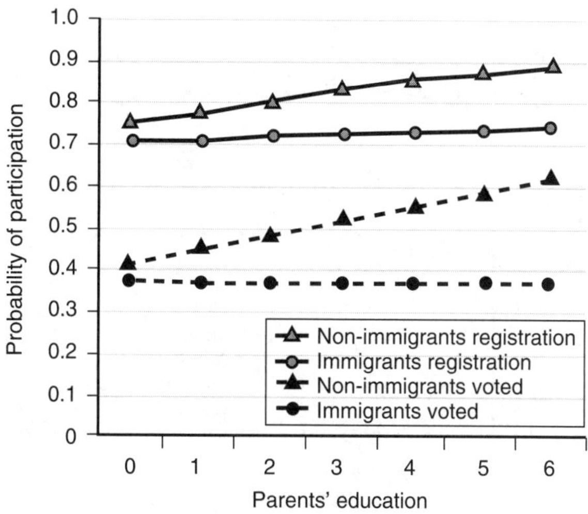

Figure 1. Differences in the Effect of Parents' Education on Civic Participation in Young Adulthood by Immigrant Status

participation while parents' education is unrelated to civic participation among the children of immigrants.

In contrast, we found that some school experiences predict the civic participation of children of immigrants, but not those of native-born parents. Again comparing otherwise "average" students, children of immigrants who accumulate more social studies credits in high school tend to be more likely to register and to vote (Figure 2). While the estimated differences between the two groups in the probabilities of registering and voting is relatively small among students with few social studies credits, the gap widens considerably around three or four credits. This represents about one course per year, which is the average amount of social studies required for high school in most schools and states. The children of immigrants who accumulate more than four social studies credits are over 10 percentage points more likely to register to vote and 20 percentage points more likely to vote than the children of native-born parents. The gap is produced because children of immigrants are more likely to register and to vote when they have taken more social studies, but taking more social studies does not appear to impact the civic participation of children of native-born parents.

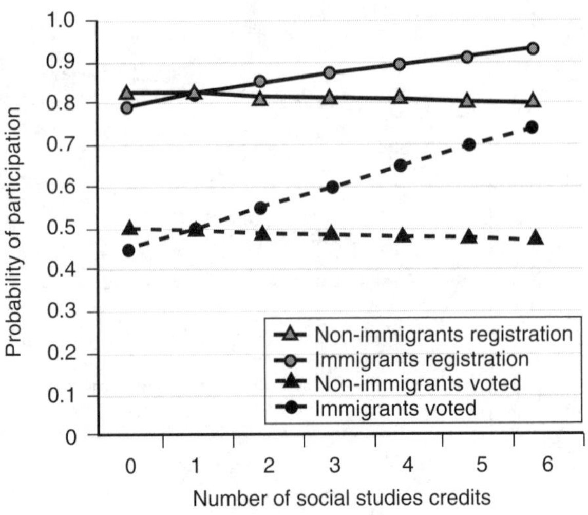

Figure 2. Differences in the Effects of Social Studies Credits on Civic Participation in Young Adulthood by Immigrant Status

Discussion and Conclusions

The findings presented above provide tangible evidence of the ways in which American high schools can, and do, plant the seeds for civic participation and ultimately the democratic citizenry necessary for the continuation of U.S. civic society. Performance in social studies coursework predicts active civic participation, an indication that our high school curriculum is in fact relevant and contributory in our increasingly disconnected society (Putnam, 2000). In an era of increasing immigration, formal education gains importance; our findings indicate that the social studies instruction students receive in high school is associated with active civic participation in early adulthood, and is even more important for children of immigrants than for children of native-born parents. While formal education in general is a known predictor of voting during young adulthood, in this study we were able to tease apart the effects of social studies coursework in particular to estimate the specific effects of formal civic education on the development of citizenry among immigrant youth.

While we understand that the social studies curriculum, as with high school curriculum generally, remains stratified, this study uses a nationally representative dataset to identify the civic benefits of social studies course taking for a key target population: immigrant young adults. This is not to say that the high school structure and curriculum is without flaw, but rather that there are specific ways in which schools prepare immigrant youth for full, active civic participation during young adulthood. This is especially important in light of the negligible effects of parental education level on immigrant youths' voting behaviors; where parent education predicts voting for the children of the native-born, it has little effect for children of immigrants. In lieu of parental knowledge of the civic system, the social studies curriculum of the schools appears to guide these students' civic development. As institutions of the state, schools have the ability to shape the civic behaviors of this growing segment of our population, children of immigrant parents.

Schools provide not only the academic base for young adults' entry into the academic, civic, and professional spheres, but also act as a source of socialization, providing a template for the organization and negotiation of adult civic society. Schools form the leaders of tomorrow not only through the formal curriculum as discussed above, but also through the informal, social curriculum. In the school, children of immigrants find the segment of American society into which they will begin to assimilate; among adolescents, schools provide the first community in which they, independent of their parents and families, begin to adopt active, participatory roles. We argue that American high schools may provide a microcosm of American society into which immigrant youth initially assimilate while simultaneously receiving their formal education and preparation for the post-secondary world awaiting them upon graduation. High schools provide adolescents with the first experience of belonging to a community outside, even independent of the home, and are thus formative in developing the next generation of active citizens. Connection to the school community as well as commitment to the larger community via community service both predict civic participation during young adulthood for all students, immigrant and third-plus generation alike. In effect, the informal realm of schooling provides the practice steps necessary during adolescence for active participation in adult civic society.

Perhaps most interesting is the importance of school climate and students' own sense of connection to the school, of belonging. At the school level, the aggregate social connection of the student body has an almost synergistic effect, increasing the likelihood of both registering and voting during young adulthood among all students. Similarly, schools with higher levels of SES (as measured by parents' education) also promote early adult civic involvement, above and beyond students' own socioeconomic background, also suggesting that there is something tangible about the school climate that may lay a foundation for a sense of social responsibility or leadership. This speaks to the importance of community building in adolescence as a bridge to civic participation during young adulthood.

Interestingly, school climate and students' social connection to school appear to apply equally to immigrant and non-immigrant students. The proportion of immigrant students in the school ultimately did not affect immigrant youths' likelihood of voting or registering to vote. Although we initially expected that immigrant students might benefit from having more immigrant classmates, either because of social connections or through the provision of curriculum tailored to their needs, this does not appear to be the case. We estimated models without other measures of school connection, and we estimated cross-level interactions to determine whether the school climate affected immigrants differently, and found no significant differences for immigrant students, leading us to conclude that our findings about the importance of a welcoming school environment in promoting civic participation apply equally well to immigrants and students with native-born parents.

Ultimately, we conclude that the formal curriculum and informal, social connections provided by schools are each important for the development of civic participation among the youth of today. However, for immigrant youth, the formal curriculum is especially critical. While children of immigrants take significantly less social studies coursework than the children of native-born parents, the *amount* of coursework they take directly predicts their registration and voting during young adulthood. Although youth voter turnout has begun to increase following the 2000 election covered in this study (Lopez et al., 2006; Lopez, Marcelo, & Kirby, 2007), there is still substantial room for improvement, especially among immigrant youth. With this study, we have identified one clear way in which schools can act to improve participation at the polls. Although we have no way to gauge the quality of their civic knowledge with our data, it is likely that the curriculum is producing *better informed* voters as well. In this way we may be underestimating the contribution of social studies curriculum to the civic preparation of immigrant students. Improving immigrant students' access to social studies curriculum and greater social studies coursework will not only promote their overall academic preparation for the adult world, but will also likely directly bolster their civic contributions as young adults.

Notes

1. After adding in the interaction terms, the coefficient for non-Mexican Latino/as becomes statistically significant at the .05 level. However, the p-value remains so close to .05 that we are reluctant to make much of this finding.
2. The patterns are remarkably substantively similar if a reduced sample of only those registered to vote is used for predicting differences in the likelihood of voting. The only two exceptions are (a) the coefficient for Asian descent is never statistically significant and (b) the interaction between social studies credits and generational status is not statistically significant. In both cases, the increase in standard errors relative to the decrease in the gamma coefficient indicates that the difference may be simply due to the smaller sample size.

References

Alba, R. D., & Nee, V. (2003). *Remaking the American mainstream: Assimilation and contemporary immigration.* Cambridge, MA: Harvard University Press.

Atherton, H. (2000). We the people . . . project citizen. In S. Mann & J. J. Patrick (Eds.), *Education for civic engagement in democracy: Service learning and other promising practices.* (pp. 93–102). Bloomington, IN: ERIC Clearinghouse for Social Studies/Social Science Education.

Barreto, M. A., & Munoz, J. A. (2003). Reexamining the "politics of in-between": Political participation among Mexican immigrants in the United States. *Hispanic Journal of Behavioral Sciences, 25*(4), 427–447.

Bearman, P. S., Jones, J. & Udry, J. R. (1997). *The National Longitudinal Study of Adolescent Health: Research design.* University of North Carolina at Chapel Hill: Carolina Population Center.

Cassel, C. A. (2002). Hispanic turnout: Estimates from validated voting data. *Political Research Quarterly, 55*(2), 391–408.

Chaffee, S. (2000). Education for citizenship: Promising effects of the Kids' Voting curriculum. In S. Mann & J. J. Patrick (Eds.), *Education for civic engagement in democracy: Service learning and other promising practices* (pp. 87–92). Bloomington, IN: ERIC Clearinghouse for Social Studies/Social Science Education.

Cho, W. K. T. (1999). Naturalization, socialization, participation: Immigrants and (non-) voting. *The Journal of Politics, 61*(4), 1140–1155.

Cosentino de Cohen, C., Deterding, N., & Clewell, B. C. (2005). *Who's left behind? Immigrant children in high- and low-LEP schools.* Washington, DC: Urban Institute.

Cremin, L. A. (1951). *The American common school: An historic conception.* New York: Teachers College Press.

Delli Carpini, M. X. (2000). Gen.com: Youth, civic engagement, and the new information environment. *Political Communication, 17*(4), 341–349.

Deschenes, S., Cuban, L., & Tyack, D. B. (2001). Mismatch: Historical perspectives on schools and students who don't fit them. *Teachers College Record, 103*(4), 525–547.

DeSipio, L. (2002). *Immigrant organizing, civic outcomes: Civic engagement, political activity, national attachment, and identity in Latino immigrant communities* (Paper No. CSD 02-08). Irvine, CA: Center for the Study of Democracy, University of California, Irvine.

Finn, C. E., & Vanourek, G. (1995). Charity begins at school. *Commentary, 100*(4) 46–48.

Gamoran, A. (1987). The stratification of high school learning opportunities. *Sociology of Education, 60*(3), 135–155.

Goodlad, J. (1984). *A place called school.* New York: McGraw Hill.

Hallinan, M. T. (1994). School differences in tracking effects on achievement. *Social Forces, 72*(3), 799–820.

Hart, D., Donnelly, T. M., Youniss, J., & Atkins, R. (2007). High school community service as a predictor of adult voting and volunteering. *American Educational Research Journal, 44*(1), 197–219.

Hernandez, D. J. (2004). Demographic change and the life circumstances of immigrant families. *The Future of Children, 14*(2), 17–47.

Jones-Correa, M. (2001). Institutional and contextual factors in immigrant naturalization and voting. *Citizenship Studies, 5*(1), 41–56.

Junn, J. (1999). Participation in liberal democracy: The political assimilation of immigrants and ethnic minorities in the United States. *American Behavioral Scientist, 42*(9), 1417–1438.

Leal, D. L. (2002). Political participation by Latino non-citizens in the United States. *British Journal of Political Science, 32*(2), 353–370.

Lopez, M. H., Levine, P., Both, D., Kiesa, A., Kirby, E., & Marcelo, K. B. (2006). *The 2006 civic and political health of the nation: A detailed look at how youth participate in politics and communities.* College Park, MD: CIRCLE: Center for Information and Research on Civic Learning and Engagement, School of Public Policy, University of Maryland.

Lopez, M. H., Marcelo, K. B., & Kirby, E. H. (2007). *Youth voter turnout increases in 2006.* College Park, MD: CIRCLE: The Center for Information and Research on Civic Learning and Engagement, School of Public Policy, University of Maryland.

McFarland, D. A., & Thomas, R. J. (2006). Bowling young: How youth voluntary associations influence adult political participation. *American Sociological Review, 71*(3), 401–425.

Muller, C., Pearson, J., Riegle-Crumb, C., Requejo, J.H., Frank, K.A., Schiller, K.S., et al. (2007). *National Longitudinal Study of Adolescent Health: Wave III Education Data:* Carolina Population Center, University of North Carolina at Chapel Hill.

Nie, N. H., Junn, J., & Stehlik-Barry, K. (1996). *Education and democratic citizenship in America.* Chicago: University of Chicago Press.

Niemi, R. G., & Junn, J. (1998). *Civic education: What makes students learn.* New Haven, CT: Yale University Press.

Oakes, J. (1985). *Keeping track: How schools structure inequality.* New Haven, CT: Yale University Press.

Olsen, L. (2000). Learning English and learning America: Immigrants in the center of a storm. *Theory into Practice, 39*(4), 196–202.

Parker, W. C. (2001). Educating democratic citizens: A broad view. *Theory into Practice,* 40(1), 6–13.

Portes, A., & Rumbaut, R. G. (2001). *Legacies: The story of the immigrant second generation.* Berkeley and Los Angeles, California: University of California Press.

Putnam, R. D. (2000). *Bowling alone: The collapse and revival of American community.* New York: Simon & Schuster.

Ramakrishnan, S. K., & Espenshade, T. J. (2001). Immigrant incorporation and political participation in the United States. *International Migration Review, 35*(3), 870–909.

Raudenbush, S. W., & Bryk, A. S. (2002). *Hierarchical linear models: Applications and data analysis methods.* Thousand Oaks, CA: Sage Publications.

Riehl, C, Pallas, A. M., & Natriello, G. (1999). Rites and wrongs: Institutional explanations for the student course-scheduling process in urban high schools. *American Journal of Education, 107*(2), 116–154.

Rumberger, R. W., & Willms, J. D. (1992). The impact of racial and ethnic segregation on the achievement gap in California high schools. *Educational Evaluation and Policy Analysis, 14*(4), 377–396.

Sherrod, L. R. (2003). Promoting the development of citizenship in diverse youth. *PS: Political Science and Politics, 36*(2), 287–292.

Shin, H., & Bruno, R. (2003). *Language use and English-speaking ability: Census 2000 brief* (No. C2KBR-29). Washington, DC: U.S. Census Bureau U.S. Department of Commerce, Economics and Statistics Administration, U.S. Census Bureau.

Smith, E. A. (1999). The effects of investments in the social capital of youth on political and civic behavior in young adulthood: A longitudinal analysis. *Political Psychology, 20*(3), 553–580.

Stevenson, D. L., Schiller, K. S., & Schneider, B. (1994). Sequences of opportunities for learning. *Sociology of Education, 67*(3), 184–198.

Torney-Purta, J. (2002). The school's role in developing civic engagement: A study of adolescents in twenty-eight countries. *Applied Developmental Science, 6*(4), 203–212.

Torney-Purta, J., Lehmann, R., Oswald, H., & Schulz, W. (2001). *Citizenship and education in twenty-eight countries: Civic knowledge and engagement at age fourteen.* Amsterdam: IEA.

Tyack, D. B. (1974). *The one best system: A history of American urban education.* Cambridge, MA: Harvard University Press.

Tyack, D. B. (2003). *Seeking common ground: Public schools in a diverse society.* Cambridge, MA: Harvard University Press.

Wortham, S., Murillo, E., & Hamann, E. T. (2002). *Education in the new Latino diaspora: Policy and the politics of identity.* Westport, CT: Ablex Publishing.

Younis, J., McLellan, J. A., & Yates, M. (1997). What we know about engendering civic identity. *American Behavioral Scientist, 40*(5), 620–631.

Reading Analytically

1. According to previously performed research cited in this piece, what effect do high school civics classes seem to have upon the general population of students? Make a list of at least five effects.
2. Look closely at the section of this essay called "Research Questions." In what ways does this section provide a specific focus for the study? How might you use this technique in your own research?
3. This study's results are presented in a number of ways, one of which is through tables and graphs. Study at least one of these visual aids, and summarize the findings that are presented there. Then consider whether presentation of this material in visual display is more or less effective than a summary of findings in words.

Reading Across Disciplinary Communities

1. As noted in the introduction to this essay, scholars often build their own study upon previously conducted research. Summarize the findings of previous studies that these authors draw upon, and articulate the ways in which the methodologies of this study build upon that previous work.
2. While most studies in the social sciences are built upon primary research—survey data, interviews, field studies, ethnographies, focus groups, and so forth—this essay draws heavily upon secondary research. Secondary research, studying the published work of other scholars, can be useful not only for surveying previous work in a review of the literature, but as a guide to the contributions made by a new study of the topic. Note three places in which these authors make use of previously published studies and discuss how those studies are used to inform their own work.

GORDON H. HANSON

The Economic Logic of Illegal Immigration

This essay examines whether there is any evidence to support the "strong consensus that if the United States could simply reduce the number of illegal immigrants in the country, either by converting them into legal residents or deterring them at the border, U.S. economic welfare would be enhanced." As an essay that questions assumptions that are strongly held, it illustrates one of the key facets of scholarly research—to check, using reliable methods, whether commonly accepted beliefs are supported by real evidence.

In this case, Gordon H. Hanson, a professor of economics at the University of California, San Diego, uses the literature and methods of his field—a field driven by quantitative data—to test these assumptions. As you read this essay, you might note the ways that he draws upon the analysis of previous studies to build his case, and how numerical information is given priority in making decisions about the viability of the "strong consensus" he is examining. You might also consider how the analysis of statistical data here confirms the importance of statistical literacy as it is discussed in Richard L. Scheaffer's essay in Chapter 1 of this book.

Introduction

Illegal immigration is a source of mounting concern for politicians in the United States. In the past ten years, the U.S. population of illegal immigrants has risen from five million to nearly twelve million, prompting angry charges that the country has lost control over its borders.[1] Congress approved measures last year that have significantly tightened enforcement along the U.S.-Mexico border in an effort to stop the flow of unauthorized migrants, and it is expected to make another effort this year at the first comprehensive reform of immigration laws in more than twenty years.

Legal immigrants, who account for two-thirds of all foreign-born residents in the United States and 50 to 70 percent of net new immigrant arrivals, are less subject to public scrutiny. There is a widely held belief that legal immigration is largely good for the country and illegal immigration is largely bad. Despite intense differences of opinion in Congress, there is a strong consensus that if the United States could simply reduce the number of illegal immigrants in the country, either by converting them into legal residents or deterring them at the border, U.S. economic welfare would be enhanced.

Is there any evidence to support these prevailing views? In terms of the economic benefits and costs, is legal immigration really better than illegal immigration? What should the United States as a country hope to achieve economically through its immigration policies? Are the types of legislative proposals that Congress is considering consistent with these goals?

This Council Special Report addresses the economic logic of the current high levels of illegal immigration. The aim is not to provide a comprehensive review of all the issues involved in immigration, particularly those related to homeland security. Rather, it is to examine the costs, benefits, incentives, and disincentives of illegal immigration within the boundaries of economic analysis. From a purely economic perspective, the optimal immigration policy would admit individuals whose skills are in shortest supply and whose tax contributions, net of the cost of public services they receive, are as large as possible. Admitting immigrants in scarce occupations would yield the greatest increase in U.S. incomes, regardless of the skill level of those immigrants. In the United States, scarce workers would include not only highly educated individuals, such as the software programmers and engineers employed by rapidly expanding technology industries, but also low-skilled workers in construction, food preparation, and cleaning services, for which the supply of U.S. native labor has been falling. In either case, the national labor market for these workers is tight, in the sense that U.S. wages for these occupations are high relative to wages abroad.

Of course, the aggregate economic consequences of immigration policy do not account for other important considerations, including the impact of immigration on national security, civil rights, or political life.[2] Illegal immigration has obvious flaws. Continuing high levels of illegal immigration may undermine the rule of law and weaken the ability of the U.S. government to enforce labor-market regulations. There is an understandable concern that massive illegal entry from Mexico heightens U.S. exposure to international terrorism, although no terrorist activity to date has been tied to individuals who snuck across the U.S.-Mexico border.[3] Large inflows of illegal aliens also relax the commitment of employers to U.S. labor-market institutions and create a population of workers with limited upward mobility and an uncertain place in U.S. society. These are obviously valid complaints that deserve a hearing in the debate on immigration policy reform. However, within this debate we hear relatively little about the actual magnitude of the costs and benefits associated with illegal immigration and how they compare to those for legal inflows.

This analysis concludes that there is little evidence that legal immigration is economically preferable to illegal immigration. In fact, illegal immigration responds to market forces in ways that legal immigration does not. Illegal migrants tend to arrive in larger numbers when the U.S. economy is booming (relative to Mexico and the Central American countries that are the source of most illegal immigration to the United States) and move to regions where job growth is strong. Legal immigration, in contrast, is subject to arbitrary selection criteria and bureaucratic delays, which tend to disassociate legal inflows from U.S. labor-market conditions.[4] Over the last half-century, there appears to be little or no response of legal immigration to the U.S. unemployment rate.[5] Two-thirds of legal permanent immigrants are admitted on the basis of having relatives in the United States. Only by chance will the skills of these individuals match those most in demand by U.S. industries. While the majority of temporary legal immigrants come to the country at the invitation of a U.S. employer, the process of obtaining a visa is often arduous and slow. Once here, temporary legal workers cannot easily move between jobs, limiting their benefit to the U.S. economy.

There are many reasons to be concerned about rising levels of illegal immigration. Yet, as Congress is again this year set to consider the biggest changes to immigration laws in two decades, it is critical not to lose sight of the fact that illegal immigration has a clear economic logic: It provides U.S. businesses with the types of workers they want, when they want them, and where they want them. If policy reform succeeds in making U.S. illegal immigrants more like legal immigrants, in terms of their skills, timing of arrival, and occupational mobility, it is likely to lower rather than raise national welfare. In their efforts to gain control over illegal immigration, Congress and the administration need to be cautious that the economic costs do not outstrip the putative benefits.

Benefits and Costs of Immigration

Are the gains that illegal immigration brings in terms of labor market flexibility offset by other economic costs? Critics of illegal immigration argue that an influx of illegal immigrants brings high economic costs by lowering domestic wages and raising expenditures on public services such as health care and education. If those costs are sufficiently high, the economic case for restricting illegal immigration would be strengthened.

Overall, immigration increases the incomes of U.S. residents by allowing the economy to utilize domestic resources more efficiently. But because immigrants of different types—illegal, legal temporary, and legal permanent—have varying skill levels, income-earning ability, family size, and rights to use public services, changes in their respective inflows have different economic impacts. Immigration also affects U.S. incomes through its impact on tax revenue and public expenditure.

Immigrants with lower incomes and larger families tend to be a bigger drain on public spending. Immigrants pay income, payroll, sales, property, and other taxes, with lower-skilled immigrants making smaller contributions. Immigrants use public services by sending their kids to public schools, demanding fire and police protection, driving on roads and highways, and receiving public assistance, with families that have larger numbers of children absorbing more expenditure. Adding the pretax income gains from immigration to immigrants' net tax contributions—their tax payments less the value of government services they use—allows for a rough estimate of the net impact of immigration on the U.S. economy.

Immigration generates extra income for the U.S. economy, even as it pushes down wages for some workers. By increasing the supply of labor, immigration raises the productivity of resources that are complementary to labor. More workers allow U.S. capital, land, and natural resources to be exploited more efficiently. Increasing the supply of labor to perishable fruits and vegetables, for instance, means that each acre of land under cultivation generates more output. Similarly, an expansion in the number of manufacturing workers allows the existing industrial base to produce more goods. The gain in productivity yields extra income for U.S. businesses, which is termed the immigration surplus. The annual immigration surplus in the United States appears to be small, equal to about 0.2 percent of GDP in 2004.[6]

These benefits, however, are not shared equally. Labor inflows from abroad redistribute income away from workers who compete with immigrants in the labor market. George Borjas estimates that over the period 1980 to 2000 immigration contributed to a decrease in average U.S. wages of 3 percent.[7] This estimate accounts for the total change in the U.S. labor force due to immigration, including both legal and illegal sources. Since immigration is concentrated among the low-skilled, low-skilled natives are the workers most likely to be hurt. Over the 1980 to 2000 period, wages of native workers without a high school degree fell by 9 percent as a result of immigration.[8] On the other hand, lower wages for low-skilled labor mean lower prices for labor-intensive goods and services, especially those whose prices are set in local markets rather than through competition in global markets. Patricia Cortes finds that in the 1980s and 1990s U.S. cities with larger inflows of low-skilled immigrants experienced larger reductions in prices for housekeeping, gardening, child care, dry cleaning, and other labor-intensive, locally traded services.[9] Lower prices for goods and services raise the real incomes of U.S. households, with most of these gains going to those in regions with large immigrant populations.

Immigration, by admitting large numbers of low-skilled individuals, may exacerbate inefficiencies associated with the country's system of public finance.[10] If immigrants pay more in taxes than they receive in government benefits, then immigration generates a net fiscal transfer to native taxpayers. The total impact of immigration on U.S. residents—the sum of the immigration surplus (the pretax income gain) and the net fiscal transfer from immigrants—would be unambiguously positive. This appears to be the case for immigrants with high skill levels, suggesting that employment-based permanent immigrants and highly skilled temporary immigrants have a positive net impact on the U.S. economy.[11] They generate a positive immigration surplus (by raising U.S. productivity) and make a positive net tax contribution (by adding to U.S. government coffers).[12]

On the other hand, if immigrants pay less in taxes than they receive in government benefits, then immigration generates a net fiscal burden on native taxpayers—native households would be making an income transfer to immigrant households. Paying for this fiscal transfer would require tax increases on natives, reductions in government benefits to natives, or increased borrowing from future generations (by issuing government debt). If immigrants are a net fiscal drain, the total impact of immigration on the United States would be positive only if the immigration surplus exceeded the fiscal transfer made to immigrants. For low-skilled immigration, whether legal or illegal, this does not appear to be the case. . . .[13]

The net economic impact of immigration on the U.S. economy appears to be modest. Available evidence suggests that the immigration of high-skilled individuals has a small positive impact on the incomes of U.S. residents, while the arrival of low-skilled immigrants, either legal or illegal, has a small negative impact. Given that the estimates in question require strong assumptions and in the end are only a fraction of a percent of U.S. GDP, one cannot say that they differ significantly from zero. For the U.S. economy, immigration appears to be more or less a wash.

From an economic perspective, the question for policymakers then becomes whether the costs of halting illegal immigration would significantly outweigh the possible benefits. This paper has already discussed the benefits that come from having a flexible supply of low-skilled labor, which would be jeopardized by some of the reforms being considered.

In addition, the enforcement costs of reducing the flow of illegal migrants are substantial and growing. President George W. Bush's budget proposal for 2008 calls for spending $13 billion to strengthen border security and immigration enforcement, including $1 billion to construct fences and undertake other security measures on the border with Mexico. Since 2001, Congress has increased funding for border security by 145 percent and immigration enforcement by 118 percent.[14]

For the sake of argument, take literally the estimate that illegal immigration was costing the economy the equivalent of 0.07 percent of GDP annually as of 2002. In that year, the Immigration and Naturalization Service spent $4.2 billion (or 0.04 percent of GDP) on border and interior enforcement, including the detention and removal of illegal aliens, in a year in which half a million net new illegal immigrants entered the country.[15] The $13 billion in proposed border security spending for next year is already two-and-a-half times that figure at 0.10 percent of GDP. With the already huge increases in spending, the flow of illegal immigrants across the southern border (as measured by apprehensions) is estimated to have fallen by about 27 percent last year. How much money would be required to reduce illegal immigration to zero? Even far short of sealing the borders, the funds spent on extra enforcement would vastly exceed the income gained from eliminating the net fiscal transfer to households headed by illegal immigrants. One should keep in mind, however, that this cost-benefit calculation is based purely on the economic consequences of illegal immigration. There may be gains to increased border enforcement associated with enhanced national security that would justify the expense, but they are not economic gains.

While the aggregate impacts of both legal and illegal immigration are small, the intensity of the public debate about the economic impacts of immigration is not a reflection of its aggregate consequences. Business, which is the biggest winner from high levels of immigration, is the strongest defender of the status quo. Low-skilled workers and select high-skilled workers whose wages are depressed by immigration, at least in the short run, want to see tougher enforcement. Nationally, the less educated tend to be the most opposed to immigration, with their opposition being stronger in states with larger immigrant populations.[16]

Taxpayers in high-immigration states have also been vocal opponents of illegal immigration. States pay most of the costs of providing public services to immigrants, which include public education to immigrant children and Medicaid to poor immigrant households (whose U.S.-born children and naturalized members are eligible to receive such assistance).[17] The federal government, in contrast, appears to enjoy a net fiscal surplus from immigration.[18] Washington is responsible for many activities, including national defense and managing public lands, whose cost varies relatively little with the size of the population. Since immigrants (including many illegals) pay federal income and withholding taxes, the federal government enjoys an increase in revenue from immigration but does not incur much in the way of additional expenses, which are borne primarily at the state and local level. Part of the political opposition to immigration comes from the uneven burden sharing associated with labor inflows. Governors in high-immigration western states, regardless of their party affiliation, have been among the strongest critics of lax federal enforcement against illegal entry.

Results from public opinion surveys bear out this analysis. College graduates, while generally more supportive of immigration, are less supportive in states that have larger populations of low-skilled immigrants and more generous welfare policies, which in combination tend to produce larger tax burdens on high-income individuals.[19]

Final Considerations

The contentiousness surrounding immigration deters many politicians from tackling the issue. While specific groups of workers, employers, and taxpayers may have much to gain or lose if policies governing illegal immigration are changed, the aggregate economic effects of policy reform do not appear to be large. In revising admission and entry restrictions, members of Congress face the unenviable choice of dramatically altering the welfare of a few voters while having a nearly imperceptible effect on aggregate welfare. This dilemma may explain why it has taken policymakers so long to get around to addressing illegal immigration. For over a decade, the net inflow of unauthorized entrants has been close to 500,000 individuals a year. Yet, it is only in the last year or two that Congress has felt compelled to reexamine the issue.

In weighing the various proposals under discussion, policymakers would do well to separate the distributional impacts of immigration from its aggregate effects. No initiative under consideration has the potential to substantially increase the overall income of U.S. residents. Because the aggregate gains or losses are small, any new policy that requires a major outlay of funds would be likely to lower U.S. economic well-being. In a rush to secure U.S. borders, some policymakers insist that major efforts are needed to prevent continued illegal inflows from abroad. While the goals of reducing illegality and establishing greater border control are laudable, it would be difficult to justify massive new spending in terms of its economic return.

Illegal immigration is a persistent phenomenon in part because it has a strong economic rationale. Low-skilled workers are increasingly scarce in the United States, while still abundant in Mexico, Central America, and elsewhere. Impeding illegal immigration, without creating other avenues for legal entry, would conflict with market forces that push for moving labor from low-productivity, low-wage countries to the high-productivity, high-wage U.S. labor market. The acceptance of these market pressures is behind proposals for a large-scale expansion of temporary legal immigration. For many elected officials, temporary legal immigration is still immigration, so they have sought to regulate guest workers in a manner that insulates U.S. labor markets from economic repercussions. But highly regulated inflows of temporary low-skilled foreign labor would be unlikely to attract much interest from U.S. employers. If foreign labor wants to come to the United States and U.S. business wants to hire these workers, then creating cumbersome legal channels through which labor could flow would give employers an incentive to eschew the new guest workers and continue to hire unauthorized workers instead. Were new legislation to combine stronger border and interior enforcement with an unattractive guest worker program, it would be pitting policy reform against itself, with only one of these components likely to survive in the long run.

What provisions might a successful guest worker program entail? To reduce demand for illegal-immigrant labor, a new visa program would have to mimic current beneficial aspects of illegal immigration. Employers would have to be able to hire the types of workers they desire. One way to achieve this would be for the Department of Homeland Security to sanction the creation of global temp agencies, in which U.S. employers posted advertisements for jobs and foreign workers applied to fill these jobs. As with the legal temporary labor market in the United States, intermediaries would likely arise to provide the services of screening workers and evaluating their applications. With illegal labor, screening happens informally. Illegal immigrants from Mexico help friends or relatives get jobs in the United States by vouching for their qualifications. Informal job networks help integrate the U.S. and Mexican labor markets. Formalizing these networks by allowing employers and employees in the two countries to match legally would deepen U.S.-Mexico integration.

Matching foreign workers to U.S. employers efficiently would require flexibility in the number of guest workers admitted. During U.S. economic expansions, there would be more employers searching for foreign workers. Similarly, during economic contractions in Mexico and elsewhere, there would be more foreign workers advertising their availability to take jobs abroad. Keeping the number of visas fixed over time, as is the case now, means that during boom times U.S. employers have a stronger incentive to seek out illegal labor. One way to make the number of visas granted sensitive to market signals would be to auction the right to hire a guest worker to U.S. employers. Congress would determine the appropriate number of visas to issue under normal macroeconomic conditions. The auction price that clears the market would reflect the supply of and demand for foreign guest workers. Increases in the auction price would signal the need to expand the number of visas available; decreases in the price would indicate that the number of visas could be reduced. By setting a range in which the auction price for a visa right would fluctuate, Congress could ensure that flows of guest workers into the U.S. economy would help stave off demand for unauthorized labor.

Perhaps the most important provision of any new visa program would be to allow guest workers to move between jobs in the United States. Currently, H-1 and H-2 visa holders are tied to the employer that sponsors them. Without mobility between employers, guest workers would lack the attractiveness of illegal laborers. They would also be exposed to abuse by unscrupulous bosses. One way to facilitate mobility for guest workers would be to allow existing visa holders to apply for new job postings, along with prospective guest workers abroad.[20] U.S. employers could then hire either existing guest workers or new guest workers, depending on who best matched their needs. In this way, guest workers could move between industries and regions of the country in response to changes in economic conditions, much as illegal laborers do now. What would differ between illegal and temporary legal employment is that the latter would enjoy the protection of U.S. labor laws and regulations.

None of the provisions discussed would be easy to implement, either administratively or politically. However, absent a bold redesign of U.S. guest worker programs, temporary legal immigrants would be unlikely to displace illegal labor.

In the Immigration Reform and Control Act of 1986, Congress voted to increase enforcement without creating a mechanism for the continued legal inflow of low-skilled labor. Under steady pressure from business, immigration authorities ultimately gutted or redirected IRCA's major enforcement provisions. The end result was that illegal labor has continued to find a way into the country. As Congress again wrestles with immigration reform, one would hope that it will pay heed to the failures of IRCA by designing a framework that allows for the dynamic participation of legal immigrant workers in the U.S. economy. Otherwise, the United States is likely to find itself with even larger illegal populations in the very near future.

Notes

1. Jeffrey S. Passel, "Estimates of the Size and Characteristics of the Undocumented Population," Pew Hispanic Center, 2006. Estimates of the illegal immigrant population are imprecise. They are based on comparing the actual number of immigrants (as enumerated in household population surveys) with the number of immigrants admitted through legal means. The stock of illegal immigrants is taken to be the difference between these two values (after accounting for mortality and return migration). See Jennifer Van Hook, Weiwei Zhang, Frank D. Bean, and Jeffrey S. Passel, "Foreign-Born Emigration: A New Approach and Estimates Based on Matched CPS Files," *Demography*, Vol. 43, No. 2 (May 2006), pp. 361–82, for a discussion of recent academic literature on estimation methods and on how existing estimates of the stock of illegal immigrants may not fully account for emigration among this population.
2. See Samuel P. Huntington, *Who Are We? The Challenges to America's National Identity* (New York: Simon and Schuster, 2004), and Patrick J. Buchanan, *State of Emergency: The Third World Invasion and Conquest of America* (New York: Thomas Dunne, 2006).
3. According to Rep. Tom Tancredo (R–CO), a leading congressional opponent of immigration, "There are nine to eleven million illegal aliens living amongst us right now, who have never had a criminal background check and have never been screened through any terrorism databases. Yet the political leadership of this country seems to think that attacking terrorism overseas will allow us to ignore the invitation our open borders presents to those who wish to strike us at home" (http://www.house.gov/tancredo/Immigration/, accessed on October 31, 2006). Former presidential candidate Pat Buchanan adds, "The enemy is already inside the gates. How many others among our eleven million 'undocumented' immigrants are ready to carry out truck bombings, assassinations, sabotage, skyjackings?" ("U.S. Pays the High Price of Empire," *Los Angeles Times*, September 18, 2001.) See also Steven A. Camarota, *The Open Door: How Militant Islamic Terrorists Entered and Remained in the United States*, Center for Immigration Studies Paper No. 21 (2002).

4. Susan Martin, "U.S. Employment-Based Admissions: Permanent and Temporary," Migration Policy Institute Policy Brief No. 15 (January 2006).
5. James Hollifield and Valerie F. Hunt find that, over the period of 1891–1945, there is a negative correlation between U.S. legal immigration and the U.S. unemployment rate, indicating that immigrant inflows are larger when U.S. labor markets are tighter. After 1945, this relationship breaks down. See James F. Hollifield and Valerie F. Hunt, "Immigrants, Markets, and Rights: The US as an Emerging Migration State," paper prepared for presentation at the Migration Ethnicity Meeting (MEM) at IZA in Bonn, Germany, May 13–16, 2006.
6. The formula for the immigration surplus, expressed as a share of GDP (in 2004), is given by -0.5 times the product of labor's share of national income (0.7), the square of the fraction of the labor force that is foreign-born (the ratio 21.2 million/146.1 million squared), and the percentage change in wages due to a one-percent increase in the labor force (0.3). See George J. Borjas, *Heaven's Door: Immigration Policy and the American Economy* (Princeton, NJ: Princeton University Press, 1999). Estimates of the immigration surplus should be viewed with caution, as this calculation treats labor as homogeneous and ignores the consequences of immigration for capital accumulation and technological innovation. Even incorporating such considerations, it would be difficult to produce a plausible estimate of the immigration surplus that was much larger than a fraction of one percent of U.S. GDP.
7. George J. Borjas, "The Labor Demand Curve is Downward Sloping: Reexamining the Impact of Immigration on the Labor Market," *Quarterly Journal of Economics*, Vol. 118, No. 4 (June 2003), pp. 1335–74. This wage impact should be viewed as temporary. In the long run, one would expect immigration to raise the incentive for capital accumulation, which could negate immigration's impact on wages. Other research suggests that the wage consequences of immigration are minimal—see David Card, "Is the New Immigration Really So Bad?" NBER Working Paper No. 11547 (August 2005). Were this the case, the immigration surplus would be even smaller than the above estimates suggest.
8. Consistent with these effects, Kenneth F. Scheve and Matthew J. Slaughter find that opposition to immigration in the United States is most intense among native workers with less than a high school degree. See Kenneth F. Scheve and Matthew J. Slaughter, *Globalization and the Perceptions of American Workers* (Washington, DC: Institute for International Economics, 2001).
9. Patricia Cortes, "The Effect of Low-Skilled Immigration on U.S. Prices: Evidence from CPI Data" (mimeo, MIT, November 2005). Based on her estimates, a 10 percent increase in the local immigrant population is associated with decreases in prices for labor-intensive services of 1.3 percent and other non-traded goods of 0.2 percent.
10. Also, immigration-induced population growth may worsen distortions due to poorly defined property rights over air, water, and public spaces. More people means more pollution and more congestion.

11. James P. Smith and Barry Edmonston, eds., *The New Americans: Economic, Demographic, and Fiscal Effects of Immigration* (Washington, DC: National Academies Press, 1997).
12. An additional potential benefit from immigration is that it may help the government manage unfunded pension liabilities. See Alan J. Auerbach and Philip Oreopoulos, "Analyzing the Fiscal Impact of U.S. Immigration," *American Economic Review*, Vol. 89, No. 2 (May 1999), pp. 176–180.
13. See Smith and Edmonston, *The New Americans;* and Steven A. Camarota, *The High Cost of Cheap Labor: Illegal Immigration and the Federal Budget* (Center for Immigration Studies, 2004). Illegal immigrants do contribute to tax revenues. They pay sales taxes on their consumption purchases and property taxes on dwellings they own or rent. In addition, many contribute to Social Security and federal and state income taxes. As of 1986, U.S. law requires employers to record the Social Security number and visa information of each immigrant employee. Many illegal immigrants present employers with Social Security cards that have invalid numbers. Between 1986 and 2000, annual Social Security contributions with invalid numbers rose from $7 billion to $49 billion (Social Security Administration, 2003). While the Social Security Administration does not immediately release these funds, they are eventually rolled into the general funds of the federal government.
14. See Office of Management and Budget, Department of Homeland Security, http://www.whitehouse.gov/omb/budget/fy2008/homeland.html.
15. See the Budget of the United States Government at http://origin.www.gpoaccess.gov.
16. Scheve and Slaughter, *Globalization and the Perceptions of American Workers.*
17. Frank D. Bean and Gillian Stevens, *America's Newcomers and the Dynamics of Diversity* (New York: Russell Sage Foundation, 2005).
18. Smith and Edmonston, *The New Americans.*
19. Gordon H. Hanson, *Why Does Immigration Divide America? Public Finance and Political Opposition to Open Borders* (Washington, DC: Institute for International Economics, 2005); Gordon Hanson, Kenneth Scheve, and Matthew Slaughter, "Public Finance and Individual Preferences over Globalization Strategies," *Economics and Politics*, forthcoming.
20. Hiring an existing guest worker would require the new employer to compensate the worker's existing employer by paying the amortized price of the visa right purchased when the worker was originally hired.

References

Auerbach, Alan J. and Philip Oreopoulos. "Analyzing the Fiscal Impact of U.S. Immigration." *American Economic Review*, Vol. 89, No. 2 (May 1999), pp. 176–80.

Bean, Frank D. and Gillian Stevens. *America's Newcomers and the Dynamics of Diversity.* New York: Russell Sage Foundation, 2005.

Borjas, George J. *Heaven's Door: Immigration Policy and the American Economy.* Princeton, NJ: Princeton University Press, 1999.

Borjas, George J. "The Labor Demand Curve is Downward Sloping: Reexamining the Impact of Immigration on the Labor Market." *Quarterly Journal of Economics,* Vol. 118, No. 4 (June 2003), pp. 1335–74.

Buchanan, Patrick J. *State of Emergency: The Third World Invasion and Conquest of America.* New York: Thomas Dunne, 2006.

Buchanan, Patrick J. "U.S. Pays the High Price of Empire." *Los Angeles Times,* September 18, 2001.

Bureau of International Labor Affairs. *Effects of the Immigration Reform and Control Act: Characteristics and Labor Market Behavior of the Legalized Population Five Years Following Legalization.* Washington, DC: U.S. Department of Labor, 1996.

Calavita, Kitty. *Inside the State: The Bracero Program, Immigration and the I.N.S.* New York: Routledge, Chapman and Hall, 1992.

Camarota, Steven A. *The Open Door: How Militant Islamic Terrorists Entered and Remained in the United States.* Center for Immigration Studies Paper No. 21 (2002).

Camarota, Steven A. *The High Cost of Cheap Labor: Illegal Immigration and the Federal Budget.* Center for Immigration Studies, 2004.

Card, David. "Is the New Immigration Really so Bad?" NBER Working Paper No. 11547 (August 2005).

Card, David and Ethan G. Lewis. "The Diffusion of Mexican Immigrants During the 1990s: Explanations and Impacts." In George J. Borjas, ed., *Mexican Immigration to the United States.* Chicago: University of Chicago and National Bureau of Economic Research, forthcoming.

Cornelius, Wayne A. "Death at the Border: Efficacy and Unintended Consequences of U.S. Immigration Control Policy." *Population and Development Review,* Vol. 27, No. 4 (December 2001), pp. 661–85.

Cortes, Patricia. "The Effect of Low-Skilled Immigration on U.S. Prices: Evidence from CPI Data." Mimeo, MIT, November 2005.

Hanson, Gordon H. *Why Does Immigration Divide America? Public Finance and Political Opposition to Open Borders.* Washington, DC: Institute for International Economics, 2005.

Hanson, Gordon H. "Illegal Migration from Mexico to the United States." *Journal of Economic Literature,* Vol. 44, No. 4 (December 2006), pp. 869–924.

Hanson, Gordon H. and Antonio Spilimbergo. "Illegal Immigration, Border Enforcement, and Relative Wages: Evidence from Apprehensions at the U.S.-Mexico Border." *American Economic Review,* Vol. 89, No. 5 (December 1999), pp. 1337–57.

Hanson, Gordon H., Kenneth F. Scheve, and Matthew J. Slaughter. "Public Finance and Individual Preferences over Globalization Strategies." *Economics and Politics,* forthcoming.

Hollifield, James F. and Valerie F. Hunt. "Immigrants, Markets, and Rights: The US as an Emerging Migration State." Paper prepared for presentation at the Migration Ethnicity Meeting (MEM) at IZA in Bonn, Germany, May 13–16, 2006.

Huntington, Samuel P. *Who Are We? The Challenges to America's National Identity.* New York: Simon and Schuster, 2004.

Jasso, Guillermina and Mark R. Rosenzweig. "Selection Criteria and the Skill Composition of Immigrants: A Comparative Analysis of Australian and US Employment Immigration." Mimeo, New York University and Yale University, 2005.

Katz, Lawrence F. and David H. Autor, "Changes in the Wage Structure and Earnings Inequality." In Orley Ashenfelter and David Card, eds., *Handbook of Labor Economics, Vol. 3A,* Amsterdam: Elsevier Science, 1999, pp. 1463–1555.

Kossoudji, Sherrie A. and Deborah A. Cobb-Clark. "Coming out of the Shadows: Learning about Legal Status and Wages from the Legalized Population." *Journal of Labor Economics,* Vol. 20, No. 3 (July 2002), pp. 598–628.

Lowell, B. Lindsay. "H-1B Temporary Workers: Estimating the Population." Mimeo, Institute for the Study of International Migration, Georgetown University, 2000.

Martin, David A. "Twilight Statuses: A Closer Examination of the Unauthorized Population." Migration Policy Institute Policy Brief No. 2 (June 2005).

Martin, Susan. "U.S. Employment-Based Admissions: Permanent and Temporary." Migration Policy Institute Policy Brief No. 15 (January 2006).

Passel, Jeffrey S. "Estimates of the Size and Characteristics of the Undocumented Population." Pew Hispanic Center, 2006.

Scheve, Kenneth F. and Matthew J. Slaughter. *Globalization and the Perceptions of American Workers.* Washington, DC: Institute for International Economics, 2001.

Smith, James P. and Barry Edmonston, eds. *The New Americans: Economic, Demographic, and Fiscal Effects of Immigration.* Washington, DC: National Academy Press, 1997.

U.S. Department of Homeland Security. "2005 Yearbook of Immigration Statistics." Office of Immigration Statistics, 2006.

U.S. Government Accountability Office. "Immigration Enforcement: Preliminary Observations on Employment Verification and Worksite Enforcement." GAO-05-822T (June 21, 2005).

Van Hook, Jennifer, Weiwei Zhang, Frank D. Bean, and Jeffrey S. Passel. "Foreign-Born Emigration: A New Approach and Estimates Based on Matched CPS Files." *Demography,* Vol. 43, No. 2 (May 2006), pp. 361–82.

Zimmerman, Wendy and Karen C. Tumlin. "Patchwork Policies: State Assistance for Immigrants under Welfare Reform." Urban Institute Paper No. 21 (April 1999).

Reading Analytically

1. The questions surrounding illegal immigration are numerous and various—starting from the illegality itself. After all, if it is illegal, it is for some simply wrong and should be stopped. How does Hanson's essay avoid that simple conclusion and instead approach the topic from a very different perspective? What is that perspective? Where in this essay does he acknowledge that he is not examining all facets of the issue?
2. The section entitled "Benefits and Costs of Immigration" uses a comparison/contrast model to examine the relative positives and negatives of illegal immigration upon economics of the country. Trace this argument paragraph by paragraph, and describe the way that he organizes this section to show both benefits and costs. What kinds of transitions between paragraphs does he use?
3. In the "Final Considerations" section of the essay, Hanson builds an argument for the centrality of economic matters in our policy making. Summarize his key recommendations for future policy and the rationale that he presents for these conclusions.

Reading Across Disciplinary Communities

1. Economics is a field of study that relies heavily upon cost/benefit analysis. Do some research on the concept of cost/benefit analysis, and describe the way that this author uses that methodology as an organizational tool for his essay.
2. Though this is in some ways a scholarly study of an economic issue, this piece is also an applied genre; that is, it goes beyond merely looking at issues theoretically, and develops recommendations within the form of a "Special Report." What parts of this piece suggest that it is meant to spur action rather than merely to present and analyze data, and therefore make it a piece of applied, rather than theoretical, science?

TIM KANE AND KIRK A. JOHNSON

The Real Problem with Immigration . . . and the Solution

This essay suggests that "the real problem presented by illegal immigration is security, not the supposed threat to the economy," and develops an argument as to what steps need to be taken in an age of terrorism to ensure the security of Americans. As such, it goes beyond the straight, quantitative economic analysis offered in the previous piece by Gordon H. Hanson, and instead looks at the issue from a wider perspective of its impact upon our culture.

Tim Kane, Ph.D., is Bradley Fellow in Labor Policy and Kirk A. Johnson, Ph.D., is a Senior Policy Analyst in the Center for Data Analysis at the Heritage Foundation, a conservative think tank. As such, this piece, though clearly drawing upon the considerable expertise of its authors, has a political and social agenda as well. That, of course, does not mean that it is not of value. Quite to the contrary, it offers a set of recommendations that are based upon conditions that these authors suggest already exist and a set of beliefs held by many Americans. Still, you might consider as you read how the data and statistics presented here interact with the political agenda of its authors and the organization for whom it was written. To learn more about this organization, you can visit its Web site at www.heritage.org.

America's exceptional status as a "nation of immigrants" is being challenged by globalization, which is making both migration and terrorism much easier. The biggest challenge for policymakers is distinguishing illusory immigration problems from real problems. One thing is quite clear: The favored approach of recent years—a policy of benign neglect—is no longer tenable. Members of both the Senate and the House of Representatives recognize this and deserve credit for striving to craft a comprehensive law during this session of Congress.

In 2005, immigration policy received far more genuine attention on Capitol Hill, and Members of Congress from both sides of the aisle are now considering what to do about immigration policy. Their various efforts have focused on a wide variety of changes in current policy, including improving border security, strengthening employer verification of employment, establishing a new temporary guest worker program, and offering some level of amnesty to illegal immigrants currently living in the United States. At present, these proposals are working their way through the legislative process.

However, to achieve results, immigration reform must be comprehensive. A lopsided, ideological approach that focuses exclusively on border security while ignoring migrant workers (or vice versa) is bound to fail. If Congress passes another law that glosses over the fundamental contradictions in the status quo, then the status quo will not change. Thinking through the incentives is the key to success.

The Real Problem

Illegal immigration into the United States is massive in scale. More than 10 million undocumented aliens currently reside in the U.S., and that population is growing by 700,000 per year.[1] On one hand, the presence of so many aliens is a powerful testament to the attractiveness of America. On the other hand, it is a sign of how dangerously open our borders are.

Typical illegal aliens come to America primarily for better jobs and in the process add value to the U.S. economy. However, they also take away value by weakening the legal and national security environment. When three out of every 100 people in America are undocumented (or, rather, documented with forged and faked papers), there is a profound security problem. Even though they pose no direct security threat, the presence of millions of undocumented migrants distorts the law, distracts resources, and effectively creates a cover for terrorists and criminals.

In other words, the real problem presented by illegal immigration is security, not the supposed threat to the economy. Indeed, efforts to curtail the economic influx of migrants actually worsen the security dilemma by driving many migrant workers underground, thereby encouraging the culture of illegality. A non-citizen guest worker program is an essential component of securing the border, but only if it is the right program.

It is important to craft a guest worker program intelligently. While there are numerous issues involved in such a program, many of which are beyond the scope of this paper, the evidence indicates that worker migration is a net plus economically. With this in mind, there are 14 principles—with an eye toward the economic incentives involved—that should be included as part of a guest worker program.

Immigration Benefits and Costs

An honest assessment acknowledges that illegal immigrants bring real benefits to the supply side of the American economy, which is why the business community is opposed to a simple crackdown. There are economic costs as well, given America's generous social insurance institutions. The cost of securing the border would logically exist regardless of the number of immigrants.

The argument that immigrants harm the American economy should be dismissed out of hand. The population today includes a far higher percentage (12 percent) of foreign-born Americans than in recent decades, yet the economy is strong, with higher total gross domestic product (GDP), higher GDP per person, higher productivity per worker, and more Americans working than ever before. Immigration may not have caused this economic boom, but it is folly to blame immigrants for hurting the economy at a time when the economy is simply not hurting. As Stephen Moore pointed out in a recent article in *The Wall Street Journal:*

> The increase in the immigration flow has corresponded with steady and substantial reductions in unemployment from 7.3 percent to 5.1 percent over the past two decades. And the unemployment rates have fallen by 6 percentage points for blacks and 3.5 percentage points for Latinos.[2]

Whether low-skilled or high-skilled, immigrants boost national output, enhance specialization, and provide a net economic benefit. The 2005 *Economic Report of the President* (ERP) devotes an entire chapter to immigration and reports that "A comprehensive accounting of the benefits and costs of immigration shows the benefits of immigration exceed the costs."[3] The following are among the ERP's other related findings:

- Immigrant unemployment rates are lower than the national average in the U.S.;
- Studies show that a 10 percent share increase of immigrant labor results in roughly a 1 percent reduction in native wages—a very minor effect;
- Most immigrant families have a positive net fiscal impact on the U.S., adding $88,000 more in tax revenues than they consume in services; and
- Social Security payroll taxes paid by improperly identified (undocumented) workers have led to a $463 billion funding surplus.

The macroeconomic argument in favor of immigration is especially compelling for highly educated individuals with backgrounds in science, engineering, and information technology. The increasing worry about outsourcing jobs to other nations is just one more reason to attract more jobs to America by insourcing labor. If workers are allowed to work inside the U.S., they immediately add to the economy and pay taxes, which does not happen when a job is outsourced. Therefore, capping the number of H-1B visas limits America's power as a brain "magnet" attracting highly skilled workers, thereby weakening U.S. firms' competitiveness.

Congress increased the number of H-1B visas by 20,000 in November 2004 after the annual cap was exhausted on the first day of fiscal year (FY) 2005.[4] On August 12, 2005, the U.S. Citizenship and Immigration Service announced that it had already received enough H-1B applications for FY 2006 (which began October 1, 2005) and would not be accepting any more applications for the general selection lottery.[5] These and other numbers show that more workers from abroad, not fewer, are needed.

Still, critics of this type of insourcing worry that jobs are being taken away from native-born Americans in favor of low-wage foreigners. Recent data suggest that these fears are overblown. While the nation's unemployment rate generally has remained just above 5 percent over the past year, unemployment in information technology now stands at a four-year low of 3.7 percent.[6]

While the presence of low-skill migrant workers can be construed as a challenge to low-skill native workers, the economic effects are the same as the effects of free trade—a net positive and a leading cause of economic growth. A National Bureau of Economic Research study by David Card found that "Overall, evidence that immigrants have harmed the opportunities of less educated natives is scant."[7] The consensus of the vast majority of economists is that the broad economic gains from openness to trade and immigration far outweigh the isolated cases of economic loss. In the long run, as has been documented in recent years, the gains are even higher.[8]

A simple example is instructive in terms of both trade and immigration. An imaginary small town has 10 citizens: some farmers, some ranchers, a fisherman, a tailor, a barber, a cook, and a merchant. A new family headed by a young farmer moves to town. His presence is resented by the other farmers, but he also consumes from the other business in town—getting haircuts, eating beef and fish, having his shirts sewn and pressed, and buying supplies at the store, not to mention paying taxes. He undoubtedly boosts the supply side of the economy, but he also boosts the demand side. If he were run out of town for "stealing jobs," his demand for everyone's work would leave with him.

The real problem with undocumented immigrant workers is that flouting the law has become the norm, which makes the job of terrorists and drug traffickers infinitely easier. The economic costs of terrorism can be very high and very real, quite apart from the otherwise positive economic impact of immigration. In order to separate the good from the bad, there is no substitute for a nationwide system that identifies all foreign persons present within the U.S. It is not sufficient to identify visitors upon entry and exit; rather, all foreign visitors must be quickly documented.

Economic Principles for an Effective Guest Worker Program

To this end, 14 economic principles should be borne in mind in crafting an effective guest worker program:

1. **All guest workers in the U.S. should be identified biometrically.** Technologically, a nationwide system of biometric identification (fingerprints, retina scans, etc.) for visitors has already been developed for the US–VISIT program. A sister "WORKER–VISIT" program is essential for enforcement efforts and would help American companies to authenticate guest workers efficiently. There is at present no effective system of internal enforcement, but the Department of Homeland Security (DHS) has in place a "basic pilot employment verification program"[9] that demonstrates the potential effectiveness of using such technology with guest workers to discourage undocumented work arrangements. Employers who want to hire guest workers should be required to verify electronically that the particular worker has registered with WORKER–VISIT and is eligible to work in the United States.
2. **Existing migrant workers should have incentives to register with the guest worker program.** A guest worker program that is less attractive to migrant workers than the status quo will fail. Therefore, the new law for guest workers should include both positive incentives for compliance and negative incentives (punishments) for non-compliance. For example, a program that caps the tenure of guest workers at six years can be expected to experience massive noncompliance at the six-year point because a hard cap on tenure is essentially an incentive to skirt the law. If the goal is to limit the number of *undocumented* foreign workers, then renewable short-term work permits have a greater likelihood of success than a single permit with an inflexible expiration date.
3. **U.S. companies need incentives to make the program work.** Immigration reform will be successful if—and probably only if—American companies support its passage and enforcement. A new law must

therefore avoid both onerous red tape (e.g., requiring an exhaustive search of native workers before a job can be offered to migrants) and any provision that would make it easier to hire guest workers than it is to hire natives (e.g., waiving payroll taxes on guest workers that must be paid on native worker payrolls). Perhaps the most important incentive is a negative one: The new law should include funding for a system of internal enforcement to police and prosecute companies that break the law.

4. **Guest worker status should not be a path to citizenship and should not include rights to U.S. social benefits.** If the incentive to work in the U.S. is artificially enhanced with a promise of potential citizenship, foreign migrants will be oversupplied. Citizenship carries with it tremendous benefits (e.g., social spending and entitlement programs) that should be provided only to American citizens. For example, unemployment insurance benefits should never go to foreign visitors. Providing benefits such as unemployment insurance, welfare, Head Start, and other payments to visiting workers will significantly distort the incentives to migrate to the U.S. The legal status equivalent of guest workers is that of tourists—people who reside in America temporarily and are bound by U.S. law but do not have any claim on citizenship or its benefits.
5. **Efficient legal entry for guest workers is a necessary condition for compliance.** Existing illegal migrants should be required to leave the U.S. and then allowed a system of entry through border checkpoints with strict conditions for identification, documentation, and compliance with U.S. law. If the guest worker program instead involves prolonged waits for reentry or a lottery for work visas, existing migrant workers will have little incentive to comply with the law. Moreover, such reforms will be perceived as attempts to shrink the supply of migrant labor and will be resisted. However, a program of efficient *legal* entry for migrants who comply with biometric identification will not deter compliance and will encourage migrants to utilize the formal channels of entry rather than jumping the border.
6. **Efficient legal entry should be contingent upon a brief waiting period** to allow law enforcement agencies the time needed to screen incoming workers. A waiting period of at least a few days will give law enforcement agencies time to screen incoming visitors' biometrics against criminal and terrorist databases.
7. **Provisions for efficient legal entry will not be amnesty,** nor will they "open the floodgates." Such a system will actually encourage

many migrants to exit, knowing that they will be able to return under reasonable regulations. This is in stark contrast to the status quo, in which the difficulty and uncertainty of reentering the U.S. effectively discourage aliens from leaving. Documented migrant workers would enter a new status: not citizen, not illegal, but rather temporary workers.

As for opening the floodgates, the reality is that they are already open. More to the point, labor markets operate effectively to balance supply and demand, and those markets are currently in balance. Creating a new category of legal migrants would not change that equilibrium, provide unfair benefits to undocumented aliens over others, or be tied to citizenship, but it would enhance security.

8. **Government agencies should not micromanage migrant labor.** Any federal attempt to license migrants by occupation—micromanaging the market for migrant labor—would be a dangerous precedent and would likely fail. Socialized planning of any market is inferior to the free market, and its implementation is dangerous on many levels. First, allowing government management of the migrant labor market would be terrible precedent for later intrusion into all U.S. labor markets. Second, it would be open to abuse, vulnerable to corruption, and inefficient even if run by angels.

   For example, in the case of a worker certified as an avocado picker who has carpentry skills that his employer would like to utilize and promote, why should the worker and his employer have to petition a Labor Department bureaucrat just to revise the worker's *skill* certification? Equally implausible is a program that requires migrants and businesses to know one another prior to entry and file the relevant paperwork. Labor markets do not work this way. Such schemes would quickly prove ineffective and lead right back to the status quo. Real labor markets work informally, and the power of the market should be utilized to make the guest worker program function efficiently.

9. **The guest worker program should not be used as an excuse to create another large federal bureaucracy.** The inherent risk of authorizing a new guest worker program is that it will establish a new, unwieldy federal bureaucracy that outgrows its budget and mandate. Critics contend that the federal government is ill-equipped to handle the substantial influx of people who would enter the U.S. through a guest worker program. They further cite

the long backlogs that plague other immigration programs, most notably the green card program.

One way to alleviate this problem is to involve the private sector in the guest worker visa process, much as gun retailers are integrated into the criminal background checks of gun buyers. Many parts of the guest worker visa process could be facilitated by contracting out certain parts of the process, including paperwork processing, interviewing of visa candidates (if necessary), coordinating with the DHS and federal law enforcement agencies on background checks, facilitating placement with prospective employers, and facilitating the exit upon expiration of the visa. As long as the private contractor has no conflict of interest in the visa selection or placement process, such a system should be better than another federal bureaucracy.

10. **Bonds should be used to promote compliance after entry.** There are many smart ways that bonds could be used to manage the immigrant pool. In one system, guest workers would pay upon entry for a bond that is redeemable upon exit. An individual who wanted to recoup the money would comply with the overall guest worker system and other U.S. laws, effectively acting as part of a self-enforcing network that discourages non-bonded, undocumented migrants. An alternative arrangement would have U.S. companies paying for the bonds as a right to hire some number of workers. If Congress felt compelled to cap the number of guest workers, the bonds could be treated like property rights and bid on to establish the market value of a guest worker. In both cases, the dollar value of the bond would be repaid after the migrant exited the U.S. but would be forfeit if the migrant went into the black market economy.
11. **Guest workers should be required to find a sponsoring employer** within one month (or some other reasonable period of time). The employer would verify via WORKER–VISIT that the particular worker is eligible to be employed in the United States. If the migrant cannot locate an employer within the time frame, the law should require that he or she leave the country. A sponsorship system is an efficient alternative to government management of the supply of and demand for migrant labor. It would be self-checking because employers could be required to submit payroll records regularly for automated review, which would identify the guest workers at each location. If employment with a sponsor

ended, the worker would be allowed a similar reasonable period of time to find a new employer. Existing undocumented workers should find it relatively easy to get sponsorship with current employers, so the act of leaving the country and reentering would neither discourage their compliance nor come at the expense of legal migrants.

12. **Day laborers should be required to find long-term sponsoring employers.** The presence of tens of thousands of day laborers in the U.S.[10] may seem to pose a challenge to immigration reform, but the day labor market should not be given an exemption. A functioning WORKER–VISIT program would likely motivate the creation of intermediary firms that employ day laborers and connect them with customers in a more formal market that develops along the lines of subcontracting firms that are already active in gardening, house-cleaning, janitorial services, accounting, and night security. Intermediary firms could offer day laborers in teams of variable sizes, allowing the hiring firms to avoid the hassles of sponsoring and documentation paperwork. Skeptics might protest that most subcontracted jobs are routine (even regularly scheduled), whereas day labor is by nature last-minute and unpredictable. However, that is not really true in the aggregate, especially when compared with other last-minute industries like plumbing/flood control or emergency towing. Competitive firms can meet demand with very little slack as long as free-market incentives are in place.
13. **Migrants and employers who do not comply with the new law should be punished.** Migrants who decline to register and are subsequently apprehended inside the U.S. should be punished with more than deportation. Deportation is not a disincentive. The Cornyn–Kyl bill (S. 1438) contains a good proposal along these lines: a 10-year ban on guest worker participation for migrants who do not comply with the new program.[11] Congress should also consider a lifetime prohibition on violators' applying for and receiving U.S. citizenship. The law should introduce steep penalties as well, including prison time and seizure of assets of undocumented workers and their employers. There is no justification for working outside the system, especially a system that allows free entry. The law would establish a date certain after which all migrants in the U.S. must be registered or face these penalties. The lifetime ban on the opportunity to acquire U.S. citizenship

would be a strong incentive for undocumented immigrants to enter the process of documentation. Likewise, firm, consistent, *enforced* penalties against employers would create the proper incentives for compliance.

14. **All migrants should respect American law and traditions.** The requirement to obey all laws is not optional for new citizens and should not be optional for visitors. While we encourage and insist on the primacy of American values for those who join our workforce, we should also remember the full spectrum of values ourselves. The Statue of Liberty reminds us that we are all equal, regardless of ethnicity, origin, or even state of wretchedness, and that America will continue to be a land of opportunity.

Conclusion

The century of globalization will see America either descend into timid isolation or affirm its openness. Throughout history, great nations have declined because they built up walls of insularity, but America has been the exception for over a century. It would be a tragedy if America were to turn toward a false sense of security just when China is ascending with openness, Western Europe is declining into isolation, and the real solution is so obvious from our own American heritage.

Notes

1. Congressional Budget Office, "The Role of Immigrants in the U.S. Labor Market" November 2005, at *www.cbo.gov/ftpdocs/68xx/doc6853/11-10-Immigration.pdf* and Jeffrey S. Passel, "Unauthorized Migrants: Numbers and Characteristics," Task Force on Immigration and America's Future, Pew Hispanic Center, June 14, 2005 at *pewhispanic.org/files/reports/46.pdf.*
2. Stephen Moore, "More Immigrants, More Jobs," *The Wall Street Journal,* July 13, 2005, p. A13.
3. Council of Economic Advisers, *Economic Report of the President* (Washington, D.C.: U.S. Government Printing Office, 2005), pp. 93–116.
4. These additional visas are available only to individuals who have master's degrees or higher from a U.S. university.
5. Press release, "USCIS Reaches H-1B Visa Cap," U.S. Department of Homeland Security, U.S. Citizenship and Immigration Service, August 12, 2005, at *uscis.gov/graphics/publicaffairs/newsrels/H-1Bcap_12Aug05.pdf* (December 27, 2005).
6. Eric Chabrow, "IT Employment on Upswing," *Information Week,* April 4, 2005, at *www.informationweek.com/story/showArticle.jhtml?articleID=160403526* (December 27, 2005).

7. David Card, "Is the New Immigration Really So Bad?" National Bureau of Economic Research *Working Paper* No. 11547, August 2005.
8. See IDG News Service, "Study: Offshore Outsourcing Helps U.S. Economy," March 30, 2004, at *www.itworld.com/Career/1826/040330outsourcing* (December 27, 2005).
9. Associated Press, "Firms Test Web Immigration Check," September 5, 2005, at *www.wired.com/news/privacy/0,1848,68761,00.html* (November 3, 2005). See also U.S. Department of Homeland Security, U.S. Citizenship and Immigration Service, "SAVE Program: Employment Verification Pilot Programs," at *uscis.gov/graphics/services/SAVE.htm#two* (December 27, 2005).
10. Abel Valenzuela, Jr., "Working on the Margins: Immigrant Day Labor Characteristics and Prospects for Employment," University of California at San Diego, Center for Comparative Immigration Studies *Working Paper* No. 22, May 2000.
11. The Cornyn–Kyl bill is a good start, but it also has a number of flaws that could be fixed. See James Jay Carafano, Ph.D., Janice L. Kephart, and Alane Kochems, "The Cornyn–Kyl Immigration Reform Act: Flawed But Fixable," Heritage Foundation *Executive Memorandum* No. 982, September 23, 2005, at *www.heritage.org/Research/HomelandDefense/em982.cfm.*

Reading Analytically

1. As with Gordon H. Hanson's essay, this essay has a section titled "benefits and costs." Compare this section in each of the two pieces, and compare their approaches to this form of analysis and the conclusions reached by each.
2. Despite this organization's impulses to protect the borders and heritage of the United States, the authors suggest that fully stemming the tide of immigrants might worsen the problem. Why? How do these authors differentiate between closing the doors of the country and allowing for dangerously open access? Upon what is this opinion based?
3. Find at least three instances in which these authors refute contrary viewpoints held by others, and demonstrate how they go about addressing counterarguments. Illustrate this by providing specific examples.

Reading Across Disciplinary Communities

1. Although this piece is meant for a relatively general audience of citizens, it still takes on many of the attributes of a scholarly article, including the citation of sources. Describe the way that these well-educated authors use the methodologies and knowledge base of their discipline while still writing in an accessible style. Give at least five examples of how the authors translate complex information into a style that could be read by nonexperts.

2. Analyze the ways that these authors present their "Economic Principles for an Effective Guest Worker Program." How do they support each of the principles with specific rationales that are based upon their disciplinary knowledge? Choose at least three of these principles and discuss whether you find the rationale for each to be sufficient to build the case. Why or why not?

STEVEN SALAITA

Ethnic Identity and Imperative Patriotism

Arab Americans Before and After 9/11

This excerpt from Salaita's Anti-Arab Racism in the USA *considers the reception of Arab Americans in the United States both before and after 9/11, and examines the status of Arab Americans within the politics of minority groups more generally. Though discussing an issue that is largely within fields like law, economics, history, and political science, Salaita writes his piece from his background as a professor of American and Ethnic literature; he also draws upon his own experiences as an Arab American.*

As a scholar of literature, Salaita brings with him expertise in textual analysis as well as recent literary theory, which is much more deeply involved in social and cultural concerns than that of previous generations of literary critics. As you read, you might consider how both the style and the methodology of this piece of cultural critique reflects this scholar's disciplinary and personal backgrounds. You might also note the ways in which this essay introduces another dimension to the debate about immigration and the status of this ethnic group as American citizens who face a great many biases after 9/11.

This essay will examine the effects of 9/11 on Arab Americans and other minorities, with emphasis on pedagogy and literature. It altered nearly all aspects of American life; even the so-called restoration of "the American lifestyle" is a contrived metamorphosis given the deliberate manner in which American leaders urged its convalescence. The events of 9/11 and their aftermath leave social critics with a remarkably broad range of issues to examine, primary among them a more patriotic—some might say more defensive—sensibility among students and educators. This sensibility is especially *apropos* in relation to what are often referred to as ethnic or multicultural studies. (Even though both terms are problematic, I will use the more common designation *ethnic studies* to describe the area studies of non-White American ethnic groups.) Ethnic critics have long invoked and then challenged centers of traditional (White) American power. They also have maintained strong ties to radical politics; ethnic critics, in fact, have been pivotal in unmasking the workings of American imperialism and in turn formulating alternative politics in response to that imperialism, both domestic and international (for instance, Edward Said, Vine Deloria Jr., Robert Warrior, Elizabeth Cook-Lynn, Barbara Christian, Angela Davis, Lisa Suhair Majaj).

Because ethnic critics challenge the production and reproduction of American hegemony, we must explore how those challenges function in a newly reactive—indeed, at times oppressive—American atmosphere. After 9/11, dissent, a cornerstone of ethnic studies, was attacked as unpatriotic, a serious accusation in today's society. In modern American universities, which increasingly are seen as investments that ultimately must pay dividends, dissent—i.e., lack of patriotism—is conceptualized as irresponsible by enraged parents and conservative groups. Since dissent is inherent in ethnic studies, it is usually the target of the attacks (NoIndoctrination.org, for example, is filled with students complaining about professors who utilize minority discourses). An American Indian Studies professor put it to me this way in a recent conversation: "How do we get people to understand the reality of American imperialism in Indian communities when imperialism is such a taboo topic now?" With the appropriate variations, this is a crucial question for any scholar dealing with domestic or international communities that are in some sort of conflict with the United States.

As an Arab American critic, I feel particularly affected by the question enunciated above. If we alter it a bit, we are left with the following: how do instructors of Arab American culture and society comprehend the position of the Arab American community in the aftermath of 9/11? How have Arab American culture and society changed? How, in turn, has the pedagogy of Arab America changed? And how, most important, do we find a viable space to develop Arab American Studies now that Arab Americans receive the sort of attention for which our scholars once clamored?

The last question is resonant, albeit extraordinarily complex. While Arab American critics once lamented a lack of Arab American issues in various disciplines, the sudden inclusion of those issues across the academic spectrum is at best ambivalent. Before 9/11, Arab American scholars were only beginning to theorize the relationship between Arab Americans and the field of ethnic studies (as well as other fields and area studies). We therefore have little prior scholarship with which to work in speculating how to position in the Academy what has become a highly manifold community after 9/11. In the following sections, I will summarize relevant issues in Arab America before and after 9/11; analyze the post-9/11 terminology that shapes mainstream perceptions of Arabs and Arab Americans; discuss theoretical issues that influence both the production and reception of Arab American scholarship; and assess possible relationships among Arab American politics and the politics of other ethnic or minority groups.

Arab Americans Before and After

It perhaps is foolish to discuss the development of a communal scholarship in the aftermath of a particular event. We would like to think, after all, that scholarship—its production and reception—is shaped by more than reaction. Many of us also promote the semi-idealized notion that scholarship shapes events just as much as it is shaped by them. Literary critics, in particular, have attended to questions of influence and resistance for decades, a process that raised more questions with few answers. The recent ascendancy of ethnic literatures has both informed and complicated longstanding debates about the uses and usefulness of literature, which, before the rise of multiculturalism, focused almost exclusively on White authors of the traditional canon. That ascendance is especially resonant after 9/11, an event whose sociopolitical implications scholars and philosophers are only beginning to understand. I mention literature here because it is so often a site where cultural and moral conflicts are invoked and analyzed, indeed encoded. I want to explore those conflicts on their own in the hope that, later, we can better apply them to discussion of literature or the pedagogy of literature. More than anybody, Arab Americans experienced far-reaching sociopolitical implications following 9/11 without, unfortunately, generating a corresponding body of internally constructed—i.e., Arab American-produced—scholarship to examine the rapid transformations occurring in the community. These sociopolitical implications are only now starting to develop into analyzable phenomena. Most important, though,

Arab Americans did not have a mature scholarly apparatus before 9/11. It has proved challenging to develop one in response to an event that so drastically affected the make-up of the Arab American community.

The last point warrants some attention because it will be of central concern to this chapter. In the years preceding 9/11, Arab American scholars from a variety of disciplines were discussing Americans of Middle Eastern background as *Arab Americans—a* development whose importance should not be underestimated—and assessing some possibilities of coalescing a distinct area study around that category. Literary critics undertook a majority of the attempts, but were buttressed—sometimes conjointly—by the work of historians, anthropologists, creative writers, psychologists, philosophers, sociologists, lawyers, demographers, pollsters, and others. Although academic circles and American society in total occasionally acknowledged an Arab American entity, the community was largely, in Nadine Naber's words, "the 'invisible' racial/ethnic group" of the United States.[1] But 9/11 dramatically altered this reality. Arab Americans evolved from invisible to glaringly conspicuous (whether or not the conspicuousness was welcomed).

Such a drastic evolution in some cases reinforced the salience of pre-9/11 scholarship, but in other cases rendered it antiquated or, worse, useless. Before 9/11 scholars examined Arab American invisibility or marginality—or whatever other term they employed to denote peripherality—but after 9/11 they were faced with a demand to transmit or translate their culture to mainstream Americans. The demand was matched by an insatiable curiosity about Arabs and Arab Americans; everybody from "everyday" Americans to high-ranking politicians wanted to know about the people who had irrevocably altered American life. Arab Americans suddenly were visible, and because of the pernicious intentions of various law and intelligence agencies, that visibility was not necessarily embraced. Indeed, it was often feared and deplored. These issues suddenly forced Arab Americans into a paradigm shift whose implications are enormous because there was no stable paradigm from which to shift emphasis in the first place. An area study that had been exploratory immediately became too much in demand for its own good.

Another competing but no less relevant factor deals with the political sensibilities of the Arab American community. Michael Suleiman, Alixa Naff, Eric Hooglund, Nabeel Abraham, and Nadine Naber all agree that before the 1967 Arab–Israeli War, Arab Americans, who were overwhelmingly Christian at that point, tended to assimilate even while maintaining cultural features of the so-called Old World (e.g., food, theology, childrearing, family ties–the Arabic language, for the most part, was not passed down from immigrants to children). After 1967, however, many Arab Americans reclaimed a sense of nationalism. The nationalism, sparked in large part by glaring Arab dispossession, was reinforced by a new wave of Muslim Arab immigrants who had been politicized already in the Arab World and had no need, given America's fairly protected civil liberties, to hide their ethnic-religious identities. Newly arrived Christian and Druze Arabs did the same. A steady appearance of "pro-Arab" or "revisionist" historiography on the Near East in the following years helped to instill ethnic pride in Arab Americans, who, prior to 1967, had virtually no representation in popular and political American culture. By the 1990s, a thoroughly *Arab* consciousness existed among Arab immigrants and American-born Arabs, who rapidly were expressing that consciousness intellectually and creatively.

Although no single form of consciousness—or conception of *Arab American*—can be said to have existed during this period, scholars were on the verge of critical breakthroughs in the years directly preceding 9/11. This fact was evident in the publication of Michael Suleiman's edited volume *Arabs in America: Building a New Future*, Khaled Mattawa and Munir Akash's *Post Gibran: Anthology of New Arab American Writing*, and a series of theoretically sophisticated articles by Lisa Suhair Majaj. In the literary arena, Diana Abu-Jaber and Rabih Alameddine received wide acclaim for novels that invoked both Arab American and Near Eastern themes. Vibrant gatherings to celebrate Arab cultures and discuss Arab American concerns occurred across the United States, in large cities and rural towns. College students with half or quarter Arab blood, some three or four generations removed from the Arab World (usually Syria or Lebanon), suddenly found value in being Arab American and reclaimed their ethnicity by visiting the Near East to learn Arabic or work for NGOs in villages and refugee camps. This phenomenon can only be understood if we situate it with similar phenomena occurring with individuals from other ethnic groups—N. Scott Momaday's famous example of his mixedblood mother "choosing" to be Cherokee, for instance. It is no accident that such ethnic valuations, whatever their merits and problems, corresponded with the rise of the Black and Indian power movements of the 1960s and 1970s, as well as the National Association for the Advancement of Colored People (NAACP), the Southern Christian Leadership Conference (SCLC), and various anti-war organizations (even virulently anti-Arab groups like Meir

Kahane's Jewish Defense League helped to create an atmosphere in which ethnic identity assumed great importance). While it is difficult to comprehend fully the effects of those movements, they often gave marginalized, lonely, or ambivalent youth (or adults in some cases) the illusion of stable identity or a feeling of belonging to communities distinguishable from mainstream society. The feeling was especially powerful for those displeased with certain American politics. This motivation has been particularly resonant in Arab America.

The reclamation or recovery of an Arab American identity is in many ways analogous to the social trajectories of other ethnic groups, and can therefore be considered typical of modern American acculturation and deculturation. And yet international relations have played a prominent role in the construction and consolidation of Arab America as a social and political unit. Nothing has been of more concern to Arab Americans since 1967 than the Israel–Palestine conflict, although Iraq has also been pivotal since 1990. American support for Israel has long enraged Arab Americans (and others), thereby providing Arab Americans with a tangible rallying cry and political purpose. The support also has been an important binding force for a community that, despite popular perception, is far from homogeneous, containing as it does people with over 20 national backgrounds, a multitude of linguistic dialects, and numerous religions. Therefore, while Palestine may have expedited the coalescence of an Arab American identity, it in no way exclusively dictates or maintains it. Like any other ethnic group, Arab Americans function as a communal entity based on innumerable factors, both cultural and political.

Ultimately, though, it can be said that no single event shaped the destiny of Arab Americans more than 9/11. After 9/11, the Arab American community was thrust into the spotlight. This attention represented a drastic change from the community's previous position, for during the times that Arab Americans attempted to be noticed—times generally related to our flagship issue, Palestinian independence—it was rare for mainstream forums to acknowledge us. When Arab Americans were acknowledged, it was usually in the form of ridicule, dismissal, or an outright racism that had long been considered an unacceptable way to address other ethnic groups. It is a general rule that ambivalence will follow when a once-ignored or outright slandered community is suddenly offered unceasing attention and is asked to define and redefine itself daily. The peculiar nature of the sudden attention after 9/11 only did more to catalyze Arab Americans into serious introspective glances. That attention was simultaneously an outpouring of hostility and kindness. On the day of the attack, Rudy Giuliani and George W. Bush urged Americans not to engage in racial violence and to prevent any that might occur, as did practically every television commentator and politician of significance. For every racist comment and report of harassment, there were ten stories about "average" Americans going out of their way to make their Arab neighbors feel safe and welcome.

But what do those pronouncements actually reveal about the culture from which they were produced and the community at which they were directed? And what were their effects on both? First, while they were in some cases sincere when uttered by politicians and probably sincere in every case when uttered by ordinary citizens, the cultural impulses inspiring them cannot be considered altogether pure since they drew tacitly from a tradition of forced assimilation. (It is also problematic that such pronouncements needed constant repeating to begin with.) While the goodwill of everyday Americans cannot be called into question, one might look upon aspects of the discourse of American leaders with suspicion. They attempted to urge Arab Americans, before 9/11 generally anti-assimilationist and radical, into total assimilation. In this case, it was not a forced assimilation that other ethnic groups, primarily Natives, have experienced. It took the form of the repeated statements: "They're American, too"; "They're American, just like you"; "They also love this country." The suspicion I cite should be drawn out briefly. A community can accept the call, whether or not it was solicited, to be absorbed fully into the politics of its surrounding society only if it assumes that the surrounding society's politics are amenable to the community. This has never been the case with Arab Americans because the American government has long been involved in the Arab World in a way that most Arab Americans find invasive and unjust. Moreover, draconian legislation like the USA Patriot Act wholly contradicts the occasionally inclusive language of Congress and the Bush administration.

The Patriot Act, however, is only the first legislative initiative of what many legal scholars fear will be a series of federal resolutions that might severely limit civil liberties. In January 2003, Bill Moyers posted on the *NOW* website the text for the Domestic Security Enhancement Act (DSEA) (also known as Patriot Act II), which would further enable federal agents and intelligence officials to intrude in people's private lives and detain them for indefinite periods of time without legal counsel based solely on suspicion. This type of legislation may soon not be limited to visitors, immigrants, aliens, or permanent residents. American citizens also are under scrutiny. In February 2003, *The Nation*'s David Cole revealed the purpose of the DSEA. He writes.

> If the Patriot Act was so named to imply that those who question its sweeping new powers of surveillance, detention and prosecution are traitors, the DSEA takes that theme one giant step further. It provides that any citizen, even native-born, who supports even the lawful activities of an organization the executive branch deems "terrorist" is presumptively stripped of his or her citizenship. To date, the "war on terrorism" has largely been directed at noncitizens, especially Arabs and Muslims. But the DSEA would actually turn citizens associated with "terrorist" groups into aliens.

Cole later notes that suspect citizens "would then be subject to the deportation power, which the DSEA would expand to give the Attorney General the authority to deport any noncitizen whose presence he deems a threat to our 'national defense, foreign policy or economic interests.'"

The domestic environment, then, is one that terrifies many Arab Americans and keeps us from politics, especially Palestinian politics, because the fear of being harassed or arrested is more than mere paranoia. At the same time, numerous Arab Americans feel that we have no real leadership on which we can rely. Nobody genuinely speaks our concerns in the media and nobody has adequate power to protect us from FBI investigations should our names become suspicious to American officials. Arab Americans, and many others, are under the impression that speaking too loudly against the war on terror or American support for Israel is a viable cause for suspicion. In addition, Arab Americans cannot discuss on campus the conditions of Palestinian life in the Occupied Territories without harassment, complaints of anti-Americanism, or, worse, accusations of anti-Semitism.

All the issues enumerated above have appeared in Arab American literature. Directly following 9/11, Palestinian American poet Suheir Hammad penned a widely circulated poem, "First Writing Since," that explored her shared ethnicity with the hijackers and her shared nationality with their victims. The Arab American literary journal *Mizna* has run poems, short stories, and essays that deal with the effects of 9/11 on Arab American identity and on the relationship between Arab Americans and our Arab brethren (the first issue after 9/11 was devoted entirely to the attacks). The themes are constant and usually didactic: the authors feel closer to the American polity and concurrently isolated from it. That sort of theme denotes, as Bill Ashcroft and Pal Ahluwalia have described in relation to Edward Said, the paradox of identity.[12] In the year after 9/11, no critical study of identity in the Arab American community was published in a sociological, psychological, historical, or literary journal, with one exception: a *Middle East Report* devoted to the influence of 9/11 on Arab and Muslim Americans.[13] This lack of critical inquiry is, of course, highly problematic, as the Arab American community continues to enhance our ambivalence by allowing the dominant society to define us and speak on our behalf. Arab Americans seem on the verge of borrowing from the sensibilities common among scholars of other ethnic groups in proclaiming that no matter how well-intentioned the speaker, when it comes to community issues, it should be Arab Americans who have priority in speaking. One often finds this sentiment expressed in literature, since numerous Arab Americans find it the last haven of articulation that still belongs to them. Cultural journals such as *Mizna*, *JUSOOR*, and *al-Jadid* have therefore assumed great importance in the community during the past few years.

"The American Way of Life"

Some years back, I published a column in the *Palestine Chronicle* urging Arab Americans to reformulate a self-image by rejecting the vocabulary of *terrorism* employed so uncritically in today's United States. My columns for the paper usually elicited passionate reactions, but this one provoked outright anger from a few American readers whose vocabulary I had attacked. One reader demanded to know why I "split time between the United States and the Middle East," as my author bio explained. The message claimed that discomfiting motivations were evident in my article: "Apparently your dislike for the American way of life and the [policy of the] current administration to keep it that way, even if it means war, is a problem for you."

This formulation in many ways accurately highlights the relationship between Arab Americans and the larger society in which we live. Often accused of dual sympathies, Arab Americans feel sometimes as if we are removed (of our own accord) from the Arab World, but equally removed (not of our own accord) from the United States. Xenophobia certainly plays a role in the isolation many Arab Americans feel, but it would be foolish to limit our analysis to either xenophobia or racism. While the respondent to my article is most likely xenophobic and perhaps racist—would she have objected had I split time between the United States and, say, Britain?—her sensibilities can be attributed to a more profound phenomenon dating to the settlement of the New World.

I speak about a particular type of discourse that, with technical and temporal variations, has existed continuously in the United States, which I term *imperative patriotism*. Imperative patriotism assumes (or demands) that dissent in matters of governance and foreign affairs is unpatriotic and therefore unsavory. It is drawn from a longstanding sensibility that nonconformity to whatever at the time is considered to be "the national interest" is unpatriotic. Imperative patriotism is most likely to arise in settler societies, which usually need to create a juridical mentality that professes some sort of divine mandate to legitimize their presence on indigenous land. The juridical mentality impresses conformity on the settlers, who might otherwise demur when being asked to slaughter indigenes or when absorbing attacks by them. Hilton Obenzinger demonstrates that this mentality existed in early America, where settlers "invested New England settlement, and by extension all of America, with a sense of religious destiny: that the new society extinguishing the various indigenous peoples' claims to land and independence was a re-creation of the scriptural narrative of covenantal, chosen-people identity."

This sensibility has evolved into a detectable feature of modern American politics. When one hears George W. Bush present war on Iraq as a "war for civilization" and make statements such as "either you are for us or against us" and "God is on America's side," it becomes clear that the early settler ethos, in which the settlers had a divine mission conferred upon them, continues to influence American discourse—and, more important, American morality. Imperative patriotism arises in this context. I prefer the phrase *imperative patriotism* to the unmodified *patriotism* because the word *imperative* insinuates necessity and purpose. It further denotes a particular set of American desires (enumerated below) that connects to a historical dynamic. In modern America, while imperative patriotism functions at the levels of discourse and philosophy, it generates its strength most consistently at the level of morality. Imperative patriotism manifests itself most explicitly during wartime or domestic unrest. Ethnic nationalist movements, such as the American Indian Movement and Black Panthers, were widely considered to be inimical to American values and therefore also caused the manifestation of imperative patriotism. (Even movements using less nationalist rhetoric, such as the SCLC and Cesar Chavez's United Farm Workers, evoked fear in many Americans.) Moreover, imperative patriotism both informs and is derived from colonial discourse. Politicians frequently speak about the need to occupy Arab countries and "civilize" them by introducing the natives to "democracy." (Like the colonial discourse before it, this one rarely mentions the actual motivation for intervention: the plunder of resources, in this case oil.) Americans today hear so much about the need for their government's "leadership" in all areas of the world that most, like the Europeans before them, automatically equate colonization with generosity and moral strength.

Yet perhaps the most crucial (and discomfiting) feature of imperative patriotism is its relationship with xenophobia. While imperative patriotism has a symbiotic moral association with colonial discourse, it is more disconnected from xenophobia because it does not actually arise from xenophobia, which is a phenomenon that, to a degree, has its roots in European contact with Indians, but more traditionally has resulted from animosity over (perceived or real) economic disparity. On one level, xenophobia is a less vicious form of colonial discourse, but it more often results from a certain type of fear that is generated when people feel that their economic stability (or the possibility of it) is threatened—as, for instance, when laborers battle with immigrants over blue-collar jobs or when middle-to-upper-class Whites complain to city councils about immigrants moving into their neighborhoods. Imperative patriotism, however, tends to inform xenophobia, a fact that is expressed in statements such as, "If you don't like America, go back to where you came from"; "If you don't agree with the United States, why don't you just leave?"; and "A real American works hard and doesn't complain." These statements insinuate that "American" is a stable, fixed identity rooted in a physical and cultural Whiteness for which many immigrants do not qualify. They also indicate that in xenophobia narrow political suppositions often govern social behavior: to dissent from the imagined mores of America is to forfeit identification as American. Leaving the United States then becomes the only logical option.

It is easy to see how these suppositions are played out in the reader's complaint that I "dislike the American way of life." The reader assumes that only one or a few forms of thought and/or behavior constitute "the American way of life." This sensibility has long been common in the United States and has proliferated since 9/11, in no small part because of the colonial discourse arising from hawks in Washington. And yet it would be reductionist to attribute the sensibility to a crude xenophobia informed by imperative patriotism. It is better conceptualized as an articulation of imperative patriotism that appears at first glance to be crude xenophobia, but in reality brings to mind remnants of settler discourse with its rigid juridical undercurrents. One might argue that it is impossible to define "the American way of life" since the United States is a multicultural society with thousands of subcultures (not to mention the fact that numerous Central and South Americans also consider themselves to be "American"). Nevertheless, at the popular level, it is assumed that a "true" American is (or should be) patriotic and capitalistic, and, less explicitly, Christian and White.

Arab Americans exist as a composite of postmodern Americana and American subculture in this complex of issues. To various degrees, our positioning in the United States has been highly complex for some time, but 9/11 exacerbated the complexities by simultaneously endowing the community with sympathetic gestures and amplifying xenophobic outpourings of imperative patriotism, a mindset that is by its very nature antithetical to the Arab American experience. The irony of this positioning became evident when a church in Jacksonville, which has a sizeable Arab American population, posted a sign claiming that Mohammad condoned murder. While Arab Americans protested this stereotype, it was another Christian conservative, radio columnist Andy Martin of Florida, who offered the most vocal response: "I thought we were past that kind of bigotry and ignorance in Florida. But apparently not . . . Any religious leader who fosters bigotry is not a religious leader; he or she is espousing evil."

It is difficult to determine whether the discourse seen in the Jacksonville church sign might accurately be construed as racism. *Racism* is a complicated term, and ethnic studies scholars do their communities few favors by applying it loosely and uniformly to a wide range of discursive phenomena. In defining the Jacksonville discourse as racist, one also must contemplate whether all agents of imperative patriotism are racist. We are then left with questions about whether forms of racism expressed unconsciously are as pernicious, in intent and action, as outright racism. The same concern exists with xenophobia. It would be foolish to decontextualize these issues from the founding narratives of the United States. If ethnic cleansing and slavery, among other odious practices, played a salient role in the physical and psychological formation of the United States, then it should be no surprise that various types of racism survive. Indeed, one could claim that the United States has a collective sickness that results from never having officially confronted its destruction of Indian nations, and that this sickness accounts, however abstractly, for many persisting social problems (imperative patriotism, xenophobia, racism, sexism, discrimination). Rather than arguing whether various types of racism exist, we are better served interrogating the actual extent of their existence.

Arab Americans are in a special position to assist in that understanding. First of all, I would argue that the Jacksonville discourse is racist precisely because it cannot be decontextualized from (admittedly more noxious) incidents in the American past. When considering this sort of argument, our analytical framework should include the peculiar amalgam of premillenialism, Messianism, and extremism that marked European settlement of the New World, particularly in New England. Modern American racism developed as a result of the imagery of Indians and Africans promulgated by White settlers—a process that continues into the present—in addition to foreign intervention and biological determinism. Indeed, the covenantal Messianism with which early American settlers invested their identity invents and reinvents itself based on deeply encoded notions of racial superiority. Those notions have been modernized, sometimes disguised as pragmatism, and manage to pervade a surprisingly large portion of mainstream American discourse. The label of *racism* can thus be applied to anti-Arab vitriol independent of the severe dehumanization that occurs by construing a religious group's prophet as a murderer. If, after all, Mohammad is portrayed as subhuman, what does it imply about those who follow his religion?

Obviously, Arab Americans interact with the dominant American culture based on the specifics of Arab immigration and the subsequent development of the Arab American community. But once Arabs formed a distinct communal identity, as do all American ethnic minorities, we inherited a centuries-old history of ethnic-mainstream conflict that has yet to be assessed in detail, either before or after 9/11. Settlement, dispossession, slavery, and overseas imperialism all are included in that inheritance. The overseas imperialism has traditionally been most resonant in the Arab American community and is the centerpiece of the community's current reorganization. Like most other minorities, Arab Americans "piggyback" the ethnic tensions that were developed uniquely in the United States based primarily on the oppression of Blacks and Indians. Imperialism, however, is the most immediate issue facing Arab Americans, since much of the imperialism is directed at the Arab World (especially if we consider, as I do, Israel's occupation of the West Bank and Gaza Strip to be an aspect of American imperialism).

Based on this formulation, I reject the notion that anti-Arab racism was formed and has evolved based solely on social features (primarily geopolitics) detectable in the interaction of Arabism and Americana. We are better served looking at that racism as being on a continuum with America's roots in settler colonialism. A correlative settler colonialism in the West Bank, after all, accounts for much of the tension among the United States and Arab nations—and, by extension, Arab Americans. American racism had thrived for years before the first Arab arrived in North America; Arab Americans have faced an evolution of that racism since we began to vocally articulate a Middle Eastern identity after 1967 (which rehashed some of the tensions developed between the Founding Fathers and Muslim pirates off the Barbary Coast 200 years earlier). It is not necessarily a modern racism, but one that has been perpetually reformulated based on contemporary popular and political sentiment and a failure by American leaders to adequately confront the past, in philosophy by apologizing and erecting monuments, or in practice by eliminating colonization and dispossession in other parts of the world.

Thus 9/11, according to this analysis, did not really disrupt anti-Arab racism in any momentous way. Rather, it polarized attitudes that had been in place years before the word *terrorism* entered common parlance. While 9/11 forced most Americans to confront issues—foreign policy, civil liberties, immigration, minority rights—that had often been muted or ignored, a detectable pre-9/11 trajectory has reasserted itself: Those who were prone to racism or xenophobia before 9/11 (mainly the advocates of imperative patriotism) found a justification for them; conversely, those who were prone to support multiculturalism (mainly left-liberals and liberal arts academics) have used the 9/11 backlash against Arab Americans to argue in favor of cosmopolitanism and the retention of civil liberties. *New Republic* editor Martin Peretz, for example, has consistently conflated Islam and terrorism. In 1995, he proclaimed "that there is a convulsion in Islam, whose particular expression is terror." Alerting Americans to "the very real phenomenon of an international killer jihad," he later wrote, "So much of the spate of terror the world has witnessed [in the past] had been wrought by Arabs."

These sentiments played an enormous role in creating the sort of xenophobic culture that prompted physical attacks—leading, in some cases, to murder—on Arab Americans and those perceived to be Arab American (Sikhs, South Asians, Central Asians, Hispanics) by Americans determined to preserve imperative patriotism. Four years after Peretz's article, in a piece chillingly titled "Terrorism at the Multiplex," Joshua Muravchik echoed Peretz by announcing that "the image of Middle Eastern terrorists wreaking havoc in the streets of America is both compelling and only too plausible." After 9/11, the same set of stereotypes expressed with an almost childish vocabulary—"international killer jihad"?—continued unmolested, only this time with a rhetorical trope the authors considered infallible. Congressman Howard Coble (R-NC) stated on a radio call-in program that internment of Arab Americans is worth discussion because "some of these Arab Americans are probably intent on doing harm to us." Coble's use of the pronoun "us" is noteworthy. It indicates, much like the message I received in response to my *Chronicle* article, that according to the ethnography of imperative patriotism Arab Americans are not actually American. "Us" denotes difference, alterity, even though Coble contradicted his own grammar by adding "American" after "Arab" in juxtaposition with the pronoun "us." Coble's invocation of Japanese Americans also illustrates, with frightening clarity, that negative attitudes about Arab Americans exist in a historical continuum that in many cases led to horrifying behavior.

Reading Analytically

1. What are Salaita's opening assumptions about American culture and its relationship with nonwhites? How does he support those assumptions? Are they likely to bias his arguments and conclusions, or are they backed up well enough to support a reasonable argument?
2. Salaita suggests that "it perhaps is foolish to discuss the development of a communal scholarship in the aftermath of a particular event" because "we would like to think, after all, that scholarship ... is shaped by more than reaction." Why does he begin his own analysis of post-9/11 treatment of Arab Americans with this self-critique? Does he manage to overcome this problematic approach as the essay proceeds?
3. Salaita develops the term *imperative patriotism* as part of his argument. What does he mean by that term? How does it differ from other definitions of patriotism?

Reading Across Disciplinary Communities

1. As a scholar of literary studies, Salaita is trained in textual analysis—in interpreting the deeper meanings of words. How does he use that skill in this essay? Give at least three examples of his textual interpretation of the words of others, and demonstrate how this technique is used to build his argument.
2. Salaita's essay is quite likely to cause discomfort—and perhaps strong reactions—in many Americans. In fact, his work has spurred a great many angry responses on Web sites and blogs. Consider whether his status as a professor of ethnic literature, and its methods as illustrated in this excerpt from his book, provides him with a strong enough basis upon which to make the claims he does. Do any of these claims cross the line from "scholarship" to personal attack?

Writing Across Disciplines: Interdisciplinary Writing Opportunities

1. Though this chapter is based in the ideals of citizenship and immigration, it also touches on issues related to race and ethnicity, discussing the specific challenges faced by our culture toward embracing diversity. Focusing upon a particular racial or ethnic group, research the various challenges faced by that group in finding their way into the American culture.
2. The social sciences perform much of their work through observation and interviews. If you have access to a particular immigrant community in your area, perform some primary research by visiting community organizations or interviewing recent immigrants. Then write a report that raises what you find to be some of the key challenges—and methods used to overcome those challenges—of that group in becoming Americans.
3. One of the most important ways that citizenship is fostered is through educational systems. Study the practices of teachers in areas that have a large immigrant population, and describe the methods used to socialize immigrants to the American form of government and way of life.
4. The article by Gordon H. Hanson and that by Tim Kane and Kirk A. Johnson address the economic impact of illegal immigration on America. Do some further research on this topic, and create a pamphlet for U.S. employers that highlights the ways that hiring undocumented workers can affect the U.S. economy.

5. One of the things that holds a culture together is its language. As such, there has been much debate about whether English should be made the "official language" of the country (as it is for the majority of states). Do some research on the debate about this topic, and lay out the benefits and disadvantages of institutionalizing English—or of bilingualism—to the ideals of the American republic.

5 CHAPTER

Studying the New Face of War

Definitions, Causes, and Effects Across Disciplines

As is noted by Pertti Joenniemi in his essay included below, "the concept of war no longer conveys meaning the way it formerly did." Wars used to have clear beginnings and ends, recognizable victors and vanquished, and clear(er) missions. In an age of terrorism and long-standing tribal and religiously based wars, it is more difficult to understand not only what we mean by war, but what peace might look like. The selections in this chapter create an interdisciplinary gallery of thought, demonstrating the ways that writers within and across disciplines address these key concepts from a number of perspectives and through a number of methodologies. As you read the selections here, you can not only learn more about what we mean by war and peace in our times, but also how each of these areas of study contribute to the attempt to better understand one of the great nemeses of human society.

But the word *war* is also used in many other ways by our culture: We are fighting wars on racism, illegal immigration, terror, AIDS, poverty, drugs, crime, cyberpredators. . . . The list seems endless. We are also seeking peace in the Middle East, peace in our lives, domestic peace,

peace of mind. ... What are we to make of all this talk about war and peace?

Of course, the "real" war, war that involves armed conflict (and the peace that signals the end of that) should be easier to define. But even that most basic version of war is muddied in a time when our armed conflicts are geared against multinational terrorism, whose perpetrators are not directly associated with a particular government. At the time of this writing, America has been at war *in* Iraq (though not *with* Iraq) for over six years, and even longer *in* Afghanistan. That was one of the key problems our country faced when we were attacked on September 11, 2001: How do we strike back, or even defend ourselves, when those responsible are such an amorphous group? We face similar problems with respect to finding peace. How do we know when such a war has been won or lost, or even when it is over, when there is not a clear group to wave a white flag or bring us to peace talks?

As the selections in this chapter demonstrate, this new kind of war raises a great many questions for a great many communities. Those in the media and those in politics debate the political gains and losses of war as well as its place in history; those in the empirical sciences try to assess the causes, effects, and costs of war in ways that stem from direct observation; those in the humanities evaluate the ethical dilemmas caused by war, and especially in wars that carry so few moral absolutes; and those who study the law sort through the thorny debates about the war on terror that have tested the adaptability of our constitution in an age when others don't follow law.

The chapter begins with two classic philosophical investigations on the circumstances under which war can be considered just, the first by Roman rhetorician and statesman Marcus Tullius Cicero and the second by Roman Catholic theologian Thomas Aquinas. These two statements are among the most influential within a large body of philosophical and ethical considerations of whether such a violent course is sometimes necessary. If you would like to read more on this topic, search for information on "just war theory," and you will find a great deal more.

Following these historical statements on the topic, Pertti Joenniemi brings the conversation into the 21st century. Drawing upon her expertise as a foreign relations scholar, she addresses the changing definitions of war in a post Cold War and post-9/11 world—and why those definitions matter a great deal. Then political scientist Jason Royce Lindsay extends the discussion about contemporary warfare, suggesting that wars like the current ones are less likely to directly affect the U.S. populace, and so may not have domestic pressures to avoid or cease them.

Studies of this broad set of social topics, however, are not limited to those disciplines directly involved in the study of politics. Thomas Pogge, a Professor of Philosophy, explores the ethical implications of the worlds' reactions to terrorism, asking how the "collateral damage" of war upon innocent citizens can somehow be justified by those who wage it. A group of social scientists, Samir Quota, Raija-Leena Punamaki, Thomas Miller, and Eyad El-Sarraj, use survey methodology typical of their discipline to gauge the effects, rather than the causes, of war. They study the effect of growing up in a perpetual war zone, the Gaza strip, upon a generation of children. And the final piece in the chapter, written by a law professor, asks whether the rights of individuals accused of terrorism have been violated by policies that label them as "enemy combatants"—a question that is very much on the mind of U.S. citizens as we reflect upon the way the war on terror was carried out.

Taken as a whole, then, this array of disciplinary and interdisciplinary explorations of one of the defining factors of the human experience demonstrates not only the importance of this topic to our time, but also the varied ways writers have attempted to come to grips with its meaning, its causes, and its effects.

MARCUS TULLIUS CICERO

Occasions that Justify War

Marcus Tullius Cicero (106 B.C.E. – 43 B.C.E.) was a Roman statesman and rhetorician. He lived during the period when Rome was transitioning from a republic to an empire. A staunch proponent of republican rule over monarchy, Cicero was known for his oratorical skills, and wrote a series of works that are classics in the rhetorical tradition. In the end, his defense of republican rule over the imperial forces led to his execution by order of Marc Antony, who also ordered that his hands were to be cut off and nailed to the rostra (speaking platform) in the Roman forum for having written against Antony's rule.

In this passage from his work De Officiis (On Obligations), *Cicero uses the methods of rhetoric to reason out the situations within which war could be considered just. This passage is presented in the context of the wider set of "occasions" within which one's duty as a good man becomes complicated by circumstances. In this way, Cicero is drawing upon both the philosophical method of investigating ethics and the rhetorical tradition of treating each case (as Aristotle suggested) within its given occasion. Note the ways that Cicero limits a just war to a very specific set of circumstances.*

X

Occasions often arise, when those duties which seem most becoming to the just man and to the "good man," as we call him, undergo a change and take on a contrary aspect. It may, for example, not be a duty to restore a trust or to fulfil a promise, and it may become right and proper sometimes to evade and not to observe what truth and honour would usually demand. For we may well be guided by those fundamental principles of justice which I laid down at the outset: first, that no harm be done to anyone; second, that the common interests be conserved. When these are modified under changed circumstances, moral duty also undergoes a change and it does not always remain the same. For a given promise or agreement may turn out in such a way that its performance will prove detrimental either to the one to whom the promise has been made or to the one who has made it. If, for example, Neptune, in the drama, had not carried out his promise to Theseus, Theseus would not have lost his son Hippolytus; for, as the story runs, of the three wishes/a that Neptune had promised to grant him the third was this: in a fit of anger he prayed for the death of Hippolytus, and the granting of this prayer plunged him into unspeakable grief. Promises are, therefore, not to be kept, if the keeping of them is to prove harmful to those to whom you have made them; and, if the fulfilment of a promise should do more harm to you than good to him to whom you have made it, it is no violation of moral duty to give the greater good precedence over the lesser good. For example, if you have made an appointment with anyone to appear as his advocate in court, and if in the meantime your son should fall dangerously ill, it would be no breach of your moral duty to fail in what you agreed to do; nay, rather, he to whom your promise was given would have a false conception of duty if he should complain that he had been deserted in time of need. Further than this, who fails to see that those promises are not binding which are extorted by intimidation or which we make when misled by false pretences? Such obligations are annulled in most cases by the praetor's edict in equity,/a in some cases by the laws.

Injustice often arises also through chicanery, that is, through an over-subtle and even fraudulent construction of the law. This it is that gave rise to the now familiar saw, "More law, less justice." Through such interpretation also a great deal of wrong is committed in transactions between state and state; thus, when a truce had been made with the enemy for thirty days, a famous general/a went to ravaging their fields by night, because, he said, the truce stipulated "days," not nights. Not even our own countryman's action is to be commended, if what is told of Quintus Fabius Labeo is true—or whoever it was (for I have no authority but hearsay): appointed by the Senate to arbitrate a boundary dispute between Nola and Naples, he took up the case and interviewed both parties separately, asking them not to proceed in a covetous or grasping spirit, but to make some concession rather than claim some accession. When each party had agreed to this, there was a considerable strip of territory left between them. And so he set the boundary of each city as each had severally agreed; and the tract in between he awarded to the Roman People. Now that is swindling, not arbitration. And therefore such sharp practice is under all circumstances to be avoided.

XI

Again, there are certain duties that we owe even to those who have wronged us. For there is a limit to retribution and to punishment; or rather, I am inclined to think, it is sufficient that the aggressor should be brought to repent of his wrong-doing, in order that he may not repeat the offence and that others may be deterred from doing wrong.

Then, too, in the case of a state in its external relations, the rights of war must be strictly observed. For since there are two ways of settling a dispute: first, by discussion; second; by physical force; and since the former is characteristic of man, the latter of the brute, we must resort to force only in case we may not avail ourselves of discussion. The only excuse, therefore, for going to war is that we may live in peace unharmed; and when the victory is won, we should spare those who have not been blood-thirsty and barbarous in their warfare. For instance, our forefathers actually admitted to full rights of citizenship the Tusculans, Acquians, Volscians, Sabines, and Hernicians, but they razed Carthage and Numantia to the ground. I wish they had not destroyed Corinth; but I believe they had some special reason for what they did—its convenient situation, probably—and feared that its very location might some day furnish a temptation to renew the war. In my opinion, at least, we should always strive to secure a peace that shall not admit of guile. And if my advice had been heeded on this point, we should still have at least some sort of constitutional government, if not the best in the world, whereas, as it is, we have none at all. Not only must we show consideration for those whom we have conquered by force of arms but we must also ensure protection to those who lay down their arms and throw themselves upon the mercy of our generals, even though the battering-ram has hammered at their walls. And among our countrymen justice has been observed so conscientiously in this direction, that those who have given promise of protection to states or nations subdued in war become, after the custom of our forefathers, the patrons of those states.

As for war, humane laws touching it are drawn up in the fetial code of the Roman People under all the guarantees of religion; and from this it may be gathered that no war is just, unless it is entered upon after an official demand for satisfaction has been submitted or warning has been given and a formal declaration made. Popilius was general in command of a province. In his army Cato's son was serving on his first campaign. When Popilius decided to disband one of his legions, he discharged also young Cato, who was serving in that same legion. But when the young man out of love for the service stayed on in the field, his father wrote to Popilius to say that if he let him stay in the army, he should swear him into service with a new oath of allegiance, for in view of the voidance of his former oath he could not legally fight the foe. So extremely scrupulous was the observance of the laws in regard to the conduct of war. There is extant, too, a letter of the elder Marcus Cato to his son Marcus, in which he writes that he has heard that the youth has been discharged by the consul, when he was serving in Macedonia in the war with Perseus. He warns him, therefore, to be careful not to go into battle; for, he says, the man who is not legally a soldier has no right to be fighting the foe.

XII

This also I observe—that he who would properly have been called "a fighting enemy" (perduyellis) was called "a guest" (hostis), thus relieving the ugliness of the fact by a softened expression; for "enemy" (hostis) meant to our ancestors what we now call "stranger" (peregrinus). This is proved by the usage in the Twelve Tables: "Or a day fixed for trial with a stranger" (hostis). And again: "Right of ownership is inalienable for ever in dealings with a stranger" (hostis). What can exceed such charity, when he with whom one is at war is called by so gentle a name? And yet long lapse of time has given that word a harsher meaning: for it has lost its signification of "stranger" and has taken on the technical connotation of "an enemy under arms."

But when a war is fought out for supremacy and when glory is the object of war, it must still not fail to start from the same motives which I said a moment ago were the only righteous grounds for going to war. But those wars which have glory for their end must be carried on with less bitterness. For we contend, for example, with a fellow-citizen in one way, if he is a personal enemy, in another, if he is a rival: with the rival it is a struggle for office and position, with the enemy for life and honour. So with the Celtiberians and the Cimbrians we fought as with deadly enemies, not to determine which should be supreme, but which should survive; but with the Latins, Sabines, Samnites, Carthaginians, and Pyrrhus we fought for supremacy. The Carthaginians violated treaties; Hannibal was cruel; the others were more merciful. From Pyrrhus we have this famous speech on the exchange of prisoners:

> Gold will I none, nor price shall ye give; for I ask none;
> Come, let us not be chaff'rers of war, but warriors embattled.
> Nay; let us venture our lives, and the sword, not gold, weigh the outcome.
> Make we the trial by valour in arms and see if Dame Fortune
> Wills it that ye shall prevail or I, or what be her judgment.
> Hear thou, too, this word, good Fabricius: whose valour soever
> Spared hath been by the fortune of war—their freedom I grant them.
> Such my resolve. I give and present them to you, my brave Romans;
> Take them back to their homes; the great gods' blessings attend you.

A right kingly sentiment this and worthy a scion of the Aeacidae.

XIII

Again, if under stress of circumstance individuals have made any promise to the enemy, they are bound to keep their word even then. For instance, in the First Punic War, when Regulus was taken prisoner by the Carthaginians, he was sent to Rome on parole to negotiate an exchange of prisoners; he came and, in the first place, it was he that made the motion in the Senate that the prisoners should not be restored; and in the second place, when his relatives and friends would have kept him back, he chose to return to a death by torture rather than prove false to his promise, though given to an enemy.

And again in the Second Punic War, after the Battle of Cannae, Hannibal sent to Rome ten Roman captives bound by an oath to return to him, if they did not succeed in ransoming his prisoners; and as long as any one of them lived, the censors kept them all degraded and disfranchised, because they were guilty of perjury in not returning. And they punished in like manner the one who had incurred guilt by an evasion of his oath: with Hannibal's permission this man left the camp and returned a little later on the pretext that he had forgotten something or other; and then, when he left the camp the second time, he claimed that he was released from the obligation of his oath; and so he was, according to the letter of it, but not according to the spirit. In the matter of a promise one must always consider the meaning and not the mere words. Our forefathers have given us another striking example of justice toward an enemy: when a deserter from Pyrrhus promised the Senate to administer poison to the king and thus work his death, the Senate and Gaius Fabricius delivered the deserter up to Pyrrhus. Thus they stamped with their disapproval the treacherous murder even of an enemy who was at once powerful, unprovoked, aggressive, and successful.

With this I will close my discussion of the duties connected with war. But let us remember that we must have regard for justice even towards the humblest. Now the humblest station and the poorest fortune are those of slaves; and they give us no bad rule who bid us treat our slaves as we should our employees: they must be required to work; they must be given their dues. While wrong may be done, then, in either of two ways, that is, by force or by fraud, both are bestial: fraud seems to belong to the cunning fox, force to the lion; both are wholly unworthy of man, but fraud is the more contemptible. But of all forms of injustice, none is more flagrant than that of the hypocrite who, at the very moment when he is most false, makes it his business to appear virtuous. This must conclude our discussion of justice.

Reading Analytically

1. In this passage, Cicero makes it clear that war (or any kind of force) is to be used only in limited cases. After reading this excerpt, describe the circumstances under which going to war might be just according to Cicero. You might also develop examples that seem to justify going to war.
2. Even when war is necessary, Cicero suggests, there are certain obligations that those who wage war must uphold in order to be just.

List as many of those obligations as you can, and discuss whether they apply to modern warfare as well.

3. In this passage, Cicero refers to what he calls an "old saw" or proverb, "More law, less justice." What is meant by this proverb? In what ways are law and justice different from one another? Why might some (including modern libertarians) suggest that, as Thoreau put it, "The government is best that governs least"?

Reading Across Disciplinary Communities

1. One of the keys to rhetorical methodology is that each topic examined is studied within a set of contexts or "occasions." What context for Cicero's discussion of war is provided by the first three paragraphs of this passage?
2. Rhetorical method also draws frequently upon examples. Find at least two instances when Cicero uses specific examples as a form of proof, and discuss how the examples are presented in a way meant to support his argument.
3. Cicero, though discussing war in the context of politics, ethics, and rhetoric, does also bring up the topic of religion. How does he bring together his secular discussions with religious principles? How is that method similar to, and different from, the combination of secular philosophy and religion in Thomas Aquinas' discussion of just war in the passage that follows?

THOMAS AQUINAS

Of War

Thomas Aquinas (1225–1274) was an influential Catholic theologian. Much of his work helped to bridge the gap between classical philosophers such as Aristotle and Christian theology, helping to develop what would later be called "Christian humanism." As both a theological voice and a philosophical one, Aquinas uses methods of proof that draw upon both of those disciplines—sometimes using methods of logic, and other times drawing upon scriptural evidence. If you read closely, you will see examples of both.

In this passage from the Summa Theologica *(Summary of Theology), Aquinas (like Cicero) takes on the question of whether war can ever be considered justified. But unlike Cicero, Aquinas also asks whether war is "sinful," whether it is right and lawful for clergy to fight in wars, whether tactics of war such as ambushes should be allowable, and whether Christians should fight on holy days. Thus, Aquinas is not only examining the justness of war in terms of logic and ethics, but at the same time considering whether war can be justified with Catholic theology. His method, though, is one frequently used by philosophers and rhetoricians such as Cicero, looking first at the contrary perspective on an issue, and then answering each of those objections in order to make his case.*

We must now consider war, under which head there are four points of inquiry:

- Whether some kind of war is lawful?
- Whether it is lawful for clerics to fight?
- Whether it is lawful for belligerents to lay ambushes?
- Whether it is lawful to fight on holy days?

Whether it is always sinful to wage war?

Objection 1

It would seem that it is always sinful to wage war. Because punishment is not inflicted except for sin. Now those who wage war are threatened by Our Lord with punishment, according to Mt. 26:52: "All that take the sword shall perish with the sword." Therefore all wars are unlawful.

Objection 2

Further, whatever is contrary to a Divine precept is a sin. But war is contrary to a Divine precept, for it is written (Mt. 5:39): "But I say to you not to resist evil"; and (Rm. 12:19): "Not revenging yourselves, my dearly beloved, but give place unto wrath." Therefore war is always sinful.

Objection 3

Further, nothing, except sin, is contrary to an act of virtue. But war is contrary to peace. Therefore war is always a sin.

Objection 4

Further, the exercise of a lawful thing is itself lawful, as is evident in scientific exercises. But warlike exercises which take place in tournaments are forbidden by the Church, since those who are slain in these trials are deprived of ecclesiastical burial. Therefore it seems that war is a sin in itself.

On the contrary, Augustine says in a sermon on the son of the centurion [*Ep. ad Marcel, cxxxviii]: "If the Christian Religion forbade war altogether, those who sought salutary advice in the Gospel would rather have been counselled to cast aside their arms, and to give up soldiering altogether. On the contrary, they were told: 'Do violence to no man ... and be content with your pay' [*Lk. 3:14]. If he commanded them to be content with their pay, he did not forbid soldiering."

I answer that, In order for a war to be just, three things are necessary. First, the authority of the sovereign by whose command the war is to be waged. For it is not the business of a private individual to declare war, because he can seek for redress of his rights from the tribunal of his superior. Moreover it is not the business of a private individual to summon together the people, which has to be done in wartime. And as the care of the common weal is committed to those who are in authority, it is their business to watch over the common weal of the city, kingdom or province subject to them. And just as it is lawful for them to have recourse to the sword in defending that common weal against internal disturbances, when they punish evil-doers, according to the words of the Apostle (Rm. 13:4): "He beareth not the sword in vain: for he is God's minister, an avenger to execute wrath upon him that doth evil"; so too, it is their business to have recourse to the sword of war in defending the common weal against external enemies. Hence it is said to those who are in authority (Ps. 81:4): "Rescue the poor: and deliver the needy out of the hand of the sinner"; and for this reason Augustine says (Contra Faust. xxii, 75): "The natural order conducive to peace among mortals demands that the power to declare and counsel war should be in the hands of those who hold the supreme authority."

Secondly, a just cause is required, namely that those who are attacked, should be attacked because they deserve it on account of some fault. Wherefore Augustine says (Questions. in Hept., qu. x, super Jos.): "A just war is wont to be described as one that avenges wrongs, when a nation or state has to be punished, for refusing to make amends for the wrongs inflicted by its subjects, or to restore what it has seized unjustly."

Thirdly, it is necessary that the belligerents should have a rightful intention, so that they intend the advancement of good, or the avoidance of evil. Hence Augustine says (De Verb. Dom. [*The words quoted are to be found not in St. Augustine's works, but Can. Apud. Caus. xxiii, qu. 1]): "True religion looks upon as peaceful those wars that are waged not for motives of aggrandizement, or cruelty, but with the object of securing peace, of punishing evil-doers, and of uplifting the good." For it may happen that the war is declared by the legitimate authority, and for a just cause, and yet be rendered unlawful through a wicked intention. Hence Augustine says (Contra Faust. xxii, 74): "The passion for inflicting harm, the cruel thirst for vengeance, an unpacific and relentless spirit, the fever of revolt, the lust of power, and such like things, all these are rightly condemned in war."

Reply to Objection 1

As Augustine says (Contra Faust. xxii, 70): "To take the sword is to arm oneself in order to take the life of anyone, without the command or permission of superior or lawful authority." On the other hand, to have recourse to the sword (as a private person) by the authority of the sovereign or judge, or (as a public person) through zeal for justice, and by the authority, so to speak, of God, is not to "take the sword," but to use it as commissioned by another, wherefore it does not deserve punishment. And yet even those who make sinful use of the sword are not always slain with the sword, yet they always perish with their own sword, because, unless they repent, they are punished eternally for their sinful use of the sword.

Reply to Objection 2

Such like precepts, as Augustine observes (De Serm. Dom. in Monte i, 19), should always be borne in readiness of mind, so that we be ready to obey them, and, if necessary, to refrain from resistance or self-defense. Nevertheless it is necessary sometimes for a man to act otherwise for the common good, or for the good of those with whom he is fighting. Hence Augustine says (Ep. ad Marcellin. cxxxviii): "Those whom we have to punish with a kindly severity, it is necessary to handle in many ways against their will. For when we are stripping a man of the lawlessness of sin, it is good for him to be vanquished, since nothing is more hopeless than the happiness of sinners, whence arises a guilty impunity, and an evil will, like an internal enemy."

Reply to Objection 3

Those who wage war justly aim at peace, and so they are not opposed to peace, except to the evil peace, which Our Lord "came not to send upon earth" (Mt. 10:34). Hence Augustine says (Ep. ad Bonif. clxxxix): "We do not seek peace in order to be at war, but we go to war that we may have peace. Be peaceful, therefore, in warring, so that you may vanquish those whom you war against, and bring them to the prosperity of peace."

Reply to Objection 4

Manly exercises in warlike feats of arms are not all forbidden, but those which are inordinate and perilous, and end in slaying or plundering. In olden times warlike exercises presented no such danger, and hence they were called "exercises of arms" or "bloodless wars," as Jerome states in an epistle.

Whether it is lawful for clerics and bishops to fight?

Objection 1

It would seem lawful for clerics and bishops to fight. For, as stated above (Article [1]), wars are lawful and just in so far as they protect the poor and the entire common weal from suffering at the hands of the foe. Now this seems to be above all the duty of prelates, for Gregory says (Hom. in Ev. xiv): "The wolf comes upon the sheep, when any unjust and rapacious man oppresses those who are faithful and humble. But he who was thought to be the shepherd, and was not, leaveth the sheep, end flieth, for he fears lest the wolf hurt him, and dares not stand up against his injustice." Therefore it is lawful for prelates and clerics to fight.

Objection 2

Further, Pope Leo IV writes (xxiii, qu. 8, can. Igitur): "As untoward tidings had frequently come from the Saracen side, some said that the Saracens would come to the port of Rome secretly and covertly; for which reason we commanded our people to gather together, and ordered them to go down to the seashore." Therefore it is lawful for bishops to fight.

Objection 3

Further, apparently, it comes to the same whether a man does a thing himself, or consents to its being done by another, according to Rm. 1:32: "They who do such things, are worthy of death, and not only they that do them, but they also that consent to them that do them." Now those, above all, seem to consent to a thing, who induce others to do it. But it is lawful for bishops and clerics to induce others to fight: for it is written (xxiii, qu. 8, can. Hortatu) that Charles went to war with the Lombards at the instance and entreaty of Adrian, bishop of Rome. Therefore they also are allowed to fight.

Objection 4

Further, whatever is right and meritorious in itself, is lawful for prelates and clerics. Now it is sometimes right and meritorious to make war, for it is written (xxiii, qu. 8, can. Omni timore) that if "a man die for the true faith, or to save his country, or in defense of Christians, God will give him a heavenly reward." Therefore it is lawful for bishops and clerics to fight.

On the contrary, It was said to Peter as representing bishops and clerics (Mt. 16:52): "Put up again thy sword into the scabbard [Vulg.: 'its place'] [*"Scabbard" is the reading in Jn. 18:11]." Therefore it is not lawful for them to fight.

I answer that, Several things are requisite for the good of a human society: and a number of things are done better and quicker by a number of persons than by one, as the Philosopher observes (Polit. i, 1), while certain occupations are so inconsistent with one another, that they cannot be fittingly exercised at the same time; wherefore those who are deputed to important duties are forbidden to occupy themselves with things of small importance. Thus according to human laws, soldiers who are deputed to warlike pursuits are forbidden to engage in commerce [*Cod. xii, 35, De Re Milit.].

Now warlike pursuits are altogether incompatible with the duties of a bishop and a cleric, for two reasons. The first reason is a general one, because, to wit, warlike pursuits are full of unrest, so that they hinder the mind very much from the contemplation of Divine things, the praise of God, and prayers for the people, which belong to the duties of a cleric. Wherefore just as commercial enterprises are forbidden to clerics, because they unsettle the mind too much, so too are warlike pursuits, according to 2 Tim. 2:4: "No man being a soldier to God, entangleth himself with secular business." The second reason is a special one, because, to wit, all the clerical Orders are directed to the ministry of the altar, on which the Passion of Christ is represented sacramentally, according to 1 Cor. 11:26: "As often as you shall eat this bread, and drink the chalice, you shall show the death of the Lord, until He come." Wherefore it is unbecoming for them to slay or shed blood, and it is more fitting that they should be ready to shed their own blood for Christ, so as to imitate in deed what they portray in their ministry. For this reason it has been decreed that those who shed blood, even without sin, become irregular. Now no man who has a certain duty to perform, can lawfully do that which renders him unfit for that duty. Wherefore it is altogether unlawful for clerics to fight, because war is directed to the shedding of blood.

Reply to Objection 1

Prelates ought to withstand not only the wolf who brings spiritual death upon the flock, but also the pillager and the oppressor who work bodily harm; not, however, by having recourse themselves to material arms, but by means of spiritual weapons, according to the saying of the Apostle (2 Cor. 10:4): "The weapons of our warfare are not carnal, but mighty through God." Such are salutary warnings, devout prayers, and, for those who are obstinate, the sentence of excommunication.

Reply to Objection 2

Prelates and clerics may, by the authority of their superiors, take part in wars, not indeed by taking up arms themselves, but by affording spiritual help to those who fight justly, by exhorting and absolving them, and by other like spiritual helps. Thus in the Old Testament (Joshua 6:4) the priests were commanded to sound the sacred trumpets in the battle. It was for this purpose that bishops or clerics were first allowed to go to the front: and it is an abuse of this permission, if any of them take up arms themselves.

Reply to Objection 3

As stated above (Question [23], Article [4], ad 2) every power, art or virtue that regards the end, has to dispose that which is directed to the end. Now, among the faithful, carnal wars should be considered as having for their end the Divine spiritual good to which clerics are deputed. Wherefore it is the duty of clerics to dispose and counsel other men to engage in just wars. For they are forbidden to take up arms, not as though it were a sin, but because such an occupation is unbecoming their personality.

Reply to Objection 4

Although it is meritorious to wage a just war, nevertheless it is rendered unlawful for clerics, by reason of their being deputed to works more meritorious still. Thus the marriage act may be meritorious; and yet it becomes reprehensible in those who have vowed virginity, because they are bound to a yet greater good.

Whether it is lawful to lay ambushes in war?

Objection 1

It would seem that it is unlawful to lay ambushes in war. For it is written (Dt. 16:20): "Thou shalt follow justly after that which is just." But ambushes, since they are a kind of deception, seem to pertain to injustice. Therefore it is unlawful to lay ambushes even in a just war.

Objection 2

Further, ambushes and deception seem to be opposed to faithfulness even as lies are. But since we are bound to keep faith with all men, it is wrong to lie to anyone, as Augustine states (Contra Mend. xv). Therefore, as one is bound to keep faith with one's enemy, as Augustine states (Ep. ad Bonif. clxxxix), it seems that it is unlawful to lay ambushes for one's enemies.

Objection 3

Further, it is written (Mt. 7:12): "Whatsoever you would that men should do to you, do you also to them": and we ought to observe this in all our dealings with our neighbor. Now our enemy is our neighbor. Therefore, since no man wishes ambushes or deceptions to be prepared for himself, it seems that no one ought to carry on war by laying ambushes.

On the contrary, Augustine says (Questions. in Hept. qu. x super Jos): "Provided the war be just, it is no concern of justice whether it be carried on openly or by ambushes": and he proves this by the authority of the Lord, Who commanded Joshua to lay ambushes for the city of Hai (Joshua 8:2).

I answer that, The object of laying ambushes is in order to deceive the enemy. Now a man may be deceived by another's word or deed in two ways. First, through being told something false, or through the breaking of a promise, and this is always unlawful. No one ought to deceive the enemy in this way, for there are certain "rights of war and covenants, which ought to be observed even among enemies," as Ambrose states (De Officiis i).

Secondly, a man may be deceived by what we say or do, because we do not declare our purpose or meaning to him. Now we are not always bound to do this, since even in the Sacred Doctrine many things have to be concealed, especially from unbelievers, lest they deride it, according to Mt. 7:6: "Give not that which is holy, to dogs." Wherefore much more ought the plan of campaign to be hidden from the enemy. For this reason among other things that a soldier has to learn is the art of concealing his purpose lest it come to the enemy's knowledge, as stated in the Book on Strategy [*Stratagematum i, 1] by Frontinus. Such like concealment is what is meant by an ambush which may be lawfully employed in a just war.

Nor can these ambushes be properly called deceptions, nor are they contrary to justice or to a well-ordered will. For a man would have an inordinate will if he were unwilling that others should hide anything from him.

This suffices for the Replies to the Objections.

Whether it is lawful to fight on holy days?

Objection 1

It would seem unlawful to fight on holy days. For holy days are instituted that we may give our time to the things of God. Hence they are included in the keeping of the Sabbath prescribed Ex. 20:8: for "sabbath" is interpreted "rest." But wars are full of unrest. Therefore by no means is it lawful to fight on holy days.

Objection 2

Further, certain persons are reproached (Is. 58:3) because on fast-days they exacted what was owing to them, were guilty of strife, and of smiting with the fist. Much more, therefore, is it unlawful to fight on holy days.

Objection 3

Further, no ill deed should be done to avoid temporal harm. But fighting on a holy day seems in itself to be an ill deed.

Therefore no one should fight on a holy day even through the need of avoiding temporal harm.

On the contrary, It is written (1 Machab 2:41): The Jews rightly determined . . . saying: "Whosoever shall come up against us to fight on the Sabbath-day, we will fight against him."

I answer that, The observance of holy days is no hindrance to those things which are ordained to man's safety, even that of his body. Hence Our Lord argued with the Jews, saying (Jn. 7:23): "Are you angry at Me because I have healed the whole man on the Sabbath-day?" Hence physicians may lawfully attend to their patients on holy days. Now there is much more reason for safeguarding the common weal (whereby many are saved from being slain, and innumerable evils both temporal and spiritual prevented), than the bodily safety of an individual. Therefore, for the purpose of safeguarding the common weal of the faithful, it is lawful to carry on a war on holy days, provided there be need for doing so: because it would be to tempt God, if notwithstanding such a need, one were to choose to refrain from fighting. However, as soon as the need ceases, it is no longer lawful to fight on a holy day, for the reasons given: wherefore this suffices for the Replies to the Objections.

Reading Analytically

1. Thomas Aquinas' formulation of the three requirements that must be met for a war to be considered just has become a classic articulation of "just war theory." What are those three conditions? Try to explain them in your own words.

2. Though some had argued that clergy can justifiably take part in warfare, Aquinas argues against this position. What are his main arguments in refuting that position?
3. Though it might seem counterintuitive, even warfare has limits and rules—though in recent days of terrorism and counter-terrorism, those rules have been strained quite a bit. In Aquinas' discussion of whether ambushes can be justified in wartime, we can see parallels to recent discussions of methods of warfare that some have considered questionable. Could any of Aquinas' methods be applied to recent discussions about what we should, or should not, do to combat terrorism? Keep this in mind, also, as you read other selections in this chapter.

Reading Across Disciplinary Communities

1. The classic philosophical technique of "answering objections" is used by Aquinas in this passage. Describe how that method of argument seems to work.
2. As is noted in the introduction to this passage, Aquinas has one foot in classical philosophical method, and another in Christian doctrine. Using examples from the text, demonstrate how Aquinas draws upon both techniques to build his argument.
3. As a theologian, Aquinas uses scripture as one of his major forms of evidence. Drawing upon several examples from the text, describe how the use of sacred writings is similar to, and different from, other forms of evidence.

PERTTI JOENNIEMI

Toward the End of War?

Peeking Through the Gap

This essay by a foreign relations scholar explores the changing definitions of war, especially those in a post–Cold War and post-9/11 world. Pertti Joenniemi is the Senior Research Fellow at the Department for European Affairs of the Danish Institute of International Studies in Denmark. He is the author of The Changing Face of European Conscription *and* The Nordic Peace.

In this essay, Joenniemi asks readers to consider how our definitions of the concept are more than just linguistic issues, but in fact influence deeply our public policies and our opinions about the nature of war and peace. He also discusses ways that consideration of how we define war can help us to think about its uses and its future direction. As you read this piece, you might question your own assumptions about war as well, attempting to broaden your understanding of this important social concept, its causes, and its relation to America's recent history.

Abstract: The concept of war is clearly not its old self. The recent debate indicates with considerable clarity that there no longer exists a superior position from which to authoritatively enforce a dominant and broadly accepted definition. The most profound challenges consist of the claims that the concept has had its days and should accordingly be abandoned. In addition to exploring the background of this critique, the article aims to evaluate what accounts for the openness in the first place. The effort is to probe the broader constellations underpinning war and in particular the nexus between war and the state in order to trace possible changes. The article argues that these broader constellations provide a firmer basis for arriving at conclusions about both the nature of the debate and the future of war as a fundamental political and social concept.

The abstract lays out the key argument that is being made. Though the article uses very complex disciplinary terminology, at its heart, the argument is that it has become increasingly difficult to have a single definition of war. Knowing that is the basic argument can help you to read this difficult piece.

The concept of war no longer conveys meaning the way it formerly did. It is no longer of help, the argument goes, if one is to make sense of recent events. With the breakdown of many certainties constructed in the name of war, a static concept is unlikely to be an adequate guide for future challenges. Pressure to unravel established ways of comprehending war is building. The discursive structures underpinning the concept have become less restrained, allowing it to be questioned on both ontological and epistemological grounds.

Note how the opening line sets up the main argument as it is portrayed in the abstract.

This term means the language used to describe war, the "discourse" that people use to define it.

Ontological means the referring to the nature of being; *Epistemological* means referring to the "nature of knowledge." So the author will examine war in terms of both its actual nature and how we come to understand it in our minds.

This critique is accompanied by efforts to rename and differentiate among various forms of political violence. A variety of voices have asserted that a breaking point has emerged. Their claims indicate, with considerable clarity, that the concept of war is not just routinely reproduced and naturalized, but also challenged through profound counterdiscourses. Critics find the concept unconvincing and assert that it is out of touch with the essence of contemporary conflicts. The commonplace understanding is, therefore, to be relegated to the dustbin of history to make room for other, and so far less-established, forms of meaning. War, as a concept, is understood to have become "obsolete"; it is seen as being on its way to "dying out," or being regarded as having entered the process of being "disinvented."[1] Allegedly, "War is not only in transition, it is in a crisis."[2]

By *counterdiscourses,* the author is suggested that there are conflicting definitions of war.

Suggesting that war is in "crisis" seems to suggest that it is increasingly difficult to know what we mean by war. Note the way that this author uses this quotation, and the accompanying footnote, to make his point about the changing nature and understanding of war.

The recent debate concerning the essence of war clearly indicates that a superior position from which to authoritatively enforce a dominant and broadly accepted definition no longer exists. The previous self-evidence of the concept of war, and its assumed contingency, has become unsustainable; what remains are multiple, contending conceptualizations. Rather than a fixed, "single point" concept, with considerable resilience, war has become unfixed and "multiperspectival." Several constitutive logics simultaneously struggle with each other over the meaning of war. In fact, one might speak of a certain "postmodernization" of war or, for that matter, of developments that reach beyond modernity wherein war appears in both pre- and postmodern forms. The emergence of many new coinages indicates varied attempts to grasp the essence of war. For instance, phrases such as "new wars," "cyber wars," "asymmetric wars," "post-Clausewitzian wars," "postnational wars," "hybrid wars," "pre-emptive wars," "immanent wars," "liberal wars," "humanitarian wars," and "global wars" point to the notion that contemporary wars are understood differently from earlier ones. "War" is no longer to be treated as an "ideal type" concept in a Weberian sense. The meaning of this fundamental category of political and social discourse is shifting.

That is, there are many competing definitions of war.

Note all the ways that we use the term *war* in our times. Can you think of other uses of this term?

This conceptual renewal—part of the search for new, interpretative categories—also includes coinages such as "network wars," a phrase developed to stay current with rapid societal and technological transformation.[3] The concept of "network wars" echoes talk of a "revolution in military affairs" and has had a considerable impact on military machineries. Likewise, the phrase "fourth-generation war" emphasizes changes in the sphere of information technology, complexity science, and the organizational logic of network society."[4] The concepts "spectacle war" and "virtual war"[5] stress images as a major product of military encounters rather than information Slavoj Zizek speaks somewhat similarly about "war without casualties." He suspects that there might be "war without warfare," or warless war, something resembling coffee without caffeine.[6]

What does this analogy suggest? How do all the various uses of the term *war* make it like "coffee without caffeine"?

In general, the concept of war is no longer used as unreflectively as often used to be the case. The blurring of many fundamental distinctions (including those between inside and outside, politics and economy, public and private, as well as peace and war) requires a brand-new vocabulary if one is to differentiate between various forms of collective violence.

Here, the author explains why arguments like this one are necessary—why we need to expand our definitions of war.

The conceptual diffusion and fragmentation that have, over the recent years, been conducive to efforts of redefinition include the collaborative scholarly platform called Dictionary of War.[7] This web endeavor departs quite explicitly from the idea that (modern) war, as an armed confrontation between sovereign states, is outdated. At the same time, the project asserts that there is no "peace" as current developments are rife with political violence of various kinds. War is not seen as an isolated occurrence disrupting a state of peace, but a constant presence imbricated and deeply rooted in social relations. In viewing the almost ever-present war "as a constitutive form of a new order," the dictionary challenges established perceptions by coining one hundred articulations regarding the issue of war. In other words, it generates a plentitude of terms for war, thereby adding considerably to the linguistic resources available. This allows one to remain abreast of the many unprecedented developments that increasingly exceed established definitions. The dictionary asserts that new and increasingly rich vocabularies are needed now that war exists as a plurality. Modernity has lost control in a dual sense: War is neither disappearing nor taking expected forms.

Again, note how the argument suggests that old understandings of war are no longer adequate.

The dictionary project signals, more generally, that, with the proliferation and blurring of established borderlines, war does not mean the same thing in all times and places. Rather than being confined to its own place and time, it permeates the normality of the political process. No doubt, the dictionary approaches the issue in a productive manner. This approach differs from

In the midst of the difficult language and terms, you can find direct and clear statements of the problem like this one.

other critics, such as Christopher Coker, Kalevi Holsti, or Martin van Crevald. While the dictionary celebrates the virtues of complexity and broadens the repertoire of linguistic resources and meanings useful to learning what war is about, the critics tend to favor parsimony and opt for the return of precise and stable meanings. Perhaps they find the plentitude aspired for through endeavors such as the Dictionary of War quite disturbing. In their view, the concept of war has been deprived of any real substance through the banishment of crucial limits and boundaries. Rather than being broadened and made increasingly fluid, they suggest that it needs further restraints and increasing distinctions; that it needs to be redrawn and fixed within the context of other conceptual departures. In Foucaultian terms, the critics claim that a certain age marked by a specific mode of reflection (*episteme*) has come to an end. A rather unexpected gap has emerged, they think, through a break in the discursive order that traditionally carried the concept of war across time and space. War no longer has a perpetual presence in social and political life. It is no longer reproduced and reinforced through undisputed and intersubjectively shared meanings. One is, consequently, asked to imagine change reaching beyond what has been imaginable within war's previously established meaning and attendant social continuities.

Here, the author explains the reason for this article—to show us why we need to imagine all the ways to think about war.

A Key Constellation of Concepts

My aim is not to pass judgment on these two approaches and ways of reacting to war, but to investigate the gap that has emerged since the discourse on war lost its power to categorically oust alternative articulations. I attempt to explore these openings through the controversy over established ways of thinking about war.

The author further clarifies the purpose and scope of the article.

The increasingly contested nature of the concept of war signals the extensive change it is undergoing. The question of how far-reaching these changes are remains unanswered. Are we basically talking about a cyclical phenomenon observed many times before with contestation and the telling of dystopies in fact contributing to the survival of the concept? Can the concept accommodate these pressures in its established form without collapsing as a meaningful communicative device? Or, does the more recent discord really point to a genuine implosion? Has this crucial signifier been fractured beyond repair, thus indicating that war as a commonly understood concept is well on its way to becoming history?

This series of questions lays out the points of inquiry of the article, which is to examine whether the term *war*, with all its meaning, is still useful.

In examining these questions, I neither want to privilege nor stake out a particular definition of war. Instead, I approach the concept as socially constructed. Since war is historically negotiated and culturally dependent, it may well display signs of contingency over a considerable period of time. It is part of a discourse (such as the Hobbesian emphasis on the state of nature being inherently violent and conflictual) that renders war as something largely inevitable. It remains, nonetheless, adjustable and malleable to changing circumstances. These qualities require that war is, from time to time, opened up and repacked.[8] The concept has to be re-found to remain vital and of value.

To call something "socially constructed" means that rather than being a natural phenomenon (ontological—what is real) it is created by the way we think about the concept (epistemological). This same question is asked about the concept of race in Chapter 3: Is it a natural phenomenon or is it socially constructed?

Here, the author argues that the term, despite its many meanings, is still important.

There is, therefore, nothing particularly surprising about the doubts surrounding the concept of war since the Cold War and 9/11. Previously well-established fault lines have been thrown into doubt and begun to falter. It is equally unsurprising that a number of contending claims concerning the "real" essence of war have emerged. These contending claims make it increasingly difficult to adjudicate among various assertions.

What is more difficult to account for, however, is the claim that the concept is no longer applicable in an intellectually legitimate context. This type of discourse differs in that it fails to contribute to increasing the number of options. Such an approach neither attempts to stake out a particular definition, nor does it aspire to coin new possibilities for restabilizing the meaning of war. Instead, it openly raises an ontological question about war as a major aspect of being. The core issue to be addressed is, therefore, how talk of rupturing the surface emerges at all. What provides such articulations with legitimacy in the discourse? Do these claims have any chance of gaining broader credibility?

Here, the question of war's actual being is contrasted with its nature as a concept or "epistemology."

The alleged demise of war tends to lack credibility because, among other reasons, it would undermine a considerable number of certainties constructed in its name. A breakdown would bring, in addition to considerable ontological anxiety, difficulties for many other key concepts essential to defining what politics is about. If war becomes ambivalent or outdated, a variety of contemporary security practices, as well as a considerable number of other, more general efforts of ordering, would run into trouble. The concept would no longer be productive in thinking about a contingent future. From a different perspective, the rupture would also open up new modes of thinking. Even more forcefully than has already been the case, articulations that pertain to particular instances (9/11, for instance) would take precedence over more neutral terms, such as "conflict," "campaign," or concepts like "risk," and "crime." Such specific articulations are bound to grow in significance in order to fill the void that has emerged.

Here, the author seems to suggest that though war as a concept has multiple meanings, we can learn a great deal by examining those multiple meanings.

Through questioning this alleged gap, my approach treats the concept of war as part of a distinct discursive structure and constellation of core ideas that regulate what can be meaningfully said.[9] Such deep connections to conceptions in other fields make the concept of war convincing and easy to reproduce over a long period of time. These links, or overarching codes, consist of a large collection of concepts such as "politics," "reason," and "international." In other words, the meaning of war is established and upheld—or, for that matter, thrown out of balance—within this discursive universe of related ideas.

This statement summarizes his point: by examining the multiple meanings of war, we can get closer to understanding its most crucial elements.

In this context, focusing on a plurality of key ideas would provide a very detailed and comprehensive picture. It would also significantly contribute to the complexity of analyses. My aim is to delimit the constellation of concepts to the extreme, thereby condensing the analysis of relationality to a nucleus of meaning. I do so by adopting the idea of the state as a basic form of communality. This analysis departs from the notion that war can be meaningfully and convincingly spoken of if the state is integrally included in its core concepts. Over a considerable period of time, war and the state have been the pair that determines contingency and fragility. War is resilient if the link between war and the state remains unproblematic. Conversely, the concept of war can no longer be articulated with the same level of confidence if it is severed from the concept of the state.

Framing Early War

Like many scholarly articles, this one begins by framing the concept historically.

Clearly, regulation and differentiation have the greatest impact on various descriptions of the historical trajectory of war. These two ways of framing are used in many historiographic efforts of outlining what war is about and how it has evolved. They create a rather linear rendition of the concept, despite the presence of some conflicting elements. This narrative presents war as undergoing a process of narrowing down. War moves from being something rather unconstrained into various, more regulated, instrumental, and modern forms. Overall, the initial expressive, as well as existential, forms are minimized so that war may appear easier to frame and comprehend."[10]

This suggests that over time, the concept of war became more specifically defined.

There is some degree of differentiation present in the historiography of war from the very beginning. This allows the concept of war to refer to something more organized and sanctioned than individual acts of killing, murder, or random forms of massacre. Widespread use of the term *primitive* in various efforts to categorize the early phases of war indicates, however, that this differentiation remains quite mild. The accounts primarily comprise descriptions of a broad variety of cases of violent conflict without narrowing the cases down into any specific pattern or form of "war."[11] With little regularity in tracing the entities involved in the conduct of violence—or the grievances fought about—there is scarce ground for a nuanced framing of war. Similarly, wars far back in history have often been cast as "chaotic" or regarded as generally part of the human condition. Additionally, factors such as bravery, chivalry, and heroic self-sacrifice have dominated these renditions, which contribute to an understanding of war as purposeful and instrumental. Unsurprisingly, concepts such as "feud" are used in parallel with "war" in the vocabularies adopted in these accounts.[12]

Furthermore, in depictions of war as part of a plurality of concepts, the connections among terms are often regarded as weak. War has been presented as a natural and ever-present perpetration of deliberate violence. It has, to some extent, been essentialized and granted immanence rather than restrained and bound by related concepts, despite the fact that many of these same concepts have subsequently been crucial to providing war with a distinct and far more regulated meaning. Notably, efforts to define war (during its early phases) through exclusion have not fared much better. In its modern form, the concept refers to a crisis, points to a moment of existential danger, or aims at outlining something extraordinary. In the context of historical accounts, however, it has been much more difficult to differentiate the norm from the exception.[13] Likewise, defining war through its productive effects has yielded unsatisfactory results. In large part, this is because the link

Becoming "essentialized" suggests that the concept was seen as a natural, inevitable thing. The article then goes on to argue against the "essential" nature of war.

between war and community building has remained obscure, although this link has occasionally been pointed out, as in the case of ancient wars fought by the Greek city-states. It was widely known that their fighting was conducive to border drawing. The practice took place, however, in regards to "barbarians," thereby depicting and singling out the Greeks as a more "civilized" community.[14]

A crucial step of differentiation occurred once factors such as religion, morality, and ethics became increasingly important in terms of the assumed underlying causes. With authors such as Saint Augustine and Saint Aquinas providing the intellectual ground for the move, war became differentiated in terms of "just" and "unjust." This distinction bolstered regulative efforts in the sense that some forms of war were regarded as excessive, whereas others were understood as tolerable, if not justified. This distinction also implied, in ontological terms, that the exceptional could be kept separate from the norm. Such moral and ethical distinctions also contributed to various law-based approaches and framings. Authors such as Vatel, Pufendorf, and Grotius built on this initial differentiation by turning the previous, predominantly theological, approach into an explicit legal category. This increasingly identified states as the sole legitimate authority and bounded political community to make decisions concerning peace and war. This move was quite important in narrowing down the ambiguity, doubt, and uncertainty that had previously surrounded ways of defining war.

This paragraph introduces another stage in the development of the concept of war.

Here, the author demonstrates how the concept of war became specifically associated with conflicts that are waged by political units—and that war wasn't always seen in that narrow way, but included other kinds of conflicts.

Toward a Modern Reading

Though we sometimes think of "modern" as meaning contemporary, here it refers to the period before our own "postmodern" period.

In accounting for the ontological and epistemic development of the concept of war, it is essential to address the work of Gad von Glausewitz. He wrote his seminal work *On War* at the end of the Napoleonic wars.[15]

Rather than emphasize legal, moral, or ethical aspects, which render war outside of politics, Glausewitz placed politics at the very core of the equation. Instead of developing a systematic theory, he stressed the complexity of war. Glausewitz viewed war as an expression of its political and social milieu, wherein the state replaced societies with pervasive warlike relations. War was viewed as a reflection of broader societal constellations, rather than something autonomous and premised by laws of its own. The state—equipped with military institutions and a monopoly over the means of violence—was located as the basic unit of an international order composed of sovereign states. War, within the context of the Clausewitzian comprehension, thus allows for differentiation between the domestic sphere of politics and the relations between state entities as a major form of human agency.

The author further develops the ways that war became associated with specific "states" (i.e., political units).

Notably, the classical model of war, introduced by Clausewitz, presents war as a duel between equal sovereignties. War is comprehended as a means of settling interstate conflicts of interest, where states have something of a monopoly on war. When, for example, Herfried Münkler argues that "war" has more recently become a politically controversial concept, his vantage point consists, in essence, of the classical Clausewitzian understanding.[16] It is necessary, therefore, to recapitulate some key aspects of the story of classical war in order to capture the structuring logic that has profoundly impacted the concept of war.

Here, the author suggests that when war became associated with states, it lost some of its original meaning, which was not always based on political units battling each other. See how this moves us closer to understanding how current concepts of war—which are more diffuse—are actually closer to its original meanings?

The classical idea of war replaced earlier, far more anarchic and unbound conceptualizations. Generally, the concept of war had included clashes and the collective use of violence. Various moral or religious justifications were abandoned in the process of subordinating war to modern reason. Within the new comprehensions, war boiled down to a duel in which no state could claim to have righteousness on its side. Since the enemy was recognized as an equal, and also provided with the right to self-defense, war was no longer—as could be the case in earlier times—understood as a prime form of self-expression. This meant that the aims of classical war could be regarded as limited, since war no longer required the elimination, submission, nor resocialization of the opponent. With politics (governed by calculable reason) steering war, its exercise could, in principle, be restrained to a balance of interests.

Along similar lines, a spatial delimitation took place with regard to classical war. The recognition of war as a statist affair ratified and sanctioned the establishment of homogenous and stabilized insides. This process located difference and contingency outside—that is, the sphere of anarchy and unpredictability. The spatial differentiation of an inside and an outside, specifically outlining the outside as the space of war, has been conducive to making the modern world legible and instructive.

This rule-bound approach allowed, more generally, for war to be discussed as an institution, or a "regime." War may also be comprehended through the use of generalizations, such as "war system." Another example of an institutionalization is the practice of formally declaring war. The notion *of Justus fiostis* presumes that the two parties will wage regulated war by limiting their hostilities to attacks against combatants and military objects. Once furnished with recognition, they may negotiate various rules and norms that govern the practice of war. These agreements have included some rather specific rules of war. The actors involved have, for instance, been able to pursue activities such as arms control. In a similar vein, they have also been able to confer about peace.

The conclusion the author draws here is that in "modern" times, the definition of war became very limited and specific.

Here, the author shows how "Institutionalized," state-related war brought about the "rules" of warfare. Since war has changed, reliance on rules has become less prevalent in our own times. War in our time isn't always about one country against another, as is the case, for example, in the "war on terror."

What is crucial here is the close interconnection established between war and states in the context of the Clausewitzian comprehension.[17] This framing does not, however, merely outline a connection. In fact, it entails recognition of the states as core actors in politics and international relations. The states are not just seen as preexisting actors advancing their interests through a relationship of instrumental rationality. They are viewed, above all, as entities that prevail through their central prerogative of deciding over war and peace, and, in this context, their opposition to each other. This relationship has, in short, been depicted as co-constitutive with war waged in the name of the sovereign whose interests are at stake.

Incidentally, this connectedness that forms one of the baselines of modern life may also be found in more current discussions about failed states. The requirement of equal dignity, with all states having a generally recognized monopoly of war, has become increasingly questionable due to growing conditionality. The introduction of a more hierarchic set of norms and rules underpinning recognition appears to invite more denial, disrespect, and denigration. One may subsequently note, in this context, that it is not only the concept of war that is in trouble: statehood is also questioned and diversified through categories such as failed, rogue, anaemic, collapsed, aborted, predatory, kleptocratic, phantom, and so forth.[18] Crucially, these are terms of misrecognition implying that states, as the key constitutive units of the international system, are no longer, a priori, alike. Instead, they are subject to considerable norms-based differentiation that allows some states to position themselves above others. Superior states may gain the right to resort to violence in the name of protection, rescue, care, democracy, or progress. Therefore, the norms prohibiting recognition on an equal basis also allow for invasion.

A Discriminatory Concept of War

Although the classical concept quickly developed into a template, and, for a long time, has been treated as the most advanced and true expression of what war is about, it has also been controversial and a cause of internal disputes. As noted by Wilhelm Grewe, "The most significant difference between international law in the 19th century and the Anglo-American Age is the turn towards a discriminatory concept of war."[19] Such a norms-based approach imposes a certain inhibition on the unfolding of war. This development may reflect a move from the teachings of Realpolitik to a more liberal stance. It may also be interpreted as replicating crucial tensions within the Realpolitik school of thought itself.

In his writings toward the end of the 1930s, Carl Schmitt pointed out that disciplining war through the creation of normative rules transfers decisions about the legality and illegality of war from states to a supranational institution.[20] According to Schmitt, this actually deprives states of one of their central prerogatives: the decision over war and peace.

Here, the author draws upon the writings of Carl Schmitt to show how creating rules for war institutionalized a limited definition of war. Note how he continues to draw upon this basic principle of Schmitt's theories.

Within such a context, war is no longer premised on the right of states to make autonomous decisions. Instead, they are constrained by the collective interests of the international community. With autonomy gone, the option of an authentic disclosure of political space also vanishes. Similarly, decisions about the just nature of war no longer rest with states, as war is "collectivized and denationalized."

Schmitt argued that war, therefore, takes on a very different nature.[21] It no longer stands for an extension of national politics by other means; instead, it is fought in the name of a higher order. In fact, this ruptures the previously coherent concept into two contradictory concepts that ultimately abolish the concept of war altogether. Schmitt asserted that either war is legitimate and just or it is unjust and illegitimate.

This understanding of war as "just" or "unjust" has become a common question we ask about war.

Introduced, to some extent, during the years of the League of Nations, a discriminatory concept of war ultimately abolishes the classical one, albeit without eliminating violence. Schmitt argued that the turn from instrumental to righteous war unravels various restrictions built into the classical concept, which could open the floodgates to "total war." From this, he concluded that there is no viable alternative to the classical concept of war.

These Schmittian warnings notwithstanding, war has been collectivized and denationalized over time. The Clausewitzian stress on rationality, cost-benefit calculations, and the primacy of politics has allowed for a different reading within Realpolitik and, more generally, an increasingly liberal way of thinking. As Timothy Dunne has pointed out, concern about the possibilities of peace, rather than the inevitability of war; with order, rather than anarchy; and with progress, instead of repetition allowed liberal thinkers in the twentieth century (particularly in view of the nuclear threat) to challenge what he calls "pure war"-related views as an ideology and a theory of choice.[22] Reason has become a restraint and an obstruction for war to overcome. Recent developments, since the century's traumatic conflicts and the period of the Cold War, have considerably strengthened arguments to restrict war through various normative measures. In other words, it is possible to trace a rather crucial disruption in contingency since the conceptual link between the state and war has become far weaker than before.

Again, as war has come to mean something more than one state against another, it has become much more difficult to define—and the rules have begun to disappear.

The Decay of States

By now, you can understand that the "decay of states" is likely to change the meaning of war as well. Consider, for example, the difficulty of retaliating after 9/11, since we were not attacked by a single country.

With the monopoly of states being undermined in the discourse, waging war has become increasingly anchored in terms of "global" and "cosmopolitan" approaches. It has also become attached to entities such as "humanity." The two latter epithets tend to stand for openly normative approaches that view the use of collective violence as potentially creating positive consequences. Terms such as *transnational networks, society*, and *local actors* also figure frequently in the analysis of "new wars." In this context, entities such as "warlords" and "terrorists" are occasionally furnished with agency.[23] Another way of anchoring the concept of war regards it as a "grand theater." Crucially, viewing war as a spectacle, devoid of specific meaning, disconnects and deprives it of external bonds. Consequently, when understood in this wholly self-centered manner, war spins rather wildly; its detached and autonomous stature then contributes to the inevitable dissolution and demise of other key categories of political order (states in particular).

There is little agreement on the transformations under way and no clear consensus around any particular points. For some observers, the fragmented, nonregular, and scattered nature of wars creates an emphasis on "local" actors and conditions. Others draw the opposite conclusion, claiming that underlying causes may be found in worldwide patterns. This claim, then, mandates "global" action to cope with the challenges. "Global" and "humanitarian" ways of framing war are often underpinned and strengthened by "liberal" approaches.

To the extent that any shared and unifying marker is invoked, it consists of the "global." The "global" figures in the discourse as an explanation as well as an outcome. It also stands out as a major factor in efforts to account for the alleged disjunctures pertaining to war. Pointing out the various corrosive effects of "globalization" constitutes a major way of accounting for the assumed weakening and declining position of the states. In other words, "globalization" is often identified as a major reason why the ability of the states to govern and exercise their power, including the waging of wars, has declined. For example, in his more general study on the interrelated processes of war-making and state-making in the context of globalization, Herfried Mùnkler argues that "Economic globalization has turned post-colonial state-building into state-decay." Statemaking has been crushed, he contends, by the twin forces of globalization and tribalism.[24]

See how this sentence, introduced by "In other words," attempts to summarize the previous and complex discussion in simpler terms. Look for those moments to help understand difficult readings like this one.

Despite frequent mention of "new" wars, the emergence of such "nonregular" wars is not, necessarily, unprecedented. The "newness" does not always imply novelty nor does it point to linear development. The claim is, rather, that various conflicts, which previously existed in the shadow of regular, political wars waged between great powers, have now entered a much more central stage in international politics. To state it differently, what was previously viewed as excessive and seen as constituting a relatively unimportant residue in regard to the way modern war was unfolding has more recently, and unexpectedly, gained ground. What was before viewed as exceptional has been reconfigured and is now seen as part of normality. The previous norm, where wars between states were regarded as "proper" wars, has become the exception.

Here, we can see why the author began his essay by reminding us that modern concepts of war as one state against another were not always the norm; what we are experiencing now, he suggests, is a return to broader definition of war.

What used to be viewed as a residue has not disappeared from the scene. Instead, it has gained significance and now dominates the discourse on contemporary wars. Rather than remaining in the shadows as something "irregular" or "unconventional," such wars occupy a key constitutive position in more recent efforts to account for crucial forms of political violence. In this context, Münkler refers to an "ironic" relapse into pre-modern times.[25] This argument is also, occasionally, taken to the point of a "medievalization" of war. In this regard, a return to (neo) medieval times is yet another way of accounting for the loss of distinctiveness among interconnections between war and the state.

With 9/11 defined as "the day that changed the world," it is clear that discussions about terrorism have had the most destabilizing impact. Instead of the calculable and well-delineated threats to power in the political era, the discourse has focused on "pathological" dangers that make the classical, statist forms of war outdated. Terrorism has, for the most part, been viewed as something unprecedented. Therefore, the terms break established borders in a profound way. Past experiences and delineations are not much help in determining the essence of contemporary terrorism because it is something quite future-orientated. In the first place, it is diffused and detached from usual statist reason: Terrorist attacks may happen at an unspecified point of time. As a form of violence, they are void of the usual regularities that characterize traditional forms of war. Established discourses are undermined in many ways: "guerillas" become "terrorists," "civil wars" are termed "terrorist" wars, nuclear weapons (seen as constituting traditional-power, political arsenals) are called "terror weapons," and some states (like Iran) are slotted into the category of "terror states." Actors previously at the fringes of the debate are acknowledged. The coining of concepts, such as "homeland security," grant the nation, and society more generally, considerable agency in the "war on terror." In fact, the discourse on terrorism signals that crucial categories of differentiation are being undermined; yet the concept of war seems malleable enough to persist.

Here, the author explicitly discusses how concepts like "the war on terror" require new definitions of war—or a return to the broader past definitions of war.

* * *

Overall, the categories used to differentiate various forms of war have become quite blurred. Standard vocabularies appear increasingly insufficient to serve as reliable points of reference. Historically

This statement introduces the concluding part of the essay by reminding us of its overall point.

drawn distinctions have resurfaced in the discourse, and a rich repertoire of very new concepts has been thrown into the debate.

Inevitably, we reach the conclusion that war is no longer its former self. In the first place, there is much doubt to be found in these debates. Clearly, the concept is not treated as generally valid, stable, nor descriptive in nature. Instead, it is a contested object of a considerable amount of critical scholarship. Moreover, there is much more awareness of the concept's historicity. Various efforts to rescue the concept do not work in the way intended, and war has become part of an expanding list of contested concepts.[26] Rather than restore war's traditionally uncontested and stable nature, these debates testify to the increasing fragility of the concept. They add to, rather than reduce, the signs of contingent disruption. Instead of erasing doubt, efforts of restoration increase the noise. As stated by Anna Leander, they "wreak havoc on the established fundamental categories through which we see the world."[27]

Does this warrant the conclusion that the concept of war has basically become intellectually illegitimate? Has it had its day? Is it well on its way out of the discourse?

After concluding that war is "no longer its former self," the author now asks key questions about how we should react to that situation—which lead to the answers proposed in its final paragraphs.

Confining the analysis to mere changes in the concept does not constitute a sufficient effort for more durable answers to emerge. The concept may no longer signify as strongly as it did in its Clausewitzian form. Nonetheless, it is able to resurface in another context. The emergence of exit-talk among scholars of war also signals some weakening. It severely challenges the usual self-evidence and ideal-type nature of the concept; still, much of the symbolic power remains and may be capitalized by opening up new, noncyclical, and openly hybrid meanings of the term.

To gain more profound answers effort needs to focus on the broader conceptual constellations and discursive structures that provide war with its distinctiveness. My analysis here has focused, in particular, on the nexus between the concepts of war and the state—a connection that has been crucial for the credibility and stability that war, as a concept, has enjoyed throughout the modern era.

This is an argument of "exigency": that is, it shows why it is important and timely to think about the concept of war as this article suggests.

Against this background, it appears that there is more at stake than simply updating the concept. These changes point to more than just a cyclical phenomenon wherein the concept is revised, every now and then, in order to remain relevant to changing circumstances. Efforts of renewal and the search for alternative articulations do not currently occur in the context of an established and unchanged constellation of broader conceptual departures. There is a basis, in that sense, for discussions of profound change including a way out of the current dilemma. Clearly, an extensive reshuffling is underway that includes changes to the nexus between war and the state.

This is not to say that the state will have lost out altogether. It is still part of a broader constellation of key concepts that underpin war; however, it does not have its former eminence. Instead, the state has to compete with other departures, in particular "humanity," "cosmopolitan," and the "global." The concept of war is less autonomous; it is reliant on, paired with, or borrows from other concepts. There are a multitude of options competing with the state for an alliance with war. Clearly, there is no hierarchy to be traced where the state would occupy a self-evident primacy. On the contrary, the various bonds have become quite diffuse and fluent. This allows war to be expressed and named in a multifaceted manner, including the possibility that the concept of war may be dropped altogether.

Creative efforts of renaming and coining a broader linguistic repertoire, rather than aspiring for a return to a strictly unilinear, precise, and stable meaning, are warranted. At the same time, returning to war in its traditional conceptual guise also requires a restoration of the nexus between war and the state. In principle, the various voices calling for the state to be brought back into the discourse on war along neo-Weberian lines are correct. The prospects for such a move to succeed appear quite slim since the discourse is moving toward completely severing the concept of war from the concept of the state. Indeed, a significant chasm has developed and will, presumably, increase rather than decrease in the years to come.

Here, the author concludes by suggesting that how we think and talk about the concept of war influences the way we act as well.

Notes

1. Arguments along these lines have been presented by a number of authors. See, for example, Christopher Coker, "Post-modernity and the End of the Cold War: Has War Been Disinvented?" *Review of International Studies* 18, no. 3 (1992): 189–198; Martin van Crevald, *The Transformation of War* (New York: Free Press, 1991); Chris Hables Gray, *Postmodern War: The Politics of Conflict* (London: Routledge, 1997); Kalevi Holsti, *The State, War, and the State of War* (Cambridge: Cambridge University Press, 1996); John Lynne, *Battle: A History of Combat and Culture* (Boulder, Colo.: Westview, 2003). For

a summary of the discourse, see Michael Brzoska, "'New Wars' Discourse in Germany," *Journal of Peace Research* 41, no. 1 (2004): 107–117. The idea that political and social concepts are historical rather than fixed has been made and elaborated, on a more general level, by Reinhart Koselleck, *Futures Past: On the Semantics of Historical Time,* trans. Keith Tribe (Cambridge, Mass.: MIT Press, 1985).

2. Gray, note 1, p. 3.
3. This concept has been used in particular by Mary Kaldor, "American Power: From 'Compellance' to 'Cosmopolitanism'?" *International Affairs* 79, no. 1 (2003): 1–22. Also Ulrich Beck has contributed to the debate with a number of new coinages, such as "post-national wars" or "humanitarian wars"; see Beck, "Über den postnationalen Krieg," *Blätter für deutsche und Internationale Politik* 8 (1999): 984–990.
4. See, for example, William Lind, "Understanding Fourth Generation Warfare," *Anti-War.com:* http://antiwar.com/lind/?articleid=1702.
5. The concept has been used by Jean Baudrillard, *The Gulf War Did Not Take Place* (Sydney: Power Publications, 1995).
6. Slavoj Zizek, *Welcome to the Desert of the Real* (New York: Verso, 2002), p. 10. On the concept of "virtual war," see Andreas Behnke, "'vvv.nato.int.': virtuousness and virtuosity in NATO's representation of the Kosovo campaign," in Peter van Ham and Sergei Medvedev, eds., *Mapping European Security After Kosovo* (Manchester, UK: Manchester University Press, 2002), pp. 26–144. On the refusal of most Western leaders to use the concept of war in the context of the Kosovo "campaign," see Pertti Joenniemi, "Kosovo and the End of War," in van Ham and Medvedev, note 6, pp. 48–65.
7. See http:/ /www. woerterbuchdeskrieges. de/
8. For this argument, see Azar Gat, *A History of Military Thought from Enlightenment to the Cold War* (Oxford: Oxford University Press, 2001); John Keegan, *History of Warfare* (London: Pimlico, 1993); or Peter Paret, *Makers of Modern Strategy: From Machiavelli to the Nuclear Age* (Princeton: Princeton University Press, 1986), p. 5.
9. For a similar effort applied to the concept of power, see Stefano Guzzini, "The Concept of Power: A Constructivist Analysis," *Millennium* 33, no. 3 (2005): 455–521. On a more general level, see Martin Bulmer, "Concept in the Analysis of Qualitative Data," *Sociological Review* 27, no. 4 (1979): 651–677.
10. Among numerous works, see, for example, Claudio Cioffi-Revilla, "Ancient Warfare: Origins and Systems," in Magnus I, Midlarsky, ed., *The Handbook of War Studies II* (Ann Arbor: University of Michigan Press, 1999), pp. 223–245.
11. Along these lines, see Keith F. Otterbein, *Feuding and Warfare: Selected Works of Keith F. Otterbein* (Langhorne: Gordon & Breach Science Publishers, 1994).
12. See for example Keegan, note 8.

13. On the relation between the norm and the exception, see Jef Huysmans, "International Politics of Insecurity: Normativity, Inwardsness, and the Exception," *Security Dialogue* 37, no. 1 (2006): 11–29.
14. Otterbein, note 11.
15. Carl von Clausewitz, *On War*, ed. and trans. Michael Howard and Peter Paret (Princeton: Princeton University Press, 1976).
16. Herfried Münkler, *The New Wars* (Cambridge, UK: Polity, 2005), p. 4.
17. The link has been stressed in particular by Charles Tilly, "War Making and State Making as Organized Crime," in P. B. Evans, D. Rueschermeyer, and T. Skoçpol, eds., *Bringing the State Back In* (Cambridge: Cambridge University Press, 1985), pp. 164–185. See also Vivienne Jabri, *Discourses on Violence. Conflict Analysis Reconsidered* (Manchester, UK: Manchester University Press, 1996).
18. See Anna Leander, "External Determinants of Local Violent Conflict: The Transnational Nature of Contemporary Warfare," in *Interdépendences et Aide Publique au Dévelopment: Actes de Séminaire DgCiD-Iddri, 2005–6* (Paris: Ministère des Affaires Etrangères, 2006); as well as Vivienne Jabri, *War and the Transformation of Global Politics* (Houndmills, Basingstoke, UK: Palgrave, 2007).
19. Wilhelm Grewe, *Epochen der Völkerrechtgeschichtliche* (Baden-Baden: Nomos Verlagsgesellschaft, 1988), p. 728.
20. Carl Schmitt, *Die Wendung zum diskriminierenden Kriegsbegriff* (Berlin: Duncker & Humblot, 1988 [1938]).
21. Ibid., p. 35.
22. Timothy Dunne, "Liberalism," in John Baylis and Steve Smith, eds., *Globalization: An Introduction to World Politics* (Oxford: Oxford University Press, 1997), p. 148.
23. Mary Kaldor's various writings on "new" wars are a case in point: Mary Kaldor, *New and Old Wars: Organized Violence in the Global Era* (Oxford, UK: Polity, 1999). See also note 3.
24. Münkler, note 16, pp. 19–21. See also note 11.
25. Ibid., p. 72. For an analysis with stress on local and postcolonial wars, see Tarak Barkawi and Mark Laffey, "The Postcolonial Moment in Security Studies," *Review of International Studies* 32, no. 2 (2002): 329–352.
26. On "essentially contested concepts," see W. B. Gallie, "Essentially Contested Concepts," *Proceedings of the Aristotelian Society*, n.s., vol. 56 (London: 1956), pp. 171–172.
27. Leander, note 18, p. 17. See note 16.

Reading Analytically

1. Part of Joenniemi's essay discusses the various ways that we have used the term *war* recently, including news wars, network wars, and so on. Add to that list other uses of the word that you have heard (e.g., "the war on poverty"), and speculate on how those uses of the word affect our overall understanding of its purposes.

2. According to Joenniemi, what are some of the key arguments that have been made by nations in support of war efforts? How have those arguments changed over time?
3. One section of Joenniemi's essay is titled "The Decay of States." In what ways has the "global" environment—in which we think in wider terms than merely country by country—changed the nature of war according to this author?

Reading Across Disciplinary Communities

1. In order to discuss contemporary definitions and concepts of war, Joenniemi provides a historical survey of past ways that this term has been constructed. In your estimation, what is the relationship between an understanding of the past and an understanding of the present? Must a political scientist have a firm foundation in the past, or can she base her research largely on an analysis of the present?
2. Though this piece is written by a foreign relations expert, its topic and method also draws upon rhetorical analysis (the ways that words are used to persuade and to frame reality) and philosophy (attempting to arrive at an understanding of war through a logical analysis). Point out some spots in the essay where you find the author using those methodologies.

JASON ROYCE LINDSEY

America and the New Dynamics of War

In this essay, Jason Royce, a faculty member in the Department of Political Science at St. Cloud University, explores what he calls the "compartmentalization" of war in America—the ways that war has been moved outside the mainstream of our cultural dialogue, and so out of our day-to-day discussions even as we are at war. This piece was first published in Peace Review: A Journal of Social Justice.

More specifically, this political scientist explores the world of war as it relates to the United States' new ability to "deploy with less domestic political cost to the American government," a change that he argues is "profound for the United States and the world." Using disciplinary methods for analyzing the relationship between war and political processes, the author is able to demonstrate the ways in which war is often predicated on the political costs to decision-makers. As you read, you might consider the degree to which recent wars have affected your own day-to-day life, and if they have in fact been kept out of the mainstream of our culture in ways that were not true of previous wars.

> The importance of domestic political pressure as a restraint on America's use of force has become more apparent with the current conflict in Iraq. In our post–Cold War international environment, there is no large rival to inhibit U.S. action. Current international organizations are unable to serve as a substitute source of pressure. Thus, while the United States is without an equal international rival, only American citizens can provide an effective political check to their government's use of force. Many Americans, however, seem remarkably apathetic. This irony is due to recent developments in the structure and technology of the American military establishment. What is emerging is a military structure that the United States can deploy with less domestic political cost to the American government. The consequences of this change are profound for the United States and the world.

One of the key trends within this troubling change is the increasing compartmentalization of the military from the rest of American society. Many observers, especially abroad, are puzzled by the small amount of political protest in the United States over the war in Iraq. What this point of view fails to see are the changes that have occurred within the U.S. armed forces and American society since the 1970s. The critical difference is that, unlike the past, today's military practically constitutes a separate social class within American society. As an all-volunteer body, with many life-long members, deployment of this professional military force does not create domestic political opposition like the 1960s conscript army that was sent to Vietnam.

Instead, the modern American military relies on a core of full-time military personnel who have chosen the service as a career. Many Americans choose the military career path in an effort to move up in society from poorer backgrounds. Studies of military recruitment consistently show that the service's most significant appeal to young people is its educational benefits. Individuals enlisting in the military after high school earn college tuition credits for each year they serve. Although feelings of patriotism are also important to military recruitment, studies consistently show that the military's chief attraction is the social mobility it brings. Surveys show, for example, that high school students with college educated parents and higher grades in school are less likely to enlist. In addition, traditionally poorer ethnic minorities, specifically African Americans and Hispanics, are more likely to enlist than their white peers are. Thus, military service often provides a path to college and social advancement for individuals with less affluent origins in American society.

Although this professional volunteer force is ethnically and regionally diverse, it remains concentrated in specific, cohesive communities. This slice of the American population lives on or near military installations across the United States, and learns to expect deployment as a possibility. Divisions within this community do exist, such as that between higher-level officers from the prestigious American military academies and lower ranking soldiers. The neighborhoods near military bases across the United States, however, are some of the most racially integrated in the country. This social cohesion sets these communities apart from others across the United States. In surveys of opinion, military personnel drawn from similar backgrounds in American society and with similar career paths show significant attitudinal differences from civilians. From this perspective, U.S. military personnel live in tight knit communities that are supportive of soldiers and families, but are also disconnected from the average American's daily life.

On this point, it is noticeable that the major source of resentment toward the current war is from the National Guard and Reserve members' families. These reservists traditionally support full-time soldiers as needed during emergencies. The Iraq conflict, however, has seen many National Guard units deployed for 12 or more months at a time, depending on the unit and its specialization. This group is drawn from a much more inclusive cross-section of the citizenry compared to the compartmentalized career soldiers. As a result, deployment of the National Guard has been one of the more politically difficult aspects of the war for the current administration.

Further deployments of reserve units would be necessary if the professional army were not also supported by so-called contract soldiers serving with U.S. forces in Iraq. Contract soldiers are employees of private American companies under contract with the U.S. Department of Defense. Currently, these contract soldiers are one of the largest contingents of coalition troops in Iraq and are almost equal in size to the British contribution. These mercenary forces perform a broad range of functions that used to be the exclusive responsibility of U.S. troops. The most elastic of these duties, security, allows contract soldiers to fill critical gaps in the overstretched volunteer army. Given this group's monetary motive for being in Iraq, it is not plausible to expect any political pressure from the public over casualties in this group. Indeed, the casualties from the contract forces are largely invisible because the media does not give them the same attention as other battlefield deaths. So far, the only controversy surrounding these mercenary troops has been the implication of some "contractors" in the questionable interrogation techniques used at Abu Ghraib.

Besides these structural changes to the military's composition, improvements in weaponry and battlefield medicine have held American casualties in Iraq to a minimum. Compared to the Vietnam conflict, fewer American soldiers die on the battlefield or are permanently incapacitated. Improvements that cost the United States less lives on the battlefield make the overall likelihood of using force more likely. This tragic paradox stems from the simple political calculation that force is easier to apply the lower its cost in American lives. Thus, fewer casualties increase the likelihood of some lives being lost because all deployments are politically cheaper.

The decline in American military deaths through better battlefield medicine also corresponds to an increased effectiveness on the battlefield. With improvements in military weaponry and technology, fewer soldiers can cover larger areas of occupation. Thus, American military forces can occupy a country the size of Iraq, at least tenuously, with a relatively small force of about 160,000 troops. The result of these two trends is fewer forces deployed and fewer casualties from that smaller force.

Another irony of this situation is that improvements in battlefield medicine and weapons technology that save the life of the common American soldier also increase the odds of collateral damage affecting foreign civilians. For example, reliance on cruise missiles and air strikes reduces American military deaths, but this is offset by the likelihood of injuring innocent bystanders. Estimates of Iraqi civilian deaths range in the tens of thousands. Yet, large numbers of Iraqi civilian deaths have so far failed to make a strong impression on the American public. The moral logic of distinguishing between the two groups is tragically nearsighted. Even by conservative estimates, the total number of Iraqi civilian deaths since the American-led invasion began is far beyond the number of U.S. military casualties. Besides the immediate suffering these deaths represent for the people of Iraq, this violence has triggered an exodus of the country's middle class and best educated.

Thus, Iraq will continue to feel the consequences of this population loss for decades to come.

Nonetheless, American politicians know that American military casualties are significant in domestic politics, not the innocents caught in the fray a world away from their constituents. So, as the political costs for using military force come down through fewer battlefield deaths and the deployment of smaller, compartmentalized forces, it is easier for this and future American administrations to use force.

Further technological developments are likely to continue this political trend. Recent reports in the news media and scholarly sources, for example, reveal that the U.S. Department of Defense is investing heavily in robotics research. This priority is supported by an enthusiastic U.S. Congress that has consistently increased funding in this area over the last few years. The military already uses robots to help with bomb disposal and other dangerous tasks. Most impressive to date has been the increased use of robotic aircraft, drones, for aerial reconnaissance and remotely controlled air strikes.

Besides robotics, reports of even more bizarre military research, with far-reaching ethical consequences and questions, have appeared in the American and British media. The research arm of the Department of Defense, DARPA, has been experimenting with the remote control of animals. Apparently, one of their largest experiments has involved using sharks for naval reconnaissance. The sharks have electronics implanted in them allowing an operator to steer them toward a chosen target. DARPA has pioneered this line of research because using a living organism, like a shark, saves much time and cost over developing a machine to do the same task (that is, to swim like a shark). The research is attempting to ascertain the feasibility of using sharks and other modified animals for dangerous reconnaissance missions.

The instrumental logic driving these developments in technology and capability raise a fundamental question for a democratic state. If robots, machines, and modified animals make up an increasingly significant element of United States fighting forces, then what will happen to the politics of military action?

One obvious point is that the use of machines and other substitutes for human soldiers reduces the political pressure on policymakers. The publics' tolerance for casualties is an important calculation when a democracy goes to war. With the increased use of machines, this political pressure can be reduced in future wars. Therefore, current trends within the American military establishment may make it much easier for politicians to support future wars. This possibility represents a challenge to long held assumptions about democracies and war.

In political philosophy, theorists have long assumed that one of the responsibilities of democratic citizens is defense of the state. Modern political scientists, who have been concerned with the public's lack of interest in foreign policy, knew that voters would at least pay attention on issues of war and peace. This traditional assumption is often cited as an important advantage of democracy. Many argue that democratic governments are more pacific since citizen armies will only support wars that are vital for self-defense. Yet, this traditional assumption, already debatable, is made even less plausible by career, volunteer armies and technologies that replace human soldiers.

Therefore, all of us face a future where the responsibility of defense and the cost of war will be shifted to machines and become a more technocratic area of policy. Although this may sound far fetched, a straightforward logic drives the U.S. Department of Defense. We see today that the use of a compartmentalized volunteer force, military contractors, and new technologies is reducing the political costs of war in Iraq. This same line of reasoning, when connected with future robotic technology, will transform the issue of war and its costs even more dramatically in the years to come.

This shift in how wars are fought will exacerbate the gap in power that exists in the world. It is easy to imagine a future where developed, wealthy countries can easily threaten military action by risking machines rather than citizens in combat. On the other side, poorer, less developed states would be faced with the less credible threat of putting their citizens on the line to face military machines. In such a scenario, it is easy to see that the power gap between developed and underdeveloped states will only widen in years to come.

How will poorer and developing states react to this dynamic? We already see one strategy in the actions of Iran and North Korea. If poorer states cannot hope to compete with the United States and other developed countries by conventional means, then the logical move is to look for a cheap equalizer: nuclear and ballistic missile programs. In the future, if one cannot hope to match a state of the art military like that of the United States on the battlefield, then the only logical deterrent are weapons that threaten its homeland citizens.

What should be the reaction of citizens in the United States and its allies to these trends? As the military power of the United States and other developed countries accelerates, the moral responsibility for using it will shift more and more to the citizenry. In a sense, this moral obligation is increasing proportionally to the ease with which government officials can apply force. As future policymakers face fewer traditional restraints on the use of military force, the burden for filling this gap with new domestic political pressure rests with the citizenry. This same dynamic will spread to other developed countries that can emulate the structure and technology of America's military.

Thus, the fate of a shrinking group of domestic professional soldiers and a growing throng of civilians everywhere depends on the action of citizens in the United States and other developed countries. To address this emerging dynamic, urgent debate is needed on the broad but interrelated topics discussed here. If citizens engage their political leaders on this issue, then perhaps the old assumption about democracies being averse to war will continue. Otherwise, this next century will see the wealthiest and most powerful states, in the absence of domestic political pressure, free to use force as never before.

Recommended Readings

Adams, Thomas K. 2001–2002. "Future Warfare and the Decline of Human Decision Making," *Parameters* 31 (Winter): 57–71.

Bekey, George A. 2005. *Autonomous Robots: From Biological Inspiration to Implementation and Control.* Cambridge, MA: MIT Press.

Brown, Susan. 2006. "Stealth Sharks to Patrol the High Seas." *The New Scientist.* 2541, March 1:30.

Eighmey, John. 2006. "Why Do Youth Enlist: Identification of Underlying Themes." *Armed Forces and Society* 32 (2): 307–328.

Engelhardt, Tom. 2006. "Shark and Awe." *Salon.* Accessed on March 10, 2006. Available at http://www.salon.com/opinion/feature/2006/03/10/sharks/

Fever, Peter D. and Gelpi. Christopher. 2004. *Choosing Your Battles: American Civil-Military Relations and the Use of Force.* Princeton, NJ: Princeton University Press.

Gray, Chris Hables. 1997. *Postmodern War: The New Politics of Conflict.* New York: Guilford Press.

Holsti, Ole R. 1998–1999. "A Widening Gap between the U.S. Military and Civilian Society? Some Evidence, 1976–1996." *International Security* 23 (3) (Winter): 5–42.

Roland, Alex and Shiman, Philip. 2002. *Strategic Computing: DARPA and the Quest for Machine Intelligence.* Cambridge, MA: MIT Press.

Segal, David R. and Mady Wechsler Segal. 2004. "America's Military Population," *Population Bulletin* 59 (4) (December): 3–17.

Singer, P.W. 2003. *Corporate Warriors: The Rise of the Privatized Military Industry*. Ithaca: Cornell University Press.

Xu, Shaohua Xu, Talwar. Sanjiv K., Hawley, Emerson S. Li, Lei and Chapin John K. 2004. "A Multi-Channel Telemetry System for Brain Microstimulation in Freely Roaming Animals." *Journal of Neuroscience Methods* 133 (1–2) (February): 57–63.

Reading Analytically

1. This piece seems to have a clear thesis and message, both in its introduction and in its conclusion. Summarize what you take to be the thesis of the piece, and what attitudes it is trying to shape in its readers.
2. What kinds of evidence are used by the author of this article? List some of the key pieces of support for his case.
3. One of the central arguments made by Lindsey is that war has been "compartmentalized," and so moved outside the realm of everyday life of American citizens; to consider the differences in how this war is being treated, you might talk to people from other generations to see if they notice this type of change, and report on their perspectives.

Reading Across Disciplinary Communities

1. This essay was originally published in a journal called *Peace Review: A Journal of Social Justice*. Though this journal publishes scholarly work, such a focus may also lead to some biases against the practice of war. After reading this piece, do you find it to live up to the standard of true scholarship; that is, does it seem to base its conclusions on the evidence available? Does the evidence seem sufficient? Or are there any signs that this piece is more of an opinion article? To form your thoughts, you might also see what you can find out about this journal from its Web site.
2. As is suggested by the previous question, there is a split between the methodologies of many of the social sciences. This split is especially evident in political science, where some practitioners are more reliant than others on quantitative information. Do some research on the state of methodology in political science—or in your own major field of study—and summarize any debates you find about current methodologies. You might also discuss current methodologies in your field with some of the professors in that field at your college.

THOMAS POGGE

Making War on Terrorists

Reflections on Harming the Innocent*

This essay, originally published in The Journal of Political Philosophy, explores the ethical implications of the world's reactions to terrorism. Its author, Thomas Pogge, is currently the Leitner Professor of Philosophy and International Affairs at Yale University, and has written extensively on global justice.

This piece, drawing upon that background, examines the willingness to treat the effect of the "war on terror" upon innocent individuals as morally justifiable, and the implications of a moral code that can justify such actions. It also illustrates the analytical methods used by the discipline of philosophy as it is applied to political issues; you might note the differences in this methodology, comparing it with the more directly argumentative methods of Jason Royce Lindsey. Which of these methods do you find most convincing?

I

The countries of the developed West are fighting a war on terror. More accurately: the governments of some of these countries are conducting a war against terrorists. This war effort was stepped up dramatically after the terrorist attack of September 11, 2001, which killed about 3,000 people in New York, Virginia, and Pennsylvania. The most notable attack until then was the car bomb attack on the US embassies in Dar es Salaam and Nairobi of August 7, 1998, which killed about 257 people including 12 US citizens. Since the September 11 attack, 202 people, including 88 Australians, were killed in Kuta on the Indonesian island of Bali on October 12, 2002; some 191 people were killed in the Madrid bombing of March 11, 2004; and the terrorist attack of July 7, 2005, in London killed 52 people.

Why wage war against these terrorists? Offhand, one might think that such a grand response to terrorism is undeserved. This thought is supported by comparisons with other threats to our life

*This lecture was presented in Oxford on February 24, 2006. I am grateful for written comments and suggestions I received from Jeff McMahan, Chris Miller, Rekha Nath, Matt Petersen, Michael Ravvin, Ling Tong, Leif Wenar, and Andrew Williams. This essay is dedicated to David Álvarez García in gratitude for his numerous translations of my work into Spanish.

and well-being—cardiovascular disease and cancer, for instance, annually kill some 250,000 and 150,000 people, respectively, in the UK alone (940,000 and 560,000 in the US), while traffic accidents kill over 3,000 each year (43,000 in the US). In the UK, only about one per 10,000 deaths in 2005 was due to terrorism. And even in the US in 2001, the corresponding ratio was about one in 750, that is, 0.13 percent. It would seem that even a small increase in the effort to combat cardiovascular disease, cancer, road accidents, or any of several other, similar threats would do much more to protect our survival and well-being, at lower cost, than revving up the war on terror.

This point has been made repeatedly with dramatic facts and figures.[1] Since 2001, the Global Fund to Fight AIDS, Tuberculosis, and Malaria, funded by all willing governments and devoted to combating diseases that kill about 6 million people each year, has committed about $6.9 billion and spent about $4.4 billion.[2] This expenditure comes to roughly $120 per fatality. Between 2001 and 2006, the US government alone has spent $438 billion on the war on terror.[3] This amount comes to roughly $146 million per US fatality—over a million times more per fatality. Many millions of deaths from extreme poverty and curable diseases could be avoided each year, if the world's governments were willing to spend even one quarter as much on combating these scourges as they are now spending on their war on terror. Such a war on poverty and disease would also avoid the substantial human costs of the war on terror: Some 5000 coalition soldiers have been killed and several ten thousand wounded in Iraq and Afghanistan. Fatalities among Iraqi and Afghan civilians have been vastly higher.

So why is terrorism being taken so seriously? This question requires nuances. We need to distinguish reasons and causes. And we need to differentiate the various groups involved in this war.

I see two main explanations. One is that public attention to terrorism serves important domestic constituencies. It serves most obviously the news media. Their economic success depends on their ability to attract the public's attention; and it is vastly easier to attract the public to stories about terrorists and their plans and victims than to stories about cancer and cancer victims or to stories about traffic accidents.[4]

Public attention to terrorism also serves the interests of politicians, especially incumbents. They can gain greatly increased attention, authority, and respect from a frightened public as well as acquiescence when they withhold information, increase surveillance, disrespect civil liberties, and curb political opposition. Many Western government policies—from the invasion of Iraq to the secret monitoring of citizens and the detention of political opponents at home and abroad—have been marketed as anti-terror measures.[5] Many non-Western governments have eagerly followed our example, often defending severe violations of basic human rights as necessary responses to terrorist threats.

The politicians of some countries derive a further benefit from a major war on terror also in the international arena, namely the benefit that this war strengthens the political power of their country. Assume simplistically that a country's political power depends on three components: military might (capacity for violence), economic might, and international moral standing. Countries differ in regard to the composition of their political power: Russia and the US are strong militarily relative to their moral and economic strength. Japan is strong economically relative to its military and moral strength. And Iceland's moral standing in the world is strong relative to its military and economic strength. Now, how much each of the three components contributes to political power depends on the regional or global environment. Military strength will be a much larger contributor to political power in the midst of a world war than in a time of universal peace; and a country's moral reputation will matter much more in peaceful times than in a period of war or conflict. Therefore, governments of countries whose military strength is relatively larger than their economic and moral strengths will tend to benefit from heightened insecurity and tension by enjoying greater freedom of action due to greater acquiescence on the part of their own citizens and other countries. The political leaders of such countries with comparatively greater military strength therefore have a further incentive to foster an international climate of conflict and hostility. Such a climate stands to enhance not only their domestic standing, but also the power they wield on their country's behalf internationally.

These points are worth further thought because, by playing up terrorism in pursuit of their own ends, our media and politicians are helping the terrorists achieve exactly what they want: attention and public fear. By helping to ensure that terrorist attacks are successful in the way their perpetrators want them to be successful, the media and politicians are multiplying the damage our societies suffer from terrorism and also encouraging further terrorist attacks.

II

Those ordinary citizens in the UK and US who have been supporting the war effort, at least tacitly, are a different matter. Why have they been so supportive of the new war? One reason is, of course, that such citizens have been persuaded that this war enhances the security of themselves and their friends and relatives from terrorist attacks. But this more prudential reason does not explain the enormous public attention paid to terrorism, nor the great cost, in terms of money and basic freedoms, that many citizens seem willing to bear to combat terrorism, because the war on terror is not a cost-effective way of protecting our health and survival. Of course, citizens are not fully informed and perfectly rational. They may not realize how small the threat really is, and how costly the counter-measures. But I think an important part of the explanation is our moral judgment that these terrorist attacks are exceptionally heinous. This judgment lends special urgency to fighting this terrorism as the effort promises not merely a reduction in the risk of harm each of us is exposed to, but also the suppression of a dreadful moral evil. Because we perceive these terrorist attacks as so exceptionally heinous, we attach to their suppression an importance that is greatly disproportional to the immediate harm they inflict.

Is it correct to consider these terrorist attacks especially heinous and thus to attach such disproportional importance to suppressing them?

Before examining this question, let us address a prior concern. Some find such an examination offensive. They find it obvious that these terrorist attacks are very wrong. And they feel that the self-evidence of this proposition is denied when we examine its meaning and grounds. They feel that the question: "What is wrong with these terrorist attacks?" suggests that these attacks are among the things about which people can reasonably disagree. And they firmly reject this suggestion.

Let me be clear then that, by asking what is wrong with these terrorist attacks, I am not suggesting that people can reasonably disagree about their wrongness, but merely that it is important to understand why these attacks are wrong. Even if we are perfectly certain they are wrong, understanding why is still important for two reasons. I will state one reason now, the other in section V.

The first reason has to do with moral theorizing. We are often faced with moral questions or decisions that are difficult to resolve. When this happens, we engage in moral reflection. Such reflection looks at relevant empirical evidence and also at other, less difficult moral questions or decisions that may be analogous or related in some way to the problem at hand. John Rawls has analyzed this ordinary method in some detail and has compared it to how we make difficult judgments in linguistics: When we are doubtful whether some particular phrase is proper English, we can hypothetically formulate grammatical rules that would forbid or allow it and then test these general hypotheses against other phrases whose status is certain. In this way, some of the rules we try out will be confirmed and others refuted. Confirmed rules can then be brought to bear on the questionable phrase to resolve our doubt.[6]

With this method, which Rawls calls reflective equilibrium, our most firmly held convictions, collectively, are the standard by which we judge difficult questions. But the method can work only if we can bring some of our most firmly held convictions to bear on the difficult question or decision we confront. This requires that we generalize from these most firmly held convictions. We can do this by hypothetically formulating more general moral principles that may then be confirmed or refuted by our firmest moral convictions, such as the conviction that these terrorist attacks are wrong. A confirmed moral principle helps us understand why these attacks are wrong, or what makes them wrong. And such a principle can then also be used to help resolve other, more difficult moral questions or decisions.

III

So what is wrong with terrorist attacks such as the five I described at the outset? In first approximation we might say that what makes these attacks presumptively wrong is that, foreseen by the agent, they harm and even kill innocent people. I assume it is clear enough for present purposes what it means to harm or kill people. By calling a person innocent, I mean that this person poses no threat and has done nothing that would justify attacking her with lethal force. To be sure, the terrorists may have believed that some of those they attacked were not innocent in this somewhat technical sense and were thus justifiably subject to lethal attack. But they could not have believed this of the great majority of the people they attacked. They clearly foresaw that their conduct would harm and kill many innocent people. In fact, the time of day they chose for their attacks, and the lack of any prior warnings such as were often issued by the IRA and the ETA, strongly suggest that they not merely foresaw but even intended to harm and kill many innocent people.

We need not claim that it is always wrong to do what one foresees will harm or kill innocent people. It is enough that there is a firm presumption against it, which may be overcome by showing that so acting is necessary to achieve some greater good (which may consist in the prevention of some greater harm).

Justifications of this kind come in two types. Justifications of the first type assert that those who will be harmed stood to gain from the action ex ante. We can give this type of justification for a doctor who administers a live vaccine to 10,000 children while knowing statistically that roughly one or two of them will die from the resulting infection. This doctor's conduct is nonetheless permissible if each child's prospects of survival are expected to increase relative to no treatment and also relative to other feasible treatment options. With justifications of this type, it is enough that the expected good should outweigh the expected harm so that there is a net expected gain for each person affected. Since it is plainly false that each of the persons attacked by the terrorists stood to gain from this attack ex ante, we can set aside this type of justification in what follows.

Justifications of the second type assert that the harm done to innocent people is outweighed—not by some good for these same people, but—by a greater good of some other kind. Some philosophers reject justifications of this second type altogether. But I find such absolutism implausible. If the brutal reign of a tyrant who is killing many thousands can be ended with a violent strike that unavoidably also kills an innocent child, then this strike seems morally acceptable, perhaps mandatory, if indeed it can save thousands from being murdered and millions from being oppressed and brutalized. Similarly, the aerial bombardment of cities may be justifiable when this is the only means of defense against a horrible aggressor state. At the opposite end of the spectrum, some philosophers hold that justifications of the second type can succeed even when the greater good just barely outweighs the harm foreseen. Such philosophers might approve of killing 19 children when this is the only way of saving 20 others. Like most, I find such an act-consequentialist standard too permissive. When the greater good an agent intends to achieve with her action will not be a good for the innocent persons this action will harm, then that good can justify the action only if it *greatly* outweighs the harm this action foreseeably inflicts. (This requirement is often thought to be especially significant when the harm to be inflicted is a means to attaining the purported good, rather than a foreseeable side effect.) In addition, a successful such justification also requires, of course, that the harm be *necessary* for achieving the greater good in question, so that the same good could not have been achieved using any other less harmful means.

Can such a justification be provided for the terrorist attacks at issue? I believe not. To show this conclusively, one would need to run through indefinitely many candidate "greater goods" that might be offered. This we cannot do. Instead, let us focus on three such candidate greater goods that have actually been appealed to by the terrorists or their supporters. This exercise may give us a clearer sense of how we might respond to other such justifications yet to be advanced.

One justification refers to various regimes in the Middle East—that of Saudi Arabia prominently included—which are regarded as dictatorial or un-Islamic or pro-Western. The terrorist attacks were meant to discourage the US and other Western countries from supporting these regimes, especially through the stationing of troops in their territories, and to boost the morale of those who are seeking to overthrow these regimes. A second justification appeals to the alleged good of weakening Israel by discouraging other governments from supporting it and by boosting the morale of Palestinians resisting the occupation of their lands. A third justification appeals to the alleged good of punishing Western countries for their past and present support of Israel and/or of dictatorial and un-Islamic Middle Eastern regimes.

To succeed, any such justification must discharge four burdens of proof: it must show that the alleged good really is a good; it must show that the terrorist attacks in question contribute to this good, at least probabilistically; it must show that the value of this contribution greatly outweighs the foreseen harms to innocent people; and, finally, any such justification must also show that all these harms were really necessary for the intended contribution to the greater good.

The quickest and clearest way of seeing that these justifications fail focuses on the fourth burden of proof. Equivalent contributions to all three candidate greater goods could have been achieved with far less harm to clearly innocent people. In fact, the manner and timing of the attacks suggest that such harm was intended. In any case, the terrorists at minimum displayed great disregard for what is often euphemistically called collateral damage. The terrorists could have attacked their US targets early on a Sunday morning, for instance, when the World Trade Center area would have been nearly deserted. Such a palpable effort to spare innocent people would not have reduced attention to the terrorists' cause. On the contrary: By signaling clearly their intent to spare innocent people as far as reasonably possible, the terrorists would have made local and Western citizens less unreceptive to their ends and grievances, and would still have demonstrated their terrifying capabilities and willingness to die for their cause. Most of the harm the terrorists inflicted on innocent people was not necessary for promoting the alleged good they sought and quite possibly even counterproductive.

We might remember in this context that the disregard for the lives of innocent persons is not a defining feature of terrorism and is in fact absent from much historical terrorism. The IRA and ETA frequently issued bomb warnings beforehand in order to minimize harm to persons. And some of the 1905–06 Russian terrorists—sometimes called moral-imperative terrorists and immortalized by Albert Camus in his play *The Just* as well as in his essay *The Rebel*—were absolutely determined not to harm innocents. Thus Kaliaev abandoned his first attempt to kill Sergei Aleksandrovich when he saw that the Grand Duke had his niece and nephew, two children, in his carriage.[7]

Moral justifications of the terrorist attacks fail, then, because the fourth burden of proof cannot be discharged: The attacks inflicted great harms on far more innocent people than was, given the goal, reasonably unavoidable.

To this it may be objected that the terrorists and their supporters may feel that no justification is needed for their killing of innocent people. They see themselves as involved in a war in which their opponents have inflicted even greater harms upon the innocent. When one's enemy in war employs immoral methods, then it is morally permissible to employ the same methods in return.

In earlier work, I have discussed this objection under the label "sucker exemption."[8] The basic idea is that an agent in a competitive context is not required to observe constraints that other, competing agents fail to observe. I believe that this idea can indeed be plausible, but only when the victims of an agent's constraint violations are themselves previous violators of the constraint. If you have various agreements with another person, for instance, and he turns out routinely to violate these agreements whenever it suits him, then you are not morally required to honor your agreements with him when it does not suit you.

The sucker exemption is distinctly implausible, however, when those whom the agent's conduct would victimize are distinct from those who have victimized her. You are not morally permitted to violate your agreements with one person because some other person has violated his agreements with you. Similarly, an agent is not morally permitted to harm the friends or relatives of someone who has harmed her friends and relatives. A man is not permitted, for example, to rape the daughter of his own daughter's rapist. And likewise for the terrorists and their supporters: They are not morally permitted fortuitously to harm and kill innocent compatriots of people who have harmed innocent compatriots or associates of theirs. A person can forfeit ordinary moral protections against being harmed only through something she herself has done, not through the actions of another. Therefore, whatever wrongful harms the terrorists or their associates or compatriots may have suffered do not alter their moral relations to third parties who are not culpable for those wrongful harms.

Interestingly, Osama bin Laden has professed to share these sentiments in his early denials of any involvement in 9/11. Thus he is reported as saying, in his *Daily Ummat* interview dated September 28, 2001: "I have already said that I am not involved in the 11 September attacks in the United States. As a Muslim, I try my best to avoid telling a lie. I had no knowledge of these attacks, nor do I consider the killing of innocent women, children and other humans as an appreciable act. Islam strictly forbids causing harm to innocent women, children and other people. Such a practice is forbidden even in the course of a battle."[9] That bin Laden's interpretation of Islam is at least a plausible one is confirmed by various passages in the Quran, such as this one: "whosoever kills a human being for other than manslaughter or corruption upon earth, it shall be as if he had killed all mankind."[10]

IV

To show that the terrorist attacks were morally unjustifiable, I have focused on the weakest link in the purported justifications for them: Any plausible purpose of the attacks could have been achieved with much less harm to innocent civilians. This focus on the fourth burden of proof should not be taken to suggest that the other three burdens can be met. I do not believe that they can be met, but lack the space to discuss this here. I conclude that the five terrorist attacks in focus were morally unjustifiable acts of mass homicide. This conclusion could be further disputed. Other candidate greater goods might be adduced, or modifications of my account of what a successful justification would need to show might be proposed. A clever philosopher might be able to keep this game going a good while longer, and I cannot anticipate, let alone respond in advance to, all the moves such a philosopher might make.

But this is no reason for us to suspend moral judgment. These attackers and their supporters have made clear that they take themselves to be engaged in justifiable political violence. Their pronouncements are laden with moral and religious language that presents their conduct as justifiable, even noble, and urges others to follow their example. Such statements give them a responsibility to justify their attacks. They may not owe such a justification to just anyone. But they do owe a justification to their innocent victims and to the innocent friends and families of such victims. And they owe a justification also to the sincere adherents of their religion, in whose name they have attacked their targets.

Put yourself in the position of someone who is involved in planning an attack that he foresees will kill many innocent civilians. And imagine this person to be someone who takes morality seriously—understanding morality broadly here as including any religion that provides moral guidance and constraints. Such a moral person would think very hard indeed before killing large numbers of innocent people. He would not do this without having assured himself, up to a very high level of confidence, that his planned action is really justifiable—in one of the ways I have sketched or in some other way he finds compelling on reflection. For a religious person, especially when he is about to act in the name of his religion, there is the further need to make quite certain that he has really used his God-given capacities to the fullest so as to reassure himself that his planned action really accords with God's will. For a seriously religious person, what could be more terrifying than the possibility that one might not be careful enough and therefore make a mistake by killing, against God's will but in God's name, hundreds of innocent human beings?

With the cases before us, this is not a far-fetched possibility. As bin Laden has said, these attacks killed innocent human beings and Islam strictly forbids harming innocent human beings even in war. So it is—to put it mildly—not obvious that these attacks are permitted, let alone that they are God's will. Some serious thought is certainly required for a genuinely religious person conscientiously to reach the conclusion that these attacks accord with God's will.

Now suppose a genuinely religious person has conscientiously reached this conclusion. He would want to give his reasons, at least after the fact, perhaps posthumously. He would feel a responsibility to explain to his innocent victims and their innocent friends and relatives why he felt compelled to harm them. He would want other Muslims not merely to follow his example, but to do so with a full appreciation of why this really is the will of God. And, perhaps most important, he would want any mistake in his understanding of Islam to be identified and corrected. A genuinely religious person seeks to live in accordance with God's will, in accordance with what his religion requires. This is distinct from seeking to live in accordance with what one *believes* to be God's will and *believes* to be required by one's religion. These two goals are distinct because of the possibility of error. To deny this possibility is to claim infallibility for oneself. This would be hubris in regard to morality, and blasphemy in any theistic religion.[11]

Now it is true that all we have are our beliefs. We have no belief-independent access to the truth. Still, beliefs can be more or less well founded. To the person who seeks to live in accordance with what she *believes* to be God's will, it does not matter whether her beliefs are well founded or not. To the person who seeks to live in accordance with God's will, by contrast, nothing matters more. The more pains she takes to examine and correct her understanding and beliefs, the more likely she is to get it right. And even when she gets it wrong nonetheless, she will at least have done her best to get it right by making full use of the faculties and other resources God had endowed her with.

It is then of great importance to a genuinely moral or religious person to have a full justification for an action that he knows will kill many innocent civilians, and also to present this justification, at least after the fact, perhaps posthumously. Such a full justification will then be examined and discussed by others whom it will help either to follow the agent's example conscientiously, with full appreciation of the reasons why it may or should be followed, or else to avoid the error he had committed in good faith.

It is stunning how far the terrorists and their supporters fall short of the conduct of persons with genuine moral or religious commitments and scruples. They traffic heavily in the language of morality and holiness, but there is no evidence that they have seriously thought about what their religion requires of them. What they give us are simple moral colorations of the world along with fervent professions of sincerity and commitment. They do indeed seem strongly committed—many of them are willing to die for the success of their attacks. But for this commitment to be a sincere commitment *to Islam*, there would need to be a serious effort substantively to connect their activities and colorations to Islamic teachings. There would need to be reflective answers to questions such as: Why is this a holy war? Who counts as an enemy in this holy war, and why? What is one allowed to do in a holy war to enemies and to the uninvolved? There is, and has been for centuries, sophisticated treatment of such questions among Islamic scholars.[12] But the terrorists and their supporters are conspicuously absent from this discourse, even though their pronouncements and actions are highly controversial within it. They seem to be quite unconcerned to rule out what I have called the most terrifying possibility for a genuine believer: the possibility that one might be mistakenly killing, in God's name but against God's will, hundreds of innocent human beings who, no less than oneself, are God's creation.

V

I have discussed two moral failings of those involved in the five terrorist attacks. It was wrong of them to harm large numbers of innocent civilians without sufficient justification. And they did wrong to perpetrate these attacks in the name of a religion without taking great care to work out whether their religion really justifies such attacks. Placing these two wrongs side-by-side, you may think that the latter pales to insignificance. But I will try to show that the latter wrong, too, is of great importance. This discussion will also bring out the second reason why it is so very important for us not merely to be certain *that* these terrorist attacks are wrong, but also to understand *why* they are wrong. We are in the same boat with the terrorists in this sense: We use moral language just as they do. Our moral judgments are fallible just as theirs are. And we have a moral responsibility, just as they do, to take great care to ensure that the important decisions we make are not merely ones that we, however sincerely, believe to be morally justifiable, but also ones that we can actually justify.

Moral language is all around us—praising and condemning as good or evil, right or wrong, just or unjust, virtuous or vicious. In all too many cases, however, such language is used only to advance personal or group interests. The speaker expresses the narrowest judgment that allows her to score her point while avoiding any further normative commitments that might encumber herself now or in the future. This is quite common in politics. Politician A criticizes politician B as unethical for accepting a free trip to a conference in Brighton courtesy of Shell Oil. Without any further explanation of what makes B's behavior unethical, this is rather too easy a way of scoring political points. B gets tarred with the label *unethical,* while A can look good for her ethical concern without imposing any ethical constraints on her own conduct. A remains at liberty, should she be found to have accepted some free trip herself, to say that her conduct was not unethical because of its different purpose, different destination, different sponsor, or whatever.

A's conduct is not atypical in our culture. Many seek to take advantage of morality to influence the sentiments and conduct of others while avoiding any interference by morality in the pursuit of their own ends. This is a moral failing, but one that may seem rather mild. And yet, this common abuse of morality is of great importance, as we recognize when we consider it, as I will now do, from the perspective of morality itself, from the perspective of agents, and from the perspective of our society and culture.

The imperative to take morality seriously is not a command merely of this or that morality, but one that any plausible morality—and again I include religions—must make central. Though substantive in content, this central imperative flows from understanding what it means to have—not some particular moral commitments, but—any moral commitments at all.

In first approximation we might say that the central imperative to take morality seriously involves at least these three injunctions: One must try to integrate one's moral judgments through more general moral principles, one's religious beliefs, and commitments in order to form a coherent account of how to live. One must work out what this unified system of beliefs and commitments implies for one's own life. And one must make a serious effort to honor these implications in one's own conduct and judgments.

Some agents who disregard the central imperative are ones who simply set aside moral considerations and moral language altogether, typically behaving badly as a result. Let us set them aside, for they are fringe groups in the contemporary world. Much more important and much more numerous are those who take no interest in morality as such—in working out its content and living in conformity with it—but nonetheless employ moral language to influence the sentiments and conduct of others. They appeal to morality in bad faith, without a sincere willingness to work out what morality requires and thus in defiance of its central imperative. In order to advance their own ends, they falsely present themselves as friends of morality, as speaking on morality's behalf. Abusing morality in this way, they are not merely bad people, behaving badly, but unjust people, behaving unjustly.[13] Such people are the analogue to judges or police officers who use the law to advance their own ends: a judge who decides in the name of the people, but on the basis of what enriches himself or what advances his sectarian ideology; a police officer who falsely arrests a young woman for his own entertainment or to prevent her from expressing political views he dislikes. Such actions are not the worst violations of the law. And yet, committed under color of law, they are in one sense the most pernicious. Similarly, acting *under color of morality*—misrepresenting oneself as motivated by a sincere commitment to morality in order to advance one's own ends—is not the worst violation of morality, but one that strikes at its very heart. Acting under color of Islam or under color of Christianity are instances of this—acts of supreme defiance where the agent puts himself in the place of God. The content of religion becomes whatever the agent declares it to be. The agent is not seeking the guidance of his religion but merely uses its moral language to color the world as suits his separate purposes.

Imagine a society whose public culture is dominated by such people—trafficking heavily in moral language without any respect for morality's central imperative. There we get endless repetitions of specific moral assertions ("The United States is the great Satan" or "To withdraw our troops now would be a cowardly capitulation to terrorism"), and endless repetitions of unexamined generalities ("We must fight the infidels wherever they dishonor what is sacred" or "We must defend freedom against the enemies of freedom"). Such moral appeals are made on all sides. But since they remain unexplicated and unjustified, there is no substantive moral debate. The political effect of all the moral language thrown around depends then on media access and acting skills. To have an impact, one must manage to intone the relevant sentences with an honest face and a good show of profound conviction, conveying to the audience that one cares deeply about moral considerations and is sincerely convinced that one is defending the moral policy. And to remain unencumbered with regard to other policies one might want to defend simultaneously or in the future, one must do all this without assuming any further, possibly inconvenient substantive moral commitments.

This imagined society is not so far from what we find in the real world today. We find it in much of the Arab world. And we find it in the UK and in the US as well. The model also resembles current international society pretty closely. To be sure, there is a great deal of serious moral discourse going on, not merely in universities, but also within other (for instance religious) associations and in political fora such as in some committees of the United Nations and of various national legislatures. But the public visibility and impact of such serious moral discourse is small and diminishing, and the political fora in which it takes place are therefore increasingly shunned and marginalized. This may not seem like a calamity comparable to terrorism. Yet, such moral corruption may be a more profound danger.

When moral language degenerates into just one more tool in the competitive struggle for advantage, then this struggle becomes ultimately unconstrained. To be sure, the power of political leaders and factions is limited by the power of other leaders and factions, and is restricted also by procedural checks and balances. But all these constraints are soft and flexible, themselves subject to indefinite modification through the use of political power. Insofar as political players understand that their competitive struggle for power is always also a struggle over the rules governing this competition, they tend to be ruthless in this competition because there is no other long-term protection of their interests and values. This problem is well explicated in Rawls's discussion of a *modus vivendi*. Rawls's preferred alternative model is that of an overlapping consensus focused on firm, widely recognized social rules to which all major groups, perhaps for diverse reasons, have a principled moral commitment.[14] But even without such an overlapping consensus, there can at least be that trust among adversaries which comes from recognizing one another as genuinely moral agents who are at least committed to *their own* morality. The moral importance of avoiding a world without trust and without shared social rules gives us further moral reasons to honor morality's central imperative in our applications of moral language to both domestic and international issues.

VI

We can now appreciate the promised second reason for considering it important—even if we have not the slightest doubt—to articulate our understanding of what makes these attacks wrong, as I have tried to do earlier. We must do this to honor morality's central imperative, which requires us to elaborate and extend our moral commitments so that they impose clear constraints on our own conduct. This is crucial for being moral persons, rather than persons acting under color of morality, and for being recognized as having genuine moral commitments that we are willing to discuss and are determined to live up to.

There is much skepticism outside the affluent West about the moral fervor with which we have condemned the terrorists and prosecuted our war against them. Occasionally, such skepticism comes with sympathy and even celebration of the terrorists. Far more frequently, however, the skeptics share our conviction that those terrorist attacks were very wrong—but believe that we are moralizing in bad faith, that we are using morality to win support or sympathy but have no interest in the moral assessment or adjustment of our own conduct and policies.

In my view, these skeptics are essentially correct. But before presenting some evidence to support their case, I should state clearly two points that I am not making and in fact strongly reject. I reject the view that wrongful conduct by our governments renders the terrorist attacks any less unjustifiable. My moral condemnation of such attacks is based on the harms they inflict on innocent civilians, who do not become permissible targets for lethal attack by wrongful policies of (even their own) governments. I also do not claim that it is impermissible for those who are doing wrong to fight the wrongs done by others. My main point in discussing our governments' conduct and policies is to show that our politicians take momentous action, in our name, without any effort to apply the morality they profess in our name to decisions that cry out for moral justification. That they can get by, comfortably, without any such effort is our fault as citizens.

Let me illustrate the point by recalling some well-known highlights of the "global war on terror" (GWOT) as orchestrated by the US and UK governments. Central to the GWOT as they conceive it is the doctrine that the terrorist danger justifies pervasive secrecy and disinformation towards the media and the general public, and even towards the legislature. The suggestion was, and still is, that the success of the war effort requires that most of this effort be exempt from public scrutiny and that even the scope of this exemption should not be disclosed.[15] A well-known and typical example is UK Attorney General Lord Peter Goldsmith threatening British media with criminal prosecution for reporting that President Bush had proposed to bomb the Al Jazeera television station in peaceful Qatar.[16]

An early episode in the GWOT was the overthrow of the Taliban regime in Afghanistan. In this initiative, our governments chose to rely heavily on the United Islamic Front for the Salvation of Afghanistan. This "Northern Alliance" had been losing the civil war against the Taliban, but massive Western air support, funding, and US teams of special forces turned the situation around in its favor. Thousands of Taliban fighters, who had laid down their arms in exchange for a promise of safe passage to their home villages in an orderly surrender negotiated with the participation of US military personnel, were instead crammed into metal shipping containers without air or water for several days. Between 960 and 3000 of them died in agony from heat, thirst, and lack of oxygen. Some of the survivors were shot dead and all bodies buried in a huge mass grave.[17] The commander of Northern Alliance forces, Abdul Rashid Dostum, later used murder and torture to intimidate witnesses to the atrocity.[18] While insisting on a full investigation of the mass graves at Srebrenica, Western governments blocked any official inquiry into the mass grave at Dasht-e Leili; and the mass murder of surrendering Taliban has now been largely forgotten in most parts of the world. Implicated also in systematic and horrific crimes against women and girls,[19] Dostum currently serves as Chief of Staff to Hamid Karzai, Commander-in-Chief of the Afghan Armed Forces.[20]

The US and UK governments defended their 2003 invasion of Iraq, once again, as a necessary component of the GWOT. But the evidence for their claims that Saddam Hussein had weapons of mass destruction and ties to Al-Qaida was flimsy, and these claims are now known to have been false and preparations for the invasion are known to have been made well before 9/11. Hussein's regime had been responsible for horrendous human rights violations, including massive chemical weapons attacks against Iraqi and Iranian civilians. But these were most severe in the 1980s when Iraq, with Western encouragement and chemicals delivered by Western states, fought a nine-year war against Iran. Then our governments were on friendly terms with Saddam Hussein—though the US, eager to prolong the war, sold weapons and intelligence to Iran as well (the "Iran-Contra Affair").

The US and UK quickly took over the prisons of the defeated regimes and filled them with thousands of people they had taken captive in their war on terror. Labelled "unprivileged combatants," "unlawful enemy combatants" or "security detainees," these people have been routinely humiliated and degraded at will by coalition personnel: stripped naked, forced to masturbate and to simulate sex acts, abused with dogs, shackled in stressful positions, kicked and beaten with electric cables, and tortured with electric shocks, drugs, sleep deprivation, induced hypothermia and "waterboarding" (simulated drowning).[21]

Such abuse is partly explained by the large and increasing number of "moral waivers" that allow people with serious criminal records to join the US armed forces.[22] Accounts from former prison personnel make clear that much of the abuse was systematic and deliberate, encouraged and condoned up the chain of command,[23] with the objective of breaking resistance to the occupation trumping any concern for protecting the innocent. This is confirmed by former US Army interrogator Tony Lagouranis who, in his *Hardball* interview with Chris Matthews, estimated that 90 percent of the people he interrogated were wholly innocent—not merely in the technical sense of innocent until proven guilty, but really innocent of any armed resistance to the occupation of Iraq or any serious crime that might conceivably justify their horrendous treatment.[24] Many were arrested for having once visited Afghanistan, for having had some association to an Islamic charity with suspected links to terrorists or their sympathizers, or even to help extract information from an incarcerated relative.

There are many facilities outside of Afghanistan and Iraq where perceived enemies of the West are held indefinitely. Best known among these is the US-operated compound at Guantánamo Bay, Cuba. United Nations officials have been trying to inspect this prison since it opened in 2002, but have declined the option to visit without full access and the opportunity to conduct private interviews with detainees.[25] The US Defense Department has been compelled by the judiciary to issue a list of the people it has been holding at Guantánamo Bay, and several people released from there have provided graphic accounts of how prisoners are treated.[26]

The US government asserts that the prisoners it holds at Guantánamo Bay are not entitled to Geneva Convention protections[27] and intends to try them by military commissions. But the US Supreme Court overruled the government on both counts, emphasizing the severe flaws of the constituted military commissions:

> The accused and his civilian counsel may be excluded from, and precluded from ever learning what evidence was presented during, any part of the proceeding that either the Appointing Authority or the presiding officer decides to "close." . . . not only is testimonial hearsay and evidence obtained through coercion fully admissible, but neither live testimony nor witnesses' written statements need be sworn.[28]

The Court concluded that trial by military commission, as envisioned, violates both the Geneva Conventions and the US *Uniform Code of Military Justice*, whose article 36(b) requires that all pre-trial, trial, and post-trial procedures must be uniform with those applied to crimes allegedly committed by US military personnel.[29] The Court also found that trial by military commission as contemplated violates Article 3, common to all four Geneva Conventions, which requires that any punishments must be pursuant to a "judgment pronounced by a regularly constituted court affording all the judicial guarantees which are recognized as indispensable by civilized peoples."[30] In response to the Court's decision, Congress has since passed the Military Commissions Act attempting to reinstate trial by military commission in modified form.[31] Whether this legislation will survive impending Supreme Court scrutiny remains to be seen.[32]

Coalition forces have also maintained secret detention facilities around the world, reportedly in Jordan, Pakistan, Qatar, Thailand, Uzbekistan, various locations in Eastern Europe, and on the British island of Diego Garcia.[33] At these "black sites" our governments are imprisoning so-called ghost detainees—unknown numbers of unknown persons for unknown reasons under unknown conditions. Our governments are telling us that nothing untoward is going on at such sites. But it would be irrational and irresponsible to trust that basic human rights are being respected in locations no one else has access to when such rights are not being respected in locations from which a fair amount of information is leaking out. Common sense suggests that, once persons have been caught in the secret prison system, their captors are reluctant to release them even when they become convinced of their innocence: Wholly unaccountable for their actions, these captors prefer innocent persons to remain missing indefinitely over their resurfacing with information about conditions in the secret facilities and possibly with knowledge that might be used to identify particular torturers, interrogators, or collaborating doctors.

The UK is the main "partner country" in this system of secret detention and torturous interrogation whose victims have no rights of any sort. UK officials sit with their US counterparts on the Joint Detention Review Board in Iraq, UK officials have participated in coercive interrogations, and UK officials have asserted that human rights law does not bind UK forces in Iraq.[34] The US government relied, in the first few years of the GWOT, on a 50-page memorandum signed by Assistant Attorney General Jay S. Bybee. This memorandum comments at length on the legal obligations of US military personnel under the *International Covenant on Civil and Political Rights* and the *Convention Against Torture and Other Cruel, Inhuman, or Degrading Treatment or Punishment*—both ratified by the US—and under implementing national legislation. Appealing to a Reagan Administration precedent, Bybee declared it a defining characteristic of torture that it should result in "excruciating and agonizing" pain, such as "the needle under the fingernail, the application of electric shock to the genital area, the piercing of eyeballs"[35]: "Torture ... covers only extreme acts.... Where the pain is physical, it must be of an intensity akin to that which accompanies serious physical injury such as death or organ failure. Severe mental pain requires suffering not just at the moment of infliction, but it also requires lasting psychological harm, such as seen in mental disorders like posttraumatic stress disorder.... Because the acts inflicting torture are extreme, there is significant range of acts that though they might constitute cruel, inhuman, or degrading treatment or punishment fail to rise to the level of torture." The Bybee memo also asserts that, even when torture in this narrow sense is used, "necessity or self-defense could provide justifications that would eliminate any criminal liability" and that judicial review of "interrogations undertaken pursuant to the President's Commander-in-Chief powers may be unconstitutional."[36] The memo proposes that the government should deny that extreme forms of torment count as torture, should declare clear-cut torture justifiable by appeal to necessity or self-defense, and should argue that the courts lack authority to stop torture ordered by the President.

The Bybee memo was superseded by a memo signed by Acting U.S. Assistant Attorney General Daniel Levin on December 30, 2004, stating that "we have reviewed this Office's prior opinions addressing issues involving treatment of detainees and do not believe that any of their conclusions would be different under the standards set forth in this memorandum."[37] The main change from the Bybee memo is that the second and third lines of defense are now declared superfluous: Because the President has directed US personnel not to engage in torture, it is unnecessary to consider whether torture is justifiable and whether the courts have the authority to stop torture ordered by the President. The memo reiterates at great length that only the most extreme forms of inhuman and degrading treatment should count as torture. It thereby follows the Bybee memo in ignoring that what the US has signed and ratified is a convention against torture *and other cruel, inhuman, or degrading treatment or punishment*, and in ignoring as well that the US has signed and ratified the *Geneva Conventions* whose common Article 3 prohibits not only torture but also "cruel treatment" and "outrages upon personal dignity, in particular humiliating and degrading treatment."[38] This article is common to all four Geneva conventions, and its application can therefore not be refuted by claiming that detainees fail to qualify as prisoners of war.[39]

Among the treatments coalition partners use and officially classify as acceptable are:

Long Time Standing.
This technique is described as among the most effective. Prisoners are forced to stand, handcuffed and with their feet shackled to an eye bolt in the floor for more than 40 hours. Exhaustion and sleep deprivation are effective in yielding confessions.

The Cold Cell.
The prisoner is left to stand naked in a cell kept near 50 degrees F. Throughout the time in the cell the prisoner is doused with cold water.

Water Boarding.
The prisoner is bound to an inclined board, feet raised and head slightly below the feet. Cellophane is wrapped over the prisoner's face and water is poured over him. Unavoidably, the gag reflex kicks in and a terrifying fear of drowning leads to almost instant pleas to bring the treatment to a halt.[40]

Another instrument in our war on terror is "extraordinary rendition" in which persons are transferred, without any legal process, to regimes known to practice even more severe forms of torture. According to former CIA officer Robert Baer, the CIA captures individuals it suspects of ties to terrorism and puts them on a plane. "The ultimate destination of these flights are places that, you know, are involved in torture. . . . If you send a prisoner to Jordan, you get a better interrogation. If you send a prisoner, for instance, to Egypt, you will probably never see him again, the same way with Syria."[41] Maher Arar, software engineer and Canadian citizen, was fortunate enough to be seen again. Coming from Tunis and headed for Montreal, he was detained during a stop-over at John F. Kennedy Airport and delivered to Syria where he was held in solitary confinement and brutally tortured on a regular basis. He was released more than a year after his arrest, completely cleared of any terrorism charges by a Canadian commission of inquiry.[42] The US ambassador to Canada, Paul Cellucci, commented that "the US government will continue to deport Canadian citizens to third countries if they pose a risk to American national security."[43] Khaled el-Masri, a German citizen abducted by the CIA while vacationing in Macedonia, also resurfaced after five months of detention in Afghanistan where he was shackled, beaten, and injected with drugs. He was released somewhere in Albania when his captors realized that his abduction was a case of mistaken identity.[44]

As with regard to the terrorist attacks, we should ask whether all this barbarity, much of it inflicted on innocents, is necessary to protect our societies from terrorist attacks. If we did examine this question, we would find that most of it is actually counterproductive by inciting more terrorism than it deters.[45] In fact, however, the moral costs are barely noted in the media, and George W. Bush, the person bearing greatest responsibility for these costs, can safely convey the nation's sentiments on the UN International Day in Support of the Victims of Torture: "The victims often feel forgotten, but we will not forget them. America supports accountability and treatment centers for torture victims . . . We stand with the victims to seek their healing and recovery, and urge all nations to join us in these efforts to restore the dignity of every person affected by torture."[46]

VII

What is remarkable is that our governments show so little interest in justifying, in moral terms, the great harms they are clearly inflicting on innocent persons. Of course, they traffic heavily in moral and specifically religious rhetoric, on both sides of the Atlantic. But is there any evidence that those who design and implement coalition methods in the global war on terror have thought carefully about their moral justifiability? Such serious reflection is what they would engage in if they were genuinely concerned that their conduct—or let me say, *our* conduct, for they are acting as our elected representatives in our names—be morally justifiable. And had they engaged in such serious moral reflection and convinced themselves that these methods are indeed morally justifiable under existing conditions, would they not want this justification to be publicly known so that we all can appreciate that what is being done in our names is, appearances notwithstanding, really morally justifiable?

The conduct of our politicians is better explained by their desire to act under color of morality. This requires no more than the bald assertion that we are doing the right thing, presented in appealing tones of sincerity and commitment. What is most astonishing here again is that our politicians get away with this so easily. This is astonishing not merely in the GWOT case here under discussion, but in US and UK foreign policy more generally.

In the 1990's, the United Nations maintained a stringent regime of economic sanctions against Iraq. These sanctions greatly reduced access to foodstuffs and medicines for poor Iraqis and further degraded Iraq's heavily damaged infrastructure, preventing the provision of electricity, water, and sanitation with devastating effects on the incidence of contagious diseases. Madeline Albright, then US Ambassador to the UN, defended the sanctions regime on *60 Minutes:*

> **Lesley Stahl:** We have heard that a half a million children have died. I mean, that's more children than died in Hiroshima. . . . Is the price worth it?

Albright: I think this is a very hard choice, but the price—we think the price is worth it. . . . It is a moral question, but the moral question is even a larger one. Don't we owe to the American people and to the American military and to the other countries in the region that this man [Saddam Hussein] not be a threat?

Stahl: Even with the starvation?

Albright: I think, Lesley, it is hard for me to say this because I am a humane person, but my first responsibility is to make sure that United States forces do not have to go and re-fight the Gulf War.[47]

The interviewer left it at that, and the remarks drew scant media attention in the US and Europe and were not noted in Albright's Senate confirmation hearings for Secretary of State that same year. The remarks were much reported and discussed in the Arab world, however, and apparently motivated at least one of the terrorists.[48] In her biography, Albright expresses deep regret about her remarks: "Nothing matters more than the lives of innocent people. I had fallen into a trap and said something that I simply did not mean."[49]

But if nothing matters more than the lives of innocent people, then why were these very severe sanctions continued without regard to their effects on Iraqi civilians? Despite considerable variation in the estimates, it was clear from the start that the sanctions' health impact on Iraqi civilians would be devastating.[50] The most careful studies I have found are Richard Garfield's, who estimates that mortality among children under 5 rose from about 40–45 per 1000 in 1990 to about 125 per 1000 during 1994–1999 and stresses that many of the surviving children sustained lasting damage to their health.[51] Garfield estimates excess deaths among children under 5 at around 3000 per month for the 1991–2002 period, with a confidence interval of 343,900 to 525,400 deaths for this entire period.[52]

In 1998, Denis Halliday, co-ordinator of humanitarian relief to Iraq and Assistant Secretary-General of the United Nations, resigned after 34 years with the UN. Explaining his resignation, he wrote: "I am resigning, because the policy of economic sanctions is totally bankrupt. We are in the process of destroying an entire society. It is as simple and terrifying as that . . . Five thousand children are dying every month . . . I don't want to administer a programme that results in figures like these."[53] He added in an interview: "I had been instructed to implement a policy that satisfies the definition of genocide: a deliberate policy that has effectively killed well over a million individuals, children and adults. We all know that the regime, Saddam Hussein, is not paying the price for economic sanctions; on the contrary, he has been strengthened by them. It is the little people who are losing their children or their parents for lack of untreated water. What is clear is that the Security Council is now out of control, for its actions here undermine its own Charter, and the Declaration of Human Rights and the Geneva Convention. History will slaughter those responsible."[54] In 2000, Halliday's successor, Hans von Sponeck, also resigned, after 32 years of UN service, while harshly criticizing the sanctions regime as well as the dishonesty of the relevant officials in the Blair and Clinton governments.[55] Jutta Burghardt, director of the UN World Food program in Iraq, also resigned for the same reasons.[56]

Nothing matters more than the lives of innocent people. Most of us would agree with Albright on this point. Most of us would also agree that her, and our, first responsibility is to our own country. And most of us endorse these two commitments in such a shallow way that, like Albright, we do not even notice the tension. Then, when a choice must be made between promoting the interests of our country—our government, citizens, or corporations—and those of innocent people abroad, we routinely prioritize the former without so much as examining the cost that our choices will impose on the lives of the innocent.

In this spirit, the US and UK governments have stated that they do not track civilian deaths in the aftermath of their invasions and occupations of Afghanistan and Iraq.[57] And in the same spirit our governments press their favored economic rules and policies upon the rest of the world: Structural adjustment programs required by the IMF have deprived millions of African children of elementary schooling.[58] Protectionist trade barriers are unfairly depriving poor populations of a decent livelihood.[59] Loans and arms sales are keeping brutal and corrupt rulers in power in developing countries, and lax banking laws facilitate massive embezzlement by these countries' public officials.[60] Intellectual property rights mandated by the WTO cut off hundreds of millions of poor patients worldwide from cheap generic medicines.[61] In these cases and many more, our politicians take momentous action, in our name, without any effort to apply the morality they profess in our name to decisions that cry out for moral justification. Their bald assurances that their conduct is alright, morally, are accepted by the vast majority of citizens who are similarly inclined to avoid further thought about how our "first responsibility" to benefit our own might be constrained by the interests of innocent people abroad. It appears that, outside a few insulated fora, the distinction between what is morally right and what is believed and proclaimed to be so has all but collapsed. This is a disastrous flaw in our public culture—one that, quite apart from its horrific effects, fundamentally undermines our ambition to be a civilization that strives for moral decency.

Notes

1. See Erica Frank, "Funding the public health response to terrorism," *British Medical Journal*, 331 (2005), 526–27, arguing that recent shifts of public funds into counter-terrorist efforts have a large negative impact on morbidity and mortality from natural disasters and common medical conditions, and Nick A. Wilson and George Thomson, "Deaths from international terrorism compared with road crash deaths in OECD countries," *Injury Prevention*, 11 (2005), 332–3.
2. The Global Fund to Fight AIDS, Tuberculosis and Malaria, "Current grant commitments and disbursements," available at: www.theglobalfund.org/en/funds_raised/commitments.
3. Amy Belasco, *The Cost of Iraq, Afghanistan, and Other Global War on Terror Operations Since 9/11*, Congressional Research Service Report for Congress (Washington: Library of Congress, 2006), available at: www.fas.org/sgp/crs/natsec/RL33110. pdf.
4. This is not a pitch for censorship, of course, but for responsible and intelligent journalism and reporting.
5. A considerable diversity of Western responses should, however, be noted. See Dirk Haubrich, "Civil liberties in emergencies," *Governments of the World: A Global Guide to Citizens' Rights and Responsibilities*, ed. C. Neai Tate, 4 vols, (Farmington Hills, MI: Macmillan Reference, 2005), pp. 199–205.
6. John Rawls, *A Theory of Justice* (Cambridge, Mass.: Harvard University Press, 1999), sec. 9.
7. Later, Voinarovski declares with respect to the planned assassination of Admiral Dubasov, the Governor-General of Moscow, that "if Dubasov is accompanied by his wife, I shall not throw the bomb" (Albert Camus, *The Rebel: An Essay on Man in Revolt*, trans. Anthony Bower (New York: Vintage, 1956), p. 140; Richard B. Spence, *Boris Savinkov—Renegade on the Left* (Boulder, CO: East European Monographs, 1991, pp. 45f.). Savinkov similarly opposes an attempt to kill Dubasov on the St. Petersburg-Moscow Express on the ground that "if there were the least mistake, the explosion could take place in the carriage and kill strangers" (Camus, *The Rebel*, p. 140). Later, when escaping from a Czarist prison, the same Savinkov reportedly "decides to shoot any officers who might attempt to prevent

his flight, but to kill himself rather than turn his revolver on an ordinary soldier" (ibid.).

8. Thomas Pogge, "Historical wrongs: the other two domains," *Justice in Time, Responding to Historical Injustice*, ed. Lukas Meyer (Baden-Baden, Germany: Nomos, 2004).
9. Interview with Osama bin Laden, *Daily Ummat* (Karachi), September 28, 2001; frequently reprinted, e.g., at www.robert-fisk.com/usama_interview_ummat.htm.
10. Quran 5:32.
11. It might be objected that the possibility of error might not be a serious possibility in some cases. In the case of Moses, perhaps, when God appeared to him, or in the cases of Jesus or Mohammad or even their immediate followers or disciples. It is well to recall then that Mohammad, the final prophet according to Islamic teaching, lived some 1400 years ago. So the possibility of errors in understanding the Divine will as revealed by Muhammad is certainly a real possibility in our time, as the diversity of schools and interpretations amply confirms. Exempting oneself from this possibility would be to claim the status of prophet for oneself or for some contemporary from whom one is receiving direct instruction.
12. See, for example, Khaled Abou El Fadl, "Islam and the theology of power," *Middle East Report*, 221 (2001), 28–33.
13. Thomas Pogge, "Justice," *Encyclopedia of Philosophy*, ed. Donald M. Borchert, 2nd edn (Farmington Hills, MI: Macmillan Reference, 2006).
14. John Rawls, *Political Liberalism*, 2nd ed. (New York: Columbia University Press, 2005), lecture 4.
15. In 2005, the FBI issued 47,211 national security letter (NSL) requests requiring businesses to turn over private data about their customers. The Justice Department's public report stated that the FBI issued 9,254 NSL requests in calendar year 2005. "The number of NSL requests we identified significantly exceeds the number reported in the Department's first public annual report on NSL usage, issued in April 2006, because the Department was not required to include all NSL requests in that report" ("A review of the Federal Bureau of Investigation's use of national security letters," Department of Justice Office of the Inspector General, March 2007, p. xix, www.usdoj.gov/oig/special/s0703b/final.pdf). See also American Civil Liberties Union: *Hundreds of New Documents Reveal Expanded Military Role in Domestic Surveillance* (October 14, 2007), www.aclu.org/safefree/nationalsecurityletters/32145prs20071014.html.
16. Kevin Maguire and Andy Lines, "Exclusive: Bush plot to bomb his Arab ally," *Mirror*, November 22, 2005, www.mirror.co.uk/news/tm_objectid=16397937&method=full&siteid=94762&headline=exclusive-bush-plot-to-bomb-his-arab-ally-name_page.html; and CNN, *Critique of Worldwide Media Coverage*, aired November 26, 2005, transcripts.cnn.com/TRAN-

SCRIPTS/0511/26/i_c.01.html. The US had bombed Al Jazeera stations twice before: 2001 in Kabul and 2003 in Bagdad, killing one reporter.

17. See Babak Dehghanpisheh, John Barry, and Roy Gutman, "The death convoy of Afghanistan," *Newsweek*, August 26. 2002, (www.globalpolicy.org/security/issues/afghan/2002/0826memo.htm), reporting on the surrender at Konduz of November 25, 2001; Physicians for Human Rights, *Preliminary Assessment of Alleged Mass Gravesites in the Area of Mazar-I-Sharif, Afghanistan* (Boston and Washington: 2002), physiciansforhumanrights.org/library/documents/reports/report-massgraves-afghanistan.pdf, and the documentary film *Afghan Massacre: The Convoy of Death* (2002), directed by Jamie Doran, www.informationclearinghouse.info/article3267.htm.
18. Valerie Reitman, "UN probes claims of violence against Afghan witnesses: reports of torture and killings are tied to case of dead Taliban fighters," *Los Angeles Times*, November 15, 2002, p. A13. Rory McCarthy, "US Afghan ally 'tortured witnesses to his war crimes,'" *Guardian*, November 18, 2002, www.guardian.co.uk/international/story/0,3604,842082,00.html.
19. David Filipov, "Warlord's men commit rape in revenge against Taliban," *Boston Globe*, February 24, 2002, p. Al. The rapes targeted the Pashtun community from which the Taliban had derived much of their political support.
20. Andrew North, "Dostum gets Afghan military role," *BBC News*, March 2, 2005, available at: news.bbc.co.uk/2/hi/south_asia/4308683.stm. On the evolution of the situation in Afghanistan generally, see reports by Amnesty International (www.amnestyusa.org/countries/afghanistan/reports.do) and Human Rights Watch, *Fatally Flawed: Cluster Bombs and Their Use by the United States in Afghanistan* (2002), hrw.org/reports/2002/us-afghanistan; *"Killing You is a Very Easy Thing for Us": Human Rights Abuses in Southeast Afghanistan* (July 2003), www.hrw.org/reports/2003/afghanistan0703; *"Enduring Freedom": Abuses by U.S. Forces in Afghanistan* (March 2004), hrw.org/reports/2004/afghanistan0304; *Afghanistan: Killing and Torture by US Predate Abu Ghraib* (May 20, 2005), hrw.org/english/docs/2005/05/20/afghan10992.htm. See also Uranium Medical Research Center, *UMRC's Preliminary Findings from Afghanistan and Operation Enduring Freedom* (April 2003), www.umrc.net/os/downloads/AfghanistanOEF.pdf, foreseeing "a potential public health disaster for Afghanistan" from massive coalition use of non-depleted uranium in bombs and missiles.
21. Coalition personnel took hundreds of photographs and video clips of the abuses they inflicted on their captives; the most horrific ones were never published, but shown at closed hearings to members of the US Congress. See Marian Wilkinson, "Photos show dead Iraqis, torture and rape," *The Age*, May 14, 2004, www.theage.com.au/articles/2004/05/13/1084289818093.html; Neil McKay, "Iraq's child prisoners," *Sunday Herald* (Glasgow), August 1, 2004, www.globalpolicy.org/security/issues/iraq/attack/law/2004/ 0801childprison.htm, reporting over 100 children in coalition custody, subjected to rape and

torture; Deborah Pearlstein and Priti Patel, *Behind the Wire* (New York: Human Rights First, 2005), www.humanrightsfirst.org/us_law/PDF/behind-the-wire-033005.pdf; Human Rights Watch, *Leadership Failure: Firsthand Accounts of Torture of Iraqi Detainees by the U.S. Army's 82nd Airborne Division* (September 2005), hrw.org/reports/2005/us0905 and "U.S. Operated Secret 'Dark Prison' in Kabul," *Human Rights News*, December 19, 2005, hrw.org/english/docs/2005/12/19/afghan12319.htm; Amnesty International, *United Kingdom Human Rights: A Broken Promise* (February 23, 2006), web.amnesty.org/library/Index/ENGEUR450042006, and *Beyond Abu Ghraib: Detention and Torture in Iraq* (March 6, 2006), web.amnesty.org/library/index/engmde140012006; Eric Schmitt and Carolyn Marshall, "Task Force 6–26: inside Camp Nama; in secret unit's 'black room,' a grim portrait of U.S. abuse," *New York Times*, March 19, 2006, p. A1, available at: select.nytimes.com/gst/abstract.html?res=F30617FC34550C7A8DDDAA0894DE404482.

22. Rick Maze, "Rise in moral waivers troubles lawmaker," *Navy Times*, February 20, 2007, available at: www.navytimes.com/news/2007/02/apWaived Recruits070213/. In 2006, 20 percent of army recruits, over 50 percent of marine recruits, 18 percent of navy recruits, and 8 percent of air force recruits needed moral waivers to enlist (Lolita C. Baldor, "Military grants more waivers to recruits," abcnews.go.com/Politics/wireStory?id=2873006 &page=3).
23. Human Rights Watch, *Leadership Failure* (note 21) and *"No Blood, No Foul": Soldiers' Accounts of Detainee Abuse in Iraq* (July 2006), available at: hrw.org/reports/2006/us0706.
24. MSNBC, *Hardball: Tactics of Interrogation*, aired January 16, 2006, available at: www.msnbc.msn.com/id/10895199.
25. United Nations, *Human Rights Experts Issue Joint Report on Situation of Detainees in Guantanamo Bay*, press release, February 16, 2006. The ICRC has been visiting Guantánamo Bay since January 2002, accompanied by efforts of the American Red Cross to appease its more blindly patriotic US donors: "It seems a horror to many Americans that anyone—especially the Red Cross—would be interested in the welfare of the Afghan war detainees being held by the U.S. military in Guantanamo Bay, Cuba. However, it is our very own government that requested the International Committee of the Red Cross (ICRC) to visit with the detainees" (www.redcross.org/news/in/intllaw/guantanamo1.html). ICRC visits take place on the understanding that its reports remain confidential and are conveyed only to select US authorities. One such report was leaked. Its contents are described in Neil A. Lewis, "Red Cross finds detainee abuse in Guantánamo," *New York Times*, November 30, 2004, p. A1, www.nytimes.com/2004/11/30/politics/30gitmo.html?ex=1259470800&en=825f1aa04c65241f&ei=5088&partner=rssnyt.
26. Center for Constitutional Rights, *Report on Torture and Cruel, Inhuman, and Degrading Treatment of Prisoners at Guantánamo Bay, Cuba*, July 2006 (www.ccr-

ny.org/v2/reports/docs/Torture_Report_Final_version.pdf) and *Detention in Afghanistan and Guantanamo Bay: Composite Statement of Shafiq Rasul, Asif Iqbal, and Rhubel Ahmet*, July 26, 2004 (www.ccr-ny.org/v2/legal/September_11th/docs/Guantanamo_composite_statement_FINAL. pdf); Moazzam Begg and Victoria Brittain, *Enemy Combatant: A British Muslim's Journey To Guantanamo and Back* (London: Free Press, 2006). See also the extensive testimony of Jumah al-Dossari in Amnesty International, *USA: Days of Adverse Hardship in US Detention Camps*, 16 December 2005, web.amnesty.org/library/index/ENGAMR511072005 and "The David Hicks affadavit," *Sydney Morning Herald*, December 10, 2004, available at: www.smh.com.au/news/World/David-Hicks-affidavit/2004/12/10/1102625527396.html.

27. See Mike Wiser, "The torture question: sidelining Geneva," *Frontline*, October 18, 2005, available at: www.pbs.org/wgbh/pages/frontline/torture/themes/sideline.html.
28. *Hamdan v Rumsfeld*, 548 U.S. (2006), pp. 50–51, majority opinion written by Justice Stevens, available at: www.supremecourtus.gov/opinions/05pdf/05-184.pdf.
29. Ibid. pp. 5, 59–62.
30. Ibid. p. 67.
31. *Military Commissions Act of 2006*, Public Law 109–366, 120 STAT. 2600 (October 17, 2006), available at: www.loc.gov/rr/frd/Military_Law/pdf/PL-109-366.pdf.
32. Robert Barnes, "Justice to weigh detainee rights," *Washington Post*, June 30, 2007, p. A1, available at: www.washingtonpost.com/wp-dyn/content/article/2007/06/29/AR2007062900743.html?hpid=topnews.
33. Amnesty International, *United States of America/Yemen: Secret Detention in CIA "Black Sites,"* November 8, 2005, available at: web.amnesty.org/library/Index/ENGAMR511772005.
34. See "United Kingdom" in Amnesty International, *Amnesty International Report 2005: The State of the World's Human Rights* (New York: Amnesty International, 2005), available at: web.amnesty.org/report2005/gbr-summary-eng.
35. See Jay S. Bybee, *Standards of Conduct for Interrogation under 18 U.S.C. sects.* 2340–2340A, Office of Legal Counsel, U.S. Department of Justice, August 1, 2002, pp. 19–20, available at: fl1.findlaw.com/news.findlaw.com/hdocs/docs/doj/bybee80102mem.pdf.
36. Ibid. p. 46.
37. See Daniel Levin, *Standards of Conduct for Interrogation under 18. U.S.C. sects.* 2340–2340A, Office of Legal Counsel, U.S. Department of Justice, December 30, 2004, available at: www.usdoj.gov/olc/18usc23402340a2.htm, n.8.
38. Text of the *Geneva Conventions* at: www.icrc.org/Web/Eng/siteengo.nsf/html/genevaconventions.
39. John Yoo, a major contributor to the Levin memo, provided this defense on May 2, 2005 (webcast.berkeley.edu/event_details.php?webcastid=12285). In

its Article 4, the *Fourth Geneva Convention* specifies that "persons protected by the Convention are those who, at a given moment and in any manner whatsoever, find themselves, in case of a conflict or occupation, in the hands of a Party to the conflict or Occupying Power of which they are not nationals"—excepting only "Nationals of a state which is not bound by the convention" (www.icrc.org/ihl.nsf/7c4d08d9b287a42141256739003e636b/6756482d86146898c125641e004aa3c5).

40. Brian Ross and Richard Esposito, "CIA's harsh interrogation techniques described," *ABC News*, November 18, 2005, available at: abcnews.go.com/WNT/Investigation/story?id=1322866&page=1. These techniques were used and refined by the Nazi Gestapo, and waterboarding was a technique commonly used by Pol Pot's Khmer Rouge in Cambodia.
41. BBC, *File on 4: Rendition*, aired February 8, 2005, available at: news.bbc.co.uk/nol/shared/bsp/hi/pdfs/15_02_05_renditions.pdf. Cf. Adrian Levy and Cathy Scott-Clark, "One huge US jail," *Guardian*, March 19, 2005, available at: www.guardian.co.uk/afghanistan/story/0,1284,1440836,00.html: "Robert Baer, a CIA case officer in the Middle East until 1997, told us how it works. 'We pick up a suspect or we arrange for one of our partner countries to do it. Then the suspect is placed on civilian transport to a third country where, let's make no bones about it, they use torture. If you want a good interrogation, you send someone to Jordan. If you want them to be killed, you send them to Egypt or Syria. Either way, the US cannot be blamed as it is not doing the heavy work'."
42. See Commission of Inquiry into the Actions of Canadian Officials in Relation to Maher Arar, *Report of the Events Relating to Maher Arar: Analysis and Recommendations* (Ottawa: Public Works and Government Services Canada, 2006), available at: www.ararcommission.ca/eng/AR_English.pdf.
43. See *CBC News*, "U.S. won't change policy on deportations to third countries: ambassador," December 4, 2003, available at: www.cbc.ca/news/story/2003/12/04/cellucci_passport031204.html.
44. See Neil A. Lewis, "Man mistakenly abducted by C.I.A. seeks reinstatement of suit," *New York Times*, November 29, 2006, p. A15, available at: select.nytimes.com/gst/abstract.html?res=F10C14FC3A5A0C7A8EDDA8 0994DE404482.
45. A secret poll conducted in Iraq for the UK Ministry of Defence and later leaked to the media found that "forty-five per cent of Iraqis believe attacks against British and American troops are justified—rising to 65 per cent in the British-controlled Maysan province; 82 per cent are 'strongly opposed' to the presence of coalition troops; less than one per cent of the population believes coalition forces are responsible for any improvement in security; 67 per cent of Iraqis feel less secure because of the occupation; 43 per cent of Iraqis believe conditions for peace and stability have worsened; 72 per cent do not have confidence in the multi-national forces" (Sean Rayment,

"Secret MoD poll: Iraqis support attacks on British troops," *Daily Telegraph*, October 22, 2005, available at: www.telegraph.co.uk/news/main.jhtml?xml=/news/2005/10/23/wirq23.xml).

46. On June 26, 2004, www.whitehouse.gov/news/releases/2004/06/20040626-19. html.
47. CBS, *60 Minutes: Punishing Saddam*, aired May 12, 1996.
48. Mohamed Rashed Daoud al-'Owhali, who was given a life sentence for his involvement in the 1998 bombing of the US Embassy in Nairobi. See Phil Hirshkorn, "Bomber's defense focuses on U.S. policy in Iraq," *CNN International*, June 4, 2001, available at: edition.cnn.com/2001/LAW/06/04/embassy.bombings.02.
49. Madeline Albright, *Madam Secretary: A Memoir* (New York: Miramax Books, 2003), p. 275.
50. See Campaign Against Sanctions on Iraq, *Starving Iraq: One Humanitarian Disaster We Can Stop*, March 1999, table 7, www.casi.org.uk/briefing/pamp_ed1.html, for a tabulation of the various estimates.
51. Richard Garfield, interview by *Columbia News*, March 3, 2000, available at: www.columbia.edu/cu/news/media/00/richardGarfield/index.html.
52. See www.pbs.org/frontlineworld/stories/iraq/sanctions.html, also reporting Garfield's earlier estimate that the sanctions had killed 227,713 children in the 91 months from August 1990 until March 1998.
53. Quoted in John Pilger, "Squeezed to death," *Guardian*, March 4, 2000, available at: www.guardian.co.uk/weekend/story/0,3605,232986,00.html.
54. Ibid.
55. See Hans von Sponeck, *A Different Kind of War: The UN Sanctions Regime in Iraq* (Oxford: Berghahn Books, 2006).
56. Burghardt's reasons (described in Anthony Arnove, "Sanctions on Iraq: the 'propaganda campaign'," *ZNET Daily Commentaries*, 1 April 2000, www.zmag.org/ZSustainers/ZDaily/2000-04/01arnove.htm) are more fully articulated in her essay, "The humanitarian situation in Iraq, the humanitarian program 'Oil for Food,' and human rights," *CSCA Web*, July 2001, available at: www.nodo50.org/csca/english/petxalim-ddhh-eng.html.
57. "The Pentagon . . . has no plans to determine how many Iraqi civilians may have been killed or injured or suffered property damage as a result of U.S. military operations in Iraq" (Bradley Graham and Dan Morgan, "U.S. has no plans to count civilian casualties," *Washington Post*, April 15, 2003, p. A13, available at: www.washingtonpost.com/ac2/wp-dyn/A26305-2003Apr14). Jack Straw, UK Secretary of State for Foreign and Commonwealth Affairs, concurred, stating that "in the conditions that exist in Iraq . . . it would be impossible to make a reliably accurate assessment . . . of the overall civilian casualties" and that, in any case, the UK has no obligation under international humanitarian law to make such an assessment (Jack Straw, written ministerial comment, 17 November 2004, *Hansard*, 426/57 (2004), available

at: http:/ /www.cbc.ca/news/background/iraq/casualties.html). Unofficial tallies of civilian deaths in Iraq record some 75,000 reported deaths since the 2003 invasion with the assumption that the true number is considerably larger (www.iraqbodycount.org). A recent survey estimates 654,965 excess civilian deaths between March 18, 2003, and June 2006 (with a 95% confidence interval of 392,979 to 942,636), including 601,027 deaths from violence. See Gilbert Burnham, Riyadh Lafta, Shannon Doocy, Les Roberts, "Mortality after the 2003 invasion of Iraq: a cross-sectional cluster sample survey," *Lancet*, October 11, 2006, available at: www.thelancet.com/webfiles/images/journals/lancet/s0140673606694919.pdf, p. 6. This survey was roundly rejected by the US and UK governments, but found to be well-grounded in internal communications within the UK government. See Owen Bennett-Jones, "Iraqi deaths survey 'was robust'," BBC News, 26 March 2007, available at: news.bbc.co.uk/2/hi/uk_news/politics/6495753.stm.

58. Joseph E. Stiglitz, *Globalization and Its Discontents* (New York: W.W. Norton, 2002).
59. Nicholas Stern, "Making trade work for poor people," speech at the National Council of Applied Economic Research, New Delhi, November 28, 2002, available at: siteresources.worldbank.org/INTRES/Resources/stern_speech_makingtrworkforpoor_nov2002.pdf.
60. Raymond W. Baker, *Capitalism's Achilles Heel* (Hoboken NJ: John Wiley & Sons, 2005).
61. See Carlos M. Correa, "Implications of bilateral free trade agreements on access to medicines," *Bulletin of the World Health Organization*, 84 (2006), 399–404, available at: www.who.int/bulletin/volumes/84/5/399.pdf; Carlos M. Correa, "Public health and intellectual property rights," *Global Social Policy*, 2 (2002), 261–78, http://gsp.sagepub.com/cgi/reprint/2/3/261; and Thomas Pogge, *World Poverty and Human Rights*, 2nd ed. (Cambridge: Polity, 2008), ch. 9.

Reading Analytically

1. How does Pogge develop his argument that terrorism is not as serious a threat as it has been made to seem? Who does he suggest is behind this overstatement of the terrorist threat?
2. On the other hand, Pogge goes to a great deal of trouble to suggest that the actions of the terrorist are morally unjustifiable. What evidence and reasoning does he use to demonstrate this lack of moral behavior? After suggesting that terrorism is not a grave threat, or at least not of the magnitude of other threats, why does he go on to show how immoral and irreligious this behavior is?
3. Based upon these two very different perspectives on the terrorist threat, what in the end would you take to be Pogge's main "thesis" or

argument in this article? Try to develop, in your own words, the full thrust of Pogge's purpose in writing this piece.

Reading Across Disciplinary Communities

1. While Pogge's piece clearly draws upon techniques of moral philosophy, examining the justifications for the behavior of both terrorists and Western countries involved in the "war on terror," he also uses many techniques of political analysis. List at least three pieces of evidence that he uses from the political decisions of these groups that are presented in order to help develop his argument.
2. This piece was first published in the *Journal of Political Philosophy*. Discuss the ways that these two disciplines, political science and philosophy, are brought together in this piece. What makes it "philosophical"? What makes it "political"? As you discuss this you should develop working definitions that express the main purpose of each of those disciplines.

SAMIR QOUTA, RAIJA-LEENA PUNAMÄKI, THOMAS MILLER, AND EYAD EL-SARRAJ

Does War Beget Child Aggression?

Military Violence, Gender, Age, and Aggressive Behavior in Two Palestinian Samples

As social scientists, the authors of this essay use the methodologies of their discipline—mental health—to add to what they call a "scarce and conflicting" pool of empirical evidence to support the common belief that "children and adolescents living in war zones are . . . a lost generation, aggressive and revengeful." These researchers are practicing psychologists; that is, though this piece is based in the methodologies usually associated with scholarly studies—using surveys of randomized samples—their background and influence in conducting this research was based in their own day-to-day observations of the effects of the ongoing war zone that is the Gaza Strip.

Sampling 640 children and adolescents from the Gaza Child Health Sample, these researchers studied the effect of "military behaviors" upon aggressive tendencies and parenting practices. Unlike the essay by philosopher Thomas Pogge, this study (first published in a journal called Aggressive

Behavior) *puts emphasis upon the generation of quantitative information; as such, it can help us better understand the evidence valued by this disciplinary community. As you read, you might consider why these mental health workers felt the need to conduct this empirically based study rather than just report on their observations. What is gained in that methodology?*

We examined, first, the relations between children's exposure to military violence and their aggressive behavior and the role of age and gender in that relation in two Palestinian samples. Second, we tested parenting practices as a moderator of the relation between exposure to military violence and aggressive behavior, and third, whether exposure to military violence of a different nature (direct victimization versus witnessing) has specific associations with different forms of aggression (reactive, proactive and aggression-enjoyment). Study I was conducted in a relatively calm military-political atmosphere in Palestine-Gaza, and included 640 children, aged 6–16 years whose parents (*N*=622) and teachers (*N*=457) provided reports. Older children (≥12 years) provided self-reports (*N*=211). Study II included 225 Palestinian children aged 10–14-year, who participated during a high-violence period of the Al Aqsa Intifada characterized by air raids, killing and destruction. Results showed that witnessing severe military violence was associated with children's aggressive and antisocial behavior (parent-reported) in study I, and with proactive, reactive and aggression-enjoyment (child-reported) in the study II. As hypothesized, good and supporting parenting practices could moderate the link between exposure to military violence and aggressive behavior. Aggr. Behav. 34:231–244, 2008.

Introduction

Children and adolescents living in war-zones are sometimes described as a lost generation, aggressive and revengeful. Empirical evidence substantiating the claim about aggressiveness among war-traumatized children is, however, scarce and conflicting. Instead, anecdotal arguments are numerous, based on the intuitive view that the human mind is a reflection of outside reality—when you live with violence, you become violent yourself, too. This kind of "reflection theory" is generally considered invalid in child development. On the contrary, environmental experiences are mediated through culturally agreed meanings and symbols [Vygotsky, 1978] and personality, activity and coping capacity of the person [Lazarus, 1993]. Also in life-endangering conditions of war and military violence, various moderating factors related to the child, family and community protect mental health, and explain considerable differences in children's vulnerability to traumatic events [Pfefferbaum, 1997; Punamäki, 2002]. Finally, the belief that war violence begets individual aggression is based on the implicit logic that revenge and animosity determine the victims' responses. Yet, alternative responses are also possible, as are illustrated by the international peace movement, the Japanese Hibacusas group and the South African Truth and Reconciliation committee.

In the Palestinian community, however, parents and teachers have expressed deep concern about the developmental consequences of constant life threat, military violence and destruction. They especially worry about children's aggressive behavior. Therefore, two important questions are, whether aggressive responses are more common among Palestinian children exposed to severe military violence and whether good parenting can protect exposed children from aggressive development? Palestinian children have been the targets of killing, beating and detention by the Israeli army and they have witnessed destruction and fighting [B'Tselem, 1998; Human.Right.Watch, 2004]. Fortunately, there has been some variation in the intensity of military violence in the Gaza Strip, which allowed us to examine the violence as a risk for aggressive behavior in two military-political contexts differing in the levels of life threat and destruction.

The discussion of war begetting child aggression has concentrated on developmental risks for physical fighting, although the concept of aggression is more comprehensive. Traditionally, aggression is conceptualized as a behavior intended to injure someone physically or psychologically [Berkowitz, 1993; p 3], which may take different forms. Reactive aggression involves overt and often physical action of harming with angry outbursts in response to actual or perceived provocations. Proactive aggression does not require provocation or anger, but it is used to reach other goals through violent means [for review, see Archer and Coyne, 2005; Little et al., 2003]. Aggressive behavior may also be direct or indirect. In school settings, for instance, direct aggression often involves hitting or cursing at peers or destroying their property. Indirect aggression involves using social manipulation and intriguing to inflict suffering, ridicule and to exclude others [Björkqvist et al., 1992; Lagerspetz et al., 1988].

Despite substantial overlap between reactive and proactive aggression [r=.70; Vitaro and Brengden, 2005], different early childhood and environmental factors foster their development, and distinct temperamental, physiological and genetic factors correlate with the two types of aggression. Reactive aggression is expected to originate from harsh, threatening and unpredictable environments, whereas proactive aggression develops in more supportive environments, where the child is, however, encouraged to use aggression as a way of achieving his or her goals [Dodge, 1991; Vitaro et al., 2006]. We expect that the nature of a child's experience with military violence, i.e. whether the child is the direct target or simply a witness of atrocities, may be important for the occurrence of reactive or proactive aggression. Both theory and earlier research suggest that personal war experiences such as losing family members and being wounded are associated with reactive aggression, whereas threat from war and observing war violence are not related to reactive aggression [Keresteš, 2006; Punamäki, 1987].

We could find few studies that explicitly examined the association between war experiences and children's and adolescents' aggressiveness. A study among Croatian preschoolers compared physical and verbal aggression before and during the major war and atrocities, and found no changes in either type of aggression during the war [Raboteg-Šaric et al., 1994]. However, 10 years later in post-war conditions, the children and adolescents exposed to severe war trauma in preschool age showed a higher level of aggressive behavior than less exposed [Keresteš, 2006]. A study among Israeli preschoolers confirmed that children who witnessed terrorist attack showed an increased level of aggressive behavior [Greenbaum, 2005]. Other studies have made implicit conclusions of children's aggressive versus prosocial development, and the results are conflicting. Lack of aggressive responses has been reported among war traumatized Ugandan adolescents [Raundalen et al., 1987] and Lebanese children [Macksoud and Aber, 1996], whereas personal exposure to severe losses and military violence was found to associate with aggressive responses among Palestinian children [Punamäki, 1987].

Research on children living in adverse conditions of community and family violence emphasizes that violence as such cannot be the reason for aggressive development. Impressive amounts of research show that community violence, involving chronic poverty, losses, criminality and gang fights, forms a risk for aggressiveness through multiple dysfunctional cognitive and emotional processes [Schwartz and Proctor,

2000] and failed or inadequate coping strategies and social support [Tolan et al., 1997]. Community violence has effects on child development through shaping their interpretations, norms, fantasies and cognitive scripts resulting in violent problem solving and aggressive behavior [Guerra et al., 2003]. In contrast, there is evidence that good family relations and optimal parenting practices can prevent aggressive development among children living in violent communities [Proctor, 2006]. Similarly, family violence does not predict children's aggressive and antisocial behavior, if they are not over involved and use flexible coping strategies and adequate emotional and psychophysiological processing of their experiences [Haj-Yahia and Abdo-Kaloti, 2003; Rogers and Holmbeck, 1997].

Thus, the sole existence of war violence in children's lives may not be sufficient to predict aggressiveness and antisocial behavior. To our knowledge, only the study by Keresteš [2006] has tested the hypothesis whether favorable child- and family-related factors moderate the association between traumatic war experiences and children's aggressive behavior. However, in her representative sample of 12–15-year-old Croatians, positive, loving, warm and supporting parenting was not able to protect war-victimized children from engaging in high levels of reactive and proactive aggression. Our aim is to test the role of non-punitive and supportive parenting practices as a moderator between exposure to military violence and aggressive and antisocial behavior among Palestinian children.

There are important developmental changes and gender differences in the expression of aggression. Physical aggression and fights are most common among toddlers [Tremblay, 2000]. Aggressive behavior decreases with age, especially in middle childhood when there are considerable improvements in social skills, perspective taking, empathy and understanding of human relationships [Burks et al., 1999; Little et al., 2003]. However, another peak of aggressive behavior occurs in early adolescence, around 12–14 years of age. Thereafter physical fighting decreases considerably through adolescence and early adulthood [Loeber and Stouthamer-Loeber, 1998; Tremblay, 2000]. The aggressive behavior in early adolescence has been explained by the simultaneous occurrence of demanding psychosocial and biological changes. Teens engage in intensive emotional relationships with peers and parents, meet increasingly challenging cognitive tasks at school and oscillate between maturity and child-likeness. These changes concur with highly negative emotions and parent–teen conflicts [Steinberg and Morris, 2001].

Recent sophisticated and comprehensive longitudinal studies have doubted the existence of an "aggression peak" in early adolescence [Vitaro et al., 2006]. It is as likely that the "late starters" of aggressive and especially antisocial behavior are those children who were highly physically aggressive already in their toddlerhood [Brame et al., 2006]. Although our knowledge is limited, it is plausible that the general and steady decrease in reactive and physical aggression from early years, through middle childhood into adolescence is counteracted by an increase in proactive instrumental aggression in adolescence [Tremblay, 2000; Vitaro et al., 2006].

The distinct developmental changes in aggression are informative when analyzing children's aggression when they are exposed to war conditions. The normative decrease in aggressive behavior requires personal resources and support from the family, school and society. The simultaneous occurrence of severe and provocative military violence and psychological and biological changes places great burden for cognitive, emotional and psychophysiological processes that underlie developmental decrease in aggressiveness. Therefore age-graded decrease in aggression may not occur among children exposed to severe military violence. In support of this idea, children living in violent communities have showed an increase in their aggressive behavior, fantasies and acceptance of aggressive solutions during the years from 5 to 12 [Guerra et al., 2003]. In other words, while in a peaceful environment aggression (especially reactive) decreased with age, in a violent environment aggression increased with age. Accordingly, we hypothesize that older children will show more aggressiveness (especially reactive aggressiveness) than younger when personally exposed to severe military violence in Palestine.

Boys and girls express aggression differently. Reactive, physical and direct aggression is more typical of boys and proactive, instrumental and indirect aggression of girls [Lagerspetz et al., 1988; Tapper and Boulton, 2000]. However, studies on relations between community violence and aggression in middle childhood have not found gender differences, rather exposure to violence increased aggression among both girls and boys [Guerra et al., 2003; Schwartz and Proctor, 2000]. As gender differences increase in adolescence, we may expect also gender-specific responses to military violence: the exposure is associated with reactive and direct aggression among boys and with proactive and indirect aggression among girls.

In the present work, we use two sets of data of Palestinian children and adolescents, collected in Gaza at times characterized by different degree of military violence, life threat, human losses and property destruction. *Study I* was conducted in 1997 during a relatively calm period of the Palestinian National Authority after the Israeli military had withdrawn from 65% of the occupied Gaza Strip, no fighting was going on and there were some hopes for a peaceful solution. On the contrary, *study II* was conducted during times of intensive violence in 2005 during the Al Aqsa Intifada that was characterized by extensive Israeli air raids, bulldozing and destruction of residential areas, targeted killing, cutting the Gaza Strip area in three by checkpoints and imposing a complete siege on the area.

Our research questions are: first, is exposure to severe military violence associated with children's aggression, indicated by aggressive and antisocial behavior (study I) and reactive, proactive, direct and enjoyment aggression (study II). Second, we examine whether supportive and non-punitive parenting practices moderate the possible link between exposure to military violence and aggression. Third, we analyze how child age and gender are associated with aggression in general and when the child is exposed to severe military violence. We hypothesize that younger children show generally higher levels of aggression than older, whereas older children show more aggression when exposed to severe military violence. Concerning gender, we hypothesize that girls show more proactive and boys reactive aggression, and especially so when exposed to severe military violence. Finally, we explore whether the nature of trauma has specific associations with different types of aggression. Direct victimization from military violence, involving being wounded and loss of family members, should be associated with reactive aggression, whereas witnessing of military violence, e.g., killing and destruction, should be associated with proactive aggression. Our general hypothesis also is that direct victimization from physical military violence is more likely to be associated with aggression than simply witnessing violence.

Study I

Participants and Procedure of the Study

The sample consists 640 children and adolescents from the Gaza Child Health Sample [Miller et al., 2000]. They were 6–16-year-old pupils ($M=10.51\pm2.45$), and 54.7% were girls and 45.3% boys. Information was collected from parents and teachers concerning children of all ages, and 12–16-year-old children and adolescents reported also themselves. The sample sizes differ for complete data of this analysis: 622 parent reports, 457 teacher reports and 211 self-reports by 12–16-year-old pupils.

A two-stage random sampling method was applied. First, schools were selected from a list of all schools in the Gaza Strip based on a stratified geographic location (town, refugee camp, village, resettled area). Second, a list was prepared from all pupils in these schools, using the stratification based on gender and age, and the allocated numbers of students were selected randomly from that list. Eight field workers (seven women) visited the homes of the selected pupils, obtained parental consent and then administrated the questionnaires to one of the parents and the child (if older than 11 years). In most cases the informant was mother (78%) or other female family member (7.9%) and the rest (16.1%) were the father or other male family member. Thereafter, the field workers met the principal teacher of the child at the school.

Measures

Military violence was assessed by an 18-event list, including ten items of the child being personally the victim of violence, e.g., being detained, wounded and beaten, losing family members and home demolition, and eight events of the child witnessing killing, fighting and destruction. The parent and child (if 12 years or older) were asked whether the child had been exposed to each of these events during the First Intifada: (0) no, (1) yes. If yes, they were also asked to estimate how many times the event occurred. Respondents had difficulty remembering the frequencies, and therefore a sum variable was constructed by counting only the occurrences of the traumatic events. Two scales were constructed from these data: *the child's victimization from one military violence*—a scale consisting of ten events, ranging between 0 and 8 in the sample, and *the child's witnessing of military violence*—a scale consisting of eight events, ranging between 0 and 5 in the sample. There was a correlation between the parent and child reports of the child's victimization from military violence (r=.57, P<0001, N=192) and between their reports of the child's witnessing of military violence (r=.64, P<0001, N=192). However, parent and child reports could not be combined into one variable because only children older than 11 years were interviewed. In this study only the parent-reported variables of military violence are used because of the larger sample size.

Aggressiveness was measured by scales of aggressive and antisocial behavior in Ontario Child Health Scale, an interviewer-administered checklist for parents, children and teachers [Boyle et al., 1987]. The scale consists of 34 questions that cover symptoms indicating conduct and emotional disorders, and attention deficit hyperactive disorder, formulated by using DSM-III criteria for disorders. The parents and teachers were asked to rate how well the items describe the child's behavior, and children and adolescents were asked how well the items describe their own behavior. The alternatives were: (0) never true, (1) sometimes or somewhat true or (2) often or very true. For the purpose of this study, parent-reported, teacher-reported and children's self-reported aggression sum variables were constructed. They included (a) nine symptoms of aggressive behavior, such as cruelty, bullying or meanness to others, physically attacks people, gets in many fights, and destroys things, and (b) nine symptoms of antisocial behavior such as disobedience at school, threatens people, lies or cheats, steals outside home and runs away from home. Aggressive behavior scales ranged between 0 and 29 (M=3.87±4.06) for parent reports, between 0 and 33 (M=3.65±4.73) for teacher reports, and between 0 and 13 (M=2.94±2.94) for child reports. The Cronbach's α values are .87 for parents, .86 for teachers and .71 for children themselves.

Parenting practices were assessed by a nine-item scale applied from Barber [1999] indicating parents' punitive, controlling and negotiating disciplining practices in a situation when the child has broken a rule. The choices were, for instance, ignoring the child's behavior, making threats of punishment or calmly discussing the problem. Parents evaluated their own behavior toward the child, and children and adolescents evaluated their parents' behavior toward themselves on a 3-point Likert scale: (1) never or rarely, (2) sometimes or (3) often or always. Parent-reported and child-reported sum variables were constructed, and they reached only moderate reliability (Cronbach α=.64 for parents' report and α=.69 for children's report). A high score on the scale indicates a negative (punitive) disciplining style and a low score indicates a positive (negotiating) style. In this study, only the parent-reported variable was used due to the larger sample size.

Results

Descriptive Statistics

Table I shows the distribution of demographic variables in study I. Half of the families lived in urban areas and a quarter in refugee camps, which corresponded to the population distribution in Gaza [Unicef,

TABLE I Percentages and Frequencies of Demographic Factors in the Sample in the Study I

	Sample	
	%	*N*
Age groups (years)		
6–10	54.5	348
11–13	24.1	154
14–16	21.4	137
Place of residency		
Urban area	46.3	295
Refugee camp	24.6	157
Village	20.6	131
Resettled area	8.5	54
Mother education		
No education	13.2	84
Elementary school (Gr 1–6)	20.2	129
Preparatory school (Gr 7–9)	26.1	167
Secondary school (Gr 10–12)[a]	34.5	220
Post secondary[b]	6.0	38
Father education		
No education	7.9	51
Elementary school (Gr 1–6)	26.7	170
Preparatory school (Gr 7–9)	22.2	142
Secondary school (Gr 10–12)[a]	24.4	156
Post secondary[b]	18.7	119

Sample sizes differ due to missing values.
[a]Includes vocational school and gymnasium.
[b]Includes also university education.

1992]. Concerning parental education, a fifth of fathers and a quarter of mothers had primary education. Of the fathers 12.5% and of the mothers 2.6% had the highest education, including a university degree, and 13% of mothers and 8% of fathers had no formal education. The educational level of the sample accords the national statistics [Unicef, 1992]. Typical to the Gaza Strip, families were large and households relatively crowded: The mean number of children under 16 was 6±2.40, and mean number of people living in a household was 7.7±2.95.

Table II presents the correlations between the key variables separately for boys and girls. The correlations with age show that older boys

TABLE II Correlations for Girls and Boys in the Study I (Boys Above the Diagonal and Girls Below the Diagonal)

Independent and dependent variables		1	2	3	4	5	6	7
					Boys[a]			
1. Age			.24**	.42***	–.08	–.08	.10	.11
2. Victimized directly by military violence: parent reports		.15**		.50***	.14*	.09	.06	–.05
3. Witnessing military violence: parent reports		.22**	.43***		.42***	.09	.19*	–.04
4. Child aggressive behavior: parent reports[c]	**Girls**[b]	.15	.20**	.24**		.21**	.36***	.32***
5. Child aggressive behavior: teacher reports[c]		–.06	.08	.02	.32**		.36**	.19*
6. Child aggressive behavior: child reports[c]		.06	.13	.02	.35**	–.03		.11
7. Punitive parenting practices: parent reported[d]		.20**	.01	.11	.33***	.14*	.12	

[a]N=290 for boys.
[b]N=350 for girls.
[c]The parent and teacher-reported aggression involves children of all ages and the child-reported the 12–1-year olds.
[d]High values indicate punitive and low values supportive parenting practices.
*$P < .05$; **$P < .01$; **$P < .001$.

and girls had been more directly victimized by military violence and had witnessed more military violence than younger children. However, age was not correlated with aggressive behavior whether reported by parents, teachers or children themselves. Among both girls and boys being victimized directly and witnessing military violence were both correlated positively with parent-reported aggressive behavior, and among boys witnessing military violence also was correlated with self-reported aggressive behavior (r=.19, P<.05). In both gender groups being victimized directly and witnessing military violence were correlated positively, indicating that witnessing violence and being victimized are related.

Concerning parenting practices, older girls reported more punitive parenting than younger girls (r=.22, P=.01), whereas age was not correlated with parenting among boys. Children's aggressive and antisocial behaviors (parent- and teacher-reported) were correlated positively with punitive parenting practices among both boys and girls. Exposure to military violence did not correlate with parenting practices, however.

Positive significant correlations were found between aggressive and antisocial behavior variables that were based on parents', teachers' and children's reports. There were no differences in the levels of parent-perceived, teacher-perceived and self-reported aggressive behavior according to paired t-tests (t=0.76, N=452, P=ns, not significant between parents and teacher, t=0.84, N=173, P=ns between parents and children and t=0.96, N=135, P=ns. between teachers and children).

Military Violence, Gender, Age, Parenting and Aggressive Behavior

Hierarchical multiple regression analyses with main and interaction effects were used to examine the associations between military violence and aggressive behavior, and the moderator role of gender, age and parenting practices in the possible association. The dimensions of parent-, teacher- and child-reported aggressive and antisocial behavior were the dependent variables. The model included three main effect and two interaction effect steps. In the step 1 gender and age were entered, in step 2 parent-reported variables of the child being victimized directly by and witnessing military violence were entered, and in step 3 the parent-reported punitive parenting practices variable was entered. In step 4 the interaction terms between demographic (gender and age) and military violence (being victimized directly and witnessing) were entered. Finally, in step 5 the military violence × parenting practices

TABLE III Hierarchical Linear Regressions Predicting Different Measures of Child Aggression From the Child's Exposure to Military Violence and Parenting Practices

	Child aggressive behavior								
	Parent reports[a]			Teacher reports[a]			Child reports[a]		
	R^2	Change in R^2	β[b]	R^2	Change in R^2	β[b]	R^2	Change in R^2	β[b]
Step 1. Demographic	.04	.04***		.03	.03**		.02	.02	
Gender (1=boys, 2=girls)			–.19***			–.16***			–.13
Age			–.17***			–.09****			–.03
Step 2. Parent-reported military trauma	.09	.05***		.03	.00		.03	.01	
Victimized directly by military violence			.01			.10			.03
Witnessing military violence			.11*			.03			.13
Step 3. Punitive parenting practices	.11	.02*	.13*	.04	.01**	.16**	.04	.01	.12
Step 4. Demographic × military violence interactions	.13	.02*		.04	.00		.05	.01	
Gender × victimized directly			–.01			.04			.17
Gender × witnessing violence			.03			–.06			–.06
Age × victimized directly			–.12*			–.01			–.10
Age × witnessing violence			–.06			.05			–.05
Step 5. Military violence × punitive parenting practices interactions	.13	.00		.06	.02*		.08	.03****	
Victimized directly × punitive parenting			.02			–.18**			–.31*
Witnessing violence × punitive parenting			.03			–.15*			–.11
Total model	$F(11,537)=7.10$, $P<.0001$, 13% of the variance explained			$F(11,428)=2.66$, $P<.003$, 6% of the variance explained			$F(11,154)=1.22$, $P=$ns, 8% of the variance explained		

[a]The parent and teacher reported aggression involves children of all ages and the child-reported the 12–16-year olds.

[b] β values from the final step in the total model.

$^{*}P<.05$; $^{**}P<.01$; $^{***}P<.001$; $^{****}P<.10$.

interaction terms were entered. All predictors in the interaction terms were first centered to avoid multicollinearity between variables, as recommended by Aiken and West [1991].

The results in Table III show that the models for children's aggressive and antisocial behavior differed according to the nature of military violence and the source of the information. The model explained 13% of the variation of the parent-reported and only 6% of the teacher-reported child aggression. The model was non-significant for children's own reported aggression.

A significant association was found between children witnessing military violence and their parent-reported aggressive behavior (β = .11, t=2.09, $P < .04$). Children who had witnessed high levels of military violence expressed a higher level of aggressive and antisocial behavior than children exposed to lower levels of witnessing violence. The significant age × victimized directly by military violence interaction effect (b=-.12, t=-2.35, P<.02) further revealed that younger children showed especially high-level aggressive behavior (parent-reported) when they were highly victimized directly by military violence, illustrated in Figure 1. Our general hypothesis that being victimized directly by military violence would be associated with aggressive and antisocial behavior was thus supported only among the younger children.

As hypothesized, boys showed more aggressive behavior than girls, as perceived by parents and teachers. Association between exposure to military violence and aggression was not gender specific, as the non-significant gender × military violence interaction effects show. Against our hypothesis younger children showed more aggressive and antiso-

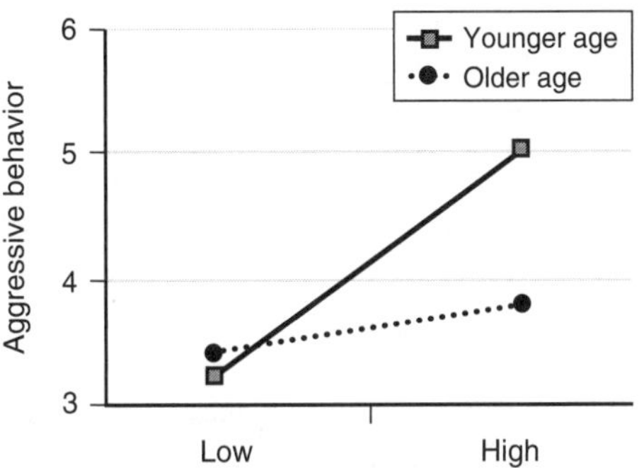

Figure 1. The association between a child being victimized directly by military trauma and the child's aggression as reported by the parents as a function of the child's age.

cial behavior than older, and especially so when directly victimized by military violence.

The hypothesis that parenting practices would moderate the relation between experiencing military violence and aggression was supported. Significant interaction effects indicate that both being directly victimized ($\beta = -.18$, $t = -2.51$, $P < .01$) and witnessing ($\beta = -.15$, $t = -2.31$, $P < .02$) military violence were associated with teacher-reported aggression more among children whose parents were punitive and non-supportive. The moderator effects are illustrated in Figures 2 and 3. Although the model for child-reported aggression was non-significant, a significant negative interaction effect ($\beta = -.31$, $t = -2.30$, $P < .02$) indicates that being victimized directly by military violence was associated with aggressive and antisocial behavior more among children with

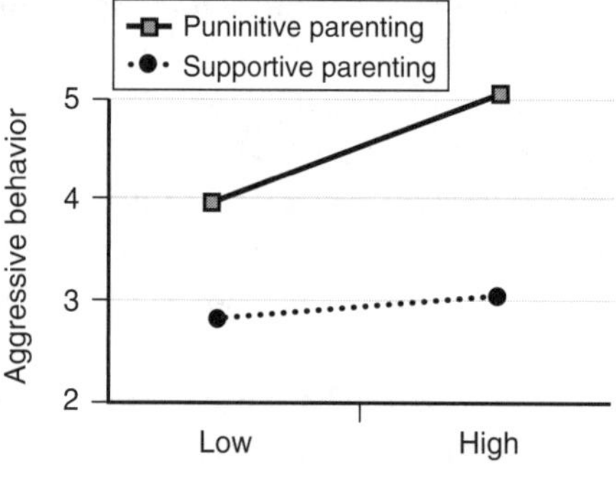

Figure 2. The interactive effect of a child being directly victimized by military violence and parenting practices on the child's aggression (teacher-reported)

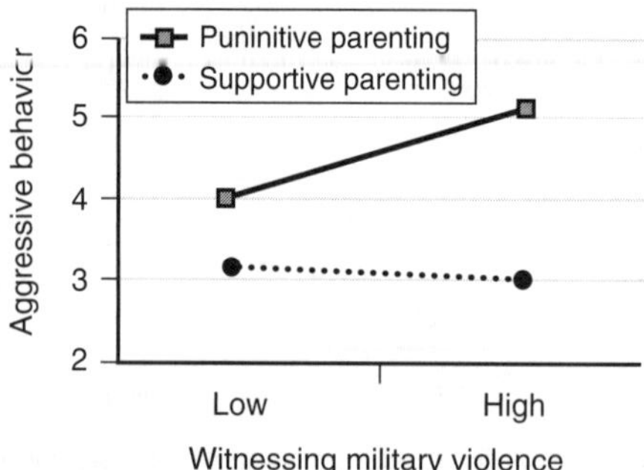

Figure 3. The interactive effect of a child witnessing military violence and parenting practices on the child's aggression (teacher-reported)

punitive and non-supportive parents. Main effects confirmed that high punitive parenting practices were associated with children's aggressive and antisocial behavior as perceived by parents and teachers.

Study II

Participants and Procedure of the Study

The participants were 225 Palestinian school children in the Gaza Strip. Of them 39% were girls and 64% boys, and their age ranged between 10 and 15 years ($M=11.37 \pm 1.1$). The data were collected as a part of an intervention study, and the analysis for study II is based on the base line assessment for the intervention. Four school classes in two schools in Northern Gaza were recruited to participate in the study. A majority of children (60.9%) lived in urban areas, 20.9% in refugee camps, 9.3% in a village and 8.9% in resettled areas.

Two of the schools were located in areas where the Israeli fighter jets, tanks and bulldozers had caused considerable destruction during the Al Aqsa Intifada, and two schools were situated in safer areas. The whole Gaza Strip has suffered a high toll of victims since 2001 when the confrontations started. According to the Palestinian Center for Human Right [PCHR-Report, 2006], 2,268 people have been killed and 36,589 have been injured. The total number of children killed is 931 as results of shelling their homes and schools, and shooting at checkpoints. Substantial restriction of moment has been imposed, and consequently a number of deaths are due to delayed first aid. For instance, 31 infants have died at checkpoints because of prevented delivery. With regard to the impact of the military violence on education, 576 of the students had been killed and 669 injured, and more than 200 of teachers have been detained, injured or killed. Of the originally small area of the Gaza Strip, 249,729 Dunum of land had been confiscated and 64,043 Dunum had been razed down (Dunum=1,000m^2) [PCHR-Report, 2006]. In other words the sample II represents children who live in an acutely life-endangering environment.

Measures

Military trauma was measured by a 25-item event list developed by the Gaza Community Mental Health Programme to catch typical experiences of Gaza Palestinians during the Al-Aqsa Intifada [Qouta et al., 2005]. The questionnaire involves 12 items of being victimized directly by the military violence the target of violence (e.g., shelling of home, being detained, wounded and beaten, losing a family member) and 13 events of witnessing military violence such as killing, injuring, house demolition and bulldozing orchards. The children responded by indicating whether they had been exposed to the event (1 = yes) or not (0=no). Similar to study I, two sum variables were formed for the purpose of this study: *the child's victimization directly by military violence*—a scale consisting of 12 events, ranging between 0 and 9 in the sample, and *the child's witnessing of military violence*—a scale consisting of 13 events, ranging between 0 and 11 in the sample.

Aggressiveness was measured by a Multiple Aggression questionnaire developed and standardized in Arab populations by Amal Abaza from Tanta University, Egypt [Abaza, 2003]. The questionnaire consists of 41 descriptions of behavior, thinking and feelings, and children estimated on a 4-point scale how well they fit them (1) not at all, (2) to some extent, (3) quite well, and (4) very well. The Multiple Aggression questionnaire depicts three qualitatively different aggression dimensions: reactive, proactive and aggression enjoyment. We conducted a factor analysis (Varimax with orthogonal rotation) to confirm the dimensionality in our data, and it turned out to be technically adequate explaining 40.6% of the variation. The *reactive aggression* subscale consists of 14 items, such as "Sometimes I toss and harm my classmate without any reason," "I prefer to fight with children who are less strong or more miserable than I," "I destroy things in the class, although I would be punished for that." The reactive aggression dimension accounts for 17.3% of the total variance of the scale, and the Cronbach's α value was .85. The *proactive aggression* dimension also has 14 items, such as "I easily start to humiliate verbally my school mates," "I feel happy when any school mate makes mistakes and the teacher scolds him," "I like playing tricks to other pupils." The proactive aggression dimension accounts 12.2% of the variance, and the Cronbach's α value was .83. Finally, the *aggression-enjoyment* dimension involves 13 items describing a kind of vicarious enjoyment of aggression, e.g., "I prefer war and risk-taking actions," "I feel happy when I see animals fighting" and "It is easy to let my classmates to be afraid." The aggression-enjoyment dimension accounted 11.1% of the variation and the Cronbach's α value was .73.

Results

Correlations

Table IV shows correlations between the key variables separately for boys and girls. Results show that older boys had been more directly victimized

TABLE IV Correlations for Girls and Boys in Study II (Boys Above the Diagonal and Girls Below the Diagonal)

Independent and dependent variables		1	2	3	4	5	6
					Boys[a]		
1. Age			.21**	.13	.04	-.05	-.05
2. Victimized directly by military violence		.13		.48****	.22**	.14*****	.12
3. Witnessing military violence	**Girls**[b]	.36***	.58****		.26**	.23**	.17*
4. Reactive aggression: child-reported		.04	.01	.15		.69****	.65****
5. Proactive aggression: child-reported		-.06	.07	.26*	.68****		.75****
6. Enjoyment of aggression: child-reported		-.21*****	.10	.27**	.43****	.60****	

[a]N=144 for boys

[b]N=81 for girls.

*P<.05, **P<.01, ***P< .001, ****P< .0001.

by military violence than younger boys ($r=.21$, $P<.01$), and older girls had witnessed more military violence than younger girls ($r=.36$, $P<.001$). Age did not significantly correlate with aggression among boys, but among girls there was a marginally significant negative correlation between age and aggression-enjoyment ($r=-.21$, $P<.06$), indicating a decreasing enjoyment of aggression. Witnessing military violence was correlated positively with all three aggression measures among boys, and with proactive aggression and aggression-enjoyment among girls. For boys being victimized directly by military violence was correlated positively with reactive aggression ($r=.22$, $P=.009$) and marginally with proactive aggression ($r=.14$, $P<.09$).

Among both genders being victimized directly by military violence and witnessing violence correlated significantly as expected. All three aggression measures also significantly correlated, indicating an overlap, for instance, between reactive and proactive aggression among both boys ($r=.69$, $P<.0001$) and girls ($r=.68$, $P<.0001$).

Military Violence, Gender, Age and Aggressive Behavior

Similar to study I, associations between military violence and aggressiveness and the role of gender and age in this association were tested with hierarchical multiple regression analyses with main and interaction effects. The dimensions of proactive, reactive aggression and aggression-enjoyment were the dependent variables. The model included two main effect and one-interaction effect steps. In step 1 gender and age were added, in step 2 being victimized directly and witnessing military violence were added, and in step 3 interaction terms between the demographic and military violence variables were entered. Parenting variables were not available in this study; so they could not be included in the regressions. As in study I all predictors in the interaction terms were first centered to avoid multi-collinearity between variables, as recommended by Aiken and West [1991].

Results in Table V show that the models were significant for all three aggression measures and the explained variance varied between 18 and 20%. Children exposed to high level of witnessing of military violence reported higher levels of proactive aggression ($\beta=.20$, $t=2.57$, $P<.01$), reactive aggression ($\beta=.23$, $t=3.11$, $P<.002$) and enjoyment of aggression ($\beta=.17$, $t = 2.19$, $P<.03$) than those exposed to lower levels. However, being victimized directly by military violence was not associated significantly with any of the three child aggression measures.

TABLE V Hierarchical Linear Regressions Predicting Different Measures of Child Aggression From the Child's Gender, Age, and Exposure to Military Violence

	Child aggression								
	Proactive aggression			Reactive aggression			Enjoyment of aggression		
	R^2	Change in R^2	β^a	R^2	Change in R^2	β^a	R^2	Change in R^2	β^a
Step 1. Demographic	.10	.10****		.14	.14****		.15	.15****	
Gender (1=boys, 2=girls)			–.27****			–.32****			–.33****
Age			–.12^{+}			–.02			–.04
Step 2. Child-reported military trauma	.16	.06***		.19	.05**		.18	.03*	
Victimized directly by military violence			.03			.01			.01
Witnessing military violence			.20**			.23**			.17*
Step 3. Demographic × military violence interactions	.18	.02		.20	.01		.19	.01	
Gender × victimized directly			–.05			–.06			.01
Gender × witnessing violence			.08			–.03			–.03
Age × victimized directly			–.08			–.10			–.09
Age × witnessing violence			–.01			.01			–.03
Total model	$F(8,215)=5.96$, $P<.0001$, 18% explained variance			$F(8,215)=6.55$, $P<.0001$, 20% explained variance			$F(8,215)=6.20$, $P<.0001$, 19% explained variance		

[a]β -values from the final step in the total model.

$^{+}P<.10$, $^{*}P<.05$, $^{**}P<.01$, $^{***}P<.001$, $^{****}P<.0001$.

Boys reported higher levels of all types of aggression than girls, including proactive aggression that we had expected to be higher among girls. The non-significant gender × military violence interaction effects indicate that the association between military violence and aggression did not depend on gender. In other words, witnessing military violence had similar associations with aggressiveness among both girls and boys.

Our general hypothesis of older children showing more aggressive behavior, especially reactive aggression, was not confirmed. On the contrary, younger children reported marginally more proactive aggression than older ($b=-.12$, $t=1.75$, $P<.08$). The interaction effects between age and military violence on aggression were non-significant, indicating that the association between witnessing military violence and children's aggression was present for all ages.

Discussion

The results of study I among Palestinian children confirmed that exposure to severe military violence was associated with higher levels of aggressive and antisocial behavior. Although both victimization and witnessing violence correlated with aggressive behavior among both genders, regression models with main and interaction effects revealed that only the witnessing of killing and destruction predicted aggression when demographics were included in the model. As hypothesized, supportive and non-punitive parenting practices protected children from aggressive and antisocial behavior, even if they were severely victimized by or witnessing military violence.

Similar to Keresteš' [2006] study the association between military violence and child aggression was dependent on the source of information, i.e. whether children themselves, their parents or teachers reported their aggressive behavior. In our data, exposure to military violence was associated only with parent-perceived aggressive behavior, whereas in the Croatian sample severe war trauma predicted child-reported aggressiveness. In our study, the protective role of optimal parenting practices in turn was evident in teacher- and child-reported aggression, but not in parent-perceived, whereas parenting had no protective role in the Keresteš' study.

Similar to research in peaceful societies [Leinonen et al., 2002; Pakaslahti, 2000], punitive parenting practices were significantly associated with aggressive behavior among both girls and boys. Military violence was not, however, associated with punitive parenting practices. This finding contradicts our observations during the First Intifada that intensified military trauma interferes with parenting resources. In that study in highly traumatized Palestinian families, children were found to perceive their parents more punitive and harsh, which in turn negatively affected children's cognitive resources and psychological adjustment [Punamäki et al., 1997]. Study I was conducted during a calmer and safer period than the First Intifada, and it is possible that then parenting practices were recovering from harsh experiences of military violence.

The results of study II based on cross-sectional single-report setting confirmed the results of the study I that children who had witnessed severe military violence showed more aggression than less exposed children. Witnessing killing, wounding and destruction or being victimized during the Al Aqsa Intifada was generally associated with both reactive and proactive aggression, as well as with aggression-enjoyment though there were some differences between genders as summarized below.

Correlation analyses revealed some gender-specific phenomena. First, boys were more likely to be victimized as they got older, whereas girls were more likely to witness violence as they got older. The gender roles in the Palestinian national struggle determine that boys are more active, participate more often in military actions and are more often targets of the enemy fire, whereas girls witness atrocities befalling their close ones [Punamäki et al., 1997]. Second, as hypothesized, military violence was correlated positively with proactive but not with reactive aggression among girls. However, among boys being victimized by military violence was associated with higher levels of both reactive and proactive aggression, thus opposing our gender-specific hypothesis concerning the type of aggression.

Implications

War and military violence signify a shattering and nightmarish reality for children: life threat, loss of home, killing and detention of family members, and witnessing humiliation of trusted and admired adults. According to psychoanalytical view, human beings have two possibilities to deal with pain and bewilderment that overwhelms their cognitive-emotional processing capacity: to turn them inside and suffer subsequently from depression and anxiety or target them outside in the form of aggression and acting out [Pedder, 1992]. Contemporary conceptualization of children's psychiatric distress as internalizing and externalizing symptoms [Achenbach, 1997; Rutter, 1967] concurs with these alternatives given for humans when facing devastating events.

We have a substantial amount of research showing that war and military violence increase risks for depressive symptoms and anxiety disorders, including posttraumatic stress disorder characterized by intrusive, avoidant and arousal symptoms [Brajša-Zganec, 2005; Smith et al., 2002; Thabet et al., 2005]. Researchers thus implicitly expect victims of war to turn their pain inwards into themselves rather than to act it out into the environment. The current two studies add a different dimension. Our results confirm that exposure to military violence also promotes acting out and aggressive behavior in both boys and girls. We found consistent associations between Palestinian children's aggressive responses and their personal exposure to military violence. The association was valid both in periods of relative calm and intensified military activity in Gaza. Yet, we also witnessed the power of favorable family relations in mitigating the negative impact of war on child aggression and antisocial behavior.

The association between exposure to military violence and aggressiveness did not depend on the intensity and acuteness of objective external danger. The study I was conducted in conditions of a very rare lull in fighting and destruction in Gaza, and, on the contrary, the study II in the midst of shelling, fighting, sonic bombing and bulldozing houses and land. What is remarkable is that in both studies it was the witnessing of atrocities toward others that was decisive for child aggression, rather than being victimized themselves. In both studies the direct victimization and witnessing military violence were correlated positively, but in regression models the witnessing proved to be a more important determinant of aggression.

Thus, our hypothesis that direct child-targeted victimization from military violence is more dangerous and thus a better candidate for predicting aggression may not correspond with experiences of children living in chronic violence. The underlying mechanisms and subsequent outcomes are apparently different among witnessing destruction, cruelties, and humiliation and harming family members. Being victimized by military actions, although harsh, can involve secondary gains such as heroism and belonging in national struggle against foreign occupation. The victims may receive social support, admiration and encouragements, which further encourage their endurance [Qouta et al., 2003]. On the contrary, witnessing violence to others can evoke feelings of frustration, impotence and cowardliness, which then find expression in aggression. Although direct victimization is collective, visible and pride-evoking, witnessing violence toward family members, for instance, often involves feelings of shame, disillusion and helplessness.

The vulnerability to aggressive and antisocial behavior in war conditions illustrates an intensive interplay between child characteristics and violence environment. Developmental demands, such as emotion regulation and adequate anger expression, are highly demanding even in normal and safe childhood conditions. With age children develop qualitatively new cognitive, emotional and social activities, which result in a decrease in physical aggression. For instance, adolescents' brain development is characterized by intensifying of complex associative connections, which allows a wider repertoire of problem solving and memorizing, emotion regulation and understanding of one's own and others' complex emotional and motivational processes [Kagan, 2003; Spear, 2000]. They in turn form the preconditions for highly sophisticated moral reasoning and consideration for peaceful values, social justice and empathy. However, children and adolescents need societal support and encouragement to succeed in these developmental changes, which makes possible the decrease in aggression and increase in prosocial behavior.

War and national struggle as a context for child development do not provide these societal preconditions for decreased aggressiveness. Freud and Burlingham [1943] argued during the Second World War that the outside reality of bombardments, filled with destruction, cruelty and aggression is in concordance with preschoolers' inner world. They described how excessive external destruction and violence made it difficult for toddlers to regulate their angry impulses, and made them therefore prone to aggressive development. Children who simultaneously face demands of both developmental transitions and war trauma are especially vulnerable to dysfunctional emotion regulation, including aggression. Contemporary longitudinal studies confirm that physical aggression is most evident in the first 3 years of life [Trembley et al., 2004]. Tremblay [2002], opposing the social learning theory [Bandura, 1973], suggests that children do not learn to be physically aggressive, but that they rather learn not to be physically aggressive under the combined effects of socialization and brain maturation. Subsequently, we may hypothesize that war and violence are especially harmful for children who struggle with their developmental transitions, and the belligerent scenes interfere with their age-graded learning of non-aggression.

The importance of the concordance between aggressive development and external reality was well illustrated by Guerra et al. [2003]. They showed an increase of aggressive schemes and behavior in elementary school years among children who witnessed and were victimized by community violence. Normative beliefs and acceptance of aggressive solutions became thus stable personality features during children's formative years. The results by Keresteš [2006] are important because they show a long-term impact of war and atrocities on child development. The Croatian children who were exposed to war trauma in their preschool years showed more reactive and proactive aggression when entering their adolescence. It is possible that the transition to adolescence among post-war youth is activating their earlier childhood traumatic memories, which explains the longitudinal link between being victimized by war violence and aggression.

Society at war sends double messages to children who until early adolescence face difficulties in interpreting them: the aggression, defiance and revenge are encouraged toward the enemy, but discouraged or even punished when directed toward their own family and peers. Similarly, research on children's war attitudes and moral development point out dilemmas and conflicts: children learn that war is generally bad and immoral, but our own war is heroic, legitimate and moral and our fighters are pure and honorable, whereas enemy soldiers are cruel and coward-like [Punamäki, 1987; Tolley, 1973].

We should, however, be careful not to ignore alternative explanations for children's aggression than military trauma. Three major issues are relevant. First, proximal influence of parents, siblings and peers might be more powerful than more distal military violence. We confirmed that punitive parenting both associated with child aggression and strengthened the violence-aggression link. For deeper understanding, the analyses should include parental norms about the appropriateness of aggression as well as ways of solving conflicts between siblings and peers. Second, a more sophisticated model is needed to reveal the child-related mechanisms that explain the occurrence of aggression in wartime societies. The information processing model provides an integrative framework and can explain why some children in a similar violent and life-endangering environment are aggressive, whereas others are proactive, show depression or remain intact [Anderson and Bushman, 2002; Crick and Dodge, 1994]. There is a multi-stage process by which the interplay between child characteristics (e.g. age, gender, temperament, trait hostility, attitudes to war, emotional regulation and physiological stress reactions) and situational factors (e.g. nature and meaning of trauma, degree and significance of humiliation and life danger) leads to aggressive behavior. Aggression, in turn needs specific changes and preconditions in children's cognitive, affective and arousal states. Future study settings should answer how being a target or witnessing military violence in certain age influence children's cognitions like attention, memory and attributions, and emotions like fear, anger and hostility. Third, societal and cultural determinants of aggressive behavior should be analyzed. We do not know how national history interpretation of collective experiences and cultural codes can prime or hinder aggressive thoughts and scripts, increase hostile feelings and regulate anger expression on an individual level.

The study deserves further criticism for conceptual and measurement issues. The results of the study II are based on single-informant setting leading to possible biased response tendencies. Children might have exaggerated or belittled both their traumatic experiences and aggressive responses. Although the study I was based on a multi-informant setting, the significant direct relation between violence exposure and aggressive behavior was found in parents' reports thus again raising concern of same-informant bias. Naturally, reliance on parents' and children's self-reports about traumatic events in conditions of military occupation deserves criticism. To have a more reliable and objective data, we should have consulted international and local human rights organizations that document events of military violence. Despite our efforts in study I, we failed to obtain more detailed information about the timing, intensity, duration and subjective appraisal about the severity of traumatic events. Furthermore, the conceptualization and measurements of aggression differed in the two samples. Therefore, we cannot genuinely answer the question whether the objective level of military violence, life threat and destruction has an impact on the level of child aggression.

Our study should be regarded as a first explorative step, the next being the hypothesis testing about underlying mechanisms explaining how collective level phenomena, war violence, is processed in individual levels of cognitive, emotional, social and brain functioning, and in turn transferred into political and military activity. Advances in aggression research, such as psychophysiological and genetic findings [Caspi et al., 2002] should be applied for the question about war begetting aggression. Understanding of multilevel and dynamic psychological processes that military violence activates is necessary for tailored, developmentally and culturally adequate intervention and prevention among traumatized children and for peace education.

References

Abaza A. 2003. Questionnaire to Measure Multiple Types of Aggression. Tanta Egypt: Tanta University Press (In Arabic).

Achenbach TM. 1997. What is normal? What is abnormal? Developmental perspectives on behavioral and emotional problems. In: Luthar SS, Burack JA, Cicchetti D, Weisz JR, (eds): Developmental Psychopathology: Perspectives on Adjustment, Risk and Disorder. Cambridge: Cambridge University Press, pp 93–114.

Aiken LS, West SG. 1991. Multiple regression: Testing and interpreting interactions. Thousand Oaks: Sage.

Anderson CA, Bushman BJ. 2002. Human aggression. Annu Rev Psychol 53:27–51.

Archer J, Coyne SM. 2005. An integrated review of indirect, relational, and social aggression. Pers Soc Psychol Rev 9:212–230.

Bandura A. 1973. Aggression: A social learning analysis. Englewood Cliffs, NJ: Prentice-Hall.

B'Tselem. 1998. 1987–1997 A Decade of Human Right Violations; Information Sheet: January 1998. Jerusalem: B'Tselem—The Israeli Information Centre for Human Rights in the Occupied Territories.

Barber BK. 1999. Youth experience in the palestinian intifada: A case study in intensity, complexity, paradox, and competence. In: Youniss AYJ, (ed): Roots of Civic Identity: International Perspectives on Community Service and Activism in Youth. New York: Cambridge University Press, pp 178–204.

Berkowitz L. 1993. Aggression. Its Causes, Consequences, and Control. New York: McGraw-Hill.

Björkqvist K, Lagerspetz K, Kaukiainen A. 1992. Do girls manipulate and boys fight? Developmental trends in regard to direct and indirect aggression. Aggress Behav 18:117–127.

Boyle MH, Offord DR, Hofman HG, Catlin GP, Byles JA, Dadman DT, Crawford JW, Links PS, Rae-Grant NI Szatmari P. 1987. Ontario child health study: Methodology. Arch Gen Psychiatry 44:826–831.

Brajša-Zganec A. 2005. The long-term effects of war experiences on children's depression in the republic of croatia. Child Abuse Negl 29:31–43.

Brame B, Nagin SD, Tremblay RE. 2006. Developmental trajectories of physical aggression from school entry to late adolescence. J Child Psychol Psychiatry 42:503–512.

Burks VS, Laird RD, Dodge KA, Pettit GS, Bates JE. 1999. Knowledge structures, social information processing, and children's aggressive behavior. Soc Dev 8:220–236.

Caspi A, McClay J, Moffitt TE, Mill J, Martin J, Craig IV, Taylor A, Poulton R. 2002. Role of genotype in the cycle of violence in maltreated children. Science 297:851–854.

Crick NR, Dodge KA. 1994. A review and reformulation of social information processing mechanisms in children's social adjustment. Psychol Bull 115:74–101.

Dodge KA. 1991. The structure and function of reactive and proactive aggression. In: Pepler DJ, Rubin KH, (eds): The Development and Treatment of Childhood Aggression. Hillsdale, NJ: Lawrence Earlbaum Associates, pp 201–218.

Freud A, Burlingham DT. 1943. War children. New York: Medical War Books, Ernest Willard.

Greenbaum C. 2005. Aggressive behavior among israeli kindergarten children witnessing terrorist attack. Personal communication.

Guerra NG, Huesmann RL, Spindler A. 2003. Community violence exposure. Social cognition, and aggresssion among uban elementary school children. Child Dev 74:1561–1576.

Haj-Yahia M, Abdo-Kaloti R. 2003. The rates and correlates of the exposure of palestinian adolescents to family violence: Toward an integrative-holistic approach. Child Abuse Negl 27:781–806.

Human Right Watch. 2004. Razing Rafah: Mass Home Demolitions in the Gaza Strip. New York: Human Rights Watch.

Kagan J. 2003. Biology, context, and developmental inquiry. Annu Rev Psychol 54:1–23.

Keresteš G. 2006. Children's aggressive and prosocial behavior in relation to war exposure: Testing the role of perceived parenting and child's gender. Int J Behav Dev 30:227–239.

Lagerspetz K, Björkqvist K, Peltonen T. 1988. Is indirect aggression typical for girls? Gender differences in aggressiveness in 11- to 12-year-old children. Aggress Behav 14:403–414.

Lazarus RS. 1993. Coping theory and research: Past, present, and future. Psychosomat Med 55:234–247.

Leinonen JA, Solantaus T, Punamäki RL. 2002. The specific mediating paths between economic hardship and the quality of parenting. Int J Behav Dev 26:423–435.

Little T, Heinrich C, Jones S, Hawley. 2003. Disentangling the "whys" from the "whats" of aggressive behavior. Int J Behav Dev 27:122–133.

Loeber R, Stouthamer-Loeber M. 1998. Development of juvenile aggression and violence: Some common misconceptions and controversies. Am Psychologist 53:242–259.

Macksoud MS, Aber JL. 1996. The war experiences and psychosocial development of children in lebanon. Child Dev 67:70–88.

Miller T, El Masri M, Qouta S. 2000. Health of Children in War Zones: Gaza Child Health Survey. McMaster: McMaster University Press.

Pakaslahti L. 2000. Children's and adolescent's aggressive behavior in context: The developmental and application of aggressive problem solving. Aggression Violent Behav 5:467–490.

PCHR-Report. 2006. Weekly Report on Israeli Human Rights Violations in the Occupied Palestinian Territory. Ramallah: Palestinian Center for Human Rights.

Pedder J. 1992. Psychoanalytic views of aggression: Some theoretical problems. Br J Med Psychol 65:95–106.

Pfefferbaum B. 1997. Posttraumatic stress disorder in children. A review of the past 10 years. J Am Acad Child Adolesc Psychiatry 36:1503–1511.

Proctor LJ. 2006. Children growing up in a violent community: The role of the family. Aggression Violent Behav 11:558–576.

Punamäki RL. 1987. Childhood Under Conflict. The Attitudes and Emotional Life of Israeli and Palestinian Children. Vol. 32. Tampere: Tampere Peace Research Institute.

Punamäki RL. 2002. The uninvited guest of war enters childhood: Developmental and personality aspects of war and military violence. Traumatology 8:45–63.

Punamäki RL, Qouta S, El Sarraj E. 1997. Models of traumatic experiences and children's psychological adjustment: The roles of perceived parenting, and the children's own resources and activity. Child Dev 68:718–728.

Qouta S, Punamäki RL, El Sarraj E. 2003. Prevalence and determinants of PTSD among Palestinian children exposed to military violence. Eur Child Adolesc Psychiatry 12:265–272.

Qouta S, Punamäki RL, El Sarraj E. 2005. Mother-child expression psychological distress in acute war trauma. Clin Child Psychol Psychiatry 10:135–156.

Raboteg-Šaric Z, Zuzul M, Kerestěs G. 1994. War and children's aggressive and prosocial behaviour. Eur J Pers 8:201–212.

Raundalen M, Lwanga J, Mugisha C, Dyregrow A. 1987. Four investigations on stress among children in uganda. In: Dodge MRCP, (ed): War, Violence, and Children in Uganda. Oslo: Norvegian University Press, pp 83–108.

Rogers MJ, Holmbeck GN, 1997. Effects of interparental aggression on children's adjustment: The moderating role of cognitive appraisal and coping. J Fam Psychol 11:125–130.

Rutter M. 1967. A children's behaviour questionnaire for completion by teachers: Preliminary findings. J Child Psychol Psychiatry 8:1–11.

Schwartz D, Proctor LJ. 2000. Community violence exposure and children's social adjustment in the school peer group: The mediating roles of emotion regulation and social cognition. J Consult Clin Psychol 68:670–683.

Smith P, Perrin S, Yule W, Hacam B, Stuvland R, 2002. War exposure among children from bosnia-hercegovina: Psychological adjustment in a community sample. J Trauma Stress 15:147–156.

Spear LP, 2000. The adolescent brain and age-related behavioral manifestations. Neurosci Biobehav Rev 24:417–463.

Steinberg L, Morris AS, 2001. Adolescent development. Annu Rev Psychol 52:83–110.

Tapper K, Boulton M. 2000. Social representations of physical, verbal, and indirect aggression in children: Sex and age differences. Aggress Behav 26:442–454.

Thabet AA, Mousa AY, Vostanis P. 2005. Comorbidity of PTSD and depression among refugee children during war conflict. J Child Psychol Psychiatry 45:533–542.

Tolan PH, Guerra NG, Montaini-Klovdahl LR. 1997. Staying out of harm's way: Coping and development of inner-city children. In: Sandler S.A.W.A.I.N., (ed): Handbook of Children's Coping: Linking Theory and Intervention. New York: Plenum, pp 453–479.

Tolley H, 1973. Children and War; Political Socialization to International Conflict. New York: Teachers' College Publisher.

Tremblay RE, 2000. The development of agressive behaviour during childhood: What have we learned in the past century? Int J Behav Dev 24:129–141.

Unicef. 1992. The Situation of Palestinian Children in the West Bank and Gaza Strip. Jerusalem: Unicef.

Vitaro F, Brendgen M, Barker ED. 2006. Subtypes of aggressive behaviors: A developmental perspective. Int J Behav Dev 30:12–19.

Vygotsky LS, 1978. Mind in Society. The Development of Higher Psychological Processes. Cambridge, MA: Harvard University Press.

Reading Analytically

1. In some ways, positing that children in a war zone are more likely to behave in aggressive ways seems intuitive; however, these researchers find that hypothesis worth testing scientifically. Why? What do they hope to gain by conducting this elaborate study? What reasons do they provide for the *exigency* of this study (i.e., why it must be conducted)?
2. Before introducing their own study and its findings, the authors first present their review of the literature—a survey of past research on similar topics. After reading this review of the literature, describe the stated reasons why this study is still necessary—what is sometimes called a "gap statement," or a statement that expresses, in the context of the other studies, what is lacking in what has been done so far. What is the "gap" in the literature here?
3. While this study is, most generally, studying the likelihood that war zones produce children with a predilection to violent behavior, it also attempts to sort out the effect on specific groups of children. What are the main categories that are parsed out here, and how is the data collected and sorted in order to draw specific conclusions about each group? What are some of the key "correlations," i.e., important relationships between variables, that are discovered in this study?

Reading Across Disciplinary Communities

1. Although the methodology section of empirical studies like this one might seem rather technical and drawn out, the use of a reliable way to collect data is central to this discipline and throughout the social sciences. After reading the methodology section, try to articulate the reasoning behind the ways that this study was formed, and what variables it was trying to control that otherwise might have tainted the results.
2. Despite the somewhat clinical and scientific methodologies of this study, this article also shows the human face behind those numbers. Point out at least three examples in this essay where the style and language reveal the attitudes of the authors through the use of emotional, rather than analytical, language. What does this inclusion suggest about the ultimate purpose of social scientists like these, and of the discipline more generally?

MARY ELLEN O'CONNELL

What Is War?

In this opinion column, Mary Ellen O'Connell, a professor of law at the Ohio State University, uses methods crucial to her discipline of legal studies to build a case that "the claim of global war"—and the denial of rights to enemy combatants based upon that claim—are not legally justified. This piece was originally published in the legal education network publication called Jurist.

As you read the piece, try to gain some insight into the analytical methods that are used in the legal discipline, as well as the methods of argument that are most likely to convince her audience—other professionals in the field. You might also consider the larger, more public, purposes of this piece. Does it seem to have a political agenda as well as a legal one?

On March 19, 2003, the United States went to war in Iraq. On October 7, 2001, the United States went to war in Afghanistan. President Bush also declared a global war on terrorism following the attacks of September 11.[1] He said the global war would last "until every terrorist group of global reach has been found, stopped and defeated."[2] The Bush Administration claims this third war is as much a war as the other two. It claims the Geneva Conventions apply, just as in the other two, along with the other legal rights and obligations of wartime. Important Bush Administration policies turn on this legal claim, including its enemy combatant policy[3] and the policy of targeted killing.[4] Yet, even a cursory review of international law quickly reveals that as a matter of law, the United States is not involved in a global war.

At one time a formal declaration of war meant a state was legally at war whether or not a single shot had been fired. Those days of formalism, however, are long over. Since the adoption of the United Nations Charter in 1945, declarations of war have little or no legal meaning. What matters is the reality of fighting, not formal declarations. No US president has formally declared war since Franklin Roosevelt. In international law today, it is the fact of fighting and the nature of the fighting that are all-important. For the privileges of war to apply, the fighting must be among organized armed groups, and it must reach a certain threshold of intensity, enduring for more than a brief period.[5] We tend to refer to fighting below this threshold as "lawlessness" or criminality when it occurs within a state. It is an "incident" when it occurs between two states.[6] We were at war in Iraq and Afghanistan. But we are not engaged in intense fighting everywhere in the world.

Thus, there is no global war. And because there is no global war, the US has no global right to invoke wartime legal privileges. Nevertheless, soon after September 11, 2001, some in the Bush Administration became aware that in wartime, certain human rights are suspended and certain actions in violation of human rights are permitted. As DoD's top lawyer, William Haynes has pointed out: "War implicates legal powers and rules that are not available during peacetime."[7] Relevant to the Bush policies: in wartime enemy combatants may be attacked without warning; ships and planes may be stopped and searched and cargoes seized; and people may be detained without trial until the end of hostilities.

These are emphatically wartime, not peacetime, privileges. They are necessitated by the exigencies of military conflict. They come at the expense of peacetime rights. It follows that international law establishes conditions—strict conditions—in which wartime privileges may be claimed. The characteristics of the American struggle against terrorism generally do not meet those conditions. We do not see military operations in multiple theaters around the world as we did in World War II. What we see today in the struggle against terrorism is a massive law enforcement effort, operating under the law of peace.

Despite the plain facts, the Bush Administration has steadily put in place policies that could only be lawful in global war:

- Detainees at Guantanamo Bay will be held until the end of the global war, not the hostilities in Afghanistan or Iraq.
- The CIA launched a Hellfire missile against a vehicle in remote Yemen; killing six alleged enemy combatants in the global war, not six criminal suspects.
- A US citizen, arrested in Chicago, is removed from the civilian justice system and placed in a military prison as an enemy combatant until the end of the global war.
- Prosecutors seek to suppress evidence because this is "wartime."[8]

These and other incidents, involving the lives of hundreds of people already, prove the claim of global war is not mere rhetoric for the Bush Administration. But claiming global war and making a case for it under law are two different things. Under the legal definition of war, self-evidently most of the world is at peace, not war. Although Al Qaeda has been active in Kenya, Germany, Morocco, Spain, Yemen, and elsewhere, none of these countries recognize an armed conflict on their territories. Spain did not declare war following the March 11, 2004 train bombings in Madrid. In all of these countries, government institutions are functioning normally. They have not proclaimed martial law. The International Committee of the Red Cross (ICRC) has not set up operations in any of them. They are pursuing the struggle against terrorism through police methods. Germany has already tried two defendants, in civilian courts, for aiding the September 11 attackers.

The United States, like these other states, has been the victim of a terrorist attack but is not a zone of war. Following the September 11 attack and others against us from Afghanistan, the United States had the legal right to take the fight to that country. We had the right to use force in self-defense. Afghanistan became a zone of active military operations, a theater of war. But the United States did not. The law of war became the operative law in Afghanistan, not in the US.[9] The United States did not have a defensible legal argument for waging war in Iraq; nevertheless, the law of war became operative once the threshold to war was crossed on March 19, 2003. At that point the law of war applied on the territory of Iraq.[10]

All this is not to say that we know with scientific precision what is war and what is peace. Certain territory, at certain times, under certain circumstances, can surely fall in a gray zone between war and peace. However, we do know with precision that where a situation is not clearly characterized as "war," international law demands that individuals enjoy the greater legal protection of peace. The Bush Administration, however, is not even struggling with gray zone cases. Claiming that Chicago's O'Hare Airport was a war zone for purposes of detaining José Padilla is a simple absurdity that the law cannot sustain.

In defending the Administration's legal position regarding Padilla and other so-called enemy combatants, Judge Alberto Gonzales, the White House Counsel, relies on a single legal authority: the 1942 United States Supreme Court decision, *Ex Parte Quirin*.[11] *Quirin*, however, is inapplicable to the question of whether the United States is today involved in a global war and may claim wartime privileges everywhere. The facts, issues, and law in *Quirin* are unrelated to this central question. *Quirin* was decided prior to the adoption of the United Nations Charter and prior to the 1949 Geneva Conventions. It involved defendants who were members of the regular armed forces of a sovereign state in a declared war—when declared war meant something. World War II was a very real war that did in fact reach around the globe. The *Quirin* defendants were all charged with violations of the law of war. Further, and most significantly, the issue before the *Quirin* court was whether the President had the authority to try the defendants on the charges against them before a military tribunal rather than in the regular civilian courts.

Today's enemy combatant cases raise very different questions. The US has not charged and is not seeking to try Padilla, Hamdi, or the vast majority of detainees at Guantanamo Bay. Their cases do not, therefore, involve the issue raised in *Quirin*. Rather, they raise the question what is war and when may a government claim wartime privileges? *Quirin* does not speak to these questions. Yet, *Quirin* is all the Administration invokes.

By contrast, ample authority in the international law on the use of force and human rights law proves definitively that the claim of global war is unjustified. The President and the Courts should see the claim for what it is—too good to be true: The US gets to declare global war, claim wartime privileges everywhere, and at the same time enjoy peacetime rights? It cannot work that way.

"Global war" is fine rhetoric for rallying a nation. It is no justification for denying rights.

Notes

1. *See* George W. Bush, President's Address to the Nation on the Terrorist Attacks, 37 *Weekly Comp. Pres. Doc.* 1301 (Sept. 11, 2001); President's Address to a Joint Session of Congress on the United States Response to the Terrorist Attacks of September 11, 37 *Weekly Comp. Pres. Doc.* 1432 (Sept. 20, 2001); Training Camps and Taliban Military Installations in Afghanistan, 37 *Weekly Comp. Pres. Doc.* 1432 (Oct. 7, 2001); President's Address Before a Joint Session of the Congress on the State of the Union, 39 *Weekly Comp. Pres. Doc.* 109 (Jan. 28, 2003), http://www.whitehouse.gov
   This essay is adapted from Mary Ellen O'Connell, *Ad Hoc War*, in Krisensicherung und Humanitärer Schutz-Crisis Management and Humanitarian Protection 399 (Horst Fischer et al, eds., forthcoming 2004).
2. Presidential Address to a Joint Session of Congress, *supra* note 1, at 1348.
3. Judge Alberto Gonzales confirmed in remarks on February 24, 2004, to a meeting of the ABA's Standing Committee on Law and National Security that the policy of declaring individuals "enemy combatants" is based on the view that "our conflict with al Qaeda is clearly a war." http://www.abanet.org/natsecurity/ at 3; *see also* Memorandum from William J. Haynes II, General Counsel of the Department of Defense, Enemy Combatants, http://www.cfr.org/publication.php?id=5312.
   Three cases involving the enemy combatant policy are now pending at the Supreme Court: Padilla v. Rumsfeld, 352 F.3d 695 (2nd Cir. 2003), *cert. granted* 72 USLW 3533 (U.S. Feb. 20, 2004)(No. 03-6696); Hamdi v. Rumsfeld, 316 F.3d 450 (4th Cir. 2003), *cert. granted* 72 USLW 3446 (U.S. Jan. 9, 2004)(No. 03-334); Al Odah v. United States, 321 F.3d 1134 (D.C. Cir. 2003) *cert. granted*, 72 USLW 3327 (U.S. Nov. 10, 2003)(No. 03-343). *See also* Gherebi v. Rumsfeld, 352 F. 3d 1278 (9th Cir. 2003).
4. Following a "targeted killing" in Yemen in November 2002, National Security Adviser Condoleeza Rice stated, "We're in a new kind of war. And we've made very clear that it is important that this new kind of war be fought on different battlefields." *Fox News Sunday* (Fox News television broadcast, Nov. 10, 2002), 2002 WL 7898884, at 9. The Deputy General Counsel of the Department of Defense for International Affairs, Charles Allen, made even clearer how the Bush Administration viewed the Yemen killings. He said the U.S. can target "Al Qaeda and other international terrorists around the world and those who support such terrorists *without warning.*" Anthony Dworkin, *Official Examines Legal Aspects of Terror War*, http://hsm.intellibridge.com/summary?view_id=117201800 (on file with author). He also said the US has the legal right to target and kill an Al Qaeda suspect on the streets of a city like Hamburg, Germany. Anthony Dworkin, *Law and the Campaign against Terrorism: The View from the Pentagon* (Dec. 16, 2002), http://www.crimesofwar.org/print/onnews/pentagon-print.html at 6.

Aspects of the Proliferation Security Initiative may also be based on the global war justification. When the policy was first announced in the summer of 2003, the Administration said it had a right to search and seize cargo from vessels on the high seas without consent of the flag state. *See* Rebecca Weiner, *Proliferation Security Initiative to Stem Flow of WMD Material* (July 16, 2003), http://cns.miis.edu/pubs/week/030716.htm; Michael Evans, *U.S. Plans to Seize Suspects at Will,* The Times (London), July 11, 2003, at 23. In February 2004, however, the Administration signed an agreement with Liberia and is seeking a similar agreement with Panama providing consent to search vessels. These agreements indicate that PSI will now operate under peacetime rules.

5. In *Prosecutor v. Tadic* before the International Criminal Tribunal for the Former Yugoslavia, the Tribunal defined "armed conflict" as existing "whenever there is a resort to armed force between States or protracted armed violence between governmental authorities and organized armed groups or between such groups within a state." *Prosecutor v. Tadic,* Decision on the Defense Motion for Interlocutory Appeal on Jurisdiction, No. IT-94-1, para. 70 (Oct. 2, 1995).

The Geneva Conventions similarly incorporate a standard of intensity that must be reached to trigger the application of certain minimum rules found in Common Article 3 (common to all four Geneva Conventions). These rules apply in armed conflicts not of an international character, in other words, in civil war. For Common Article 3 to apply, such conflicts must amount to "more than situations of internal disturbances and tensions such as riots and isolated and sporadic acts of violence." IV Commentary to the 1949 Geneva Convention Relative to the Protection of Civilian Persons in Time of War 3–9 (Jean Pictet ed., 1958). In *Hamdi v. Rumsfeld,* 316 F. 3d 450 (4th Cir. 2003), a U.S. circuit court decided that the law of war applied-and not U.S. (or presumably Afghan) criminal law—because a suspect was apprehended in a "zone of active military operations," *id.* at 462, or "active hostilities," *id.* at 476. *See also* Dinstein: "War in the material sense unfolds regardless of any formal steps. Its occurrence is contingent only on the eruption of hostilities between the parties, even in the absence of a declaration of war. . . . The decisive factor here is deeds rather than declarations. What counts is not a *de jure* state of war, but *de facto* combat. Granted, even in the course of war in the material sense, hostilities do not have to go on incessantly and they may be interspersed by periods of cease-fire. . . . But there is not war in the material sense without some acts of warfare. . . . Warfare means the use of armed force, namely, violence." Yoram Dinstein, War, Aggression and Self-Defence 9 (3d ed. 2001). *Accord* Leslie C. Green, The Contemporary Law of Armed Conflict 70 (2d ed. 1999). *See also* Kenneth Roth, *The Law of War in the War on Terror, Washington's Abuse of Enemy Combatants,* For. Aff. (Jan/Feb. 2004) at 2; Gabor Rona, *Interesting Times for*

International Humanitarian Law: Challenges from the 'War on Terror,' 27 Fletcher Forum of World Affairs 55, 57 (2003).

6. *See, e.g.,* Military and Paramilitary Activities in and Against Nicaragua (Nicar. v. U.S.), 1986 I.C.J. 14, paras. 194–95.
7. Haynes, *supra* note 3; *see also,* Anthony Dworkin, *Law and the Campaign against Terrorism: The View from the Pentagon* (Dec. 16, 2002), http://www.crimesofwar.org/print/onnews/pentagon-print.html
8. Larry Margasak, *Uncertainty Shrouds Terror Prosecutions,* AP Online, Sept. 8, 2003, 2003 WL 63460199
9. It is worth emphasizing that war or armed conflict begins when there is an exchange. Thus the war with Afghanistan did not begin on September 11, 2001. It began on October 7, 2001 when the US and UK began the counter-attack. The September 11 attacks, the bombing of the *Cole,* the East African embassy bombings, and the 1993 World Trade Center bombing were all armed attacks on the United States that created a right of self-defense. Each attack may have been sufficient in itself to create the right. The four taken together make a very strong case. Yet, these armed attacks, even all four together, did not amount to armed conflict. Armed conflict or hostilities only began when armed forces of the United States and the United Kingdom engaged the armed forces of the Taleban, together with Al Qaeda fighters, on the territory of Afghanistan. The US and UK had the right to launch hostilities against Afghanistan as a lawful exercise of self-defense. Under UN Charter Article 51, states may use force in individual and collective self-defense if an armed attack occurs, against those responsible for the attack. Self-defense consists of the right to take proportional and necessary retaliatory military action, including action on the territory of the responsible state for the purpose of defense. The essence of self-defense is destroying the armed attacker's ability to attack again. In the case of Afghanistan, the right of self-defense entitled significant numbers of US and UK armed forces to engage the armed forces of the Taleban and Al Qaeda in hostilities. For more on the law of self-defense, see, Mary Ellen O'Connell, *Lawful Self-Defense to Terrorism,* 63 U. of Pitt. L.R. 889 (2002).

   Judge Gonzales invokes references to the American right of self-defense by the Security Council, NATO, ANZUS and the Rio Treaty Organization as further support for the argument that the United States is in a worldwide war. Gonzales, Remarks, *supra* note 3, at 3. References to self-defense indicate the right to take necessary and proportional armed action against an attacker. They do not support an argument for characterizing every corner of the globe as a war zone. The members of these various organizations do not view their own territory as war zones. Together they make up a very large segment of the planet.
10. For discussions of the legality of the war in Iraq, see the American Journal of International Law, vol. 97, nos. 3 & 4; *see also,* Mary Ellen O'Connell,

Addendum to Armed Force in Iraq: Issues of Legality http://www.asil.org/insights/insigh99a.htm

11. 317 U.S. 1 (1942). *See* Gonzales, Remarks, supra note 3, at 4. *See also*, Haynes, *supra* note 7.

Reading Analytically

1. The first three paragraphs attempt to build the argument that the war on terrorism does not in fact constitute a "global war." Why does O'Connell develop this legal argument so carefully? Why is it so crucial for her to establish this point before proceeding?
2. O'Connell does admit, in the midst of her argument, that "all this is not to say that we know with scientific precision what is war and what is peace." In light of some of the other essays earlier in this chapter, why is it so difficult to determine whether we are at war, and with whom, in the present political climate?
3. What actions conducted by the United States under President George W. Bush does O'Connell most scrutinize? Why does she find these actions legally and ethically specious? Cite some specific examples and summarize O'Connell's argument against their justifications.

Reading Across Disciplinary Communities

1. One of the key elements of the legal discipline is its use of "precedent"—previous cases that establish the common practices that should also be followed in future decisions. What precedents does O'Connell look to as she builds her argument?
2. Though this piece uses many techniques of argument that one would expect in the forming of legal opinions, it also frequently takes on the tone and style of an editorial. Point out at least three examples in which you find O'Connell stepping outside the purer legal logic to inject political opinion.

Writing Across Disciplines
Interdisciplinary Writing Opportunities

1. One of the key questions of this chapter involves the changing definitions of war in a rapidly changing world. One of the ways to investigate the questions posed by authors in this chapter is to talk to people across generations to see how age and experience influences one's views on war. Perform a series of interviews, surveys, or both with individuals of various age groups, gathering perspectives on war's causes, effects, and purposes, asking similar questions to each group.

You might glean some of those questions from the readings in this chapter. Then write an essay that draws some conclusions about what facets of "war" have remained intact, and what facets seem to have changed.

2. Not only the concept of war, but the concepts of "victory" and "peace" have been affected by the changing global landscape. Study the history of some recent conflict (the Vietnam War, either of the conflicts in Iraq, the conflicts between Arabs and Israelis in the Middle East, the Cold War, etc.) and speculate upon reasons why the concept of victory or peace in any of these conflicts is so elusive. What has changed? How is it that, in the past, we could celebrate "Victory in Europe Day," or "Armistice Day," but now we have little chance of such a defining moment in any recent conflicts? What key elements of "war" have changed? How have historical events influenced these changes?
3. As is noted in the introduction to this chapter, the word *war* has been applied not only to armed conflicts, but to attempts to overcome a great many other social ills as well: the "War on Poverty," "War on Drugs," "War on Illiteracy," "War on Cancer," "War on Illegal Immigration," and so on are all common phrasings. What is the effect of calling these efforts *wars*? Write a position paper that investigates the history of such usages, and which speculates upon the use of the word *war* in such social initiatives.
4. War is often called "inhumane." However, war is a distinctively human activity. Drawing upon the pieces in this chapter, and the work of other philosophers, social scientists, and/or natural scientists, write an essay that explores the reasons why human beings have allowed themselves to become embroiled in these clearly destructive activities. You might either focus upon one discipline (psychological studies, philosophical studies, genetic predispositions, sociological or anthropological studies) or present an interdisciplinary study that draws upon multiple disciplines. In either case, attempt to cast light upon the reasons why we choose to go to war.
5. Clearly, war is based in human divisions. Some of those divisions are, in turn, based in other issues that are discussed by authors in this book. Write an essay that discusses the effects upon human conflict that arise as a result of race, ethnicity, attempts to control resources such as oil, religious conflict, and so forth. Drawing upon some of the discussions in other chapters, demonstrate the interconnectedness of issues surrounding war with another issue or set of issues.

CHAPTER 6

Beyond Petroleum

Finding a Sustainable Energy Future

One thing is clear: the time of peak oil is coming (if, as some experts claim, it is not already here). *Peak oil* is a term used to describe the moment when the rate at which we are extracting oil from the earth reaches its maximum; that moment, looked at another way, signals the moment that the rate of oil production will go into "terminal decline." As such, one of the key challenges facing the world is transitioning from an oil-driven energy system and economy to new alternatives. The writers in this chapter each address this central question; but they do so from a wide range of disciplinary and interdisciplinary angles.

There are many potential solutions being offered to address this looming challenge, from hybrid cars that can preserve our oil economy for the present to new energy alternatives that can move us into the future. Finding and agreeing upon solutions to this national and global challenge is a problem that requires the expertise of many communities. For natural scientists, this challenge requires a new understanding of the nature of energy and how it affects our eco-system; for the applied sciences such as engineering and business, it requires attention to new methods of generating energy through the development of methods that can use energy efficiently—and doing so at a cost that consumers can afford and will buy into. After all, as the article from *The Economist* included below suggests, this moment has tremendous potential as a new profit center for the business world. Understanding what it is that Americans are likely to support, both as citizens and as consumers, is the work of social scientists who use their methodologies to gather public opinion. And for ethicists and others in the humanities, there are many important questions that must be asked in order to evaluate a course of action that will fulfill our obligation to behave in ways that are not only pragmatically sound, but morally sound as well.

The first two articles in this section present an overview of the problem and possible paths toward solutions. Michael T. Klare's "Beyond the Age of Petroleum" lays out the challenges we face in addressing our energy needs, focusing especially on the things policy-makers will need to consider in that process. Then, an excerpt from T. Boone Picken's Web site, "The Pickens Plan," demonstrates how a successful businessman has attempted to influence public energy policy and take the lead on finding sustainable sources of energy that will be at once financially viable and a way to break our "addiction" to foreign oil.

Energy policy has more specific implications for various disciplinary communities as well, as the rest of the articles in this chapter illustrate. First, M. Balat and H. Balat offer a review of recent engineering research into the potential of biogas—the byproducts of organic processes—to provide a scientifically viable solution to our energy needs. Of course a viable solution isn't just based on technologies; it is based upon what consumers are likely to support. Geoffrey Carr thus challenges those in business-based disciplines to see the energy problem as a business opportunity. His essay, originally appearing in *The Economist*, discusses the ways that any possible solution will be driven by investors—and helps readers consider which of the alternatives is most likely to be the best bet. Then, Berenice Baker, in an essay originally written for the trade journal *The Engineer*, provides information on one of many discoveries that might contribute to alleviating the problem we face. Written in a style that is meant to make complex engineering accessible, it demonstrates the ways that the latest discoveries in specific disciplines are brought into professional communities. Likewise, Michael E. Weber's article, first published in an edition of *Scientific American* about alternative energies, provides to non-experts a look at another problem we face as we pursue new technologies—the growing use of fresh water, which is also in short supply. Since so many of the new technologies depend upon water, Weber suggests, we need to be wary of depleting one resource to find another.

The final two pieces in this section ask you to evaluate one direction that the search for sustainable and viable alternative energies has taken—toward "biofuels." This is a particularly exigent topic, since biofuels are already being employed on a large scale. Biofuels have long been touted as a form of "sustainable" energy, since the energy they produce comes from materials that do not, like oil, take millions of years to go from living things to a source of combustion. Ethanol derived from corn is perhaps the most well-known of biofuels, as it has been used in combination with petroleum for decades. However, more recently, biofuels have come under greater scrutiny as some experts point out environmental, engineering, and ethical flaws in our reliance upon them. In this way, the future of energy is not merely a problem for the natural sciences to study, but one that ranges within, and among, all disciplinary communities. And because the problem is so public, these disciplinary debates have found their way into varied media outlets, from the mainstream magazines such as *TIME* to a wide variety of Web sites and blogs on which the topic is hotly debated and through which specific plans (such as that of T. Boone Pickens's) are promoted. As you read these pieces, it also would be worthwhile for you to listen to the various conversations in both "old" and "new" media. The *TIME Magazine* story by Michael Grunwald, "The Clean Energy Scam," will introduce you to some of the issues that environmentalists and ethicists have raised regarding biofuels. Since this essay has caused a great deal of public debate, you can find many responses to it available on the Web. C. Ford Runge and Benjamin Senauer then address one of the most frequent criticisms of biofuels—its effect upon the world food supply and food prices.

Taken as a group, the reading you will do in this section can demonstrate the ways that this key national and international challenge has found its way into a wide range of disciplines, genres, and debates among our citizenry. And by becoming informed as a reader, you can enter into that dialogue as well, considering especially how energy policy might affect the work that you are doing now as a student and that which you will do in the future as a professional.

MICHAEL T. KLARE

Beyond the Age of Petroleum

This journalistic essay, first published in the left-leaning magazine, The Nation, *draws upon the expertise of those in public policy and governmental agencies to make its argument for a more coherent energy policy. Michael T. Klare is the Five College Professor of Peace and World Security Studies, based at Hampshire College in Amherst, Massachusetts, and has written widely on world conflicts surrounding the struggle for oil, including his most recent book,* Blood and Oil. *He teaches courses on global resource policies and political and international relations.*

As you read this piece, you might consider how it combines reporting—describing the situation with "peak oil" that is discussed in the introduction to this essay—with political opinion, especially those held by Democrats. Since, in the current age of journalism, the line between news and opinion has grown increasingly thin, you might consider which parts of this piece seems to be "objective" or "factual," and which parts seem more aimed at persuading its audience.

In May 2007, in an unheralded and almost unnoticed move, the Energy Department signaled a fundamental, near epochal shift in US and indeed world history: we are nearing the end of the Petroleum Age and have entered the Age of Insufficiency. The department stopped talking about "oil" in its projections of future petroleum availability and began speaking of "liquids." The global output of "liquids," the department indicated, would rise from 84 million barrels of oil equivalent (mboe) per day in 2005 to a projected 117.7 mboe in 2030—barely enough to satisfy anticipated world demand of 117.6 mboe. Aside from suggesting the degree to which oil companies have ceased being mere suppliers of petroleum and are now purveyors of a wide variety of liquid products—including synthetic fuels derived from natural gas, corn, coal and other substances—this change hints at something more fundamental: we have entered a new era of intensified energy competition and growing reliance on the use of force to protect overseas sources of petroleum.

To appreciate the nature of the change, it is useful to probe a bit deeper into the Energy Department's curious terminology. "Liquids," the department explains in its International Energy Outlook for 2007, encompasses "conventional" petroleum as well as "unconventional" liquids—notably tar sands (bitumen), oil shale, biofuels, coal-to-liquids and gas-to-liquids. Once a relatively insignificant component of the energy business, these fuels have come to assume much greater importance as the output of conventional petroleum has faltered. Indeed, the Energy Department projects that unconventional liquids production will jump from a mere 2.4 mboe per day in 2005 to 10.5 in 2030, a fourfold increase. But the real story is not the impressive growth in unconventional fuels but the stagnation in conventional oil output. Looked at from this perspective, it is hard to escape the conclusion that the switch from "oil" to "liquids" in the department's terminology is a not so subtle attempt to disguise the fact that worldwide oil production is at or near its peak capacity and that we can soon expect a downturn in the global availability of conventional petroleum.

Petroleum is, of course, a finite substance, and geologists have long warned of its ultimate disappearance. The extraction of oil, like that of other nonrenewable resources, will follow a parabolic curve over time. Production rises quickly at first and then gradually slows until approximately half the original supply has been exhausted; at that point, a peak in sustainable output is attained and production begins an irreversible decline until it becomes too expensive to lift what little remains. Most oil geologists believe we have already reached the midway point in the depletion of the world's original petroleum inheritance and so are nearing a peak in global output; the only real debate is over how close we have come to that point, with some experts claiming we are at the peak now and others saying it is still a few years or maybe a decade away.

Until very recently, Energy Department analysts were firmly in the camp of those wild-eyed optimists who claimed that peak oil was so far in the future that we didn't really need to give it much thought. Putting aside the science of the matter, the promulgation of such a rose-colored view obviated any need to advocate improvements in automobile fuel efficiency or to accelerate progress on the development of alternative fuels. Given White House priorities, it is hardly surprising that this view prevailed in Washington.

In just the past six months, however, the signs of an imminent peak in conventional oil production have become impossible even for conservative industry analysts to ignore. These have come from the take-no-prisoners world of oil pricing and deal-making, on the one hand, and the analysis of international energy experts, on the other.

Most dramatic, perhaps, has been the spectacular rise in oil prices. The price of light, sweet crude crossed the longstanding psychological barrier of $80 per barrel on the New York Mercantile Exchange for the first time in September, and has since risen to as high as $90. Many reasons have been cited for the rise in crude prices, including unrest in Nigeria's oil-producing Delta region, pipeline sabotage in Mexico, increased hurricane activity in the Gulf of Mexico and fears of Turkish attacks on Kurdish guerrilla sanctuaries in Iraq. But the underlying reality is that most oil-producing countries are pumping at maximum capacity and finding it increasingly difficult to boost production in the face of rising international demand.

Even a decision by the Organization of the Petroleum Exporting Countries (OPEC) to boost production by 500,000 barrels per day failed to halt the upward momentum in prices. Concerned that an excessive rise in oil costs would trigger a worldwide recession and lower demand for their products, the OPEC countries agreed to increase their combined output at a meeting in Vienna on September 11. "We think that the market is a little bit high," explained Kuwait's acting oil minister, Mohammad al-Olaim. But the move did little to slow the rise in prices. Clearly, OPEC would have to undertake a much larger production increase to alter the market environment, and it is not at all clear that its members possess the capacity to do that—now or in the future.

A warning sign of another sort was provided by Kazakhstan's August decision to suspend development of the giant Kashagan oil region in its sector of the Caspian Sea, first initiated by a consortium of Western firms in the late '90s. Kashagan was said to be the most promising oil project since the discovery of oil in Alaska's Prudhoe Bay in the late '60s. But the enterprise has encountered enormous technical problems and has yet to produce a barrel of oil. Frustrated by a failure to see any economic benefits from the project, the Kazakh government has cited environmental risks and cost overruns to justify suspending operations and demanding a greater say in the project.

Like the dramatic rise in oil prices, the Kashagan episode is an indication of the oil industry's growing difficulties in its efforts to boost production in the face of rising demand. "All the oil companies are struggling to grow production," Peter Hitchens of Teather & Greenwood brokerage told the *Wall Street Journal* in July. "It's becoming more and more difficult to bring projects in on time and on budget."

That this industry debilitation is not a temporary problem but symptomatic of a long-term trend was confirmed in two important studies published this past summer by conservative industry organizations.

The first of these was released July 9 by the International Energy Agency (IEA), an affiliate of the Organization for Economic Cooperation and Development, the club of major industrial powers. Titled *Medium-Term Oil Market Report,* it is a blunt assessment of the global supply-and-demand equation over the 2007–12 period. The news is not good.

Predicting that world economic activity will grow by an average of 4.5 percent per year during this period—much of it driven by unbridled growth in China, India and the Middle East—the report concludes that global oil demand will rise by 2.2 percent per year, pushing world oil consumption from approximately 86 million barrels per day in 2007 to 96 million in 2012. With luck and massive new investment, the oil industry will be able to increase output sufficiently to satisfy the higher level of demand anticipated for 2012—barely. Beyond that, however, there appears little likelihood that the industry will be able to sustain any increase in demand. "Oil look[s] extremely tight in five years' time," the agency declared.

Underlying the report's general conclusion are a number of specific concerns. Most notably, it points to a worrisome decline in the yield of older fields in non-OPEC countries and a corresponding need for increased output from the OPEC countries, most of which are located in conflict-prone areas of the Middle East and Africa. The numbers involved are staggering. At first blush, it would seem that the need for an extra 10 million barrels per day between now and 2012 would translate into an added 2 million barrels per day in each of the next five years—a conceivably attainable goal. But that doesn't take into account the decline of older fields. According to the report, the world actually needs an extra 5 million: 3 million to make up for the decline in older fields plus the 2 million in added requirements. This is a daunting and possibly insurmountable challenge, especially when one considers that almost all of the additional petroleum will have to come from Iran, Iraq, Kuwait, Saudi Arabia, Algeria, Angola, Libya, Nigeria, Sudan, Kazakhstan and Venezuela—countries that do not inspire the sort of investor confidence that will be needed to pour hundreds of billions of dollars into new drilling rigs, pipelines and other essential infrastructure.

Similar causes for anxiety can be found in the second major study released last summer, *Facing the Hard Truths About Energy*, prepared by the National Petroleum Council, a major industry organization. Because it supposedly provided a "balanced" view of the nation's energy dilemma, the NPC report was widely praised on Capitol Hill and in the media; adding to its luster was the identity of its chief author, former ExxonMobil CEO Lee Raymond.

Like the IEA report, the NPC study starts with the claim that, with the right mix of policies and higher investment, the industry is capable of satisfying US and international oil and natural gas demand. "Fortunately, the world is not running out of energy resources," the report bravely asserts. But obstacles to the development and delivery of these resources abound, so prudent policies and practices are urgently required. Although "there is no single, easy solution to the multiple challenges we face," the authors conclude, they are "confident that the prompt adoption of these strategies" will allow the United States to satisfy its long-term energy needs.

Read further into the report, however, and serious doubts emerge. Here again, worries arise from the growing difficulties of extracting oil and gas from less-favorable locations and the geopolitical risks associated with increased reliance on unfriendly and unstable suppliers. According to the NPC (using data acquired from the IEA), an estimated $20 trillion in new infrastructure will be needed over the next twenty-five years to ensure that sufficient energy is available to satisfy anticipated worldwide demand.

The report then states the obvious: "A stable and attractive investment climate will be necessary to attract adequate capital for evolution and expansion of the energy infrastructure." This is where any astute observer should begin to get truly alarmed, for, as the study notes, no such climate can be expected. As the center of gravity of world oil production shifts decisively to OPEC suppliers and state-centric energy producers like Russia, geopolitical rather than market factors will come to dominate the marketplace.

"These shifts pose profound implications for U.S. interests, strategies, and policy-making," the NPC report states. "Many of the expected changes could heighten risks to U.S. energy security in a world where U.S. influence is likely to decline as economic power shifts to other nations. In years to come, security threats to the world's main sources of oil and natural gas may worsen."

The implications are obvious: major investors are not likely to cough up the trillions of dollars needed to substantially boost production in the years ahead, suggesting that the global output of conventional petroleum will not reach the elevated levels predicted by the Energy Department but will soon begin an irreversible decline.

This conclusion leads to two obvious strategic impulses: first, the government will seek to ease the qualms of major energy investors by promising to protect their overseas investments through the deployment of

American military forces; and second, the industry will seek to hedge its bets by shifting an ever-increasing share of its investment funds into the development of nonpetroleum liquids.

The New 'Washington Consensus'

The need for a vigorous US military role in protecting energy assets abroad has been a major theme in American foreign policy since 1945, when President Roosevelt met with King Abdul Aziz of Saudi Arabia and promised to protect the kingdom in return for privileged access to Saudi oil.

In the most famous expression of this linkage, President Carter affirmed in January 1980 that the unimpeded flow of Persian Gulf oil is among this country's vital interests and that to protect this interest, the United States will employ "any means necessary, including military force." This principle was later cited by President Reagan as the rationale for "reflagging" Kuwaiti oil tankers with the American ensign during the Iran-Iraq War of 1980–88 and protecting them with US warships—a stance that led to sporadic clashes with Iran. The same principle was subsequently invoked by George H.W. Bush as a justification for the Gulf War of 1991.

In considering these past events, it is important to recognize that the use of military force to protect the flow of imported petroleum has generally enjoyed broad bipartisan support in Washington. Initially, this bipartisan outlook was largely focused on the Persian Gulf area, but since 1990, it has been extended to other areas as well. President Clinton eagerly pursued close military ties with the Caspian Sea oil states of Azerbaijan and Kazakhstan after the breakup of the USSR in 1991, while George W. Bush has avidly sought an increased US military presence in Africa's oil-producing regions, going so far as to favor the establishment of a US Africa Command (Africom) in February.

One might imagine that the current debacle in Iraq would shake this consensus, but there is no evidence that this is so. In fact, the opposite appears to be the case: possibly fearful that the chaos in Iraq will spread to other countries in the Gulf region, senior figures in both parties are calling for a reinvigorated US military role in the protection of foreign energy deliveries.

Perhaps the most explicit expression of this elite consensus is an independent task force report, *National Security Consequences of U.S. Oil Dependency*, backed by many prominent Democrats and Republicans. It was released by the bipartisan Council on Foreign Relations

(CFR), co-chaired by John Deutch, deputy secretary of defense in the Clinton Administration, and James Schlesinger, defense secretary in the Nixon and Ford administrations, in October 2006. The report warns of mounting perils to the safe flow of foreign oil. Concluding that the United States alone has the capacity to protect the global oil trade against the threat of violent obstruction, it argues the need for a strong US military presence in key producing areas and in the sea lanes that carry foreign oil to American shores.

An awareness of this new "Washington consensus" on the need to protect overseas oil supplies with American troops helps explain many recent developments in Washington. Most significant, it illuminates the strategic stance adopted by President Bush in justifying his determination to retain a potent US force in Iraq—and why the Democrats have found it so difficult to contest that stance.

Consider Bush's September 13 prime-time speech on Iraq. "If we were to be driven out of Iraq," he prophesied, "extremists of all strains would be emboldened. . . . Iran would benefit from the chaos and would be encouraged in its efforts to gain nuclear weapons and dominate the region. Extremists could control a key part of the global energy supply." And then came the kicker: "Whatever political party you belong to, whatever your position on Iraq, we should be able to agree that America has a vital interest in preventing chaos and providing hope in the Middle East." In other words, Iraq is no longer about democracy or WMDs or terrorism but about maintaining regional stability to ensure the safe flow of petroleum and keep the American economy on an even keel; it was almost as if he was speaking to the bipartisan crowd that backed the CFR report cited above.

It is very clear that the Democrats, or at least mainstream Democrats, are finding it exceedingly difficult to contest this argument head-on. In March, for example, Senator Hillary Clinton told the *New York Times* that Iraq is "right in the heart of the oil region" and so "it is directly in opposition to our interests" for it to become a failed state or a pawn of Iran. This means, she continued, that it will be necessary to keep some US troops in Iraq indefinitely, to provide logistical and training support to the Iraqi military. Senator Barack Obama has also spoken of the need to maintain a robust US military presence in Iraq and the surrounding area. Thus, while calling for the withdrawal of most US combat brigades from Iraq proper, he has championed an "over-the-horizon force that could prevent chaos in the wider region."

Given this perspective, it is very hard for mainstream Democrats to challenge Bush when he says that an "enduring" US military presence is needed in Iraq or to change the Administration's current policy, barring a major military setback or some other unforeseen event. By the same token, it will be hard for the Democrats to avert a US attack on Iran if this can be portrayed as a necessary move to prevent Tehran from threatening the long-term safety of Persian Gulf oil supplies.

Nor can we anticipate a dramatic change in US policy in the Gulf region from the next administration, whether Democratic or Republican. If anything, we should expect an increase in the use of military force to protect the overseas flow of oil, as the threat level rises along with the need for new investment to avert even further reductions in global supplies.

The Rush to Alternative Liquids

Although determined to keep expanding the supply of conventional petroleum for as long as possible, government and industry officials are aware that at some point these efforts will prove increasingly ineffective. They also know that public pressure to reduce carbon dioxide emissions—thus slowing the accumulation of climate-changing greenhouse gases—and to avoid exposure to conflict in the Middle East is sure to increase in the years ahead. Accordingly, they are placing greater emphasis on the development of oil alternatives that can be procured at home or in neighboring Canada.

The new emphasis was first given national attention in Bush's latest State of the Union address. Stressing energy independence and the need to modernize fuel economy standards, he announced an ambitious plan to increase domestic production of ethanol and other biofuels. The Administration appears to favor several types of petroleum alternatives: ethanol derived from corn stover, switch grass and other nonfood crops (cellulosic ethanol); diesel derived largely from soybeans (biodiesel); and liquids derived from coal (coal-to-liquids), natural gas (gas-to-liquids) and oil shale. All of these methods are being tested in university laboratories and small-scale facilities, and will be applied in larger, commercial-sized ventures in coming years with support from various government agencies.

In February, for example, the Energy Department announced grants totaling $385 million for the construction of six pilot plants to manufacture cellulosic ethanol; when completed in 2012, these "biorefineries" will produce more than 130 million gallons of cellulosic ethanol per year.

(The United States already produces large quantities of ethanol by cooking and fermenting corn kernels, a process that consumes vast amounts of energy and squanders a valuable food crop while supplanting only a small share of our petroleum usage; the proposed cellulosic plants would use nonfood biomass as a feedstock and consume far less energy.)

Just as eager to develop petroleum alternatives are the large energy companies, all of which have set up laboratories or divisions to explore future energy options. BP has been especially aggressive; in 2005 it established BP Alternative Energy and set aside $8 billion for this purpose. This past February the new spinoff announced a $500 million grant—possibly the largest of its kind in history—to the University of California, Berkeley, the University of Illinois and Lawrence Berkeley National Laboratory to establish an Energy Biosciences Institute with the aim of developing biofuels. BP said the institute "is expected to explore the application of bioscience [to] the production of new and cleaner energy, principally fuels for road transport."

Just about every large oil company is placing a heavy bet on Canadian tar sands—a gooey substance found in Canada's Alberta province that can be converted into synthetic petroleum—but only with enormous effort and expense. According to the Energy Department, Canadian bitumen production will rise from 1.1 mboe in 2005 to 3.6 mboe in 2030, an increase that is largely expected to be routed to the United States. Hoping to cash in on this bonanza, giant US corporations like Chevron are racing to buy up leases in the bitumen fields of northern Alberta.

But while attractive from a geopolitical perspective, extracting Canadian tar sands is environmentally destructive. It takes vast quantities of energy to recover the bitumen and convert it into a usable liquid, releasing three times as much greenhouse gases as conventional oil production; the resulting process leaves toxic water supplies and empty moonscapes in its wake. Although rarely covered in the US press, opposition in Canada to the environmental damage wreaked by these mammoth operations is growing.

Environmental factors loom large in yet another potential source of liquids being pursued by US energy firms, with strong government support: shale oil, or petroleum liquids pried from immature rock found in the Green River basin of western Colorado, eastern Utah and southern Wyoming. Government geologists claim that shale rock in the United States holds the equivalent of 2.1 trillion barrels of oil—the same as the original world supply of conventional petroleum. However, the only way to recover this alleged treasure is to strip-mine a vast wilderness area and heat the rock to 500 degrees Celsius, creating mountains of waste material in the process. Here too, opposition is growing to this massively destructive assault on the environment. Nevertheless, Shell Oil has established a pilot plant in Rio Blanco County in western Colorado with strong support from the Bush Administration.

Life After the Peak

And so we have a portrait of the global energy situation after the peak of conventional petroleum, with troops being rushed from one oil-producing hot spot to another and a growing share of our transportation fuel being supplied by nonpetroleum liquids of one sort or another. Exactly what form this future energy equation will take cannot be foreseen with precision, but it is obvious that the arduous process will shape American policy debates, domestic and foreign, for a long time.

Reading Analytically

1. What two reasons does Klare offer in the essay that suggest that the current situation with oil reserves is more than a temporary problem?
2. Why, according to Klare, do we have a vital and ongoing interest in political stability in the Middle East? According to the author, why is maintaining this interest particularly hard for any political leaders to contest?
3. What other "liquids" are being offered as alternatives to our dependence upon oil? What is the likelihood that these "liquids" will supplant the need for oil? Consider Klare's view; as you read other articles, you might continue to critique the vision presented here, evaluating its viability in order to gain a variety of perspectives on the topic that you might evaluate further through research.

Reading Across Disciplinary Communities

1. Review the experts who are cited in Klare's article, listing the various disciplines that seem to be involved in this topic. How is this an engineering problem? A political one? One that needs to be alleviated by business interests? In what ways can you imagine these various experts working together?
2. What types of disciplinary research and knowledge do citizens and government officials rely upon to attempt to solve what is, at its heart, also a political and practical problem? What facets of this issue would people in your own major or prospective career field need to consider?

America Is Addicted to Foreign Oil

This excerpt from T. Boone Pickens's Internet site demonstrates the ways that this businessman has used a variety of arguments—economic, environmental, and political—to build the case for his plan for a sustainable energy future. The site also features sections on research, resources, community action, and a blog through which the issues can be debated.

T. Boone Pickens is an intriguing character. He is a geologist, a wealthy oil baron who also has interests in natural gas, water as a resource, and, most recently, his own brand of environmentalism that is carried out through industry. In 2008, he launched a huge media campaign to publicize his "Pickens Plan" to develop alternative energies that can take us beyond dependence on oil. As you consider the tenets of his plan presented here, you might take some time to also find out more about this man and his perspectives on government, politics, and business.

America is addicted to foreign oil.

It's an addiction that threatens our economy, our environment and our national security. It touches every part of our daily lives and ties our hands as a nation and as a people.

The addiction has worsened for decades and now it's reached a point of crisis.

In 1970, we imported 24% of our oil.
Today, it's more than 65% and growing.

Oil prices have come down from the staggering highs of last summer, but lower prices have not reduced our dependence on foreign oil or lessened the risks to either our economy or our security.

If we are depending on foreign sources for nearly two-thirds of our oil, we are in a precarious position in an unpredictable world.

In additional to putting our security in the hands of potentially unfriendly and unstable foreign nations, we spent $475 billion on foreign oil in 2008 alone. That's money taken out of our economy and sent to foreign nations, and it will continue to drain the life from our economy for as long as we fail to stop the bleeding.

Projected over the next 10 years the cost will be $10 trillion - it will be the greatest transfer of wealth in the history of mankind.

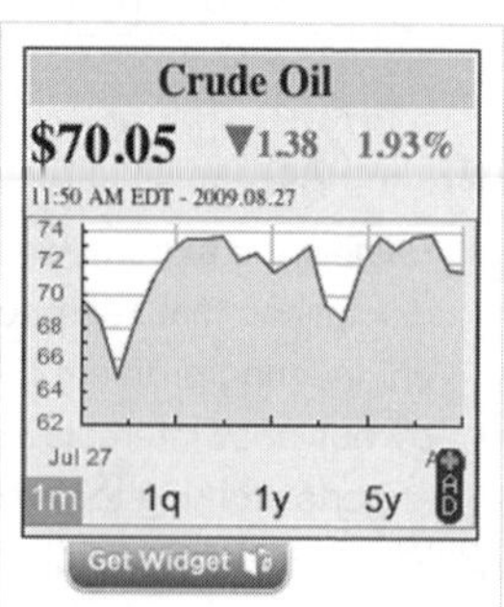

Can't we import more oil?

America uses a lot of oil. Every day 85 million barrels of oil are produced around the world. And 21 million of those are used here in the United States.

That's 25% of the world's oil demand. Used by just 4% of the world's population.

Can't we just produce more oil?

Consider this: America imports 12 million barrels a day, and Saudi Arabia only produces 9 million a day. Is there really more undiscovered oil here than in all of Saudi Arabia?

World oil production peaked in 2005. Despite growing demand and an unprecedented increase in prices, oil production has fallen over the last three years. Oil is getting more expensive to produce, harder to find and there just isn't enough of it to keep up with demand.

The simple truth is that cheap and easy oil is gone.

But America is focused on another crisis: The economy.

All Americans are feeling the effects of the recession. And addressing the economy is the top priority of our nation. This is more than bailing out a bank, an insurance firm or a car company. The American economy is huge and has many facets.

To make a real and lasting impact we must seek to do more than create new jobs and opportunities today, we must build the platform on which our economy can continue to grow for decades to come.

There is nothing more important to the present and future of our economy than energy. Any effort to address our economic problems will require a thorough understanding of this issue and willingness to confront our dependence on foreign oil and what domestic resources we can use.

It is a crisis too large to be addressed piecemeal. We need a plan of action on scale with the problems we face. That is the spirit in which the Pickens Plan was conceived. The Pickens Plan is a collection of coordinated steps that together form a comprehensive approach to America's energy needs.

The Pickens Plan.

There are several pillars to the Pickens Plan:

- Create millions of new jobs by building out the capacity to generate up to 22 percent of our electricity from wind. And adding to that with additional solar generation capacity;
- Building a 21st century backbone electrical transmission grid;
- Providing incentives for homeowners and the owners of commercial buildings to upgrade their insulation and other energy saving options; and
- Using America's natural gas to replace imported oil as a transportation fuel in addition to its other uses in power generation, chemicals, etc.

While dependence on foreign oil is a critical concern, it is not a problem that can be solved in isolation. We have to think about energy as a whole, and that begins by considering our energy alternatives and thinking about how we will fuel our world in the next 10 to 20 years and beyond.

New jobs from renewable energy and conservation.

Any discussion of alternatives should begin with the 2007 Department of Energy study showing that building out our wind capacity in the Great Plains - from northern Texas to the Canadian border - would produce 138,000 new jobs in the first year, and more than 3.4 million new jobs over a ten-year period, while also producing as much as 20 percent of our needed electricity.

Building out solar energy in the Southwest from western Texas to California would add to the boom of new jobs and provide more of our growing electrical needs - doing so through economically viable, clean, renewable sources.

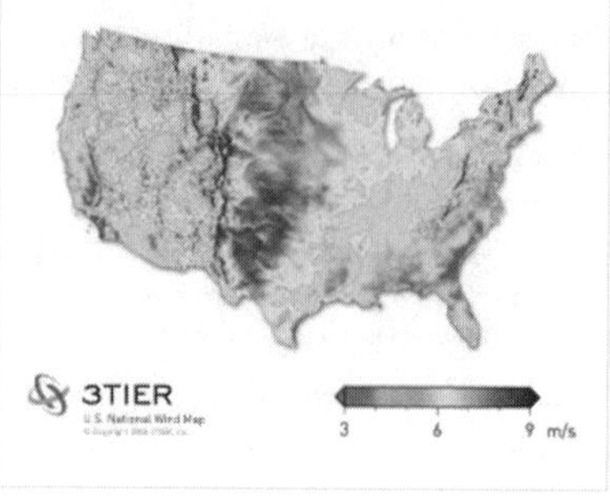

To move that electricity from where it is being produced to where it is needed will require an upgrade to our national electric grid. A 21st century transmission grid which will, as technology continues to develop, deliver power where it is needed, when it is needed, in the direction that it is needed, will be the modern equivalent of building the Interstate Highway System in the 1950's.

Beyond that, tremendous improvements in electricity use can be made by creating incentives for owners of homes and commercial buildings to retrofit their spaces with proper insulation. Studies show that a significant upgrading of insulation would save the equivalent of one million barrels of oil per day in energy by cutting down on both air conditioning costs in warm weather and heating costs in winter.

A domestic fuel to free us from foreign oil.

Conserving and harnessing renewable forms of electricity not only has incredible economic benefits, but is also a crucial piece of the oil dependence puzzle. We should continue to pursue the promise of electric or hydrogen powered vehicles, but America needs to address transportation fuel today. Fortunately, we are blessed with an abundance of clean, cheap, domestic natural gas.

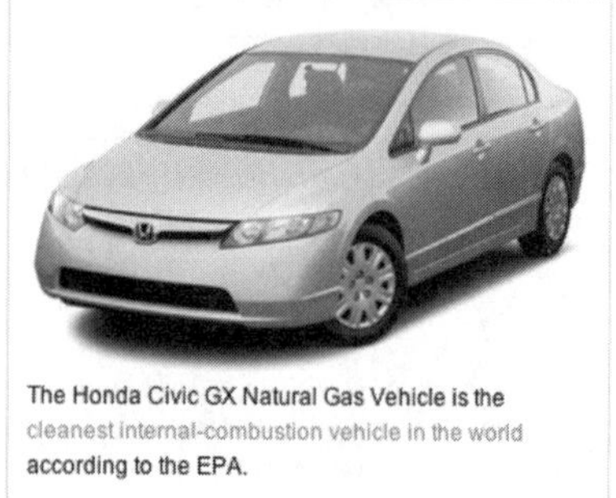

The Honda Civic GX Natural Gas Vehicle is the cleanest internal-combustion vehicle in the world according to the EPA.

Currently, domestic natural gas is primarily used to generate electricity. It has the advantage of being cheap and significantly cleaner than coal, but this is not the only use of our natural gas resources.

By aggressively moving to shift America's car, light duty and heavy truck fleets from imported gasoline and diesel to domestic natural gas we can lower our need for foreign oil - helping President Obama reach his goal of zero oil imports from the Middle East within ten years.

Nearly 20% of every barrel of oil we import is used by 18-wheelers moving goods around and across the country by burning imported diesel. An over-the-road truck cannot be moved using current battery technology. Fleet vehicles like buses, taxis, express delivery trucks, and municipal and utility vehicles (any vehicle which returns to the "barn" each night where refueling is a simple matter) should be replaced by vehicles running on clean, cheap, domestic natural gas rather than imported gasoline or diesel fuel.

A plan that brings it all together.

Natural gas is not a permanent or complete solution to imported oil. It is a bridge fuel to slash our oil dependence while buying us time to develop new technologies that will ultimately replace fossil transportation fuels. Natural gas is the critical puzzle piece that will help us to keep more of the $350 to $450 billion we spend on imported oil every year at home, where it can power our economy and pay for our investments in wind energy, a smart grid and energy efficiency.

It is this connection that makes The Pickens Plan not just a collection of good ideas, but a plan. By investing in renewable energy and conservation, we can create millions of new jobs. Developing new alternative energies while utilizing natural gas for transportation and energy generation; securing our economy by reducing our dependence on foreign oil, and keeping more money at home to pay for the whole thing.

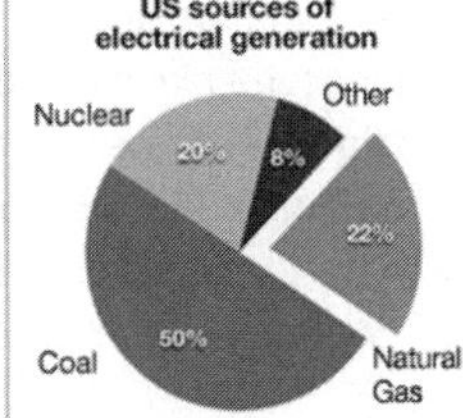

How do we get it done?

The Pickens Plan is a bridge to the future - a blueprint to reduce foreign oil dependence by harnessing domestic energy alternatives, and to buy us time to develop even greater new technologies.

Building new wind generation facilities, conserving energy and increasing the use of our natural gas resources can replace more than one-third of our foreign oil imports in 10 years. But it will take leadership.

We're organizing behind the Pickens Plan now to ensure our voices will be heard.

Together with President Obama and the Congress, we can take down the old barriers and provide energy security for generations to come, while helping to dig us out of the recession we are in today.

As the President has said, "Yes, we can." And together, as never before, we will.

Reading Analytically

1. What context does the Pickens Plan Web site set for his suggestions for going beyond oil by calling it an "addiction"? What other parts of this site support that vision of oil and the consequences of what is termed an addiction?
2. What is the effect of the graphs and charts that are used on this site? Do they lend credibility? How are they linked to the text itself?
3. In what ways does this argument take advantage of the styles of writing and argument that are unique to an Internet site? That is, imagining yourself as a user of the web looking for information, how does the way the information is organized here suit the ways that users "read" a Web site?

Reading Across Disciplinary Communities

1. Since the Pickens Plan is funded and organized by a person who has an economic interest in our adoption of it, some might be skeptical of its purposes. On the other hand, wealthy individuals have often done great public good. If you wanted to verify the information and consider the credibility and value of these suggestions, to what disciplines might you turn? What kinds of research, and what fields, would you be likely to look to for further information? What questions would you ask?

2. One of the ways that the Pickens plan—and many other plans for energy independence—are framed is within a capitalist system of economics: that is, if the plans can breed profit while they serve the larger good, they are likely to be followed. In this way, business and environmentalists can work together. What new business possibilities does this site suggest exist in order to drive this change? Consider this question, also, in light of the other articles in this chapter.

M. BALAT[1] AND H. BALAT[1]

Biogas as a Renewable Energy Source—A Review

This essay, written by two scientists in search of technical solutions for the very practical need to replace oil as our central energy source, demonstrates one possible avenue in the search for alternative energies. The essay overviews previous research on the potential of biogas, the gas generated as a result of organic processes, as a source of energy.

This essay is called a "review" because it is largely a summary of past research that has been done by other scientists. These experts in energy engineering draw largely on secondary source information to build their argument. As you read, then, you might study the writing techniques they use to organize the large amount of data they present. Those techniques can inform your own academic writing, since much of the writing you will do as an undergraduate involves similar processes of reading and synthesizing previous research. While parts of the essay use somewhat complex scientific explanations and descriptions of its potential, the piece also attempts to build an argument for further research in this area. As you read, consider the authors' need to address several types of audiences to achieve their ultimate purpose.

Abstract: This article reviews the production processes and characterization of biogas as an alternative energy source. Biogas, the gas generated from organic digestion under anaerobic conditions by mixed population of microorganisms, is an alternative energy source, which has been commenced to be utilized both in rural and industrial areas at

[1]Sila Science, University Mahallesi, Trabzon, Turkey

least since 1958. Biogas technology offers a very attractive route to utilize certain categories of biomass for meeting partial energy needs. Unlike other forms of renewable energy, biogas neither has any geographical limitations and required technology for producing energy and it is neither complex or monopolistic.

Address correspondence to Mustafa Balat, H. Osman Yucesan Cad. Zambak Sok. Polatoglu Ap. Kat 6, Besikduzu, Trabzon, Turkey. E-mail: mustafabalat@yahoo.com

Introduction

Energy demand forecasting is one of the most important policy tools used by the decision makers all over the world (Ediger and Akar, 2007). The high energy demand in the industrialized world as well as in the domestic sector, and pollution problems caused due to the widespread use of fossil fuels make it increasingly necessary to develop the renewable energy sources of limitless duration and smaller environmental impact than the traditional one (Meher et al., 2006). Renewables such as solar, wind, hydropower, and biogas are potential candidates to meet global energy requirements in a sustainable way (Muneer et al., 2006; Balat, 2007).

Biogas technology offers a very attractive route to utilize certain categories of biomass for meeting partial energy needs. In fact, proper functioning of biogas systems can provide multiple benefits to the users and the community resulting in resource conservation and environmental protection (Santosh et al., 2004). But what makes biogas distinct from other renewable energies is its importance in controlling and collecting organic waste material and at the same time producing fertilizer and water for use in agricultural irrigation. Unlike other forms of renewable energy, biogas neither has any geographical limitations and required technology for producing energy and it is neither complex or monopolistic (Taleghani and Kia, 2005).

Definition of Biogas

Biogas, a clean and renewable form of energy, could very well be a substitute (especially in the rural sector) for conventional sources of energy (fossil fuels, oil, etc.), which are causing ecological–environmental problems and at the same time depleting at a faster rate (Santosh et al., 2004). The most important biogas components are methane (CH_4), carbon dioxide (CO_2), and sulfuric components (H_2S) (Coelho et al., 2006). The gas is

TABLE 1 Composition of biogas

	Typical analysis (% by volume)
Methane (CH_4)	55–65
Carbon dioxide (CO_2)	35–45
Hydrogen sulphide (H_2S)	0–1
Nitrogen (N_2)	0–3
Hydrogen (H_2)	0–1
Oxygen (O_2)	0–2
Ammonia (NH_3)	0–1

TABLE 2 Typical combustion properties of biogas

Ignition point	700°C
Density (dry basis)	1.2 kg/m^3
Ignition concentration gas content	6–12%
Heat value	5.0–7.5 k Wh/m^3

generally composed of methane (55–65%), carbon dioxide (35–45%), nitrogen (0–3%), hydrogen (0–1%), and hydrogen sulfide (0–1%) (Anunputtikul and Rodtong, 2004). Composition of biogas is presented in Table 1.

Due to its elevated methane content, resultant of the organic degradation in the absence of molecular oxygen, biogas is an attractive source of energy. The physical, chemical, and biological characteristics of the manure are related to diet composition, which can influence the biogas composition (Mogami et al., 2006). Natural gas is about 90–95% methane, but biogas is about 55–65% methane. So biogas is basically low-grade natural gas (House, 2007). The biogas composition is an essential parameter, because it allows identifying the appropriate purification system, which aims to remove sulfuric gases and decrease the water volume, contributing to improve the combustion fuel conditions (Coelho et al., 2006). Biogas has a heat value of approximately 5.0–7.5 kWh/m^3. Table 2 shows typical combustion properties of biogas.

Sources for Biogas

Biogas production has usually been applied for waste treatment, mainly sewage sludge, agricultural waste (manure), and industrial organic waste streams (Hartmann and Ahring, 2005). Table 3 cites some potential feedstocks in anaerobic digestion processes. The primary source, which delivers the necessary microorganisms for biomass biodegradation and

TABLE 3 Possible feedstock in anaerobic processes

Origins		
Agricultural origin	**Industrial origin**	**Municipal origin**
Animal waste	Wastewater	Sewage sludge
Crop waste	Sludge	Municipal solid waste
Dedicated energy crops	By-products	

Source: Buekens, 2005.

as well one of the largest single sources of biomass from the food/feed industry, is manure from animal production, mainly from cows and pig farms. In the EU-27, more than 1,500 million tons (Mt) is produced every year (Nielsen et al., 2007). Table 4 depicts the amount of cattle and pig manure produced every year in the European Union. Table 5 shows the biogas and energy potential of pig and cattle manure in the EU-27.

Anaerobic digestion of organic fraction municipal solid waste (OFMSW) has been studied in recent decades, trying to develop a technology that offers waste stabilization with resources recovery (Nguyen et al., 2007). The anaerobic digestion of municipal solid waste (MSW) is a process that has become a major focus of interest in waste management throughout the world. In India, the amounts of MSW generated in urban areas range from 350 to 600 g per capita/day (Elango et al., 2006). MSW stream in Asian cities is composed of a high fraction of organic material of more than 50% with high moisture content (Juanga et al., 2005).

Currently, biogas production is mainly based on the anaerobic digestion of single energy crops. Maize, sunflower, grass, and sudan grass are the most commonly used energy crops. In the future, biogas production from energy crops will increase and requires to be based on a wide range of energy crops that are grown in versatile, sustainable crop rotations (Bauer et al., 2007).

A specific source of biogas is landfills. In a typical landfill, the continuous deposition of solid waste results in high densities and the organic content of the solid waste undergoes microbial decomposition (Filipkowska and Agopsowicz, 2004). The production of methane-rich landfill gas from landfill sites makes a significant contribution to atmospheric methane emissions. In many situations the collection of landfill gas and production of electricity by converting this gas in gas engines is profitable and the application of such systems has become widespread. The benefits are obvious: useful energy carriers are produced from gas that would otherwise contribute to a build-up of methane greenhouse gas (GHG) in the atmosphere, which has stronger GHG impact than the CO_2 emitted from the power plant. This makes landfill gas utilization, in general, a very attractive GHG mitigation option that is widely adopted throughout the EU and North America and increasingly deployed in other world regions (Faaij, 2006).

TABLE 4 Estimated amounts of animal manure in EU-27

Country	Cattle (1,000 heads)	Pigs (1,000 heads)	Cattle (1,000 livestock units)	Pigs (1,000 livestock units)	Cattle manure, Mt	Pig manure, Mt	Total manure, Mt
Austria	2,051	3,125	1,310	261	29	6	35
Belgium	2,695	6,332	1,721	529	38	12	49
Bulgaria	672	931	429	78	9	2	11
Cyprus	57	498	36	42	1	1	2
Czech R.	1,397	2,877	892	240	20	5	25
Denmark	1,544	13,466	986	1,124	22	25	46
Estonia	250	340	160	28	4	1	4
Finland	950	1,365	607	114	13	3	16
France	19,383	15,020	12,379	1,254	272	28	300
Germany	13,035	26,858	8,324	2,242	183	49	232
Greece	600	1,000	383	83	8	2	10
Hungary	723	4,059	462	339	10	7	18
Ireland	7,000	1,758	4,470	147	98	3	102
Italy	6,314	9,272	4,032	774	89	17	106
Latvia	371	436	237	36	5	1	6
Lithuania	792	1,073	506	90	11	2	13
Luxembourg	184	85	118	7	3	0	3
Malta	18	73	11	6	0	0	0
Netherlands	3,862	11,153	2,466	931	54	20	75
Poland	5,483	18,112	3,502	1,512	77	33	110
Portugal	1,443	2,348	922	196	20	4	25
Romania	2,812	6,589	1,796	550	40	12	52
Slovakia	580	1,300	370	109	8	2	11
Slovenia	451	534	288	45	6	1	7
Spain	6,700	25,250	4,279	2,107	94	46	140
Sweden	1,619	1,823	1,034	152	23	3	26
U.K.	10,378	4,851	6,628	405	146	9	155
EU-27	91,364	160,530	58,348	13,399	1,284	295	1,578

Source: Nielsen et al., 2007.

TABLE 5 Energy potential of pig and cattle manure in EU-27

Total manure, Mt	Biogas, Mm^3	Methane, Mm^3	Potential, PJ	Potential, Mtoe
1,578	31,568	20,519	827	18.5

Mt (million tons), Mm^3 (million cubic meter); Mtoe (million tons oil equivalent); 1 Mtoe = 44.8 PJ.
Methane heat of combustion: 40.3 MJ/m^3; Assumed methane content in biogas: 65%.
Source: Nielsen et al., 2007.

Biogas Production Processes

Biogas, the gas generated from organic digestion under anaerobic conditions by mixed population of microorganisms, is an alternative energy source, which has been commenced to be utilized both in rural and industrial areas at least since 1958 (Anunputtikul and Rodtong, 2004). In the complex process of anaerobic digestion, hydrolysis/acidification and methanogenesis are considered as rate-limiting steps (Juanga et al., 2005; Nguyen et al., 2007). Figure 1 illustrates the three stages involved in the combined anaerobic digestion process (Nguyen et al., 2007). Since hydrolytic/acidogenic bacteria and methanogens have different growth requirements, it may not be possible to use a single-phase system, especially in high-solid digestion where substrates are concentrated and volatile fatty acids are produced in high amounts inhibiting the growth of methanogens. Thus, separation of hydrolysis/acidogenesis and methanogenesis would possibly enhance the process. Growth of hydrolytic and acidogenic bacteria can be optimized in the first stage where methanogenesis can be optimized in the second stage. In parallel, the rate of pre-stage reaction can be optimized by applying microaeration (Juanga et al., 2005). Typical reactions during anaerobic digestion are (Ostrem et al., 2004):

$$\underset{\text{(organic compound)}}{C_6H_{12}O_6} \longrightarrow \underset{\text{(ethanol)}}{2C_2H_5OH} + \underset{\text{(carbon dioxide)}}{2CO_2} \qquad (1)$$

$$\underset{\text{(ethanol)}}{2C_2H_5OH} + \underset{\text{(carbon dioxide)}}{CO_2} \longrightarrow \underset{\text{(methane)}}{CH_4} + \underset{\text{(acetic acid)}}{2CH_3COOH} \qquad (2)$$

$$\underset{\text{(acetic acid)}}{CH_3COOH} \longrightarrow \underset{\text{(methane)}}{CH_4} + \underset{\text{(carbon dioxide)}}{CO_2} \qquad (3)$$

$$\underset{\text{(carbon dioxide)}}{CO_2} + \underset{\text{(hydrogen)}}{4H_2} \longrightarrow \underset{\text{(methane)}}{CH_4} + \underset{\text{(water)}}{2H_2O} \qquad (4)$$

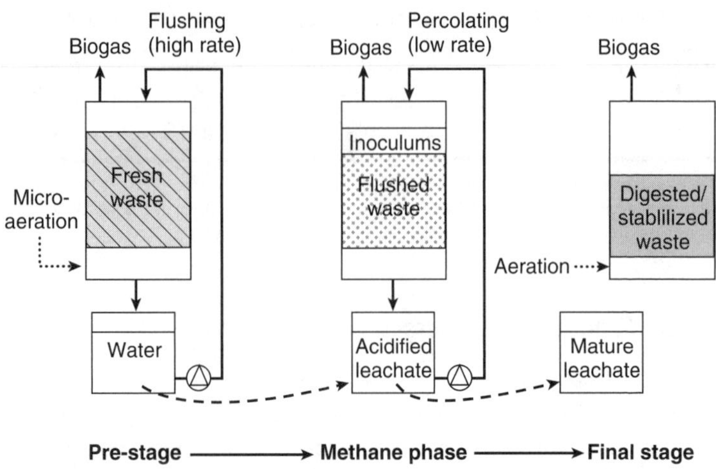

Figure 1. Schematic diagram of the three-stage anaerobic digestion system.
Source: Nguyen et al., 2007.

The biogas produced in anaerobic digestors could contain methane concentrations of until 80% in volume, and its quality would depend on its origin (drain, anaerobic digestion of residual waters, or treatment of residuals) (Benito et al., 2007). The end products of anaerobic digestion are biogas and digestate, a moist solid, which is normally dewatered to produce a liquid stream and a drier solid. The components of the biogas depend on the process of digestion, but are predominately methane and CO_2. The solid is a humus-like, stable, organic material, the quality and subsequent use of which is determined by the characteristics of the feedstock to the anaerobic digestion process. The liquid contains soluble materials, including dissolved organic compounds. In a typical anaerobic digestion facility processing OFMSW, the gas mass comprises about 15% of the output stream and the liquid and solid compose approximately equal parts, or 42.5% each (Ostrem, 2004).

Anaerobic digestion offers an effective way to manage dairy manure by addressing the principal problems of odor and environmental control while offering an opportunity to create energy from conversion of biogas with a system of combined heat and power (CHP). The use of biogas as an energy source has numerous applications. However, all of the possible applications require knowledge about the composition and quantity of constituents in the biogas stream (Scott et al., 2006).

The most widely employed systems are granular sludge-based bioreactors, such as the upflow anaerobic sludge blanket (UASB), expanded granular sludge bed, and the anaerobic hybrid reactor, which consists of a granular sludge bed and an upper fixed bed section (Pender et al., 2004). The advantage of the UASB design is the ability to retain high biomass concentrations despite the upflow velocity of the wastewater and the production of biogas. Consequently, the reactor can operate at short hydraulic retention times since the sludge retention time is almost independent of the hydraulic retention time. In UASB reactors, the biomass is retained as granules, formed by the natural self-immobilization of the bacteria (Trnovec and Britz, 1998). Most of the anaerobic reactor types tried have achieved quite satisfactory removals of chemical oxygen demand (COD) (Gelegenisa et al., 2007). Throughout the recent years the performance of biogas reactors has been increased through a better control of the process and improved reactor design based on a better understanding of the process mechanisms and inhibiting factors. On a worldwide basis, the biogas process will still have its significance as a robust and easily to establish low-cost technology for the treatment of organic waste. Especially in developing countries like China, India, and Africa thousands of simple small-scale reactors are under operation and will still, in the future, have their benefit of waste management combined with decentralized energy production (Hartmann and Ahring, 2005).

Although most full-scale anaerobic treatment plants are operated at mesophilic temperatures (typically 35°C–37°C), many wastewaters are discharged at relatively high temperatures making these effluents potentially attractive for thermophilic anaerobic treatment. In recent years, thermophilic systems have become a more common option for medium- and high-strength wastewaters since they are capable of handling very high organic loading rates while maintaining high treatment efficiency. However, significant drawbacks of thermophilic processes include: (a) they are reported to be more sensitive to environmental perturbations than mesophilic systems and (b) the formation of granular sludge is not straightforward under thermophilic conditions (Pender et al., 2004).

Parameters in Anaerobic Digestion

The performance of biogas plants can be controlled by studying and monitoring the variation in parameters like pH, temperature, carbon/nitrogen ratio, retention time, etc. Any drastic change in these can adversely affect the biogas production. So these parameters should be varied within a desirable range to operate the biogas plant efficiently (Santosh et al., 2004).

pH

pH is a major variable to be monitored and controlled. The range of acceptable pH in digestion is theoretically from 5.5 to 8.5. However, most methanogens function only in a pH range between 6.7 and 7.4 (Buekens, 2005). A falling pH can point toward acid accumulation and digester instability. Gas production is the only parameter that shows digester instability faster than pH (Ostrem, 2004). For an anaerobic fermentation to proceed normally, concentration of volatile fatty acids, acetic acid in particular, should be below 2,000 mg/l (Santosh et al., 2004).

Temperature

Bacteria have a limited range of temperature in which they are active (Elango et al., 2006). Methane production has been documented under a wide range of temperatures, but bacteria are most productive in either mesophilic conditions, at 25°C–40°C, or in the thermophilic range, 50°C–65°C. A mesophilic digester must be maintained between 30°C and 35°C for optimal functioning. A thermophilic digester is maintained near 50°C (Ostrem et al., 2004).

C/N Ratio

It is necessary to maintain proper composition of the feedstock for efficient plant operation so that the C/N ratio in feed remains within a desired range. It is generally found that during anaerobic digestion microorganisms utilize carbon 25–30 times faster than nitrogen. Thus, to meet this requirement, microbes need a 20–30:1 ratio of C to N with the largest percentage of the carbon being readily degradable (Santosh et al., 2004). A high C/N ratio is an indication of rapid consumption of nitrogen by methanogens and results in lower gas production. On the other hand, a lower C/N ratio causes ammonia accumulation and pH values exceeding 8.5, which is toxic to methanogenic bacteria. Optimum C/N ratios of the digester materials can be achieved by mixing materials of high and low C/N ratios, such as organic solid waste mixed with sewage or animal manure (Verma, 2002).

Retention Time

In anaerobic digestion technology, two types of reactors are used: the batch process and the continuous process. In the batch process, the substrate is put in the reactor at the beginning of the degradation period and sealed for the duration of digestion. All of the reaction stages occur more or less consecutively and therefore the production of biogas follows a bell curve. Retention time ranges from 30–60 days and only about 1/3 of the tank volume is used for active digestion (Ostrem et al., 2004).

If anaerobic digestion is to compete with other MSW disposal options, the retention time must be lower than the current standard of 20 days. The retention time is determined by the average time it takes for organic material to digest completely, as measured by the chemical and biological oxygen demand (COD and BOD) of exiting effluent. Speeding up the process will make the process more efficient. Microorganisms that consume organic material control the rate of digestion that determines the time for which the substrate must remain in the digestion chamber, and therefore the size and cost of the digester (Ostrem et al., 2004).

Reducing retention time reduces the size of the digester, resulting in cost savings. Therefore, there is incentive to design systems that can achieve complete digestion in shorter times. A shorter retention time will lead to a higher production rate per reactor volume unit, but a lower overall degradation. These two effects have to be balanced in the design of the full-scale reactor. Several practices are generally accepted as aiding in reducing retention time. Two of these are continuous mixing and using low solids (Ostrem, 2004).

Biogas and Methane Yields

Accumulated biogas yields over the retention time were fitted by regression analysis with an exponential form of the Chapman function (Mahnert et al., 2002; Prochnow et al., 2005):

$$y(t) = y_{max}\,(1 - e^{-a \times t})^{b} \tag{5}$$

where $y(t)$ = biogas yield at time t (1N/kg VS); y_{max} = maximum biogas yield (1N/kg VS); t = time (d); and a, b = coefficients.

Methane contents in the biogas were also fitted by regression analysis using an empirical equation of the Hill function (Mahnert et al., 2002; Prochnow et al., 2005):

$$p_{CH_4}(t) = p_0 + a\frac{t^b}{c^b + t^b} \tag{6}$$

where p_{CH_4} = methane content at time t (vol%); p_o = minimum content of methane (vol%); a, b, c = coefficients. Accumulated methane yields over the retention time can be calculated by multiplication of Eqs. (5) and (6).

Up to now the preferred cultivated energy crops are maize (*Zea mays*), different cereals like rye (*Secale cereale*) and triticale (*Triticum X Secale*), and to some extent sugar beet (*Beta vulgaris*). In addition to the cereals already in use wheat (*Triticum aestivum*) and barley (*Hordeum vulgare*) are of interest as input material. Viewing on growing conditions, plants like hemp (*Cannabis sativa*) or alfalfa (*Medicago sativa*) are remarkable substrates as well. Experiments have demonstrated that maize and cereals harvested at milk ripeness gain the highest yields in biogas. Under laboratory conditions these crops produce within approx. 28 days 450 to 920 m^3 biogas per ton dry matter (DM) with an average methane content of 50 to 60% (Table 6). These yields of energy crops compare to the biogas yields obtained from animal manure and animal slurry, which ranges from 370 m^3 per ton DM cattle manure to 450 m^3/ton DM pig manure with average methane contents of 60 to 65%. In Table 7 dry matter content and organic dry matter as well as methane or biogas yields are summarized for a whole range of tropical substrates (Plöchl and Heiermann, 2006).

With biogas production, the key factor to be optimized is the methane yield per hectare. This may result in different harvesting strategies when growing energy crops for anaerobic digestion compared to growing them as a forage source for ruminants. Specific harvest and processing technologies and specific genotypes are required when crops are used as a renewable energy source. Table 8 compares energy yields from specialized and integrated crop rotations from arable land in EU-25. The total arable land is 93 million hectares. In the specialized crop rotation, it is assumed that 20% of arable land is

TABLE 6 Biogas and/or methane yields from energy crops

Energy crop	DM (% FM)	ODM (% DM)	Biogas yield (Nm^3 t^{-1} ODM)	Methane yield (Nm^3 t^{-1} ODM)
Forage mix	10–16	86–91		297–370
Paddock mix	10	88		246
Clover	9–17	88–91		290–390
Alfalfa	14–35	84–88	514–737	283–405
Maize	30–48	96–97		247–375
Barley	25–38	90–93	694–920	382–506
Rye	33–46	91–93	733–734	403–404
Triticale	27–41	93–95	740–807	407–444
Sugar beet	22	90	840	504
Turnip	23	95		400
Hemp	28–36	92–93	452–485	250–267

DM = dry matter; FM = fresh matter; ODM = organic dry matter, Nm^3 = norm cubic meter, i.e., volume is standardized to norm conditions of 0°C, 1,023 mbar air pressure and 0% relative humidity.
Source: Plöchl and Heiermann, 2006.

TABLE 7 Biogas and/or methane yields from different tropical substrates

Substrate	DM (% FM)	ODM (% DM)	Methane yield ($Nm^3\ t^{-1}$ ODM)	Biogas yield ($Nm^3\ t^{-1}$ ODM)
Bagasse				165
Banana peel		87–94	243–322	
Citrus waste		89–97	433–732	
Coriander waste		80–86	283–325	
Mango peel		89–98	370–523	
Oil palm fibre	37	94	183	
Onion peels		88	400	
Pine apple waste		93–95	355–357	
Pomegranate		87–97	312–430	
Rice				
Straw	87	86	210	
Seed hull	86	84	17–22	
Sapote peels		96	244	
Tomato waste		93–98	211–384	
Water hyazinth	7	81	211–310	

DM = dry matter; FM = fresh matter; ODM = organic dry matter, Nm^3 = norm cubic meter, i.e., volume is standardized to norm conditions of 0°C, 1,023 mbar air pressure and 0% relative humidity.
Source: Plöchl and Heiermann, 2006.

TABLE 8 Annual energy yields of specialized and integrated crop rotation from arable land in EU-25 (Arable land in EU-25: 93 million ha)

Specialized crop rotation	Integrated crop rotation
Specialized energy crop production on 20% of the arable land 18.6 million ha	Integrated energy crop production on the whole arable land: 93 million ha
Energy yield (methane): 234 GJ $ha^{-1}\ a^{-1}$	Energy yield (methane): 20.5 GJ $ha^{-1}\ a^{-1}$
	Energy yield (ethanol): 76.1 (109.1) GJ $ha^{-1}\ a^{-1}$
Energy production: 4,352,400 TJ a^{-1} 104 Mtoe a^{-1}	Energy production: 9,727,800 (13,122,300) TJ a^{-1} 232 (313) Mtoe a^{-1}

Total energy demand of road traffic in EU-25: 334 Mtoe a^{-1}.
Source: Bauer et al., 2007.

used for energy crop production, and that a mean of 234 GJ energy $ha^{-1}\ a^{-1}$ is produced. This results in an energy production in EU-25 of 4,352,400 TJ a^{-1}. This amount of energy corresponds to 104 Mtoe a^{-1} (Bauer et al., 2007).

The energy of the biogas comes from the methane. Methane has an energy value of 37.78 MJ/m_n^3. Allowing for 55% methane, then the energy value of biogas is about 21 MJ/m_n^3 (Murphy, 2005).

Categories of Biogas Plants

The biogas plants studied were in one of two categories. The first was farm-based plants (Table 9), and the other was community-based, or co-operative plants (Table 10). The farm-based plants were located on farms, but some were solely operated by the farm owner, while others involved partnerships between two or three farm owners. Others were located at the farm site, but were owned and operated by companies separate from the farm. The community and co-operative sites were large commercial sites collecting manure from as many as 200 farms, digesting it, and then returning it to the farms to be land applied. Two research station plants were also visited (Table 11) (House, 2007).

Uses of Biogas

The produced biogas may be utilized for CHP production or for transport fuel production as CH_4-enriched biogas. When used to produce transport fuel some of the biogas is used in a small CHP unit to meet electricity demand on site. This generates a surplus thermal product (Murphy and McKeogh, 2004).

Traditionally, biogas has been burned in internal combustion engines for the electricity production and heat, but its potential use in fuel cells could increase its electric efficiency, especially in applications at low scale, diminishing the NOx emissions to the atmosphere (Benito et al., 2007).

To use biogas as a transport fuel, the carbon dioxide, impurities and water content of the gas should be removed. This process of cleaning the biogas is known as scrubbing and is carried out to increase the calorific value of the gas. To utilize the gas as a transport fuel, the gas is usually scrubbed to a methane content of more than 97%. Once the biogas is cleaned, it is known as CH_4-enriched biogas. CH_4-enriched biogas has an energy value of 36.6 MJ/m_n^3 and replaces 1 liter of petrol (Murphy, 2005).

Typically 1 m_n^3 of biogas will generate 0.57 m_n^3 of CH_4-enriched biogas and replace 0.57 liters of petrol. In April 2005, 1 liter of petrol cost approximately €1; thus biogas may generate a revenue of €0.47/m_n^3 (excluding VAT at 21%). In terms of electricity production, 1 m_n^3 of biogas will generate 2 kWh of electricity, which will generate a revenue of €0.14 (allowing €0.07/kWh from biogas). A significant revenue advantage (€0.33/m_n^3) is

TABLE 9 Farm-based biogas plants

Biogas plant	Company	Feedstock	BG production, m^3/day	Methane content, %	Genset, kW	Energy production, kWh/day
Eissen Dairy	PlanET	50% hog manure		54	2 × 625	20,000
		50% dairy manure				
		Corn silage				
Beeston	Lipp	75% hog manure			190	
		25% beef cattle	1,680	52	250	10,000
		Ground corn				
Spargelhof Querdl	Bio Energy	Turkey manure		52	120	
		Corn silage			190	
Bioenergie Ahden	Biogas Nord	30% hog manure		65–70	750	
		70% food waste				
Hohne	Archea	Corn silage			500	
		Wheat in secondary				
RWG Jameln	Biogas Nord	Manure	7,000	53	250	
		Corn silage			300	
Agrarenergie Kaarben	BioConstruct	Dairy manure	28,800	51–52	2 × 1,416	
		Corn silage				
Hegndal	Skaaning	Hog manure	3,600		300	11,500
		Fish waste				
Skovbaekgaard Diary	Skaard	Dairy manure				
		Vegetable fats			625	8,000
		Glycerine				
SNO	PlanET	Dairy manure				
		Hog manure	1,600		200	
		Vegetables				

Source: House, 2007.

TABLE 10 Community and co-operative biogas plants

Biogas plant	Company	Feedstock	BG production, m3/day	Methane content, %	Genset, kW	Energy production, kWh/day
Bio Energie Haestal	Schmack	Manure Corn silage	10,000	52–55	10 × 80	19,200
Wertle	Krieg & Fischer	60% manure 40% food waste	25,000	60–65	2 × 1,250	10,000
Ribe	Kruger	Manure Food waste	13,150		2 × 1,000	
Juhnde Village	Haas Anlagenbau	Dairy manure Corn silage Ground corn	7,800	50–52	700	

Source: House, 2007.

TABLE 11 Other biogas plants

Biogas plant	Company	Feedstock	BG production, m^3/day	Methane content, %	Genset, kW	Energy production, kWh/day
Futterkamp Research Station	Envitec	Dairy manure Corn silage			330	
Nij Bosma Zathe	Krieg & Fischer	Dairy manure Silage crops Food wastes		Up to 75%	37	

Source: House, 2007.

available in utilizing biogas as a transport fuel in Ireland rather than as a raw material for the production of electricity (Murphy, 2005).

Conclusions

Biogas is most commonly produced by using animal manure mixed with water, which is stirred and warned inside an airtight container, known as a digester. The most important biogas components are methane, carbon dioxide, and sulfuric components. The is gas generally composed of methane (55–65%), carbon dioxide (35–45%), nitrogen (0–3%), hydrogen (0–1%), and hydrogen sulfide (0–1%).

Anaerobic processes could either occur naturally or in a controlled environment such as a biogas plant. Organic waste such as livestock manure and various types of bacteria are put in an airtight container called digester so the process could occur. In the complex process of anaerobic digestion, hydrolysis/acidification and methanogenesis are considered as rate-limiting steps.

The performance of biogas plants can be controlled by studying and monitoring the variation in parameters like pH, temperature, carbon/nitrogen ratio, retention time, etc. Any drastic change in these can adversely affect the biogas production. So these parameters should be varied within a desirable range to operate the biogas plant efficiently.

Acknowledgment

The authors would like to thank the Sila Science for their financial support.

References

Anunputtikul, W., and Rodtong, S. 2004. Laboratory scale experiments for biogas production from cassava tubers. *The Joint International Conference on "Sustainable Energy and Environment (SEE),"* Hua Hin, Thailand, December 1–3.

Balat, H. 2007. A renewable perspective for sustainable energy development in Turkey: The case of small hydro-power plants. *Renew. Sustain. Energy Rev.* 11:2152–2165.

Bauer, A., Hrbek, R., Amon, B., Kryvoruchko, V., Machmüller, A., Hopfner-Sixt, K., Bodiroza, V., Wagentristl, H., Pötsch, E., Zollitsch, W., and Amon, T. 2007. Potential of biogas production in sustainable biorefinery concepts. *5th Research and Development Conference of Central- and Eastern European Institutes of Agricultural Engineering*, Kiev, Ukraine, June 20–24.

Benito, M., Garcia, S., Ferreira-Aparicio, P., Garcia Serrano, L., and Daza, L. 2007. Development of biogas reforming Ni-La-Al catalysts for fuel cells. *J. Power Sources* 169:177–183.

Buekens, A. 2005. Energy Recovery from Residual Waste by Means of Anaerobic Digestion Technologies. *Conference "The Future of Residual Waste Management in Europe,"* Luxemburg, November 17–18.

Coelho, S. T., Velazquez, S. M. S. G., Pecora, V., and Abreu, F. C. 2006. Energy generation with landfill biogas. *Proceedings of RIO6, World Climate & Energy Event*, Rio de Janeiro, Brazil, November 17–18.

Ediger, V. Ş., and Akar, S. 2007. ARIMA forecasting of primary energy demand by fuel in Turkey. *Energy Policy* 35:1701–1708.

Elango, D., Pulikesi, M., Baskaralingam, P., Ramamurthi, V., and Sivanesan, S. 2006. Production of biogas from municipal solid waste with domestic sewage. *Energy Sources, Part A* 28:1127–1134.

Faaij, A. 2006. Modern biomass conversion technologies. *Mitigation and Adaptation Strategies for Global Change* 11:335–367.

Filipkowska, U., and Agopsowicz, M. H. 2004. Solids waste gas recovery under different water conditions. *Polish J. Environ. Stud.* 13:663–669.

Gelegenisa, J., Georgakakisb, D., Angelidakic, I., and Mavris, V. 2007. Optimization of biogas production by co-digesting whey with diluted poultry manure. *Renew. Energy* 32:2147–2160.

Hartmann, H., and Ahring, B. K. 2005. The future of biogas production. *Risø; International Energy Conference on Technologies for Sustainable Energy Development in the Long Term, Riso-R-1517(EN)*, Roskilde, Denmark, May 23–25, pp. 163–172.

House, H. 2007. Alternative Energy Sources—Biogas Production. *London Swine Conference—Today's Challenges . . . Tomorrow's Opportunities*, London, April 3–4, pp. 119–128.

Juanga, J. P., Kuruparan, P., and Visvanathan, C. 2005. Optimizing combined anaerobic digestion process of organic fraction of municipal solid waste. *International Conference on Integrated Solid Waste Management in Southeast Asian Cities*, Siem Reap, Cambodia, July 5–7, pp. 155–192.

Mahnert, P., Heiermann, M., Pöchl, M., Schelle, H., and Linke, B. 2002. Alternative use for grassland cuts—Forage grasses as biogas co-substrates. *Landtechnik* 57:260–261.

Meher, L. C., Sagar, D. V., and Naik, S. N. 2006. Technical aspects of biodiesel production by transesterification—A review. *Renew. & Sustain. Energy Rev.* 10:248–268.

Mogami, C. A., Souza, C. F., Paim, V. T., Tinoco, I. F., Baeta, F. C., and Gates, R. S. 2006. Methane concentration in biogas produced from dejections of milk goats fed with different diets. Paper no. 064068. *ASABE Annual Meeting*, Portland, Oregon, July 9–12.

Muneer, T., Maubleu, S., and Asif, M. 2006. Prospects of solar water heating for textile industry in Pakistan. *Renew. Sustain. Energy Rev.* 10:1–23.

Murphy, J. D., and McKeogh, E. 2004. Technical, economic and environmental analysis of energy production from municipal solid waste. *Renew. Energy* 29:1043–1057.

Murphy, J. D. 2005. CH_4-enriched biogas utilised as a transport fuel: The case for the utilisation of biogas as a transport fuel. *Engineers J.* 59:571–576.

Nguyen, P. H. L., Kuruparan, P., and Visvanathan, C. 2007. Anaerobic digestion of municipal solid waste as a treatment prior to landfill. *Biores. Technol.* 98:380–387.

Nielsen, J. B. H., Oleskowicz-Popiel, P., and Al Seadi, T. 2007. Energy crops potentials for bioenergy in EU-27. *15th European Biomass Conference & Exhibition From Research to Market Deployment*, Berlin, Germany, May 7–11.

Ostrem, K. 2004. *Greening waste: Anaerobic digestion for treating the organic fraction of municipal solid waste.* M.S. Thesis, Department of Earth and Environmental Engineering, Columbia University, New York, NY.

Ostrem, K., Millrath, K., and Themelis, N. J. 2004. Combining anaerobic digestion and waste-to-energy. *12th North American Waste To Energy Conference*, Savannah, Georgia, May 17–19.

Pender, S., Toomey, M., Carton, M., Eardly, D., Patching, J. W., Colleran, E., and O'Flaherty, V. 2004. Long-term effects of operating temperature and sulphate addition on the methanogenic community structure of anaerobic hybrid reactors. *Water Res.* 38:619–630.

Plöchl, M., and Heiermann, M. 2006. Biogas farming in central and northern Europe: A strategy for developing countries?. *Agricultural Engineering International: The CIGR Ejournal*, Invited Overview No. 8, Vol. VIII.

Prochnow, A., Heiermann, M., Drenckhan, A., and Schelle, H. 2005. Seasonal pattern of biomethanisation of grass from landscape management. *Agricultural Engineering International: the CIGR Ejournal*, Manuscript EE 05 011, Vol. VII.

Santosh, Y., Sreekrishnan, T. R., Kohli, S., and Rana, V. 2004. Enhancement of biogas production from solid substrates using different techniques—A review. *Biores. Technol.* 95:1–10.

Scott, N. R., Zicari, S., Saikkonen, K., and Bothi, K. 2006. Characterization of dairy-derived biogas and biogas processing. Paper no. 064177. *ASABE Annual Meeting*, Portland, Oregon, July 9–12.

Taleghani, G., and Kia, A. S. 2005. Technical-economical analysis of the Saveh biogas power plant. *Renew. Energy* 30:441–446.

Tmovec, W., and Britz, T. J. 1998. Influence of organic loading rate and hydraulic retention time on the efficiency of a UASB bioreactor treating a canning factory effluent. *Water SA* 24:1147–1152.

Verma, S. 2002. Anaerobic digestion of biodegradable organics in municipal solid wastes. M.S. Thesis, Columbia University, New York, NY.

Reading Analytically

1. The authors begin their piece by claiming that biogas "could very well be a substitute . . . for conventional sources of energy." Upon what specific features of this energy source is this claim based?
2. The authors are careful to begin their argument by defining what they mean by biogas. After reading this part of the essay, write your own definition of that term. Try to develop it in language that you might use if you were explaining this energy source to someone without a strong background in science.
3. Later in this chapter you will find an article entitled "How Biofuels Could Starve the Poor" which suggests that some alternative energies might be creating more problems than they are solving. Read that piece, and then take a position on whether biogas is likely to present the same kind of challenges as other forms of biofuel, or whether biogas has the potential to overcome some of those issues. Use specific evidence to support your position.

Reading Across Disciplinary Communities

1. In many cases, scientific information is best presented in tables or charts rather than in paragraph format. Look over the tables and charts in this article, and speculate as to why the authors decided upon that technique for a specific set of data.
2. While this piece is certainly based in scientific methodologies, its beginning and end are more argumentative, taking a clear position on the topic. Does that in any way taint the fact-based nature of science? Can science take sides, or should it just present facts? Could advocating for the potential of a particular kind of research potentially represent a conflict of interest?

GEOFFREY CARR

The Power and the Glory

This essay, originally published in The Economist, *a journal of international business, was written by its science editor. Geoffrey Carr, who joined this publication in 1991, specializes in topics that include disease, climate science, evolution, genetics, neuroeconomics, neuroscience, and synthetic biology.*

In this piece, Carr places the issue of alternative energy into the perspective of the applied sciences. He explores the ways that the need for new energy sources, in combination with the most promising technologies, provides an opportunity for investors who can most aptly predict the direction our energy decisions will take. As you read, you might consider how these disciplines—natural science, engineering, and business—interact with one another to drive decision-making.

Everyone loves a booming market, and most booms happen on the back of technological change. The world's venture capitalists, having fed on the computing boom of the 1980s, the internet boom of the 1990s and the biotech and nanotech boomlets of the early 2000s, are now looking around for the next one. They think they have found it: energy.

Many past booms have been energy-fed: coal-fired steam power, oil-fired internal-combustion engines, the rise of electricity, even the mass tourism of the jet era. But the past few decades have been quiet on that front. Coal has been cheap. Natural gas has been cheap.

The 1970s aside, oil has been cheap. The one real novelty, nuclear power, went spectacularly off the rails. The pressure to innovate has been minimal.

In the space of a couple of years, all that has changed. Oil is no longer cheap; indeed, it has never been more expensive. Moreover, there is growing concern that the supply of oil may soon peak as consumption continues to grow, known supplies run out and new reserves become harder to find.

The idea of growing what you put in the tank of your car, rather than sucking it out of a hole in the ground, no longer looks like economic madness. Nor does the idea of throwing away the tank and plugging your car into an electric socket instead. Much of the world's oil is in the hands of governments who have little sympathy with the rich West. When a former head of America's Central Intelligence Agency allies himself with tree-hugging greens that his outfit would once have suspected of subversion, you know something is up. Yet that is one tack James Woolsey is trying in order to reduce his country's dependence on imported oil.

The price of natural gas, too, has risen in sympathy with oil. That is putting up the cost of electricity. Wind- and solar-powered alternatives no longer look so costly by comparison. It is true that coal remains cheap, and is the favoured fuel for power stations in industrialising Asia. But the rich world sees things differently.

In theory, there is a long queue of coal-fired power stations waiting to be built in America. But few have been completed in the past 15 years and many in that queue have been put on hold or withdrawn, for two reasons. First, Americans have become intolerant of large, polluting industrial plants on their doorsteps. Second, American power companies are fearful that they will soon have to pay for one particular pollutant, carbon dioxide, as is starting to happen in other parts of the rich world. Having invested heavily in gas-fired stations, only to find themselves locked into an increasingly expensive fuel, they do not want to make another mistake.

That has opened up a capacity gap and an opportunity for wind and sunlight. The future price of these resources—zero—is known. That certainty has economic value as a hedge, even if the capital cost of wind and solar power stations is, at the moment, higher than that of coal-fired ones.

The reasons for the boom, then, are tangled, and the way they are perceived may change. Global warming, a long-range phenomenon, may not be uppermost in people's minds during an economic downturn. High fuel prices may fall as new sources of supply are exploited to fill rising demand from Asia. Security of supply may improve if hostile governments are replaced by friendly ones and sources become more diversified. But none of the reasons is likely to go away entirely.

Global warming certainly will not. "Peak oil," if oil means the traditional sort that comes cheaply out of holes in the ground, probably will arrive soon. There is oil aplenty of other sorts (tar sands, liquefied coal and so on), so the stuff is unlikely to run out for a long time yet. But it will get more expensive to produce, putting a floor on the price that is way above today's. And political risk will always be there—particularly for oil, which is so often associated with bad government for the simple reason that its very presence causes bad government in states that do not have strong institutions to curb their politicians.

A prize beyond the dreams of avarice

The market for energy is huge. At present, the world's population consumes about 15 terawatts of power. (A terawatt is 1,000 gigawatts, and a gigawatt is the capacity of the largest sort of coal-fired power station.) That translates into a business worth $6 trillion a year—about a tenth of the world's economic output—according to John Doerr, a venture capitalist who is heavily involved in the industry. And by 2050, power consumption is likely to have risen to 30 terawatts.

Scale is one of the important differences between the coming energy boom, if it materialises, and its recent predecessors—particularly those that relied on information technology, a market measured

A dance to the music of time

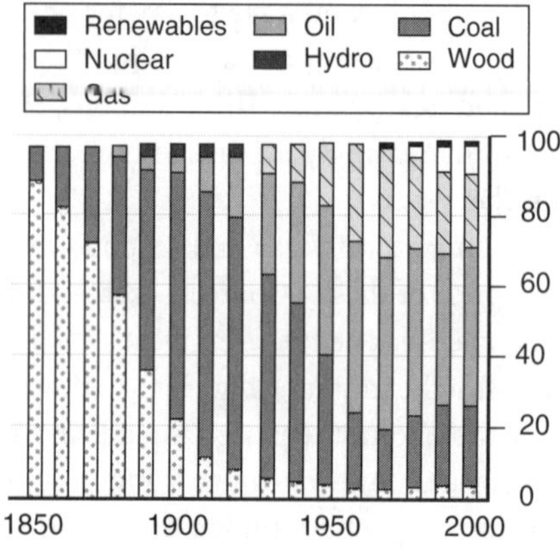

in mere hundreds of billions. Another difference is that new information technologies tend to be disruptive, forcing the replacement of existing equipment, whereas, say, building wind farms does not force the closure of coal-fired power stations.

For both of these reasons, any transition from an economy based on fossil fuels to one based on renewable, alternative, green energy—call it what you will—is likely to be slow, as similar changes have been in the past (see chart 1). On the other hand, the scale of the market provides opportunities for alternatives to prove themselves at the margin and then move into the mainstream, as is happening with wind power at the moment. And some energy technologies do have the potential to be disruptive. Plug-in cars, for example, could be fuelled with electricity at a price equivalent to 25 cents a litre of petrol. That could shake up the oil, carmaking and electricity industries all in one go.

The innovation lull of the past few decades also provides opportunities for technological leapfrogging. Indeed, it may be that the field of energy gives the not-quite-booms in biotechnology and nanotechnology the industrial applications they need to grow really big, and that the three aspiring booms will thus merge into one.

The possibility of thus recapturing the good times of their youth has brought many well-known members of the "technorati" out of their homes in places like Woodside, California. Energy has become supercool. Elon Musk, who co-founded PayPal, has developed a battery-powered sports car. Larry Page and Sergey Brin, the founders of Google, have started an outfit called Google.org that is searching for a way to make renewable energy truly cheaper than coal (or RE<C, as they describe it to their fellow geeks).

Vinod Khosla, one of the founders of Sun Microsystems, is turning his considerable skills as a venture capitalist towards renewable energy, as are Robert Metcalfe, who invented the ethernet system used to connect computers together in local networks, and Mr Doerr, who works at Kleiner Perkins Caufield & Byers, one of Silicon Valley's best-known venture-capital firms. Sir Richard Branson, too, is getting in on the act with his Virgin Green Fund.

This renewed interest in energy is bringing forth a raft of ideas, some bright, some batty, that is indeed reminiscent of the dotcom boom. As happened in that boom, most of these ideas will come to naught. But there could just be a PayPal or a Google or a Sun among them.

More traditional companies are also taking an interest. General Electric (GE), a large American engineering firm, already has a thriving wind-turbine business and is gearing up its solar-energy business. The energy researchers at its laboratories in Schenectady, New York, enjoy much of the intellectual freedom associated with start-up firms, combined with a secure supply of money.

Meanwhile, BP and Shell, two of the world's biggest oil companies, are sponsoring both academic researchers and new, small firms with bright ideas, as is DuPont, one of the biggest chemical companies. Not everyone has joined in. Exxon Mobil, the world's largest oil company not in government hands, is conspicuously absent. But in many boardrooms renewables are no longer seen as just a way of keeping environmentalists off companies' backs.

Some people complain that many existing forms of renewable energy rely on subsidies or other forms of special treatment for their viability. On the surface, that is true. Look beneath, though, and the whole energy sector is riddled with subsidies, both explicit and hidden, and costs that are not properly accounted for. Drawing on the work of people like Boyden Gray, a former White House counsel, Mr Woolsey estimates that American oil companies receive preferential treatment from their government worth more than $250 billion a year. And the Intergovernmental Panel on Climate Change (IPCC), a United Nations-appointed group of scientific experts, reckons that fossil fuels should carry a tax of $20–50 for every tonne of carbon dioxide they generate in order to pay for the environmental effects of burning them (hence the fears of the power-generators).

So the subsidies and mandates offered to renewable sources of power such as wind turbines often just level the playing field. It is true that some

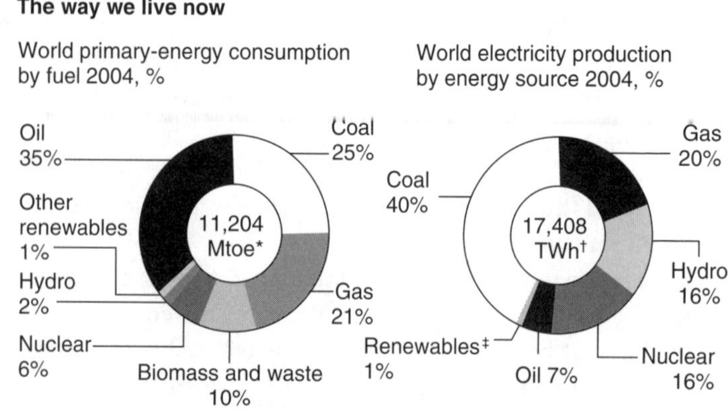

subsidies amount to unwarranted market-rigging: examples include those handed by cloudy Germany to its solar-power industry and by America to its maize-based ethanol farmers when Brazilian sugar-based ethanol is far cheaper. Others, though, such as a requirement that a certain proportion of electricity be derived from non-fossil-fuel sources, make no attempt to pick particular technological winners. They merely act to stimulate innovation by guaranteeing a market to things that actually work.

If the world were rational, all of these measures would be swept away and replaced by a proper tax on carbon—as is starting to happen in Europe, where the price arrived at by the cap-and-trade system being introduced is close to the IPCC's recommendation. If that occurred, wind-based electricity would already be competitive with fossil fuels and others would be coming close. Failing that, special treatment for alternatives is probably the least bad option—though such measures need to be crafted in ways that favour neither incumbents nor particular ways of doing things, and need to be withdrawn when they are no longer necessary.

The poor world turns greener too

That, at least, is the view from the rich world. But poorer, rapidly developing countries are also taking more of an interest in renewable energy sources, despite assertions to the contrary by some Western politicians and businessmen. It is true that China is building coal-fired power stations at a blazing rate. But it also has a large wind-generation capacity, which is expected to grow by two-thirds this year, and is the world's second-largest manufacturer of solar panels—not to mention having the largest number of solar-heated rooftop hot-water systems in its buildings.

Brazil, meanwhile, has the world's second-largest (just behind America) and most economically honest biofuel industry, which already provides 40% of the fuel consumed by its cars and should soon supply 15% of its electricity, too (through the burning of sugarcane waste). South Africa is leading the effort to develop a new class of safe and simple nuclear reactor—not renewable energy in the strict sense, but carbon-free and thus increasingly welcome. These countries, and others like them, are prepared to look beyond fossil fuels. They will get their energy where they can. So if renewables and other alternatives can compete on cost, the poor and the rich world alike will adopt them.

That, however, requires innovation. Such innovation is most likely to come out of the laboratories of rich countries. At a recent debate at Columbia University, which *The Economist* helped to organise, Mr

Khosla defended the proposition, "The United States will solve the climate-change problem." The Californian venture capitalist argued that if cheaper alternatives to fossil fuels are developed, simple economics will ensure their adoption throughout the world. He also insisted that the innovation which will create those alternatives will come almost entirely out of America.

As it happens, he lost. But that does not mean he is wrong. There are lots of terawatts to play for and lots of money to be made. And if the planet happens to be saved on the way, that is all to the good.

Reading Analytically

1. What new perspectives on the "energy problem" are added by this business-oriented publication? According to this essay, what is most likely to drive the move toward solving this problem?
2. Consider the tone of this piece: How is this piece geared toward the specific audience of a publication like *The Economist* in its phrasing, its word choice, and its organization? Provide several examples of how this writer accommodates his audience.
3. What are the implications of the section title, "A Prize beyond the Dreams of Avarice," and that section of the essay? Look up the meaning of the word *avarice,* and consider how that meaning is altered here.

Reading Across Disciplinary Communities

1. How is the concept of innovation, here framed as a business issue, different from the way it might be treated in the natural sciences? In engineering? In what ways is it similar?
2. What basic economic principles and beliefs underlie the argument here? Try to list a few specific assumptions that those in this discipline generally hold that inform this argument. Then speculate on the ways that this essay draws its conclusions based on those assumptions.

BERENICE BAKER

Power Play

This essay, written for the trade journal The Engineer *provides a good example of how a specific discipline—in this case, engineering—presents its research in more public forums. This piece was written by a business marketing specialist, Berenice Baker.*

Like many articles in such publications, this piece provides news of recent developments in the field. As you read, you might note the ways that the piece uses some degree of specialized language, but also provides a less technical style and tone in order to be accessible to a wider audience. You might also consider how the background of the author as a marketing specialist might inform the tone and the message of this piece—as well as the connection between two applied sciences: business and engineering.

As the cost of petrol and domestic energy bills hit the roof, a system that produces and stores hydrogen that can fuel your car and heat your home—and remains affordable and green—sounds like a gift from the technology gods.

Sadly for motorists and householders, the much-vaunted hydrogen economy has remained an elusive dream, dogged by high costs and a lack of infrastructure.

Alternative energy innovator ITM Power, based in Saffron Walden, believes part of the solution may lie in its fridge-freezer-sized domestic electrolyser, the Green Box. The device, soon to enter production, produces affordable hydrogen using water and solar or wind energy, which can fuel vehicles and power homes.

Jim Heathcote, ITM's chief executive, says the system overcomes one of the fundamental problems of renewable energy, whether for domestic or commercial use.

He claims renewable energy is not a substitute for a reliable grid system and is impracticable without storage. ITM's vision is to store hydrogen produced by wind or solar energy, or off-peak electricity. 'You can't run a factory just when the wind blows, and countries with a large wind penetration have to run fossil-fuel plants in parallel in case the wind drops. So renewable energy systems don't do the job without storage,' said Heathcote.

'What we have to do is take this intermittent renewable energy and make a useful fuel. The battle for energy security is based on whether we can make hydrogen cost-competitive with the competing fuels, and that is what we are attempting to do.'

The heart of ITM's technology is a polymer membrane that it claims is superior to existing alternatives.

Heathcote says electrolysis technology can be difficult because of the aggressive chemical environment it entails, which has so far made a low-cost endurable electrolyser impossible. Alkaline electrolysers use a liquid electrolyte that can absorb some of the gases produced, making it

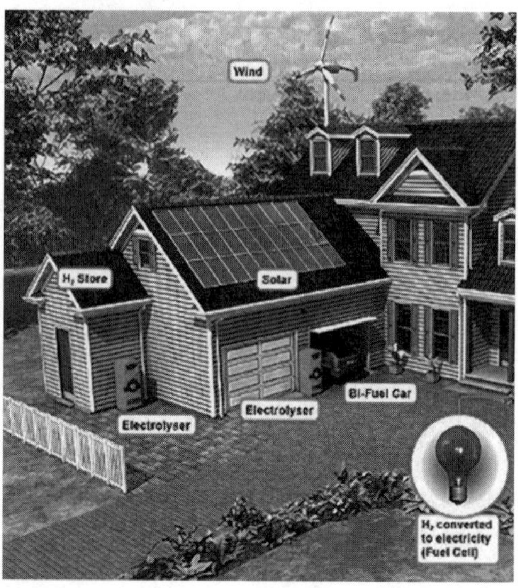

Hydrogen power may hold the key to practical renewables, with applications for the home and car, according to ITM

potentially explosive and requiring the extra cost of degasification plant. Acid chemistry electrolysers use a fluorinated polymer membrane to keep the hydrogen and oxygen separate, but the polymer and the platinum catalyst used in the process are too expensive.

Standard membrane materials cost about £250/m^2, but ITM Power's membrane could be produced for about £2.50/m^2, the company claims.

ITM has developed a new class of material called an ionically conducting hydrophilic cross-linked polymer, which it claims costs one per cent of the price of current polymers and its high ionic conductivity gives increased gas output.

The materials start as liquids, which are poured into a mould and made to cross link using gamma or ultraviolet radiation. The molecules join together in 3D so there are no ends that would be susceptible to end-chain degradation and no need for fluorine. 'We have made a low-cost, endurable polymer,' said Heathcote, and after years of testing, we have not been able to identify a failure mode for it.

'Because our materials start as liquids, we are able to add an alkaline component or an acid component before we polymerise it, so we got rid of the degasification of the traditional alkaline electrolysers and the platinum from the acid electrolysis.'

The electrolyser could have a significant impact in transportation. ITM is collaborating with Roush Technologies to build a system incorporating the Green Box to refuel a car so it can go 25 miles (40km)—the average US commute—on hydrogen before switching to petrol in the same engine. Roush is adapting internal combustion engines to run on hydrogen.

Heathcote claims this approach means there would be little cost in converting a petrol engine car to run on hydrogen. The most expensive part would be the fuel tank, costing £3,000, which could get cheaper with volume production. 'It is unlikely fuel cells will be able to compete with the internal combustion engine in the near future,' said Heathcote. 'The first step is evolution, not revolution. If you could travel 25 miles on hydrogen, you would have a remarkable impact on our energy dependency for petrol, and a dramatic impact on emissions.'

He also claims the battery alternative is unsustainable. 'One of our scientists calculated that if you tried to move cars to nickel cadmium batteries, you would need more than twice the known cadmium inside the planet. Within one major car programme, you would run into resource problems with cadmium.'

The eventual aim of the deal with Roush is to produce dual-fuel commercial vehicles that go further on hydrogen than cars because they can carry bigger tanks. ITM has developed a hydrogen-fuelled Ford Focus with PhD researchers at Hertfordshire University, which it plans to launch with a refueller soon.

As well as vehicles, the Green Box could also be used to enable zero-carbon housing, which Heathcote also describes as energy independence or grid independence. Electricity from renewable sources would be used to produce hydrogen and fill a propane-style tank. A single unit could produce enough for direct cooking and heating, to use in a generator for grid-independent electricity and to fill a car.

The first systems will be commercially available this year after 10 or 15 years of development. The launch model will be able to produce hydrogen with a pressure of about 75 bar, enough to fill the car tanks Heathcote envisages. 'The higher the pressure, the more expensive it becomes,' he said. 'Commercial companies may want a lower-pressure system, but a with hydrogen compressor to take it up to 300 bar.'

ITM had a low-pressure stack using its technology independently costed and claims the unit would cost £82 kW. 'If it were 50 per cent efficient and it lasted an hour, it would cost £164 for a kilowatt-hour's worth of hydrogen.' said Heathcote. 'But the economy comes through the cost-of-life calculation—at 10,000 hours, it comes down to 3,28 cents [less that two pence] per kilowatt-hour.' Domestic electricity bills range from two to 10 pence/kWh.

ITM's initial target market will be large units to fuel vehicles for local authorities and commercial companies interested in reducing their energy dependence and to power forklift trucks that cannot use fossil fuels in an enclosed warehouse.

'We've made a low-cost endurable polymer and after years of testing we haven't been able to identify a failure mode for it'

Jim Heathcote, ITM Power

The company also plans to go into production in the second half of 2009 with a 1W–2W domestic electrolyser that would be used to refuel a metal hydride cylinder. This could be used with a fuel cell to give backup electricity for essential appliances, or users could buy several to use with solar panels to power a hydrogen home.

Although other manufacturers are making electrolysers, ITM claims its model is more affordable and more environmentally friendly, because the polymer is made from common hydrocarbons with no fluorine, which would cause disposal problems.

ITM has been testing its electrolyser technology for more than 10 years. Durability and chemistry testing has already been completed, and pressure testing is under way.

The first fuel-cell stacks are achieving power densities of about $1W/cm^2$, says ITM, which claims its internal tests are giving power densities in excess of published figures for other systems. It has not revealed specific efficiency figures, but believes its technology will be at least as efficient as existing PEM (proton exchange membrane) alternatives.

Turning wind or solar energy into a fuel that can be stored and is cheaper than fossil fuels is more important than overall efficiency, says Heathcote. 'The primary driver will be economics, not thermodynamics. The only issue for a viable hydrogen economy is that the cheapest pump has to be the hydrogen pump. To quote one of the US speakers at a conference attended, thermodynamics is for sissies.'

Reading Analytically

1. What specific critiques does this article offer for some of the proposed alternative energy options? What are the ongoing engineering challenges for the implementation and use of those techniques?

2. Summarize the main advantages of the new technologies that are presented here. What problems might they solve?
3. What questions are you left with as regards this technology? How might you go about doing further research into its potential?

Reading Across Disciplinary Communities

1. One of the individuals interviewed for this piece suggests that "the primary driver will be economics, not thermodynamics." What does this suggest about the relationship between science and business in the applied fields of engineering?
2. This piece was written for a "trade journal," a publication that is designed to keep members of a professional community up on the most recent developments in the field. How does this piece serve that purpose? What parts of it seem most oriented toward other professionals in the industry?

MICHAEL E. WEBBER

Catch-22

Water Versus Energy

This article, originally published in a special edition of Scientific American *on sustainable energy, provides another set of issues in the debate about how to address our needs for alternative energies—its effect upon our water supply. Its author, Michael E. Webber, is the associate director of the Center for International Energy & Environmental Policy at the Jackson School of Geosciences at the University of Texas at Austin. He holds a B.A. in liberal arts and a B.S. in Aerospace Engineering from the University of Texas at Austin, and a M.S and Ph.D. in Mechanical Engineering from Stanford University. This broad background of study, from liberal arts to engineering, provides him with a deeply interdisciplinary perspective on this issue.*

In the article, Webber adds another challenge to the development of new energy technologies: many of them tend to deplete our reserves of fresh water, creating new problems as they attempt to solve existing ones. As you read this piece, you might consider how this expert in engineering who also has a background in the liberal arts weighs out the options and helps readers to consider the larger picture in proposed new energy alternatives. You might also consider that T. Boone Pickens, whose plan is excerpted earlier in this chapter, also has financial holdings in the water industry. How might that help you think about the motivations and viability of his plan?

In June the state of Florida made an unusual announcement: it would sue the U.S. Army Corps of Engineers over the corps's plan to reduce water flow from reservoirs in Georgia into the Apalachicola River, which runs through Florida from the Georgia-Alabama border. Florida was concerned that the restricted flow would threaten certain endangered species. Alabama also objected, worried about another species: nuclear power plants, which use enormous quantities of water, usually drawn from rivers and lakes, to cool their big reactors. The reduced flow raised the specter that the Farley Nuclear Plant near Dothan, Ala., would need to shut down.

Georgia wanted to keep its water for good reason: a year earlier various rivers dropped so low that the drought-stricken state was within a few weeks of shutting down its own nuclear plants. Conditions had become so dire that by this past January one of the state's legislators suggested that Georgia move its upper border a mile farther north to annex freshwater resources in Tennessee, pointing to an allegedly faulty border survey from 1818. Throughout 2008 Georgia, Alabama and Florida have continued to battle; the corps, which is tasked by Congress to manage water resources, has been caught in the middle. Drought is only one cause. A rapidly growing population, especially in Atlanta, as well as overdevelopment and a notorious lack of water planning, is running the region's rivers dry.

Water and energy are the two most fundamental ingredients of modern civilization. Without water, people die. Without energy, we cannot grow food, run computers, or power homes, schools or offices. As the world's population grows in number and affluence, the demands for both resources are increasing faster than ever.

Woefully underappreciated, however, is the reality that each of these precious commodities might soon cripple our use of the other. We consume massive quantities of water to generate energy, and we consume massive quantities of energy to deliver clean water. Many people are concerned about the perils of peak oil—running out of cheap oil. A few are voicing concerns about peak water. But almost no one is addressing the tension between the two: water restrictions are hampering solutions for generating more energy, and energy problems, particularly rising prices, are curtailing efforts to supply more clean water.

The paradox is raising its ugly head in many of our own backyards. In January, Lake Norman near Charlotte, N.C., dropped to 93.7 feet, less than a foot above the minimum allowed level for Duke Energy's McGuire Nuclear Station. Outside Las Vegas, Lake Mead, fed by the

Colorado River, is now routinely 100 feet lower than historic levels. If it dropped another 50 feet, the city would have to ration water use, and the huge hydroelectric turbines inside Hoover Dam on the lake would provide little or no power, potentially putting the booming desert metropolis in the dark.

Research scientist Gregory J. McCabe of the U.S. Geological Survey reiterated the message to Congress in June. He noted that an increase in average temperature of even 1.5 degrees Fahrenheit across the Southwest as the result of climate change could compromise the Colorado River's ability to meet the water demands of Nevada and six other states, as well as that of the Hoover Dam. Earlier this year scientists at the Scripps Institution of Oceanography in La Jolla, Calif., declared that Lake Mead could become dry by 2021 if the climate changes as expected and future water use is not curtailed.

Conversely, San Diego, which desperately needs more drinking water, now wants to build a desalination plant up the coast, but local activists are fighting the facility because it would consume so much energy and the power supply is thin. The mayor of London denied a proposed desalination plant in 2006 for the same reason, only to have his successor later rescind that denial. Cities in Uruguay must choose whether they want the water in their reservoirs to be used for drinking or for electricity. Saudi Arabia is wrestling with whether to sell all its oil and gas at record prices or to hold more of those resources to generate what it doesn't have: freshwater for its people and its cities.

We cannot build more power plants without realizing that they impinge on our freshwater supplies. And we cannot build more water delivery and cleaning facilities without driving up energy demand. Solving the dilemma requires new national policies that integrate energy and water solutions and innovative technologies that help to boost one resource without draining the other.

Vicious Cycle

The earth holds about eight million cubic miles of freshwater—tens of thousands of times more than humans' annual consumption. Unfortunately, most of it is imprisoned in underground reservoirs and in permanent ice and snow cover; relatively little is stored in easily accessible and replenishable lakes and rivers.

Furthermore, the available water is often not clean or not located close to population centers. Phoenix gets a large share of its freshwater via a 336-mile aqueduct from, of course, the Colorado River. Municipal supplies are also often contaminated by industry, agriculture and wastewater effluents. According to the World Health Organization, approximately 2.4 billion people live in highly water-stressed areas. Two primary solutions—shipping in water over long distances or cleaning nearby but dirty supplies—both require large amounts of energy, which is soaring in price.

Nationwide, the two greatest users of freshwater are agriculture and power plants. Thermal power plants—those that consume coal, oil, natural gas or uranium—generate more than 90 percent of U.S. electricity, and they are water hogs. The sheer amount required to cool the plants impacts the available supply to everyone else. And although a considerable portion of the water is eventually returned to the source (some evaporates), when it is emitted it is at a different temperature and has a different biological content than the source, threatening the environment. Whether this effluent should be processed is contentious; the Supreme Court is set to hear a consolidation of cases about the Environmental Protection Agency's requirements that power plants retrofit their systems to minimize impact on local water supplies and aquatic life.

Any switch from gasoline to electric vehicles or biofuels is a strategic decision to switch our dependence from foreign oil to domestic water.

At the same time, we use a lot of energy to move and treat water, sometimes across vast distances. The California Aqueduct, which transports snowmelt across two mountain ranges to the thirsty coastal cities, is the biggest electricity consumer in the state. As convenient resources become tapped out, providers must dig deeper and reach farther. Countries that have large populations but isolated water sources are considering daunting megaprojects. China, for example, wants to transport water from three river basins in the water-rich south over thousands of miles to the water-poor north, consuming vast energy supplies. Old-guard investors such as T. Boone Pickens who made their billions from oil and natural gas are now putting their money into water, including one project to pipe it across Texas. Cities such as El Paso are also trying to develop desalination plants positioned above salty aquifers, which require remarkable amounts of energy—and money.

In addition, local municipalities have to clean incoming water and treat outgoing water, which together consume about 3 percent of the nation's electricity. Health standards typically get stricter with time, too, so the degree of energy that needs to be spent per gallon will only increase.

From Imported Oil to Domestic Water

The strains between the resources manifest themselves in tough choices at the local level—especially in land- and water-locked regions such as the desert Southwest. Is it better for a city to import freshwater or to import electricity to desalinate brackish water in deep aquifers below? Or is it better yet to move the people to where the water is? With infinite energy, freshwater can be reached, but even if the public coffers were unlimited, policymakers are under pressure to limit carbon emissions. And with climate change possibly altering the cycles of droughts, floods and rainfall, burning more energy to get more water might be doubly dire. The challenges get even tougher because the U.S. has finally conceded that the best way to fix its energy and security problems is to break its dependence on imported oil. This new view is reflected in the Energy Independence and Security Act of 2007 and other legislation. Because the transportation sector is a major oil consumer—and a major carbon emitter—it is on the short list of targets for radical change by policymakers, innovators and entrepreneurs. The two most popular choices to replace gasoline appear to be electricity for plug-in vehicles and biofuels. Both paths have merits, but both are more water-intensive than our current system.

Plug-in vehicles are particularly appealing because it is easier to manage the emissions from 1,500 power plants than from hundreds of millions of tailpipes. The electrical infrastructure is already in place. But the power sector swallows water. Compared with producing gasoline for a car, generating electricity for a plug-in hybrid-electric or all-electric vehicle withdraws 10 times as much water and consumes up to three times as much water per mile, according to studies done at the University of Texas at Austin.

Biofuels are worse. Recent analyses indicate that the entire production cycle—from growing irrigated crops on a farm to pumping biofuel into a car—can consume 20 or more times as much water for every mile traveled than the production of gasoline. When scaling up to the 2.7 trillion miles that U.S. passenger vehicles travel a year, water could well become a limiting factor. Municipalities are already fighting over water supplies with the booming biofuels industry: citizens in the Illinois towns of Champaign and Urbana recently opposed a local ethanol plant's petition to withdraw two million gallons a day from the local aquifer to produce 100 million gallons of ethanol a year. Resistance will grow as ranchers' wells run dry.

Whether proponents realize it or not, any plan to switch from gasoline to electricity or biofuels is a strategic decision to switch our dependence from foreign oil to domestic water. Although that choice might seem more appealing than reducing energy consumption, we would be wise to first make sure we have the necessary water.

New Mind-set Needed, Too

Regardless of which energy source the U.S., or the world, might favor, water is ultimately more important than oil because it is more immediately crucial for life, and there is no substitute. And it seems we are approaching an era of peak water—the lack of cheap water. The situation should already be considered a crisis, but the public has not grasped the urgency.

The public has indeed become more open-minded about the risks of peak oil, which vary from the dire (mass starvation and resource wars) to the blasé (markets bring forth new technologies that save the day). Supply shortages and skyrocketing prices have ratcheted up confidence in the claims of the "peakers." Policy levers and market forces are being deployed to find a substitute for affordable oil.

What will it take for us to make the leap for water and, better yet, to consider both issues as one? When the projections for declining oil production are overlaid with the increasing demand for water, the risks become severe. Because water is increasingly energy-intensive to produce, we will likely be relying on fossil fuels for pumping water from deeper aquifers or for moving it through longer pipelines. Any peak in oil production could force a peak in water production. Peak oil might cause some human suffering, but peak water would have more extreme consequences: millions already die every year from limited access to freshwater, and the number could grow by an order of magnitude.

Perhaps signposts will wake our collective minds. Kansas lost a lawsuit to Missouri recently over interstate water use, causing Kansan farmers to reconfigure how they will grow their crops. Rationing should certainly put society on notice, and it is beginning. My hometown of

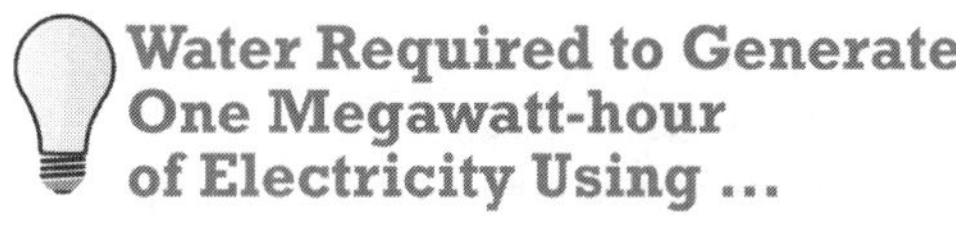

Gas/steam combined cycle 7,400–20,000 gallons

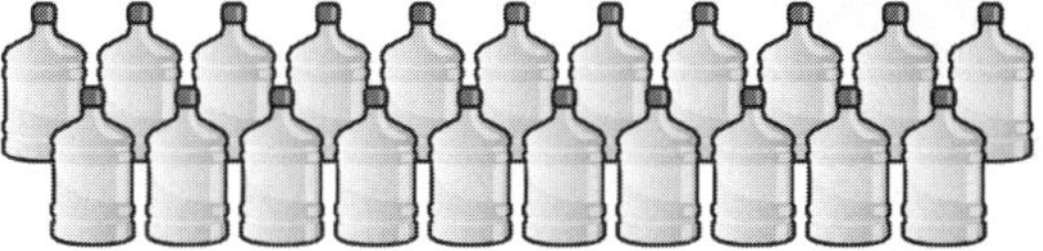

Coal and oil 21,000–50,000

Nuclear 25,000–60,000

Data are for plants that draw and dump water; plants with cooling towers use less
Lucy Reading-Ikkanda for Scientific American Earth 3.0 Magazine. Reprinted with permission.

Austin, Tex., now imposes strict lawn-watering restrictions. California, suffering record low snowfalls, has issued statewide requirements for municipal water conservation and rationing of water that are reminiscent of gasoline controls in the 1970s.

Someday we might look back with a curious nostalgia at the days when profligate homeowners wastefully sprayed their lawns with liquid gold to make the grass grow, just so they could then burn black gold to cut it down on the weekends. Our children and grandchildren will wonder why we were so dumb.

Forcing Solutions

The rising tension between water and energy is troubling, but it also presents an opportunity. We can tackle the problem. The first step is to integrate U.S. policy-making processes. Although the two resources are highly interdependent, energy and water regulators operate separately, with different funding streams, accountability mechanisms, government oversight and legislative committees. Instead of water planners assuming they will have all the energy they need and energy planners assuming they will have all the water they need, we must get them in the same room to make decisions.

Energy Required to Deliver One Million Gallons of Clean Water from ...

Lake or river 1,400 kilowatt-hours

Groundwater 1,800

Wastewater 2,350–3,300

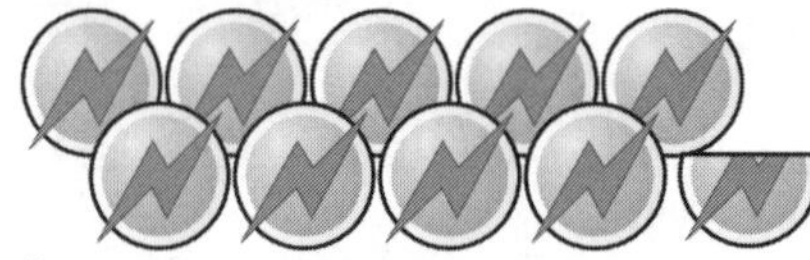

Seawater 9,780–16,500

The federal government has long had a Department of Energy but does not have a Department of Water. The EPA oversees water quality, and the U.S. Geological Survey is responsible for collecting data and monitoring supply, but no federal agency ensures the effective use of water. Congress should create a single overseer, possibly in the Department of the Interior (because of water's environmental importance) or the Department of Commerce (because of its role in the economy). Partly because water has historically been produced locally, most regulatory responsibility has been pushed down to the state and municipal levels. Local policies can readily fail, however, when aquifers, rivers and watersheds span multiple cities or states. What happens when another city takes your water?

The federal government should create a single overseer of water, and Congress should then develop a plan for integrated water and energy policy making.

Federal energy and water agencies should then develop a plan for integrated policy making. For example, when power plant owners seek building permits for a given site they must show that the new installations will meet EPA air-quality standards; similar requirements from a new agency should have to be met for water usage. Energy planners should be in the room when their counterparts debate issuing water permits, to raise concerns about greater electricity demand. When siting and permitting are considered for power plants, water experts should be there to comment on any potentially elevated risk of scarcity. These interactions can take the form of simple collaborations.

The same cross talk should inform climate change legislation. In May, Michael Arceneaux, deputy executive director of the Association of Metropolitan Water Agencies, began a one-person campaign to educate Congress that high-profile bills under consideration, notably those involving carbon cap-and-trade systems, had serious effects on water supplies that were not being considered.

As the U.S. better coordinates policy making, innovative technologies can reduce the amount of freshwater that society extracts and consumes. Agriculture is the place to start. Drip irrigation (instead of spraying water onto fields, allowing much of it to evaporate) requires much less water and delivers it directly to a crop's roots. Farmers in the high plains due east of the Colorado River should switch to drip irrigation for their own good. Nearly all of them tap the Ogallala aquifer, the largest in the U.S., and it is being depleted at a rate of 15 billion cubic yards a year—much more than the rainfall and runoff that reaches it to recharge it. Irrigation now accounts for 94 percent of the groundwater used in the entire region.

Consumption by power plants can be significantly reduced by switching from water cooling to air cooling or at least hybrid air-water cooling. Although air systems are more expensive and are less efficient during operation, they virtually eliminate water withdrawal.

Reusing municipal and industrial wastewater will also save supplies and reduce energy consumed to transport them. Although many people cringe at the thought of "toilet to tap" cycles that convert wastewater to drinking water, astronauts onboard the space station and residents in Singapore readily drink treated wastewater every day with no ill effects. Even if that option remains unpalatable to many consumers, municipalities can certainly use reclaimed water for agriculture and industry and, indeed, for cooling power plants.

Engineering advances can also make water treatment much less energy-intensive. For example, Stonybrook Purification in Stony Brook, N.Y., is developing advanced membranes that more efficiently clean wastewater and desalinate saltwater. The inventor who discovered a way to purify water using minimal energy could become the world's richest person and be forever enshrined.

Intelligent monitors can reduce residential and commercial waste. It is not uncommon to see sprinkler systems spraying lawns at full force in the heat of the afternoon—when evaporation is maximized and irrigation effects are minimized—and in the middle of a rainstorm. Companies such as Accuwater in Austin combine sensors, smart software and Internet connectivity for real-time weather information to better control such systems.

Residents can also spare the energy spent to heat water by widely implementing solar water heating. The simple technology is affordable, reliable, time-tested and pays for itself. But perhaps because the technology doesn't seem cutting-edge and doesn't have much backing from the federal government, its market penetration remains small.

We may have to make social choices, too. Conserving energy and water means we might need to give up our young love affair with corn-based ethanol.

More than anything, however, we need to value water. We must move away from a long-standing expectation that water should be free or cheap. If we think water is important, we should put a realistic price on it. Without that, we send a confusing signal that everyone can be blasé about wasting water.

Once true pricing is in place, the U.S. can perhaps go further and show consumers and regulators how much the price of water raises the price of energy and how much the price of energy raises the price of water. These two metrics will bring us face to face with the dilemma of conserving both resources, prompting effective solutions.

Reading Analytically

1. What is the opening narrative in this piece meant to illustrate? Why does the author choose to begin with this story?
2. What relationship exists between alternative energy sources and our freshwater supply? Which alternative energies seem to be the largest draw upon that supply of water?
3. Is this piece suggesting that because of the strain these energy technologies will place upon the water supply, we ought to abandon them? What action is he suggesting?

Reading Across Disciplinary Communities

1. As an engineer, Webber has a strong disciplinary background in the various technologies he describes. But in this piece, he is writing for a nonexpert audience, readers of *Scientific American*, a popular science magazine. What techniques does he use to transfer that knowledge to this wider audience? Provide at least three examples of his methods.
2. While Webber is an engineer, he is also trained in the humanities. How does that humanities background show through in this piece? In particular, how is Webber writing not only as an engineer, but as a member of the civic community? What solutions does he propose that suggest that membership?

MICHAEL GRUNWALD

The Clean Energy Scam

Just the title of this piece does a good deal to reveal its perspective, calling the movement toward "clean energy," and particularly toward biofuels, a "scam." Its author, Michael Grunwald is an award-winning senior correspondent for Time Magazine *and author of* The Swamp, *a history of the Everglades and attempts to preserve its ecology.*

This story, first published in Time Magazine, *caused a good deal of debate both within and outside of scientific and political circles. Examining one movement within the rush to find sustainable energy sources—the use of biofuels—Grunwald labels these technologies "part of the problem." As you read, consider the ways that Grunwald draws upon the scientific community's findings to make arguments meant to influence public opinion and policy. You might also consider his personal and professional commitments to environmentalism and other forms of social justice.*

From his Cessna a mile above the southern Amazon, John Carter looks down on the destruction of the world's greatest ecological jewel. He watches men converting rain forest into cattle pastures and soybean fields with bulldozers and chains. He sees fires wiping out such gigantic swaths of jungle that scientists now debate the "savannization" of the Amazon. Brazil just announced that deforestation is on track to double this year; Carter, a Texas cowboy with all the subtlety of a chainsaw, says it's going to get worse fast. "It gives me goose bumps," says

Carter, who founded a nonprofit to promote sustainable ranching on the Amazon frontier. "It's like witnessing a rape."

The Amazon was the chic eco-cause of the 1990s, revered as an incomparable storehouse of biodiversity. It's been overshadowed lately by global warming, but the Amazon rain forest happens also to be an incomparable storehouse of carbon, the very carbon that heats up the planet when it's released into the atmosphere. Brazil now ranks fourth in the world in carbon emissions, and most of its emissions come from deforestation. Carter is not a man who gets easily spooked—he led a reconnaissance unit in Desert Storm, and I watched him grab a small anaconda with his bare hands in Brazil—but he can sound downright panicky about the future of the forest. "You can't protect it. There's too much money to be made tearing it down," he says. "Out here on the frontier, you really see the market at work."

This land rush is being accelerated by an unlikely source: biofuels. An explosion in demand for farm-grown fuels has raised global crop prices to record highs, which is spurring a dramatic expansion of Brazilian agriculture, which is invading the Amazon at an increasingly alarming rate.

Propelled by mounting anxieties over soaring oil costs and climate change, biofuels have become the vanguard of the green-tech revolution, the trendy way for politicians and corporations to show they're serious about finding alternative sources of energy and in the process slowing global warming. The U.S. quintupled its production of ethanol—ethyl alcohol, a fuel distilled from plant matter—in the past decade, and Washington has just mandated another fivefold increase in renewable fuels over the next decade. Europe has similarly aggressive biofuel mandates and subsidies, and Brazil's filling stations no longer even offer plain gasoline. Worldwide investment in biofuels rose from $5 billion in 1995 to $38 billion in 2005 and is expected to top $100 billion by 2010, thanks to investors like Richard Branson and George Soros, GE and BP, Ford and Shell, Cargill and the Carlyle Group. Renewable fuels has become one of those motherhood-and-apple-pie catchphrases, as unobjectionable as the troops or the middle class.

But several new studies show the biofuel boom is doing exactly the opposite of what its proponents intended: it's dramatically accelerating global warming, imperiling the planet in the name of saving it. Corn ethanol, always environmentally suspect, turns out to be environmentally disastrous. Even cellulosic ethanol made from switchgrass, which has been promoted by eco-activists and eco-investors as well as by President Bush as the fuel of the future, looks less green than oil-derived gasoline.

Meanwhile, by diverting grain and oilseed crops from dinner plates to fuel tanks, biofuels are jacking up world food prices and endangering the hungry. The grain it takes to fill an SUV tank with ethanol could feed a person for a year. Harvests are being plucked to fuel our cars instead of ourselves. The U.N.'s World Food Program says it needs $500 million in additional funding and supplies, calling the rising costs for food nothing less than a global emergency. Soaring corn prices have sparked tortilla riots in Mexico City, and skyrocketing flour prices have destabilized Pakistan, which wasn't exactly tranquil when flour was affordable.

Biofuels do slightly reduce dependence on imported oil, and the ethanol boom has created rural jobs while enriching some farmers and agribusinesses. But the basic problem with most biofuels is amazingly simple, given that researchers have ignored it until now: using land to grow fuel leads to the destruction of forests, wetlands and grasslands that store enormous amounts of carbon.

Backed by billions in investment capital, this alarming phenomenon is replicating itself around the world. Indonesia has bulldozed and burned so much wilderness to grow palm oil trees for biodiesel that its ranking among the world's top carbon emitters has surged from 21st to third according to a report by Wetlands International. Malaysia is converting forests into palm oil farms so rapidly that it's running out of uncultivated land. But most of the damage created by biofuels will be less direct and less obvious. In Brazil, for instance, only a tiny portion of the Amazon is being torn down to grow the sugarcane that fuels most Brazilian cars. More deforestation results from a chain reaction so vast it's subtle: U.S. farmers are selling one-fifth of their corn to ethanol production, so U.S. soybean farmers are switching to corn, so Brazilian soybean farmers are expanding into cattle pastures, so Brazilian cattlemen are displaced to the Amazon. It's the remorseless economics of commodities markets. "The price of soybeans goes up," laments Sandro Menezes, a biologist with Conservation International in Brazil, "and the forest comes down."

Deforestation accounts for 20% of all current carbon emissions. So unless the world can eliminate emissions from all other sources—cars, power plants, factories, even flatulent cows—it needs to reduce deforestation or risk an environmental catastrophe. That means limiting the expansion of agriculture, a daunting task as the world's population keeps expanding. And saving forests is probably an impossibility so long as vast expanses of cropland are used to grow modest amounts of fuel. The biofuels boom, in short, is one that could haunt the planet for generations—and it's only getting started.

Why the Amazon Is on Fire

This destructive biofuel dynamic is on vivid display in Brazil, where a Rhode Island–size chunk of the Amazon was deforested in the second half of 2007 and even more was degraded by fire. Some scientists believe fires are now altering the local microclimate and could eventually reduce the Amazon to a savanna or even a desert. "It's approaching a tipping point," says ecologist Daniel Nepstad of the Woods Hole Research Center.

I spent a day in the Amazon with the Kamayura tribe, which has been forced by drought to replant its crops five times this year. The tribesmen I met all complained about hacking coughs and stinging eyes from the constant fires and the disappearance of the native plants they use for food, medicine and rituals. The Kamayura had virtually no contact with whites until the 1960s; now their forest is collapsing around them. Their chief, Kotok, a middle-aged man with an easy smile and Three Stooges hairdo that belie his fierce authority, believes that's no coincidence. "We are people of the forest, and the whites are destroying our home," says Kotok, who wore a ceremonial beaded belt, a digital watch, a pair of flip-flops and nothing else. "It's all because of money."

Kotok knows nothing about biofuels. He's more concerned about his tribe's recent tendency to waste its precious diesel-powered generator watching late-night soap operas. But he's right. Deforestation can be a complex process; for example, land reforms enacted by Brazilian President Luiz Inácio Lula da Silva have attracted slash-and-burn squatters to the forest, and "use it or lose it" incentives have spurred some landowners to deforest to avoid redistribution.

The basic problem is that the Amazon is worth more deforested than it is intact. Carter, who fell in love with the region after marrying a Brazilian and taking over her father's ranch, says the rate of deforestation closely tracks commodity prices on the Chicago Board of Trade. "It's just exponential right now because the economics are so good," he says. "Everything tillable or grazeable is gouged out and cleared."

That the destruction is taking place in Brazil is sadly ironic, given that the nation is also an exemplar of the allure of biofuels. Sugar growers here have a greener story to tell than do any other biofuel producers. They provide 45% of Brazil's fuel (all cars in the country are able to run on ethanol) on only 1% of its arable land. They've reduced fertilizer use while increasing yields, and they convert leftover biomass into electricity. Marcos Jank, the head of their trade group, urges me not to lump biofuels together: "Grain is good for bread, not for cars. But sugar is different." Jank expects production to double by 2015 with little effect on the Amazon. "You'll see the expansion on cattle pastures and the Cerrado," he says.

So far, he's right. There isn't much sugar in the Amazon. But my next stop was the Cerrado, south of the Amazon, an ecological jewel in its own right. The Amazon gets the ink, but the Cerrado is the world's most biodiverse savanna, with 10,000 species of plants, nearly half of which are found nowhere else on earth, and more mammals than the African bush. In the natural Cerrado, I saw toucans and macaws, puma tracks and a carnivorous flower that lures flies by smelling like manure. The Cerrado's trees aren't as tall or dense as the Amazon's, so they don't store as much carbon, but the region is three times the size of Texas, so it stores its share.

At least it did, before it was transformed by the march of progress—first into pastures, then into sugarcane and soybean fields. In one field I saw an array of ovens cooking trees into charcoal, spewing Cerrado's carbon into the atmosphere; those ovens used to be ubiquitous, but most of the trees are gone. I had to travel hours through converted Cerrado to see a 96-acre (39 hectare) sliver of intact Cerrado, where a former shopkeeper named Lauro Barbosa had spent his life savings for a nature preserve. "The land prices are going up, up, up," Barbosa told me. "My friends say I'm a fool, and my wife almost divorced me. But I wanted to save something before it's all gone."

The environmental cost of this cropland creep is now becoming apparent. One groundbreaking new study in Science concluded that when this deforestation effect is taken into account, corn ethanol and soy biodiesel produce about twice the emissions of gasoline. Sugarcane ethanol is much cleaner, and biofuels created from waste products that don't gobble up land have real potential, but even cellulosic ethanol increases overall emissions when its plant source is grown on good cropland. "People don't want to believe renewable fuels could be bad," says the lead author, Tim Searchinger, a Princeton scholar and former Environmental Defense attorney. "But when you realize we're tearing down rain forests that store loads of carbon to grow crops that store much less carbon, it becomes obvious."

The growing backlash against biofuels is a product of the law of unintended consequences. It may seem obvious now that when biofuels increase demand for crops, prices will rise and farms will expand into nature. But biofuel technology began on a small scale, and grain surpluses were common. Any ripples were inconsequential. When the scale becomes global, the outcome is entirely different, which is causing cheerleaders for biofuels to recalibrate. "We're all looking at the numbers in an entirely new way," says the Natural Resources Defense Council's Nathanael Greene, whose optimistic "Growing Energy" report in 2004 helped galvanize support for biofuels among green groups.

Several of the most widely cited experts on the environmental benefits of biofuels are warning about the environmental costs now that they've recognized the deforestation effect. "The situation is a lot more challenging than a lot of us thought," says University of California, Berkeley, professor Alexander Farrell, whose 2006 Science article calculating the emissions reductions of various ethanols used to be considered the definitive analysis. The experts haven't given up on biofuels; they're calling for better biofuels that won't trigger massive carbon releases by displacing wildland. Robert Watson, the top scientist at the U.K.'s Department for the Environment, recently warned that mandating more biofuel usage—as the European Union is proposing—would be "insane" if it increases greenhouse gases. But the forces that biofuels have unleashed—political, economic, social—may now be too powerful to constrain.

America the Bio-Foolish

The best place to see this is America's biofuel mecca: Iowa. Last year fewer than 2% of U.S. gas stations offered ethanol, and the country produced 7 billion gal. (26.5 billion L) of biofuel, which cost taxpayers at least $8 billion in subsidies. But on Nov. 6, at a biodiesel plant in Newton, Iowa, Hillary Rodham Clinton unveiled an eye-popping plan that would require all stations to offer ethanol by 2017 while mandating 60 billion gal. (227 billion L) by 2030. "This is the fuel for a much brighter future!" she declared. Barack Obama immediately criticized her—not for proposing such an expansive plan but for failing to support ethanol before she started trolling for votes in Iowa's caucuses.

If biofuels are the new dotcoms, Iowa is Silicon Valley, with 53,000 jobs and $1.8 billion in income dependent on the industry. The state has so many ethanol distilleries under construction that it's poised to become a net importer of corn. That's why biofuel-pandering has become virtually mandatory for presidential contenders. John McCain was the rare candidate who vehemently opposed ethanol as an outrageous agribusiness boondoggle, which is why he skipped Iowa in 2000. But McCain learned his lesson in time for this year's caucuses. By 2006 he was calling ethanol a "vital alternative energy source."

Members of Congress love biofuels too, not only because so many dream about future Iowa caucuses but also because so few want to offend the farm lobby, the most powerful force behind biofuels on Capitol Hill. Ethanol isn't about just Iowa or even the Midwest anymore. Plants are under construction in New York, Georgia, Oregon and Texas, and the ethanol boom's effect on prices has helped lift farm incomes to record levels nationwide.

Someone is paying to support these environmentally questionable industries: you. In December, President Bush signed a bipartisan energy bill that will dramatically increase support to the industry while mandating 36 billion gal. (136 billion L) of biofuel by 2022. This will provide a huge boost to grain markets.

Why is so much money still being poured into such a misguided enterprise? Like the scientists and environmentalists, many politicians genuinely believe biofuels can help decrease global warming. It makes intuitive sense: cars emit carbon no matter what fuel they burn, but the process of growing plants for fuel sucks some of that carbon out of the atmosphere. For years, the big question was whether those reductions from carbon sequestration outweighed the "life cycle" of carbon emissions from farming, converting the crops to fuel and transporting the fuel to market. Researchers eventually concluded that yes, biofuels were greener than gasoline. The improvements were only about 20% for corn ethanol because tractors, petroleum-based fertilizers and distilleries emitted lots of carbon. But the gains approached 90% for more efficient fuels, and advocates were confident that technology would progressively increase benefits.

There was just one flaw in the calculation: the studies all credited fuel crops for sequestering carbon, but no one checked whether the crops would ultimately replace vegetation and soils that sucked up even more carbon. It was as if the science world assumed biofuels would be grown in parking lots. The deforestation of Indonesia has shown that's not the case. It turns out that the carbon lost when wilderness is razed overwhelms the gains from cleaner-burning fuels. A study by University of Minnesota ecologist David Tilman concluded that it will take more than 400 years of biodiesel use to "pay back" the carbon emitted by directly clearing peat lands to grow palm oil; clearing grasslands to grow corn for ethanol has a payback period of 93 years. The result is that biofuels increase demand for crops, which boosts prices, which drives agricultural expansion, which eats forests. Searchinger's study concluded that overall, corn ethanol has a payback period of about 167 years because of the deforestation it triggers.

Not every kernel of corn diverted to fuel will be replaced. Diversions raise food prices, so the poor will eat less. That's the reason a U.N. food expert recently called agrofuels a "crime against humanity." Lester Brown of the Earth Policy Institute says that biofuels pit the 800 million people with cars against the 800 million people with hunger problems. Four years ago, two University of Minnesota researchers predicted the ranks of the hungry would drop to 625 million by 2025; last year, after adjusting for the inflationary effects of biofuels, they increased their prediction to 1.2 billion.

Industry advocates say that as farms increase crop yields, as has happened throughout history, they won't need as much land. They'll use less energy, and they'll use farm waste to generate electricity. To which Searchinger says: Wonderful! But growing fuel is still an inefficient use of good cropland. Strange as it sounds, we're better off growing food and drilling for oil. Sure, we should conserve fuel and buy efficient cars, but we should keep filling them with gas if the alternatives are dirtier.

The lesson behind the math is that on a warming planet, land is an incredibly precious commodity, and every acre used to generate fuel is an acre that can't be used to generate the food needed to feed us or the carbon storage needed to save us. Searchinger acknowledges that biofuels can be a godsend if they don't use arable land. Possible feedstocks include municipal trash, agricultural waste, algae and even carbon dioxide, although none of the technologies are yet economical on a large scale. Tilman even holds out hope for fuel crops—he's been experimenting with Midwestern prairie grasses—as long as they're grown on "degraded lands" that can no longer support food crops or cattle.

Changing the Incentives

That's certainly not what's going on in Brazil. There's a frontier feel to the southern Amazon right now. Gunmen go by names like Lizard and Messiah, and Carter tells harrowing stories about decapitations and castrations and hostages. Brazil has remarkably strict environmental laws—in the Amazon, landholders are permitted to deforest only 20% of their property—but there's not much law enforcement. I left Kotok to see Blairo Maggi, who is not only the soybean king of the world, with nearly half a million acres (200,000 hectares) in the province of Mato Grosso, but also the region's governor. "It's like your Wild West right now," Maggi says. "There's no money for enforcement, so people do what they want."

Maggi has been a leading pioneer on the Brazilian frontier, and it irks him that critics in the U.S.—which cleared its forests and settled its frontier 125 years ago but still provides generous subsidies to its farmers—attack him for doing the same thing except without subsidies and with severe restrictions on deforestation. Imagine Iowa farmers agreeing to keep 80%—or even 20%—of their land in native prairie grass. "You make us sound like bandits," Maggi tells me. "But we want to achieve what you achieved in America. We have the same dreams for our families. Are you afraid of the competition?"

Maggi got in trouble recently for saying he'd rather feed a child than save a tree, but he's come to recognize the importance of the forest. "Now I want to feed a child and save a tree," he says with a grin. But can he do all that and grow fuel for the world as well? "Ah, now you've hit the nail on the head." Maggi says the biofuel boom is making him richer, but it's also making it harder to feed children and save trees. "There are many mouths to feed, and nobody's invented a chip to create protein without growing crops," says his pal Homero Pereira, a congressman who is also the head of Mato Grosso's farm bureau. "If you don't want us to tear down the forest, you better pay us to leave it up!"

Everyone I interviewed in Brazil agreed: the market drives behavior, so without incentives to prevent deforestation, the Amazon is doomed. It's unfair to ask developing countries not to develop natural areas without compensation. Anyway, laws aren't enough. Carter tried confronting ranchers who didn't obey deforestation laws and nearly got killed; now his nonprofit is developing certification programs to reward eco-sensitive ranchers. "People see the forest as junk," he says. "If you want to save it, you better open your pocketbook. Plus, you might not get shot."

The trouble is that even if there were enough financial incentives to keep the Amazon intact, high commodity prices would encourage deforestation elsewhere. And government mandates to increase biofuel production are going to boost commodity prices, which will only attract more investment. Until someone invents that protein chip, it's going to mean the worst of everything: higher food prices, more deforestation and more emissions.

Advocates are always careful to point out that biofuels are only part of the solution to global warming, that the world also needs more energy-efficient lightbulbs and homes and factories and lifestyles. And the world does need all those things. But the world is still going to be fighting an uphill battle until it realizes that right now, biofuels aren't part of the solution at all. They're part of the problem.

Reading Analytically

1. As a journalist, Grunwald knows the importance of beginning with a good "lead"—an opening to his piece that will hook the audience into reading on. What is the effect of his opening narrative?
2. The title and thesis of this article label the use of biofuels as a "scam." Name three pieces of evidence that Grunwald presents to support that charge.
3. If, as Grunwald contends, biofuels are a "scam," what is driving their use? What does Grunwald suggest is the source of this movement? Are his views supported by other writers in this chapter and in other articles you might find on the topic?

Reading Across Disciplinary Communities

1. Grunwald, a journalist, is also clearly deeply interested in environmentalism and in social justice; in fact, many of his publications (including an award-winning piece on the aftermath of Hurricane Katrina) draw upon concepts from the field of ethics. What are the underlying ethical assumptions he makes that cause him to judge this movement in energy policy a "scam?"
2. Scan the various experts that Grunwald cites in this journalistic piece. What disciplines do they represent? If you wanted to check on the credibility of this argument, who might you interview? What disciplinary experts might you turn to that may not be adequately represented here? You might also do a search of the Internet to read some of the discussion that this piece has bred on blogs and in other articles and letters to the editor.

C. FORD RUNGE AND BENJAMIN SENAUER

How Biofuels Could Starve the Poor

This essay, originally published in Foreign Affairs, *argues that the biofuel movement has not been driven by market forces or science, but instead by "politics and the interests of a few large companies." This essay's argument is based in the ethics of the biofuel movement, linking the growth of biofuels to an increasing food shortage in developing nations. As you read, you might consider one of the more difficult facets of ethical decision-making: deciding between courses of action that each have some negative consequences. In this case, how is one to balance the need for new energy sources with the need to consider the good of other, developing nations?*

C. Ford Runge is Distinguished McKnight University Professor of Applied Economics and Law at the University of Minnesota. Benjamin Senauer is Professor of Applied Economics at the University of Minnesota. The place of original publication, Foreign Affairs *is devoted to issues of international relations and is published by the Council on Foreign Relations, a private sector group with the mission "of promoting understanding of foreign policy and America's role in the world."*

The Ethanol Bubble

In 1974, as the United States was reeling from the oil embargo imposed by the Organization of Petroleum Exporting Countries, Congress took the first of many legislative steps to promote ethanol made from corn as an alternative fuel. On April 18, 1977, amid mounting calls for energy independence, President Jimmy Carter donned his cardigan sweater and appeared on television to tell Americans that balancing energy demands with available domestic resources would be an effort the "moral equivalent of war." The gradual phase out of lead in the 1970s and 1980s provided an additional boost to the fledgling ethanol industry. (Lead, a toxic substance, is a performance enhancer when added to gasoline, and it was partly replaced by ethanol.) A series of tax breaks and subsidies also helped. In spite of these measures, with each passing year the United States became more dependent on imported petroleum, and ethanol remained marginal at best.

The opening sets the current argument in an historical context, providing the reader with important background information.

The paragraph ends by stating one important element of the thesis—ethanol hasn't solved our dependence on foreign oil.

This transition helps move the reader from the survey of past actions to the present situation.

Now, thanks to a combination of high oil prices and even more generous government subsidies, corn-based ethanol has become the rage. There were 110 ethanol refineries in operation in the United States at the end of 2006, according to the Renewable Fuels Association. Many were being expanded, and another 73 were under construction. When these projects are completed, by the end of 2008, the United States' ethanol production capacity will reach an estimated 11.4 billion gallons per year. In his latest State of the Union address, President George W. Bush called on the country to produce 35 billion gallons of renewable fuel a year by 2017, nearly five times the level currently mandated.

> The use of quantitative data supports the claim that "ethanol has become the rage."

The push for ethanol and other biofuels has spawned an industry that depends on billions of dollars of taxpayer subsidies, and not only in the United States. In 2005, global ethanol production was 9.66 billion gallons, of which Brazil produced 45.2 percent (from sugar cane) and the United States 44.5 percent (from corn). Global production of biodiesel (most of it in Europe), made from oilseeds, was almost one billion gallons.

> This paragraph expands the previous one about U.S. production, demonstrating how ethanol production has spread to other countries.

The industry's growth has meant that a larger and larger share of corn production is being used to feed the huge mills that produce ethanol. According to some estimates, ethanol plants will burn up to half of U.S. domestic corn supplies within a few years. Ethanol demand will bring 2007 inventories of corn to their lowest levels since 1995 (a drought year), even though 2006 yielded the third-largest corn crop on record. Iowa may soon become a net corn importer.

> Note how using the words "feed the huge mills" contrasts with the title—starving the poor.

The enormous volume of corn required by the ethanol industry is sending shock waves through the food system. (The United States accounts for some 40 percent of the world's total corn production and over half of all corn exports.) In March 2007, corn futures rose to over $4.38 a bushel, the highest level in ten years. Wheat and rice prices have also surged to decade highs, because even as those grains are increasingly being used as substitutes for corn, farmers are planting more acres with corn and fewer acres with other crops.

> This paragraph transitions the reader from the causes to the effects of ethanol production—and toward the real topic of the essay: how biofuel production is impacting food production and prices.

This might sound like nirvana to corn producers, but it is hardly that for consumers, especially in poor developing countries, who will be hit with a double shock if both food prices and oil prices stay high. The World Bank has estimated that in 2001, 2.7 billion people in the world were living on the equivalent of less than $2 a day; to them, even marginal increases in the cost of staple grains could be devastating. Filling the 25-gallon tank of an SUV with pure ethanol requires over

450 pounds of corn—which contains enough calories to feed one person for a year. By putting pressure on global supplies of edible crops, the surge in ethanol production will translate into higher prices for both processed and staple foods around the world. Biofuels have tied oil and food prices together in ways that could profoundly upset the relationships between food producers, consumers, and nations in the years ahead, with potentially devastating implications for both global poverty and food security.

Notice how this sentence contrasts the two uses of corn: filling an SUV once or feeding a person for a year—suggesting the key ethical dilemma being investigated.

Notice how this main thesis—the direct statement of the article's point—is built from the previous paragraphs' information. A thesis is not always presented at the very beginning of an essay. Why is it delayed here?

The Oil and Biofuel Economy

In the United States and other large economies, the ethanol industry is artificially buoyed by government subsidies, minimum production levels, and tax credits. High oil prices over the past few years have made ethanol naturally competitive, but the U.S. government continues to heavily subsidize corn farmers and ethanol producers. Direct corn subsidies equaled $8.9 billion in 2005. Although these payments will fall in 2006 and 2007 because of high corn prices, they may soon be dwarfed by the panoply of tax credits, grants, and government loans included in energy legislation passed in 2005 and in a pending farm bill designed to support ethanol producers. The federal government already grants ethanol blenders a tax allowance of 51 cents per gallon of ethanol they make, and many states pay out additional subsidies.

The discussion of government subsidies suggests that the production of biofuels is being directly encouraged by government, not by supply and demand.

Consumption of ethanol in the United States was expected to reach over 6 billion gallons in 2006. (Consumption of biodiesel was expected to be about 250 million gallons.) In 2005, the U.S. government mandated the use of 7.5 billion gallons of biofuels per year by 2012; in early 2007, 37 governors proposed raising that figure to 12 billion gallons by 2010; and last January, President Bush raised it further, to 35 billion gallons by 2017. Six billion gallons of ethanol are needed every year to replace the fuel additive known as MTBE, which is being phased out due to its polluting effects on ground water.

The European Commission is using legislative measures and directives to promote biodiesel, produced mainly in Europe, made from rapeseeds and sunflower seeds. In 2005, the European Union produced

890 million gallons of biodiesel, over 80 percent of the world's total. The EU's Common Agricultural Policy also promotes the production of ethanol from a combination of sugar beets and wheat with direct and indirect subsidies. Brussels aims to have 5.75 percent of motor fuel consumed in the European Union come from biofuels by 2010 and 10 percent by 2020.

Note how the author once again demonstrates how this is a global, not just an American, issue.

Brazil, which currently produces approximately the same amount of ethanol as the United States, derives almost all of it from sugar cane. Like the United States, Brazil began its quest for alternative energy in the mid-1970s. The government has offered incentives, set technical standards, and invested in supporting technologies and market promotion. It has mandated that all diesel contain two percent biodiesel by 2008 and five percent biodiesel by 2013. It has also required that the auto industry produce engines that can use biofuels and has developed wide-ranging industrial and land-use strategies to promote them. Other countries are also jumping on the biofuel bandwagon. In Southeast Asia, vast areas of tropical forest are being cleared and burned to plant oil palms destined for conversion to biodiesel.

Words like *required* once again reinforce the idea that this move toward biofuels is being driven by government regulation—identifying a key cause of the problem being argued.

This trend has strong momentum. Despite a recent decline, many experts expect the price of crude oil to remain high in the long term. Demand for petroleum continues to increase faster than supplies, and new sources of oil are often expensive to exploit or located in politically risky areas. According to the U.S. Energy Information Administration's latest projections, global energy consumption will rise by 71 percent between 2003 and 2030, with demand from developing countries, notably China and India, surpassing that from members of the Organization for Economic Cooperation and Development by 2015. The result will be sustained upward pressure on oil prices, which will allow ethanol and biodiesel producers to pay much higher premiums for corn and oilseeds than was conceivable just a few years ago. The higher oil prices go, the higher ethanol prices can go while remaining competitive—and the more ethanol producers can pay for corn. If oil reaches $80 per barrel, ethanol producers could afford to pay well over $5 per bushel for corn.

This short, pithy sentence shows the extent of the problem in a strong, declarative way.

Notice how dependent this argument is on quantitative data—numbers, statistics, projections, etc.—for support. What kind of authority do such numbers hold? Why is it important for consumers to have "statistical literacy" as they read such arguments (as is contended by Richard L. Scheaffer in Chapter 1)?

Notice how this transition once again moves from causes to potential—and negative—effects.

With the price of raw materials at such highs, the biofuel craze would place significant stress on other parts of the agricultural sector. In fact, it already does. In the United States, the growth of the biofuel industry has triggered increases not only in the prices of corn, oilseeds, and other grains but also in the prices of seemingly unrelated crops and products. The use of land to grow corn to feed the ethanol maw is reducing the acreage devoted to other crops. Food processors who use crops such as peas and sweet corn have been forced to pay higher prices to keep their supplies secure—costs that will eventually be passed on to consumers. Rising feed prices are also hitting the livestock and poultry industries. According to Vernon Eidman, a professor emeritus of agribusiness management at the University of Minnesota, higher feed costs have caused returns to fall sharply, especially in the poultry and swine sectors. If returns continue to drop, production will decline, and the prices for chicken, turkey, pork, milk, and eggs will rise. A number of Iowa's pork producers could go out of business in the next few years as they are forced to compete with ethanol plants for corn supplies.

This sentence uses an "If/then" structure, creating a logic that suggests *if* one condition continues, *then* there is likely going to be negative consequences. This kind of structure is important for speculating on possible future effects.

Proponents of corn-based ethanol argue that acreage and yields can be increased to satisfy the rising demand for ethanol. But U.S. corn yields have been rising by a little less than two percent annually over the last ten years, and even a doubling of those gains could not meet current demand. As more acres are planted with corn, land will have to be pulled from other crops or environmentally fragile areas, such as those protected by the Department of Agriculture's Conservation Reserve Program.

In addition to these fundamental forces, speculative pressures have created what might be called a "biofuel mania": prices are rising because many buyers think they will. Hedge funds are making huge bets on corn and the bull market unleashed by ethanol. The biofuel mania is commandeering grain stocks with a disregard for the obvious consequences. It seems to unite powerful forces, including motorists' enthusiasm for large, fuel-inefficient vehicles and guilt over the ecological consequences of petroleum-based fuels. But even as ethanol has created opportunities for huge profits for agribusiness,

Calling this a "biofuel mania" suggests that the trend is being driven by unreasonable, emotional attachment to this solution to energy needs, rather than the logical argument he is presenting with the quantitative data.

The word *commandeering,* which means "to take arbitrary or forcible possession of" suggests that foodstuffs are being diverted from their proper use.

speculators, and some farmers, it has upset the traditional flows of commodities and the patterns of trade and consumption both inside and outside of the agricultural sector.

Once again, the suggestion is that government action and biofuel "mania" has caused the natural supply/demand structure to be subverted.

Note how words like *craze* and *mania* continue to emphasize the irrational nature of the use of biofuels.

This craze will create a different problem if oil prices decline because of, say, a slowdown in the global economy. With oil at $30 a barrel, producing ethanol would no longer be profitable unless corn sold for less than $2 a bushel, and that would spell a return to the bad old days of low prices for U.S. farmers. Undercapitalized ethanol plants would be at risk, and farmer-owned cooperatives would be especially vulnerable. Calls for subsidies, mandates, and tax breaks would become even more shrill than they are now: there would be clamoring for a massive bailout of an overinvested industry. At that point, the major investments that have been made in biofuels would start to look like a failed gamble. On the other hand, if oil prices hover around $55–$60, ethanol producers could pay from $3.65 to $4.54 for a bushel of corn and manage to make a normal 12 percent profit.

Whatever happens in the oil market, the drive for energy independence, which has been the basic justification for huge investments in and subsidies for ethanol production, has already made the industry dependent on high oil prices.

Cornucopia

One root of the problem is that the biofuel industry has long been dominated not by market forces but by politics and the interests of a few large companies. Corn has become the prime raw material even though biofuels could be made efficiently from a variety of other sources, such as grasses and wood chips, if the government funded the necessary research and development. But in the United States, at least, corn and soybeans have been used as primary inputs for many years thanks in large part to the lobbying efforts of corn and soybean growers and Archer Daniels Midland Company (ADM), the biggest ethanol producer in the U.S. market.

Note how this transition returns the argument to further "causes" of the problem—stressing once again the negative effects of government regulation over "market forces."

Since the late 1960s, ADM positioned itself as the "supermarket to the world" and aimed to create value from bulk commodities by transforming them into processed products that command heftier prices. In the 1970s, ADM started making ethanol and other products resulting from the wet-milling of corn, such as high fructose corn syrup. It quickly grew from a minor player in the feed market to a global powerhouse. By 1980, ADM's ethanol production had reached 175 million gallons per year, and high fructose corn syrup had become a ubiquitous sweetening agent in processed foods. In 2006, ADM was the largest producer of ethanol in the United States: it made more than 1.07 billion gallons, over four times more than its nearest rival, VeraSun Energy. In early 2006, it announced plans to increase its capital investment in ethanol from $700 million to $1.2 billion in 2008 and increase production by 47 percent, or close to 500 million gallons, by 2009.

ADM owes much of its growth to political connections, especially to key legislators who can earmark special subsidies for its products. Vice President Hubert Humphrey advanced many such measures when he served as a senator from Minnesota. Senator Bob Dole (R-Kans.) advocated tirelessly for the company during his long career. As the conservative critic James Bovard noted over a decade ago, nearly half of ADM's profits have come from products that the U.S. government has either subsidized or protected.

This paragraph continues the argument of the previous one, suggesting the "political connections" of ADM, not real need, is causing this trend.

Partly as a result of such government support, ethanol (and to a lesser extent biodiesel) is now a major fixture of the United States' agricultural and energy sectors. In addition to the federal government's 51-cents-per-gallon tax credit for ethanol, smaller producers get a 10-cents-per-gallon tax reduction on the first 15 million gallons they produce. There is also the "renewable fuel standard," a mandatory level of nonfossil fuel to be used in motor vehicles, which has set off a political bidding war. Despite already high government subsidies, Congress is considering lavishing more money on biofuels. Legislation related to the 2007 farm bill introduced by Representative Ron Kind (D-Wis.) calls for raising loan guarantees for ethanol producers from $200 million to $2 billion. Advocates of corn-based ethanol have rationalized subsidies by pointing out that greater ethanol demand pushes up corn prices and brings down subsidies to corn growers.

Notice how the author continually comes back to "government support" as the key problem.

The word *rationalized* has negative consequences, suggesting that arguments for biofuels are not sound, but explained in ways that try to make positives out of negatives.

The ethanol industry has also become a theater of protectionism in U.S. trade policy. Unlike oil imports, which come into the country duty-free, most ethanol currently imported into the United States carries a 54-cents-per-gallon tariff, partly because cheaper ethanol from countries such as Brazil threatens U.S. producers. (Brazilian sugar cane can be converted to ethanol more efficiently than can U.S. corn.) The Caribbean Basin Initiative could undermine this protection: Brazilian ethanol can already be shipped duty-free to CBI countries, such as Costa Rica, El Salvador, or Jamaica, and the agreement allows it to go duty-free from there to the United States. But ethanol supporters in Congress are pushing for additional legislation to limit those imports. Such government measures shield the industry from competition despite the damaging repercussions for consumers.

This final sentence makes one of the key exigencies of the argument—the reason why the argument is timely: according to the author, we need to avoid further "protectionism" of this industry.

Starving the Hungry

This section title makes an emotional argument.

This section now introduces another, "even more devastating" effect of encouraging biofuel production.

Biofuels may have even more devastating effects in the rest of the world, especially on the prices of basic foods. If oil prices remain high—which is likely—the people most vulnerable to the price hikes brought on by the biofuel boom will be those in countries that both suffer food deficits and import petroleum. The risk extends to a large part of the developing world: in 2005, according to the UN Food and Agriculture Organization, most of the 82 low-income countries with food deficits were also net oil importers.

Even major oil exporters that use their petrodollars to purchase food imports, such as Mexico, cannot escape the consequences of the hikes in food prices. In late 2006, the price of tortilla flour in Mexico, which gets 80 percent of its corn imports from the United States, doubled thanks partly to a rise in U.S. corn prices from $2.80 to $4.20 a bushel over the previous several months. (Prices rose even though tortillas are made mainly from Mexican-grown white corn because industrial users of the imported yellow corn, which is used for animal feed and processed foods, started buying the cheaper white variety.) The price surge was exacerbated by speculation and hoarding. With about half of Mexico's 107 million people living in poverty and relying on tortillas as a main source of calories, the public outcry was fierce. In January 2007, Mexico's new president, Felipe Calderón, was forced to cap the prices of corn products.

Note how the author again presents key figures to support the new claims.

The International Food Policy Research Institute, in Washington, D.C., has produced sobering estimates of the potential global impact of the rising demand for biofuels. Mark Rosegrant, an IFPRI division director, and his colleagues project that given continued high oil prices, the rapid increase in global biofuel production will push global corn prices

The author bolsters his own ethos by citing other experts.

up by 20 percent by 2010 and 41 percent by 2020. The prices of oilseeds, including soybeans, rapeseeds, and sunflower seeds, are projected to rise by 26 percent by 2010 and 76 percent by 2020, and wheat prices by 11 percent by 2010 and 30 percent by 2020. In the poorest parts of sub-Saharan Africa, Asia, and Latin America, where cassava is a staple, its price is expected to increase by 33 percent by 2010 and 135 percent by 2020. The projected price increases may be mitigated if crop yields increase substantially or ethanol production based on other raw materials (such as trees and grasses) becomes commercially viable. But unless biofuel policies change significantly, neither development is likely.

Notice how the transition moves the reader to a new, but related topic, while also reminding the reader of the overall point of this section.

The production of cassava-based ethanol may pose an especially grave threat to the food security of the world's poor. Cassava, a tropical potato-like tuber also known as manioc, provides one-third of the caloric needs of the population in sub-Saharan Africa and is the primary staple for over 200 million of Africa's poorest people. In many tropical countries, it is the food people turn to when they cannot afford anything else. It also serves as an important reserve when other crops fail because it can grow in poor soils and dry conditions and can be left in the ground to be harvested as needed.

Thanks to its high-starch content, cassava is also an excellent source of ethanol. As the technology for converting it to fuel improves, many countries—including China, Nigeria, and Thailand—are considering using more of the crop to that end. If peasant farmers in developing countries could become suppliers for the emerging industry, they would benefit from the increased income. But the history of industrial demand for agricultural crops in these countries suggests that large producers will be the main beneficiaries. The likely result of a boom in cassava-based ethanol production is that an increasing number of poor people will struggle even more to feed themselves.

These three sentences work together to create an argument: "If" one thing happens it would be positive; "But" that is not likely; so, the "more likely result" is more poverty.

Participants in the 1996 World Food Summit set out to cut the number of chronically hungry people in the world—people who do not eat enough calories regularly to be healthy and active—from 823 million in 1990 to about 400 million by 2015. The Millennium Development Goals established by the United Nations in 2000 vowed to halve the proportion of the world's chronically underfed population from 16 percent in 1990 to eight percent in 2015. Realistically, however, resorting to biofuels is likely to exacerbate world hunger. Several studies by economists at the World Bank and elsewhere suggest that caloric consumption among the world's poor declines by about half of one percent whenever the average prices of all major food staples increase by one percent. When one staple becomes more expensive, people try to replace it with a cheaper one, but if the prices of nearly all staples go up, they are left with no alternative.

Notice the use of the first-person plural to state the findings of the author and his own associates—and differentiate his own primary research from the secondary research that he cites.

In a study of global food security we conducted in 2003, we projected that given the rates of economic and population growth, the number of hungry people throughout the world would decline by 23 percent, to about 625 million, by 2025, so long as agricultural productivity improved enough to keep the relative price of food constant. But if, all other things being equal, the prices of staple foods increased because of demand for biofuels, as the IFPRI projections suggest they will, the number of food-insecure people in the world would rise by over 16 million for every percentage increase in the real prices of staple foods. That means that 1.2 billion people could be chronically hungry by 2025—600 million more than previously predicted.

The world's poorest people already spend 50 to 80 percent of their total household income on food. For the many among them who are landless laborers or rural subsistence farmers, large increases in the prices of staple foods will mean malnutrition and hunger. Some of them will tumble over the edge of subsistence into outright starvation, and many more will die from a multitude of hunger-related diseases.

The section ends with a strong emotional appeal.

The Grass Is Greener

And for what? Limited environmental benefits at best. Although it is important to think of ways to develop renewable energy, one should also carefully examine the eager claims that biofuels are "green." Ethanol and biodiesel are often viewed as environmentally friendly because they are plant-based rather than petroleum-based. In fact, even if the entire corn crop in the United States were used to make ethanol, that fuel would replace only 12 percent of current U.S. gasoline use. Thinking of ethanol as a green alternative to fossil fuels reinforces the chimera of energy independence and of decoupling the interests of the United States from an increasingly troubled Middle East.

This sentence fragment is used to add punch to the opening of the concluding section—and force the reader to think about whether the negative results are worth the current course of action.

This question draws the reader in to the examination of a key question of the article.

Should corn and soybeans be used as fuel crops at all? Soybeans and especially corn are row crops that contribute to soil erosion and water pollution and require large amounts of fertilizer, pesticides, and fuel to grow, harvest, and dry. They are the major cause of nitrogen runoff—the harmful leakage of nitrogen from fields when it rains—of the type that has created the so-called dead zone in the Gulf of Mexico, an ocean area the size of New Jersey that has so little oxygen it can barely support life. In the United States, corn and soybeans are typically planted in rotation, because soybeans add nitrogen to the soil, which corn needs to grow. But as corn increasingly displaces soybeans as a main source of ethanol, it will be cropped continuously, which will require major increases in nitrogen fertilizer and aggravate the nitrogen runoff problem.

Notice the shift to another argument, this one based on environmental concerns.

Nor is corn-based ethanol very fuel efficient. Debates over the "net energy balance" of biofuels and gasoline—the ratio between the energy they produce and the energy needed to produce them—have raged for decades. For now, corn-based ethanol appears to be favored over gasoline, and biodiesel over petroleum diesel—but not by much. Scientists at the Argonne National Laboratory and the National Renewable Energy Laboratory have calculated that the net energy ratio of gasoline is 0.81, a result that implies an input larger than the output. Corn-based ethanol has a ratio that ranges between 1.25 and 1.35, which is better than breaking even. Petroleum diesel has an energy ratio of 0.83, compared with that of biodiesel made from soybean oil, which ranges from 1.93 to 3.21. (Biodiesel produced from other fats and oils, such as restaurant grease, may be more energy efficient.)

Once again, the author uses a short, pithy sentence to make his case strongly and directly. The unusual use of *Nor* (which is usually a coordinating conjunction) also connects his new argument to the one in the previous paragraph.

Similar results emerge when biofuels are compared with gasoline using other indices of environmental impact, such as greenhouse gas emissions. The full cycle of the production and use of corn-based ethanol releases less greenhouse gases than does that of gasoline, but only by 12 to 26 percent. The production and use of biodiesel emits 41 to 78 percent less such gases than do the production and use of petroleum-based diesel fuels.

This transition shows the connection of the previous paragraph's discussion of effects to those about to be introduced.

Another point of comparison is greenhouse gas emissions per mile driven, which takes account of relative fuel efficiency. Using gasoline blends with 10 percent corn-based ethanol instead of pure gasoline lowers emissions by 2 percent. If the blend is 85 percent ethanol (which only flexible-fuel vehicles can run on), greenhouse gas emissions fall further: by 23 percent if the ethanol is corn-based and by 64 percent if it is cellulose-based. Likewise, diesel containing 2 percent biodiesel emits 1.6 percent less greenhouse gases than does petroleum diesel, whereas blends with 20 percent biodiesel emit 16 percent less, and pure biodiesel (also for use only in special vehicles) emits 78 percent less. On the other hand, biodiesel can increase emissions of nitrogen oxide, which contributes to air pollution. In short, the "green" virtues of ethanol and biodiesel are modest when these fuels are made from corn and soybeans, which are energy-intensive, highly polluting row crops.

The benefits of biofuels are greater when plants other than corn or oils from sources other than soybeans are used. Ethanol made entirely from cellulose (which is found in trees, grasses, and other plants) has an energy ratio between 5 and 6 and emits 82 to 85 percent less greenhouse gases than does gasoline. As corn grows scarcer and more expensive, many are betting that the ethanol industry will increasingly turn to grasses, trees, and residues from field crops, such as wheat and rice straw and cornstalks. Grasses and trees can be grown on land poorly suited to food crops or in climates hostile to corn and soybeans. Recent breakthroughs in enzyme and gasification technologies have made it easier to break down cellulose in woody plants and straw. Field experiments suggest that grassland perennials could become a promising source of biofuel in the future.

For now, however, the costs of harvesting, transporting, and converting such plant matters are high, which means that cellulose-based ethanol is not yet commercially viable when compared with the economies of scale of current corn-based production. One ethanol-plant manager in the Midwest has calculated that fueling an ethanol plant with switchgrass, a much-discussed alternative, would require delivering a semitrailer truckload of the grass every six minutes, 24 hours a day. The logistical difficulties and the costs of converting cellulose into fuel, combined with the subsidies and politics currently favoring the use of corn and soybeans, make it unrealistic to expect cellulose-based ethanol to become a solution within the next decade. Until it is, relying more on sugar cane to produce ethanol in tropical countries would be more efficient than using corn and would not involve using a staple food.

Notice the logic of the way that these two paragraphs are connected: It is possible that biofuels could be viable in the future, but they are not now.

This transition reinforces the "not yet" argument that is important to this part of the article.

The future can be brighter if the right steps are taken now. Limiting U.S. dependence on fossil fuels requires a comprehensive energy-conservation program. Rather than promoting more mandates, tax breaks, and subsidies for biofuels, the U.S. government should make a major commitment to substantially increasing energy efficiency in vehicles, homes, and factories; promoting alternative sources of energy, such as solar and wind power; and investing in research to improve agricultural productivity and raise the efficiency of fuels derived from cellulose. Washington's fixation on corn-based ethanol has distorted the national agenda and diverted its attention from developing a broad and balanced strategy. In March, the U.S. Energy Department announced that it would invest up to $385 million in six biorefineries designed to convert cellulose into ethanol. That is a promising step in the right direction.

After all the negative arguments, the author leaves the reader with a sense that things can be better if we act now. This keeps the article from being too overwhelmingly negative, and calls the reader to action.

Reading Analytically

1. While this essay, like Grunwald's, points out potential problems with the movement toward the use of biofuels, it has a very different focus. Compare the two essays, and identify the differences in their concerns as well as areas of agreement. You might also consider whether the technologies of biogas, discussed by Balat and Balat, offer a potential solution.
2. According to the authors, the biofuels movement is not truly being driven by "market needs," but by other forces. What are those other forces that are identified here?
3. Does this piece go on to propose a solution to the problem? If so, what is the potential solution presented here?

Reading Across Disciplinary Communities

1. One question you might ask is why such an article would be written by two professors of applied economics? What is their interest in this topic? What disciplinary expertise in the field of economics is demonstrated here? How is their economic perspective different from that of Geoffrey Carr's piece, written for *The Economist?*
2. How do these economists rely upon quantitative and statistical information in this piece? List at least three instances in which the support for claims is found in numbers.

Writing across Disciplines
Interdisciplinary Writing Opportunities

1. This chapter's readings are based upon the contention that fossil fuels such as oil are on their way out as the primary source of our energy.

However, many citizens and political leaders believe that we ought not rush to that conclusion, and should pursue methods of research and development that allow us to extend our oil-based economies. In order to assess this set of arguments, do some research to see if this underlying assumption—that we are rapidly running out of oil—is viable and exigent. What is the future of oil-based energy, based upon the best scientific opinion? What business policies suggest that we are moving in that direction, and which suggest that oil is still quite viable? What types of discoveries and research in engineering and other applied sciences suggest that we have not yet given up on oil?

2. Much of the debate about recent wars and conflicts in the Middle East surround that region's importance in supplying oil. Consider whether the pursuit of alternative energies might reduce the need for, and incidence of, armed conflict. Research the role of oil-based economies upon recent wars and foreign policies, and write an essay that discusses the topic of alternative energy in the context of alleviating world conflict. You might also consider whether protecting our oil-based economy is indeed a viable reason to go to war, as has been argued by many political and public policy experts. To do so, review some of the readings in Chapter Five.
3. After surveying the various alternative energies discussed in this chapter, focus upon those discoveries that you find most promising. After doing some further research on the science, engineering, and business possibilities of one of those discoveries, write an essay that supports more research and development for that particular path. Be sure to take into account both the science that demonstrates the importance of this particular line of development as well as its potential for economic support by businesses. You should also consider the ethical implications raised by writers in this chapter.
4. As is clear from the multidisciplinary readings in this chapter, questions about the future of energy are of great concern not only for those in the natural and applied sciences, but for those in the social sciences and humanities as well. Drawing upon your own field of study, develop a set of key questions that members of your disciplinary or professional community must ask with regard to the future of alternative energies. Using the methods of that field, write an essay that argues for the importance of this topic for those in your own field of study.
5. As is illustrated by the excerpt from "The Pickens Plan" for energy independence and by campaigns like British Petroleum's new meaning for BP (formerly meaning "British Petroleum," now being marketed as "Beyond Petroleum"), those in business fields are busily engaged not only in developing new markets, but in public relations campaigns to forward their new business plans. Set up your own public relations

campaign to argue for a particular type of alternative energy that you find to be most viable. You can construct this campaign using an editorial, a Web site, blog, or wiki (including visuals), a video or audio presentation, a brochure, or a PowerPoint/oral presentation; you might also create a multimedia campaign using a combination of those various modes of composing.

credits

American Society of Human Genetics, "ASHG Statement on Direct-to-Consumer Genetic Testing in the United States" from *The American Journal of Human Genetics* 81.3, Sept. 2007, pages 635–37.

John W. Ayers, "Changing Sides: 9/11 and the American Muslim Voter" from *Review of Religious Research* 2007, Vol. 49; Number 2. Reprinted with permission of Religious Research Association.

Berenice Baker, "Power Play" from *The Engineer*, June 2–15, 2008. Copyright © 2009 Centaur Media Plc. All rights reserved. Reprinted with permission.

M. Balat and H. Balat, "Biogas as a Renewable Energy Source—A Review" from *Energy Sources, Part A: Recovery, Utilization, and Environmental Effects*, 31:14 published by Taylor & Francis. Reprinted by permission of Taylor & Francis Group, http://www.informaworld.com

Rebecca M. Callahan, Chandra Muller, and Kathryn S. Schiller, "Preparing for Citizenship: "Immigrant High School Students' Curriculum and Socialization" from *Theory and Research in Social Education*, v36 n2, pages 6–31, Spring 2008.

Arthur Caplan, "Mind Reading" from *The American Prospect*, Volume 19, Number 7: June 23, 2008. http://www.prospect.org. All right reserved. Reprinted with permission.

Geoffrey Carr, "The Power and the Glory" from *The Economist*, June 19, 2008. Copyright © The Economist Newspaper Limited, London, 2008. Reprinted with permission.

Elizabeth Daley, "Expanding the Concept of Literacy" from a paper delivered at the 2002 Aspen Symposium of the Forum for the Future of Higher Education. Reprinted with permission.

Michael Grunwald, "The Clean Energy Scam" from *Time Magazine*, March 27, 2008. Copyright TIME INC. Reprinted by permission. TIME is a registered trademark of Time Inc. All rights reserved.

Sheldon Hackney, "The Elements of American Identity" from *One America Indivisible*. Copyright © 1997 by The National Endowment for the Humanities.

Gordon H. Hanson, "The Economic Logic of Illegal Immigration." Copyright © 2007 by the Council on Foreign Relations Press. Reprinted with permission.

Pertti Joenniemi, "Toward the End of War? Peeking through the Gap" from *Alternatives* 33 (2008). Reprinted by permission of Lynne Rienner Publishers.

Jonathan Kahn, "Race in a Bottle" from *Scientific American*, August, 2007. Reprinted with permission. Copyright © 2007 by Scientific American, Inc. All rights reserved.

Tim Kane and Kirk A. Johnson, "The Real Problem with Immigration . . . and the Solution" from *Backgrounder*, No. 1913, March 1, 2006. The Heritage Foundation. Reprinted with permission.

Philip Kitcher, "Does 'Race' Have a Future?" from *Philosophy and Public Affairs*, 35.4, Fall 2007.

Michael T. Klare, "Beyond the Age of Petroleum" from *The Nation*, October 25, 2007. Reprinted with permission from the October 25, 2007 Issue of *The Nation*. For subscription information, call 1-800-333-8536. Portions of each week's Nation magazine can be accessed at http://www.thenation.com.

Loretta M. Kopelman, "Using the Best Interests Standard to Decide Whether to Test Children for Untreatable, Late-Onset Genetic Diseases" from *Journal of Medicine and Philosophy* 32, 2007, pages 375–394. Used with permission.

Eric Lane, "America 101: How We Let Civic Education Slide" from *Democracy: A Journal of Ideas*, Vol. 10, Fall 2008. Reprinted by permission.

Ricki Lewis, "Stem Cells and Genetic Testing: The Gap Between Science and Society Widens" from *The American Journal of Bioethics* 8.4, Nov. 4, 2008. Reprinted by permission of Taylor & Francis Group, http://informaworld.com

Jason Royce Lindsey, "America and the New Dynamics of War" from *Peace Review: A Journal of Social Justice*, Volume 19, January 4, 2007. Reprinted by permission of Taylor and Francis Group, http://informaworld.com.

Patricia McCann-Mortimer, Martha Augoustinos, and Amanda LeCouteur, "'Race' and the Human Genome Project: Constructions of Scientific Legitimacy" from *Discourse and Society*, Sage Publishers, Volume 15, Issue 4, July 1, 2004. Copyright © 2004 by Sage Publications. Reprinted by permission of SAGE.

Daniel V. Meegan, "Neuroimaging Techniques for Memory Detection: Scientific, Ethical, and Legal Issues" from *The American Journal of Bioethics* 8.1, Jan. 1, 2008. Reprinted by permission of Taylor & Francis Group, http://www.informaworld.com

Ashley Montagu, "The Origin of the Concept of Race" from *Man's Most Dangerous Myth: The Fallacy of Race*, Sixth Edition: Altamira Press, Sage Publications. Reprinted by permission of Rowman & Littlefield Publishing Group.

Melissa Moreno, "Lessons of Belonging and Citizenship Among Hijas/os de Inmigrantes Mexicanos" from *Social Justice*, Spring 2008, Vol. 35, Issue 1. Copyright © 2008 by Social Justice. Reprinted with permission.

Carol Mukhopadhyay and Rosemary C. Henze, "How Real Is Race: Using Anthropology to Make Sense of Human Diversity" from *Phi Delta Kappan*, Jan. 14, 2008 at http://www.pdkintl.org/kappan/k0305muk.htm.

National Council of Teachers of English, "21st Century Curriculum and Assessment Framework" adopted by the NCTE Executive Committee, November 19, 2008 from http://www.ncte.org/positions/statements/21stcentframework.

Mary Ellen O'Connell, "What is War?" from *Jurist*, University of Pittsburgh School of Law, March 17, 2004 at http://www.jurist.law.pitt.edu.

Robert Orrill, "Humanism and Quantitative Literacy" from *Calculation vs. Context*. Reprinted with permission.

The Pickens Plan, "America is Addicted to Foreign Oil" at http://www.pickensplan.com. Reprinted with permission.

Thomas Pogge, "Making War on Terrorists—Reflections on Harming the Innocent" from *The Journal of Political Philosophy* 16.1 (March 2008): 1–25.

Public Broadcasting System, "Ten Things Everyone Should Know about Race" courtesy, *Race-The Power of an Illusion*, on DVD from California Newsreel. http://www.newsreel.org; www.pbs.org/Race. Reprinted with permission.

Samir Quota, Raija-Leena Punamaki, Thomas Miller, and Eyad El-Sarraj, "Does War Beget Child Aggression? Military Violence, Gender, Age, and Aggressive Behavior in Two Palestinian Samples" from *Aggressive Behavior*, 34.3 (May/June 2008): 231–244.

Susan Rippberger and Kathleen Staudt, "Teaching Citizenship and Values on the Border" from *Aztlan: A Journal of Chicano Studies*, 32.1, Spring 2007, pages 87–112. Reprinted with permission of The Regents of the University of California, UCLA Chicano Studies Research Center. Not for further reproduction.

Barbara Rockenbach and Carole Ann Fabian, "Visual Literacy in the Age of Participation" from *Art Documentation* 27.2 2008. Reprinted with permission.

Beatrix P. Rubin, "Therapeutic Promise in the Discourse of Human Embryonic Stem Cell Research" from *Science as Culture* 17.1, March 2008. Reprinted by permission of Taylor & Francis Group, http://www.informaworld.com.

C. Ford Runge and Benjamin Senauer, "How Biofuels Could Starve the Poor" from *Foreign Affairs* 86.3 (May/June 2007). Reprinted by permission of *Foreign Affairs*, May/June 2007. Copyright © 2007 by the Council on Foreign Relations, Inc. http://www.ForeignAffairs.com.

Steven Salaita, "Ethnic Identity and Imperative Patriotism: Arab Americans Before and After 9/11" from *Anti-Arab Racism in the USA*, published 2006 by Pluto Press. Reprinted with permission.

Vincent Sarich and Frank Miele, "Race and the Law" from *Race: The Reality of Human Differences*, 2004. Reprinted by permission of Westview Press, a member of the Perseus Books Group.

Richard L. Sheaffer, "Statistics and Quantitative Literacy." Reprinted by permission of the author.

O. Carter Snead, "Neuroimaging and the 'Complexity' of Capital Punishment" from *Notre Dame Lawyer*, Fall 2007. Reprinted with permission.

Michael E. Weber, "Catch 22: Water Versus Energy" from *Scientific American* Special Issue, September 2009. Reprinted with permission. Copyright © 2009 by Scientific American, Inc. All rights reserved.

index

A

AASL Standards for 21st-Century Learners (American Association of School Libraries), 37–39
America 101 (Lane), 67–79
America and the New Dynamics of War (Lindsey), 498–505
America is Addicted to Foreign Oil (The Pickens Plan), 590–594
American Society of Human Genetics, ASHG Statement on Direct-to-Consumer Genetic Testing in the United States, 119–128
American Association of School Librarians and the American Library Association, AASL Standards for 21st-Century Learners, 37–39
Aquinas, Thomas, Of War, 470–479
ASHG Statement on Direct-to-Consumer Genetic Testing in the United States (American Society of Human Genetics), 119–128
Augoustinos, Martha, Patricia McCann-Mortimer and Amanda LeCouteur, Race and the Human Genome Project, 277–307

B

Background Readings on Race in America (Online Texts), 224–225
Baker, Berenice, Power Play, 618–623
Balat, H. and M. Balat, Biogas as a Renewable Energy Source—A Review, 594–612
Balat, M. and H. Balat, Biogas as a Renewable Energy Source—A Review, 594–612
Beyond the Age of Petroleum (Klare), 580–589
Biogas as a Renewable Energy Source—A Review (Balat and Balat), 594–612

C

Callahan, Rebecca M., Chandra Muller and Kathryn S. Schiller, Preparing for Citizenship, 400–418
Caplan, Arthur L., Mind Reading, 134–139
Carr, Geoffrey, The Power and the Glory, 612–618
Catch 22 (Webber), 623–633
Cicero, Marcus Tullius, Occasions that Justify War, 464–470
Classic Texts Online: Background Readings on Race in America, 224–225
Clean Energy Scam, The (Grunwald), 633–642

D

Daly, Elizabeth, Expanding the Concept of Literacy, 54–67
Does Race Have a Future? (Kitcher), 252–276
Does War Beget Childhood Aggression? (Qouta, Punamäki, Miller and El-Sarraj), 538–568

E

The Economic Logic of Illegal Immigration (Hanson), 418–433
The Elements of American Identity (Hackney), 335–345
Ethnic Identity and Imperative Patriotism (Salaita), 445–460
Expanding the Concept of Literacy (Daly), 54–67
El-Sarraj, Eyad, Samir Qouta, Raija-Leena Punamäki and Thomas Miller, Does War Beget Childhood Aggression?, 538–568

F

Fabian, Carole Anne and Barbara Rockenbach, Visual Literacy in the Age of Participation, 39–53

G

Grunwald, Michael, The Clean Energy Scam, 633–642

H

Hackney, Sheldon, The Elements of American Identity, 335–345
Hanson, Gordon H., The Economic Logic of Illegal Immigration, 418–433
Henze, Rosemary C. and Carol Mukhopadhyay, How Real is Race?, 307–323
How Biofuels Could Starve the Poor (Runge and Senauer), 642–655
How Real is Race? (Mukhopadhyay and Henze), 307–323
Humanism and Quantitative Literacy (Orrill), 98–111

J

Joenniemi, Pertti, Toward the End of War?, 479–498
Johnson, Kirk A. and Tim Kane, The Real Problem with Immigration . . . and the Solution, 433–445

K

Kahn, Jonathan, Race in a Bottle, 323–331
Kane, Tim and Kirk A. Johnson, The Real Problem with Immigration . . . and the Solution, 433–445
Kitcher, Philip, Does Race Have a Future?, 252–276
Klare, Michael T., Beyond the Age of Petroleum, 580–589
Kopelman, Loretta M., Using the Best Interests Standard to Decide Whether to Test Children for Late-Onset Genetic Diseases, 163–186

L

Lane, Eric, America 101, 67–79
LeCouteur, Amanda, Patricia McCann-Mortimer and Martha Augoustinos, Race and the Human Genome Project, 277–307
Lessons of Belonging and Citizenship Among *Hijas/os de Immigrantes Mexicanos* (Moreno), 367–400
Lewis, Ricki, Stem Cells and Genetic Testing, 128–134
Lindsey, Jason Royce, America and the New Dynamics of War, 498–505

M

Making War on Terrorists (Pogge), 505–538
McCann-Mortimer, Patricia, Martha Augustinos, and Amanda LeCouteur, Race and the Human Genome Project, 277–307
Meegan, Daniel V., Neuroimaging Techniques for Memory Detection, 186–212
Miele, Frank and Vincent Sarich, Race and the Law, 239–252
Miller, Thomas, Samir Qouta, Raija-Leena Punamäki and Eyad El-Sarraj, Does War Beget Childhood Aggression?, 538–568
Mind Reading (Caplan), 134–139
Moreno, Melissa, Lessons of Belonging and Citizenship Among *Hijas/os de Immigrantes Mexicanos*, 367–400
Montagu, Ashley, The Origin of the Concept of Race, 225–236
Mukhopadhyay, Carol and Rosemary C. Henze, How Real is Race?, 307–323
Muller, Chandra, Rebecca M. Callahan and Kathryn S. Schiller, Preparing for Citizenship, 400–418

N

National Council of Teachers of English, 21st Century Literacies: Curriculum and Assessment, 29–37
Neuroimaging and the "Complexity" of Capital Punishment (Snead), 212–220
Neuroimaging Techniques for Memory Detection (Meegan), 186–212

O

Occasions that Justify War (Cicero), 464–470
O'Connell, Mary Ellen, What is War?, 568–575
Of War (Aquinas), 470–479
Online Resources for Understanding the Human Genome Project and Neuroimaging, 117–119
The Origin of the Concept of Race (Montagu), 225–236
Orrill, Robert, Humanism and Quantitative Literacy, 98–111

P

Pickens Plan, The, America is Addicted to Foreign Oil, 590–594
Pogge, Thomas, Making War on Terrorists, 505–538
Power and the Glory, The (Carr), 612–618
Power Play (Baker), 618–623
Preparing for Citizenship (Callahan, Muller, and Schiller), 400–418
Public Broadcasting System, Ten Things Everyone Should Know about Race, 236–239
Punamäki, Raija-Leena, Samir Qouta, Thomas Miller and Eyad El-Sarraj, Does War Beget Childhood Aggression?, 538–568

Q

Qouta, Samir, Raija-Leena Punamäki, Thomas Miller, and Eyad El-Sarraj, Does War Beget Childhood Aggression?, 538–568

R

Race and the Human Genome Project (McCann-Mortimer, Augoustinos and LeCouteur), 277–307
Race and the Law (Sarich and Miele), 239–252
Race in a Bottle (Kahn), 323–331
The Real Problem with Immigration . . . and the Solution (Kane and Johnson), 433–445
Rippberger, Susan and Kathleen Staudt, Teaching Citizenship and Values on the U.S.–Mexico Border, 345–367
Rockenbach, Barbara and Carole Anne Fabian, Visual Literacy in the Age of Participation, 39–53
Rubin, Beatrix P., Therapeutic Promise in the Discourse of Human Embryonic Stem Cell Research, 140–162
Runge, C. Ford and Benjamin Senauer, How Biofuels Could Starve the Poor, 642–655

S

Salaita, Steven, Ethnic Identity and Imperative Patriotism, 445–460
Sarich, Vincent and Frank Miele, Race and the Law, 239–252
Scheaffer, Richard L., Statistics and Quantitative Literacy, 79–98
Schiller, Kathryn S., Rebecca M. Callahan and Chandra Muller, Preparing for Citizenship, 400–418
Senauer, Benjamin and C. Ford Runge, How Biofuels Could Starve the Poor, 642–655

Snead, O. Carter, Neuroimaging and the "Complexity" of Capital Punishment, 212–220
Statistics and Quantitative Literacy (Scheaffer), 79–98
Staudt, Kathleen and Susan Rippberger, Teaching Citizenship and Values on the U.S.–Mexico Border, 345–367
Stem Cells and Genetic Testing (Lewis), 128–134

T

Teaching Citizenship and Values on the U.S.–Mexico Border (Rippberger and Staudt), 345–367
Ten Things Everyone Should Know about Race (Public Broadcasting System), 236–239
Therapeutic Promise in the Discourse of Human Embryonic Stem Cell Research (Rubin), 140–162
Toward the End of War? (Joenniemi), 479–498
21st Century Literacies: Curriculum and Assessment Workshop, 29–37

U

Using the Best Interests Standard to Decide Whether to Test Children for Late-Onset Genetic Diseases (Kopelman), 163–186

V

Visual Literacy in the Age of Participation (Rockenbach and Fabian), 39–53

W

Webber, Michael E., Catch 22, 623–633
What is War? (O'Connell), 568–575